How John Wrote the Book of Revelation:

From Concept to Publication

by
Kim Mark Lewis

Library of Congress Control Number: 2015918062

Photo of the wax tablet was taken by Martin Rulsch under the CC-by-sa 4.0 license.
Picture taken in the Roman history museum in Osterburken.

Cover designed by Six Penny Graphics.

Editing services done by Jennifer Faylor who I regard as the magical girl with the red wand.

Paperback Version:
ISBN-13: 978-1943325009 (Kim Mark Lewis)
ISBN-10: 1943325006

e-Book Version
ISBN-13: 978-1-943325-02-3 (Kim Mark Lewis)
ISBN-10: 1-943325-02-2

Lewis, Kim Mark.
  How John wrote the Book of Revelation : from concept to publication / Kim Mark Lewis.
    pages cm
  ISBN: 978-1-943325-00-9 (pbk.)
  ISBN: 978-1-943325-02-3 (e-book)
  1. Bible. Revelation—Criticism, interpretation, etc. 2. Bible. Revelation—Commentaries. 3. Bible. New Testament—Criticism, interpretation, etc. 4. Translating and interpreting.   I. Title.
BS2825.52 .L48 2015
228`.06—dc23
                                                                                            2015918062

Dedication and Thanks

The writing of this book has taken many years. It has been more than a project, it has been a journey. It all started with my return to Revelation after years of neglect. As I read it and then diagrammed it I was amazed at how it was structured. I tried to nail down exactly how it was written, to see if I could find the key that unlocked the structure of Revelation. There were so many wild goose chases I pursued, that I quickly learned not to say anything about my findings.

Fortunately for me I have a wonderful wife, in which I could be jealous of if she was someone else's wife. I came to her one day with a diagram of an overarching theme and explained it to her. She looked at me, smiled, and said, "You should write a book on this." Being the fool I am I said "Great idea!" So if you like this book and it adds value to your study of Revelation, I give her all the credit for it being published. If, on the other hand, you hate the book, then the credit is all mine.

In the beginning, I thought this project would be easy. I wanted to write something around 200-pages long, which showed Revelation in its simplest form while being void of any theological (eschatological[1]) frameworks attached to it. I wanted something that a non scholar could pick up, read, and walk away with the knowledge of how Revelation is interconnected. So I wrote, translated Revelation, and thought I came up with something. There were many false starts along the way and sometimes there were times I just wanted to give up.

What I know now and wish I knew then, is that the most important thing when writing a book is to see it to the end. There have been many ups and downs in the writing of this book. For one, the book you are reading now is not the book I wanted to write. One does not wake up one morning and plan to write a book on how Revelation was written. It is only in writing 250 pages for another book on Revelation that I discovered exactly how John wrote Revelation. At that moment, I had to decide whether to finish the book that I'd already started or to write an entirely different book that would change everything. I chose the latter. It is now, more than ever, that I appreciate all the friends who supported me. They not only encouraged me through this book, but through the last book that I failed to complete as well. They put up with thousands upon thousands of emails, hundreds of drafts, and scores of editing. All along this process they encouraged me to continue and words cannot express my appreciation for all of their efforts.

The first friend who helped me was Mackensie Glander, who without fail transformed what I would call English into what the rest of the world would call English. She has been with me from nearly the beginning and stayed with me towards the end of this project. The second friend who helped me greatly was Aaron Wicklund. The insight and direction he gave was instrumental in the production of this book. Though I sometimes considered his critiques harsh, in the end I have a better book because of it. He helped transform this book into something I would want to keep on my shelf even if I didn't write it myself.

---

1   A theological word meaning the study of end times.

My last friend whom I will mention is Mary Economos. Writing a book is a lonely effort, but she encouraged me and read my stuff. She offered insight and though we were thousands of miles apart she was someone I could always reach out to and talk about the book with.

I have been truly blessed with a great wife and great friends. Their encouragement during this project has been stellar and their patience goes above and beyond. Along the way I have had other friends that have helped to a lesser degree, but nonetheless pages have been added because of their encouragement. I even have to thank my dog. He may be old, and I like to think that he is smarter than the average dog, but his help was in the walks he forced me to take. There were many times that I would write a two-sentence paragraph and believed I'd sufficiently covered the topic. Upon taking him for a walk however, hundreds of thoughts would go through my head, and those two sentences would be further developed and fleshed out.

This book is dedicated to my daughter Chloe who, from the ages of five to fourteen, generously helped me balance my time with her and this book. Through those years they both have improved, but she has enriched my life beyond my wildest dreams. I am so blessed to have her as my daughter.

Contents

Abbreviations . . . . **xv**

The Introduction . . . . **.xix**

What You Need to Know Before You Read This Book. . . . . **xix**

The Translation Used in This Book xix

How This Book References Scripture Citations xix

How This Book Views the Date and Authorship of Revelation xx

Key Concepts Regarding the Quality of the Greek Language Found Within Revelation xx

Literary Concepts the Reader Needs to Understand xx

Parallels xxi

Synonyms xxii

Antonyms xxii

Hebrew Poetry as a Means of Writing xxii

Genetic Literary Reconstruction . . . . **xxiii**

How Genetic Literary Reconstruction Will Change How We Do Things xxiii

We Get to Know the Author(s) . . . . *xxiv*

A New Dynamic to Source Criticism. . . . . *xxiv*

Approximation Drafts Versus Manuscripts . . . . *xxiv*

A Literary Genetic Tree of Scripture . . . . *xxv*

Precision of Meaning on Words, Phrases, and Symbols . . . . *xxv*

The Scope and Limitations of Genetic Literary Reconstruction xxvi

The Process of Genetic Literary Reconstruction xxvi

Source Identification. . . . .*xxvi*

Source Parallel Formation . . . . *xxvii*

Parallel Formation and Deconstruction . . . . *xxviii*

Rethinking Parallel Formation . . . . *xxviii*

Parallels: A Literary Time Machine . . . . *xxix*

Other Literary Patterns . . . . *xxxiii*

Conflation . . . . *xxxiii*

How Material Is Split in Revelation . . . . *xxxvi*

How Books Were Written in John's Time . . . . **xxxvii**

The Use of Wax Tablets xxxvii

The Way They Wrote in John's Time xxxix

How Books Were Published in John's Time xxxix

How John Wrote Revelation xl

The Advantage of Writing in the Horizontal . . . . *xlii*

The Disadvantage of Writing in the Horizontal . . . . *xliii*

How John Formed Each Sentence . . . . *xliv*

Revelation: An Unfinished Work xlvi

John Was Most Likely a Skilled Writer but Rushed to Publish xlvi

Many Illustrations . . . . **xlvi**

Chapter 1: How John Wrote Revelation 1

Introduction to the Revelation Draft Hypothesis **1**

The Drafts **3**

The Ezekiel-Isaiah Draft (EID) 4

The Zechariah Draft (ZrD) 4

The Deuteronomy-Joshua Draft (DJD) 5

The Exodus Draft (ExD) 6

The Daniel Draft (DnD) 6

Chapter 2: The Ezekiel-Isaiah Draft (EID) 13

What the Ezekiel-Isaiah Draft Looked Like **14**

The Ezekiel-Isaiah Draft: From Exile to Heaven to Commissioning (EP1-2, IP1-2) **15**

Ezekiel's and John's Calling and Visitation to Heaven (Ezek 1:1 - 2:2; Ezek 2:8 - 3:3; Rev 1:9-10; 4:1-11) 15

Ezekiel's and Isaiah's Heavenly Adventure as John's Heavenly Adventure (Isa 6:1-8; Rev 4:1-11) 16

The Mission of Ezekiel, Isaiah and John (EP2, IP2) **17**

Ezekiel, Sent to God's People to Say "Thus Says the Lord" (Ezek 2:1-8; Rev 2:1-3:22; 9:3; 10:11) 17

The Two Missions: The Call of the Watchman and the Birth of a Child (EP3, IP3) **17**

Ezekiel Called to Be a Watchman (Ezek 2:6; 3:4-27) 18

God's People are like Briers, Thorns and Scorpions and the Hardening of Ezekiel's Head (Ezek 2:6; 3:8-9) 18

Ezekiel's Journey to Tel Aviv and Being Appointed as a Watchman (Ezek 3:4-27) 18

The End of One Ministry and the Birth of Another (Ezek 4:5-8; Isa 6:13-9:19) 18

The Length of the Siege of Jerusalem Changed From Years of Sin to Years of Ministry (Ezek 4:5-8; Rev 11:2-3, 9) . . . 20

Jesus as the Child (Isa 7:14 - 9:21; Rev 12:1-17) 20

How John Added Catastrophes to the Ezekiel-Isaiah Parallel (Ezek 5:2; Isa 7:1 - 9:21 ; Rev 8:7-12; 12:1-17) . . . 21

The Judgments (EP4, IP4) **22**

John's First Major Content Alignment Corrections 22

The Glory of God Flees and Fights (EP5, IP5) **26**

The Father and Mother of God's People (EP6, IP6) **28**

Jesus Depicted as Eliakim and the Birth of the Church in Philadelphia 28

The Two Wealth's of Tyre (EP7, IP7) **28**

The Tyre Found in Ezekiel and in Revelation (Ezek 27:1-36; Rev 18:1-19) 28

Tyre Found in Isaiah and Revelation (Isa 23:1 - 25:6; Rev 3:18; 18:2-6; 19:1-9) 29

Jesus as the Certain King (Isa 23:15-7; Rev 18:2-6, 22) 29

The Birth of the Content for the Church in Laodicea (Isa 23:16-8; Rev 3:17-8) 29

The Birth of the Saints Praising God Over Babylon's Destruction and the Wedding Feast of the Lamb (Isa 25:1-6; Rev 19:1-9) . 30

It Takes Two to Slay the Great Dragon (EP8, IP8) **30**

Jesus Depicted as the Shoot and Root of Jesse (Isa 11:1-16; Rev 19:11-22) 30

The Plight of Two Peoples and Two Rivers 31

Gog and Magog and the Attack by the Multitude of Nations (EP9, IP9) 31

The City of God and the Holy City of Jerusalem (EP10, IP10) 32

The Ezekiel Account of the City of God (Ezek 40:1 - 48:35; Rev 21:1 - 22:5) 32

The Differences Between the City of God in Ezekiel and in the New Jerusalem 32

The Contrast Between Jerusalem as the Harlot and Tyre as the City of Wealth Within the New Jerusalem 32

Transition From the City of God (Ezek 40:1-48:35) in Judaism to the New Jerusalem in Christianity 33

The Holy City of Jerusalem (Isa 25:8, 42:9, 60:19, 65:17, 22, 66:17, 20, 22) 34

The Two Accounts of the New Jerusalem Descending 34

Final Thoughts. 35

The Ezekiel-Isaiah Draft Approximation Text 37

Chapter 3: The Zechariah Draft (ZrD) **65**

The Process That John Used to Construct the Zechariah Draft **65**

Z1 - Whom They Have Pierced (Zech 12:9-10; Rev 1:9) 66

Z2 - The Oratories to God's People as the Birth of the Letters to Seven Churches (Zech 7:1 - 12:8; Rev 2:1 - 3:22) 67

Defining the Structure of the Letters to the Churches. 71

Defining the Content and the Recipients of the Letters to the Churches 71

The First Use of the Author's Notation. 72

Z3 - The Coronation of Jesus as the High Priest (Zech 6:9-15; Rev 5:1-14) 74

Z4 - The Four Chariots/Four Horsemen and the Four Winds/First Four Trumpets (Zech 6:1-8; Rev 6:1-8; 8:7-12) 75

How the Four Winds/First Four Trumpets Were Constructed. 75

Z5 - Two Women in the Basket (Zech 5:5-11; Rev 12:1-17; 17:1-18). 78

Z6 - The Flying Scroll (Zech 5:1-4; Rev 5:1-2, 7-8; 10:1-11).. 79

The Mighty Angel Author's Notation 80

The Conflation of the Primary Mighty Angel Text (Rev 10:1-11) 84

Z7 - The Building of the Encoded-Complex Parallel (Zech 2:1 - 4:14; Rev 11:1 - 12:17) 86

The Creation of Satan in the Zechariah Draft. 86

Satan Defeated in Heaven and the Great Dragon Locked in the Abyss and How Satan Got so Many Names 87

Other Places That Provide Content for Satan Outside of the Zechariah Draft. 88

Satan, Balaam, and Phinehas (Num 22:1 - 25:18; Rev 2:13-5) 89

Satan in Heaven as the Adversary to Job (Job 1:6 - 2:6; Rev 12:10). 90

The Creation of the Temple and its Courtyard Trampled by Gentiles (Zech 2:1-4; Rev 11:1-2) 90

The Creation of the Nations Are Angry Against Israel (Zech 2:9-13; Rev 11:15-8; Rev 12:15-6) . . . 91

The Creation of the Two Prophets 91

Z8 - The Creation and Placement of the Four Horns/First Four Bowls (Zech 1:18-21; Rev 16:1-9) . . . 92

The Harlot as Judah, Israel, and Jerusalem (Zech 1:18-21; Rev 17:1-18) 93

Z9 - The Final Segment of Zechariah 93

God Pleads for His People to Return to Him (Zech 1:3, 12-5; Rev 18:4-20). 94

How Long Will God Not Have Mercy on Jerusalem (Zech 1:12-5)? 94

The Destruction of Tyre and the Rejoicing of the Saints (Zech 1:12; Rev 19:1-9) 94

The Destruction of the Dragon and the Two Riders of the Red and White Horses (Zech 1:7-16; Rev 19:11-21) 95

The Nations Attack Jerusalem or The Remaking of Jerusalem (Zech 1:7-16; Rev 20:4-15) . . . 96

The Remaking of Jerusalem (Zech 1:1-6; Rev 21:1 - 22:5) 96

Final Thoughts. **97**

The Zechariah Approximation Draft **99**

Chapter 4: The Deuteronomy-Joshua Draft (DJD) **131**

The Purpose and Scope of the Deuteronomy-Joshua Draft 131

The Purpose of the Deuteronomy-Joshua Draft 131

The Scope of the Deuteronomy-Joshua Draft 133

Let's Build the Deuteronomy-Joshua Draft (DJD) 133

The Epilogue is Born 134

The Birth of the Warning for Those Who Wish to Modify Revelation. 135

The Blessings and the Curses, the Story of Gog and Magog, and the New Jerusalem. . . . 135

The Song of Moses and the Lamb/Jesus 139

The People Swear Allegiance to the Lamb/Jesus 139

The Sending of the Two Spies Into Jericho/Jerusalem 140

The Crossing of the Jordan River 140

The Circumcision of Those Born in the Wilderness 142

The First Passover Meal in the Promised Land 142

The Commander of the Lord's Army 143

The Lion From the Tribe of Judah. 143

The Worship Scene of Jesus 143

John's First Deuteronomy-Joshua Draft Dilemma 143

The Retelling of the Story of the Conquest of Jericho. 145

The Recreation of the Seven Days of Marches Around the City of Jericho 145

The Creation of the Seventh Seal 147

The Creation of the Fifth and Sixth Trumpets 147

The Seventh Trumpet: How and Why it Was Placed. 149

The Finishing Phase 149

From the Four Horns to the Seven Bowls 152

The Creation of the Alpha and Omega Parallel 152

The Beginning of the Beatitudes 155

The Prologue and Epilogue 158

The Prologue, the Seven Churches and the Epilogue 159

The Seven Churches 159

The Expanding of the ZrD's Story of Satan 160

The Two Stories of Satan and the Two Stories of God's People 160

The New Timeline for Satan 161

The Story of One Wax Tablet 162

Joshua and the Crossing of the Jordan River 162

How The Content of the Wax Tablet Was Distributed. 163

Final Thoughts. 163

The Deuteronomy-Joshua Draft Approximation Text 165

Chapter 5: The Exodus Draft (ExD) 191

The Purpose of the Exodus Draft 191

Let's Build the Exodus Draft 192

Moses, the Burning Bush, and the Name of God 192

The Believers Became the Kingdom of Priests to God 193

The Sanctifying of the New Believers 197

The Washing of the Clothes 197

Abstaining From Sexual Activity With Women 197

God Coming in the Clouds 198

The Commandments of God and the Story of the Golden Calf Retold . . . 199

The Servicing of the Tabernacle in Heaven 201

Transitioning From the Deuteronomy-Joshua Draft to the Exodus Draft . . . 201

The Servicing of the Menorah 201

The Servicing of the Bread on the Table of the Bread of Presence 202

The Four Living Creatures and the 24 When Used Together 203

The Four Living Creatures Only 203

The Absence of the Four Living Creatures and the 24 Elders in the New Jerusalem . . 206

The Servicing the Altar of Incense and the Entering the Most Holy Place . . 206

God and Jesus Become the Temple 206

Moses, Aaron, and the Ten Plagues 207

The Birth of the 144,000 and the Great Multitude 207

The Creation of the 144,000 207

The Creation of the Great Multitude 208

The Seven Letters a Transition From Jewish Cities to Gentile Cities? 209

The Changing of the Prologue 209

The Organizing of the Seven Churches 209

Final Thoughts 209

Chapter 6: The Daniel Draft (DnD) 211

Let's Build the Daniel Draft 211

The Debut of the Beast 211

How the Beast Is Organizationally on the Same Level as Jesus 212

The Beast Defeats Jesus on Earth 212

Jesus Defeats the Beast on Earth 213

The Creation of the Second Death 213

The Removal of Gog and Magog's Vulture Scene 219

The Descriptions of Jesus, John's Worshiping of the Two Angel, and Broken Parallels (Dan 10:1-21; Rev 1:9-17; 19:9-21; 22:6-15) 222

Satan and Jesus as Allies and the Origin of the 200 Million Horsemen 225

God and the Beast as Allies 227

The Merging of the Harlot and Tyre to Become Rome 227

The Changes to the Bowls 228

God's Defeat by Satan and God's Victory Over Satan 228

The Believers Versus the Beast and the Harlot 229

The End is Soon . . . . **.229**

The Two Publication Dates of Revelation and Who Is the Beast?. 231

What About 666? 231

Who Was the False Prophet? 232

The State of the Daniel Draft 232

Why Was the Daniel Draft Rushed?. 233

Revelation as the Key to the Past 234

Chapter 7: The Published Version of Revelation **235**

The Prologue (Rev 1:1-20) 238

The Chain of Custody of the Vision (Rev 1:1-3) 238

John Provides Background to His Message (Rev 1:4-8) 238

Where John Was (Rev 1:9-10) 238

The Seven Churches (Rev 2:1 - 3:22) 239

The Message to the First Church in Ephesus (Rev 2:1-7) 239

The Message to the Second Church in Smyrna (Rev 2:8-11) 239

The Message to the Third Church in Pergamum (Rev 2:12-7) 239

The Message to the Fourth Church in Thyatira (Rev 2:18-29) 240

The Message to the Fifth Church in Sardis (Rev 3:1-6) 240

The Message to the Sixth Church in Philadelphia (Rev 3:7-13) 240

The Message to the Seventh Church in Laodicea (Rev 3:14-22) 241

John's Encounter with God in Heaven (Rev 4:1-11) 241

The Removing of the Seals (Rev 6:1 - 8:5) 243

The Opening of the First Seal (Rev 6:1-2) 243

The Opening of the Second Seal (Rev 6:3-4) 243

The Opening of the Third Seal (Rev 6:5-6) 243

The Opening of the Fourth Seal (Rev 6:7-8) 243

The Opening of the Fifth Seal (Rev 6:9-11) 244

The Opening of the Sixth Seal (Rev 6:12-7). 244

The Intermission: The 144,000 Sealed on Earth (Rev 7:1-8). 244

The Intermission: The Great Multitude in Heaven (Rev 7:9-17) 245

The Opening of the Seventh Seal (Rev 8:1-5) 245

The Seven Trumpets (Rev 8:6 - 11:19) 246

The First Trumpet (Rev 8:6-7) 246

The Second Trumpet (Rev 8:8-9). 246

The Third Trumpet (Rev 8:10-1) 246

The Fourth Trumpet (Rev 8:12-13) 246

The Fifth Trumpet (Rev 9:1-12) 246

The Sixth Trumpet (Rev 9:13-21). 247

The Intermission: The Two Prophets (Rev 11:1-14) 248

Their Ministry (Rev 11:1-6) 248

Their Martyrdom (Rev 11:7-10) 248

Their Resurrection and Ascension into Heaven (Rev 11:11-4) *248*

The Seventh Trumpet (Rev 11:15-9) 249

The Woman, Child, and Satan (Rev 12:1-17) **249**

The War in Heaven (Rev 12:7-9) 249

The War on Earth (Rev 12:10-7) 250

The Beast (Rev 13:1-10) **250**

The False Prophet (Rev 13:11-8) **251**

The 144,000 in Heaven (Rev 14:1-5) **251**

The Message of the Three Angels (Rev 14:6-12) 251

The Great Harvest of the Saints (Rev 14:13-20) **252**

The Seven Bowls (Rev 16:1-20) **253**

The First Bowl (Rev 16:2) 253

The Second Bowl (Rev 16:3) 253

The Third Bowl (Rev 16:4-5) 254

The Fourth Bowl. 254

The Fifth Bowl 254

The Sixth Bowl 254

The Seventh Bowl 254

Who is the Beast. 255

The War Against the Saints on Earth 255

Who is the Harlot and What are the Ten Horns 255

The Destruction of the Harlot and the Beast (Rev 19:1-21) **257**

The Destruction of the Harlot and the Marriage of the Lamb (Rev 19:1-9) 257

The First Angel John Worships (Rev 19:9-10) 258

Jesus Avenges the Saints: The Destruction of the Beast (Rev 19:11-21) 258

The Final Defeat of Satan (Rev 20:1-15) **259**

Satan Imprisoned for a Thousand Years (Rev 20:1-3) 259

The First Resurrection: The Saints will Rule with Jesus (Rev 20:4-6). 259

Satan is Released from the Abyss (Rev 20:7-10) 259

The Second Resurrection: Satan and His Followers are Placed in the Lake of Fire (Rev 20:11-5) 259

The New Heaven, the New Earth and the New Jerusalem (Rev 21:1 - 22:5) **260**

The Epilogue (Rev 22:6-21) **261**

The Second Angel that John Worships (Rev 22:6-11) 261

Jesus Speaks (Rev 22:12-6) 262

The Spirit, Jesus and John Speaks (Rev 22:17-21) .263

Chapter 8: Reading in the Horizontal. **265**

A Different Way to Read Revelation **265**

The Finishing Phase 265

Reading the Seven Churches **266**

The Structure of the Church Letters 266

The Salutation *266*

The Body 270

The Closing 270

The Spiritual State of the Seven Churches 272

The Seven Churches and the Seven Seals 275

The First Three Churches and the Primary Beast Narrative .276

Ephesus Verses the Second Beast / False Prophet (Rev 2:1-7; 13:11-7) 278

Smyrna Taken into Captivity (Rev 2:8-11; 13:8-10) 278

Pergamum Lives with Satan (Rev 2:12-7; 13:1-7) 280

Conclusion to the Three Churches and the Beast Parallel 281

The Story of the Fifth Church 282

What is Living and What is Dying? 282

Rising to One's Height and Descending to One's Depth 283

The Anger of the Righteous and the Unrighteous 286

When Parallels Fail: The Story of the White Robes 286

The Story of the Fifth Church as Revelation was Intended to Be 287

The Story of the Sixth Church. 287

The Synagogue of Satan 287

Becoming a Fixed Pillar. 288

Kept From the Hour of Testing 288

The Story of the Seventh Church 288

Buy From Jesus Gold Refined By Fire and White Garments (Rev 3:18) 289

If They Overcome They Will Sit on Their Thrones Next to God (Rev 3:21) 289

Wealth and Earthquakes 289

The Open Door, The Closed Door, And What Is Behind the Door 293

Satan's Story **294**

How John Formed the Story of Satan. 294

The Sealing of the 144,000 and the Sealing of Satan for a Thousand Years (Rev 7:1-8; 20:1-3) 294

The Martyrdom of Believers and Their 1,000 Year Reign (Rev 7:9-17; 20:4-6) 295

The First Four Trumpets and the Four Attacks By Satan Against the Woman 295

The Twelve Tribes Conceived in Heaven and Deceived by Satan (Rev 8:12; 12:1-6) 297

The War in Heaven and the Falling Star (Rev 8:10-1; 12:7-9) 297

The Land Absorbs the Water and the Sea Absorbs the Mountain (Rev 8:8-9; 12:15-6). . . .297

Satan Wars Against Those who Keep God's Commandments and Jesus' Testimony (Rev 8:7; 12:17) 298

The Release of Satan From the Abyss (Rev 9:1-12; 20:7) 302

The Gathering of the Army of Satan (Rev 9:13-9; 20:8-10) 302

Those Who Keep on Sinning on Earth and Where They Go (Rev 9:20-2; Rev 20:11-5). . . .302

The Trumpets and the Bowls. **302**

The Formation of the Trumpets and the Bowl. 302

The 144,000 and the Great Multitude 303

The Similarities Between the 144,000 and the Great Multitude. 303

The Differences Between the 144,000 and the Great Multitude. 306

John's Placement of the 144,000 and the Great Multitude 308

The Burning of the Incense 309

Understanding the Trumpets and the Bowls 311

How the Seals, Trumpets, and the Bowls Are Connected to Each Other 311

The Unique Similarities and Differences Between the Trumpets and the Bowls 313

The First Four Trumpets and the First Four Bowls 313

The Fifth, Sixth, and Seventh Trumpet and Bowl Combinations 313

The Woman and the Harlot 314

The Alpha and Omega Parallel . . . . **.314**

Final Thoughts. . . . . **.317**

Bibliography **323**

The Stratification Charts. **325**

Abbreviations

Book Specific and General Abbreviations

Abbreviation	
42 months parallel	A complex parallel (chiasmus) in which the elements are 42 months (Rev 11:2; 13:, 1260 days (Rev 11:3; 12: and 3½ days (Rev 11:9, 11) parallel.
BCE	Before the Common Era -- The modern way of saying BC or Before Christ.
CE	Common Era -- The modern way of saying AD in calendars.
DJD	The Deuteronomy - Joshua Draft.
ExD	Exodus Draft -- The final phase of the Revelation manuscript after John incorporated the Exodus content.
DnD	Daniel Draft -- The state of Revelation was in after John included content from the book of Daniel.
GLR	Genetic Literary Reconstruction -- The process of applying literary practices to produce previous drafts of a literary work such as Revelation.
EID	Ezekiel - Isaiah Draft
LXX	The Septuagint -- The Greek translation of the Hebrew Scriptures.
PVR	The Published Book of Revelation (The final version of Revelation we have in our Bibles today).
RDH	Revelation Draft Hypothesis -- The theory in which Revelation was composed of six major sources and processes to create the book of Revelation.
ZrD	Zechariah Drat -- The state of the book of Revelation after John included Zechariah.

The Hebrew Scriptures

Abbreviation	Hebrew Scripture	Abbreviation	Hebrew Scripture
Gen	Genesis	Eccl (or Qoh)	Ecclesiastes (or Qoheleth)
Exod	Exodus	Song or (Cant)	Song of Songs (Songs of Solomon or Canticles)
Num	Numbers	Isa	Isaiah
Lev	Leviticus	Jer	Jeremiah
Deut	Deuteronomy	Lam	Lamentations
Josh	Joshua	Ezek	Ezekiel
Judg	Judges	Dan	Daniel
Ruth	Ruth	Hos	Hosea
1–2 Sam	1–2 Samuel	Joel	Joel
1–2 Kgdms	1–2 Kingdoms (LXX)	Amos	Amos
1–2 Kgs	1–2 Kings	Obad	Obadiah
3–4 Kgdms	3–4 Kingdoms (LXX)	Jonah	Jonah
1–2 Chr	1–2 Chronicles	Mic	Micah
Ezra	Ezra	Nah	Nahum
Neh	Nehemiah	Hab	Habakkuk
Esth	Esther	Zeph	Zephaniah
Job	Job	Hag	Haggai
Ps/Pss	Psalms	Zech	Zechariah
Prov	Proverbs	Mal	Malachi

Hebrew Pseudepigrapha

Abbreviation	Hebrew Pseudepigrapha
1 En	*1 Enoch*

The Christian Scriptures

Abbreviation	New Testament	Abbreviation	New Testament
Matt	Matthew	1-2 Thess	1-2 Thessalonians
Mark	Mark	1-2 Tim	1-2 Timothy
Luke	Luke	Titus	Titus
John	John	Phlm	Philemon
Acts	Acts	Heb	Hebrews
Rom	Romans	Jas	James
1-2 Cor	1-2 Corinthians	1-2 Pet	1-2 Peter
Gal	Galatians	1-2-3 John	1-2-3 John
Eph	Ephesians	Jude	Jude
Phil	Philippians	Rev	Revelation
Col	Colossians		

Ancient Literature

Eusebius

Hist. eccl.   *Historia ecclesiastica*

Ignatius

Ign. *Trall*   Ignatius, *To the Trallians*

Josephus

Ant.   *Antiquities*

Pliny the Elder

Nat.   *Naturalis historia*

Strabo

Geogr.   *Geographica*

Tacitus

Ann.   *Annales*

Hist.   *Historiae*

Modern Works

APOT   *The Apocrypha and Pseudepigrapha of the Old Testament*. Edited by R. H. Charles. 2 vols. Oxford, 1913

BDAG   Bauer, W., F. W. Danker, W. F. Arndt, and F. W. Gingrich. *Greek-English Lexicon of the New Testament and Other Early Christian Literature*. 3d ed. Chicago, 1999

ISBE   *International Standard Bible Encyclopedia*. Edited by G. W. Bromiley. 4vols Grand Rapids, 1979-1988

JBL   *Journal of Biblical Literature*

NA[27]   *Novum Testamentum Graece*, Nestle-Aland, 27th ed.

NIBCNT   New International Biblical Commentary of the New Testament

NIGTC   New International Greek Testament Commentary

WBC   Word Biblical Commentary

Modern Translations

CEB   *Common English Bible*. © Copyright 2011 Common English Bible.

ESV   *English Standard Version*. Copyright © 2001, 2007, 2011 by Crossway Bibles, a division of Good News Publishers.

KJV   *King James Version*, 1611.

NASB   *New American Standard Bible,* 1977 Copyright © 1986, both by The Lockman Foundation.

NET   The NET Bible. Copyright © 1996-2006 Biblical Studies Press, L.L.C.

NIV   *New International Version*. Copyright © 2011 by International Bible Society.

NRSV   *New Revised Standard Version Bible*. Copyright © 1989, Division of Christian Education of the National Council of the Churches of Christ in the United States of America.

RSV   Revised Standard Version of the Bible. Copyright © 1952 [2nd edition, 1971] by the Division of Christian Education of the National Council of Churches of Christ in the United States of America.

The Introduction

What You Need to Know Before You Read This Book

This book is different from any other book previously written on Revelation. It is not a commentary, nor is it a book that depicts the various views on Revelation. It is not a book that tells what others think of Revelation, if anything, it ignores them. What it is, is a book that recreates the methodology that John used to write Revelation and in turn reveals the truth behind this often misunderstood work of biblical literature.

Imagine being able to look at the first few drafts of Revelation, being able to see how it changed from one draft to the next. Imagine being able to witness where the symbols came from and how they changed. The process completely changes the dynamics of Biblical interpretation. No longer is it in the realm of guessing, but rather in the light of objectivity.

The Translation Used in This Book

This book uses a public domain version of the Bible and as a result takes advantage of the lack of licensing restrictions that are applied to commercial versions of the Bible. There are a few places where this book strays from or alters the version in order to promote consistency of word meaning. For example, it uses the word "church" rather than "assembly," even though "assembly" is closer to its original meaning. The usage of "THE LORD" instead of "Yahweh" is done to make it less offensive to many Jewish readers.

How This Book References Scripture Citations

This book cites scripture differently than most books on the Bible. Rather than parenthetically quoting scripture throughout the body of the text, this book places them in footnotes. The placement of verse references in footnotes makes it easier for the reader. There will be many times where the verses are cited and a chart which contains the verse(s) and reflects the content of the section being footnoted will be exhibited. The end result is a text that is easier to read as well as a more transparent display of the verses presented.

The method of citing referenced verses is also different in this book. When it is a single verse such as Revelation 2:12 it will be cited as Rev 2:12. When it is a block of verses being cited within a block of ten verses such as Revelation 2:12-17 it will be cited as Rev 2:12-7 instead of Rev 2:12-17. If the block of verses goes beyond the ten verses such as Revelation 2:8-11 it will be displayed as Rev 2:8-11.

How This Book Views the Date and Authorship of Revelation

The purpose of this book is to convey a theory of construction of Revelation, not to provide an exhaustive coverage of its date and authorship. This book will view the author of Revelation as John since that is who Revelation claims to be written by.[1] It is the primary view of this author that only one person wrote Revelation, therefore in this book the author will always be referred to as "John" as an individual, rather than written by a community.

Key Concepts Regarding the Quality of the Greek Language Found Within Revelation

The Greek language found within Revelation is considered bad, or as one church father said, "barbaric."[2] This is one of the few viewpoints of Revelation that there is an overwhelming consensus on within the scholarly community. Unfortunately, the agreement of why the Greek in Revelation is bad segments the scholarly community into numerous camps.

This book will add one more idea to the many that are already out there. Instead of arguing that Greek was not his thinking language,[3] or trying the many other positions, this book will present the position that Revelation was not a finished book and the process used to write Revelation and its rush to publication is the reason the Greek is bad.

Literary Concepts the Reader Needs to Understand

There are many books written to teach students the ins and outs of Semitic literature,[4] but the purpose of this book is not to burden the reader with a plethora of terms but rather to understand the concepts on a general level. This book considers Hebrew poetry to have one primary purpose—to build content in a work. The process of parallel formation—which will be discussed later in this section—is really the process of doubling the content of a work. The use of synonyms and antonyms are means to add variety to the content. Therefore this book is more concerned with how Hebrew poetry is formed and what makes it malformed rather than understanding and identifying every nuance. The book presents a methodology by first assuming that the parallel at one time was perfect and through John's writing process the parallel

---

1   Rev 1:1, 9-10; 22:8.
2   Hist. eccl. vii, xxv.
3   R. H. Charles, *A Critical and Exegetical Commentary on the Revelation of St. John.* New York: Charles Scribner's Sons, 1920, cxlii - cxliii.
4   The following books are great resources for those who wish to learn about Hebrew poetry:
     Robert Alter, *The Art of Biblical Poetry* (New York: Basic Books, 2011);
     E. W. Bullinger, *Figures of Speech Used in the Bible: Explained and Illustrated.* (Lodon: Eyre & Spottiswoode, 1898);
     David Noel Freedman, *The Dynamics of Biblical Parallelism* (Grand Rapids, MI: Eerdmans, 1985).

An Anatomy of a Simple and a Complex Parallel

Examples of simple and complex parallels are presented below, first with text in unformatted prose and then revealed in their respective parallel type. The simple parallel is represented by a parallel list while the introverted parallel looks like an outline. The marking of each element in the parallel is shown by a letter (A, B, C, D), and the corresponding element in the other list is shown by a letter and an apostrophe (A', B', C', D').

Parallel elements can either be complementary or opposite to each other. The illustration below shows all the elements in the simple parallel forming an opposite to their corresponding element. The complex parallel shows all three of the four elements as complementary. In these two small parallels consisting of only four items there can be 256 different possible combinations.

John is poor, tall, and old, but he is a great father to his daughter. Jill on the other hand is wealthy, small, and young. However, she is John's daughter.	John is poor among his family and tall in stature. He is the eldest of his brothers. He is the father to Jill and she is the daughter to John. She is the eldest among her sisters and the tallest. She is also poor.

A He is poor. A' She is wealthy.	A. He is poor.
B He is tall. B' She is small.	B. He is tall.
C He is old. C' She is young.	C. He is the eldest brother.
D He is her father. D' She is his daughter.	D. He is her father.

For the complex parallel list:

A. He is poor.
  B.   He is tall.
    C.   He is the eldest brother.
      D.   He is her father.
      D'.   She is his daughter.
    C'.   She is the eldest sister.
  B'.   She is tall.
A'. She is poor.

---

became malformed. We will examine what caused the malformed parallel and from there assess a logical order of construction for a given passage.

Parallels

Parallel formation is the primary tool that Biblical authors used to convey stories in both nearby and faraway passages. Parallels come in two basic types: the simple parallel and the complex parallel. The simple parallel can be thought of as two lists that contain similar items in the same order. The complex parallel (commonly called an introverted parallel or chiasmus) is when one list is in reverse order of the other. In both simple and complex parallels each item in each list will be seen as an element. Each element can form a complement or an opposite to its corresponding element.[5]

As with any structure the author may combine both types of parallels in order to make a composite parallel. The author may have one part of the process form a perfect parallel, and if the reader looks at the parallel in a different way it will form an offset—we will call these types of parallels offset parallels. The most complex of all parallels is the multilayer parallel in which the parallel is written in such a way that it is encoded by the source text one way and forms a parallel in the resulting text another way.

---

5   See "An Anatomy of a Simple and a Complex Parallel" on page xxi.

Synonyms

Synonyms are different words that have similar or the same meanings. In Biblical studies the focus is on why different words are used. For example, the dialogue between Jesus and Peter on whether Peter loves Jesus is perhaps one of the most famous uses of synonyms in the New Testament. In the conversation, Jesus uses one Greek word for love and Peter uses a different Greek word for love.[6] Unfortunately in most English Bibles they are both translated as the same word "love" however there are many who expound on the differences between the two words.[7] This book takes the position that synonyms are the spice to parallel construction. For example, in the parallel "An Anatomy of a Simple and a Complex Parallel" on page xxi, synonyms for "he is poor" could be "he is in poverty" or "he is destitute."

Synonyms can also be seen as a means of hiding something from the reader. For example, Jesus is often referred to as the "Lamb," and in many of those cases it is because John does not want the reader to connect Jesus as the son of God with Joshua / Jesus the son of Nunn.[8] Therefore, we are not looking at the synonym per se, we are looking at why the synonym is used.

Sometimes synonyms are used to get the writer out of a literary predicament. If the writer has already created symbolism and a definition to depict one thing, and needs to have an equal symbol with its own unique definition (to differentiate the two), they can utilize synonyms to achieve this. An example of this is how the "mighty angel" was developed as a synonym to the seraph. In the Ezekiel-Isaiah Draft (EID) John created the heaven scene as a conflation of Ezekiel and Isaiah's encounter with God in heaven. Ezekiel had powerful beings in heaven, known as the living creatures, and Isaiah had powerful creatures in heaven known as the seraphim. John combined the actions of both and assigned them to the living creatures. Later in the draft, John realized that he needed a powerful creature to match the level of the living creature and the seraphim, but he could not use the term "seraph" because the role and its descriptions were already assigned to the four living creatures. To solve this, John simply created the synonym "mighty angel" and a new heavenly host was born.[9]

Antonyms

Antonyms are different words that have the opposite meaning. Most of the antonyms found in Revelation appear within the letters to the seven churches. For example, "Laodicea" means "righteous or just people," but from the content of the letter we find that they do not possess these qualities. Another example is how "Philadelphia" means "beloved" but we learn that they are, in fact, hated. Antonyms are useful in that they provide the writer with a tool to convey opposites, and in a book such as Revelation they are used to present a dualistic world of good versus evil.

Hebrew Poetry as a Means of Writing

The use of Hebrew poetry was not used as a clever writing style overlaying a story, but rather as a clever means of writing the story itself. The author, such as John, would begin with the desire to write a story, but instead of writing the story itself, the author picks a story previously done that is similar to what the au-

---

6   John 21:15-7; Jesus used ἀγαπάω and Peter used φιλέω.

7   CEB, ESV, NASB, NET all use the English word "love" for the two Greek words, ἀγαπάω and φιλέω.

8   See "The Lamb of God" on page 134.

9   See "Z3 - The Coronation of Jesus as the High Priest (Zech 6:9-15; Rev 5:1-14)" on page 74.

How This Book Tells the Story of the Construction of Revelation

The best way to think of how this book is arranged is to think of it as an archaeological dig but in reverse. Instead of digging through the top layer to tell the story we start from the bottom layer and reveal what Revelation looked like at that stage or strata. The stages are called drafts and they are named after the principle material that was used to formulate them. As one reads each draft he or she may wish to explore how a theme developed across the drafts similar to the vertical themes shown below. The book will direct the reader in footnotes to the location of the next and previous drafts similar to a cross-section of an archaeological dig.

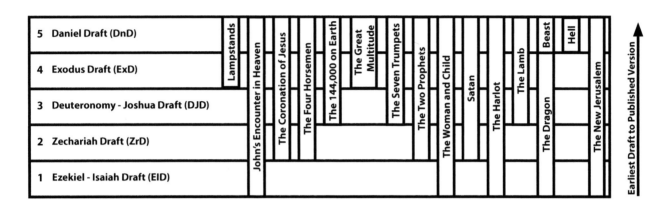

thor wishes to convey. The author will then form either a complex or simple parallel to the story and tweak each of the elements so that the story copied becomes the story the author wishes to convey. Once the story is sufficiently crafted, the author can then construct parallels to a section and thereby create a new section with only minor adjustments to the parallel. This book contains the story of how John used Hebrew poetry to construct the book of Revelation.

Genetic Literary Reconstruction

Genetic literary reconstruction (GLR) is the methodology used to produce prior drafts of a given work when no prior drafts exist. It is primarily limited to many of the Hebrew and Christian Scriptures in which the author follows a consistent process, such as, but not limited to: Genesis, Exodus, Ezekiel, Matthew, Luke-Acts, and Revelation.

How Genetic Literary Reconstruction Will Change How We Do Things

The benefits of GLR are many and this book is an example of it. Consider the Book of Revelation, which is the most difficult book in the Christian Scriptures to both understand and to write about. Prior to this book there has been no generally accepted theory of construction, and no commonly held interpretation. The only constant in those who study Revelation is that John's Greek had room for improvement.

By just following a few simple processes, the book becomes approachable—for the first time in history we have a platform upon which we can objectively interpret and understand the book of Revelation. For many this may be a bad thing, for others, the centuries of interpretation by guesswork can now be confined within a fruitful process.

We Get to Know the Author(s)

GLR allows us to become more intimate with the author through his writing process. As we follow the methodology that the author uses we relive his struggles and experience his solutions. From the earliest reconstruction of a draft to the final product, the writing habits that the author had while constructing their work is revealed. It allows us to see what was and wasn't important to the author. This is also true for documents written by multiple authors, as it allows us to focus on the authors as individuals, and reveals how later scribes treated their writings when they placed them into a collection.

A New Dynamic to Source Criticism

I am often amazed at the number of books written on Biblical literature, where the authors must have gone through numerous drafts and editing cycles themselves, but somehow they do not take that process into consideration enough to apply it to the Biblical book they are writing about. Every book in the Bible, with the possible exception of the smallest of books, had some draft stages and editing cycles. Those who utilize source criticism tend to be satisfied with just knowing that the author used a particular source. Wouldn't it be better if we not only knew the source but the actual process by which the source was incorporated into the text?

Much is debated in scholarly literature as to what the true definition of an allusion is, and how difficult it is to say that something is an allusion.[10] GLR tells us what an allusion is, because we can see the source that the author is using and how the author tweaks the source for their purposes. The problem, however, comes from how much the author tweaks the text. In each of the draft chapters we can see many examples of John changing the text to suit his needs. This is shown in how he modernizes imagery (such as changing the four chariots into the four horsemen)[11] as well as how he sometimes forms a complete opposite to the original text. It is also shown in ways such as how he changed the imagery of briers, thorns, and thistles representing evil doers (where God will burn them because of their wickedness) to imagery of green grass, representing righteous believers (where they will be burned by the wicked because of their faithfulness).[12]

Since an author has the freedom to change the text of the source document to the extent that John did, the term "allusion" is neither sufficient nor accurate enough to express this action. Describing the process as being a parallel formation provides a richer platform in communicating the literary process from the source document. It is easier for a person to link two passages together by means of a parallel rather than be shackled by the proximity of an actual quote.

Approximation Drafts Versus Manuscripts

The Bible is a book comprised of many books written across centuries. Today, most people do not realize how the words contained in the Bible were given to us. In a day in which we can electronically transmit massive amounts of data and print books on command with the aid of a computer, we forget that the

---

10   The following citations below represent the imprecise nature of what is an allusion and the difficulty in forming a census among scholars of what is an allusion and what is not. Jauhiainen, Marko. *The Use of Zechariah in Revelation*. (Tübingen: Mohr Siebeck, 2005) p 35. G. K. Beale and D. A. Carson. *Commentary on the New Testament Use of the Old Testament*. (Grand Rapids, Mich.: Baker Academic, 2007) xxiv. Grant R. Osborne. *Revelation* (Grand Rapids, Mich.: Baker Academic, 2002), 25-26.

11   See "How John Created the Four Horsemen Through Thematic Conflation" on page xlv.

12   See Isa 10:15-9 and how it maps to Rev 9:3-4 in "IP4 - The Judgments by Jesus - Part 2" on page 49.

books in the Bible were copied by hand, and due to this, mistakes inevitably resulted during the copying process. With each manuscript copied it brought over the mistakes of the previous scribe. To determine what is a mistake and what is likely belonging to the original, scholars employ a discipline known as "textual criticism." Basically, they have a set of guidelines that they follow when comparing manuscripts, with the end goal of producing something very close to the original or at least the earliest possible draft. The obvious problem with textual criticism is the limitation of the earliest manuscripts and their scarcity. Unfortunately, finding more manuscripts is more dependent on luck, which thereby leaves scholars to devise new methods of comparing manuscripts.

Genetic literary reconstruction does the same thing that textual criticism does, but backwards. Instead of producing a work that closely resembles the original manuscript, the GLR critic produces a prior draft of the work. The result is that the GLR critic can see the process used to transition from one draft to another. The process is also open and can be validated and/or corrected by others. With some works, such as Revelation, multiple complete approximation drafts can be produced, while with other works only portions of the text will yield a draft. This is in contrast to the circumstances of the textual critic, who has to hope for a discovery of a new manuscript or a better methodology (which will more than likely result in word variances and some unique quirks to the newly discovered manuscript).

One of the most important end products of textual criticism is a critical text of the Bible or books contained within it. A critical text is not a text derived from a single manuscript, but rather text that is derived from studying all of the earlier manuscripts. Generally, they contain the critical text and notations that show the significant differences between the manuscripts.

Just as the discipline of textual criticism has produced critical texts, we can do the same using GLR. How this book reconstructs the previous drafts of Revelation is only the beginning of producing critical texts of previous drafts. Imagine being able to pick up a book that used GLR to produce the critical texts to the various drafts that ultimately became the Gospel of Matthew.

A Literary Genetic Tree of Scripture

For the first time in history, we now have a tool set that allows us the ability to produce a literary genetic tree of scripture. In this book we will see that Revelation forms a first-generation parallel with Exodus and Ezekiel. We have also seen that Isaiah forms a first-generation parallel with Ezekiel and Revelation forms a first-generation parallel with Isaiah.[13] This begs the question, how many unique stories are there in the scriptures and how many of them are parallels? Thanks to GLR we can begin the quest to discovering this answer.

Precision of Meaning on Words, Phrases, and Symbols

The primary tools for determining word meanings are Greek and Hebrew grammar and lexicons. Depending upon how technical the commentaries add in more detail concerning the various interpretations and contextual information. Language tools are powerful in how they communicate possible meanings and grammar construction. Commentaries range in quality with the more technical giving more contextual information and a summation of interpretations prior to its publication. The limitations faced by language

---

13 See "Ezekiel's Exodus Draft" on page 200.

tools and most commentaries is that they are confined with their approach. If the writer being commented on follows a different approach or changes their approach, the tools will remain consistent within their approach. These tools become less important when you can see how the source text used the word or phrase and how the author tweaked them. We now have a means of both isolating possible meanings and excluding meanings by exploring the thought process from draft to draft.

When and how a phrase comes into a book is more important than its lexical meaning or grammatical structure. How and why the Lamb came into Revelation is more important than the definition of the Lamb. How the scroll came into Revelation and was split into two or how Satan became the red dragon is more important than any lexical definitions could ever be for them. There are literally hundreds more that could be mentioned and what is worse is that outside of GLR there are hundreds of scholarly opinions for what each word or phrase's meaning is, which is an incredibly misguided waste of time and effort.

The Scope and Limitations of Genetic Literary Reconstruction

Genetic literary reconstruction can only be accomplished if the author of the work being examined follows an orderly process in writing their work. The process does not need to be consistent from the first to last stage but it needs to be consistent within the various stages of the work. It can be as tiny as forming a parallel or it can be massive in how it imports its source material. The scribal practices that produced much of the Hebrew and Christian Scriptures lend themselves nicely to the GLR process.

The Process of Genetic Literary Reconstruction

In order to produce similar results on other Biblical books that this book achieves with Revelation, you will need to have a basic understanding of Hebrew poetry.[14] You will also need knowledge of the source material of the work you wish to apply this methodology to. From there, it is a simple matter of figuring out the order that the sources were added to the work and the process in which they were added. The knowledge of Hebrew poetry will both speed up and enhance the understanding of this process.

It should be noted that much of this chapter uses examples found in the book of Revelation. This is done for an obvious reason—so that the reader can see the entire process. Revelation, however, is not unique by any means. The EID is actually an example of how the author of First Isaiah created their work by forming a synonymous parallel from the whole of Ezekiel. In the Exodus draft (ExD) we discuss how the whole of Ezekiel was from the Exodus narrative beginning with Moses, prior to receiving the Decalogue, to the end of Exodus. This is only the beginning.

Source Identification

The most important part of producing prior drafts is to identify the major sources that were used to construct the draft. The priority is always to organize the material that is used from the most to the least frequent. The more a source is used the more likely a pattern will also be used. The least- used material is most likely material that was added only to support the larger material. Therefore less attention should be given to how it affected the work.

---

14   See "Literary Concepts the Reader Needs to Understand" on page xx for a description of the basic knowledge of Hebrew poetry required to implement GLR in many of the Hebrew and Christian Scriptures.

Source Parallel Formation

A source parallel formation analyzes how a work incorporated a single source. If a pattern emerges then we can assume that the author was consistent in that approach for all or most of the duration that the source was imported. As in all things there are variances that must be accounted for, such as the earlier that the material was added the more disjointed the pattern would be, since subsequent additions would cause previous material to shift around. Thus this process may have to infer based upon a consistent and yet limited set of data.

On the surface it may sound extraordinary to assume that an author like John would be consistent within the framework of adding material from a source. Yet we find this consistency in books such as Revelation, Isaiah, Ezekiel, Matthew, and Luke-Acts. For example, when we read Ezekiel and Revelation together, Revelation seems to follow Ezekiel from Revelation beginning with the encounter of the four living creatures and God on his throne in heaven and ending with being in a city of God with a river of life flowing through both cities.[15] Both cities have a tree or trees that bear twelve kinds of fruit (a different one for each month), and leaves used for healing.[16] The difference that the two exhibit is the order of things; some things follow the same order in both books while others are shifted around. Since they, for all intents and purposes, begin and end the same, we can assume that when John used Ezekiel it was a direct linear copy of selected material from Ezekiel.

The book of Zechariah is the opposite of Ezekiel in that John takes the first twelve chapters of Zechariah in reverse order and aligns Revelation by subject order.[17] We see clues for this in how the coronation of Jesus in Rev 5:1-14 is similar to that of Joshua the high priest,[18] and how the four horsemen in Revelation have the same colors as the four chariots in Zechariah.[19] We have the four winds in Revelation which are another name for the four chariots in Zechariah.[20] Revelation steps out of order when it comes to the two women in the basket who are flown into the wilderness by two stork wings,[21] because we also have the woman flown by two eagle wings into the wilderness, and the harlot flown into the wilderness by a scarlet-colored beast.[22] The parallels are restored again in the mighty angel scene[23] with the flying scroll.[24] This is not the complete list of common content between Revelation and Zechariah, nor is it the end of the parallels, but it is sufficient enough to make the assumption that when John used Zechariah he both shaped the material in the reverse order of the first twelve chapters of Zechariah and added material from Zechariah.

From John's perspective, how he uses Hebrew Scripture sources is no different than how he wrote Revelation. John's use of Ezekiel would be to consider forming a simple parallel and John's use of Zechariah would be no different than him forming a complex parallel. This is important to note because there are many other sources that John used to make Revelation and none of the sources are used differently than how he wrote Revelation. We can also make the same statement with other writers of this genre.

---

15   See "Revelation's Parallel Formation With Ezekiel" on page xxxi.
16   Ezek 47:12; Rev 22:2
17   See "Revelation's Parallel Formation With Zechariah" on page xxxii.
18   Zech 6:9-15.
19   Rev 6:1-8; Zech 6:1-8.
20   Rev 7:1-3; Zech 6:1-8.
21   Zech 5:5-11.
22   Rev 12:4; 17:3.
23   Rev 10:1-11.
24   Zech 5:1-4.

From the standpoint of reconstructing the order and what each draft might of looked like in the production of Revelation, we would need to establish the process of how each parallel formation was made with Revelation and then organize each process into an order that produces an end result similar to what we have in Revelation today.

Identifying the order of each Hebrew Scripture added will become the major means of identifying the order of passages. It is also our primary means of organizing our description of how Revelation was constructed. This is why this book is organized in terms of "drafts" based upon the primary Hebrew Scripture used.

Parallel Formation and Deconstruction

The vast majority of the Hebrew and Christian Scriptures are a product of writing in parallels. As such, parallel formation is the primary means in which we can determine how a work was written. To do this we need to think in terms of writing parallels rather than in terms of identifying them. The draft chapters of this book are a great resource for visualizing the writing of Revelation and thereby providing all the knowledge a person needs to reproduce the work that has been done in this book with another Hebrew or Christian Scripture.

Rethinking Parallel Formation

We cannot think of a parallel as something that is limited to words or sentences and that must be in close proximity with each other. We cannot even think of a parallel in terms of the book that is being examined. We have to think of parallels in terms of relationships between the information being conveyed, organized, and copied. How John created the Ezekiel-Isaiah draft, the Zechariah draft, and the Deuteronomy-Joshua draft are all examples of parallel formation. How John created the encoded parallel with the content from Zechariah 2:1 - 4:14 and Rev 11:1 - 12:17 is a parallel between two works.[25]

Additionally, we cannot think of parallels as contiguous blocks of text that neatly line up with other contiguous blocks of text. Parallels can simply be a set of wax tablets arranged in a particular order alongside another set of wax tablets in a particular order. How John created the two stories of Satan illustrates that not all parallels formed are straightforward.[26]

We have to see parallels as a means of telling a story within a story. John primarily wrote in the horizontal which means that he used parallels to tell a story—the parallels were separated by large amounts of content, but when put together they told a coherent story. The story of the fifth, sixth, and seventh church is an example of telling such a story in the horizontal.[27] For example, without looking at the parallels that formed the sixth church we would have no means of determining the meaning of the "synagogue of Satan" and yet through its parallels the answer is obvious.[28]

---

25   See "Z7 - The Building of the Encoded-Complex Parallel (Zech 2:1 - 4:14; Rev 11:1 - 12:17)" on page 86.

26   See "Satan's Story" on page 294 for how John completes a parallel with two stories of Satan by simply inserting Rev 12:1-17 into Rev 20:1-15.

27   See "The Story of the Fifth Church" on page 282, "The Story of the Sixth Church" on page 287, and "The Story of the Seventh Church" on page 288.

28   See "The Story of the Sixth Church" on page 287.

We cannot think in terms of "one parallel to rule them all" but in terms of "one parallel that ruled a draft." Many books show the different ways of outlining the book of Revelation. The reason why Revelation has no single parallel is that it was never finished and also because the former draft's organizational structures are exposed. Even books published in a finished state will have more than one structure to organize the book. The book of Matthew, for example, is organized by the portrayal of Jesus as the new Moses. Both were born at the time when babies were killed and both were saved in Egypt. Moses was the law giver and Jesus was the law fulfiller. Moses had five books and Jesus had five great sermons. Matthew is organized into a great complex parallel as well. Each of the ways of organizing Matthew was a way that the author of Matthew wrote his Gospel.[29]

Additionally, we cannot think in terms of parallel use being restricted to the actual writing of a work. A parallel can be formed in preparation of a work (we will call this type of parallel a content-preparation parallel). The Ezekiel-Isaiah parallel is a parallel that John formed as a means of content preparation to construct the ZrD.[30] The parallel existed in the form of two columns of wax tablets but not in terms of a physical writing.

Perfect parallels are only part of the story though—it is the malformed parallels that tell us the story of how a work was written. Today, scholars tend to take the safe route by only identifying perfect parallels and not malformed parallels. As a result, malformed parallels are ignored to the point that they cannot exist. Never is the question posed "why are they malformed?" That is because of one common blindness in virtually every book written about Biblical literature—scholars see a Biblical book as being written in one sitting and not as an ongoing process of construction. This type of perspective is extraordinary when you think about it, every work ever written in the field of Biblical studies goes through many iterations and yet for some reason the overwhelming majority of books written do not address the actual process of construction.

Finally, we need to see the big picture of parallel writing. A simple copy of one text is a simple parallel between the text copied and the text written. Overlaying a process or a life story, such as how John overlaid the servicing of the tabernacle onto Revelation or how Matthew overlaid the life of Moses onto the Gospel of Matthew,[31] would be considered parallel formation. How the texts were imported into Revelation has just as much to do with parallel formation as anything else.

Parallels: A Literary Time Machine

The major assumption in this book and in GLR is that when an author such as John writes parallels they are perfect. Therefore when we come across parallels that are not perfect we can assume that one or more events later in the writing process caused the parallel to become malformed. That is not to exclude the possibilities of either the writer being distracted (and therefore not finishing the parallel) or the writer realizing that the current parallel will overwrite a previously constructed essential parallel (and therefore ceasing to continue its formation). What it does mean is that the writer, in the vast majority of their work, will form perfect parallels and as those sections are modified the parallels will become malformed.

The more malformed the parallel is the more likely that it is an earlier parallel in the writing process or that it signifies many rewrites of a section. The more perfect the parallel is, is an indication that less mod-

---

29 See "Jesus as the New Moses in Matthew" on page xxx for all references to this paragraph.
30 This will be discussed in more detail in the Ezekiel - Isaiah draft chapter.
31 See "Jesus as the New Moses in Matthew" on page xxx.

Jesus as the New Moses in Matthew

The Gospel of Matthew presented Jesus as the new Moses by attributing many elements of Moses' life to Jesus. Both Moses and Jesus experience a ruler who slaughtered male infants. Both Moses and Jesus had similar situations in giving the law, for Moses, and giving the beatitudes for Jesus. Matthew, even structured the sermons to match the number of Moses' books, which positioned Jesus to be at the same level (or greater) than Moses.

The Life of Moses	The Life of Jesus in the Gospel of Matthew
Birth of Moses: Pharaoh Kills All the Hebrew Infants*	**Birth of Jesus: Herod Kills All the Infants in and Around Bethlehem**
• A scribe tells Pharaoh that there will be an Israelite born who would diminish Egypt and raise up the Israelites power (Ant 2:205).	• The chief priests and scribes tell Herod that a child would be born who will govern Judah and shepherd Israel (Matt 2:1-7).
• Pharaoh feared his loss of power and ordered the infants to be cast in the river (Ant 2:206; Exod 1:22).	• Herod slays every male child in and around Bethlehem (Matt 2:16).
• Moses is taken into the Pharaoh's house for safety (Exod 2:3-10). Moses flees from Egypt for safety from the Pharaoh (Exod 2:15).	• Jesus is taken to Egypt for safety (Matt 2:14).
• Moses returns to Egypt (Exod 4:18-31).	• Jesus returns from Egypt when it is safe (Matt 2:19).
The Giving of the Ten Commandments	**The Giving of the Nine Beatitudes (Matt 5:1 - 7:29)**
• Moses fasted for 40 days and nights (Exod 34:28).	• Jesus fasted for 40 days and nights (Matt 4:2).
• Moses came down from the mountain to give the law (Exod 34:1-10).	• Jesus went up the mountain to give the new law (Matt 5:1).
• Moses brings the 10 commandments (Exod 34:1-10).	• Jesus fulfills the law (Matt 5:17). Jesus gives 9 beatitudes to the people (Matt 5:3-11). Jesus explains 10 things about the law (Matt 5:21 - 6:19).
• Moses judges the people (Exod 32:1-35).	• Jesus instructs how to judge (Matt 6:20 - 7:29).
Moses Wrote Five Books	**Jesus Gave Five Great Sermons**
• The book of Genesis.	• Sermon on the Mount (Matt 5:1 - 7:29).
• The book of Exodus.	• Instructions to the Twelve Apostles (Matt 10:1-42).
• The book of Leviticus.	• The Kingdom of Heaven parables (Matt 13:1-53).
• The book of Numbers.	• Discourse for the Believers (Matt 18:1-35).
• The book of Deuteronomy.	• Olivet Discourse (Matt 23:1 - 25:46).

*Note: The story of the birth of Moses is the conflation of Josephus' account of the birth of Moses and Exodus' account of the birth of Moses.

---

ifications were done to that section, or that the parallel was formed later in the process. By looking at the pristine parallels and identifying malformed parallels in which there is content overlap with the pristine parallel, we can deduce that the forming of the pristine parallel is the cause of the malformed parallel. We can also continue the process with the malformed parallel and see which parallels overlapped with it. From there we can create a logical order of construction and simulate the logical order. The process combined with knowing the order of how the texts were inserted into Revelation gives us a powerful tool as well as a means of validating the process.

Sometimes parallel formations leave a trail that makes it easy to determine the logical order of construction. Suppose the author constructs a parallel between two sections (section A and section B) and as a result the parallel elements from section A are copied to section B. At some later point in time the author forms a parallel between section B and another section, section C, and as a part of the process elements that came from A to B are now copied to section C. In a later parallel development the author forms a parallel with section B and a new section, section F, and as a result the element that came from section A and was

Revelation's Parallel Formation With Ezekiel

The chart below represents the process of determining how Revelation added the content of Ezekiel into Revelation. The observation shows how major components agree between Revelation and Ezekiel. The Pattern Predicted shows the likely process that John used to incorporate Ezekiel into Revelation.

The Observation

Content in Ezekiel			Content in Revelation
1:1-3	Ezekiel exiled the priest.	1:9-11	John exiled.
1:4-26	Four living creatures (1:4-26).	4:4-11	The 24 elders and four living creatures.
1:26-2:2	Ezekiel's encounter with God.	4:1-3	John's encounter with God.
2:9-3:3	Ezekiel is given a two-sided scroll that tastes like honey to the mouth.	5:1-8 10:8-10	Jesus is given a two-sided scroll. John is given a scroll that tastes like honey.

The content from Ezekiel and Revelation below seems to follow the general pattern from beginning to end but strays from any two connecting points.

Content in Ezekiel			Content in Revelation
3:4-11	God makes Ezekiel's head harder than flint.	7:1-3	Seal of God on the forehead of the 144,000 (7:1-3).
4:1-17	Ezekiel is given a formula of days into years.	11:1-12	42 months, 1,260 days, 3½ days.
5:1-4	Jerusalem is destroyed in three parts.	8:7-12	The four trumpets.
5:5-8	God surrounds Jerusalem.	9:13-21	The sixth trumpet.
5:9-11	Those who do evil will suffer severe pain.	9:1-12	The fifth trumpet.
5:13-5	The wrath of God on Jerusalem.	9:13-21	The sixth trumpet.
5:16-7	Death by arrows, famine, pestilence, wild beasts, and the sword.	6:1-8	The first four seals/the four horsemen.
9:1-11	God places a mark on the righteous' forehead which protects them from impending doom.	9:4-5	Those with the mark of God on their forehead will not suffer pain.
13:1-23	They kill the good prophets and let the bad prophets live. They also give gifts to the bad prophets.	11:1-12	They kill the two prophets and give gifts (11:1-12).
16:1-58	Jerusalem the adulterous bride.	17:1-18	The harlot, part 1.
27:1-36	The lament over Tyre.	18:1-24	The harlot, part 2.
29:1-32:32	Destruction of Pharaoh.	19:11-21	Second coming of Jesus.
38:1-39:29	Gog and Magog attack Jerusalem and they are destroyed by God.	20:7-10	Gog and Magog attack Jerusalem and they are destroyed by God.
40:1-48:35	The city of God.	21:1-22:5	The New Jerusalem.

The Pattern Predicted

Looking at the table to the left we can see that Revelation's overall use of Ezekiel follows a simple pattern, much like if the content from Ezekiel was copied in order and placed into Revelation. There are many items that are out of order but that could be seen as text migrating in order to accommodate later texts being imported into Revelation.

The predicted original import pattern would be a simple parallel between the two.

Revelation's Parallel Formation With Zechariah

The chart below compares the content between Zechariah and Revelation (the Observation) and predicts the process in which Zechariah was imported into Revelation (the Pattern Predicted). By knowing the process that John used to import Zechariah into Revelation we have a powerful tool for predicting the order of construction by simply comparing and contrasting other sources John used and their importation patterns.

The Observation

The table below represents the major agreement between Zechariah and Revelation.

Content in Zechariah (Reversed)	Zech	Rev
Whom they have pierced they shall mourn (The prologue).	12:10	1:7
Coronation of Joshua the high priest (Exaltation of Jesus).	6:9-15	5:1-14
The four chariots (The four horsemen/the first four seals).	6:1-8	6:1-8
The flying scroll (The scroll).	5:1-4	5:1-2; 10:1-11

The content from Zech 2:1-4:15 forms a complex parallel with the 42 month, 1,260 days, 3½ days complex parallel from Rev 11:1-13:8. This is an example of how disciplined John was when importing Hebrew Scripture sources into Revelation. It also indicates that John intended the two prophets to represent Jesus by associating them with Joshua (Jesus in Greek) the high priest (Zech 3:3; Rev 11:3) and salvation brought to the world (Zech 3:8-10; Rev 12:10) by the child in Rev 12:3-6.

A. 42 Months
Measure Jerusalem but not its walls (Zech 2:1-5).
Measure the temple but not its courtyard (Rev 11:1-2).

B.   1,260 Days
Joshua dressed in filthy rags (Zech 3:3).
The two prophets wore sackcloth (Rev 11:3).

C.   3½ Days
The two olive trees and the lampstands represent the work of Joshua and Zerubbabel (Zech 4:11-4).
The two olive trees and the two lampstands, the two prophets do all kinds of miracles from God (Rev 11:4-7).

C.   3½ Days
The building of the temple on earth and the nations will rejoice (Zech 4:6-10)
The temple is in heaven and the nations will be angry (Rev 11:18-9).

B.   1,260 Days
Satan kicked out of Jerusalem (Zech 3:1).
Satan kicked out of heaven (Rev 12:3-10).

Sin will be removed from the land (Zech 3:8-10).
Salvation brought to the whole world (Rev 12:10).

A. 42 Months
God will protect his people and Jerusalem will be loved by all the nations (Zech 2:6-13).
The beast waged war against God's people for 42 months (Rev 13:5-9).

The four horns (The first four bowls).	1:18-20	16:2-9
The horsemen (The second coming).	1:7-17	19:11-21
The return home (The New Jerusalem).	1:1-6	21:1-22:5

The Pattern Predicted

From the observation we can assume that John formed a complex parallel between Revelation and Zechariah. John organized the book of Revelation from the reverse order of the content found in Zech 1:1 - 12:10.

We can also see that in the center of the complex parallel, John had another complex parallel organized by the 42-month parallel. This suggests that the book of Zechariah was a major contributor to the book of Revelation.

With this pattern we can compare it with previous patterns and see how the content shifts. For example, we have seen in the Importation Pattern of Ezekiel that Revelation and Ezekiel formed a simple parallel and now we can compare the complex parallel between Zechariah and Revelation and the content of Ezekiel. If we find that the content of Ezekiel was shifted to support the complex parallel with Zechariah and Revelation then we can assume that Ezekiel was used prior to the complex parallel.

copied to section C is now overwritten by the new parallel between sections B and F. In this scenario we can easily reverse engineer the construction process, thereby creating a logical order of construction as well as recovering the content of the previous parallels.

Sometimes parallels are formed and a section is rewritten so content is shifted and/or reassigned to different imagery. As a result, the original parallel is malformed with one or more of its elements drifting outside of the original parallel. By assessing the cause of the reassigned imagery we can produce a logical order of construction as well as recover the original parallel formation. The alpha and omega parallel is an example of this where the phrase "I am the first and the last" was originally ascribed to God and later assigned to Jesus.[32]

When a work is created by forming parallels, the parallels provide the means of producing previous drafts. It is not the identification of the parallel that is important but the knowledge of what that parallel changed prior to its formation or what changed that parallel after the formation. If a parallel can be formed then it can be completely or partially returned to its pre-parallel state. This is provided that we know what the prior source of one of the sides of the parallel is.

Other Literary Patterns

Parallel formation is not the only way we can produce a logical order of construction as well as a prior draft. In this section we will cover common ways of incorporating text from one source into another and how it becomes distributed to other sections. If you can visualize a student who produces a paper following a set of rules of copying and shifting work around using a variety of methods, then the remainder of the introduction will be easier to grasp.

Conflation

Conflation is simply the combining of two separate stories into a single story. In Revelation this is done in many places, but there are differences in how Revelation conflates the Hebrew Scriptures. This section is an attempt to form a system of identification and implications to forming a logical order of construction.

Identifying the conflated passages is essential in determining the order of construction of a given book. By identifying the conflated passages as well as having knowledge of how the source was imported into the text, one can simulate how the work was constructed and use the conflated text to validate the predicted order of the drafts.

Similar Content Conflation

A common type of conflation is the merging of multiple sources that have similar content into a single story. The end result of the conflation of multiple stories becomes a new story. We see this in how John's encounter in heaven is taken from two Hebrew Scripture sources: Ezekiel and Isaiah. The Ezekiel source brings in the descriptions of God and the four living creatures, while the Isaiah source ascribes the worship role to the four living creatures and an altar. Revelation retains the faces of the four living creatures found in Ezekiel but reduces their faces

---

32   See "The Creation of the Alpha and Omega Parallel" on page 152.

to only one face and gives them two wings which conforms more to Isaiah's description of the Seraph having one face and six wings.[33]

Things to observe that may help in determining the order of construction:
- The source material and particularly which is the later source added. This will identify that the creation of the conflation could not have happened earlier than the latest source added.
- The elements that remain untouched and the elements that are conflated.
- Conflicting element descriptions and numbers. Usually the new material overwrites the older material.
- The order of the sources being conflated. Sometimes the two sources are in reverse order and therefore the author will arrange one source with another.

Other examples:
- The sealing of the 144,000 on earth (Rev 7:1-8) is a conflation of the twelve tribes crossing the Jordan River to get circumcised (Josh 5:1-9), but instead of getting circumcised they get the seal of God on their forehead which comes from Ezek 3:4-15; 9:4-7.[34]
- The mighty angel (Rev 10:1-11) is a conflation of several different passages from the Hebrew Scriptures. It is God giving Ezekiel the scroll that tastes like honey (Ezek 2:9-3:3), God appointing Ezekiel as the watchman in Ezek 3:17-27, and which represents a priest crossing the Jordan River with one foot on land and one in the water (Josh 3:1-15) and Michael from Dan 12:1-7.[35]

For passages that have been over written by new material it is possible to reconstruct an approximation of the material being overwritten by comparing the new content with the source content that was overwritten. If both source and the new content can be seen as a parallel formation than it is likely that some parallel formation of the source was overwritten.
- The harlot narrative was overwritten in the last draft by text supporting the beast. The source text for the harlot is derived from Ezekiel 16:1-63 with the section that John overwrites is from Ezek 16:20-40.[36]

Content Shift Conflation

Content shift conflation is the result of text being moved from one place to another or a text being removed. When a text is moved from one section to another section the content is adjusted so that the text flows with the newly added content and thus conflating two stories that were never intended to be joined together. Likewise, when content is moved from one section to another section the non-affected areas are joined together and therefore the author must adjust the text so that the two sections can be read as a seamless story.

The production of the ZrD is a great example of how John took tablets containing Ezekiel and

---

33   See Ezek 1:5-18; Isa 6:2-8 in "The Conflation of Ezekiel and Isaiah's Encounter With God" on page xliii.
34   See "The Circumcision of Those Born in the Wilderness" on page 142.
35   See "The Mighty Angel Tells John it Will Happen Soon" on page 230.
36   "The Creation of the Beast and the False Prophet -- Part 2" on page 215.

Isaiah and used Zechariah as a key to rearrange the tablets to form the ZrD.[37] As a result, John conflated many distant passages such as the two prophets' narrative (Rev 11:1-12) which is a conflation of Ezek 4:5-8 and Ezek 13:1-23.[38]

Things to observe that may help in determining the order of construction:
- Sections of the final product having content not associated with its initial parallel formation, such as extra symbols and extra content inserted from another process.
- Content derived from a parallel formation that is distributed outside of the parallel formation.

Other examples:
- The combining of the seal of God on the forehead, the green grass, and the trees into a single statement.[39]
- Distributing the content from one wax tablet to many wax tablets.[40]

Content Simplification Conflation

Sometimes the content depicts two similar items, places, or things, and at a certain point in time the author will conflate them as one story. Today, we see this type of conflation commonly in movies where all the scenes are supposed to have occurred in a single city and in actuality they were filmed in multiple cities.

We see this in Revelation, when two nearby texts are merged into a single text such as combining the harlot as Jerusalem[41] and the city of Tyre[42] as the harlot, the conflation could happen at the time of the original parallel formation or in a later parallel formation. The source of what caused the conflation will be the determining factor of its logical placement in the order of construction.

Things to ask that may help in determining the order of construction:
- Do earlier drafts treat the items as separate entities or conflated entities?
- Which draft is most likely to have conflated the two entities into a single entity?

Thematic Conflation

Thematic conflation is when items or a process are added and content from another source is added. Thematic conflation differs from similar content conflation in that there is nothing connecting the passages being conflated other than quantity or location of the elements. The author performing thematic conflation is forcing the previous material to conform to a theme.

An example of thematic conflation can be seen in how John took the four chariots in Zechariah 6:1-8 and made them the four horsemen in Rev 6:1-8. He took the colors of the

---

37 See "The Process That John Used to Construct the Zechariah Draft" on page 65.
38 See "Z7 - The Building of the Encoded-Complex Parallel (Zech 2:1 - 4:14; Rev 11:1 - 12:17)" on page 86 for the detailed process of the creation of the two prophets.
39 See "When Wax Tablets Are Placed Together" on page 85.
40 See "How John Distributed the Content From One Wax Tablet in the Deuteronomy-Joshua Draft" on page 164.
41 Ezek 16:1-58; Rev 17:1-18.
42 Ezek 27:1.

horses found in Zech 6:1-8 and combined them with the actions of God against his people to produce the four horsemen of Revelation.[43]

The item would signify the draft sequence that the source came from and the content would most likely signify a previous source (or at least the same source that created the item). This is called structure building, because John uses the items to contain previous source material.

Other examples:
- The nesting of the seven trumpets in the seventh seal follows the same pattern that we find in Joshua's defeat of Jericho (Josh 6:10-20; Rev 6:1-18; 8:1-9:21; 11:14-9; see).[44]
- The woman and the harlot taken to the wilderness (Jerusalem in Ezek 16:1-58 and Tyre in Ezek 27:1-36) were combined into a single city when the story of the two women in the basket were flown to the wilderness by giant heron wings (Zech 5:5-15). Since the woman in Rev 12:1-17 was described as being flown into the wilderness (Rev 12:14) John had to combine the other two into one city (see Rev 17:3 for the harlot being flown into the wilderness by the beast).
- The saints in heaven imagery was derived primarily from two sources, Isa 12:1-13:15 and the tabernacle imagery from Exodus. John used both of these instances of imagery to form all the saints in heaven passages.[45]

How Material Is Split in Revelation

The inserting of material in the middle of a text is the separation of the text prior to its insertion. This is done because of content expansion and to reorganize the material in order to produce a better flowing work. Every college student who writes a paper of substantial size will move text around to accommodate new research material that has been attained. As the paper is developed a student may have followed their primary source's order but over time rearranges that order into a way that is better suited for what they want to cover. For the most part, footnotes provide the means of referencing the source of the material being inserted.

When it comes to Revelation we do not have any footnotes but we do have the original source material that John used to construct Revelation. Having both the published version of Revelation and the source materials gives us a means of exploring what John did and if he left anything that we can use in the quest for earlier formations of text.

Fortunately for us John does leave clues for some of the major splits of texts and for the minor splits (minor being an insertion of a small amount of material between the text being split). The following are the ways we will refer to the various techniques that John uses to divide source text in Revelation.

Author's Notation

In Revelation, John provides a notation mark before and after the insertion of material in a contiguous single source material or a previous draft. In this book we refer to this notation as

---

43   See the illustration "How John Created the Four Horsemen Through Thematic Conflation" on page xlv.
44   See "How John Recreates Joshua's March on Jericho" on page 146.
45   See the bottom chart in the illustration "IP8 - Jesus Slays the Great Dragon With a Great Sword" on page 59.

an Author's Notation.

- The angel with a loud voice is used by John in Rev 1:9; 4:1 to indicate that the material from Ezek 1:1-2:2 was split.[46]
- The mighty angel is used as an author's notation three times (Rev 5:2; 10:1; 18:20). The second instance is from Ezek 2:9-3:3 and Rev 5:1-2; 10:9-10 mirroring God giving the scroll to Ezekiel.[47]
- The phrase "Here is wisdom" was used to split the beast's source text from Daniel.[48]
- The phrase "Lord of Lords" was used to create a second beast's source text from Daniel.[49]

Wax Tablet Insertion

 Beyond the literary practices of parallel formation as well as noting the insertion of text with an author's notation. We have to consider the practicality of adding a content between the pages of material. If we think in terms of writing a work using paper, the author may wish to insert a story between the pages that transition from one story to another story. In John's case it is not pieces of paper but as we will learn in the next section, wax tablets.

- The temple scene and the song of Moses and the Lamb is an example of John adding a wax tablet in to satisfy the parallel formation with the source text of Deuteronomy.[50]
- The 144,000 sealed on earth, the great multitude in heaven, and the seventh seal were all added to a wax tablet that was inserted between two judgment scenes.[51]

How Books Were Written in John's Time

In the last section we covered the literary techniques to deconstruct Semitic literature prior to 150 CE. We talked about parallel formation and how it allows us to produce a logical order of construction of a work. We also covered the movement and conflation of texts. What we did not cover was the actual process of writing a book back in John's time. In this section we will briefly cover the tools and the techniques used in the writing of books because the rest of the book we will see how the book of Revelation was written in a detail that no prior work has ever produced.

The Use of Wax Tablets

Books were written similarly to how we write books today—just painfully slower. In John's time the tool for developing a story was the wax tablet. These wax tablets were boards that had their interiors chiseled out to form a cavity. Wax was then poured into the cavity, forming a sunken inlay.

To write on a wax tablet the writer used a stylus—a sharp-ended instrument used to etch into the wax. In order to erase a word or letter, the wax simply needed to be melted where the mistake had occurred, and

---

46 See "What Is an Author's Notation?" on page xxxviii.

47 See "The Mighty Angel Author's Notation" on page 80.

48 See "The Creation of the Beast and the False Prophet -- Part 1" on page 214, "The Creation of the Beast and the False Prophet -- Part 2" on page 215.

49 See "The Creation of the Beast and the False Prophet -- Part 2" on page 215 and "The Creation of the Beast and the False Prophet -- Part 3" on page 217.

50 See "The Song of Moses and the Lamb/Jesus" on page 139. See "Inserting Between the Wax Tablets" on page 144 for the big picture..

51 See "Inserting Between the Wax Tablets" on page 144.

What Is an Author's Notation?

Origin of John's Encounter With God and the Heaven Scene

The chart below has content from Ezekiel on the left side and the content that it maps to in Revelation on the right. At one time the two sections from Ezekiel were a single contiguous section and later John inserted the encounter with Jesus as well as the seven churches. When John inserted the material he created the phrase "a voice like a trumpet" before and after the inserted content. The phrase is called an author's notation because it allows the author to keep track of the change so that the author can restore the text back to its original state.

Content Found in Ezekiel	Content in Revelation
Ezekiel is an exiled priest (Ezek 1:1-3)	**John is exiled on Patmos (Rev 1:9-10)**
1:1 Ezekiel was among the captives by the river Chebar.	1:9 I was on the isle of Patmos.
1:1-3 Ezekiel the exiled priest.	1:9 John exiled because of God's Word . . . of Jesus Christ.
1:3 The Lᴏʀᴅ's word came expressly to Ezekiel the priest.	1:10 John was in the Spirit on the Lord's day, and I heard behind me a loud voice.

Author's Notation ⟶

> **A Loud Voice Like a Trumpet Speaking - 1A**
> I heard behind me **a loud voice, like a trumpet speaking with me** (1:10).

> *The Encounter With Jesus in 1:12-20*

John inserted the equivalent of 2½ chapters of content between the two author's notations. As a result the continuity of the story from Ezekiel was broken. To keep track of the Ezekiel storyline John added the phrase "like a trumpet" to the Ezekiel text that was torn apart.

> *The Seven Churches in 2:1-3:22*

Author's Notation ⟶

> **A Loud Voice Like a Trumpet Speaking - 1B**
> After these things . . . **the first voice that I heard, like a trumpet speaking with me** (4:1).

Ezekiel's encounter with God in heaven (Ezek 1:4-2:2)	John's encounter with God on his throne (4:1-11)
1:5 Out of its center came . . . living creatures.	4:6 In the middle of the throne . . . four living creatures.
1:6 Each one of them had ~~four wings.~~	4:8 Each one of them having six wings.
1:10* Face of a lion.	4:7 Like a lion.
Face of an ox.	Like a calf.
Face of a man.	Like a face of a man.
Face of an eagle.	Like a flying eagle.
1:13 Lightning went out of the fire.	4:5 Out of the throne proceeded lightning, sounds, and thunder.
1:18 The four of them had their rims full of eyes all around.	4:6 Full of eyes before and behind.
1:22 Over the head . . . was the likeness of an expanse, like the awesome crystal to look on.	4:6 Before the throne was something like a sea of glass, similar to crystal.
1:26 The likeness of a throne.	4:2 There was a throne set in heaven, and one sitting on the throne.
1:26 The appearance of a sapphire stone.	4:3 Looked like a jasper stone and a sardius.
1:28 As the appearance of the rainbow.	4:3 There was a rainbow around the throne.

* Arranged in the order found in Revelation 4:7.

then once the wax had re-hardened, the correction could be etched in. The tablet itself was reusable since the wax could be scraped out and one could pour in new wax to prepare for another task.

Today, we might ask, "Why would someone use a wax tablet instead of papyrus?" The answer is practicality. Papyrus was certainly cheaper than a wax tablet but since an author must typically make several hundred edits to a story, the tablets in the long run would, in fact, be cheaper. The ability to reuse them and the easy method for correction were the main reasons why it was the primary writing medium for everyone from the King's scribes, down to the school child doing homework.[52]

The Way They Wrote in John's Time

Writing in the time of Revelation was very different than the way we write today. Today we have punctuation, both lower and upper case letters, spaces between every word, and visual distinctions to signal separate paragraphs. All of this contributes to a more enjoyable and easeful reading experience. In the time of Revelation however, there was no concept of placing spaces between the words, all the letters were in upper case and the lettering went from margin to margin without any paragraph separation.

The cover of this book features an image of a partial wax tablet from August 4, 186 CE (about 90 years after Revelation was published). The image tells us a lot about the process of writing on wax tablets. For example, writers would score each line before writing in order to ensure consistency in letter size. They used the entirety of the wax space for their writing, which left no margin to insert comments or room for page notations. This was different than the process of writing on papyrus, because users of papyrus left ample margins for possible editorial notations, regardless of the paper's size.[53] The likely reason that wax tablets did not have wide margins is because the scribe could easily melt the wax to make corrections, whereas removing ink from papyrus was much more difficult.

How Books Were Published in John's Time

Books were published differently in John's time than today due to production aspects, as well as the fact that it was not possible to maintain intellectual rights to a work. The physical production of the books (or scrolls) was an extremely labor-intensive and time-consuming process, which was usually done in a local scribal shop. It would start with the negotiation of how much each copy would cost the author, but in order to assess that the vendor would need to count the number of letters in the manuscript (which in this case consisted of a large stack of wax tablets), and based upon that information would then calculate how much material and time it would take to produce each book. The more skilled the writer the easier it would be to determine the scope of the project. When the sizes of the letters and tablets were uniform it made it much easier for the vendor to determine how much it would cost to transcribe the wax tablets to scroll or codex.[54] From there the vendor could determine the lowest price he was willing to accept and try to negotiate the highest price the writer would be willing to pay.

---

52   Colin H. Roberts and T. C. Skeat. *The Birth of the Codex*. (London: Oxford University Press, 1983), 11.

53   Raffaella Cribiore, *Writing, Teachers and Students in Graeco-Roman Egypt* (Atlanta: Scholars Press, 1996), 59-60. It should be noted that Cribiore points out that the blank areas of paprus seldom had comments or corrections on them.

54   Colin H. Roberts and T. C. Skeat. *The Birth of the Codex*. (London: Oxford University Press, 1983), 15–22 has the earliest mention of the codex in the first century CE and common in the fourth century CE. Revelation was written in 96 CE at the time when we are aware of the codex being used.

The process of transferring the text of the wax tablet to a scroll—or for that matter making a copy of a scroll—was very labor intensive. Each letter was done by hand, and a pen had to be dipped in ink to form each letter. This process would repeat itself letter after letter until the end of the manuscript. The process was even more difficult than today's since the text was all in the same case, had no spaces between letters and no punctuation. Therefore to make it easier, the author must have used uniform wax tablets to allow the scribes to have each line of text be likewise uniform. This would also provide a means of looking at the first and last letters of each line to see if any were missed or duplicated.

Obviously if the wax tablets used to construct a manuscript were not uniform in width then the scribe would have to transfer all of the text to a set of wax tablets that were uniform in width in order to produce a publication that was pleasing to the eye. Without the source material being uniform the transferring of the text would be a nightmare for the scribe.

Once the manuscript was finished the author could then put a price on it. In John's time, the production and sale of books were factors in determining the author's profit. However, the same process that the author used to mass-produce his manuscript could be duplicated by others. So once a manuscript left the author's hand there was nothing that could stop the person who purchased it from repeating the same process that the author used, and reproduce his work. It is not too difficult to imagine some traveling merchant from Ephesus in Rome buying a newly published manuscript and upon returning to his home in Ephesus, mass-producing the manuscript, thereby making a profit without the time and expense of writing it. In this type of publishing environment, the author would want to produce as many books as he could afford for the initial sell of his work. Obviously the more books produced the more expensive it would be, and the longer it would take. This may have caused problems if financial and/or time constraints were a factor.

How John Wrote Revelation

Perhaps the greatest advantage of the wax tablet is the flexibility in how books like Revelation could be written. Revelation was written two different ways, which we will describe as being written in the "vertical" and in the "horizontal." When we refer to Revelation as being written in the vertical we can think of how we write today by formulating a short story from beginning to end. When writing in the vertical we are more concerned with how the story flows and how characters progress. Since the story is meant to be read from beginning to end, the writing and editing of it is done in a linear fashion.

When writing in the horizontal, however, the author's primary concern is forming content over several sections of a book which tells its own story. The common literary method was the use of parallels which are when the content of two sections follows either the same or a reverse order. This book will define a parallel where both sections follow the same order as a "simple parallel." Where the two sections follow a reverse order we will refer to it as a "complex parallel." In both simple and complex parallels each element of the parallel can be complementary to or form an opposite with its corresponding element.

Revelation is such a book that every section has been modified or created by the use of forming a parallel with another section. To maintain literary variety, John mixes simple and complex parallels as well as making each element either complementary or opposite to each other. Thus the complexity of documenting all the parallels in Revelation would be a monumental work in itself.

How Wax Tablets Were Used to Form Parallels

Below is an illustration adapted for the modern reader* showing how John probably used two wax tablets to form a simple and a complex distant parallel. By placing two wax tablets side by side the writer can compare one with the other and validate that the content agrees with the purpose. In this case they both contain parallels which connect the two in some way.

The Fifth Seal (Rev 6:9-11)   **The Fifth Bowl (Rev 16:10-1)**

6:9 When he opened the **fifth seal**, I saw **underneath the altar** the souls of **those who had been killed for the Word of God, and for the testimony of the Lamb** which they had. 6:10 **They cried with a loud voice, saying, "How long, Master, the holy and true, until you judge and avenge our blood on those who dwell on the earth?"** 6:11 A long white robe was given to each of them. **They were told that they should rest yet for a while**, until their fellow servants and their brothers, who would also be killed even as they were, should complete their course.

16:10 The **fifth** poured out his **bowl** on the **throne of the beast**, and his kingdom was darkened. **They gnawed their tongues because of the pain**, 16:11 and **they blasphemed the God of heaven because of their pains and their sores. They didn't repent of their works.**

How the Fifth Seal (Rev 6:9-11) Parallels the Fifth Bowl (Rev 16:10-1)

The Simple Parallel

A. The Fifth Seal (Rev 6:9).

B. Underneath the Altar (Rev 6:9).

The Complex Parallel

A. Those who had been killed for the word of God and the testimony of the Lamb (6:9).

B. They cried with a loud voice saying, "How long, Master, the holy and true, until you judge and avenge our blood on those who dwell on the earth?"

C. They were told that they should rest yet for a little while (Rev 6:11).

The Simple Parallel

A. The fifth bowl (Rev 16:10).

B. On the throne of the beast (Rev 16:10).

The Complex Parallel

C. They gnawed their tongues because of the pain (Rev 16:10).

B. They blasphemed the God of heaven because of their pains and their sores (Rev 16:11).

A. They did not repent of their works (Rev 16:11).

The chart below is another way to look at how the fifth seal and the fifth bowl relate to each other. Note the opposite positional relationship between the two groups of followers.

	The Followers of God in Heaven	The Followers of the Beast on Earth
Location	Under the altar of God in heaven.	On the throne of the beast on Earth.
Suffering	Those killed because of the word of God.	They gnawed their tongues because of their pain.
Their Response	They plea to God to bring pain on those who caused their deaths.	They blasphemed God in heaven for their pains and sores on Earth.
Their State	They were told to rest because of their faith.	They did not repent.

*Based upon Greek manuscripts and letters, Greek authors such as John would not have used spaces between the words, mixed cased letters and definitely no verse references. The wax tablet may have been bigger, containing many seals or bowls, or it may have had some notations of how it is placed in the greater picture of Revelation, we simply do not know.

The use of wax tablets made writing in the horizontal a much easier task. John simply had to keep each story on one wax tablet and when he wanted to form a parallel with one section (wax tablet) all he had to do was to lay the two wax tablets he wanted to form a parallel with side by side. To best understand the process that John used, we will examine how John harmonized the fifth seal and the fifth bowl.[55] By placing the wax tablet containing the fifth seal alongside the wax tablet containing the fifth bowl, John could easily make adjustments to both tablets to form the desired parallels. In the case of the fifth bowl and the fifth seal, John provides plenty of contrasts between those in heaven and those on earth. For those in heaven, they are beneath the altar[56] (or the lowest part of heaven) while those on earth are above the beast's throne.[57] Those in heaven cry out to God to take revenge on those who caused their deaths on earth[58] and those on earth blaspheme God because of the pain he inflicts on them.[59] There are many more parallels between the fifth seal and fifth bowl as well as there are many parallels that form between the fifth trumpet[60] and fifth church.[61] Using wax tablets made this type of writing possible and efficient.

When we talk about writing in the horizontal to form parallels we must look at it not as simply forming parallels but also as forming a story that spans the parallels. John simply wrote many stories in Revelation horizontally which go undetected today due to a lack of understanding of this method of writing. A good example of how John maintains a plot across parallels can be seen in the story of the believers and the non-believers found in the fifth church, fifth seal, fifth trumpet, fifth bowl and the marriage of the lamb.[62]

John also had the flexibility to form rich sets of simple and complex parallels to create mental stimulation for the reader. This form of writing provides a means of interweaving stories with clues that tell the reader where one story emerges again in the overall storyline. For example, John describes the time of judgment in terms of the hour or day of a particular judgment. In the sixth church, sixth seal, sixth trumpet, and sixth bowl John alternates between the hour of and the day of judgment. The alternating day and hour with the parallel of the sixth church, sixth seal, sixth trumpet, and sixth bowl provides the reader with a clue to read them as a contiguous story.[63]

So far we have only seen a very small portion of the easiest parallels. Later in this book we will explore how John formed parallels in previous drafts, and when they were removed as well as how we know they were removed. We will see how we can determine his purpose for a section by seeing how he formed parallels with other sections. After all, this is the way that John is telling the story so it only makes sense that examining the parallels would be the best way to understand John's writing.

The Advantage of Writing in the Horizontal

Beyond what we have already covered, the advantage of writing in the horizontal is twofold. First it allows the writer to bulk up his work in the formation of parallels. The author can make a parallel to an existing section or create a new section by creating a parallel with a section that already exists. Either way, material

---

55   See Rev 6:9-11; Rev 16:10-1 in the illustration"How Wax Tablets Were Used to Form Parallels" on page xli.
56   Rev 6:9.
57   Rev 16:10.
58   Rev 6:10.
59   Rev 16:11.
60   Rev 9:1-11.
61   Rev 3:1-13.
62   See "The Story of the Fifth Church" on page 282.
63   See "The Story of the Sixth Church" on page 287.

The Conflation of Ezekiel and Isaiah's Encounter With God

The chart below is an example of how John conflated Ezekiel's account in heaven and Isaiah's account in heaven. In so doing, John assigned the worshiping role of the seraphim to the living creatures (Isa 6:3). John also changed the physical characteristics of Ezekiel's living creatures from four faces to one face and from four wings to six wings to match Isaiah's encounter (Ezek 1:6; Isa 6:2; Rev 4:6, 8).

	Content Found in Ezekiel and Isaiah		Content Found in Revelation (Ordered by Isaiah and then Revelation)
Isa 6:1	I saw THE LORD sitting on a throne.	4:2	There was a throne set in heaven, and one sitting on the throne.
Ezek 1:28	A rainbow around the throne.	4:3	A rainbow around the throne.
Ezek 1:26	Throne appearance like sapphire.	4:3	Throne appearance like jasper.
Ezek 1:22	Crystal expanse.	4:6	Sea of glass like crystal.
Ezek 1:5	The living creatures with four faces.	4:6	Four living creatures.
Ezek 1:6 Isa 6:2	~~Each having four faces.~~ The seraphim had one face.	4:6	Each having one face.
Ezek 1:10	Face of a lion, ox, man, and eagle.*	4:7	Face of a lion, calf, man, and eagle.
Ezek 1:6 Isa 6:2	~~Each having four wings.~~ Each having six wings.	4:8	Each having six wings.
Ezek 1:18	Full of eyes all around.	4:8	Full of eyes around and within.
Isa 6:3	They said "Holy, holy, holy is THE LORD . . . ."	4:8	They said "Holy, holy, holy is THE LORD . . . ."
Isa 6:3	"The whole earth is filled with his glory."	4:8	God created all things.

* Arranged in the order found in Revelation 4:7

from one parallel will get copied or migrated to a second parallel and thus the work as a whole will increase in size. The second is that the author can express connections to the reader/listener in a creative way that incorporates intellectual exercises in both the creation of and consumption of the work. The end result is a book that contains many puzzles to the reader/listener to the extent that the reader cannot identify or exhaust them all. In Revelation, for example, almost every section has in some way a literary connection with several other sections which makes it extremely difficult to write an exhaustive guide to a book that has less than 10,000 Greek words.

A second advantage is that content from a later passage can be connected to content formed in an earlier passage. For example each of the seven churches is given a reward for overcoming, and the reader will encounter many of them again later in Revelation. For John it would have been easy to lay one wax tablet which described an attribute Jesus was given pertaining to salvation or a description of a saint in heaven and another tablet with one of the seven churches. Once laid, he can now copy material from one tablet to the other.

The Disadvantage of Writing in the Horizontal

The disadvantage of writing in the horizontal is that the author cannot write perfect vertical prose until the final stage of the writing process. It makes no sense to write a section in perfect vertical prose only to have that work overwritten with a new formation of a parallel between that section and another. There needs to be a finishing phase in which the sum of all the work is edited to form the desired story from a vertical perspective.

The second disadvantage of writing in the horizontal is the difficulty of keeping track of the parallels from one section with another section. As one section parallels another and the parallel of that section forms parallels with others, more and more parallels will be formed. The sheer number of parallels from section to section would cause the earlier parallels to become out of sync, thus they would have to be refreshed or abandoned. It is just impossible to form perfect parallels across the many nested parallels that John formed in Revelation. For many sections of Revelation, John has at least four separate parallels, so if he wanted to refresh all parallels after the formation of a new parallel the labor involved would have been a complete redo of the book. Even if he refreshed all the parallels, by the time he finished his original parallel formation the process would end up out of sync.

The difficulty of refreshing parallels becomes even more pronounced when John forms a parallel with the content of one section and then later removes the content from one of the parallels and thus loses the complement. Revelation has many odd descriptions that leave the reader in the dark as to what the intentions of them were. Since the vast majority of Revelation's content is expressed in at least one other place we can assume that John intended everything to be mentioned at least twice. The RDH will validate that assumption but in this section the removal of content or a radical adjustment would mean that parallels would be grossly affected by lack of complementary items.

A third disadvantage of writing in the horizontal has to do with content that repeats but expresses a different story. Imagine stacks of wax tablets from which John can remove any two, and place them side by side to adjust the text so that the two wax tablets tell a story in the parallel that links them. Now imagine when John uses multiple sources of the Hebrew Scriptures that use similar imagery or when John uses similar imagery to form content of a single action. What John will end up with are two different descriptions nearby that tell different stories of the same events. For example there are two sets of witnessing the New Jerusalem descending: one is described as "adorned like a bride" and the other described as the "bride of Lamb descending."[64]

A fourth disadvantage is a logical extension of the last chapter. As we saw, John used six primary Hebrew Scripture sources to formulate the finished product that we have today. Each draft brought a major change into the previous draft and in some of the drafts John performed many parallels. With the constant shifting of material and parallels being formed content does not always get copied but is sometimes migrated. As the process continues the connections between the source material and the finished product becomes lost or at least scattered to the point that it is difficult to reconstruct. This may or may not have been a problem for authors using this methodology, but it is a one-way process in that each draft would be more difficult to revert to an earlier draft.

How John Formed Each Sentence

When John was making drafts of Revelation he began almost every sentence with the conjunction καὶ (the Greek word for "and") with notable exceptions found at the beginning of major sections and the first chapter. Writing this way allowed him to shuffle the wax tablets or sentences around and still retain the

---

64   Rev 21:1-8 describes one scene where John witnesses the New Jerusalem descending and Rev 21:9-27 describes another scene.

How John Created the Four Horsemen Through Thematic Conflation

The bulk of the material for the four horsemen was the product of two drafts. The Ezekiel-Isaiah draft provided most of the content for each of the four horsemen. The Zechariah draft provided the imagery of the four chariots but John changed them to the four horsemen to match the weaponry of his time. The last element John added was the great sword which came from Isa 27:1.

Ezek	From the Ezekiel-Isaiah Draft	Zech	Elements Found in Zech 6:1-8	Rev	Conflated in Revelation
		6:3	Chariot with white horses (third chariot).	6:1	The rider of the white horse.
5:16	God will send evil arrows of famine.				He had a bow [a bow implies arrows].
		6:2	Chariot with red horses (first chariot).	6:4	The rider of the red horse.
				6:4	He had a great sword (from Isa 27:1).
		6:2	Chariot with black horses (second chariot).	6:5	The rider of the black horse.
5:16	God will increase the famine on them and will break the staff of bread.			6:6	A quart of wheat for a denarius (day's wage) and three quarts of barley for a denarius (day's wage).
		6:3	Chariot with dappled horses (fourth chariot).	6:8	The rider of the pale horse.
5:17	God will send famine and evil animals, and they shall bereave you; and pestilence . . . and bring the sword on them.			6:8	He will kill with the sword, famine, death, and wild animals.

flow of the text. So with each Hebrew Scripture phrase copied, John would begin it with χαὶ ("and"). We know this because of the excessive use of this word found in Revelation like those found in other writings that were constructed similarly, such as Luke-Acts. What we find in Luke-Acts is that Luke uses the word χαὶ 1,349 times out of the 19,482 total words in Luke (6.9% of the time) and in Acts 1,010 times out of 18,405 (5.5% of the time). In the book of Revelation we see excessive use of the Greek word χαὶ used mainly as a means to separate clauses. John uses χαὶ 1,109 times out of the 9,851 total words used in Revelation (11% of the time).

The process of removing the unnecessary instances of χαὶ from a work would begin in the editing of the vertical stage of writing. What we find when we read the book of Revelation in Greek is that χαὶ is used less often at the beginning of each verse in chapter 1 compared to any other portion in Revelation. This signifies that the author of Revelation stopped the editing process, or the earliest copyist stopped the clean-up process before it was finished, to leave us with this final version of Revelation. In contrast, within Luke-Acts we find a consistent presence of verses beginning with χαὶ, and this is something we expect from a finished work.

Revelation: An Unfinished Work

Revelation is by any standard an unfinished work and we can see this in a variety of ways. The final revision of Revelation would have taken place in the vertical, since with the predominant emphasis on parallel formation with every passage it would not have been an effective use of time to write perfect prose for each parallel formed only to have to rewrite it each time John formed another parallel with a different passage. The final phase of cleaning up Revelation would have been in the vertical after everything that John wanted to link together was linked via parallel formations.

Most scholars on Revelation consider the Greek to be unrefined although their opinions vary as to why. The theories range from suggesting that Greek was not John's first language, to proposing that it was because this was common for the time.[65] The RDH views the inconsistencies as the product of predominately writing in the horizontal without a proper finishing phase that focuses on the continuity of the story from a vertical perspective.

Then there is the question of why John would have published an unfinished version of Revelation. One possible answer is that John may have died before completing the final edit, and perhaps his family published it on his behalf. Another possible circumstance is that Revelation was written to express that Domitian was the beast and he died before the book was finished. Perhaps certain events unfolded which forced his hand in publishing the book. He could have had a financial backer that was willing to pay for a copy or a set of copies. Perhaps he needed to return the wax tablets he'd used to construct Revelation. The circumstances which led John to publish an unfinished version of Revelation will be explored more fully in the DnD.

John Was Most Likely a Skilled Writer but Rushed to Publish

We can assume that John was probably a skilled writer but we have no way of ever validating that. The sum of this book will explore the mechanical and literary process that John used to construct Revelation. We know at least that John was very talented in producing books in this literary style, so we can say with some certainty that he was probably a talented writer as well,[66] and that the end result would have likely been of very high quality if he'd had the time to finish the book properly.

Many Illustrations

To aid in the discovery process, this book is full of charts that are so encompassing that one could simply read the charts and ignore the text of the book. The charts are more a reflection of my vocation as a software engineer who loves charts and diagrams. In this book I wanted a means whereby the reader can see how John used the Hebrew Scriptures to formulate Revelation in a side-by-side manner. I wanted to allow the reader to see each draft and understand how each was formed. The easiest way is to illustrate them, so as a result hundreds of never-seen-before charts were created and placed in this book to assist you.

One of the major reasons why I self-published this book was so that I could have complete flexibility in and control over how I structured it. Publishers are concerned with page count, and charts increase page

---

65 Aune, WBC, Beale, *Revelation*, 101-7; Osborne, Revelation, 24-5.

66 Jürgen Roloff, *The Revelation of John: A Continental Commentary*. (Minneapolis: Fortress Press, 1993), 12. He notes that John knew Greek fairly well and that he was trying to make it sound like the Hebrew Scriptures.

count exponentially. While many of the charts can be reduced to a single sentence, pictures have their own magic and can express things that prose cannot easily convey.

As with any tool, though, there are limitations to what they present and the charts are no exception. The very purpose of this is to show how Revelation was constructed step by step. As with any book, paper, or work of writing, text will get shuffled in the process through each phase of construction. Many of the charts represent a logical snapshot in the phase that John was writing the book of Revelation, and therefore the earliest drafts will be displayed and ordered by the source material which will make the content of Revelation look disjointed. As we get to the later drafts we will see a transition from the draft text being disjointed and the text of Revelation becoming more like the published version we have today.

Chapter 1: How John Wrote Revelation

Introduction to the Revelation Draft Hypothesis

Biblical scholars are almost in unanimous agreement that John borrowed heavily from the Hebrew Scriptures in the construction of the book of Revelation. In this book I will provide a comprehensive theory as to the order and construction of Revelation which I will call: The Revelation Draft Hypothesis (RDH). My theory is that John created Revelation in five successive drafts based on the Hebrew Scriptures as follows: (1) the Ezekiel-Isaiah draft (EID), (2) the Zechariah draft (ZrD), (3) the Deuteronomy-Joshua draft (DJD), (4) The Exodus draft (ExD), and finally, (5) the Daniel draft (DnD).

Revelation is full of mystery, but John left many clues as to how he constructed it; some are fairly obvious, some more subtle, and some are deeply buried within complex parallels and reversals of the source material's original order. We will walk through his compilation process step by step. We will examine each of the five drafts for its original material, and then for how the new material's placement caused the earlier draft to be edited, dropped or rearranged (or, in a few cases, apparently, mistakenly left in place!). We must remember that since the original draft document(s) no longer exists, each draft document I refer to should be thought of as a hypothetical document.

So much of the unique imagery found within Revelation is the direct result of the process through which John created the book. For example, one of the most well-known yet least understood symbols is that of the four horsemen. When we see how they were constructed we are given a better idea of their purpose. Within just the first three drafts of Revelation we get the sense that they represent actions of God.[1] In each of the three primary drafts used to construct Revelation the actions were of God or of those who served

---

1   See "How John Created the Four Horsemen in the First Three Drafts" on page 3.

The Summary of the Drafts

The table below summarizes each of the drafts in regards to how they were imported into the final product of Revelation and the content that they brought into Revelation. Each mechanical process was different from the other drafts and consistent in the draft itself. The content added in each draft expanded the previous draft's storyline to become the Revelation that we have today.

	The Mechanical Process	**The Content Added to Revelation**
The Ezekiel-Isaiah Draft (EID)	John leveraged the simple parallel between the bulk of Ezekiel and Isaiah 6:12 - 29:21. The Ezekiel side of the Ezekiel-Isaiah parallel were judgments against Jerusalem. The Isaiah side of the Ezekiel-Isaiah parallel was the restoration through Jesus.	• The encounter in heaven. • The bulk of the judgments. • The destruction of Jerusalem and Tyre. • The defeat of the great dragon. • Gog and Magog. • The New Jerusalem. • Hope through Jesus the son. • The saints in heaven scenes. • Specific content to some of the seven churches.
The Zechariah Draft (ZrD)	John rearranged and rewrote the Ezekiel-Isaiah Draft to conform to the reverse order of Zechariah 1:1-12:10.	• Jesus as the high priest. • Satan. • The judgment passages, four horsemen (first four seals), four winds (first four trumpets) and the four horns (first four bowls).
The Deuteronomy-Joshua Draft (DJD)	John started at the end of the ZrD and inserted content from Deuteronomy 29:1 to Joshua 6:27 in between the wax tablets.	• Jesus as the military leader. • Depicted the destruction of Jerusalem with the same significance as the destruction of Jericho in Joshua. • The expansion of churches, seals, trumpets and bowls from four to seven. • The roles of the priests were given to angels.
The Exodus Draft (ExD)	John used the servicing of the tabernacle as a way of organizing the Deuteronomy-Joshua Draft.	• The making of all believers into priests and kings. • The seven candlesticks as the Menorah. • The 24 elders as two sets of the bread of presence (the twelve tribes of Israel and the twelve apostles). • The burning of the incense for the trumpets and the bowls. • The Height of the New Jerusalem to form the Most Holy Place. • The earthquakes imagery on the seventh seal, seventh trumpet, and seventh bowl.
The Daniel Draft (DnD)	John used material from Daniel to describe and identify the beast.	• Many new descriptions of Jesus. • The defining of the beast. • The addition of the book of life. • The second death.

him.[2] We have barely scratched the surface of the four horsemen within the first three drafts, but in the next three drafts a precise pictures emerges.

The RDH in essence is that John created Revelation by parallel formation from the Hebrew Scriptures and other works. The process of parallel formation was to construct a different type of parallel within each of the draft. For example, in one draft John formulated the source material to create a simple parallel, while in the next he formulated the previous draft to resemble a complex parallel with the source text. Each subsequent draft was not just limited to reshaping the previous draft into a new pattern, it also included new

---

2   Ezek 5:16-7 God's actions on the Israelites. Isa 27:1 God slays the great dragon and the four horsemen secure Israel for God.

How John Created the Four Horsemen in the First Three Drafts

The bulk of the material for the four horsemen was the product of two drafts. The Ezekiel-Isaiah draft provided most of the content for the description of each of the four horsemen. The Zechariah draft provided the imagery of the four chariots but John changed them to the four horsemen to match the weaponry of his time. The last element John added was the great sword which came from Isa 27:1.

Ezek	From the Ezekiel-Isaiah Draft	Zech	Elements Found in Zech 6:1-8	Rev	How John Combined Them in Revelation
		6:3	Chariot with white horses (third chariot).	6:1	The rider of the white horse.
5:16	God will send evil arrows of famine.				He had a bow [a bow implies arrows].
		6:2	Chariot with red horses (first chariot).	6:4	The rider of the red horse.
				6:4	He had a great sword (from Isa 27:1).
		6:2	Chariot with black horses (second chariot).	6:5	The rider of the black horse.
5:16	God will increase the famine on them and will break the staff of bread.			6:6	A quart of wheat for a denarius (day's wage) and three quarts of barley for a denarius.
		6:3	Chariot with dappled horses (fourth chariot).	6:8	The rider of the pale horse.
5:17	God will send famine and evil animals, and they shall bereave you; and pestilence . . . and bring the sword on them.			6:8	He will kill with the sword, famine, pestilence, and wild animals

imagery which expanded the story. The structural changes and content enhancement provided John with a serendipitous approach to the production of Revelation in which the process dictated how he would write it. Due to this, it is very possible that John never knew what the final text of Revelation would have looked like when he first started.

The Drafts

Each draft is a product of three literary actions starting with the form and content of the previous draft, with the exception of the first draft. First, each draft varies due to the different mechanical processes used to construct it. Second, a new draft adds content that will be used to extend the previous draft, focusing on a major point in the previous draft. Third, John consistently maintains imagery from previous drafts, and rarely drops them, so in some cases he stretches or adapts the meaning to the new material. This, as we shall see, causes some images to have multiple meanings; i.e. the sum of the previous drafts. Thus we need to look at each draft in its entirety, to see how it is formulated and what content is added, so that we may develop an understanding of the "revelation" that John was attempting to show.[3]

---

3   See "The Summary of the Drafts" on page 2.

The following sections name and provide a brief description of John's drafts in the order of construction according to the RDH. Each draft will be discussed in depth in its own chapter. Each draft will also show how John formed literary connections in the form of simple and complex parallels to connect material from various sources of the previous completed draft into what would have been, at the time of its completion, the completed book of Revelation. What we call the book of Revelation today is the final published version of the RDH process.

The Ezekiel-Isaiah Draft (EID)

The EID is in essence a simple parallel between the whole of Ezekiel and the bulk of the content within Isaiah 6:1 - 29:24, and forms an opposite.[4] The Ezekiel side of the parallel was the story of judgment against God's people for having abandoned the commandments of God. The Isaiah side of the parallel was the story of God raising a new holy people, beginning with Jesus. In order to portray Jesus, John took all the people or personifications found in Isaiah that fit John's idea and conveyed them as descriptions of Jesus. One example of this is the portrayal of the woman with child,[5] in how the child is taken to heaven before he can say "mommy" or "daddy,"[6] as well as the imagery of this child ruling and being called God.[7] Perhaps two of the most unusual descriptions of Jesus that came from Isaiah is his being identified as the bright morning star, which came from Isaiah's description of Babylon.[8] The second is the two-edged sword that came from the rod of Jesus' mouth, conflated with a synonym of the "great sword" from Isaiah's account of God defeating the great dragon.[9]

The nature of the EID was not to become a finished product but a finished parallel. In it John made numerous tweaks and a few content shifts to provide the best parallel for the ZrD. Therefore the EID should be considered not only a draft but the first phase of the ZrD.

The Zechariah Draft (ZrD)

For the ZrD, John took the EID and rearranged it to form a complex parallel (the reverse order) of Zechariah 1:1-12:10.[10] In constructing the ZrD, John drastically rearranged the previous drafts into the form we have today. This process was a lengthy one. John made many changes, and the nature of these changes required him to create a specialized notation that he used to document the shifts in material.[11] I refer to these notations as "author's notations" and discuss them in depth in later chapters. It is largely due to John's consistency in how he did this that allows us to see how he created the entire work.

---

4   See "How John Created the Ezekiel-Isaiah Draft" on page 7.

5   Isa 7:14 became "A great sign was seen in heaven: a woman . . . She was with child. She cried out in pain, laboring to give birth." Rev 12:1-2.

6   Isa 8:4 "Before the child knows how to say, 'my father,' and, 'my mother,' the riches of Damascus and the plunder of Samaria will be carried away by the king of Assyria." became before the dragon could devour him he was taken to heaven in Rev 12:4-5.

7   Isa 9:6-7 tells us that a child is born and that child becomes God and rules forever which becomes "She gave birth to a son, a male child, who is to rule all the nations with a rod of iron. Her child was caught up to God, and to his throne." in Rev 12:5.

8   Isa 14:12; Rev 22:16.

9   "Rod of his mouth" from Isa 11:4; "Great sword" from Isa 27:1.

10   See "How John Created the Zechariah Draft (ZrD)" on page 8.

11   See "The First Use of the Author's Notation" on page 72.

With the ZrD John added a great deal of content and structure to the EID by focusing on the rewards for those who serve Jesus and those who "pierced him."[12] Jesus was given a coronation similar to that of Joshua the high priest of Zechariah, where people would come from all corners of the world to serve in the temple being built in heaven.[13]

The origin and placement of the judgments came from the ZrD, however there were, at this time, only three sets of four judgments; the four horsemen,[14] the first four trumpets[15] and the first four bowls.[16] The later three were added in the DJD.

The ZrD was also the first draft to include Satan, portraying him as being kicked out of heaven and attacking a woman in Revelation 12:1-17. The imagery of Isaiah 14:12-7 is where the King of Babylon is trying to make himself higher than God and thus he was thrown out of heaven and placed into Sheol. The ZrD simply takes the imagery of Satan being kicked out of Jerusalem[17] and conflates it with Isa 14:12-7 where we have the imagery of Satan kicked out of heaven[18] and placed in the abyss.[19]

The Deuteronomy-Joshua Draft (DJD)

The DJD is the opposite of the ZrD in that John starts from the end of the ZrD and reads Deuteronomy 29:1 to Joshua 6:27 forward. As he reads forwards in the selected Deuteronomy and Joshua passages he is looking for places to put them in as he goes backwards in the ZrD. Sometimes, John can make adjustments while other times he inserts wax tablets between the ZrD to form new content.[20]

When John arrives at the coronation of Jesus from the ZrD,[21] he then goes forward making the four horsemen and the four winds into the four seals and the four trumpets. After that, he expands the seals to seven judgments with the seventh containing the seven trumpets. By arranging the seven trumpets nested in the seven seals John is recreating the seven marches around Jericho and the seven priests blowing the seven trumpets prior to the destruction of Jericho.

After John imported the texts from Deuteronomy and Joshua, he then began the procedure of making everything in the DJD link to other passages via multiple parallels. Each parallel allowed John to add more content within the DJD and also revealed the passages that he thought should be connected together. In this phase John must have created hundreds of parallels. As each parallel was created, unfortunately, a previous parallel would become malformed, which reveals the process of his writing methodology.

---

12   Zech 12:10; Rev 1:7.
13   Zech 6:9-15; Rev 5:1-14.
14   Zech 6:1-8 as the four chariots; Rev 6:1-8.
15   Zech 6:1-8 as the four winds; Rev 8:7-12.
16   Zech 1:18-21.
17   Zech 3:1-2.
18   Rev 12:7-9.
19   Rev 20:1-3.
20   See "How John Created the Deuteronomy-Joshua Draft" on page 9 for the path that John used to create the DJD. It should be noted that each of the texts derived from Deuteronomy and Joshua in the illustration were placed on new wax tablets and inserted between existing wax tablets from the ZrD.
21   Rev 5:1-14.

The Exodus Draft (ExD)

For the ExD John uses the story of the coronation of Joshua (the high priest from the book of Zechariah) and attributes it to Jesus. He then uses material from Exodus which details the duties of the high priest in servicing the tabernacle (and later the temple).[22] He expands this by taking God's promise to Moses that the Israelites will be a kingdom of priests,[23] to making all believers kings and priests.[24] From this we get the phrase "the kingdom of the world is now the kingdom of God."[25] Exodus 19:6 was specifically used to extend the DJD by equating the destruction of Jerusalem with the destruction of Jericho.

The ExD takes the imagery of the lightning, sounds, thunder and earthquake which are present when Moses receives the ten commandments on Mount Sinai and uses them in the seventh seal, seventh trumpet and seventh bowl. However, since John had already used the trumpet as a symbol (the seven trumpets) he used hail and the earthquake to increase the intensity of the judgments.[26]

The Daniel Draft (DnD)

The DnD was the last draft and added two key items: identification of the beast and clues to the date of the vision and subsequently the book itself.[27] The DnD added the majority of the beast's imagery as well as many of the descriptions of Jesus found in both the beginning and end of the book.[28] Daniel became the source of all texts dealing with eternal punishment as well as a few of the references to the Lamb's Book of Life, which became the primary encouragement to remain faithful to the message of Revelation.

One of the most intriguing additions was the clues about the beast's identity,[29] and therefore the urgency of the events that were to unfold for the contemporary readers of Revelation. John creates this urgency by incorporating the imagery of Daniel into the mighty angel passage in Revelation.[30] It is there where the angel swears that the events which are foretold in Revelation will happen in the near future if not immediately.[31] It is the placement of Revelation 10:6 before the destruction of Jerusalem (Rev 11:8) which enables us to correctly identify who the beast is in Revelation 13:8; 17:9-12.[32]

22　See "How John Created the Exodus Draft (ExD)" on page 10.
23　Exod 19:6.
24　Rev 1:5; 5:10.
25　Rev 11:15; 12:10.
26　Exod 19:16-9; Rev 8:5; 11:19; 16:18-21.
27　See "How John Created the Daniel Draft (DnD)" on page 11.
28　Rev 1:12 - 3:22; 20:11-7; see "The Descriptions of Jesus, John's Worshiping of the Two Angel, and Broken Parallels (Dan 10:1-21; Rev 1:9-17; 19:9-21; 22:6-15)" on page 222.
29　See "The Two Publication Dates of Revelation and Who Is the Beast?" on page 231.
30　Dan 12:1-9; Rev 10:1-11.
31　Rev 10:6.
32　See "The Two Publication Dates of Revelation and Who Is the Beast?" on page 231.

How John Created the Ezekiel-Isaiah Draft

The Ezekiel-Isaiah draft was a simple parallel comprised of two columns of wax tablets based upon common content found within Ezekiel and Isaiah. The Ezekiel side of the parallel is one of judgment against a rebellious people and how God dealt with them with the destruction of Jerusalem and the temple. The Isaiah side of the parallel tells the story of God raising a new holy seed beginning with Jesus and ending with the triumph of the faithful.

Ezekiel Side	Isaiah Side

Ezekiel Introduce (Ezek 1:1-3)

EP1 Ezekiel's Experience in Heaven • God on the throne (Ezek 1:26-2:2). • The living creatures (Ezek 1:4-26). • The scroll (Ezek 2:8 - 3:3).	**IP1 Isaiah's Experience in Heaven** • God on the throne (Isa 6:1). • The seraphim (Isa 6:2-7). • The altar that removes iniquity (Isa 6:6-7).
EP2 Ezekiel's Mission • Gods do not hear or understand (Ezek 3:4-7). • Say "Thus says the Lord" (Ezek 2:4; 3:27).	**IP2 Isaiah's Mission** • God's people do not hear or understand (Isa 6:9-10). • "Go, and tell this people" (Isa 6:9).
EP3 Ezekiel Appointed as a Watchman • God's people are like briers, thorns and scorpions (Ezek 2:6), God hardens Ezekiel's head (Ezek 3:8-9). • Ezekiel appointed as a watchman (Ezek 3:16-27). • End of three ministries and its relation to the siege of Jerusalem (Ezek 4:5-8).	**IP3 The New Seed (Jesus the Child)** • When a tenth of the city is burned God will raise up a new holy seed (Isa 6:10-13). • The sign of a woman with child (Isa 7:14-6). • Three phases of the child's life is connected to the destruction of Jerusalem (Isa 7:14 - 10:34).
EP4 The Judgments by the Nations • The nations will strike in thirds (Ezek 5:2). • God's people give evil decrees (Ezek 5:6-10). • The day of the Lord (Ezek 7:7) where God will destroy those without the mark of God on their forehead (Ezek 9:1-11).	**IP4 The Judgments by Jesus** • Jesus will strike in thirds (Ezek 5:16-7). • God's people receive evil decrees (Isa 10:1-19). • The day of the Lord (Isa 13:9) where God will darken the sky (Isa 13:10; Ezek 32:7-10).
EP5 The Glory of God Flees Jerusalem • Babylon comes, the glory of God flees (Ezek 10:1- 22). • Israel at war with nations (Ezek 11:1-13). • The Israelites are taken to all nations (Ezek 11:16 - 12:28).	**IP5 The Glory of God Triumphs in Heaven (Jesus the True Morning Star)** • The glory of God triumphs in heaven (Isa 14:1- 12). • The nations are at peace (Isa 14:18). • The remnants of Israel return (Isa 14:32).
EP6 Jerusalem the Mother of God's Children • The harlot wears expensive clothing (Ezek 16:10-1). • The harlot kills God's children (Ezek 16:20). • The harlot is the mother of God's children (Ezek 16:20).	**IP6 Jesus as Eliakim the Father of God's Children** • Eliakim wears expensive clothing (Isa 22: 21). • Eliakim saves God's children (Isa 22:21). • Eliakim is the father of God's children (Isa 22:21).
EP7 Tyre • Wealth from trading with other nations (Ezek 27:12-22). • Their riches became what ruined them (Ezek 27:27). • Merchants lamenting, Tyre's destruction (Ezek 27:27-28:2).	**IP7 Tyre (Jesus, a Certain King)** • Wealth from trading with other nations (Isa 23:1-17). • Post-destruction's wealth will be righteousness (Isa 23:18). • Saints rejoicing over Tyre's destruction (Isa 25:1-6).
EP8 The Slaying of the Great Dragon • With a sword (Ezek 29:8). • The great dragon finds comfort in his army (Ezek 32:31).	**IP8 Jesus Slays the Great Dragon** • The rod of his mouth (Isa 11:4), a great sword (Isa 27:1). • Jesus musters his army from the whole world (Isa 11:10-6).
EP9 Jerusalem Attacked by Gog and Magog • Nations come from the north to destroy Jerusalem and God destroys the nations (Ezek 38:1 - 39:29).	**IP9 Jerusalem Attacked by a Multitude of Nations** • Nations come from all over the world to destroy Jerusalem and God destroys the nations (Isa 29:1-21).
EP10 The City of God • Jerusalem will be a city that God and the righteous will live in (Ezek 40:1 - 48:35).	**IP10 The Holy City of Jerusalem** • Various descriptions of the Holy City of Jerusalem scattered throughout Isaiah.

How John Created the Zechariah Draft (ZrD)

In this illustration the left two columns represent the order and process in which John dealt with the EID wax tablets shown on page 7. The right column represents how the wax tablets were moved to satisfy the content found in the left column. At this point in the construction, the bulk of Ezekiel is arranged in the order that we find in the PVR.

The Order and Process John Moved the Wax Tablets	The Tablets John Moved or Used

Z1   Whom They Have Pierced They Shall Mourn (Zech 12:10; Rev 1:9)
John began a new wax tablet with Zechariah 12:10 at the beginning.

Z2   Oratories to God's People (Zech 7:1-12:9; Rev 2:1 - 3:22)
John conflated the wax tablets EP2 and IP2 to form the template to the letters of the seven churches.

John took the whole wax tablet IP6 and a phrase in IP7 as the first unique content to the seven churches.

EP2	Ezekiel's Mission
IP2	Isaiah's Mission
IP6	Jesus as Eliakim
IP7	Tyre (Jesus as a Certain King)

Z3   The Coronation of Joshua the High Priest (Zech 6:9-15; Rev 4:1 - 5:14)
John conflated both Ezekiel's and Isaiah's experience in heaven and then adds the coronation of Jesus.

EP1	Ezekiel's Experience in Heaven
IP1	Isaiah's Experience in Heaven

Z4   The Four Chariots and the Four Winds (Zech 6:1-8; Rev 6:1-8; 8:7 - 9:21)
John took the two wax tablets (EP4, IP4) and made IP4 the four chariots and appended EP4 afterwards making it the four winds.

IP4	The Judgments by Jesus
EP4	The Judgments by the Nations

Z5   A Woman in the Basket (Zech 5:5-11; Rev 12:1-17; 17:1-18)
John took the pregnant woman and the harlot and made them both the city of Jerusalem. The pregnant woman represented the righteous and the harlot represented the wicked. He then constructed a simple parallel between the two.

IP3	The New Seed (Jesus the Child)
EP7	Jerusalem the Harlot

Z6   The Flying Scroll (Zech 5:1-4; Rev 10:1-11)
John split the scroll from EP1(Ezek 2:8 - 3:3), leaving a portion in the coronation of Jesus scene and moving the rest to this location.

EP1	Ezekiel and the Scroll
IP7	Tyre (Jesus, a Certain King)

Z7   Jerusalem Will be Blessed, Joshua the High Priest, and the Two Anointed (Zech 2:1 - 4:15; Rev 11:1 - 12:17)
John took the wax tablets (EP3, EP5, IP3, IP5) and creatively infused Zechariah 2:1 - 4:15 to form the 42 month, 1,260 day, 3½ day parallel (see "Z7 - The Zechariah-Encoded Parallel: How it Was Built (Part 1)" on page 117).

EP3	Ezekiel Appointed as a Watchman	IP3	The New Seed
EP5	The Glory of God Flees Jerusalem	IP5	Babylon Pursues God's Glory

Z8   The Four Horns (Zech 1:18-20; Rev 16:1 - 18:19)
John made the four horns by copying the four winds from EP4 and changing them from affecting a third to affecting all.

EP4	Judgment by the Nations (John copied)
EP6	Jerusalem the Harlot

Z9   The Return Home (1:1-17; Rev 18:20 - 20:15)
John used Zechariah 1:1-17 to tell the following stories:
- God, after 70 years, is angry with the nations (Zech 1:12, IP7, EP8, IP8).
- God's cities will once again flow with prosperity (1:17, EP9, IP9, EP10, IP10).
- God calls his son to return to him (Zech 1:3; EP8).

EP7	Tyre		
IP7	Tyre (Jesus, a Certain King) (Isa 23:15-7; 25:1-6)		
EP8	God Slays the Great Dragon	IP8	Jesus Slays the Great Dragon
EP9	Attacked by Gog and Magog	IP9	Jerusalem Attacked by the Nations
IP10	The Holy City of Jerusalem		
EP10	The City of God		

How John Created the Deuteronomy-Joshua Draft

John created the DJD by starting at the end of the ZrD and integrating Deuteronomy 29:1 to Joshua 5:13 backwards. From there John integrated Joshua 6:1-27 forwards into the ZrD as shown below. The solid boxes represents the text (wax tablets) from the ZrD and the dashed line boxes represents the wax tablets John inserted and in the order that he inserted them (DJ1 being the first). The two dashed line boxes that contain two items (DJ6 and DJ7, DJ5 and DJ8) represents one wax tablet in which John added content going backwards in the ZrD and then appended the content to the wax tablet when John went forwards in the ZrD.

Z3 - The Coronation of Jesus the High Priest (Zech 6:9-15; Rev 4:1 - 5:8)

DJ6 - The Commander of the Lord's Army (Josh 5:13-5; Rev 5:9-14)
- Jesus given a title "The Lion who is of the tribe of Judah." (Josh 5:14; Rev 5:5).
- They were in a holy place and all worshiped him. (Josh 5:14-5; Rev 5:8-14).

DJ7 - The Destruction of Jericho (Josh 6:1 - 8; Rev 6:1-17)
- Created the seven seals imagery as seven marches around Jericho (Rev 5:1; 6:1-17; 8:1-6).
- Made existing content into two additional seals (Rev 6:9-17).

Z4.1 - The Four Chariots/First Four Seals (Zech 6:1-8; Rev 6:1-17)

DJ5 - Entering the Promised Land (Josh 4:1 - 5:12; Rev 7:1-17)
- The sealing of the 144,000 on their foreheads in lieu of circumcision (Josh 5:1-8; Rev 7:1-8).
- The passover meal (Josh 5:9-12; Rev 7:9-17).

DJ8 - The Seventh Day March (Josh 6:1-16; Rev 8:1-6)
- There was silence (Josh 6:10; Rev 8:1).
- The seal contained the seven trumpets (Josh 6:10-15; Rev 8:1-2).
- The four winds became the seven trumpets with angels representing priests (Josh 6:10-6; Rev 8:1-9:21).

Z4.2 - The Four Winds/First Four Trumpets (Zech 6:1-8; Rev 8:7 - 9:11)

DJ4 - Crossing the Jordan River (Josh 3:1-17; Rev 9:13-21)
- The great river Euphrates dried up and an army walks across it (Josh 3:1-17; Rev 9:14; 16:12).
- Added "right foot on the sea, and his left on the land" as the priests carrying the ark and crossing the Jordan (Josh 3:13, 5; Rev 10:2).

Z6 - The Flying Scroll (Zech 5:1-4; Rev 10:1-11)

Z7.1 - The Two Prophets (Zech 2:1 - 4:14; Rev 11:1-12)

DJ9 - The Destruction of Jericho (Josh 6:11-27; Rev 11:15-9)
- Modified that the city was destroyed by fire to destroyed by an earthquake to conform with the destruction of Jericho (Josh 6:20; Rev 11:13).
- The seventh trumpet blown (Josh 6:20; Rev 11:15).
- Great voices in heaven are heard (Josh 6:20; Rev 11:15).
- The ark of the covenant is seen (Josh 6:12; Rev 11:18).

Z7.2 - The Woman, the Child, and Satan (Zech 2:1 - 4:14; Rev 11:1-12)

DJ3 - The Allegiance to Joshua (Josh 1:1-18; Rev 14:1-5)
- They followed the Lamb (Josh 1:16; Rev 14:4).
- They obeyed his commandments (Josh 1:16-8; Rev 14:4-5).

Z7.3 - Non-Zechariah Encoded Passage (Zech 2:1 - 4:14; Rev 14:1-20)

DJ2 - The Song of Moses (Deut 31:15-9; Rev 15:1-8)
- Song of Moses and the Lamb (Deut 31:18; Rev 15:3-5).
- God was angry and hid in the tabernacle until the judgments were complete (Deut 31:15-8; Rev 15:6-8).

Z8 - The Four Horns (Zech 1:18-20; Rev 16:1 - 17:18)

Z9 - The Return Home (Zech 1:1-17 ; Rev 18:20 - 22:5)

DJ1 - Follow God or Receive the Curses in This Book (Deut 29:1-28; Rev 22:6-21)
- They have seen all of what God will do (Deut 29:1-5; Rev 22:6).
- Remain faithful and prosper or practice idolatry and fail (Deut 29:9-19; Rev 22:7, 14-5).
- The curses in this book (Deut 29:18-28; Rev 22:18-9).

DJD Starts Here

Left vertical label: The Final Days of Moses to Joshua Crossing the Jordan River (Deuteronomy 29:18 to Joshua 5:15)

Right vertical label: The Destruction of Jericho (Joshua 5:13 - 6:27)

How John Created the Exodus Draft (ExD)

John takes several items from Exodus and applies them to the Deuteronomy-Joshua draft (DJD). First he introduces God the same way God introduced himself from the burning bush (Exod 3:6; Rev 1:4) and then he tells all believers that they are kings and priests (Exod 19:6; Rev 1:5-6).

John then overlaid the DJD with the imagery of a priest servicing the tabernacle beginning with the servicing of the menorah and ending with the entering of the Most Holy Place. This can be seen in the illustration below which shows the tabernacle floor plan numbered in the order that the priest would have serviced it on the day of atonement. The table below it illustrates how John overlaid the duties of the priest in Revelation.

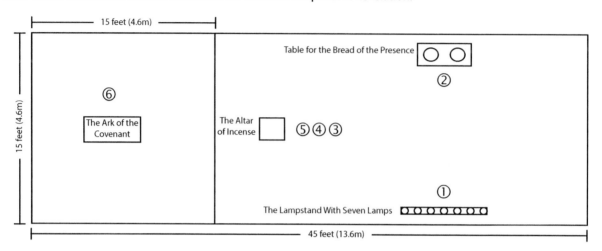

Below is how John distributed the servicing of the tabernacle throughout Revelation.

	Revelation Depiction of Exodus	Exod	Rev
①	Jesus servicing the Menorah as portrayed by the seven candlesticks.	25:31-40	1:12-20
②	God being nourished at the table of the bread of presence by the worshiping of the 24 elders and the 4 living creatures. The 24 elders are divided into four groups of six by the placement of the living creatures similar to how the bread of presence was divided up into stacks of six loaves. Twelve of the twenty-four elders represent the twelve tribes of Israel and the other twelve represent the twelve apostles. Table overlaid with pure gold / twenty-four elders wearing gold crowns.	Lev 24:5-9; 25:23-30; 37:10-6	4:4-11
③	The preparing of the incense through the sacrifice of Jesus, and the altar of incense.	30:1-5; 37:25-9	5:8-11
④	The burning of the incense by God.	30:7-10	8:1-6
⑤	The cleansing of the tabernacle.	Lev 16:1-13	15:1-5
⑥	The entering of the Most Holy Place as portrayed by the New Jerusalem. Both the Most Holy Place and the New Jerusalem are represented by a cube.	 26:15-29	21:1-22:5 21:16

How John Created the Daniel Draft (DnD)

The Daniel draft (DnD) brought the imagery of the beast (Dan 7:2-25; Rev 13:1-18; 17:9-18) along with the urgency of the end of the events that are about to unfold. John however reverses the presentation in Daniel to reflect the destruction of Jerusalem as the trigger mechanism for the words to be unsealed.

The Mighty Angel (Rev 10:1-11)

John used the last chapter of Daniel to set the date for the reader to calculate who the beast is. He conflated the imagery of the mighty angel passage (Rev 10:1-11) and the destruction of Jerusalem (Rev 11:1-13) with Michael in Dan 12:1-11. John expressed the urgency of when these things will happen (Rev 10:6-7) and set the stage with the chronometer set prior to the destruction of Jerusalem.

The Daniel 12 and Revelation 10	Dan	Rev
The angel above the waters.	12:7	10:8
He had a hand lifted towards the sky.	12:7	10:5
He swore by him who lives forever.	12:7	10:6
There will be no more delay.	12:7	10:6-7
"Seal up seal up these words."	12:9	10:4
Angel above the water.	12:7	10:8
The angel swore by he who lives forever.	12:7	10:6
In Daniel 1,290 days, in Revelation 1,260 days.	12:11	11:3, 12:6

The Beast Added and Revealed (Rev 13:1-18; 17:9-18)

John then created Rev 13:1-18; 17:9-18 with the description of the beast and the formula for determining who the beast was.

The Beast in Revelation and Daniel	Dan	Rev
The beast comes from the sea.	7:2	13:1
Described as a lion, bear, leopard and destroyer.	7:4-7	13:2, 4-7
The beast had ten horns.	7:7	13:1
He made war with the saints and won.	7:21	13:7
He spoke words against the Most High	7:25	13:5-6
Formula for identifying the beast	7:16-23	13:18; 17:9-18
The beast will devour its enemies.	7:23	17:16, 18

The Identification of the Beast (Rev 17:10-11)

John set the stage in Revelation 10:1-11 as the time Revelation was written and described the scenes moving forward in time to identify the beast, using Revelation 17:10-11 as the text:

17:10 *They are seven kings.* **Five have fallen, the one is, the other has not yet come. When he comes, he must continue a little while. 17:11 The beast that was, and is not, is himself also an eighth**, *and is of the seven; and he goes to destruction.*

Roman Emperors From the Destruction of Jerusalem	Reign
Vespasian as the emperor when Jerusalem was destroyed. He set up his sons Titus and Domitian as co-rulers (see Rev 17:11).	69-79 CE
Titus reigned for only two years (see Rev 17:10).	79-81 CE
Domitian fits Revelation 17:10-1 as well as being killed by the sword (Rev 13:3).	81-96 CE

Chapter 2: The Ezekiel-Isaiah Draft (EID)

The Ezekiel-Isaiah Draft (EID) is in essence a simple parallel between common content found in Ezekiel and Isaiah. Since the bulk of the material used to form the parallel is found within Ezekiel 1:4 – 32:32 and Isaiah 6:1 – 29:24 we will refer to this as the Ezekiel-Isaiah parallel. The reason for the specific phrase (Ezekiel-Isaiah parallel) is because they form a parallel in the strictest sense of the term. The items mentioned mostly follow the same order. There are some items out of alignment but they still have their complements and a means that connect them to their original place with which they would form a perfect parallel. The only real difference is that the majority of the parallel elements form opposites of each other. The Ezekiel side of the parallel depicts judgment against God's people because of their sins, and shows God rallying the nations to defeat Israel and scatter the people throughout the nations. The Isaiah side of the parallel tells of how God will preserve his righteous followers and will gather them from all parts of the world to defeat the nations that performed evil actions against his people.

This chapter will serve two purposes. First, it will show how John wrote this phase of Revelation, and second, it will demonstrate how John will leverage a parallel already created between Ezekiel and Isaiah. The result of the parallel is a demonstration that someone used the same method of book writing that John incorporated in the EID. This chapter will show how John formed his own version of the Ezekiel-Isaiah parallel by setting the text side by side and tweaking the content to tell his story better. We will see how he formed opposites in symbols and migrated text from one side of the Ezekiel-Isaiah parallel to the other to improve his story. In all aspects of how John formed the parallel, it will be abundantly clear that either Ezekiel or Isaiah patterned their work from the other.[1]

---

1   Although it is not important to understand this book a few comments need to be made regarding who copied from who. First there is the historical background and at the time that Isaiah was written (720 BCE), Assyria was the nation that ruled, so references such as Babylon would have been more likely made during or after the Babylonian captivity. Also Isaiah 6:1 - 29:24 strays from the content of Ezekiel 1:4 - 32:32 in that Isaiah has three scenes of the conquest of Egypt (Isa 11:15; 21:1-6; 27:1-14) and Ezekiel only has one (Ezek 28:1- 32:32). It is more likely that the copier would simply copy directly and later rearrange the text than consolidate.

How to Get the Most out of Reading This Book

When reading a draft chapter, the reader should be aware that each draft chapter, except the ExD and the DnD, is composed of a narrative portion and an approximation draft. The narrative portion describes the process or the material with limited examples of the text. The approximation draft shows what the source material looks like as well as what the PVR has in the order that the text must have looked like.

The narrative portion and the approximation draft portion are separate because there will be a time when the reader may want to read only the approximation draft sections in each chapter to get the feel of how Revelation flowed from one draft to another. The reader may just want to read the narrative portion in its entirety and read the draft portion later. For a first-time reading I recommend that the reader take the time to look at the approximation drafts as they read each narrative portion. The combination of the two will make it much easier to understand the complexities of each draft.

Since each of the draft chapters is a snapshot in time, there will be items or events that at first glance may not make sense in the PVR. Therefore there will be citations to later and/or earlier drafts that will allow the reader to see how a theme transitions from draft to draft. This will allow the reader to develop a cross-section view of the theme in how it transitions from one draft to another. However, it is probably best to read the book once to understand how John constructed Revelation and then follow the theme from draft to draft.

What the Ezekiel-Isaiah Draft Looked Like

The EID would not be viewed as a story but more as two columns of wax tablets arranged side by side. One side was the Ezekiel content which tells of God's judgment of sinful people and the other side was the Isaiah content which depicted God's restoration of his people from all nations. John took elements from Isaiah that were part of each major parallel and made them descriptions of Jesus. John introduced Jesus as the central figure to restore God's people.

We know that John kept the connection between the Ezekiel and Isaiah parallels together because in the ZrD he moved and conflated much of the parallel content in unison. This would suggest that they were stored together—perhaps two wax tablets were tied together like a book, or he utilized a marking system etched into the wax.[2]

The arrangement of the wax tablets in the EID could be to depict one of two stories. The first is to convey the transition of God's people with the end of one holy seed and the birth of a new holy seed. It can also represent transition between the ministry of Jesus to the ministry of John. Whereas Jesus ministered to the Jews and as a result the faithful were spared, and Jerusalem was destroyed, John will take up the mission to the world and Rome will be destroyed and God's people will be spared.

At the end of this chapter an approximation of the text of EID is presented which gives the reader the text of both Ezekiel (on the left) and Isaiah (on the right). Both sides will also show the Revelation text that represents the final resting place for the text.[3] The text will also be broken in logical parallels and some-

---

However, in this chapter we will see that John consolidates the material but it is based upon having both sides of the equation and writing a book that is significantly shorter than Ezekiel or Isaiah.

2   See "How John Created the Ezekiel-Isaiah Draft" on page 7 for an overview of how the wax tablets were laid out.

3   See "How the Ezekiel-Isaiah Draft Will Be Displayed" on page 37.

times places that do not appear to form natural breaks. The reason for this is because of how the text is rearranged in the ZrD.[4]

The Ezekiel-Isaiah Draft: From Exile to Heaven to Commissioning (EP1-2, IP1-2)

This is the first place where we look at the content and placement of the wax tablets and how it differs from what we have today in the published version of Revelation (PVR). In this section we will concentrate on Ezekiel because Ezekiel has three chapters of text compared to ten verses found in Isaiah. Therefore, John used more from Ezekiel than from Isaiah. This is not to suggest that Isaiah is less important—because its contribution is significant—it is only because the more content there is, the more there is to draw upon.

Ezekiel's and John's Calling and Visitation to Heaven (Ezek 1:1 - 2:2; Ezek 2:8 - 3:3; Rev 1:9-10; 4:1-11)

The EID began in the same way that Ezekiel began. Ezekiel, an exiled priest, was by a river one certain day when he received a vision which took him up to a cloud, and he experienced the presence of God on his throne.[5] There were strange living creatures which each had four different faces—one of a man, one of a lion, one of an ox and one of an eagle. The living creatures had four wings and eyes all around them.[6] There were a few words about the decor of heaven, such as a great expanse of something that resembled magnificent crystal looming over Ezekiel's head, as well as the presence of lightning.[7]

In Revelation, John is imprisoned on the isle of Patmos because of his faith. Then on one certain day he received a vision which took him into the presence of God sitting on his throne. There was a crystal sea around the throne and lots of lightning. John saw four living creatures each with a single face and yet a different face from each other. One had a face like a lion, the other like a calf, the third like a man and the fourth like a flying eagle. The living creatures had eyes all around them similar to as in Ezekiel, but they had six wings instead of the four that were seen in Ezekiel. The four living creatures in Revelation also took on a worship role which is something not found in Ezekiel.[8]

How Ezekiel and John described their account in heaven are the opposite of each other. John describes the situation from the perspective of the throne of God outward and Ezekiel tells of his journey toward the throne. Ezekiel has a scene where God speaks and he falls down, but John never falls down before God in the entirety of Revelation. John does have three accounts which are similar to Ezekiel's account though— one where he falls down before Jesus, and two where he falls down before angels (on separate occasions).[9]

Ezekiel's account begins with his introduction of being exiled in the space of three verses and in the fourth verse he is in heaven. John's account of being exiled to the isle of Patmos begins in the middle of the first chapter of Revelation and his adventure in heaven is three chapters away.

---

4   To see more on how the text is presented see and the following pages for the approximation of the draft.
5   See "The Ezekiel Prototype for the Calling of John" on page 38 and "EP1 - Ezekiel's Experience in Heaven - Without the Scroll" on page 38 for what the very first draft of John's calling and his experience in heaven with God looked like.
6   Ezek 1:6, 18.
7   Ezek 1:1-27.
8   Rev 1:10-1; 4:1-11.
9   Rev 1:17; 19:9-10; 22:8.

When we read more of Ezekiel and Revelation we encounter other similarities and subtle differences. One example of this is the two-sided scroll that Ezekiel and John both eat, and it tastes sweet to both of them. John has the scroll in two places, as if Ezekiel's account of the scroll was cut in two and the top half went to one location while the bottom half went to another.[10]

Ezekiel's and Isaiah's Heavenly Adventure as John's Heavenly Adventure (Isa 6:1-8; Rev 4:1-11)

So why was John's account so similar to Ezekiel and yet still so very different? The simple answer is that they were the same in Revelation's first draft, but it is a little more complex than that. John began the EID with Ezekiel's account (which we already discussed) and with Isaiah's encounter with God in heaven. Both accounts included the throne of God, divine beings and a call to serve. Additionally both accounts had something touch the protagonist's lips (resulting in a positive outcome) as well as the protagonist being sent to preach to God's people. The differences in the accounts were due to the size of the text. Ezekiel devotes three chapters to the subject, while Isaiah devotes only ten verses.

What John did was to segment the material as best as possible and create at least four wax tablets—two on the Ezekiel side and two on the Isaiah side. The Ezekiel side had the totality of Ezekiel's experience with God and the scroll scene. The Isaiah side had Isaiah's experience told from his encounter with God and his receiving coal from God's altar.[11] John then formed a set of tablets having both Ezekiel's and Isaiah's mission.[12]

This simple process of examining the text from Ezekiel with the text from Isaiah and forming a wax tablet from each in the Ezekiel-Isaiah parallel will become the norm for John's process. It did not mean that it always worked or was always as simple as those two accounts of heaven though. John dealt with the more difficult areas on a case-by-case basis since they were in the minority.

The end result is that the differences between the items common to Ezekiel and Revelation can be explained when we conflate Ezekiel's account with Isaiah's account. The living creatures in Ezekiel had four faces and four wings, and the Seraph had a single face and six wings.[13] The worship role of the four living creatures in Revelation is the same as what the Seraph did in Isaiah, not to mention the altar in heaven came from Isaiah.[14]

If you have not seen the EID approximation draft for this section ("The Ezekiel Prototype for the Calling of John" on page 38, "EP1 - Ezekiel's Experience in Heaven - Without the Scroll" on page 38, "IP1 -

10   Ezek 2:10 has the scroll written on both sides which can be found in Rev 5:1. Ezek 3:2-3 Ezekiel is handed the scroll and is told to eat it. Upon eating it, it tastes sweet to Ezekiel's lips. John has a similar story in which the mighty angel gave John the scroll to eat and it tasted sweet to the lips (Rev 10:9-10).

11   Ezek 1:4 - 2:2; 2:8-3:3; Isa 6:1-8. See EP1 and IP1 in "How John Created the Ezekiel-Isaiah Draft" on page 7 for a simple illustration. For a line-by-line comparison see "EP1 - Ezekiel's Experience in Heaven - Without the Scroll" on page 38, "IP1 - Isaiah's Experience in Heaven - Without the Altar" on page 39, "EP1 - Ezekiel's Experience in Heaven - The Scroll" on page 40, "IP1 - Isaiah's Experience in Heaven - The Altar That Removes Iniquity" on page 41.

12   Ezek 2:4; 3:4-27; Isa 6:9-10. See EP2 and IP2 in "How John Created the Ezekiel-Isaiah Draft" on page 7 for a simple illustration. For a line-by-line comparison see "EP2 - Ezekiel's Mission" on page 40 and "IP2 - Isaiah's Mission" on page 41.

13   Ezek 1:6, 10; Isa 6:2.

14   Isa 6:3; Rev 4:8; see "IP1 - Isaiah's Experience in Heaven - Without the Altar" on page 39 and "IP1 - Isaiah's Experience in Heaven - The Altar That Removes Iniquity" on page 41.

Isaiah's Experience in Heaven - Without the Altar" on page 39, "EP1 - Ezekiel's Experience in Heaven - The Scroll" on page 40, and "IP1 - Isaiah's Experience in Heaven - The Altar That Removes Iniquity" on page 41) it is well worth your time. The reason is that the way it is presented is not too different from how John arranged and aligned the wax tablets to write Revelation. Since this book is how John wrote Revelation, there is a part entitled "The Process of Construction" which describes what he is doing, and then there is the approximation draft that shows what he did. In order to understand the process sometimes one will be sufficient, and other times both will be needed. It is all about building context for a process of something that has never been explained before.

The Mission of Ezekiel, Isaiah and John (EP2, IP2)

Ezekiel and Isaiah both had similar missions that revolved around ministering to people who didn't want to listen. Both accounts had a dramatic exchange between God and man. Ezekiel, upon hearing and seeing God, falls down before him.[15] Isaiah, after being cleansed of sin by the coal touching his lips, hears the call from God and volunteers without hesitation.[16] Both are sent to a people who refuse to listen to them, which makes their ministry similar. Ezekiel was told to begin each speech with the phrase, "Thus says the Lord."[17]

Ezekiel, Sent to God's People to Say "Thus Says the Lord" (Ezek 2:1-8; Rev 2:1-3:22; 9:3; 10:11)

God tells Ezekiel to go to his rebellious people, who are described as scorpions, and to begin each message with the phrase "Thus says the Lord." The imagery of the scorpions and beginning each message with the phrase "Thus says the Lord" survives in two forms in the PVR. The phrase "Thus says the Lord" is found in the salutation of each of the seven letters to the churches. The scorpions are found as the tormenting device from the angel of the abyss (Satan) against all those who do not obey God.[18]

How the two got separated is simple, John moved the descriptions of God's people as scorpions to where he is called to be a watchman and from there it ended up being migrated to the fifth trumpet from a process that will be discussed in the next chapter.[19] The saying "Thus says the Lord" was retained as well and part of what makes up the EID parallel (EP2) to try to get God's rebellious people to listen to him.[20]

The Two Missions: The Call of the Watchman and the Birth of a Child (EP3, IP3)

Ezekiel and Isaiah both depict the end/destruction of God's people as well as a survival of a remnant.[21] In Ezekiel it is the call to be a watchman where he is to minister to both the righteous and the wicked. Whether or not those whom Ezekiel ministers to decide to repent, so long as he accepts the duty, it will

---

15 Ezek 1:28 - 2:2.
16 Isa 6:8.
17 Ezek 2:4; 3:11; see "EP2 - Ezekiel's Mission" on page 40.
18 Rev 9:5.
19 See "When Wax Tablets Are Placed Together" on page 85.
20 Ezek 2:4-5; 3:5-7, 11.
21 Ezek 2:3 - 32:32 shows how Babylon will destroy everything and Ezek 33:1 - 48:35 tells of Israel's restoration. Isaiah 6:10 - 29:21 tells how Israel will be destroyed and Judah will be saved.

be okay. If, however, Ezekiel decides not to minister to the righteous and wicked then their blood will be on his hands.[22]

Isaiah depicts a transition from one holy seed to another.[23] John takes that imagery and emphasizes the child born in the following chapter using that imagery. From there he takes various instances of positive imagery and one instance of negative imagery and ascribes them to Jesus.

Ezekiel Called to Be a Watchman (Ezek 2:6; 3:4-27)

Ezekiel is sent by God on a mission and then is called to be a watchman so that he may proclaim the message to the righteous and the wicked. The task has consequences if he decides not to do it in that he will be responsible for those who did not repent. Ezekiel will form the watchman passage out of three passages interrupted by the scroll narrative. The first is the defining of God's rebellious people as scorpions, the second is Ezekiel's journey to Tel Aviv[24] and the last is the actual appointment as a watchman and the consequences of refusing.

God's People are like Briers, Thorns and Scorpions and the Hardening of Ezekiel's Head (Ezek 2:6; 3:8-9)

To prepare Ezekiel for his ministry an illustration is given to show just how hard it will be. John took the descriptions of the people Ezekiel would minister to as the reasoning for why Ezekiel's head is hardened. Since God describes his people as things that prick and sting defenseless skin (like briers, thorns and scorpions) Ezekiel needed a means to protect himself from their attacks. So in order to prepare Ezekiel for the mission to Tel Aviv, as well as all subsequent missions, God hardened his head to be as tough as flint.[25]

Ezekiel's Journey to Tel Aviv and Being Appointed as a Watchman (Ezek 3:4-27)

Ezekiel's first mission was to go to Tel Aviv via the spirit. As the spirit takes him the spirit says, "Blessed be THE LORD's glory from his place." Along the journey, Ezekiel hears the thunderous noises generated by the wings of the living creatures touching together. Upon his arrival, Ezekiel goes into a state of bitterness for seven days.

All of the elements mentioned in this section become the main mighty angel narrative in Revelation. The seven days, the spirit's words and the thunderous noise of the living creatures' wings became the seven thunders and their sayings. The experience of bitterness will become the bitter taste that the scroll will leave behind in the stomach.[26]

The End of One Ministry and the Birth of Another (Ezek 4:5-8; Isa 6:13-9:19)

As the storylines in Ezekiel and Isaiah continue, John will in some places work to make them form a parallel while in others the parallels will flow more naturally. In both Ezekiel and Isaiah there is a prophesy of

---

22   Ezek 3:17-21.

23   Isa 6:10-13.

24   A different Tel Aviv than the one today (see Nancy R Bowen, *Ezekiel* (Nashville: Abingdon, 2010), 12).

25   To see how this section looked on a wax tablet and what the items eventually become go to "EP3 - Ezekiel Appointed as a Watchman - Part 1" on page 42.

26   See Ezek 3:12-16 and Rev 10:4-5; 9-10 in "EP3 - Ezekiel Appointed as a Watchman - Part 1" on page 42.

How John Made and Aligned the End of the Ministry and the Birth of a Child Parallel

John transformed the Ezekiel calculation where each year of sin represents each day of the Babylonian siege of Jerusalem to the EID where each day and month combination represent the length of the Roman siege of Jerusalem (see "EP3 - Ezekiel Appointed as a Watchman - Part 2" on page 43). The Isaiah account was interlaced with problems that Israel will face, but the Ezekiel account did not have such a pattern. The solution John came up with was to use the three attacks by the nations in Ezekiel 5:2 and the three problems found in Isaiah 7:17-22; 8: 5-17; 9:12-9.

Content Found in Ezekiel and Revelation

Content Found in Isaiah and Revelation

End of a City and the Birth of a New Holy Seed (Isa 6:10-3)

An illustration that even if the oak tree is burned (believers) and a tenth of the city is remains. The 10% will be destroyed and a new crop of believers as a holy seed will sprout from the acorns.

Years of Sin by Israel (Ezek 4:5)
- Ezekiel lay on his left side for 390 days which represents 390 years that Israel sinned against God.

Years of Service by the 2nd Temple (Rev 11:2)
- The temple courtyard will be trampled by the gentiles for 42 months.

In Isaiah 7:14-6
- The Sign of the Woman with Child (7:14-6).

In Revelation 12:1-2
- A great sign was seen in heaven: a woman . . . . She was with child. She cried out in pain, laboring to give birth.

Razor as the Alignment Text (Isa 7:20)

The First Problem for Israel (Isa 7:17-22)
- The land will go from plentiful harvest to weeds.

Years of Sin by Judah (Ezekiel 4:6)
- Ezekiel lay on his right side for 40 days which represents the 40 years Judah has sinned against God.

Years of Service by Israel (Rev 11:3)
- I will give power to my two witnesses, and they will prophesy one thousand two hundred sixty days, clothed in sackcloth.

In Isaiah 8:4
- Before the child knows how to say "father," or "mother" the riches of Damascus will be carried away by the king of Assyria (8:4).

In Revelation 12:4-5
- She gave birth to a son . . . who is to rule all the nations with a rod of iron. Her child was caught up to God, and to his throne.

The Second Problem for Israel (Isa 8:5-17)
- An army will sweep through Israel like a flood, Judah spared. (8:5-17).

The Sum of Israel and Judah's Sin (Ezek 4:8)
- The combination of 390 days + 40 days = The length of the Babylonian siege of Jerusalem.

The Ministry of the Two Prophets (Rev 11:9)
- The two prophets lay dead in the streets for 3½ days.

In Isaiah 9:6
- When the son is born the government shall be upon his shoulders (9:6).

In Revelation 12:5
- Who is to rule all the nations with a rod of iron.

The Third Problem for Israel (Isa 9:12-9)
- [Two nations] will devour Israel with an open mouth (Isa 9:12).
- The prophet who teaches lies is the tail (Isa 9:15).
- For those who lead this people lead them astray; and those who are led by them are destroyed (Isa 9:16).
- For wickedness burns like a fire. It devours the briers and thorns . . . people are the fuel for the fire (Isa 9:18-9).
- Their hunger is never satisfied, they will eat their own (9:20).

Razor as the Alignment Text (Ezek 5:2)

First Attack by the Nations (Ezek 5:2)
- You shall take a third part, and strike with the sword (5:2).

Second Attack by the Nations (Ezek 5:2)
- A third part you shall scatter to the wind, and I will draw out a sword after them (5:2).

Third Attack by the Nations (Ezek 5:2)
- A third part you shall burn in the fire in the middle of the city, when the days of the siege are fulfilled (5:2).

a city being destroyed. In Ezekiel the prophesy is centered on the number of days that Ezekiel had lain on his left side and his right, where one day equaled a year that Israel and Judah had sinned against God. The total number of days that Ezekiel had lain on both sides also represented the total number of days that Jerusalem was besieged by Babylonians.[27]

In Isaiah we learn of a change from one set of believers to another set of believers that if a city is destroyed then God will raise a new holy seed.[28] Isaiah continues and provides comfort by giving a sign of a woman with child and by the time that child grows up and can refuse evil the calamity would be no more.[29] The Isaiah narration of the child continues into two other stories in Isaiah, first that before the child can say "mother" or "father" the riches of Damascus and the plunder of Samaria will be taken away by the king of Assyria,[30] and second that a child is born that will rule forever.[31]

The Length of the Siege of Jerusalem Changed From Years of Sin to Years of Ministry (Ezek 4:5-8; Rev 11:2-3, 9)

For John to harmonize the Ezekiel and Isaiah passages he needed to tweak one of them. John first capitalized on Isaiah's rendition that if the believers of a certain city are reduced to 10% God will raise up a new seed.[32] The emphasis upon a new holy seed forced John to change the Ezekiel 4:5-8 account from years of sin to years of ministry along with adjusting the numbers to match the Roman siege of Jerusalem to agree with his time. How and what John used to illustrate the ministry and the length of the ministry we do not know. The reason we do not know this has to do with how the two chapters were changed in the ZrD[33] and EID.[34] However, the numbers and illustrations that the published version of Revelation depicts of a ministry represent either 3½ years or can be adjusted by multiplying days by years. We see that 390 days (representing years) that Judah sinned against God became the 42 months (420 years) that the second temple served. The 40 days, representing years, that Judah sinned became the 1,260 days that Israel as a nation served God. The place where Ezekiel is told to add the number of days that he laid on his left side and right side to calculate the length of the Babylonian siege became the number of days representing the years (3½ days represented 3½ years) of the Roman siege of Jerusalem. John, in the first two elements of the 42 month, 1,260 day and 3½ day complex parallel maintained the 3½ year Roman siege on Jerusalem.

Jesus as the Child (Isa 7:14 - 9:21; Rev 12:1-17)

Each of the three descriptions of the child is modified slightly to represent Jesus, such as the child being conceived in heaven instead of on earth. Another such modification is the child being taken to heaven before being devoured by Satan instead of Damascus. The last modification is a description of the child rul-

---

27   Ezek 4:5-8.

28   Isa 6:10-3.

29   Isa 7:14-6.

30   Isa 8:3-4.

31   Isa 9:6-7.

32   Isa 6:10-3.

33   The ZrD brought in the imagery of the temple (see "The Creation of the Temple and its Courtyard Trampled by Gentiles (Zech 2:1-4; Rev 11:1-2)" on page 90), the two prophets (see "EP8 - The Slaying of the Great Dragon" on page 58), Satan (see "The Creation of Satan in the Zechariah Draft" on page 86).

34   "Z7 - The Building of the Encoded-Complex Parallel (Zech 2:1 - 4:14; Rev 11:1 - 12:17)" on page 86.

ing the whole earth with God up in heaven, as opposed to ruling on the earth. In this way, John defines Jesus as the first of the new holy seeds that God raises up.[35]

John also defines Jesus as the means of escape from calamities, similar to how Judah escaped from the Assyrian invasion while Israel did not. We see this in how the child's/Jesus' actions are followed by a calamity, and the final action in each calamity consists of saving those who have followed the child/Jesus.[36]

How John Added Catastrophes to the Ezekiel-Isaiah Parallel (Ezek 5:2; Isa 7:1 - 9:21 ; Rev 8:7-12; 12:1-17)

In the Isaiah side of the parallel there are three major scenes of destruction which occur after each of the child's revelations. The first is that after the child is conceived the land will go from a harvest of plenty to a harvest of weeds.[37] The second is that before the child can speak the words "father" or "mother" an army will sweep through the land like a flood and destroy everything but Judah.[38] The last is that after the son is to rule, the destruction scenes intensify to include: 1) the army of Syria and the Philistines who will devour Israel with an open mouth, 2) the false prophets of Israel (called "tails") will lead the people and themselves into destruction, and 3) the wicked will be burned away like briers, thorns and trees.[39]

The Ezekiel side of the parallel contains the judgment scenes which occur after the destruction of Israel's illustration, thus creating a lopsided parallel. However, John could plan the parallel using the three attacks by the nations in Ezek 5:2. Perhaps the parallel is aligned by the word "razor" which is found in both passages,[40] similar to how he aligns things in many other places. Additionally, the parallel could have been aligned by combining symbols from Isaiah with symbols found in Ezekiel. Although John shifted content and changed symbols throughout the course of the draft process, he still maintained the parallel all the way to the PVR.[41]

With the calamities being added to the birth of a new ministry, John associated the birth of Jesus with ushering forth a calamity that ended the old ministry and brought forth a new one. This can be seen in how John uses the Isaiah text within Revelation. He first describes a tenth of the city being destroyed and from that action a new crop of believers sprouted.[42] He then describes the birth of Jesus and the plight of the

---

35 To see the overview of how the child is changed see "How John Made and Aligned the End of the Ministry and the Birth of a Child Parallel" on page 19. To see how the whole passage in question was changed line by line see "IP3 The New Seed (Jesus the Child)" on page 45.

36 To see the overview of how the child is changed see "How John Made and Aligned the End of the Ministry and the Birth of a Child Parallel" on page 19. To see how the whole passage in question was changed line by line see "IP3 The New Seed (Jesus the Child)" on page 45.

37 Isa 7:17-22. See "How John Made and Aligned the End of the Ministry and the Birth of a Child Parallel" on page 19 and "IP3 The New Seed (Jesus the Child)" on page 45 for all scripture references and illustrations in this section.

38 Isa 8:5-17.

39 Isa 9:12-9.

40 Both Ezek 5:1 and Isa 7:20 contain the same Hebrew and Greek words for "razor" (Hebrew תַּעַר, Greek ξυρόν) which would have been a literary way for John to align the two passages.

41 The parallel formed between the Ezekiel 5:2 and Isaiah 7:17 - 9:19 catastrophes can be seen in "How John Made and Aligned the End of the Ministry and the Birth of a Child Parallel" on page 19 which is part of the larger story of Satan found on "Z7 - The Zechariah-Encoded Parallel: How it Was Built (Part 1)" on page 117, "Z7 - The Zechariah Encoded Parallel: Satan's Entry into Revelation (Z7 -- Part 3)" on page 119, "Z7 - The Zechariah Encoded Parallel: Satan's Entry into Revelation (Part 4)" on page 120, where John forms a complex parallel between the two passages.

42 Rev 6:10-3; Rev 11:13.

woman and her children.[43] The difference is that the faithful children of the woman are those who follow the commandments of God and Jesus.[44] The army that will sweep through like a flood in Isaiah become Satan trying to flood the believers away.[45] The army of Syria and the Philistines devouring Israel from Isaiah becomes Satan trying to devour Jesus.[46] The prophet who teaches lies (referred to as the "tail") in Isaiah becomes Satan's "tail" who deceives a third of the Israelites.[47]

Two descriptions in Isaiah become their opposite in Revelation. The first is the depiction of God's anger not turning away, which becomes Satan's wrath not turning away.[48] The second instance is of the briers, thorns and trees which represent the wicked and are burned, which become the righteous beings burned by Satan's destruction.[49] These two changes are another set of examples of how John will form opposites to convey the storyline while remaining true to his writing methodology.

The Judgments (EP4, IP4)

In the previous Ezekiel-Isaiah parallel we saw how John changed the Ezekiel text from the destruction of Jerusalem being determined by the years that God's people sinned (the number of years converted into days), to the years of his faithful servants' ministry determining the days of the Roman Seige of Jerusalem (with again the number of years converted into days). We have also seen how John formed a parallel between the judgments of the nations in Ezekiel 5:2 and the nations attacks in Isaiah 7:14 - 9:19.

In this section, we will see Ezekiel 5:2 used yet again to form a third parallel and shape two major portions of the book of Revelation. This will be an example of how he consolidates material and can shift content from one side of the parallel to the other. Here, actions of God in Ezekiel are shifted over to become actions of Jesus on the Isaiah side of the Ezekiel-Isaiah parallel.

John's First Major Content Alignment Corrections

After wrapping up the previous parallel in a logical and satisfactory manner, John continued the process, but with more difficulty. The parallels between Ezekiel and Isaiah were structurally sound enough to continue but the problem that John faced was the duplication of the battle scene with Egypt[50] and the fact that the darkening of the sun, moon and stars symbolism is also found in the scene where God defeats the great dragon in Ezekiel.[51] The solution that John came up with was to move the story of God gathering his people to destroy Egypt with the Ezekiel story of God destroying in Ezekiel.[52] John, also followed his theme of

---

43   Rev 12:1-17; see "IP3 The New Seed (Jesus the Child)" on page 45

44   Rev 12:17.

45   Isa 8:5-17; Rev 12:15-6.

46   Isa 9:12; Rev 12:5.

47   Isa 9:15-6 "The prophet who teaches lies is the tail that will lead them to destruction." Rev 12:4 "Satan's tail drew one third of the stars of the sky, and threw them to the earth." The imagery of the stars in the sky comes from Joseph's dream in Gene 37:9 (see "Z7 - The Zechariah Encoded Parallel: Satan's Entry into Revelation (Z7 -- Part 3)" on page 119).

48   Isa 9:17; Rev 12:12, 16.

49   Isa 9:18-9; Rev 8:7; see "IP3 The New Seed (Jesus the Child)" on page 45.

50   In Ezek 29:1 - 32:32 God destroys the great dragon with the sword which also appears in Isa 27:1-13. However, the gathering of a great army to defeat Egypt is found in Isa 11:1-16.

51   The darkening of the sun, moon and stars appears in Ezek 32:7-10 and in Isa 13:19-22.

52   Isa 11:1 - 13:8 was moved to parallel Ezek 29:1 - 32:32; see "John's Problem with the Ezekiel-Isaiah Parallel and How He Solved It (Part 2)" on page 25 for how he moved around the passages.

redefining positive actions of people and ascribing them to Jesus, replaced the actions of God slaying the great dragon with the symbolism of the stock of Jesse slaying the great dragon.[53]

In order to equalize the text shift, John moved the darkening of the sun, moon and stars from the slaying of the great dragon passage to the darkening of Israel's glory—this paralleled the darkening of the sun, moon and stars in Isaiah.[54] This simple alignment and consolidation of text will become the framework for the darkening of the sun, moon and stars in their totality by God and the Lamb, as well as their darkening in partiality by Satan.[55]

The next problem John faced when he shifted the texts was when he moved the stock of the Jesse passages to enhance the slaying of the great dragon by Jesus (instead of God). When he did this he created a void— the three actions by God in the Ezekiel account had no complement.[56] The solution was to leverage associating the acts of God to the acts of Jesus as he had done with the slaying of the great dragon,[57] and take the actions of God performed in Ezekiel and move them to the Isaiah side of the parallel in order to complement the actions of the nations in Ezekiel. The final shifting of all the texts sets the stage for the trumpets and seals to form a parallel to each other.[58]

The Ezekiel side of the parallel has the Isaiah prototype of the first four trumpets representing actions that are done by the nations against Israel.[59] The Isaiah prototype of the fifth trumpet explains that Israel was judged because they were worse than the nations around them.[60] The Isaiah prototype of the sixth trumpet shows the final state of Israel as its glory darkens when the first two prototypes are enacted.[61]

The Isaiah side of the parallel mostly represents the actions by the people of Jesus and God, which forms an opposite to the Ezekiel side of the parallel. The Isaiah prototype of the first four seals represents actions against those who have issued harmful decrees against God's people.[62] The Isaiah prototype of the fifth seal portrays the believers who follow oppressive decrees by evil people.[63] John, however, will take the Isaiah material and form opposites to a few of the stories which emphasize the believer's triumph over tyranny. Isaiah depicts that those who make evil decrees will only change when faced with prison or death, and this

---

53   Isa 11:4-5 was also moved to Isa 27:1-13 (God slays the great dragon) complementing the account in Ezek 29:1 - 32:32. Isa 11:4-5 became the origin of the imagery of Jesus as the slayer of the great dragon (beast) in Rev 19:11-21 (see "John's Problem With the Ezekiel-Isaiah Parallel and How He Solved It (Part 1)" on page 24, "John's Problem with the Ezekiel-Isaiah Parallel and How He Solved It (Part 2)" on page 25 and "IP8 - Jesus Slays the Great Dragon With a Great Sword" on page 59).

54   Ezek 32:7-10 was combined with Ezek 8:1 - 9:11 to reflect the imagery of the darkening of Israel and to complement the darkening of the sun, moon and stars in Isa 13:9-22. See "John's Problem with the Ezekiel-Isaiah Parallel and How He Solved It (Part 2)" on page 25.

55   The wrath of God and the Lamb associated with the total darkening of the sun, moon and stars is in Rev 6:12-6. Satan strikes and darkens the sun, moon and stars by a third, seen in a complex parallel containing Rev 8:12; 12:1-4 (see "The Twelve Tribes Conceived in Heaven and Deceived by Satan (Rev 8:12; 12:1-6)" on page 300).

56   Ezek 5:16-7; Isa 11:1-16; see "John's Problem With the Ezekiel-Isaiah Parallel and How He Solved It (Part 1)" on page 24 and "John's Problem with the Ezekiel-Isaiah Parallel and How He Solved It (Part 2)" on page 25 on how he shifted the material.

57   Ezek 29:1 - 32:32; Isa 11:4-5; 27:1-13; Rev 19:11-21.

58   John moved the acts of God (Ezek 5:16-7) and made them parallel with the actions of the nations in Ezek 5:2; see "John's Problem with the Ezekiel-Isaiah Parallel and How He Solved It (Part 2)" on page 25.

59   Ezek 5:2 will become Rev 8:7-12.

60   Ezek 5:6-8.

61   Ezek 8:1 - 9:11

62   Ezek 5:16-7 is used in the context from Isa 10:1-19 (see "John's Problem with the Ezekiel-Isaiah Parallel and How He Solved It (Part 2)" on page 25).

63   Isa 10:1-2.

John's Problem With the Ezekiel-Isaiah Parallel and How He Solved It (Part 1)

Below is a representation of how the Ezekiel-Isaiah parallel is organized. The lighter text represents text/concepts that are not associated in Revelation but form elements in the Ezekiel-Isaiah parallel. We know, however, by the present text of Revelation that the parallel content is much different today than in the Ezekiel-Isaiah parallel. How John organized the parallel will be explained in part 2.

Jerusalem Gives Evil Decrees (Ezek 5:6-15)	**God's People Keeps His Decrees (Isa 10:1-19)**
• Judgment against God's people (5:6-9).	• Judgment against those who issued the evil decrees (10:1-19).
• Jerusalem changes on her own, becoming worse than the nations around her (5:6-8).	• Those who attack God's people will only change when they face prison or death (10:4).
• Those in Jerusalem will be inflicted with great pain (5:9-10).	• God will destroy those who try to deceive God's people, illustrated in the burning of all the thorns, briers and most of the trees (10:15-9).
• They continued to do evil (5:11-2).	• God's people continue to lean on God (10:20).
• God will make their land desolate for the inhabitants of Jerusalem (5:13-5).	• God will gather his people up from all over the world (10:21-34).

God Will Strike Judah (Ezek 5:16-7)	**The Stock of Jesse Will Act Towards People (Isa 11:1-16)**
• He will send evil arrows of famine (5:16).	• He will judge with righteousness (11:4).
	• Righteousness will be the belt of his waist and faithfulness the belt of his waist (11:5).
• He will break their staff of bread (5:16).	• He will strike the earth with the rod of his mouth and the breath from his lips shall kill the wicked (11:4).
• He will send upon you famine and evil animals, and they shall bereave you; and pestilence and blood shall pass through you; and I will bring the sword on you (5:17).	The wolf will live with the lamb. The leopard will lie down with the goat. The calf with the lion. The child will lead them. The cow and the bear will graze. They will not hurt or destroy in all my holy mountain (11:6-9).

God Assembles the Nations to Destroy Israel (Ezek 7:1-27)	**God Gathers His People to Destroy the Egyptians (Isa 11:10 - 13:8)**
• God gathers the nations to destroy Israel (7:24).	• God gathers the remnants from the four corners of the earth (11:12).
• God tells the story of the horrors that await Israel because of their sins (7:1-27).	• God tells the story of how he recovers the remnants and how they praise him (11:15 - 13:8).

The Glory of Israel and Judah is Darkened (Ezek 8:1 - 9:11)	**The Glory of the Sun, Moon and Stars Darkened (Isa 13:9-22)**
• In the sixth month, in the fifth day (8:1).	• Behold the day of the THE LORD comes, cruel, with wrath and fierce anger (13:9).
• The glory of Israel can be seen but it is darkened (8:3-17).	• The sun will be darkened . . . . the moon will . . . . not shine (13:10).
	• For the stars of the sky and its constellations will not give their light (13:10).
	• God will make the heavens tremble and the earth will be shaken out of place (13:13).
• In his wrath God will have no mercy to his people (8:18).	• On the day of wrath God will show no mercy to the invading army (13:13-22).
• Those without a seal on their forehead will be killed (9:4).	
• Kill utterly the old man, the young man and the virgin, and little children and women, but don't come near any man on whom is the mark, and begin at my sanctuary. Then they began at the old men that were before the house (9:6).	• Everyone who is found will be thrust through. Everyone who is captured will fall by the sword. Their infants also will be dashed in pieces before their eyes. Their houses will be ransacked, and their wives raped (13:15-6).

John's Problem with the Ezekiel-Isaiah Parallel and How He Solved It (Part 2)

In order for John to align the Ezekiel-Isaiah draft to be closer to the final published version of Revelation he would have to make a few shifts within the content. The first would have been to form a parallel with Ezekiel 5:2 by shifting Ezek 5:16-7 on the Isaiah side of the parallel, since the Ezek 5:2 passage deals with the actions of the nations and Ezek 5:16-7 deals with the actions of God.

The second and third shift would have been maintaining parallels of similar material. The darkening of the sun, moon and stars from Ezek 32:7-10 was moved to form a parallel with Isa 13:9-22 where we have the imagery of the sun, moon and stars darkening. The content from Isa 11:1-16 contains imagery of many similar elements regarding the destruction of Egypt that only parallels the Ezek 29: 1 - 32:32 stars passage (Ezek 32:7-10).

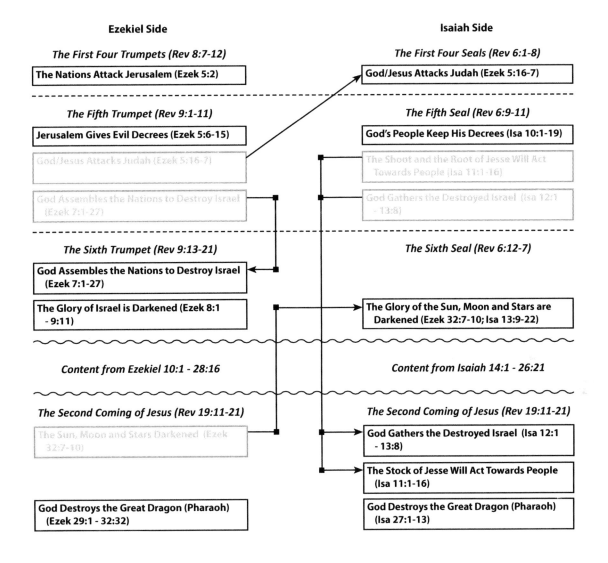

will become that the believers will remain faithful even when faced with prison or death.[64] Isaiah depicts those who perform evil against God's people as thorns, briers and trees being burned, which in Revelation will be depicted as the believers as the green grass and trees being burned by fire.[65]

John also incorporated Isaiah 12:1 - 13:8 which depicts the return of the faithful remnant from the nations. This forms an opposite to the Ezekiel side of the parallel where the nations come from all over the world to destroy Jerusalem.[66] The contrast that John forms in the Isaiah prototype of the fifth trumpet and fifth seal also fits within the description in Isaiah of God being both angry with Israel and comforting them.[67] This action will continue to be a theme across the fifth seal, fifth trumpet and fifth bowl where those who are righteous will be comforted and those who are not will be in severe pain.[68]

The depiction in Isaiah of the return of the faithful remnant will be scattered throughout Revelation, and will function as the starter material for all of the saints in heaven scenes in Revelation.[69] The scattering of this portion of the Isaiah material might provide the illusion to many scholars that John used a pair of scissors and distributed bits and pieces of Isaiah throughout Revelation haphazardly.[70]

For the Isaiah prototype of the sixth seal, John combined the imagery of the darkening of the sun, moon and stars found in Ezekiel and Isaiah to complement the darkening of the glory of Israel and Judah found in Ezekiel. Both the Ezekiel and Isaiah portion of the parallel depict the complete destruction of the unfaithful.[71]

The Glory of God Flees and Fights (EP5, IP5)

John continues building the Ezekiel-Isaiah parallel by focusing on the Ezekiel side of the glory of God fleeing the temple as Babylon advances on Jerusalem, where the nations are angry with Israel and so scatters the Israelites among the nations.

The Isaiah side of the parallel has Babylon pursuing the glory of God into the heights of heaven and being defeated and sent to Sheol. As a result, the nations are subdued and the remnants of Israel assembles from all over the world.

John conveyed this in the EID with a simple parallel that tells the story of the plight of the unrighteous on the Ezekiel side and the plight of the righteous on the Isaiah side. The difficulty in reconstructing it is that because of the changes in both sides of the parallel, the story gets shifted around in later drafts and imagery gets reassigned. Therefore we will examine the parallel itself and how the content of Ezek 10:1 - 15:8

---

64   Isa 10:4; Rev 2:9-10; 6:9; 13:10 (see "IP4 - The Judgments by Jesus - Part 3" on page 51).

65   Isa 10:15-9; Rev 7:3, 8:7; 9:4-7 (see "IP4 - The Judgments by Jesus - Part 3" on page 51).

66   Ezek 7:1-27; Isa 12:1 - 13:8.

67   Isa 12:1.

68   Rev 6:11; 9:4-6; 16:10-1 (see "EP4 - The Judgments by the Nations - Part 3" on page 50, "EP4 - The Judgments by the Nations - Part 4" on page 50, "IP4 - The Judgments by Jesus - Part 2" on page 49, "IP4 - The Judgments by Jesus - Part 3" on page 51).

69   Isa 12:1-13:8 will become Rev 6:9-11; 7:9-10; 14:1-4; 19:1-8, 14 (see "IP4 - The Judgments by Jesus - Part 3" on page 51).

70   See "The Story of One Wax Tablet" on page 162.

71   Ezek 8:1 - 9:11; 32:7-10; Isa 13:9-22.

and Isa 14:1 - 22:15 is used in Revelation today.[72] From the advantage of knowing both the source material and the final published state, we can use the process of reverse engineering to discover what John was attempting to do.

The most obvious example of this is Isaiah's depiction of Babylon trying to defeat the glory of God in heaven and being thrown into Sheol, with the nations being at rest, and how this is parallel to the story of Satan's war in heaven, his defeat, and his being locked up in the abyss so that the nations will not go to war.[73] The story of Satan is told in a previous place in Revelation, with tweaks to the symbols and imagery. In the story of the 144,000 we don't have the war in heaven but rather we have the imagery of Satan being thrown to the earth and locked in the abyss.[74] Looking at the story of Satan in the story of the 144,000 and the story of Gog and Magog we have two stories; the first is where Satan is victorious against Jerusalem and the second is where Satan is defeated by God when he attacks Jerusalem.[75]

The story of Satan was a later modification that was woven into the Ezekiel-Isaiah parallel, by combining the attacks by the nations from EP4 and IP4 with Isaiah's depiction of Babylon.[76] The Isaiah portion—where they will praise the holy one of Israel on Mount Zion and the faithful remnant is gathered from the whole world while God issues oracles against the nations—is found in chapter 14 of Revelation.[77] This will become the 144,000 praising Jesus on Mount Zion, and the gospel being preached to the whole world as the first message by an angel (oracle) against the nations with two more to follow.[78]

The second message from the angel is, "Babylon the great has fallen," which is taken from Isaiah and placed in another location in Revelation in a later parallel.[79] It is interesting to note that even though Babylon is prominent in Ezekiel and Isaiah this is the first place where Revelation references Babylon. The other citations will redefine the cities of Jerusalem and Tyre (the Harlot in the published version) to Babylon, painting the image of doom upon the city.[80]

There is one interesting connection between the portion of the Ezekiel-Isaiah draft in how Jerusalem is depicted as a useless vine where the son of man (Ezekiel) witnesses God burning the vines (which represent the inhabitants of Jerusalem). John must have shifted it to the Isaiah side of the Ezekiel-Isaiah parallel and kept the son of man portion, but instead of the vines being useless they became what the angels harvested into the grapes used for the cup of wrath's wine which destroyed the harlot.[81]

---

72 To EID version of the parallel can be found in "EP5 - The Glory of the Lord Flees Jerusalem" on page 52 and "IP5 - The Glory of the Lord Triumphs in Heaven" on page 53.

73 Rev 12:7-9; 20:1-3; 7-9.

74 Satan is depicted as:

A star thrown to earth in Rev 8:10-1 ; 12:7-9 , locked up in the abyss by an angel with a key in Rev 20:1-3 and released from the abyss in Rev 20:7-9, by an angel with a key in Rev 9:1-2, 10.
He is called the king, the angel of the abyss in Rev 9:10, and there was an angel that had the key to the abyss in Rev 9:1-2

75 See "Satan's Story" on page 294.

76 See "How John Made and Aligned the End of the Ministry and the Birth of a Child Parallel" on page 19, "Z7 - The Zechariah Encoded Parallel: Satan's Entry into Revelation (Z7 -- Part 3)" on page 119 and "Z7 - The Zechariah Encoded Parallel: Satan's Entry into Revelation (Part 4)" on page 120.

77 Isa 14:32; see "IP5 - The Glory of the Lord Triumphs in Heaven" on page 53.

78 Isa 14:32; 17:7, 10; 21:9; Rev 14:1-8; see "IP5 - The Glory of the Lord Triumphs in Heaven" on page 53.

79 Isa 21:9; Rev 14:8; see also Rev 18:2; see "IP5 - The Glory of the Lord Triumphs in Heaven" on page 53.

80 Rev 16:19; 17:5; 18:2, 10, 21.

81 Ezek 15:2-8; Rev 14:13-20; See "EP5 - The Glory of the Lord Flees Jerusalem" on page 52 and "IP5 - The Glory of the Lord Triumphs in Heaven" on page 53.

The Father and Mother of God's People (EP6, IP6)

John forms a parallel around the maternal/paternal representation of God's people with the harlot as the mother from Ezekiel[82] and Eliakim as the father of Jerusalem from Isaiah.[83] Ezekiel depicts Jerusalem as a bride of God whom he clothed and adorned with expensive clothing and jewelry,[84] but she was unfaithful to God and responsible for killing their children.[85] However, even with all the tragedy that Jerusalem brings to God and his people there will be a day when Jerusalem will be restored.[86] In contrast, Isaiah depicts a new leader, Eliakim, who is also clothed and given the title of the father of Jerusalem and Judah.[87] Unlike the depiction in Ezekiel 16:62-3, Isaiah depicts Eliakim as being nailed to the temple and overburdened with temple wares fixed to the nail, until one day when the burden would be cut off.[88] In Revelation, the imagery is rotated from pegs on the wall to pillars in the temple and the believers are the ones kept.[89]

Jesus Depicted as Eliakim and the Birth of the Church in Philadelphia

The appointment of Eliakim in Isaiah 22:20-5 represents the first text that we can conect to one of the seven churches. The appointment of Eliakim has many of the same elements that the church in Philadelphia has. It has the key of David that opens any door and lock any door. It even depicts imagery of nails on a temple wall that will break when the burden is too great. John will transform the nails on the wall and make them believers represented as pillars in the temple that will not break.[90]

The Two Wealth's of Tyre (EP7, IP7)

The next Ezekiel-Isaiah parallel formed naturally fit together. Ezekiel and Isaiah's account centers around the city of Tyre with both accounts having similarities in their depictions of wealth and destruction, as well as important differences.

The Tyre Found in Ezekiel and in Revelation (Ezek 27:1-36; Rev 18:1-19)

In Ezekiel, Tyre is depicted as a lament for a great city whose wealth is brought from trading with every nation, and is illustrated in a long list of luxury items as well as the nations that they traded with. God tells Ezekiel that in one day the city will be destroyed and the sailors and merchants will lament over her destruction.[91]

In the EID and the PVR, Ezekiel's description of Tyre and her destruction is the foundation for the second portion of the harlot in Revelation. The sheer number of items traded in the Ezekiel account is found in the harlot narrative, as well as similar imagery of the merchants lament over Tyre.[92]

---

82   Ezek 16:1-63.
83   Isa 22:20-5.
84   Ezek 16:10-8.
85   Ezek 16:20-3.
86   Ezek 16:62-3.
87   Isa 22:20-2.
88   Isa 22:23-5.
89   Rev 3:10-2.
90   See "IP6 - Jesus as the Father of God's Children (Isa 22:20-5)" on page 55.
91   Ezek 27:29-33.
92   See "EP7 - Tyre" on page 56 for a side-by-side comparison between Ezekiel and Revelation.

Tyre Found in Isaiah and Revelation (Isa 23:1 - 25:6; Rev 3:18; 18:2-6; 19:1-9)

In the Isaiah account, Tyre will have similar imagery as found in Ezekiel which will be ignored by John for the most part. The differences will produce its own portion of the Tyre narrative and content for one of the seven churches. Those differences will enrich the imagery we get from Ezekiel. For example it is in Isaiah that we get the imagery that Tyre will be forgotten just like the songs sung in honor of a prostitute, which is in contrast to Ezekiel where all will mourn her death. This can be seen in Revelation today where the music in Tyre will no longer be heard.[93]

Jesus as the Certain King (Isa 23:15-7; Rev 18:2-6, 22)

In Isaiah, Tyre's destruction is centered on the prophetic date set seventy years after the days of a certain king, who John will ascribe to Jesus in the EID and the early ZrD.[94] For the EID, the seventy years are set against two cities, Jerusalem and Tyre (Rome) based upon Jesus' birth and death. In John's mind, Jerusalem was destroyed seventy years after the birth of Jesus and Rome will be destroyed seventy years after Jesus' death. As we have discussed, John revised the prophetic formula for predicting the length of the Roman siege of Jerusalem to 3½ years.[95] The Ezekiel side of the Ezekiel-Isaiah parallel ended with the death of the two prophets, which was a later revision of something representing the death of Jesus,[96] and the birth of Jesus as the birth child of the woman.[97] In the ZrD it will become more clear as to how John moves the wax tablets around to satisfy one ZrD criteria and what and how he moves things within this section to satisfy another.[98] In each of the two movements, the number seventy and the destruction of Tyre (Rome) play an important role in the movement.

The Birth of the Content for the Church in Laodicea (Isa 23:16-8; Rev 3:17-8)

A portion of Isaiah's Tyre account became the first specific content to the church in Laodicea. The prophet Isaiah will tell that one day Tyre's merchandise will be holiness to God and her treasure will be durable clothing. This will be modified to Jesus instructing the church in Laodicea to buy gold from him that has been refined in the fire and clothing that will not reveal their nakedness.[99]

In Revelation the white robes represent acts of righteousness.[100] The "refining by fire" phrase comes from how John associates the burning of incense with saints' prayers.[101] In the ExD, John will tie the seventh seal with the refining that Jesus is talking about in his message to Laodicea.[102]

---

93 Rev 18:22.

94 See "Z6 - The Flying Scroll (Zech 5:1-4; Rev 5:1-2, 7-8; 10:1-11)." on page 79.

95 See "The End of One Ministry and the Birth of Another (Ezek 4:5-8; Isa 6:13-9:19)" on page 18.

96 The two prophets were killed by the leaders (Rev 11:7) laid dead for 3½ days (Rev 11:9, 11), resurrected by God and taken up to heaven witnessed by all (Rev 11:12) which are similar actions Jesus experienced. The final outcome of the two prophets was Christ making the kingdom of the world became the kingdom of God (Rev 11:15). The same can be said of the child who was taken to heaven to rule with God and as a result the kingdom of the world was made the kingdom of God through his Christ (Rev 12:5; 10).

97 Rev 12:1-2, 4-5, 10.

98 See "How Long Will God Not Have Mercy on Jerusalem (Zech 1:12-5)?" on page 94.

99 Isa 23:17-8; Rev 3:18. See "IP7 - Tyre (Jesus, a Certain King)" on page 57.

100 Rev 19:8.

101 Rev 5:8; 8:3.

102 See "The Wages of Righteousness (Isa 23:18; Rev 3:18)" on page 57.

treasure that cannot be burned him clothing that cannot be However, before it becomes part of the church in Laodicea, it will reflect that something positive will happen after the destruction of Tyre which we see in the saints' clothing at the marriage of the Lamb.[103]

John took one aspect from the Tyre narrative in Isaiah and used it to form the basis for the plea by Jesus to the Laodiceans to buy from him clothing that is durable.[104] We can also see that the Laodiceans are connected in some way to Tyre and in the final version of Revelation the last four churches form a complex distant parallel with the harlot.[105]

The Birth of the Saints Praising God Over Babylon's Destruction and the Wedding Feast of the Lamb (Isa 25:1-6; Rev 19:1-9)

Just prior to the second coming and after the destruction of the harlot there is a scene where the saints in heaven praise God for his righteous judgments and for destroying the harlot. This praise session ends with the marriage of the Lamb.[106] The placement of this scene as well as the placement and content of Isaiah 25:1-6 within the EID reveals where John derived the scene from. In the Isaiah narrative, the saints praise God from the mountain top, because he destroyed a strong, fortified city that will never again be built. The scene ends with righteous eating—the feast of fat things (expensive meats) and choice wines. The Revelation narration follows the order of the Isaiah account as well as its major points.[107]

It Takes Two to Slay the Great Dragon (EP8, IP8)

The slaying of the dragon represents one of the strongest parallels between Ezekiel and Isaiah. In both Ezekiel and Isaiah there is a story of God slaying the great dragon with a sword.[108] Both accounts identify the great dragon as Pharaoh[109] and both accounts have a river theme—in one the river is stopped and in the other it is opened.

The problem for John was how to incorporate Jesus into the slaying of the dragon imagery. John's methodology was to take the Ezekiel-Isaiah parallel and use descriptions of individuals from Isaiah as the basis for his descriptions of Jesus. The slaying of the dragon was different in that both sides of the parallel have God as the slayer of the great dragon. John, therefore, needed different imagery for God and Jesus. John solved this problem by shifting the text from Isaiah 11:1 - 13:8 to the slaying of the dragon in Rev 19:11 - 20:3.

Jesus Depicted as the Shoot and Root of Jesse (Isa 11:1-16; Rev 19:11-22)

The imagery of the shoot and root of Jesse did not form a direct parallel but came from another account from Isaiah in which the root of Jesse will destroy the Egyptian tongue.[110] So in an effort to consolidate the material better and form another parallel which ascribes the actions of God to Jesus, the descriptions were

---

103 Rev 19:8; see "IP7 - Tyre (Jesus, a Certain King)" on page 57 to see how the verses from Isaiah map to Revelation.
104 Isa 23:16-8.
105 Isa 23:18; Rev 3:18. See "The Wages of Righteousness (Isa 23:18; Rev 3:18)" on page 57.
106 Rev 19:1-9.
107 See "The Destruction of Tyre, the Saints Praising God and the Eating of a Meal (Isa 25:1-6; Rev 19:1-9)" on page 57.
108 Ezek 32:32; Isa 27:1. See "EP8 - The Slaying of the Great Dragon" on page 58 and "IP8 - Jesus Slays the Great Dragon With a Great Sword" on page 59 for what the EID draft looked like for this section.
109 Ezek 29:3; Isa 27:1.
110 Isa 11:15; 27:1.

added.[111] We get the symbolism of Jesus being righteous with his judgments and striking the earth with the rod (changed to sword) of his mouth.[112]

Did John intend in the EID for this to be a joint action with God or a solo action by Jesus? The only clue we have of it being a joint action can be found in the sixth seal where the great day of the wrath of God and the Lamb is mentioned.[113] The passage most likely refers to the slaying of the dragon as a cooperative process with God and the Lamb since much of the source material that formed the sixth seal came from the Ezekiel side of the beast parallel.

The most likely place for John to have merged the imagery of God and Jesus would have been in the ZrD where John expanded the judgments from sets of three to four. This is also where the great sword gets shifted to the second seal (rider of the red horse) and the rod from Jesus' mouth is changed to a sharp two-sided sword (a synonym of the great sword).[114]

The Plight of Two Peoples and Two Rivers

Both Ezekiel and Isaiah have two rivers in their slaying of the dragon accounts. The combined Isaiah passages that John moved (used to construct the EID prototype of the second coming) has God's people crossing the Euphrates River to destroy Egypt.[115] The Ezekiel account tells that God will stop the Egyptians and animals from crossing the Nile River.[116] The former will be retained in the published version of Revelation but relocated to represent the armies crossing the Euphrates River to destroy Jerusalem as well as the harlot.[117] It will also represent the believers crossing the Jordan River.[118]

In the EID version, the believers crossing the Euphrates River begins the process of the remnant of Jacob returning so that Jesus can muster the army to slay the great dragon. Therefore the texts regarding the return of the remnant of Jacob must have come prior to the slaying of the dragon. However, in later drafts the process will touch upon all aspects of the saints in heaven scenes found in Revelation 6:9 - 19:21.

Gog and Magog and the Attack by the Multitude of Nations (EP9, IP9)

The Ezekiel story of Gog and Magog attacking Jerusalem forms a parallel to the multitude of the nations attacking the encamped city of David. When the two stories are conflated in the ZrD they will form the bulk of the content from Revelation 20:4-15 containing Gog, Magog, a multitude of nations and a book where the righteous rejoice and the unrighteous are destroyed.[119] This will lay the foundation for later draft

---

111 For a summary of how John moved the text around see "John's Problem With the Ezekiel-Isaiah Parallel and How He Solved It (Part 1)" on page 24 and part 2 on page 25.

112 Judges in righteousness in Isa 11:4; Rev 19:11. Rod of his mouth in Isa 11:4; Rev 19:15. See "IP8 - Jesus Slays the Great Dragon With a Great Sword" on page 59 for all parallels in this section.

113 Rev 6:17.

114 "The Destruction of the Dragon and the Two Riders of the Red and White Horses (Zech 1:7-16; Rev 19:11-21)" on page 95.

115 Isa 11:15; 27:12.

116 Ezek 29:3-11.

117 Rev 9:14; 16:12.

118 See "Joshua and the Crossing of the Jordan River" on page 162.

119 See "When Ezekiel 38:2 - 39:20 and Isaiah 29:1-9 are Conflated You Get Revelation 20:4-15" on page 61.

material additions (such as, but not limited to): Satan leading the army of Gog and Magog,[120] as well as the first and second resurrection.[121]

The City of God and the Holy City of Jerusalem (EP10, IP10)

The parallel between the city of God and the holy city of Jerusalem is formed outside of the Ezekiel-Isaiah parallel and therefore represents a scattering of verses from Isaiah that contain a similar depiction of the city of God from Ezekiel.

The Ezekiel Account of the City of God (Ezek 40:1 - 48:35; Rev 21:1 - 22:5)

John takes Ezekiel's description and encounter with the city of God and modifies them to fit within a Christian theological view. They both begin describing the process with a vision of being taken to a high mountain to observe their respective cities,[122] though because of later parallels formed in Revelation Rev 21:10 was moved.[123]

Both Ezekiel and John meet a person/angel who measures the city they are describing in the same manner.[124] Both cities are square with each side facing either north, south, east or west and each side has three gates, for a total of 12 gates (each named after one of the twelve tribes of Israel).[125] Both describe the city as the place where God lives and those who inhabit the city are those who obey God's commandments.[126] Additionally, both describe those excluded from the city as those who have not obeyed God's commandments.[127]

The Differences Between the City of God in Ezekiel and in the New Jerusalem

We have seen the similarities between the city of God and the New Jerusalem so now we can explore the differences between the two and how they came to be. To simplify matters we will reference the differences of those within the EID and those from a later draft. Although we cannot be absolutely sure that those identified within the EID were part of the EID, we can identify the EID as the earliest draft they can appear in.

The Contrast Between Jerusalem as the Harlot and Tyre as the City of Wealth Within the New Jerusalem

The first editorial action forms a contrast between the two cities mentioned earlier in Ezekiel and the New Jerusalem. We have Jerusalem depicted as the harlot in Ezek 16:1-58 compared to the New Jerusalem de-

---

120 See "God's Defeat by Satan and God's Victory Over Satan" on page 228.

121 See "The Creation of the Second Death" on page 213.

122 Ezek 40:1; Rev 21:10; see "EP10 - The Foundation Stones of the City of God" on page 62.

123 To explore how the New Jerusalem was developed in later drafts see the following:

"The Blessings and the Curses, the Story of Gog and Magog, and the New Jerusalem" on page 135 in the DJD.

"The Servicing the Altar of Incense and the Entering the Most Holy Place" on page 206 in the ExD.

"The Creation of the Second Death" on page 213 in the DnD.

124 Isa 40:3-5; Rev 21:15.

125 Ezek 48:31-4; Rev 21:12-3.

126 Ezek 42:7-11; Rev 21:3.

127 Ezek 43:7-11; Rev 21:7-8; 22:14-5.

picted as the bride of the Lamb (Rev 21:2, 9). It is most likely that the Rev 21:9 reference is from the Ezekiel draft since that verse directly equates the New Jerusalem as the bride of the Lamb in direct contrast to Jerusalem as the harlot. The *Rev* 21:2 verse emphasizes the clothing which most likely came from the Isaiah draft.

The next city is Tyre which is reflected as a city with great wealth that is destroyed in Ezek 27:1-36, compared to the unimaginable wealth and eternal quality of the New Jerusalem.[128] For John, the city of Jerusalem and its imagery still remains in his day, Tyre on the other hand is different. Since there was no present day city of Tyre for John, the imagery had to be applied to another city, which he chose to be Rome.[129] The emphasis on Jerusalem and Rome caused John to make another change in the New Jerusalem that was both extraordinary in scale as well as accuracy in the ancient world. John expanded the size of the city of God from 1.5 miles (2.36 kilometers) on each side[130] to 1,432 miles (2,304 kilometers) on each side[131] which is roughly 1,000 times the distance and the distance between Jerusalem and Rome.[132] If John intended the size of the New Jerusalem to be the distance between Jerusalem and Rome then he is saying that the New Jerusalem is greater than both cities, as well as the wealth between them, combined.

Transition From the City of God (Ezek 40:1-48:35) in Judaism to the New Jerusalem in Christianity

The second editorial action inside the EID was to rewrite the city of God narrative and transition it from Judaism to Christianity. From a Christian perspective the City of God could not exist for several reasons. There was no reason for the continuation of the sacrifices in Ezekiel after the death of Jesus, since he was the one sacrifice that ended all the sacrifices and brought salvation to every believer.[133]

Several changes had to be made to revise the city of God to a city that would follow early Christian teachings. The first change was the transformation of the temple from a physical structure to the physical presence of God and the Lamb.[134] With this came the expansion of the priesthood from a single tribe (the Levites) to all believers.[135]

The city of God could no longer be restricted to the nation of Israel, it had to be expanded to all nations, representing the believers of all nations. This was accomplished in several ways. The first was creating twelve foundations and naming each after one of the twelve apostles, complementing the twelve children (tribes) of Jacob as the twelve gates.[136] Second, John substituted the twelve tribes around the city of God

---

128 Rev 21:3-4, 11-21; 22:5.

129 *Rev* 17:9 refers to the woman residing on seven hills which describes both Jerusalem and Rome. However *Rev* 17:18 tells of the woman that was the great city that reigns over all the kings of the earth which better describes Rome than Jerusalem.

130 Ezek 48:16 (CEB has it as 1.28 miles while NET has it at 1.5 miles).

131 Rev 21:16. A stadia is 607 feet or 182 meters (BDAG, στάδιον)

132 The distance between the map coordinates between Jerusalem and Rome is 1,432 miles (2,305 kilometers) which is the same as one equilateral side of the city of New Jerusalem. It must be stated that there is no known source of a distance calculation such as between Rome and Jerusalem to exist at the time of John. The distance agreement could possibly be an extraordinary coincidence between the two major cities in Revelation or an extraordinarily accurate guess of the distance between Jerusalem and Rome.

133 Rev 1:5-6; 5:9-10; 7:14; 14:4.

134 Ezek 40:48 - 44:14; Rev 21:22.

135 Ezek 44:15-30;Rev 1:5-6; 5:9-10; 7:14.

136 Rev 21:14 as the 12 apostles and Ezek 48:31-4; Rev 21:12-3 representing the twelve tribes of Jacob.

and made it the nations by allowing the nations to enter through the gates.[137] Third, John changed the trees the produce twelve kinds of fruits to the tree of life to represent all humanity.[138]

How John derived the twelve foundation stones was also his means of connecting the New Jerusalem with the Garden of Eden. This can be seen earlier in Ezekiel when Tyre is described as being in the Garden of Eden adorned with twelve precious stones.[139] It is likely that when John was forming the contrasting parallel between Tyre and the New Jerusalem, John took the twelve stones and enhanced a few to become the twelve foundations of the New Jerusalem (with slight modifications).[140] From there, John continued the parallel with the Garden of Eden reducing the trees in the New Jerusalem to the tree of life from the Garden of Eden, and expanded its effects from healing only Israel to healing all of humanity.[141]

The Holy City of Jerusalem (Isa 25:8, 42:9, 60:19, 65:17, 22, 66:17, 20, 22)

The Isaiah account offered many things that the Ezekiel account of the City of God did not contain, such as but not limited to:

- The creation of a new heaven and the new earth (Isa 65:17, 22; Rev 21:1)
- The name of the city as the New Jerusalem, which was the result of renaming the "Holy City of Jerusalem" the "New Jerusalem" (Isa 66:17, 20, 22; Rev 21:2).
- New Jerusalem is depicted as God clothing it as a bride adorns herself for her husband (Isa 61:10; Rev 21:2).
- The place where God will wipe away tears from their eyes (Isa 25:8; Rev 21:4)
- The place where God swallowed up death forever (Isa 25:8; Rev 21:4)
- The place where God is making all things new (Isa 42:9; Rev 21:5)
- The sun and the moon will be no more, God will be their light (Isa 60:19; Rev 21:23)

Both the Ezekiel account and the Isaiah account that God ascribes to be the New Jerusalem for the most part stayed separate from each other. The Isaiah account appears first in Revelation for two reasons: first, the placement of the new heaven and the new earth clause would make it sound silly if it were to be placed after the first description. The second reason is that John forms the parallel with the New Jerusalem in Revelation 20:1-27 as a parallel with the harlot and the city of Tyre from Ezekiel.[142]

The Two Accounts of the New Jerusalem Descending

One of the more interesting aspects about the EID expansion of the City of God/New Jerusalem is that it contains two different descriptions of the New Jerusalem descending by the same person. One reflects the Isaiah account which says that after the creation of the new heaven and the new earth John sees the city

---

137 Ezek 48:1-8; Rev 22:1.
138 Ezek 47:12; Rev 22:2.
139 Ezek 28:13.
140 See "EP10 - The Foundation Stones of the City of God" on page 62.
141 Ezek 47:12; Rev 22:2.
142 Ezek 16:1-53; Ezek 27:1-36.

descend like it was adorned as a bride.[143] The other reflects the account in Ezekiel where Ezekiel was taken to a high mountain so he can get a good view of the city descending.[144]

Final Thoughts

In this chapter we have seen how both John and Isaiah used the same methodology to write their work. Therefore, we can take the techniques that John used and see if we can reverse engineer the work in order to derive previous drafts. Scholars, for the most part, do this but not at the level that this book does. The vast majority of scholars agree that Matthew and Luke used Mark as their primary source much like John used Ezekiel. The Ezekiel-Isaiah parallel brings forth the concept that an author can copy a work but make the material an opposite to the source and thereby make it more difficult to identify the source that it was copied from.

As John finished, the EID was a transitory draft in that it was intended to be processed by the ZrD process and thus was never intended to be published. This also brings up the question "Did John create the EID as a single draft or did he start with Ezekiel and realize the Ezekiel-Isaiah parallel later?" This question can never be answered because it is easy to formulate an argument for separate drafts and for a combined construction.

The EID is, like all the drafts, simple to understand once you are aware of the process, but it was the most difficult for me to discover the process for. It is a draft which signifies that, John wanted Jesus as a central figure. It is the draft that provides the bulk of the information found with in Revelation today. It is where we get God in heaven, the New Jerusalem, most of the material for the judgments, the primary content for the saints in heaven scenes, the imagery of Jesus, and some of the content for the seven churches. It is the draft wherein we also get the primary imagery for Satan, but it is in the ZrD that we get the word "Satan" itself.

---

143 Isa 65:17-10; Rev 21:1-3.
144 Ezek 40:2; Rev 21:9-10.

The Ezekiel-Isaiah Draft Approximation Text

The Ezekiel-Isaiah approximation draft is a combination of source material, how the material is found in Revelation, and its placement in the Ezekiel-Isaiah draft, which gives the reader a feel for what the draft looked like at this stage of its development. Below is an approximation of how the wax tablets were laid out for the Ezekiel-Isaiah draft and will be used for identification purposes found in the approximation texts.

How the Ezekiel-Isaiah Draft Will Be Displayed

Throughout the Ezekiel-Isaiah draft text, sometimes material from Isaiah is moved to the Ezekiel side, and sometimes material from Ezekiel is moved to the Isaiah side. Other times John will change the meaning of an object by forming an opposite to it. This allows the reader to see two things: first how either Ezekiel and Isaiah formed their parallel with the other, and second how John took Ezekiel and Isaiah and made it his own. This gives us a rare glimpse as to the writing process of the time. Therefore, the EID will be displayed as a parallel with the Ezekiel material on the left page and the Isaiah material on the right. Each content source will also have the final resting place of the Revelation content which was derived from the source. The displaying of the EID is intended to represent something similar to how John must have arranged the wax tablets to construct the EID. For those portions that have unique content such as descriptions of persons in Isaiah (which will become imagery for Jesus), they will only be shown on their respective side.

When material from the Ezekiel (or Isaiah) portion is found on the Isaiah (or Ezekiel) side of the Ezekiel-Isaiah parallel it will be displayed in one of two ways. If the material was shifted over to the other side because no parallel existed for the content John required, then the entire source content is placed on the opposite side of the parallel. If there was the possibility of a parallel made in the EID but the source content came from only one side of the parallel and the content found in Revelation came from the other side of the parallel then the source material will be displayed on the appropriate side and mapped to the Revelation side on an opposite parallel.

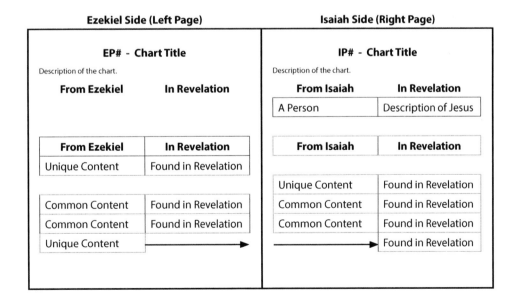

The Ezekiel Prototype for the Calling of John

The Calling of John

Ezekiel is introduced as a priest who is among the captives by a river. Then one day Ezekiel hears John used the calling of Ezekiel 1:1-3 as the calling for himself in the book of Revelation.

	Content Found in Ezekiel		Content Found in Revelation
1:1	I was among the captives by the River Chebar.	1:9	I John, your brother and partner with you in the oppression, Kingdom, and perseverance in Christ Jesus, was on the isle that is called Patmos because of God's Word and the testimony of Jesus Christ.
1:3	Ezekiel the priest.		
1:2	In the fifth of the month, which was the fifth year of king Jehoiachin's captivity.	1:10	I was in the Spirit on the Lord's day, and I heard behind me a loud voice.
1:3	THE LORD's word came expressly to Ezekiel the priest.		

EP1 - Ezekiel's Experience in Heaven - Without the Scroll

John and Ezekiel's experience in heaven were very similar to each other in what the heard and saw. They both saw living creatures, God sitting on a throne, and expanse around the throne made of crystal or glass. The differences between the two are minor such as the order of how the story is depicted and the number of faces the living creatures have.

	Content Found in Ezekiel		John's Encounter With God on His Throne (4:1-11)
Ezek 1:5	Out of its center came . . . . living creatures.	4:6	In the middle of the throne . . . . four living creatures.
Ezek 1:6	Each one of them had ~~four wings.~~	4:8	Each one of them having six wings.
Ezek 1:10*	Face of a lion.	4:7	Like a lion.
	Face of an ox.		Like a calf .
	Face of a man.		Like a face of a man.
	Face of an eagle.		Like a flying eagle.
Ezek 1:13	. . . and lightning went out of the fire.	4:5	Out of the throne proceeded lightnings, sounds and thunders.
Ezek 1:18	The four of them had their rims full of eyes all around.	4:6	Full of eyes before and behind.
Ezek 1:22	Over the head . . . . was the likeness of an expanse, like the awesome crystal to look on.	4:6	Before the throne was something like a sea of glass, similar to crystal.
Ezek 1:26	The likeness of a throne.	4:2	There was a throne set in heaven, and one sitting on the throne.
Ezek 1:26	The appearance of a sapphire stone.	4:3	Looked like a jasper stone and a sardius stone.
Ezek 1:28	As the appearance of the rainbow.	4:3	There was a rainbow around the throne.

* Arranged in the order found in Revelation 4:7.

IP1 - Isaiah's Experience in Heaven - Without the Altar

When John conflated the encounter and commission accounts by God from Ezekiel and Isaiah he chose to use the Isaiah account to determine the order. The result is that we get something very similar to the major elements found in John's encounter with God in Revelation today. The Isaiah content added several key aspects to the EID such as giving the worshiping role to the living creatures and providing an altar for the cleansing of sin.

	Content Found in Isaiah			Content Found in Revelation (Ordered by Isaiah and Then Revelation)
Isa 6:1	I saw THE LORD sitting on a throne.		4:2	There was a throne set in heaven, and one sitting on the throne.
Isa 6:2	The seraphim had one face.		4:6	Each having one face.
Isa 6:2	Each having six wings.		4:8	Each having six wings.
Isa 6:3	They said, "Holy, holy, holy is THE LORD . . . ."		4:8	They said, "Holy, holy, holy is the Lord God, the Almighty."
Isa 6:3	"The whole earth is filled with his glory."		4:8	God created all things.
Isa 6:4	The foundations of the thresholds shook at the voice of him who called.		5:2	I saw a mighty angel proclaiming with a loud voice, "Who is worthy to open the book and to break its seals?"

EP1 - Ezekiel's Experience in Heaven - The Scroll

John made the experience of Ezekiel tasting the scroll that is sweet to his lips as the commissioning scene for Ezekiel. This will later be a major portion of the coronation of Jesus (Rev 5:1-14) where he is the only one to open the scroll. The scroll will also be part of the scene in which the might angel hands John the scroll.

	Content Found in Ezekiel		Content Found in Revelation
Ezek 2:9	When I looked, behold, a hand was stretched out to me; and, behold, a scroll of a book was therein.	5:1 10:2	I saw, in the right hand of him who sat on the throne, a book he had in his hand, a little open book.
Ezek 2:10	He spread it before me: and it was written within and without.	5:2	The scroll written inside and outside.
Ezek 2:10	Written therein lamentations, and mourning, and woe.		
Ezek 3:1	He said to me, "Son of man, eat that which you find. Eat this scroll."	5:7	Jesus took the scroll from the hand of God.
		10:9	He said to me, "Take it, and eat it up. It will make your stomach bitter, but in your mouth it will be as sweet as honey."
Ezek 3:1	and go, speak to the house of Israel.	10:11	"You must prophesy again over many peoples, nations, languages and kings."
Ezek 3:2	So I opened my mouth, and he caused me to eat the scroll.		
Ezek 3:3	He said to me, "Son of man, cause your belly to eat, and fill your bowels with this scroll that I give you. Then I ate it; and it was as sweet as honey in my mouth."	10:10	I took the little book out of the angel's hand and ate it up. It was as sweet as honey in my mouth.

EP2 - Ezekiel's Mission

John extracted the following text from Ezekiel 2:3 - 3:7 to form a parallel with Isaiah's mission. As a result of selecting these passages John is creating the core concepts that will form the message to all of the seven churches.

	Content Found in Ezekiel	Content Found in Revelation
Ezek 2:3	He said to me, "Son of man, I send you to the children of Israel, to a nation of rebels who have rebelled against me. They and their fathers have transgressed against me even to this very day."	This will become the essence of the seven letters as a mixture of people rebelling and following Jesus.
Ezek 2:5	They, whether they will hear, or whether they will forbear (for they are a rebellious house), yet shall know that there has been a prophet among them.	
Ezek 3:5	For you are not sent to a people of a strange speech and of a hard language, but to the house of Israel;	This will be transformed to, "He who has ears let him hear" and placed at the end of each of the letters to the seven churches (Rev 2:7, 11, 17, 29; 3:6, 13, 22).
Ezek 3:6	not to many peoples of a strange speech and of a hard language, whose words you cannot understand. Surely, if I sent you to them, they would listen to you.	
Ezek 3:7	But the house of Israel will not listen to you; for they will not listen to me: for all the house of Israel are obstinate and hard hearted.	
Ezek 2:4	The children are impudent and stiff hearted: I am sending you to them; and you shall tell them, "Thus says THE LORD."	For Ezekiel was told to say, "Thus says THE LORD" for every letter to the seven churches begins this way: [A description of Jesus] "Thus says these things:"
Ezek 3:11	Go to them of the captivity, to the children of your people, and speak to them, and tell them, "Thus says THE LORD;" whether they will hear, or whether they will forbear.	

Scripture	Greek (Thus says)
Ezek 2:4	Τάδε λέγει
Rev 2:1, 8, 12, 18; 3:1, 7, 14	Τάδε λέγει

IP1 - Isaiah's Experience in Heaven - The Altar That Removes Iniquity

John formed a parallel with the commissioning of Ezekiel by receiving and eating the scroll with Isaiah's experience of the coal touching his lips to cleanse him of iniquity. Both accounts will become source material for the coronation of Jesus (Rev 5:1-14). Below represents how the John formed a parallel with Isa 6:4-8 and Rev 5:2-9.

	Content Found in Isaiah		Content Found in Revelation
Isa 6:4	The house was filled with smoke.	5:3	No one in heaven above, or on the earth, or under the earth, was able to open the book, or to look in it.
Isa 6:5	Then I said, "Woe is me! For I am undone, because I am a man of unclean lips, and I dwell among a people of unclean lips: for my eyes have seen the King, THE LORD of Armies!"	5:4	And I wept much, because no one was found worthy to open the book, or to look in it.
Isa 6:6	Then one of the seraphim flew to me, having a live coal in his hand, which he had taken with tongs from off the altar.	5:9	Jesus' death cleanses believers of sin.
Isa 6:7	He touched my mouth with it, and said,		
Isa 6:7	"Behold, this has touched your lips, and your iniquity is taken away, and your sin forgiven."		
Isa 6:8	"Whom shall I send, and who will go for us?" Then I said, "Here I am. Send me!"	5:2	I saw a mighty angel proclaiming with a loud voice, "Who is worthy to open the book and to break its seals?"

IP2 - Isaiah's Mission

John takes the mission of Isaiah and applies it to the letters of the seven churches. The message is in two parts, the first is that God's people need to hear him, and the second is that the cities will be destroyed.

	Content Found in Isaiah	Content Found in Revelation
Isa 6:9	Tell the people that they hear but do not understand. They see but do not perceive.	This will be transformed to, "He who has ears let him hear" and placed at the end of each of the letters to the seven churches (Rev 2:7, 11, 17, 29; 3:6, 13, 22).
Isa 6:210	Make the heart of his people fat.	
	Make their ears heavy and shut their eyes; lest they see with their eyes, and hear with their ears, and understand with their heart, and turn again and be healed."	
Isa 6:11	Then I said, "Lord, how long?"	This will set the stage for the finality of Revelation to take place when all the believers have either become martyrs or have fallen away from the faith in the seven cities.
Isa 6:12	He answered, "Until cities are waste without inhabitant, and houses without man, and the land becomes utterly waste, and THE LORD has removed men far away, and the forsaken places are many within the land.	

EP3 - Ezekiel Appointed as a Watchman - Part 1

The Ezekiel portion of the EID was considerably larger than the Isaiah portion and as a result Ezekiel had content that was not found in Isaiah. The text below represents such content in that they are two passages that John combined into one wax tablet, thus making the prototype for the mighty angel narrative.

	Content Found in Ezekiel and Isaiah		Content Found in Revelation (Ordered by Revelation)
Ezek 2:6	You, son of man, don't be afraid of them, neither be afraid of their words, though briers and thorns are with you, and you do dwell among scorpions: don't be afraid of their words, nor be dismayed at their looks, though they are a rebellious house.	9:4	They were told that they should not hurt the grass of the earth, neither any green thing, neither any tree, but only those people who don't have God's seal on their foreheads.
Ezek 3:8	Behold, I have made your face hard against their faces, and your forehead hard against their foreheads.	9:5	They were given power not to kill them, but to torment them for five months. Their torment was like the torment of a scorpion, when it strikes a person.
Ezek 3:9	As an adamant harder than flint have I made your forehead: don't be afraid of them, neither be dismayed at their looks, though they are a rebellious house.		
Ezek 3:12	Then the spirit lifted me up, and I heard behind me the voice of a great rushing, saying, "Blessed be Lord's glory from his place."	10:4	John heard the seven thunders but was told not to write what they said.
Ezek 3:13	I heard the noise of the wings of the living creatures as they touched one another, and the noise of the wheels beside them, even the noise of a great rushing.	10:4-5	[The imagery of the seven thunders was derived from the noise that the four living creatures made, the seven days of noise.]
Ezek 3:14	So the spirit lifted me up, and took me away; and I went in bitterness, in the heat of my spirit; and THE LORD's hand was strong on me.	10:9-10	The scroll tasted bitter to John's stomach.
Ezek 3:15	I sat there overwhelmed among them seven days.		
Ezek 3:16	At the end of seven days THE LORD's word came to me, saying,	10:4	When the seven thunders sounded, I was about to write but I heard a voice from the sky saying, "Seal up the things which the seven thunders said, and don't write them."
Ezek 3:17	"Son of man, I have made you a watchman to the house of Israel: therefore hear the word from my mouth, and give them warning from me."		
Ezek 3:17-27	[Ezekiel must go to the righteous and the unrighteous.]		

EP3 - Ezekiel Appointed as a Watchman - Part 2
(Ezek 4:5-8; Rev 11:2-3, 9)

The End of One Ministry and the Beginning of the New Holy Seed

The Ezekiel side of the parallel conveys the story of the plight of the unrighteous, while the Isaiah side conveys the story of the righteous. He will continue this pattern until he reaches the second passage where Ezekiel is appointed as a watchman (Ezek 33:1-8).

How John constructed this by forming a complex parallel transforming the numbers representing years of sin for Israel, Judah and the combination of the two, to parallel the days of the siege to the years of ministry for Israel, the temple, and aspects of Jesus. John then changed the numbers so they would reflect the time of the Roman siege of Jerusalem.

42 months	420 years that the second temple was in service.
	42 months = 3½ years as the length of the Roman siege of Jerusalem in 67 - 70 CE.
1,260 days	1,260 years since the exodus or Israel crossed the Jordan river.
	1,260 days = 3½ years as the length of the Roman siege of Jerusalem in 67 - 70 CE.
3½ days	*3½ days = 35 years that Jesus lived (1 BCE to 35 CE).*
	3½ days = 3 days Jesus was dead.
	3½ days = 3½ years as the length of the Roman siege of Jerusalem in 67 - 70 CE.

Ezekiel Side

A. 42 Months as the Length of the Ministry of the Temple (Ezek 4:5; Rev 11:2).

Ezekiel laid on his left side for 390 days which represents 390 years Israel has sinned against God (Ezek 4:5).

The temple courtyard will be trampled by the gentiles for 42 months = 420 years the second temple served (Rev 11:1-2).

B.　1,260 Days as the Ministry of Israel (Ezek 4:6; Rev 11:3).

Ezekiel laid on his right side for 40 days which represents the 40 years Judah has sinned against God (Ezek 4:6).

The two prophets witnessed for 1,260 days = 1,260 years since the Exodus or Israel crossing the Jordan river (Rev 11:3).

C.　3½ Days as the Days Jesus was Dead and the Length of the Siege of Jerusalem (Rev 11:9).

The combination of 390 days + 40 days = The length of the Babylonian siege of Jerusalem (Ezek 4:8).

The two prophets were dead for 3½ days then raised and taken to heaven (Rev 11:9, 12).

Isaiah Side

An illustration that even if the oak tree (believers) and a tenth of the city is burned, a new crop of believers will be sprouted from the acorns (Isa 6:10-3).

C'.　3½ Days Connected With the Conception of Jesus (Isa 7:14-5; Rev 12:1-2).

There will be a sign of a woman with child (Isa 7:14).
There was seen in heaven; a woman . . . with child . . . she cried out in pain, laboring to give birth (Rev 12:1-2).

Although there is no evidence supporting the 3½ day parallel in Revelation 12, it is likely that the 3½ was at the birth of Jesus. In this way John would complement the death of the two prophets with the birth of the child. If this was the case then the 3½ days would represent the 35 years of Jesus' life.

B'.　1,260 Days Connected With the Ascension of Jesus (Isa 8:4; Rev 12:5).

Before the child knows how to say "father" or "mother" the riches of Damascus and the plunder of Samaria will be taken by the king of Assyria (Isa 8:3).

In revelation this becomes the child is born and then taken to heaven to rule with God (Rev 12:4-5). The woman (as Jerusalem/Israel)will be taken to the wilderness for 1,260 days (Rev 12:6).

A'. 42 Months Connected With the Child Ruling the World (Isa 9:6-7; Rev 12:10).

The child will rule the world (Isa 9:6-7; 12:10).

In Revelation John connects the point where Jesus becomes ruler of (brings salvation to) the whole world (Rev 12:10-1).

Page Intentionally Left Blank

IP3 The New Seed (Jesus the Child)
The Death of a City and the Birth of a Ministry

John used the content of Isaiah 6:10 - 9:18 as the primary source material for depicting a new holy seed (the child Jesus), the destruction of a city (the woman) by military conquests from other nations (Rome). In doing so, he also portrayed the chronological order of Jesus being taken to heaven to rule with God, an army invading Judah/Israel and God's people being preserved.

It should be noted that John is using the birth of the child and the two prophets as depictions of Jesus and thereby forming a transition period where the end of the ministry ends with the death and ascension of the two prophets (Rev 11:8-12) and the birth of the second ministry begins with the birth of Jesus (Rev 12:4). Both will ascend to heaven (Rev 11:12; 12:5) and as a result the kingdom of the world will become the kingdom of God (Rev 11:15; 12:10).

Content Found in Isaiah		Content Found in Revelation	
The End of a City and a New Seed (Isa 6:10-10:17)			
6:10-3	An illustration that even if the oak tree (believers) and a tenth of the city is burned, a new crop of believers will be sprouted from the acorns.	11:13	In that day there was a great earthquake, and a tenth of the city fell. Seven thousand people were killed in the earthquake, and the rest were terrified, and gave glory to the God of heaven.
7:14-5	A sign of a woman with child (7:14-5).	12:1-2	A sign in heaven of a woman and child.
7:17-22	The land will go from plentiful harvest to weeds.	12:3-4	Satan will take a third of the stars in the sky.
8:4	Before the child knows how to say "father" or "mother" the child will be carried away by the King of Assyria.	12:4-5	Before Satan could kill the child God took him away.
8:5-17	The army will sweep through Israel like a flood but will not destroy Judah.	12:15-6	The serpent spewed water out of his mouth so that he might cause her to be carried away. The earth rescued the woman by absorbing the water.
8:19-22	God's people should consult with God and turn to the law and to the testimony.	12:17	Those who obey the commandments of God and the Lamb
	If they don't they will go hungry.	12:6, 14	God nourished the woman.
9:4	For the yoke of his burden, and the staff of his shoulder, the rod of his oppressor, you have broken as in the day of Midian.	12:5	The child is to rule all the nations with a rod of iron.
9:6-7	When the son is born the government shall be upon his shoulders. His name will be called wonderful, counselor, mighty God, everlasting father, prince of peace. Of the increase of his government and of peace there shall be no end.	12:5	The child was caught up to God, and to his throne.
		12:10	Now the salvation, the power, the kingdom of our God and the authority of his Christ has come (see also 11:15).
9:12	Syria and the Philistines will devour Israel with an open mouth.	12:4	Satan wanted to devour the child.
		12:15	Satan spewed water out of his mouth like a river.
9:15	The prophet who teaches lies is the tail.	12:4	Satan's tail drew a third of the stars of the sky and threw them to the earth.
9:16	For those who lead this people lead them astray; and those who are led by them are destroyed.	12:7-8	Satan and his angels were thrown to the earth. . .
		12:12	knowing that he has but a short time.
9:17	God's anger will not turn away.	12:12	Satan has great wrath.
		12:16	Satan grew angry with the woman to make war with the rest of her children.
9:18-9	For wickedness burns like a fire. It devours the briers and thorns . . . . people are the fuel for the fire.	8:7	The believers are burned up and described as "a third of the trees and all the green grass" (see 7:1-3; 9:4).

EP4 - The Judgments by the Nations - Part 1

John was faced with the problem that parts of the Ezekiel-Isaiah parallel did not match the parallel that he wanted to convey. John's solution was to move a few sections around to create the proper message (see "John's First Major Content Alignment Corrections" on page 22).

John recycled the Ezekiel 5:2 passage illustrating the three attacks by the nations against Judah and moved the Ezek 5:16-7 passage to the Isaiah side of the parallel making it the three attacks by Jesus.

Content Found in Ezekiel	Content Found in Revelation
	First Trumpet
5:2 A third by fire.	8:7 Hail and fire mixed with blood was thrown down to the earth, a third of the earth and trees were burnt up . . .
	Second Trumpet
5:2 A third part scattered to the wind.	8:8-9 A third of the sea became blood, and a third of the living creatures which were in the sea died. One third of the ships were destroyed.
	Third Trumpet
	[No parallel with Ezekiel found.]
	Fourth Trumpet
5:2 A third was struck with the sword.	8:12 A third of the sun, moon and stars were struck. They were darkened by day and night by a third.

IP4 - The Judgments by Jesus - Part 1

John took the attacks by God from the Ezekiel side (Ezek 5:16-7) and transformed the imagery to Jesus as a warrior. This balanced out the attacks by the nations from the Ezekiel side of the EID parallel in that both sides had three actions against Jerusalem. The end result will set the stage for two groups of people and two destructive elements where the Ezekiel side of the Ezekiel-Isaiah parallel represents the Jews who did not keep God's commandments and follow Jesus, and the Isaiah side will represent the plight of those who did.

Content Found in Ezekiel	Content Found in Revelation
	First Seal / Horseman (Rev 6:1-2)
	6:1 The Lamb (Jesus) opened one of the seven seals . . .
5:16 God will shoot evil arrows at them.	6:2 He had a bow.
	Second Seal / Horseman (6:3-4)
	6:3 He [Jesus] opened the second seal . . .
	[No parallel with Ezekiel found.]
	Third Seal / Horseman (6:5-6)
	6:5 He [Jesus] opened the third seal . . . .
5:16 God will increase their famine and break their staff of bread.	6:5 He had a balance in his hand.
	6:6 A little food will be very expensive.
	Fourth Seal / Horseman (6:7-8)
	6:7 He [Jesus] opened the fourth seal . . . .
5:17 God will send famine, evil animals, pestilence and death by the sword.	6:8 He will kill with the sword, famine, pestilence and by wild animals.

EP4 - The Judgments by the Nations - Part 2

The Ezekiel side of the Ezekiel-Isaiah parallel reflects God's people rejecting God's commandments and becoming more evil than the nations around them. As a result they will be in torment and scattered to the winds. In the end they will face the wrath of God.

Content Found in Ezekiel		Content Found in Revelation	
They Disobeyed God's Commandments		**They Disobeyed God's Commandments**	
5:5-6	Jerusalem disobeyed God's ordinances.	9:21	They didn't repent of their murders, nor of their sorceries, nor of their sexual immorality, nor of their thefts.
5:9	Because of your abominations.		
They Will Not Change Even Though		**They Will Not Change Even Though**	
5:10	Father shall eat son and their sons shall eat their fathers.	9:5	They were tormented for five months, in those days people will seek death.
5:12	The survivors are scattered to the winds.	6:15	Those remaining will hide in the caves and mountains.
5:13	They will face the wrath of God.	6:16	They will face the wrath of God and the Lamb.
God Will Destroy Those Who Deceive His People		**God Will Destroy Those Who Deceive His People**	
6:3	God will bring a sword to destroy the high places.	11:18	[God's] wrath came to those who destroy the earth.
6:6	All the dwellings, high places and alters will be destroyed.		[They polluted the land by placing idols everywhere.]
6:7	The slain shall fall among you and you will God.		
6:8	The house of Israel shall fall by the sword, famine and pestilence because of their wickedness.		
6:13	All the idols in the mountains and under every tree.		

IP4 - The Judgments by Jesus - Part 2

The Isaiah side of the Ezekiel-Isaiah parallel tells of God's people that will obey God no matter what. John did this by making a few adjustments. First, he turned the evil actions of Jacob/Israel (Isa 9:8) into the synagogue of Satan. Second, he flipped the contrast of: the evil does only repenting when confronted with threat of life, to: the true believers will remain faithful even in facing death. Third, he took the imagery of trees, thorns and briers as evil and transformed it to trees and grass representing the believers (Rev 7:3; 8:7; 9:4-7). John then used Isa 12:1 - 13:8 to depict the saints in heaven for keeping the commandments of God.

Content Found in Isaiah		Content Found in Revelation	
They Issued Evil Commandments to God's People		**They Resisted Evil Commandments**	
10:1	Woe to those who decree unrighteous decrees (Jacob/Israel; see 9:8), and those who write oppressive decrees;	2:9	"I know your works, oppression and your poverty (but you are rich), and the blasphemy of those who say they are Jews, and they are not, but are a synagogue of Satan.
10:2	To deprive the needy from justice, and to rob the poor among my people of their rights.		
	They Will Only Change When:		**They Will Remain Faithful Even When:**
10:4	They will only bow down under the prisoners, and will fall under the slain.	2:10	The devil is about to throw some of you into prison, that you may be tested. Be faithful to death.
	For all this his anger is not turned away, but his hand is stretched out still.	13:10*	If anyone is to go into captivity, he will go into captivity. If anyone is to be killed with the sword, he must be killed.
		6:9	Under the throne of God are the people who were martyred by keeping the commandments.
God Will Destroy Those Who Deceive His People		**The Wicked Will Destroy God's People Because They Obey Him**	
10:15-9	God will destroy those who try to deceive God's people illustrated in the burning of all the thorns, briers and most of the trees.	7:3	Do not harm the trees until all are sealed.
		9:4-7	In the fifth trumpet those with the seal of God on their foreheads as well as the trees and the green grass will not be harmed. The rest will be in torment for five months.
		8:7	One third of the trees were burned up, and all green grass was burned up.
		6:10	Those who martyred the saints will be avenged.
God's People Will Lean on God		**God's People Will Lean on God**	
10:20	God's people will continue to lean on God.	2:9	Be faithful to death.
		6:9	Under the altar of God were the martyrs of the faithful.
		6:11	They were given a white robe and told to rest.

*Revelation 13:10 is a parallel formation of Rev 2:10 which derives its source parallel from Isa 10:4 (see "The Church in Smyrna and the Beast Narrative" on page 279).

EP4 - The Judgments by the Nations - Part 3

The Ezekiel side of the EID parallel paints the picture that God is angry with his people because of their abominations. Therefore, God will send the worst of the nations and they will profane all their holy places. God will strip them of all their dignity, wealth and power by giving them to the nations to plunder (Ezek 7:17-21).

	Content Found in Ezekiel		Content Found in Revelation
Ezek 7:1	The end has come on the four corners of the land (or earth).	7:1	I saw four angels at the four corners of the earth.
		9:14	Free the four angels who are bound at the great River Euphrates.
Ezek 7:2-8	Various descriptions of how God is angry with them.		
Ezek 7:10	The day . . . . it comes and your doom has gone out.	6:17	The great day of his wrath has come; and who is able to stand?
Ezek 7:16	Those who escape shall be on the mountains like doves of the valleys.	6:14	They hid themselves in the caves and in the rocks on the mountains.
Ezek 7:24	The worst nations will posses their houses and their holy places will be profaned.		
Ezek 7:27	The king shall mourn, and the prince shall be clothed in desolation, and the hands of the people of the land shall be troubled.	6:14	The kings of the earth, the princes and everyone else.
Ezek 8:1	In the sixth year, in the sixth month, in the fifth day of the month.	9:15	That hour and day and month and year.

EP4 - The Judgments by the Nations - Part 4

Ezekiel provides the foundation material for John's imagery of the seal of God on believers' foreheads to protect them through crises.

	Content Found in Ezekiel		Content Found in Revelation
Ezek 9:4	Go through the middle of Jerusalem and set a mark on the foreheads of the men signed and cried over all the abominations that were done.	9:4	They were told that they should not hurt the grass of the earth, neither any green thing, neither any tree,
Ezek 9:4	To the others . . . . Go through the city after him, and strike: don't let your eye spare, neither have pity.	9:4	but only those people who don't have God's seal on their foreheads.
		9:5	They were given power not to kill them, but to torment them for five months. Their torment was like the torment of a scorpion, when it strikes a person.

IP4 - The Judgments by Jesus - Part 3

To create the Isaiah prototype to the sixth seal John consolidated the two passages found in Ezekiel and Isaiah regarding the darkening of the sun, moon and stars in the sky. The consolidating of the two passages will become the sixth seal.

	Content Found in Isaiah and Joel		Content Found in Revelation
Isa 13:9	Behold the day of THE LORD comes, cruel, with wrath and fierce anger.	6:17	The great day of his wrath has come; and who is able to stand?
		19:15	The fierceness of the wrath of God, the almighty (19:15)
Isa 13:10	The sun will be darkened . . . . the moon will . . . . not shine (Joel 2:10).	6:12	The sun became black as sackcloth made of hair and the moon became as blood.
Isa 13:10	For the stars of the sky and its constellations will not give their light.	6:13	The stars of the sky fell to the earth.
Isa 13:13	God will make the heavens tremble and the earth will be shaken out of place.	6:14	The sky was removed like a scroll when it is rolled up. Every mountain and island were moved out of their places.
Isa 13:14-22	They will flee to their own lands.	6:15-6	They will flee to the mountains.

The Ezekiel Prototype of the Sixth Seal (Ezek 32:7-10; Rev 6:12-17)

John, in an effort to consolidate symbols, combined two similar passages that were out of order in the Ezekiel-Isaiah parallel. Thus the EID was formed, the Isaiah material (Isa 13:10-22) was processed first and connected with an Ezekiel parallel. He simply conflated Ezek 32:7-10 with Isa 13:9-22.

	Content Found in Ezekiel and Joel		Content Found in Revelation
Ezek 32:6	I will also water with your blood.	6:12	The moon became as blood.
Ezek 32:7	The stars withdraw from shining.	6:12	The sun became black as sackcloth made of hair.
Ezek 32:7	The moon shall not give its light.	6:12	The moon became as blood.
Ezek 32:8	[I will] make its stars dark.	6:14	The sky was removed like a scroll.
Ezek 32:7	I will cover the heavens.		
Joel 2:10	The earth quakes before them.	6:14; 6:20	Every mountain and island were moved out of their places.
Ezek 32:10	Their kings shall be horribly afraid for you.	6:15	The kings of the earth, the princes, the commanding officers, the rich, the strong, and every slave and free person.
Ezek 32:10	They shall tremble at every moment, every man for his own life, in the day of your fall.	6:15	[They] hid themselves in the caves and in the rocks of the mountains.

EP5 - The Glory of the Lord Flees Jerusalem

The Ezekiel side of this parallel tells the story of the glory of God fleeing the temple pending the Babylonian siege of Jerusalem. The consequences are dire for the Israelites but so are the consequences of their sinning against God. As such they will be removed from their country and live among the nations. The end of the section, which John used for this wax tablet, describes the inhabitants of Jerusalem as a worthless vine. John will turn that into the description of Jerusalem and bring it to the Isaiah side of the equation.

The Glory of the Lord Flees Babylon on Earth

Content Found in Ezekiel		Content Found in Revelation	
Ezek 10:1-21	An account of the glory of THE LORD leaving the temple in Jerusalem [because of the Babylonian invasion].	11:1-2	Measure the temple but not its walls.
Ezek 11:1-13	The great men in God's house who gave wicked council will be brought down.	11:7-13	The two prophets are killed and taken to heaven.
Ezek 11:15	They said to each other, "Go far away from THE LORD. This land has been given to us for a possession."		
Ezek 11:16	God removed them to far-off nations.		
Ezek 12:1-28	They will know God because the stranger will take their house.		
Ezek 12:17-28	The judgment will not be delayed.		
Ezek 13:18	The women sew pillows and make kerchiefs for those who hunt souls.	11:10	They will give gifts to one another.
Ezek 13:19	They kill the souls that should not die.	11:7	When they have finished their testimony . . . . [they] kill them.
Ezek 13:19	They give handfuls of barley and pieces of bread to kill souls.	11:10	They will give gifts to one another.
Ezek 13:23	God will deliver his people out of their hand.	11:12	God breathed life into the two prophets.
Ezek 13:23	You will see no more false visions nor practice divination.	11:13	The rest were terrified and gave glory to God.
Ezek 15:2	Son of man,		
Ezek 15:6	The inhabitants of Jerusalem are connected to the worthless vine.		
Ezek 15:7	God will use fire against them.		
Ezek 15:8	God will make the land desolate because they have committed a trespass.		

IP5 - The Glory of the Lord Triumphs in Heaven

Below is only a representation of the Isaiah portion of the simple parallel and how it gets interwoven into Revelation. Note that Isaiah reflects the opposite content that is found in Ezekiel such as that the glory of God flees Babylon on earth (Ezek 10:1-21) and the glory of God triumphs against Babylon in heaven (Isa 4:12-5).

The Description of Jesus

	Content Found in Isaiah		Content Found in Revelation
14:12	How you have fallen from heaven, morning star, son of the dawn! How you are cut down to the ground, who laid the nations low!	22:16	Jesus as the bright morning star [signifying Jesus as the real morning star].

	Content Found in Isaiah		Content Found in Revelation
14:12	How you have fallen from heaven, morning star, son of the dawn! How you are cut down to the ground, who laid the nations low!	22:16	Jesus as the bright morning star [signifying Jesus as the real morning star].
14:13	You said in your heart, "I will ascend into heaven! I will exalt my throne above the stars of God! I will sit on the mountain of assembly, in the far north!"	12:7	There was war in the sky. Michael and his angels made war on the dragon. The dragon and his angels made war.
14:14	"I will ascend above the heights of the clouds! I will make myself like the Most High!"		
14:15	Yet you shall be brought down to Sheol, to the depths of the pit.	12:8	They didn't prevail, neither was a place found for him any more in heaven.
		12:9	The great dragon was thrown down.
		20:1	I saw an angel . . . . having the key of the abyss . . . .
		20:2	He . . . . Satan, who deceives the whole inhabited earth, and bound him . . . .
14:18	All the kings of the nations sleep in glory, everyone in his own house.	20:3	[The angel] cast him into the abyss, and shut it, and sealed it over him, that he should deceive the nations no more, until the thousand years were finished.
14:21	Prepare for slaughter of his children because of the iniquity of their fathers, that they not rise up and possess the earth, and fill the surface of the world with cities.	20:7	And after the thousand years, Satan will be released from his prison,
14:26	This is the plan that is determined for the whole earth. This is the hand that is stretched out over all the nations.	20:8	and he will come out to deceive the nations which are in the four corners of the earth, Gog and Magog, to gather them together to the war; the number of whom is as the sand of the sea.
14:27	For THE LORD has planned, and who can stop it? His hand is stretched out, and who can turn it back?		
14:29	For out of the serpent's root an adder will emerge, and his fruit will be a fiery, flying serpent.	12:9; 20:2	The old serpent, he who is called the devil and Satan, the deceiver of the whole world.
14:32	What will they answer the messengers of the nation? That THE LORD has founded Zion, and in her the afflicted of his people will take refuge.	14:1-4	The Lamb standing on Mount Zion with the 144,000 representing the first fruits to God and the Lamb.
14:32	What will they answer the messengers of the nation?	14:6	The gospel was spread to the entire world.
15:1 to 19:17	The oracles to the nations,		
17:7, 10	People will look to their maker . . . . the forgotten God of salvation.	14:7	Fear the Lord . . . . who made everything.
21:9	Fallen, fallen is Babylon and all the engraved images of her gods are broken to the ground.	14:8	Babylon the great has fallen, which has made all the nations to drink of the wine of the wrath of her sexual immorality.
		14:14	One sitting like the son of man
		14:13-6	The saints are connected to the great harvest of grapes.
		14:18	An angel who has the power of fire [no fire is used].
		14:19-20	The grapes make the wrath of God which will destroy the harlot and make her desolate (Rev 17:6; 18:5-8).

EP6 - Jerusalem as the Mother of God's Children (Ezek 16:1-63; Rev 17:1 - 18:24)

In Ezekiel, Jerusalem is depicted as an unwanted woman whom God married, adorned in riches and produced many children with. Jerusalem then became unfaithful to God to the extent that she was being paid by her suitors. She even took the children produced with God and sacrificed them which caused God to destroy her suitors and her.

John took the story of Jerusalem as the harlot and made it part of the harlot in Rev 17:1-18:24. Ezekiel depicts Jerusalem as a harlot that was clothed by God with all kinds of riches but she became worse than a prostitute––at least a prostitute asks for payment. In Ezek 16:34 she is paid for her affection, but in Revelation there are no statements that speak to this effect (although there are no statements that challenge that she pays others for services).

Content Found in Ezekiel		Content Found in Revelation	
16:10	I clothed you also with embroidered work, and shod you with sealskin, and I dressed you about with fine linen and covered you with silk.	17:4	The woman was dressed in purple and scarlet, and decked with gold and precious stones and pearls, having in her hand a golden cup full of abominations and the impurities of the sexual immorality of the earth.
16:11	I decked you with ornaments, and I put bracelets on your hands and a chain on your neck.		
16:16	You took off your garments, and made for yourself high places decked with various colors, and played the prostitute on them.		
16:17	You also took your beautiful jewels of my gold and of my silver, which I had given you, and made for yourself images of men, and played the prostitute with them.		
16:20	Moreover you have taken your sons and your daughters, whom you have borne to me, and you have sacrificed these to them to be devoured.	17:6	I saw the woman drunken with the blood of the saints, and with the blood of the martyrs of Jesus.
16:37	God will gather all her lovers and they will hate her and strip her naked.	17:16	They will make her desolate, and will make her naked.
16:41	They will burn her houses with fire.	17:16	They will burn her utterly with fire.
16:36	the blood of your children, that you gave to them.	18:24	In her was found the blood of prophets and of saints, and of all who have been slain on the earth.

IP6 - Jesus as the Father of God's Children (Isa 22:20-5)

John formed a parallel with the harlot from Ezekiel as the unfaithful mother of God's children and with Eliakim, God's faithful servant whom he will make the father of Jerusalem. They both were clothed by God and given his people to lead and then took different paths. The Ezekiel side depicts those who are unfaithful to God and the Isaiah side depicts those faithful to God.

In the published version of Revelation Jesus will be maintained as the keeper of the key of David (Isa 22:22; Rev 3:7) and addressed as the root and offspring of David (Isa 22:22; Rev 22:16). The rest of the descriptions of Tyre will become the foundation for the church in Philadelphia.

The Description of Jesus

	Content Found in Isaiah		Content Found in Revelation
22:20	It will happen in that day that I will call my servant Eliakim the son of Hilkiah.		
22:21	and I will clothe him with your robe, and strengthen him with your belt.		
	I will commit your government into his hand; and he will be a father to the inhabitants of Jerusalem, and to the house of Judah.	22:16	Jesus is "the root and the offspring of David."
22:22	I will lay the key of David's house on his shoulder. He will open, and no one will shut. He will shut, and no one will open.	3:7	He who is true, he who has the key of David, he who opens and no one can shut, and who shuts and no one opens, says these things:
22:23	I will fasten him like a nail in a sure place. He will be for a throne of glory to his father's house.	3:12	I will make him a pillar in the temple of my God.
22:25	In that day . . . . the nail that was fastened in a sure place will give way. It will be cut down and fall. The burden that was on it will be cut off.	3:10	Because you kept my command to endure, I also will keep you from the hour of testing, which is to come on the whole world, to test those who dwell on the earth.

EP7 - Tyre

The Merchandise Traded

Most of the items mentioned in Rev 18:12-3 are found in Ezek 27:12-22 with the major difference being that Ezekiel focuses on the specific nations that trade specific items (Ezek 27:12-22) and Revelation refers to them as nations (Rev 18:11).

In Ezekiel		In Revelation	
27:12	Silver	18:12	Merchandise of silver.
	Iron	18:12	Merchandise of iron.
27:13	Persons of men	18:13	People's bodies and souls.
	Vessels of brass	18:12	Every vessel made of . . . . brass.
27:14	Horses	18:13	Horses
	War horses	18:13	Chariots?
27:15	Ivory tusks	18:12	Every vessel made of ivory.
	Ebony	18:12	Expensive wood.

In Ezekiel		In Revelation	
27:16	Purple	18:12	Purple
	Fine linen	18:12	Fine linen
27:17	Oil	18:13	Olive oil
27:18	Wine of Helbon.	18:13	Wine
27:20	Lambs	18:13	Sheep
27:22	Chief of all spices.	18:13	Spices
	Precious stones.	18:12	Precious stones.
	Gold	18:12	Merchandise of gold.

The Lament of the Merchants

Below shows how both Ezekiel and Revelation cover the same material regarding how the sea merchants react to the destruction of each respective city. The two accounts differ as to the time of the destruction. Revelation has it as an hour (Rev 18:17) while Ezekiel has it as a day. In Revelation the hour and day are interchangeable, which can be seen in the alternating between hour and day in the sixth church (Rev 3: 10 - "the hour of testing"), the sixth seal (6:17 - "the great day of his wrath"), the sixth trumpet (Rev 9:15 - "that hour and day ") and the sixth bowl (Rev 16:14 - "that great day of God").

	Content Found in Ezekiel		Content Found in Revelation
	[See Ezek 27:12-22 for the various merchants and goods traded.]	18:15	The merchants of these things, who were made rich by her, will stand far away for the fear of her torment, weeping and mourning;
27:27	Your riches . . . . shall fall into the heart of the seas in the day of your ruin.	18:17	for in an hour such great riches are made desolate.
27:29	All who handled the oar, the mariners, and all the pilots of the sea, shall come down from their ships; they shall stand on the land.	18:17	Every ship master, and everyone who sails anywhere, and mariners, and as many as gain their living by sea, stood far away.
27:30	and shall cast up dust on their heads, they shall wallow themselves in the ashes	18:19	They cast dust on their heads.
	[They] shall cause their voice to be heard over you, and shall cry bitterly.		[they] cried, weeping and mourning,
27:32	In their wailing they shall take up a lamentation for you . . . . "Who is there like Tyre?"	18:18	and cried out as they looked at the smoke of her burning, saying, "What is like the great city?"
27:33	When your wares went out of the seas, you filled many peoples; you enriched the kings of the earth with the multitude of your riches and of your merchandise.	18:9	The kings of the earth, who committed sexual immorality and lived wantonly with her, will weep and wail over her, when they look at the smoke of her burning.
		18:11	The merchants of the earth weep and mourn over her, for no one buys their merchandise any more.
28:2	Because your heart is lifted up, and you have said, I am a god, I sit in the seat of God, in the middle of the seas; yet you are man, and not God.	18:7	however much she glorified herself. . . for she says in her heart, "I sit a queen, and am no widow, and will in no way see mourning."

IP7 - Tyre (Jesus, a Certain King)

John sees Jesus' lifespan as 35 years and uses the phrase "70 years from a certain king" to predict the destruction of Jerusalem and Rome. He predicts the destruction of Jerusalem being 70 years after Jesus is born and the destruction of Rome 70 years after his death. Jerusalem was destroyed by the Romans in 70 CE and given this prediction, John is predicting that the destruction of Rome will take place in 105 CE.

Content Found in Isaiah		Content Found in Revelation	
23:15	It will come to pass in that day that Tyre will be forgotten seventy years, according to the days of one king. After the end of seventy years it will be to Tyre like in the song of the prostitute.		[Removed in the ZrD (see "Z6 - The Flying Scroll Alteration" on page 116 and "The Destruction of Tyre and the Rejoicing of the Saints (Zech 1:12; Rev 19:1-9)" on page 94.)]
23:16	Take a harp; go about the city, you prostitute that has been forgotten. Make sweet melody. Sing many songs, that you may be remembered.	18:22	The voice of harpists, minstrels, flute players and trumpeters will be heard no more at all in you.

The Wages of Sin and the Destruction of Tyre (Isa 23:1 -17; Rev 18:2-6)

The following Isaiah content depicts Tyre more like the Ezekiel depiction of Jerusalem in Ezekiel 16:1-58 than Ezekiel's description of Tyre. So John will move this section closer to the placement of Jerusalem as the harlot (Rev 17:1-18).

Content Found in Isaiah		Content Found in Revelation	
23:17	It will happen after the end of seventy years that		
	THE LORD will visit Tyre, and she shall return to her wages,	18:6	Return to her just as she returned, and repay her double as she did, and according to her works.
	and will play the prostitute with all the kingdoms of the world on the surface of the earth.	18:3	All the kings of the earth committed sexual immorality with her.
23:1-12	All those on earth who have traded with Tyre will mourn over her destruction. Similar content to the Ezek 27:12-33 description of Tyre.	18:12-9	Same content found on the Ezekiel side for Rev 18:12-9.

The Wages of Righteousness (Isa 23:18; Rev 3:18)

John uses Isaiah's description that Tyre's wages and merchandise will be holiness to God and contrasts it with the wickedness of Tyre. This content will become the central message to the church in Laodicea.

Content Found in Isaiah		Content Found in Revelation	
23:18	Her merchandise and her wages will be holiness to the THE LORD. It will not be treasured nor laid up; for her merchandise will be for those who dwell before Yahweh, to eat sufficiently, and for durable clothing.	3:18	I counsel you to buy from me gold refined by fire, that you may become rich; and white garments [acts of righteousness, see Rev 19:8], that you may clothe yourself, and that the shame of your nakedness may not be revealed; and eye salve to anoint your eyes, that you may see.

The Destruction of Tyre, the Saints Praising God and the Eating of a Meal (Isa 25:1-6; Rev 19:1-9)

Below depicts the righteous on a mountain praising God and eating a meal because God destroyed a fortified city. This will eventually be the first part of the second coming from Revelation 19:1-9.

Content Found in Isaiah		Content Found in Revelation	
25:1	THE LORD, you are my God. I will exalt you! I will praise your name, for you have done wonderful things, things planned long ago, in complete faithfulness and truth.	19:1 19:2	Hallelujah! Salvation, power and glory belong to our God. True and righteous are his judgments . . . . and he has avenged the blood of his servants at her hand" (see Rev 6:9-11).
25:2	[God] made a city into a heap, a fortified city into a ruin. . . It will never be built.	19:2	For he has judged the great prostitute, who corrupted the earth with her sexual immorality.
25:3	Therefore a strong people will glorify you. A city of awesome nations will fear you.	19:1-5	The righteous praise God and the city that rules the world is destroyed by God.
25:6	In this mountain, THE LORD . . . . will make all peoples a feast of fat things, a feast of choice wines, of fat things full of marrow, of well-refined choice wines.	19:9	Blessed are those who are invited to the marriage supper of the Lamb.

EP8 - The Slaying of the Great Dragon

The destruction of the great dragon found in Ezekiel became a major portion of the destruction of the beast in Revelation. When compared to the Isaiah portion of the parallel we can see that the difference between the two accounts is well within the confines of parallel formation by forming opposites and complements. We can also see that the river drying up in the Isaiah account (Ezek 30:12; Isa 11:15-6; 27:212) was relocated in Isaiah as a result of the author of Isaiah's methodology of constructing First Isaiah.

Content Found in Ezekiel		Content Found in Revelation	
29:3	The great monster [dragon].		[See the dragon through the drafts.]
29:13	At the end of forty years will I gather the Egyptians from the peoples where they were scattered.		
30:12	God will make the rivers dry.	9:14	Free the four angels who are bound at the great River Euphrates! [See Rev 7:1 where they are the four angels holding back the four winds].
		16:12	The great river, the Euphrates. Its water was dried up, that the way might be prepared for the kings that come from the sunrise.
32:4	The birds and animals will feast on the dragon's army.		[See Ezek 39:17-20; Rev 19:17-8 below as the rest of the feast of the vulture.]
32:5	The blood of the dead will be deep enough to swim in.	14:20	The blood was as deep as a horse's bridle and as far as 180 miles.
32:10	Their kings shall be horribly afraid for you.	6:15	The kings of the earth, the princes, the commanding officers, the rich, the strong and every slave and free person.
32:10	They shall tremble at every moment, every man for his own life, in the day of your fall.	6:15	[they] hid themselves in the caves and in the rocks of the mountains.
32:21	The strong among the mighty shall speak to him out of the middle of Sheol.	20:1-3	I saw an angel coming down out of heaven, having the key of the abyss and a great chain in his hand. He seized the dragon, the old serpent, which is the devil and Satan, who deceives the whole inhabited earth, and bound him for a thousand years, and cast him into the abyss, and shut it, and sealed it over him, that he should deceive the nations no more, until the thousand years were finished.
		19:20	The beast . . . . and . . . . the false prophet . . . . These two were thrown alive into the lake of fire that burns with sulfur.
32:31	Pharaoh shall see them, and shall be comforted over all his multitude.	19:19	I saw the beast, and the kings of the earth, and their armies, gathered together to make war against him who sat on the horse, and against his army.
32:32	Those who are slain by the sword, even Pharaoh and all his multitude,	19:21	The rest were killed with the sword of him who sat on the horse.

IP8 - Jesus Slays the Great Dragon With a Great Sword

The Isaiah side of the EID of the second coming is a conflation of two remote texts in Isaiah that tell the story of the remnant of Jacob crossing the Euphrates River and the destruction of the Egyptians by the sea.

The Description of Jesus

Content Found in Isaiah		Content Found in Revelation	
11:4	With righteousness he will judge the poor.	19:11	In righteousness he judges.
11:4	He will strike the earth with the rod of his mouth.	2:27	Jesus received authority to rule over nations and a rod.
27:1	In that day, THE LORD with his hard and great sword will punish the dragon that is in the sea.	12:5	He had a rod to rule all nations.
		19:15	Out of his mouth comes a sharp two-edged sword.
11:5	Righteousness and faithfulness shall be the belt of his waist.	19:8	The fine linen is the righteous acts of the saints.
11:10-4	The root of Jesse, who stands as a banner of the peoples; and his resting place will be glorious . . . . The people will come from many nations which are outcasts from the four corners of the earth . . . . and those who persecute will be destroyed.	6:9-11	Jesus comforts his people and tells them to rest.
		7:9	Jesus with the great multitude in heaven.
		14:1-4	Jesus with the 144,000 in heaven.
		15:1-8	Jesus with both groups in heaven.
			Jesus with both groups and those that killed the saints will be destroyed (the Harlot in Rev 19:2 and the beast in Rev 19:17-21).
11:14	They will fly down and plunder the children of the east.	16:12	The beast's army crosses the Euphrates (East of Jerusalem).
		19:11-21	The saints with Jesus will swoop down and destroy the beast.

John combines the Ezekiel and Isaiah side of the parallel with the Euphrates River drying up so that the remnant can cross it wearing just sandals. The end comes from the four corners of the earth into the sixth trumpet and sixth bowl narrative (Rev 9:14; 16:12). The Ezekiel side of the Ezekiel-Isaiah parallel reveals how angry God is against his people while the Isaiah side of the parallel shows how God comforts his people. The comfort and anger motif will become the foundation for the fifth seal (Rev 6:9-11), the fifth trumpet (Rev 9:1-12) and the fifth bowl (Rev 16:10).

Content Found in Isaiah		Content Found in Revelation	
The Remnant Returns (12:1-13:8)		**Saints in Heaven Passages and the Destruction of Egypt**	
11:15	THE LORD will utterly destroy the tongue of the Egyptian sea.		
27:1	He will kill the dragon that is in the sea.		
11:15	His scorching wind he will wave his hand over the great (Euphrates) river.	9:14	Free the four angels who are bound at the great River Euphrates! (see Rev 7:1 where they are the four angels holding back the four winds).
27:12	THE LORD will thresh the River of Euphrates and he will gather the children of Israel one by one.	16:12	The great river, the Euphrates. Its water was dried up, that the way might be prepared for the kings that come from the sunrise.
11:16	Will cause men to march over in sandals There will be a highway for the remnant that is left of his people from Assyria.		
12:2	God is my salvation. I will trust and will not be afraid.	7:10	Salvation be to our God.
12:3	Therefore with joy you will draw water out of the wells of salvation.	7:17	"The Lamb . . . . leads them to springs of waters of life. And God will wipe away every tear from their eyes."
12:6	Cry aloud and shout, you inhabitant of Zion for the Holy One of Israel is great among you.	14:1	The Lamb standing on Mount Zion.
		14:2	They sounded like many waters and a great thunder.
12:2	They will sing a song of salvation.	14:3	They sing a new song before the throne.
		14:4	The were redeemed by Jesus.
12:4	In that day you will say, "Give thanks to THE LORD! Call on his name. Declare his doings among the peoples."	14:6	I saw an angel flying in mid-heaven, having eternal good news to proclaim to those who dwell on the earth, and to every nation, tribe, language and people.
12:5	Sing to THE LORD for he has done excellent things.	15:3	They sang the song of the Lamb, saying, "Great and marvelous are your works."
12:6	The Holy One of Israel.	15:4	For you only are holy.
13:1-8	God is mustering a great army from a distant land to the ends of heaven in order to battle the nations.	19:1-8	The great multitude that came from every nation (see 7:9).

EP9 - Jerusalem Attacked by Gog and Magog

The story of Gog and Magog tells of a time in Jerusalem when God will protect Jerusalem from the armies of Gog.

Content Found in Ezekiel		Content Found in Revelation	
38:2	Set your face toward Gog, of the land of Magog.	20:8	Gog and Magog.
38:14	In that day when my people of Israel dwell securely, shall you not know it?	20:7	And after the thousand years, Satan will be released from his prison.
38:15	You shall come from your place out of the uttermost parts of the north, you, and many peoples with you, all of them riding on horses, a great company and a mighty army.	20:8	He will come out to deceive the nations which are in the four corners of the earth, Gog and Magog, to gather them together to the war; the number of whom is as the sand of the sea.
38:18	It shall happen in that day, when Gog shall come against the land of Israel.	20:9	They went up over the width of the earth, and surrounded the camp of the saints and the beloved city.
38:19	For in my jealousy and in the fire of my wrath have I spoken.	20:9	Fire came down out of heaven from God and devoured them.
39:17	Speak to the birds of every sort, and to every animal of the field, assemble yourselves, and come; gather yourselves on every side to my sacrifice that I do sacrifice for you, even a great sacrifice on the mountains of Israel, that you may eat flesh and drink blood.	19:17	He cried with a loud voice, saying to all the birds that fly in the sky, "Come! Be gathered together to the great supper of God."
39:18	You shall eat the flesh of the mighty, and drink the blood of the princes of the earth.	19:18	You may eat the flesh of kings, the flesh of captains, the flesh of mighty men.
39:20	You shall be filled at my table with horses and chariots, with mighty men and with all men of war.	19:18	The flesh of horses and of those who sit on them, and the flesh of all men, both free and slave, and small and great.

IP9 - Jerusalem Attacked by a Multitude of Nations

Isaiah has a similar account of Gog, Magog and Jerusalem that Ezekiel has. Both accounts have the righteous and the unrighteous as well as God intervening at the last minute to preserve the righteous.

	Content Found in Isaiah		**Content Found in Revelation**
29:1	The city where David encamped.	20:9	The camp of the saints, the beloved city.
29:8	The multitude of all nations that fight against Mount Zion.	20:8	The nations will come from the four corners of the earth.
29:5	The multitude will be like fine dust .	20:8	Their numbers is the sand of the sea
29:6	They will be destroyed by a devouring fire.	20:9	Fire came down out of heaven from God, and devoured them.
29:11	A book that is sealed.		
29:18-9	The blind, deaf and poor will hear the words of the book and rejoice.	20:4-6	The first resurrection where those who were righteous were found in the book.
29:20-1	The unrighteous will be destroyed.	20:11-5	The second resurrection where those who did evil will be put in the lake of fire.

When Ezekiel 38:2 - 39:20 and Isaiah 29:1-9 are Conflated You Get Revelation 20:4-15

In the Zechariah Draft (ZrD), the story of Gog and Magog as well as the Isaiah account of the multitude of nations attacking Jerusalem will be conflated to form the foundation of Revelation 20:4-15. If we arrange the Ezekiel and Isaiah content in the order of Revelation we can see how John used the text to provide the primary content of Gog and Magog in Revelation.

	Content Found in Ezekiel and Isaiah		**Content Found in Revelation (Ordered By)**
Isa 29:18-9	The blind, deaf and poor will hear the words of the book and rejoice.	20:4-6	The first resurrection where those who were righteous were found in the book.
Ezek 38:14	In that day when my people of Israel dwells securely, shall you not know it?	20:7	And after the thousand years, Satan will be released from his prison.
Ezek 38:2	Gog of the land of Magog.	20:8	Gog and Magog mentioned.
Isa 29:8	Multitude of nations	20:8	Nations from the four corners of the earth.
Ezek 38:18	They shall come against Israel. The city where David encamped.	20:9	They went up over the width of the earth, and surrounded the camp of the saints, and the beloved city.
Isa 29:6	They will be destroyed by a devouring fire.	20:9	Fire came down out of heaven from God, and devoured them.
29:20-1	A book in the context and the unrighteous will be destroyed.	20:11-5	The second resurrection where those who did evil will be put in the lake of fire.

EP10 - The City of God

The chart below represents how the New Jerusalem was constructed from the content found in Ezekiel and Isaiah. As one can see, John was very selected in his parallel formation with Ezekiel, taking only the portions that would satisfy an early Christian movement.

	Content Found in Ezekiel		Content Found in Revelation (Ordered by)
Ezek 40:2	Ezekiel in a vision was carried to a high mountain in Israel where he saw the City of God.	21:10	He carried John away in spirit to a great mountain and showed him the New Jerusalem.
Ezek 40:3	[He had] a measuring reed.	21:15	He who spoke with me had for a measure, a golden reed, to measure the city, its gates and its walls.
Ezek 40:5	[He measured] the wall, all around and the thickness of the building.		
Ezek 43:7	God dwells in the temple where his throne is. He will dwell among the people of Israel forever.	21:3	I heard a loud voice out of heaven saying, "Behold, God's dwelling is with people, and he will dwell with them, and they will be his people, and God himself will be with them as their God."
Ezek 43:7-11	The house of Israel will no longer defile God's name by prostitution, sacrificing to high places and violating God's ordinances.	21:7-8 and 22:15	Those who overcome, they will live in the New Jerusalem. Outside are the dogs, the sorcerers, the sexually immoral, the murderers, the idolaters, and everyone who loves and practices falsehood.
Ezek 48:31-4	The City of God has 12 gates named after each of the twelve tribes of Israel, 3 on each side.	21:12	The New Jerusalem has twelve gates named after the twelve tribes of Israel.
		21:13	There are three gates on each side.
Ezek 48:16	The city is a square with each side measuring 4,500 cubics (1.28 miles in CB, 1.5 miles in NET).	21:16	The city is a cube with each side measuring 12,012 stadia (1,380 miles / 2,221 km).
Ezek 47:1	The waters came down from under, from the right side of the house, on the south of the altar.	22:1	A river of water of life, clear as crystal, proceeding out of the throne of God and the Lamb.
Ezek 47:12	By the river on its bank . . . . shall grow every tree for food whose leaf shall not wither, neither shall its fruit fail. It shall produce new fruit every month . . . . its leaf for healing.	22:2	On this side of the river was the tree of life, bearing twelve kinds of fruits, yielding its fruit every month. The leaves of the tree were for the healing of the nations.

EP10 - The Foundation Stones of the City of God

Ezekiel lists the twelve stones found in the Garden of Eden (Ezek 28:13). John will take the stones and use them to create the twelve foundations to the New Jerusalem.

	Content Found in Ezekiel		Content Found in Revelation
28:13	Sardius (σάρδιον).	21:20	The sixth, sardius (σάρδιον).
	Topaz (τοπάζιον).	21:20	The ninth, topaz (τοπάζιον).
	Emerald (σμάραγδος).	21:19	The fourth, emerald (σμάραγδος).
	Sapphire (σάπφειρος).	21:19	The second, sapphire (σάπφειρος).
	~~Silver and~~ Gold.	21:18	The city was pure gold.
	Amethyst (ἀμέθυστος).	21:20	The twelfth, amethyst (ἀμέθυστος).
	Chrystolite (χρυσόλιθος).	21:20	The seventh, chrystolite (χρυσόλιθος).
	Beryl (βηρύλλιον).	21:20	The eight, beryl (βήρυλλος).
		21:19	The third, chalcedony (χαλκηδών).
		21:20	The fifth, sardonyx (σαρδόνυξ).
		21:20	The tenth, chrysoprase (χρυσόπρασος).
		21:20	The eleventh, jacinth (ὑάκινθος).

IP10 - The Holy City of Jerusalem

The chart below represents how the New Jerusalem was constructed from the content found in Isaiah and placed in the order that Revelation presents it. The selection of the verses outside of the Ezekiel - Isaiah parallel represents that John searched beyond the Isaiah portion of the Ezekiel-Isaiah parallel for material to complement the Ezekiel side of the parallel.

	Content Found in Isaiah		Content Found in Revelation (Ordered by)
Isa 65:17	"For, behold, I create new heavens and a new earth; and the former things will not be remembered, nor come into mind."	21:1	I saw a new heaven and a new earth: for the first heaven and the first earth have passed away, and the sea is no more.
Isa 66:22	"For as the new heavens and the new earth, which I will make, shall remain before me."		
Isa 66:20	The holy city Jerusalem	21:2	I saw the holy city, New Jerusalem, coming down out of heaven from God.
Isa 61:10	God has clothed me . . . . as a bride adorns herself with her jewels.		Prepared like a bride adorned for her husband.
Isa 25:8	THE LORD will wipe away tears from off all faces.	21:4	He will wipe away from them every tear from their eyes.
Isa 25:8	He has swallowed up death forever!		"Death will be no more; neither will there be mourning, nor crying, nor pain anymore. The first things have passed away."
Isa 42:9	Behold, the former things have happened, and I declare new things.	21:5	He who sits on the throne said, "Behold, I am making all things new."
Isa 25:1	God has done things in complete faithfulness and truth.	21:5	These words of God are faithful and true.
		22:6	These words are faithful and true.
Isa 44:6	I am the first and I am the last.	22:13	I am . . . . the first and the last.
Isa 44:3	I will pour water on him who is thirsty.	21:6	I will give freely to him who is thirsty from the spring of the water of life.
Isa 55:1	"Hey! Come, everyone who thirsts, to the waters! Come, he who has no money, buy, and eat! Yes, come, buy wine and milk without money and without price."	22:17	He who is thirsty, let him come. He who desires, let him take the water of life freely.
Isa 60:19	The sun will be no more your light by day; nor will the brightness of the moon give light to you, but THE LORD will be your everlasting light, and your God will be your glory.	21:23	The city has no need for the sun, neither of the moon to shine, for the very glory of God illuminated it, and its lamp is the Lamb.

Chapter 3: The Zechariah Draft (ZrD)

The Process That John Used to Construct the Zechariah Draft

When John finished the EID he essentially had two columns of wax tablets. One column represented the Ezekiel side, which depicted a story of the destruction of Jerusalem by the nations as the direct result of their sins against God. The other column represented the restoration of God's people through the birth of a child. When both columns were set side by side they formed a simple parallel with other; each element had an opposite corresponding element within the other column.

In the ZrD, John increased the complexity of the EID by forming a complex parallel with the first twelve chapters of Zechariah. The process was similar to the way the EID was formed but in reverse order, and at the end of the process John would be left with one column of wax tablets instead of two. The reason he would be left with only one column is that the content from Zechariah was used as a means to organize the EID material as well as to add additional content into it. To do this John segmented Zechariah 1:1 -12:10 into sections, similar to how a good study Bible would divide Zechariah. He then went through each section, starting with the last and working backwards to the first section, looking for content from the EID that would fit each part's storyline. He put Zechariah 12:10 onto a new wax tablet and from there the process began.

As he read each section from Zechariah, in reverse order, he moved the content that transformed the section from Zechariah to the place where he was at in the process. If the Zechariah section contained material about a double-sided flying scroll, John searched the EID for something similar. Once the content from the EID was moved to the appropriate location, John would then add additional content to enhance the storyline. The entire process involved rewriting the entire EID using a set of fresh tablets and/or reusing wax tablets that were no longer needed, by melting and scoring a fresh set of lines into them. To visualize the process of how John took the EID and transformed the tablets into the ZrD, two illustrations have been created. The first shows how the wax tablets were laid out at the end of the EID, to provide content for each tablet (see "How John Made the Zechariah Draft (Part 1)" on page 68). The second shows the order and process of how John moved the EID wax tablets to create the ZrD (see "How John Made the Zechariah Draft (Part 2)" on page 69). The far-right column that contains "Z1" to "Z10" represents the order that the ZrD was created. The middle column represents the text of Zechariah and where the text eventually found its way into Revelation, as well as a description of what John did with the tablets. The far-right column represents the abbreviated form of the wax tablets from part 1 of the chart in order to visualize the shuffling that John did with the wax tablets from the EID.

What is important about the two charts (see "How John Made the Zechariah Draft (Part 1)" on page 68 and "How John Made the Zechariah Draft (Part 2)" on page 69) is how the process reordered the EID to become more aligned with the PVR. This is evident in how you see that part two follows the order of the book of Revelation.[1]

The way John moved content from Zechariah into the EID to form the ZrD will be shown as we progress in the order that John wrote the ZrD. This is due to the scale and scope of the ZrD as well as the contextual considerations that John must have struggled with.

What You Need to Understand Before You Read Further

The ZrD is a complex parallel that uses both the reverse order of Zechariah 1:1 - 12:10 as well as its content as the key to reshape the EID. We will analyze the draft the same way that John wrote it, beginning with Zech 12:10 and working backwards. We will look at the broad content similarly to how a good study Bible breaks down Zechariah's sections, and will seek out content that matched the EID and Zechariah, and describe the process as we go along. The result is that we take a collection of wax tablets from the EID and move the appropriate ones to the ZrD collection of wax tablets.

Since we are going backwards:

Instead of saying:

"As we continue to go backwards from Zechariah 1:1 - 12:10 we come to a passage about the flying scroll."

I will say:

"The next section John used was the flying scroll passage."

The numbering of the order will be sequentially increasing while conveying the content backwards. See how "Z1" to "Z9" is referenced in "How John Made the Zechariah Draft (Part 2)" on page 69.

Z1 - Whom They Have Pierced (Zech 12:9-10; Rev 1:9)

The place where John started the ZrD matched extremely well with the EID. It had the destruction of Jerusalem, the destruction of the nations that destroyed Jerusalem, and the death of Jesus,[2] all within two verses.

It will happen in that day, that I will seek to destroy all the nations that come against Jerusalem.

---

1   See also "The Zechariah Draft (ZrD) Simplified" on page 70.
2   Early Christian writings cited Zech 12:10 as referring to Jesus being pierced at his death(John 19:37; Ign. *Trall x.*).

I will pour on David's house, and on the inhabitants of Jerusalem, the spirit of grace and of supplication, and they will look to me whom they have pierced, and they shall mourn for him, as one mourns for his only son, and will grieve bitterly for him, as one grieves for his firstborn.[3]

The only problem for John was that the set of verses depicted the post-destruction of Jerusalem and in the EID John predicted that the destruction of Jerusalem and the destruction of Tyre (Rome) would occur 70 years after a certain king (Jesus).[4] Therefore, John simply left Zechariah 12:9 out of the quotation in order to retain the predictive element of Jerusalem's destruction.

John most likely began the ZrD with a blank wax tablet with only the lines scored on it. He then etched Zechariah 12:10 into the wax tablet creating the first version of the ZrD prologue as well as the first step in the creation of the ZrD. He then added the ZrD version of the first three verses describing Ezekiel/John as an exile in a place because of who he was.

Behold, he is coming with the clouds, and every eye will see him, including those who pierced him. All the tribes of the earth will mourn over him. Even so, Amen.[5]

I, John, your brother and partner with you in oppression, Kingdom, and perseverance in Christ Jesus, was on the isle that is called Patmos because of God's word and the testimony of Jesus Christ. I was in the spirit on the Lord's day, and I heard behind me a loud voice, like a trumpet saying, "What you see, write in a book and send to the cities."[6]

Z2 - The Oratories to God's People as the Birth of the Letters to Seven Churches (Zech 7:1 - 12:8; Rev 2:1 - 3:22)

John continued on with the process to the next discernible section in Zechariah, the oratories of God, which are various statements by God to his people regarding how they should behave.[7] Since the EID had nothing that matched the oratories of God in Zechariah, John had to improvise by selecting the wax tablets that had content that could be adapted into messages by God to his people.

He first merged the missions of Ezekiel and Isaiah into one message, and this became the template for all subsequent versions of the letters to the seven churches.[8] They provided the addressing to the cities, the inclusion of the phrase, "Thus says The Lord," as well as the message that they need to listen. We even get the message that the coming of God is tied to the destruction of the cities within the letters. Each of these elements are central to understanding the letters to the seven churches and the judgments.

All that John needed was to individualized content for each of the message from the EID (and possibly Zechariah). We know that John took the wax tablet that contained the story of Eliakim and fashioned it into what is now the letter to the church of Philadelphia.[9] This is because there is no trace of the Eliakim passage found outside of normal parallel formation to the placement of the letter to the Philadelphia

---

3   Zech 12:9-10; Rev 1:7.
4   Isa 23:15-7.
5   Rev 1:7.
6   Modified version of Rev 1:9-11 to reflect more closely what the ZrD looked like.
7   Zech 7:1 - 12:8.
8   See "Z2 - How The Seven Churches Were Formed" on page 103 for all citations in this paragraph.
9   Isa 22:20-5; Rev 3:7-13.

How John Made the Zechariah Draft (Part 1)

The Ezekiel-Isaiah Draft (The Wax Tablet View)

Below is a depiction of how John organized the wax tablets at the end of the EID. The left side represents the judgment against Israel for disobeying God and the right side represents those who followed Jesus.

Ezekiel Side	Isaiah Side
Ezekiel Introduce (Ezek 1:1-3)	
EP1 Ezekiel's Experience in Heaven • God on the throne (Ezek 1:26-2:2). • The living creatures (Ezek 1:4-26). • The scroll (Ezek 2:8 - 3:3).	**IP1 Isaiah's Experience in Heaven** • God on the throne (Isa 6:1). • The seraphim (Isa 6:2-7). • The altar that removes iniquity (Isa 6:6-7).
EP2 Ezekiel's Mission • Gods do not hear or understand (Ezek 3:4-7). • Say, "Thus says THE LORD" (Ezek 2:4; 3:27).	**IP2 Isaiah's Mission** • God's people do not hear or understand (Isa 6:9-10). • Until the cities are waste without inhabitant (Isa 6:10).
EP3 Ezekiel Appointed as a Watchman • God's people are like briers, thorns, and scorpions (Ezek 2:6), God hardens Ezekiel's head (Ezek 3:8-9). • Ezekiel is appointed as a watchman (Ezek 3:16-27). • End of three ministries and its relation to the siege of Jerusalem (Ezek 4:5-8).	**IP3 The New Seed (Jesus the Child)** • When a tenth of the city is burned God will raise up a new holy seed (Isa 6:10-13). • The sign of a woman with child (Isa 7:14-6). • Three phases of the child's life is connected to the destruction of Jerusalem (Isa 7:14 - 10:34).
EP4 The Judgments by the Nations • The nations will strike in thirds (Ezek 5:2). • God's people give evil decrees (Ezek 5:6-10). • The day of THE LORD (Ezek 7:7) where God will destroy those without the mark of God on their forehead (Ezek 9:1-11).	**IP4 The Judgments by Jesus** • Jesus will strike in thirds (Ezek 5:16-7). • God's people receive evil decrees (Isa 10:1-19). • The day of THE LORD (Isa 13:9) where God will darken the sky (Isa 13:10; Ezek 32:7-10).
EP5 The Glory of God Flees Jerusalem • Babylon comes, the glory of God flees (Ezek 10:1- 22). • Israel at war with nations (Ezek 11:1-13). • The Israelites are taken to all nations (Ezek 11:16 - 12:28). • They kill the souls that should not die (Ezek 13:1-23).	**IP5 The Glory of God Triumphs in Heaven (Jesus the True Morning Star)** • The glory of God triumphs in heaven (Isa 14:1- 12). • The nations are at peace (Isa 14:18). • The remnant of Israel returns (Isa 14:32).
EP6 Jerusalem the Mother of God's Children • The harlot wears expensive clothing (Ezek 16:10-1). • The harlot kills God's children (Ezek 16:20). • The harlot is the mother of God's children (Ezek 16:20).	**IP6 Jesus as Eliakim the Father of God's Children** • Eliakim wears expensive clothing (Isa 22: 21). • Eliakim saves God's children (Isa 22:21). • Eliakim is the father of God's children (Isa 22:21).
EP7 Tyre • Wealth from trading with other nations (Ezek 27:12-22) • [No parallel] • Their riches became what ruined them (Ezek 27:27). • Merchants lamenting Tyre's destruction (Ezek 27:27-28:2).	**IP7 Tyre (Jesus, a Certain King)** • Wealth from trading with other nations (Isa 23:1-17). • Tyre's destruction 70 years after certain king (Isa 23:15-7). • Post-destruction's wealth will be righteousness (Isa 23:18). • Saints rejoicing over Tyre's destruction (Isa 25:1-6)
EP8 The Slaying of the Great Dragon • With a sword (Ezek 29:8) • The great dragon finds comfort in his army (Ezek 32:31).	**IP8 Jesus Slays the Great Dragon** • The rod of his mouth (Isa 11:4), a great sword (Isa 27:1). • Jesus musters his army from the whole world (Isa 11:10-6).
EP9 Jerusalem Attacked by Gog and Magog • Nations come from the north to destroy Jerusalem and God destroys the nations (Ezek 38:1 - 39:29).	**IP9 Jerusalem Attacked by a Multitude of Nations** • Nations come from all over the world to destroy Jerusalem and God destroys the nations (Isa 29:1-21).
EP10 The City of God • Jerusalem will be a city that God and the righteous will live in (Ezek 40:1 - 48:35).	**IP10 The Holy City of Jerusalem** • Various descriptions of the Holy City of Jerusalem scattered throughout Isaiah.

How John Made the Zechariah Draft (Part 2)

The Process Used to Shuffle the Ezekiel-Isaiah Draft Wax Tablets

In this illustration the left two columns represent the order and process in which John dealt with the EID wax tablets shown in part 1. The right column represents how the wax tablets were moved to satisfy the content found in the left column.

The Order and Process John Moved the Wax Tablets	The Tablets John Moved or Used	
Z1 **Whom They Have Pierced They Shall Mourn (Zech 12:10; Rev 1:9)** John began a new wax tablet with Zechariah 12:10 at the beginning.		
Z2 **Oratories to God's People (Zech 7:1-12:9; Rev 2:1 - 3:22)** John conflated the wax tablets EP2 and IP2 to form the template to the letters of the seven churches. John took the whole wax tablet IP6 and a phrase in IP7 as the first unique content to the seven churches.	**EP2** Ezekiel's Mission **IP2** Isaiah's Mission **IP6** Jesus as Eliakim **IP7** Tyre (Jesus as a Certain King)	
Z3 **The Coronation of Joshua the High Priest (Zech 6:9-15; Rev 4:1 - 5:14)** John conflated both Ezekiel's and Isaiah's experience in heaven and then adds the coronation of Jesus.	**EP1** Ezekiel's Experience in Heaven **IP1** Isaiah's Experience in Heaven	
Z4 **The Four Chariots and the Four Winds (Zech 6:1-8; Rev 6:1-8; 8:7 - 9:21)** John took the two wax tablets (EP4, IP4) and made IP4 the four chariots and appended EP4 afterwards making it the four winds.	**IP4** The Judgments by Jesus **EP4** The Judgments by the Nations	
Z5 **A Woman in the Basket (Zech 5:5-11; Rev 12:1-17; 17:1-18)** John took the pregnant woman and the harlot and made them both the city of Jerusalem. The pregnant woman represented the righteous and the harlot represented the wicked. He then constructed a simple parallel between the two.	**IP3** The New Seed (Jesus the Child) **EP7** Jerusalem the Harlot	
Z6 **The Flying Scroll (Zech 5:1-4; Rev 10:1-11)** John split the scroll from EP1(Ezek 2:8 - 3:3), leaving a portion in the coronation of Jesus scene and moving the rest to this location.	**EP1** Ezekiel and the Scroll **IP7** Tyre (Jesus, a Certain King)	
Z7 **Jerusalem Will be Blessed, Joshua the High Priest, and the Two Anointed (Zech 2:1 - 4:15; Rev 11:1 - 12:17)** John took the wax tablets (EP3, EP5, IP3, IP5) and creatively infused Zechariah 2:1 - 4:15 to form the 42 month, 1,260 day, 3½ day parallel (see "Z7 - The Zechariah-Encoded Parallel: How it Was Built (Part 1)" on page 117).	**EP3** Ezekiel Appointed as a Watchman **EP5** The Glory of God Flees Jerusalem	**IP3** The New Seed **IP5** Babylon Pursues God's Glory
Z8 **The Four Horns (Zech 1:18-20; Rev 16:1 - 18:19)** John made the four horns by copying the four winds from EP4 and changing them from affecting a third to affecting all.	**EP4** Judgment by the Nations (John copied) **EP6** Jerusalem the Harlot	
Z9 **The Return Home (1:1-17; Rev 18:20 - 20:15)** John used Zechariah 1:1-17 to tell the following stories: • God, after 70 years, is angry with the nations (Zech 1:12, IP7, EP8, IP8). • God's cities will once again flow with prosperity (1:17, EP9, IP9, EP10, IP10). • God calls his son to return to him (Zech 1:3; EP8).	**EP7** Tyre **IP7** Tyre (Jesus, a Certain King) (Isa 23:15-7; 25:1-6) **EP8** God Slays the Great Dragon **EP9** Attacked by Gog and Magog **IP10** The Holy City of Jerusalem **EP10** The City of God	**IP8** Jesus Slays the Great Dragon **IP9** Jerusalem Attacked by the Nations

The Zechariah Draft (ZrD) Simplified

John reordered the content of the Ezekiel-Isaiah Draft to conform with the reverse order of the content found in Zech 1:1-12:10. In so doing he, in essence, made the Zechariah Draft a complex parallel of Zechariah. John also did something extraordinary, he interlaced the content found in Zechariah 2:1-4:14 with the 42 month, 1,260 day, and 3½ day parallel, so that Zechariah 2:1-5 would be the first 42-month parallel and Zech 2:6-13 would be the second 42-month parallel. He continued this where the next parallel took from the second chapter and the third parallel took from the fourth chapter of Zechariah.

Content in Zechariah and Revelation	Zech	Rev
Whom they have pierced they shall mourn (the prologue).	12:10	1:7
Oratories to God's people (the four messages/primitive form of the seven churches).	7:1-12:9	2:1-3:22
Coronation of Joshua the high priest (exaltation of Jesus).	6:9-15	5:1-14
The four chariots (the four horsemen/the first four seals).	6:1-8	6:1-8
The four winds (the first four trumpets).	6:1-8	8:7-12
Women in a basket (the woman and the harlot, both representing Jerusalem).	5:5-11	12:1-17 17:1-18
The flying scroll (the scroll).	5:1-4	5:1-2; 10:1-11

A. 42 Months
 Measure Jerusalem but not its walls (Zech 2:1-5).
 Measure the temple but not its courtyard (Rev 11:1-2).

> **B. 1,260 Days**
> Joshua dressed in filthy rags (Zech 3:3).
> The two prophets wore sackcloth (Rev 11:3).

>> **C. 3½ Days**
>> The two olive trees and the lampstands represent the work of Joshua and Zerubbabel (Zech 4:11-4).
>> The two olive trees and the two lampstands, the two prophets do all kinds of miracles from God (Rev 11:4-7).

>> **C'. 3½ Days**
>> The building of the temple on earth and the nations will rejoice (Zech 4:6-10).
>> The temple is in heaven and the nations will be angry (Rev 11:18-9).

> **B'. 1,260 Days**
> Satan is kicked out of Jerusalem (Zech 3:1).
> Satan is kicked out of heaven (Rev 12:3-10).
>
> Sin will be removed from the land (Zech 3:8-10).
> Salvation brought to the whole world (Rev 12:10).

A'. 42 Months
 God will protect his people and Jerusalem will be loved by all the nations (Zech 2:6-13).
 The woman was nourished . . . And the land (nations) rescued her (Rev 12:14-6).

	Zech	Rev
The four horns (the first four bowls).	1:18-20	16:2-9
The horsemen (the second coming).	1:7-17	19:11-21
The return home (the New Jerusalem).	1:1-6	21:1-22:5

church. Therefore we can conclude that John just moved the Eliakim wax tablet into the seven churches passages.

We also know that John took content from one wax tablet and used it to form the primary message to the church in Laodicea.[10] Since the content was only a verse or a few lines on the wax tablet, all John had to do was write the new lines on a wax tablet as a new church. Once done, he just had to melt the wax and then would have created a clean break.

John also took a message from Zechariah where God asks his people the question, "Why did the people fast and why did the people eat?" The conclusion was that they ate for themselves and they did not bother to listen to the prophets or else why would they be in the position they were in? John transformed the dialogue into, "The people are eating food sacrificed to idols because they are listening to false prophets."[11]

The approximation draft at the end of this chapter will provide the reader with what the text probably looked like. It will also provide content that will be covered later in this chapter that affected the development of the Zechariah prototype of the seven churches; namely the development of the prologue and epilogue and how it affected the seven churches.

Defining the Structure of the Letters to the Churches

To construct the message to God's people, John needed a means of communication and a structure for the communication to deliver the message to God's people. Instead of a prophetic voice or narration where John goes to God's people to deliver a message, John decided to communicate in the form of letter correspondences for each group of believers. How the letters were structured was done by a simple conflation of a pair of wax tablets that contained the missions of Ezekiel and Isaiah from the EID.[12] As a result of the conflation, we have the structure that will eventually form the seven churches.[13] In the final version, we have each letter addressed to a particular city, a description of Jesus, and the phrase, "Thus says." The final disposition of all believers is their martyrdom and thus the end of a city. Even the final phrase, "He who has an ear, let him hear what the spirit says," comes from the conflation.

Defining the Content and the Recipients of the Letters to the Churches

What we can be certain of is that there were two letters addressed to the cities of Jerusalem and to Tyre (Rome). Each letter probably contained two messages, one to the faithful and the other to those less faithful. Each letter contained text that related to the city that the source material describes. For example, the Eliakim content parallels Jerusalem, therefore it was part of the letter to Jerusalem. Likewise the wages for Tyre were holiness, and so that portion became part of Tyre.[14]

The central message to the two cities was to combat idolatry. To do this effectively John focused on the most powerful statement in the Hebrew Scriptures that there is only one God.

> *This is what* THE LORD, *the King of Israel,*

10　Isa 23:18; Rev 3:17-20; see "Z2 - The Ezekiel-Isaiah Draft Content for the Seven Churches" on page 107.

11　Zech 7:5-6; Rev 2:14,20; see "Z2 - The Letter to the City of Jerusalem: The Message to the Unrighteous -- Part 2" on page 105.

12　To see how they were laid side by side see "EP2 - Ezekiel's Mission" on page 40 and "IP2 - Isaiah's Mission" on page 41.

13　See "Z2 - How The Seven Churches Were Formed" on page 103.

14　Isa 23:18.

and his Redeemer, THE LORD, *says:*

"I am the first, and I am the last;
and besides me there is no God.

Who is like me?
Who will call,
    and will declare it,
    and set it in order for me,
        since I established the ancient people?

Let them declare the things that are coming, and that will happen.

Don't fear, neither be afraid.
Haven't I declared it to you long ago, and shown it?

You are my witnesses.
Is there a God besides me? Indeed, there is not.
I don't know any other rock."

Everyone who makes an engraved image is vain.
The things that they delight in will not profit.
Their own witnesses don't see, nor know, that they may be disappointed.[15]

He extracted the phrase "I am the first, and the last" and the testimony of God which he defines as the "true and faithful witness." These two phrases became the description of God for two of the letters.[16] How we know all of this is by looking at the ZrD as it was completed as well as seeing how the prologue and epilogue were formed. Since John created the prologue and epilogue at the end of the ZrD process, we will cover it then.

The content that formed the ZrD prototype of the letters to the seven churches gave John plenty of material to work with, which can be seen in the approximation drafts at the end of the chapter.[17] It also gave John plenty of work; he had to create new wax tablets, and migrate content from one to another, all to form the content of the believers. The days of simple tweaks to the text found in the EID are over at this point, the ZrD's construction involved a lot of redoing and creating wax tablets.

The First Use of the Author's Notation

The ZrD created two problems for John: placement and erasing old wax tablets as well as the creation of new ones with old material. This might not be obvious to us today, but the EID was composed of two sets of wax tablets forged with blank wax tablets that contained only minor modifications of the original text.

The ZrD necessitated a different approach to construction; no longer could John simply spot edit a wax tablet. With this draft he had to transfer large amounts of material from one wax tablet to another. In the

---

15   Isa 44:6-9.

16   Rev 2:8; 3:14.

17   See "Z2 - The Letter to the City of Jerusalem: The Message to the Unrighteous -- Part 1" on page 104, "Z2 - The Letter to the City of Jerusalem: The Message to the Righteous" on page 106, and "Z2 The Letter to the City of Rome: The Message to the Righteous" on page 107.

case of constructing the messages to the churches, John had to take many texts from multiple tablets and move them into a single tablet or multiple tablets to form its own storyline.

Additionally, John did not have the luxuries we have today with computers. Before any major rework of a story, he could not make a backup copy to allow him to recover the material in case the rework turned out to be a disaster. Actions like cutting a section out and pasting it into another place is a simple task with a computer, but with wax tablets it was highly labor intensive.

However, what John did with wax tablets is remarkably similar to what we do on a computer today. When material is moved to a new location, the material at both ends of the text being moved becomes joined together. Sometimes, the act of joining the material creates new ideas for stories and other times it creates a disjointed story—it all depends on the thoroughness of the author.

John used what I suspect is an ancient way of tagging material to signify the beginning and end of the content that was added. The technique is to place a catch phrase prior to and after where the material is inserted. We will define this technique as an "author's notation" and although it may be new to those who read this book, it is a process that was probably used in a lot in the writing of the Hebrew Scriptures with the final finishing phase deleting the catch phrase. In Revelation they are much more apparent because Revelation was never a finished book, which suggests that one of the final editing processes was to remove the author's notations before publications.

The best way to explain what an author's notation is, is with an illustration of how one is formed in Revelation. As discussed earlier, John moved the content that formed the letters to the seven churches in the ZrD, and inserted it between the calling of Ezekiel and Ezekiel's encounter with God in heaven. John added a phrase, "A loud voice like a trumpet speaking to me" prior to and after the content was added.[18]

At one point John made two sets of author's notations using the phrase "mighty angel" as the means of splitting the text.[19] John even used an author's notation to construct the story of Satan, which will be discussed later in this chapter.[20] The ZrD is the first draft where John used the author's notation, but it is not by any means the last place. One of the most famous phrases in Revelation is, "Here is wisdom. He who has understanding, let him calculate the number of the beast" is an author's notation.[21]

---

18 See "What Is an Author's Notation?" on page xxxviii.

19 See "Z6 - The Flying Scroll Alteration" on page 116 on how John formed the mighty angel author's notation.

20 See "Satan Defeated in Heaven and the Great Dragon Locked in the Abyss and How Satan Got so Many Names" on page 87 on how John leveraged a surviving author's notation from Isaiah to tell the story of Satan.

21 See "The Creation of the Beast and the False Prophet -- Part 1" on page 214 and "The Creation of the Beast and the False Prophet -- Part 2" on page 215 as to how John formed the author's notation.

Lost in Translation Because of Tradition

The Greek and Hebrew word for Joshua is the same word for Jesus. Traditionally only Jesus Christ is translated as Jesus and everyone else with the same name is translated as Joshua.

Jesus = Joshua = Ἰησους = יְהוֹשׁוּעַ meaning "The Lord is Salvation"

When it comes to parallel formations where the actions of Joshua the son of Nunn in Josh 1:1-6:27 become the actions of Jesus, John will use the synonym 'The Lamb.' When it comes to John creating parallel formations with Joshua the High Priest in Zech 1:1-6:15 in Revelation 5:1-12:17, John will use other synonyms.

Z3 - The Coronation of Jesus as the High Priest (Zech 6:9-15; Rev 5:1-14)

The next scene in Zechariah is the coronation of Joshua the high priest.[22] So John kept the Ezekiel and Isaiah encounter with God in heaven and conflated the two, and they became his account of John experiencing God in heaven. He synchronized the text to Isaiah's order and used Ezekiel's living creatures as the superior angelic beings by conflating the duties and activities of the seraphim and living creatures.[23] When he finished conflating the two accounts, the stage was set for the coronation of Jesus as the new high priest.

How John created the scene for the coronation of Jesus as the high priest was to take the scroll scene from Ezekiel and the altar scene from Isaiah and conflate the two into a single storyline that involved Jesus. Unfortunately, we may not know which came first, but what we can say is that they were both conflated into the coronation of Jesus the high priest.[24]

One of the more interesting aspects of the coronation of Jesus narrative is the entry of the mighty angel. In Revelation, it is the mighty angel that gives the equivalent of, "Whom shall I send, and who will go for us?"[25] by using instead, "Who is worthy to open the book, and to break its seals?"[26] The likely candidate would have been a seraph, but John already assigned the duties of the seraph to the living creatures.[27] John simply created the "mighty angel" as a synonym of the seraph, thus freeing up any constraints that Ezekiel or Isaiah had with the living creatures and the seraphim.

We know the mighty angel was used in the ZrD because of how it was distributed in three places of Revelation. This is because the "mighty angel" is the phrase that John used as an author's notation as the being that was connected to the scroll, and how he shifted the content could only be satisfied in the ZrD.[28]

John had to draw upon Zechariah for content to support the coronation of Jesus; therefore, he takes the imagery of the "branch" (Jesus) as the one who builds the Lord's temple.[29] He adds the imagery from Zech-

---

22   Zech 6:9-15.
23   See "Author's Notation" on page xxxvi.
24   "Z3 - The Coronation of Joshua/Jesus: The First Draft (Part 2)" on page 109.
25   Isa 6:8.
26   Rev 5:2.
27   Isa 6:2-3; Rev 4:6-8; See "Z3 - The Coronation of Joshua/Jesus: The First Draft (Part 1)" on page 108.
28   "Z6 - The Flying Scroll (Zech 5:1-4; Rev 5:1-2, 7-8; 10:1-11)." on page 79.
29   Zech 6:12.

ariah of Jesus being a priest and sitting on a throne.[30] Additionally he adds the imagery of the crowning of four individuals, which will become the 24 elders in the ExD who represent all believers.[31]

John now has a transition scene of God on his throne, giving a scroll to Jesus because of his sacrifice (remaining faithful to God even though he was killed), and thus God crowned him and gave Jesus a throne. Jesus then in turn crowns four individuals representing the believers who remained faithful to God and Jesus even to their deaths. Revelation as written today, however, does not have such a scene, but it did at one time and we know this because of a reward given to Laodicea if they obeyed Jesus:

> *He who overcomes, I will give to him to sit down with me on my throne, as I also overcame, and sat down with my Father on his throne.*[32]

The reward to Laodicea is connected to a reward given if they open the door, and it is a story told in the horizontal. The church of Philadelphia is told that their door has been opened by Jesus, and no one can shut it. The church of Laodicea has their door closed, and Jesus is knocking on it and telling them that they should open it. The final door imagery is when John is taken through the door to see God on his throne and what would have been Jesus on his throne and the twenty-four elders on their throne.[33]

Z4 - The Four Chariots/Four Horsemen and the Four Winds/First Four Trumpets (Zech 6:1-8; Rev 6:1-8; 8:7-12)

Next, as we continue to read Zechariah backwards, John comes to the section of the four chariots "which go out from standing before the Lord of all the earth."[34] Each of the chariots have different-colored horses and are given an additional name as the "four winds."[35] How John integrates the EID tablets into the four chariots and the four winds is a simple act of moving wax tablets in a parallel way and then appending them with the four chariots first and then the four winds second.

The four chariots become conflated with the attacks by Jesus from the Isaiah side of the EID, and the four winds become the attacks by the nations from the Ezekiel side of the EID.[36] Since the Zechariah account of the four chariots did not have any specific actions associated with it, John used the color of the horses to define the actions and attacks of Jesus from the EID as the content to the actions of the horses.[37] How the four chariots became the four horsemen is a simple editorial change, which modernized the chariot to the horsemen since the chariot was no longer a viable weapon in John's time.

How the Four Winds/First Four Trumpets Were Constructed

John constructed the content of the four winds by forming a parallel between two source passages that dealt with the attack on Israel by the nations.[38] The Ezekiel passages had only three items contained with-

30 Zech 6:13.
31 Zech 6:14; See "Z3 - The Coronation of Joshua/Jesus: The First Draft (Part 2)" on page 109.
32 Rev 3:21.
33 Rev 3:8, 20; 4:1-4; see "The Three Door Segue" on page 295.
34 Zech 6:1-8; the verse quoted is in Zech 6:5.
35 Zech 6:2-5.
36 To see a simplified version of the EID wax tablet layout see IP4 and Ep4 in "How John Made the Zechariah Draft (Part 1)" on page 68.
37 See "Z4 - The Four Chariots (Horsemen)/First Four Seals (Part 1)" on page 110.
38 See "How John Made and Aligned the End of the Ministry and the Birth of a Child Parallel" on page 19.

How John Made the Four Winds/First Four Trumpets (Part 1)

The chart below is the same one presented in the EID to illustrate how John connected the attack by the nations in Ezekiel 5:2 and the attack by the nations in Isaiah 7:17 - 9:19 with a razor. The purpose of reshowing this illustration is to better visualize the transition from what he arranged in the EID to how he arranged it in the ZrD (part 2) and finally what it looks like in the finished draft.

Content Found in Ezekiel and Revelation	Content Found in Isaiah and Revelation
	End of a City and the Birth of a New Holy Seed (Isa 6:10-3)
	An illustration that even if the oak tree is burned (believers) and a tenth of the city is burned a new crop of believers as a holy seed will be sprouted from the acorns.
Years of Sin by Israel (Ezek 4:5) • Ezekiel laid on his left side for 390 days which represents 390 years that Israel sinned against God. **Years of Service by the 2nd Temple (Rev 11:2)** • The temple courtyard will be trampled by the gentiles for 42 months.	**In Isaiah 7:14-6** • The sign of the woman with child (7:14-6). **In Revelation 12:1-2** • A great sign was seen in heaven: a woman . . . . She was with child. She cried out in pain, laboring to give birth.
	Razor as the Alignment Text (Isa 7:20)
	The First Problem for Israel (Isa 7:17-22) • The land will go from plentiful harvest to weeds.
Years of Sin by Judah (Ezekiel 4:6) • Ezekiel laid on his right side for 40 days which represents the 40 years Judah has sinned against God. **Years of Service by Israel (Rev 4:3)** • I will give power to my two witnesses, and they will prophesy 1,260 days, clothed in sackcloth.	**In Isaiah 8:4** • Before the child knows how to say "father," or "mother" the riches of Damascus will be carried away by the king of Assyria (8:4). **In Revelation 12:4-5** • She gave birth to a son . . . who is to rule all the nations with a rod of iron. Her child was caught up to God, and to his throne.
	The Second Problem for Israel (Isa 8:5-17) • The army will sweep through Israel like a flood but will not destroy Judah (8:5-17).
The Sum of Israel and Judah's Sin (Ezek 4:8) • The combination of 390 days + 40 days = the length of the Babylonian siege of Jerusalem. **The Ministry of the Two Prophets (Rev 11:9)** • The two prophets laid dead in the streets for 3½ days.	**In Isaiah 9:6** • When the son is born the government shall be upon his shoulders (9:6). **In Revelation 12:5** • Who is to rule all the nations with a rod of iron.
	The Third Problem for Israel (Isa 9:12-9) • [Two nations] will devour Israel with an open mouth (Isa 9:12). • The prophet who teaches lies is the tail (Isa 9:15). • For those who lead this people lead them astray; and those who are led by them are destroyed (Isa 9:16). • For wickedness burns like a fire. It devours the briers and thorns . . . . people are the fuel for the fire (Isa 9:18-9).

Razor as the Alignment Text (Ezek 5:2)

First Attack by the Nations (Ezek 5:2)
• A third part you shall burn in the fire in the middle of the city, when the days of the siege are fulfilled (5:2).

Second Attack by the Nations (Ezek 5:2)
• You shall take a third part, and strike with the sword (5:2).

Third Attack by the Nations (Ezek 5:2)
• A third part you shall scatter to the wind, and I will draw out a sword after them (5:2).

How John Made the Four Winds/First Four Trumpets (Part 2)

The primary way John formed the four winds (first four trumpets) is by creating a complex parallel with the four attacks by nations (Satan in the ZrD). The chart below shows how John arranged the material from part 1 (page 76) to what we have in the published version of Revelation.

The First Trumpet/Wind	The Fourth Attack by Satan
First Attack by the Nations (Ezek 5:2) • A third part you shall burn in the fire in the middle of the city, when the days of the siege are fulfilled (Ezek 5:2).	**The Third Problem for Israel (Isa 9:12-9)** • For wickedness burns like a fire. It devours the briers and thorns . . . . people are the fuel for the fire (Isa 9:18-9).

The Second Trumpet/Wind	The Third Attack by Satan
Third Attack by the Nations (Ezek 5:2) • A third part you shall scatter to the wind, and I will draw out a sword after them (5:2).	**The Second Problem for Israel (Isa 8:5-17)** • The army will sweep through Israel like a flood but will not destroy Judah (8:5-17).
	The Third Problem for Israel (Isa 9:12-9) • [Two nations] will devour Israel with an open mouth (Isa 9:12).

The Third Trumpet/Wind	The Second Attack by Satan
	Morning star fallen from heaven (Isa 14:12).
	The Third Problem for Israel (Isa 9:12-9) • For those who lead this people lead them astray, and those who are led by them are destroyed (Isa 9:16).

The Fourth Trumpet / Wind	The First Attack by Satan
	In Isaiah 7:14-6 • The sign of the woman with child (7:14-6).
Second Attack by the Nations (Ezek 5:2) • You shall take a third part, and strike with the sword (5:2).	**The Third Problem for Israel (Isa 9:12-9)** • The prophet who teaches lies is the tail (Isa 9:15). • For those who lead this people lead them astray; and those who are led by them are destroyed (Isa 9:16).

The Published Version of the First Four Trumpets and the Four Attacks by Satan

The First Four Trumpets
8:7 The First Wind/Trumpet • A third of the earth was burnt up. • A third of the trees (Jewish believers). • All the green grass was burnt up (believers).
8:8-9 The Second Wind/Trumpet • A great burning mountain was thrown into the sea. • The sea absorbed the mountain.
8:10-1 The Third Wind/Trumpet • A great star fell from the sky. • The star is called "Wormwood." • A third of the waters became poisoned.
8:12 The Fourth Wind/Trumpet • A third of the sun, moon, and stars were darkened .

The Four Attacks by Satan
12:17 The Fourth Attack by Satan • Satan wages war against the woman's children. • Those who kept God's commandments. • Those who hold to Jesus' testimony.
12:13-6 The Third Attack by Satan • Satan spewed water from his mouth to destroy the woman and her children. • The land absorbed the water.
12:7-9 The Third Wind/Trumpet • Satan thrown to earth. • Satan's four names. • Satan is out to deceive the world.
12:1-3 The Fourth Wind/Trumpet • A third of the stars in the sky are taken. The woman dressed with the sun, the moon under her feet and a crown of twelve stars.

in a single verse, while the Isaiah content spanned several chapters. It is only natural that when forming a parallel between two passages that have an imbalance of content, the one with the most content will fill in the one with the least amount of content.

The illustrations "How John Made the Four Winds/First Four Trumpets (Part 1)" on page 76 and "How John Made the Four Winds/First Four Trumpets (Part 2)" on page 77 shows what John started out with, and what he had to do to move the text in order for it to align with the PVR. It also shows how the first four trumpets (four winds) and the four attacks by Satan form a parallel with opposite elements.

Unfortunately, the illustration only shows a portion of the symbols found in the four winds/first four trumpets today. How the blood, sea, ships, sun, moon, and stars came to be a part of the four winds will be covered later in this chapter. This leads us to a question: "Did John just move the content and at the end of the ZrD to form the four winds or was it done in many edits as he progressed throughout the ZrD?"

So why did John retain the "third" from Ezekiel 5:2? The answer has to do with the concept John laid out from Isaiah where God will inflict double the damage on Jerusalem for what she inflicted on his people. If the believers represent a "third" of the population of Jerusalem and it is removed then two thirds remain which represents all who are living and twice the number of the believers to satisfy the doubling of the damage.[39]

Z5 - Two Women in the Basket (Zech 5:5-11; Rev 12:1-17; 17:1-18)

In the next section John deals with two women placed into a basket and flown to Babylon on stork wings.[40] For John, the selection possibilities were limited to two women. The first woman was pregnant and gave birth to Jesus and the second was the harlot who killed God's children.[41] Both the woman and the harlot represents different aspects of the city of Jerusalem. The woman represents the righteous aspect of Jerusalem[42] and the harlot the wicked aspect of Jerusalem.[43] Obviously the harlot was wicked, but what does one do with the woman that gave birth to Jesus? How John solved the problem was that he made the woman in Isaiah a representation of Israel by giving her the clothing that was associated with Joseph's dream.[44] Second, John had the source of the woman with child from heaven and the source of the harlot's influence from the earth.[45] Third, John tied Jerusalem from the two prophets to the woman and thereby connected the destruction of Jerusalem in Revelation 11:1-12 with the destruction of the woman.[46]

---

39   Isa 40:2.
40   Zech 5:5-11.
41   Rev 12:1-3, 4-5; 17:6.; see also "Z5 - The Two Aspects of the Same Woman in the Zechariah Draft" on page 79.
42   Isa 7:14-6; Rev 12:1-5; 15-7.
43   Ezek 16:20; Rev 17:6; see "Z8 - Jerusalem as the Harlot (Part 2)" on page 123.
44   In Joseph's dream, the sun represented his father Jacob (Israel), the moon represented his mother and the twelve stars represented his brothers (or the 12 tribes of Israel) (Gene 37:9). The likely reason for using Joseph's dream was the parallel between the story of the child in Revelation and the story of Joseph. Joseph was sent to a faraway place (Gen 37:28) where he became second to the most powerful ruler on earth (Gen 41:40). This is similar to the child being taken to heaven to rule with God (Rev 12:4-5).
45   Rev 12:1-2; 17:1-2.
46   "Z7 - The Building of the Encoded-Complex Parallel (Zech 2:1 - 4:14; Rev 11:1 - 12:17)" on page 86.

Z5 - The Two Aspects of the Same Woman in the Zechariah Draft

The woman and the harlot in Revelation represents the city of Jerusalem. The woman represents the righteous element that is preserved because they obeyed the commandments of God and the Lamb (Rev 12:17). The harlot represents the element of Jerusalem that sought to destroy those who obeyed God (Rev 17:6, 8, 13). At one point John formed a parallel between the two women and continued to keep the parallel even through later edits as seen below.

The beast did not appear until the DnD which is the last major draft in the RDH. Satan is a product of this draft (ZrD) so therefore it is likely that John had Satan interacting with the harlot instead of the beast in the ZrD.

	The Woman (Rev 12:1-17)		The Harlot (Rev 17:1-18)
12:1	She is introduced in heaven.	17:1	She is introduced as the woman who sits on many waters.
12:1	Sun, moon, and a crown of twelve stars (from Gen 37:9)	17:4	Dressed in purple and scarlet with gold and all kinds of precious stones and pearls
12:2	She is with child (conceived in heaven?).	17:2	She is committing sexual immorality with all the kings on earth.
12:4	Satan tries to devour her and her child.	17:6	She drinks the blood of the saints.
12:14	She was taken to the wilderness by the wings of a great eagle.	17:3	She rode a scarlet-colored beast to the wilderness.
12:7-9	The expulsion of Satan from heaven	17:8-	The rise of the beast from they abyss
12:10-1	The kingdom of the world became the kingdom of God.	17:9-14	The harlot, the beast, and the nations try to destroy the kingdom of God.
12:15-6	Satan tries to destroy the woman with a flood but the nations rescue her and her children.	17:16	The beast and the nations will burn her with fire.

John then added elements from the woman in the basket to both the woman-with-child passage and the harlot passage. For the woman with child he had her flown into the wilderness on two eagle wings to be nourished (protected) by God.[47] For the harlot he had the dragon fly her into the wilderness.[48]

The question remains, did John move the two passages next to each other as a possibility for the draft or did he simply form parallels between the two with no intention to keep them together? The short answer is that we really don't know; we can easily construct scenarios for both. If he simply formed a parallel between the woman who gave birth and the harlot then this would be the only time he did not move text in the ZrD. If he moved and appended the woman with child together with the harlot then the process must have caused the harlot to return back to her pre-ZrD placement.[49]

Z6 - The Flying Scroll (Zech 5:1-4; Rev 5:1-2, 7-8; 10:1-11).

The flying scroll is an example of how John not only conflates passages but also the meanings of a symbol. In Ezekiel, the scroll was written on two sides, tasted like honey, and contained the "lamentations, and mourning, and woe."[50] The flying scroll in Zechariah is written on two sides as well, but it is the size of a

---

47   Rev 12:14.
48   Rev 17:3. Note: In the ZrD the beast did not exist and most likely it was the dragon (Satan) and later changed to the beast in the DnD.
49   See "Z5 - The Two Women Flown Into the Wilderness and the Shifting of a Wax Tablet" on page 81.
50   Ezek 2:8-3:3.

billboard, flies through the whole land, and destroys the houses of the thief and the liar.[51] We do not have any of the unique elements to the flying scroll with the exception of the purpose of destroying the houses of the liars and thieves. This is evident when John describes the sins of both Jerusalem and Tyre (Rome) in Revelation. For Jerusalem it is their continued ability to steal, and he describes it as that they did not repent of "their thefts," and for Tyre it is how they deceived.[52]

The Mighty Angel Author's Notation

How John incorporated the flying scroll into Revelation was to first conflate the meanings of the scroll from Ezekiel and the flying scroll from Zechariah.[53] Second, John splits the scroll text and places the first part in Revelation 5:1-2, 7 and the second part in Rev 10:1-11. He uses the mighty angel (synonym for the seraph) as an author's notation to remind him where the material came from.[54] The reason for splitting the scroll text into two locations deals with the meaning of the scroll and how John assigns the meaning to various parts of the ZrD. For the Ezekiel meaning--in which the scroll represents "lamentations, and mourning, and woe,"--John assigns the mourning to the seals/horsemen, the woe to the trumpets/winds, and the lamentations to the merchants' lament over Tyre's destruction.[55] It is important to note that at this point in the construction of the ZrD, the judgment of the bowls has not yet been created in the ZrD. They were created when John incorporated the four horns from Zechariah into the EID.[56]

The Zechariah meaning of the scroll is that it is something that flies around and destroys the houses of the liars and thieves. John decided to use cities instead of houses, and with that decision there could only be two cities that John could have used. The first city is Jerusalem, which John symbolized in the EID as the end of a ministry and the birth of a ministry reflected with the destruction of Jerusalem, and the second city of Tyre as a symbol for Rome.[57] The problem for John is where to put the content for the second half of the scroll. He could place it before the harlot and Tyre (the EID equivalent of Rev 17:1-18 and Rev 18:1-24), but that would make it harder to incorporate Zech 1:1 - 4:15 into the EID. He could place it before the woman (Rev 12:1-17 equivalent), but that would split the association between the end of a ministry and the birth of a new holy seed.[58]

John elected to place the second part of the scroll and conflate it with the first commissioning of Ezekiel as the watchman.[59] The reason is two-fold, first it did not destroy the storyline with the EID prototype of the end of one ministry and the birth of a new holy seed. Second, it provided John a convenient location for the prediction of the destruction of Tyre based upon 70 years after the days of a certain king[60] as well as connecting the same prophecies with the destruction of Jerusalem. Since the EID saw Jesus' death

---

51   Zech 5:1-4.
52   Rev 9:21; 18:23-4.
53   Ezek 2:8 - 3:3; Zech 5:1-4.
54   See "Z6 - The Flying Scroll (Part 2)" on page 83
55   Ezek 2:8-3:3. To see how John assigns the "lamentations, the mourning, and woe" to the judgments see "How John Connected the Scroll to the Judgments in Revelation" on page 274.
56   See "Z8 - The Creation and Placement of the Four Horns/First Four Bowls (Zech 1:18-21; Rev 16:1-9)" on page 92.
57   See "Z8 - Jerusalem as the Harlot (Part 2)" on page 123 and "Z9 - God Pleads to His People to Return to Him (Part 1)" on page 124 for how the verses map.
58   See "The Two Missions: The Call of the Watchman and the Birth of a Child (EP3, IP3)" on page 17 for how John constructed the parallel.
59   Ezek 3:16-27.
60   Isa 23:15-17.

Z5 - The Two Women Flown Into the Wilderness and the Shifting of a Wax Tablet

The illustrations below show how John could have initially aligned the woman-with-child and harlot passages together to accommodate Zechariah 5:5-11. As each subsequent change took place the building of the ZrD the two passages would have returned to their original EID locations.

The Initial Composition Part 1 (Z5)	**The Initial Composition Part 2 (Z5)**
John appended the aspect of being flown into the wilderness (Babylon) on the woman with child tablet. He also prefixed the aspect of being flown into the wilderness to the Harlot tablet.	John then appended the two stories together so as to become one narrative containing two aspects of Jerusalem. One came from heaven (Rev 12:1) and the other came from earth (Rev 17:1).

Note: The below illustration shows the parallel formation after the introduction of Satan into the ZrD (see Z7).

The Woman with Child (12:1-17)	**The Harlot (17:1-18)**
	Flown to the wilderness
The woman's clothing.	The harlot's clothing.
Tries to devour the child.	Drinks saint's blood.
Satan, war in heaven.	War against the Lamb.
Short time.	Short time.
Flown to the wilderness	

The Woman with Child (12:1-17)
The woman's clothing.
Tried to devour the child.
Satan is defeated in heaven.
Satan has a short time.
Flown to the wilderness

The Harlot
Flown to the wilderness
The harlot's clothing.
She drinks the saint's blood.
War against the Lamb.
[Short time]

The Zechariah-Encoded Parallel Part 1 (Z7)	**The Zechariah-Encoded Parallel Part 2 (Z7)**
The wax tablets below represent how John laid them out when he created the Zechariah-encoded parallel.	The finished product of the Zechariah-encoded parallel created what we know as Revelation 10:1 to 12:17.

Mighty Angel and End of a Ministry	Woman
Glory of God Flees Jerusalem	Glory of God Triumphs in Heaven
	The Harlot

Mighty Angel
The Two Prophets (Z7)
The Woman and Satan (Z7)
The Leftover Content Not Encoded
The Harlot

The Adding of the Four Horns (Z8)

The wax tablets below represent how the wax tablets were arranged after John included the four horns in the ZrD.

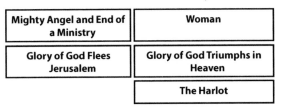

The Four Winds (Z4)
Mighty Angel
The Two Prophets
The Woman and Satan
The Leftover Content Not Encoded
The Four Horns (Z8)
The Harlot

Z6 - The Flying Scroll (Part 1)

The flying scroll in Zechariah is a two-sided large flying billboard scroll that was used to destroy the houses of the robbers and liars (Zech 5:1-4). However, John already had a previous scroll imagery which was a small scroll that was supposed to be eaten by John (Ezek 2:8-3:3). The scroll from Ezekiel also affected content in the EID containing the symbolism for the "lamentations, and mourning, and woe" (Ezek 2:10). The final resting place for the purpose of the Ezekiel scroll was to define the seals as the mourning, the trumpets as the woes, and the bowls as the lamentations (see "How John Connected the Scroll to the Judgments in Revelation" on page 274) requiring the scroll imagery to come before the judgments. John wanted to use the flying scroll imagery from Zechariah to show the destruction of the two cities: Jerusalem and Tyre. Therefore the flying scroll needed to precede Jerusalem and Tyre.

The Key Text of Zechariah:

5:1 *Then again I lifted up my eyes, and saw, and behold, a flying scroll.* **5:2** *He said to me, "What do you see?" I answered, "I see a flying scroll; its length is twenty cubits (30 feet), and its width ten cubits (15 feet)."* **5:3** *Then he said to me, "This is the curse that goes out over the surface of the whole land; for everyone who steals shall be cut off according to it on the one side, and everyone who swears falsely shall be cut off according to it on the other side.* **5:4** *I will cause it to go out," says* THE LORD*, "and it will enter into the house of the thief, and into the house of him who swears falsely by my name; and it will remain in the middle of his house, and will destroy it with its timber and its stones."*

EP1	Ezekiel's Experience in Heaven
	• God on the throne (Ezek 1:26-2:2)
	• The living creatures (Ezek 1:4-26)
	• The scroll (Ezek 2:8 - 3:3)

EP3	Ezekiel Appointed as a Watchman
	• God's people are like briers, thorns, and scorpions (Ezek 2:6), God hardens Ezekiel's head (Ezek 3:8-9).
	• Ezekiel is appointed as a watchman (Ezek 3:16-27).
	• End of three ministries and its relation to the siege of Jerusalem (Ezek 4:5-8)

IP7	Tyre (Jesus, a Certain King)
	• Wealth from trading with other nations (Isa 23:1-17)
	• Tyre's destruction 70 years after a certain king (Isa 23:15-7)
	• Post-destruction's wealth will be righteousness (Isa 23:18).
	• Saints rejoicing over Tyre's destruction (Isa 25:1-6)

as the end of the ministry of Israel and his birth as the beginning of the new holy seed of God,[61] John set the 70-year timer for the destruction of Jerusalem as 70 years after Jesus' birth and the destruction of Tyre (Rome) as 70 years after Jesus' death. We see this by comparing the source texts to what was included and what was left out and by using the author's notation to bring the separated text across Revelation together as one storyline.[62]

The way John defined the cities of Jerusalem and Tyre (Rome) as a city of thieves and a city of liars was actually an easy process. He prefixed the sin of thieving at the end of the four winds (the first six trumpets) text and just prior to the second mighty-angel scene.[63] For the city of Tyre (Rome), John simply used the space provided by moving the text:

> *"Her merchandise and her wages will be holiness to* THE LORD*. It will not be treasured nor laid up; for her merchandise will be for those who dwell before* THE LORD*, to eat sufficiently, and for durable clothing."*[64]

---

61 See "The End of One Ministry and the Birth of Another (Ezek 4:5-8; Isa 6:13-9:19)" on page 18.
62 See "Z6 - The Flying Scroll (Part 2)" on page 83.
63 John incorporated the thieving sin from Zech 5:3-4 into Rev 9:21. See "Z6 - The Flying Scroll (Part 2)" on page 83.
64 Isa 23:18.

Z6 - The Flying Scroll (Part 2)

With each scroll having a different result and imagery, John elected to keep the imagery of the Ezekiel scroll and split the context of the scroll using the mighty angel as its author's notation. This allowed him to keep a portion of the scroll before the seals (Rev 5:1-2) and a portion of the scroll prior to the destruction of Jerusalem (Rev 11:1-12). He then included the EID depiction of Jesus representing a certain king and added in the prophecy that the destruction of Jerusalem would take place 70 years after the birth of Jesus and the destruction of Rome would take place 70 years after Jesus' death. However, the adding of the four horns required John to reassess the placement of the Tyre content and therefore he created a second author's notation with the mighty angel and removed the scroll imagery.

The flying scroll destroys the houses of the thieves and liars, so John appended at the end of the judgments to Jerusalem (the seven seals and the first six trumpets) a list of sins with the last sin unique to the city. Jerusalem was assigned the sin of theft and Tyre (Rome) the sin of lying.

	Content Found in Ezekiel and Isaiah		**Content in Revelation (Ordered by Isaiah, Revelation)**
Ezek 2:10	It was written within and without	5:1	The scroll written inside and outside
Isa 6:8	"Whom shall I send, and who will go for us?"	5:2	"Who is worthy to open the scroll . . ."

Mighty Angel - 1A
The mighty angel (5:2 to 10:1)

The Seven Seals (Rev 6:1 - 8:6)

The First Six Trumpets (Rev 8:7 - 9:21)

Zech 5:3-4	Everyone who steals shall be cut off according to it on the one side.	9:21	They didn't repent of their murders, nor of their sorceries, nor of their sexual immorality, **nor of their thefts**.

Mighty Angel - 1B
The mighty angel (10:1 from 5:2)

Ezek 1:28	The appearance of a rainbow The appearance of brightness all around him	10:1	A rainbow on his head His face was like the sun.
Ezek 3:12	Ezekiel hears the living creatures making loud noises, seven days, saying: "Blessed be THE LORD's glory from his place."	10:3-4	John hears the message of the seven thunders but is told not to reveal it to anyone.
Ezek 3:1-3	Ezekiel told to take the scroll and eat it. It will taste sweet to the mouth.	10:9-10	John told to take the scroll and eat it. It was sweet to the lips.
Ezek 3:14	Ezekiel was bitter.	10:9-10	The scroll was bitter to John's stomach.
Ezek 3:16-27	Ezekiel is appointed as a watchman to tell everyone.	10:11	John is told to tell everyone.

Mighty Angel - 2A
The mighty angel (10:1, 11 to 18:21)

Mighty Angel - 2B
The mighty angel (18:21 from 10:11)

Jer 51:63	It shall be, ~~when you have finished reading this scroll~~, that you shall bind a stone to it, and cast it into the middle of the Euphrates.	18:21	A mighty angel took up a stone like a great millstone and cast it into the sea, saying,
Jer 51:64	Thus shall Babylon sink, and shall not rise again because of the evil that I will bring on her; and they shall be weary.	18:21	"Thus with violence will Babylon, the great city, be thrown down, and will be found no more at all.
Isa 23:15, 17	Tyre will be forgotten seventy years, according to the days of one king . . . after the end of seventy years that THE LORD will visit Tyre.		[see "Jesus as the Certain King (Isa 23:15-7; Rev 18:2-6, 22)" on page 29]
Isa 23:16	Take a harp; go about the city . . . . Make sweet melody. Sing many songs, that you may be remembered.	18:22	The voice of harpists, minstrels, flute players, and trumpeters will be heard no more at all in you.
Isa 23:17	She . . . will play the prostitute with all the kingdoms of the world on the surface of the earth.		
Zech 5:3-4	Everyone who swears falsely shall be cut off according to it on the other side.	18:23	With your sorcery **all the nations were deceived**.
Jer 51:49	As Babylon has caused the slain of Israel to fall, so at Babylon shall fall the slain of all the land.	18:24	In her was found the blood of prophets and of saints, and of all who have been slain on the earth.

to the location that became the message to the seven churches.[65] He then replaced the text similar to how it appears in Revelation today:

> *For with your sorcery all the nations were deceived. In her was found the blood of prophets and of saints, and of all who have been slain on the earth.*[66]

John also added the sin of murder against God's people as a means of reinforcing the "mourning" element from the Ezekiel version of the scroll.[67] The process was as simple as prefixing a line and using the space of an erased line to satisfy the process requirements of adding Zechariah into the ZrD.

What the mighty angel author's notation tells us is that John really constructed the ZrD in the order that this chapter conveys. The splitting of the scroll and the placement of its parts could only come from a progression in the production of the ZrD. The first placement represents the Ezekiel scroll location defined by the EID and conflated in the ZrD. The second placement contained parts of Isaiah concerning the 70-year prophecy as to the destruction of Tyre as well as a selection from Jeremiah, which includes scroll imagery as well as the millstone imagery that will become part of the third placement of the mighty angel author's notation.[68] It also, at this point, what became the conveyance of the message from God to Jesus, to the angel, and finally to John, which is the beginning of Revelation and the chain of custody of the vision.[69]

How the mighty angel gets a third placement has to do with John needing imagery of nations going out of their way to make God angry with them and a passage that has 70 years in it.[70] Perhaps a simpler way of explaining why it moved again was that John needed to return the passage back to the original context which supported the later portion of Zechariah.

The Conflation of the Primary Mighty Angel Text (Rev 10:1-11)

In the ZrD, the mighty angel passage is the passage in which John receives the vision that God wishes him to relay to the world.[71] Regarding the chronology of all prophetic events, the mighty angel passage is the point at which John wants the reader to believe the vision was given to him. This was true in the ZrD and is true in the PVR. We see it expressed with the mighty angel swearing before God that what will happen after the passage will occur very soon.[72] Therefore all aspects of the mighty angel's conflated text will exhibit the urgency of the coming of the prophetic message to the believers.

In order to construct the mighty angel passage, John's edits were slightly more complex than usual. He took the episode where Ezekiel was sent to Tel Aviv (not the city today) via the living creatures whose wings made a thunderous noise when they touched, while saying "Blessed be The Lord's glory from his

---

65   See "Z2 - The Ezekiel-Isaiah Draft Content for the Seven Churches" on page 107 on how John used Isa 23:18 to form the central request for the church in Laodicea.

66   Rev 18:23-24 taken from Zech 5:3-4.

67   Rev 9:21; 18:23-4.

68   Jer 51:63-4; see "Z6 - The Flying Scroll (Part 2)" on page 83; see "The Destruction of Tyre and the Rejoicing of the Saints (Zech 1:12; Rev 19:1-9)" on page 94 where John aligned the text with another seventy years mentioned in Zechariah.

69   Rev 1:1.

70   "The Destruction of Tyre and the Rejoicing of the Saints (Zech 1:12; Rev 19:1-9)" on page 94.

71   Rev 1:1

72   The mighty angel "swore by him who lives forever and ever, who created heaven and the things that are in it, the earth and the things that are in it, and the sea and the things that are in it, that there will no longer be delay" (Rev 10:6). This text was added in the DnD (see "The Mighty Angel Tells John it Will Happen Soon" on page 230).

When Wax Tablets Are Placed Together

As John moved the wax tablets around they became joined with the other tablets. Sometimes the content from one wax tablet would be better suited as content to the adjoining wax tablet. Below is an example of the content moved from one wax tablet to another.

EP4 Judgment by the Nations (Ezek 5:2)
- The nations will strike in thirds (Ezek 5:2).
- God's people give evil decrees (Ezek 5:4-15).
- *The day of the Lord (Ezek 7:10) where God will destroy those without the mark of God on their forehead (Ezek 9:4).*

To the left is how two of the wax tablets were aligned when the judgment scenes were moved prior to Ezekiel's appointment to be a watchman. The text in **bold italics** are what was conflated with the bottom tablet text moved to the upper wax tablet.

EP3 Ezekiel Appointed as a Watchman
- *God's people are like briers, thorns, and scorpions (Ezek 2:6) so God hardened Ezekiel's head to protect him (Ezek 3:8-9).*
- Ezekiel appointed as a watchman (Ezek 3:16-27)

The chart below illustrates how John combined most of the elements by tweaking the text. He kept the mark on the forehead in Ezek 9:4 as describing the righteous and used the hardening of Ezekiel's head as the alignment point. The scorpions went from being God's rebellious people to the instruments of pain found in Revelation. John formed an opposite to wickedness, as represented by the briers and thorns to the righteous people by changing the briers and thorns to greenery.

9:4	Go through the middle of Jerusalem **and set a mark on the foreheads** of the men signed and cried over all the abominations that were done.
	To the others . . . . Go through the city after him, and strike: don't let your eye spare, neither have pity;

The Fifth Trumpet (Rev 9:1-12)

9:4	They were told that they **should not hurt the grass of the earth, neither any green thing**, neither any tree, **but only those people who don't have God's seal on their foreheads.**
9:5	They were given power not to kill them, but to torment them for five months. **Their torment was like the torment of a scorpion**, when it strikes a person.

2:6	You, son of man, don't be afraid of them, neither be afraid of their words, **though briers and thorns are with you, and you do dwell among scorpions**: don't be afraid of their words, nor be dismayed at their looks, though they are a rebellious house.
3:8	Behold, **I have made your face hard against their faces, and your forehead hard against their foreheads.**
3:9	As an adamant harder than flint have I made your forehead: don't be afraid of them, neither be dismayed at their looks, though they are a rebellious house.

place." At Tel Aviv, he stayed for seven days in bitterness. John transformed the story into the seven thunders speaking to him and added the taste of bitterness to the scroll.[73]

The text that John did not use to construct the mighty angel migrated to the wax tablets that were placed before the primary mighty angel passage. John saw that the previous wax tablet had the imagery of the people with the mark on their foreheads who will be spared from the destruction of Jerusalem was similar to God hardening Ezekiel's head. Due to this, John erased the hardening of Ezekiel's head from the tablet.

---

73   Ezek 3:11-6; Rev 10:3-4, 9-10; see "Z6 - The Flying Scroll (Part 2)" on page 83.

He then moved the imagery of the briers, thorns, and scorpions to the fifth trumpet, making transformations to the imagery. The briers and thorns that represented wickedness became the greenery to symbolize the righteousness of those with the mark of God on their forehead. The scorpions that represented God's rebellious people had a dual meaning, as those who deceived God's people in rebelling against the Romans and the Romans inflicting pain on those who stayed in Jerusalem during the Roman siege.[74]

Z7 - The Building of the Encoded-Complex Parallel (Zech 2:1 - 4:14; Rev 11:1 - 12:17)

John performs one of his most creative uses of importing Hebrew Scriptures into a draft. He takes the content from Zechariah 2:1 - 4:14 and distributes it to what is now Revelation chapters 11 and 12 via the creation of the 42 months, 1,260 days, 3½ days complex parallel (also called the 42-month parallel). He places the content from Zechariah chapter 2 to form both elements of the 42-month portion of the parallel, content from chapter 3 to form both elements of the 1,260 days parallel, and content from chapter 4 to form both elements of the 3½ days complex parallel.[75] John further encoded the 42-month complex parallel by alternating each set of elements with opposites and complements. The end result was that the Zechariah content formed a simple parallel with the 42-month parallel and made each set of elements from Zechariah form a complex parallel that followed this order: opposite, complement, opposite.

As we have seen, John is building the ZrD, content from the EID in the form of wax tablets are being shifted around. So when John is rewriting the wax tablets used to construct the 42-month complex parallel he is also dealing with the content that represents the editing state of the EID such as the remaining content when the judgment scenes were relocated to another section in the ZrD. The result was that two unconnected passages from Ezekiel were joined together and two unrelated passages in Isaiah were also merged. The material from the leftover EID and from Zechariah gave John the imagery to many of the more profound portions of Revelation such as the temple imagery, some aspects of the two prophets, and the creation of Satan.[76]

The Creation of Satan in the Zechariah Draft

To best explain the conflation of the 42-month parallel, we will focus on the placement of Satan and how John conflated a series of passages from Ezekiel, Isaiah, and Zechariah to obtain what we have in Revelation today. So far we have seen how John moved wax tablets around to formulate the ZrD, and how it affected the content of the passage. There is no better spot that validates the ZrD portion of the Revelation Draft Hypothesis than the formation of the 42-month parallel and the construction of Satan. It is the place where the two sets of the Ezekiel-Isaiah parallel passages are joined together by a process used to complete all previous passages in the ZrD. When they are placed together, the result is strikingly similar to what is found in the PVR.

---

74 See "EP4 - The Judgments by the Nations - Part 3" on page 50 on how the five months is connected to the Roman siege of Jerusalem. See "When Wax Tablets Are Placed Together" on page 85 as to how they are conflated.

75 See "Z7 - The Zechariah-Encoded Parallel: How it Was Built (Part 1)" on page 117.

76 "Z7 - The Zechariah-Encoded Parallel: How it Was Built (Part 1)" on page 117 represents the state of the EID and the portions that John used to form the 42 month, 1,260 day, 3½ complex parallel. The second chart, "Z7 - The Zechariah-Encoded Parallel: How it Was Built (Part 1)" on page 117 shows how the parallel was formed and also shows how different sections of Ezekiel and Isaiah were conflated.

In the EID, John transformed Ezekiel's prophecy that relates the number of days of the Babylonian siege of Jerusalem to the sum of the days that Israel and Judah sinned against God to the number of days of each of the ministries served God. John then connected the EID prototype of the 42-month parallel with various aspects of the life of a child who John defines as Jesus, and various actions of the Assyrian army destroying Israel as the Roman army destroying Jerusalem.[77]

John took the 42-month parallel and overlaid the content from Zechariah's chapters 2, 3, and 4 on each of the corresponding parallels. So the 42-month elements contained items from Zechariah chapter 2, the 1,260 day elements contained items from Zechariah chapter 3, and the 3½ day element contained items from Zechariah chapter 4.[78] However there was one element in Zechariah that became the Isaiah side of the 42-month complex parallel and at least one element in the Ezekiel side of the 42-month complex parallel.

Satan Defeated in Heaven and the Great Dragon Locked in the Abyss and How Satan Got so Many Names

John created Satan by taking the description of Satan being forcibly removed from Jerusalem (found in Zechariah 3:1-2). When he scanned the text that comprised the 42-month parallel, he found nothing that was usable as a Satan figure. So John continued reading the remaining text from the reshaping of the EID to the Zechariah source import pattern.[79] The tablets were perfectly aligned in that the Isaiah side of the Ezekiel-Isaiah parallel told the story of Babylon chasing the glory of God in heaven and God forcing Babylon to earth and then placing Babylon in Sheol.[80] As a result of Babylon residing in Sheol, the nations became at ease, and the Israelites among the nations were finally able to come home.[81]

The assigning of Satan to the military actions that will defeat Jerusalem caused a big problem for John, namely if Satan chases Jesus into heaven, and he is defeated and thrown into the Abyss, how then will Jerusalem be destroyed? One of the solutions that John came up with was a delay between Satan being kicked out of heaven and his being locked up in the abyss.[82] Therefore, John needed a place to seal away Satan into the Abyss and the best location for that was the slaying of the great dragon (Pharaoh) found in the last Ezekiel-Isaiah parallel.[83] Since the imagery of the great dragon's final resting place is found in Sheol,[84] this made it possible to conform to how John harmonized material in each draft. To link the two separate and distant events together, John used a surviving author's notation found in Isaiah in which Isaiah repeated the same phrase twice:

---

77 See "The End of One Ministry and the Birth of Another (Ezek 4:5-8; Isa 6:13-9:19)" on page 18.

78 See "Z7 - The Zechariah-Encoded Parallel: How it Was Built (Part 1)" on page 117.

79 "Z7 - The Zechariah-Encoded Parallel: How it Was Built (Part 1)" on page 117 represents the state of the EID and the portions that John used to form the 42 month, 1,260 day, 3½ complex parallel. The second chart, "Z7 - The Zechariah-Encoded Parallel: How it Was Built (Part 1)" on page 117 shows how the parallel was formed and also shows how different sections of Ezekiel and Isaiah were conflated.

80 Isa 14:13-5 becomes the war in heaven (Rev 12:7-9) and Satan locked up in the Abyss (Rev 20:1-3).

81 Isa 14:18-9 tells of the nations sleeping in their own homes indicating peace. Revelation depicts two states of the world, one of war depicts Satan amassing an army via deception when released (Rev 9:11-22; 12:12-7; 20:7-10) and the other is when Satan is locked away so he can no longer deceive the nations (Rev 20:1-3). The beast which was Satan in the ZrD is also described as amassing an army through his deception (Rev 16:12-6).

82 Rev 12:12 where as in Rev 12:1-3 Satan is locked away for a thousand years.

83 Ezek 29:1 - 32:32; Isa 27:1-13; Rev 19:11 - 20:3.

84 Ezek 31:15-6.

"Because the rod that struck you is broken; for out of the serpent's root an adder will emerge, and his fruit will be a fiery flying serpent."[85]

In that day, THE LORD with his hard and great and strong sword will punish leviathan, the fleeing serpent, and leviathan the twisted serpent; and he will kill the dragon that is in the sea.[86]

The end result of John using the author's notation for Isaiah's serpent was the source for the descriptions of Satan as exhibited in:

The great dragon was thrown down, the old serpent, he who is called the devil and Satan, the deceiver of the whole world.[87]

In order for John to link the defeat of Satan in heaven with the defeat of Satan on earth, John had to make some adjustments to the EID and leave a notation for both Jesus and Satan by linking the changes to the storyline. The notation John left for Satan was to repeat the same descriptions of Satan, thus linking the defeat of Satan in heaven with his defeat on earth.[88] The notation for Jesus was a little more involved in that it included the changing of symbols. He first conflated the imagery of the rod of the mouth and the great sword into the sharp two-edged sword of Jesus' mouth by making the rod stand alone and replacing the sword with the original context of the rod.[89] The rod came to symbolize how Jesus will rule the nations and thus became a means of connecting Jesus ruling in heaven with Jesus defeating the great dragon on earth.[90]

The solution of Satan roaming in the gap between being defeated by Jesus in heaven and being defeated by Jesus on earth before he is locked away in the abyss will be a short one. John will later create a story that Satan will be defeated by the angel Michael around the time that Michael defeated Satan over Moses' body.[91] As a result, Satan will be sealed away in the abyss until the time of Jesus a thousand years later. Upon his release, Satan will actively seek out and destroy all the followers of God and the Lamb.[92] The end result is that we will have both stories of Satan woven together in a way that was never finished and can never be harmonized.

Other Places That Provide Content for Satan Outside of the Zechariah Draft

The addition of Satan into the ZrD would most likely inspire John to use other scriptures that talked about Satan. We have seen where John will add scriptures outside of the principle draft source already in several places such as the interjection of text containing a scroll and conflating it with the flying scroll from Zech-

---

85   Isa 14:29 as the source for "The great dragon was thrown down, the old serpent, he who is called the devil and Satan, the deceiver of the whole world" (Rev 12:9).

86   Isa 27:1 as the source for "He seized the dragon, the old serpent, which is the devil and Satan, who deceives the whole inhabited earth" (Rev 20:2).

87   Rev 12:9; 20:2.

88   "The great dragon . . . the old serpent, he who is called the devil and Satan, the deceiver of the whole world" found in Rev 12:9; 20:2.

89   The "strike the earth rod of the mouth" imagery came from Isa 11:4 and the "great sword" came from Isa 27:1 which becomes: "Out of his mouth proceeds a sharp, double-edged sword, that with it he should strike the nations. He will rule them with an iron rod" in Rev 19:15.

90   Rev 12:5; 19:15; see also Rev 2:26-7 to see how John linked the church of Thyatira with Rev 12:5; 19:15.

91   Jude 1:9.

92   The second story about Satan will be come into play in the DJD where Satan will be locked away for a thousand years. The story will undergo a major modification in the DnD where many of the places in Revelation ascribed to Satan will be ascribed to the beast.

ariah.[93] So it is not surprising that we should find passages outside of Zechariah that John uses to enhance the story of Satan within the ZrD or a later draft, and as a result, we find at least two of the places connected to Satan that are found in Revelation.

The Problem of Translating Satan

In the Hebrew Scriptures, Satan generally does not get translated well. This is due to its theological ramifications that sometimes drive a translation's marketability. The person that we know of as Satan is not the Hebrew Scriptures entity of the Christian "Satan" but the result of post-Hebrew Scripture sources. As such, translators are stuck with the reality of the Satan doctrine's development and the readers desire to see known passages that contain the word "Satan." Therefore many translations follow a few simple rules on how to translate the Hebrew word Satan (שָׂטָן) into English.

- If it can be Satan, then translate it as "Satan," and pay no attention to any other possibility (eg. Job 1:6 - 2:7; Zech 3:1).

- If it cannot be Satan, then translate it as "adversary" and downplay the Hebrew word (eg. Numbers 22:22, 23; 1 Sam 29:4; 2 Sam 19:23; 1 Kgs 5:18; 1 Kgs 11:14).

Satan, Balaam, and Phinehas (Num 22:1 - 25:18; Rev 2:13-5)

The first text containing 'Satan' in the Hebrew Scriptures has to do with the scene of an angel playing the role of Satan (adversary) against Balaam.[94] The conclusion of the Balaam account in Numbers is that the Israelite men had sexual relationships with women and ate food sacrifices to idols aligning themselves with Baal.[95] One of the Israelites was so bold as to bring a Midianite woman to their brother in front of Moses and the tent of meeting.[96] As a result of this action one of the priests, Phinehas, rose up from the middle of the congregation and pierced the man and woman through with a spear.[97] The end result is that the actions of Phinehas turned the wrath of God away and spared the people.[98]

John will leverage the story of Phinehas and form a complex parallel with it, resulting in the creation of the central message to the church of Pergamum:

> *"I know your works and where you dwell, where Satan's throne is. You hold firmly to my name, and didn't deny my faith in the days of Antipas my witness, my faithful one, who was killed among you, where Satan dwells. But I have a few things against you, because you have there some who hold the teachings of Balaam, who taught Balak to throw a stumbling block before the children of Israel, to eat things sacrificed to idols, and to commit sexual immorality. So you also have some who hold to the teaching of the Nicolaitans likewise.[99]*

The message to the church of Pergamum was changed to reflect wordplay and opposites, and additionally the story is told in reverse order of Numbers 25:1-11; instead of being in front of Moses and the tent of meeting, it is in front of Satan and his throne, placing Antipas (Phinehas in Numbers) in hostile territory

---

93   See how John used Jeremiah to enhance the scroll imagery in "Z6 - The Flying Scroll (Part 2)" on page 83.
94   Num 22:22, 32.
95   Num 25:1-5.
96   Num 25:6.
97   Num 25:7-9.
98   Num 25:10-1.
99   Rev 2:13-5.

and yet standing up. The story has Antipas die off early so the schemes of Balaam and Balak prevail and the people will follow the teachings/actions of the Midianites.

John changed the name of Phinehas to Antipas, and Midianites to Nicolaitans, because of wordplay formation. Antipas (Greek: Ἀντιπᾶς) is comprised of two Greek words ἀντί, meaning: "opposite" or "instead of"[100] and πᾶς meaning "every" or "all"[101] and thus when combined Antipas means "against everyone." With Antipas meaning "against everyone," John needed a way of saying the opposite, and thereby he chose to use the word Nicolaitans (Greek: Νικολαΐτης) which like Antipas is comprised of two words: νῖκος meaning "victory,"[102] and λαός meaning "people"[103] and when combined became "victory by everyone" or "victory by the people."

Satan in Heaven as the Adversary to Job (Job 1:6 - 2:6; Rev 12:10)

The second scene from the Hebrew Scriptures is the description of Satan found in Job. In Job, there is a council of the sons of God who meet up in heaven from time to time. One of them, "the adversary" and translated as "Satan" in most Bibles, accused Job of being righteous because he had everything. So God and Satan made a bet in which Satan can do anything to Job short of killing him and Job will not abandon God.[104]

The story of the "Accuser" in Job was probably the primary driving force to have Satan begin his journey in heaven to take on the role of the accuser against the saints in heaven.[105] The rest of the story is how he pursued the woman and child to earth and then the child to heaven and is sent back to earth; this is from his conflation of Zechariah and Isaiah as we have discussed.

The Creation of the Temple and its Courtyard Trampled by Gentiles (Zech 2:1-4; Rev 11:1-2)

On the Ezekiel side of the 42-month parallel, John had to tell a story similar to the story of Satan and keeping with the EID in depicting it as the end of a ministry.[106] He needed to consolidate elements of Zechariah, Ezekiel, and Isaiah to tell a unified story.

So John began with the story in Zechariah where an angel tells a person to measure the city of Jerusalem but not its walls, because the city will be so wealthy that it will be trampled by cattle.[107] He took the Ezekiel-Isaiah parallel that contained the Isaiah source text of Satan, that depicted the glory of God fleeing the temple and transformed the Zechariah text from Jerusalem to the temple.[108] John had in his narrative an angel that told him to measure the temple but not its courtyard because it will be trampled by the na-

---

100 BDAG, ἀντί.

101 BDAG, πᾶς.

102 BDAG, νῖκος.

103 BDAG, λαός

104 Job 1:6 - 2:6.

105 Rev 12:3-4,10.

106 See "The Two Missions: The Call of the Watchman and the Birth of a Child (EP3, IP3)" on page 17.

107 Zech 2:1.

108 See "Z7 - The Zechariah-Encoded Parallel: How it Was Built (Part 1)" on page 117, "Z7 - The Zechariah Encoded Parallel: The Two Prophets (Part 2)" on page 118, "Z7 - The Zechariah Encoded Parallel: Satan's Entry into Revelation (Z7 -- Part 3)" on page 119, and "Z7 - The Zechariah Encoded Parallel: Satan's Entry into Revelation (Part 4)" on page 120.

tions,[109] thus depicting it as a ministry and defining its ending as 42 months (representing 420 years of the second temple's service).[110]

The Creation of the Nations Are Angry Against Israel (Zech 2:9-13; Rev 11:15-8; Rev 12:15-6)

The second part of chapter 2 in Zechariah tells of a world where the nations will be blessed by Israel and share in the worship of God. In the ZrD this will become the story of the nations being angry at Israel but working in harmony with God.[111] We also see one attack by Satan seeking to destroy the woman and her children who are faithful to God; when the nations step in and rescue the faithful by absorbing the attack.[112] This makes the nations defending the faithful and destroying the unfaithful the most likely spot for the second 42-month element in the 42-month parallel. Furthermore we have textual evidence supporting this claim in the form of how John expanded the 42-month element in the DnD by simply exchanging Daniel's description of "a time, times and time, and half a time" with the ZrD description of 42 months.[113] Thereby, John in the Daniel draft associated the anger of the nations and the blaspheming of God and his people (the temple) in heaven, thus creating the perfect second half of the 42-month parallel element.

The Creation of the Two Prophets

The creation of the two prophets followed the same process of conflation as the creation of Satan and the measuring of the temple. John basically read what was in Zechariah and searched for a match in the wax tablets before him. The difference in the creation of the two prophets is that John had to read farther down the text of Ezekiel to find a suitable candidate for the "two anointed ones"[114] in Zechariah. We know that John chose the passage in Ezekiel that talked about the Israelites killing the prophets they should not kill and rewarding the prophets that they should not have rewarded because those elements are found within Revelation.

When John was moving content from Zechariah chapters 2 to 4 into the 42 month, 1,260 day, 3½ day complex parallel, he took the ideas from Zechariah and shaped the Ezekiel imagery to construct the parallel. Instead of using the two anointed ones (Joshua the high priest and Zerubabel), he decided to use the killing of the prophets from Ezekiel.[115]

The creation of the two prophets in Revelation came about with the conflation of two unrelated, distant passages from Ezekiel that came together as a result of the material between the two placed elsewhere.[116] As a result, John opted to use the imagery of the two prophets instead, since they already contained the imagery of Joshua the high priest that he wanted to portray, such as their death and the people giving gifts, as well as maintaining the Ezekiel side of the Ezekiel-Isaiah parallel.[117]

---

109 Rev 11:1-2

110 Shaye J.D. Cohen and Joshua J. Schwartz. *Studies in Josephus and the Varieties of Ancient Judaism.* (Leiden: Brill, 2007), 125-6 in footnotes, cites Clement of Alexandria stating that the temple stood for 410 years and Seder Olam claiming it stood for 420 years.

111 "The kingdom of the world has become the kingdom of our Lord, and of his Christ" in Rev 11:15; 12:10 and "the nations became angry, and your wrath came . . . to those who destroyed the earth." in Rev 11:18.

112 Rev 12:15-7.

113 Dan 7:25; see "The Expanding of the 42-Month Parallel" on page 220.

114 Zech 4:14; Ezek 13:18-9; see "Z7 - The Zechariah Encoded Parallel: The Two Prophets (Part 2)" on page 118.

115 Ezek 13:18-9; see "Z7 - The Zechariah Encoded Parallel: The Two Prophets (Part 2)" on page 118.

116 See "Z7 - The Zechariah-Encoded Parallel: How it Was Built (Part 1)" on page 117.

117 Ezek 13:1-13; Rev 11:7, 10.

This is not to say that the content from Zechariah did not add to the descriptions of the two prophets in Revelation though. The imagery of the two prophets wearing sackcloth came from the imagery of Joshua (Jesus) the high priest wearing filthy rags[118] as well as the imagery of them being the two olive trees and the two lampstands before the Lord of the earth.[119]

As far as the process of encoding Zechariah into the EID, the first part of the story of Joshua the high priest and Zerubabel form the creation of the two prophets, whereas the second part of each story is inscribed into the story of the woman. For Joshua the high priest, it is that salvation will come to the world, which is the imagery that we get after the child is taken to heaven.[120] For the second half of the story of Zerubabel, it is the building of the temple that will be seen with the temple in heaven and will become Jesus as the high priest.[121]

One of the elements that did make it into the ZrD is the two prophets' narrative, but not in the PVR was the "Lord's seven eyes, which run back and forth through the whole earth."[122] They will become the seven spirits of God, and Jesus who will "go back and forth through the whole world."[123]

Z8 - The Creation and Placement of the Four Horns/First Four Bowls (Zech 1:18-21; Rev 16:1-9)

John moves to his next topic in producing the ZrD by incorporating the four horns from Zechariah into the modified EID. In Zechariah, the four horns accomplishes the scattering of Judah, Israel, and Jerusalem.[124] John elected to place the four horns before the Ezekiel harlot passage[125] At this point in the draft process, John has only one place to put the four horns and that is before the Ezekiel depiction of the harlot passage in Revelation. This is because the placement of the four horns (which are now the first four bowls), tells us a lot of what John was thinking in the ZrD, since he placed the four horns before the harlot passage from Ezekiel.[126] The primary reason is that in order to create the imagery of two women thrown into a basket and taken to the wilderness, John formed a parallel between the woman with child and the harlot passages.[127] John defined the woman with child as the righteous element that despite Satan's effort her children sill managed to escape the calamities.[128] John defined the harlot as the unrighteous element, that no matter how hard God tried, she and her children sinned against him.[129] Since both groups were taken to the wilderness, the action would be synonymous as being scattered throughout the wilderness.

---

118 Zech 3:3-4; Rev 11:3.

119 Zech 4:2, 12, 14; Rev 11:4.

120 Zech 3:9; Rev 12:5, 10-1.

121 Temple seen in heaven in Rev 11:19; the kingdom of the world becomes the kingdom of God (Rev 12:10) and Jesus as the high priest preparing the incense with his blood in Rev 5:8-10.

122 Zech 4:10.

123 In Rev 12:5 they become the seven spirits of God, sent out into all the earth. From there the seven spirits of God can be found in Rev 1:4 as the seven spirits of God, Rev 1:20 as the "seven angels of Jesus," Rev 3:1 as the "seven spirits of God and the seven spirits of Jesus," Rev 4:5. as the "seven lamps, which are the seven spirits of God."

124 Zech 1:18-21.

125 Ezek 16:1-63; Rev 17:1-18.

126 Rev 17:1 - 18:24.

127 See "Z5 - Two Women in the Basket (Zech 5:5-11; Rev 12:1-17; 17:1-18)" on page 78.

128 Rev 12:1-17.

129 Ezek 16:1-63; Rev 17:1-18.

All John needed was content to define the four horns to his readers. Unfortunately for John there were no more wax tablets that provided content that would best fit the four horns passage in Zechariah. So John decided to create the four horns by taking the four winds/first four trumpets by parallel formation. We can see this today where they are essentially the same with only the word "third" being replaced with "all" in the four horns/first four bowls.[130] We can also see that the trumpets and bowls are connected by actions, in that whatever the trumpet affects, the corresponding bowl is poured on. The first trumpet affects the earth, and the contents of the bowl is dumped upon the earth.[131] The second trumpet affects the health of the sea, and we find that the contents of the second bowl was dumped on the sea.[132] The third trumpet affects all sources of drinking water, and the contents of the third bowl was poured on each of the sources.[133] The fourth trumpet darkens the sun, moon, and stars while the contents of the fourth bowl intensifies the heat of the sun to provide the non-believers with a severe sun burn.[134]

The Harlot as Judah, Israel, and Jerusalem (Zech 1:18-21; Rev 17:1-18)

As mentioned earlier, the harlot is derived from the EID where Jerusalem is depicted as the harlot[135] and thus the placement of the harlot in the ZrD reflects that John considered the harlot as Jerusalem. We can see this in how John formed a parallel between the woman and child passages and the harlot and beast passages in Revelation. We find that both women are introduced at the beginning at a particular location depicting their state of holiness or lack thereof. The woman is in heaven which signifies being associated with God while the harlot is introduced as being on earth which is associated with the sins of the rulers.[136] They are both taken to the wilderness; the woman is taken by the wings of an eagle,[137] and the harlot is taken by the beast, which was Satan in the ZrD.[138]

However, we know that the beast does not enter into Revelation until the DnD, so we will expect to find any statement directed at the beast to reflect statements to Satan or an unknown subordinate of Satan. Many of the descriptions of the beast resemble those of Satan but were changed due to light editing, such as the beast comes from the abyss when in the beginning the beast came from the sea.[139]

Z9 - The Final Segment of Zechariah

John is running out of content from Zechariah to organize the remaining EID wax tablets. With only sixteen verses remaining in Zechariah, John must accommodate five chapters in Revelation (chapters 18 to 22). Unfortunately for us, since it was a struggle for John it will also be a struggle for us to recover what he did and how he did it. It is possible to form the content in Revelation using a complex parallel with the

---

130 See "Z8 - Creating the Four Horns / First Four Bowls (Part 1)" on page 122.

131 Rev 8:7; 16:2.

132 Rev 8:8; 16:3.

133 Rev 810-1: 16:4.

134 Rev 8:12; 16:8-9.

135 See "The Father and Mother of God's People (EP6, IP6)" on page 28. and "EP6 - Jerusalem as the Mother of God's Children (Ezek 16:1-63; Rev 17:1 - 18:24)" on page 54 .

136 Rev 12:1-2; 17:1-2.

137 Rev 12:14.

138 Rev 12:3.

139 Dan 7:7, 24; Rev 13:1; 17:7-18 the entry place in the DnD where John gets the concept of heads and horns. See "The Creation of the Beast and the False Prophet -- Part 2" on page 215. Therefore the description of Satan having seven heads and ten horns must have come from parallel formations and incomplete transitions from Satan to the beast.

remaining content, or a simple parallel with the leftover content from Zechariah and the remaining wax tablets. It is also possible that John was simply desperate and was satisfied with any match regardless of if it formed a parallel or not. Therefore, this section will select the content from Zechariah and match it with the content in Revelation following the order of Revelation.

God Pleads for His People to Return to Him (Zech 1:3, 12-5; Rev 18:4-20)

John takes the description of God's anger against the nations who are at ease and associates it with the Ezekiel account of the nations trading with Tyre and Tyre's destruction by God.[140] He then takes God's plea to his people to return to him and makes it a plea from God requesting his people to leave Tyre/Rome.[141] He does this by adding the following line to the beginning of the wax tablet containing Ezekiel's version of Tyre:

> *I heard another voice from heaven, saying, "Come out of her, my people, that you have no participation in her sins, and that you don't receive any of her plagues."*[142]

The rest of the content of Tyre remained unaffected by Zechariah other than being moved into the ZrD.

How Long Will God Not Have Mercy on Jerusalem (Zech 1:12-5)?

In Zechariah, the question, "How long will you not have mercy on Jerusalem and on the cities of Judah, against which you have had indignation these seventy years?" is posed. God's response is that he is jealous for Jerusalem and Zion and angry with the nations that are at ease and yet they add to their calamity.[143] With the question and response, John uses three separate stories to show how the nations provoked God.

The Destruction of Tyre and the Rejoicing of the Saints (Zech 1:12; Rev 19:1-9)

The first story that John developed for the ZrD addressed the elements in the story (such as 70 years) and how long before God attacks the nation that is at peace. The solution that John came up with was to use the prophecy connected with the destruction of Tyre, 70 years after the days of a certain king that was used to formulate the flying scroll content. For John to do this, he created a second author's notation and appended it to the Tyre passage.[144] The passage that John shifted was the Isaiah portion of the destruction of Tyre so it naturally was connected to the city of Tyre and flowed well with Ezekiel's description of Tyre. He only needed to make one slight change which was to remove a phrase regarding the "scroll" from the added Jeremiah passage.[145]

The remainder of the Isaiah parallel to the destruction of Tyre became the answer to the question in Zechariah of "how long?"[146] The answer from Isaiah is that the judgment against Tyre was planned a long time

---

140 Zech 1:12-5; Rev 18:5-20. See "Z9 - God Pleads to His People to Return to Him (Part 1)" on page 124.
141 Zech 1:3; Rev 18:4.
142 Rev 18:4.
143 Zech 1:13-5.
144 Isa 23:15-6; see "Z6 - The Flying Scroll (Part 2)" on page 83 for all references for this paragraph.
145 Jer 51:63; see the strike-through text in "Z6 - The Flying Scroll (Part 2)" on page 83.
146 Zech 1:12.

ago by God, and when it happens all the saints will celebrate by eating the best foods and drinking the best wines.[147]

The Destruction of the Dragon and the Two Riders of the Red and White Horses (Zech 1:7-16; Rev 19:11-21)

John is now faced with the EID prototype of the second coming, which has two slayers of the great dragon. On the Ezekiel side, it is God who slays the great dragon with a sword while on the Isaiah side, it is Jesus who slays the great dragon with the rod/sword of his mouth.[148] For John, the process of integrating the following text from Zechariah into the EID was fairly straight forward:

1:8 *"I had a vision in the night, and behold, a man riding on a red horse, and he stood among the myrtle trees that were in a ravine; and behind him there were red, brown, and white horses.* **1:9** *Then I asked, 'My lord, what are these?'"*

The angel who talked with me said to me, "I will show you what these are."

1:10 *The man who stood among the myrtle trees answered, "They are the ones* THE LORD *has sent to go back and forth through the earth."*

1:11 *They reported to* THE LORD'S *angel who stood among the myrtle trees, and said, "We have walked back and forth through the earth, and behold, all the earth is at rest and in peace."*

1:12 *Then* THE LORD'S *angel replied, "O* THE LORD *of Armies, how long will you not have mercy on Jerusalem and on the cities of Judah, against which you have had indignation these seventy years?"*

The imagery, from Zechariah, of riding horses fits very well with the EID version of the second coming in that Jesus amasses a great army that will fly down from the mountaintop to defeat his enemies.[149] John simply exchanges the mountaintop with heaven and used the horses as a means of descending upon the great dragon's army. This is how we got the second coming where we have an image of Jesus being backed up by his entire army of followers similarly to how the rider of the red horse in Zechariah is backed up by the red, brown, and white horses, only in Revelation they all have white horses.[150] In Zechariah the horsemen go back and forth through the whole earth, and as a result, the earth is at rest and in peace, while in Revelation they go from one spot to another, with the final result being that the world is at peace.[151]

John will add the questioning by the angel into the ZrD which will become the questioning of John by one of the 24 elders. Though the questions in the PVR and the placement of the questions will be removed from both Zechariah and the second coming narrative. The patter of having a question, a stall, and the an-

---

147 Isa 25:1-6; Rev 19:1-9; see "The Destruction of Tyre and the Saints Praising God and the Eating of a Meal (Isa 25:1-6; Rev 19:1-9)." on page 125.

148 See "EP8 - The Slaying of the Great Dragon" on page 58 and "IP8 - Jesus Slays the Great Dragon With a Great Sword" on page 59.

149 Isa 11:10-4; see "IP8 - Jesus Slays the Great Dragon With a Great Sword" on page 59.

150 Zech 1:8; Rev 19:11-4. See "Z9 - The Zechariah Draft Version of the Second Coming (Part 3a)" on page 126 and "Z9 - The Zechariah Draft Version of the Second Coming (Part 3b)" on page 127 for how John constructed the ZrD's version of the second coming.

151 Zech 1:10-1; Rev 19:11-21.

swer to the question will be the same as well as both accounts have the object of the question serving day and night.[152]

The ZrD carries the rest of the EID imagery that will become the second coming of Jesus, such as God's children crossing the Euphrate's River and much of the passages that will become the saints in heaven passages.[153] How John will scattered the saints in heaven passages, to where they are in the PVR, is a story of transferring the content from one wax tablet to fill the space in several newly added wax tablets.[154]

Perhaps the more interesting part of the ZrD is the placement of the great dragon in the abyss, which we alluded to earlier.[155] The ZrD's version of the second coming is Jesus defeating the army of Satan, and it is Satan who is tossed into the abyss. So, therefore, the ZrD ending of the second coming encompasses the placing of Satan into the abyss (Rev 20:1-3).[156] It is only later in the DnD that we get the story of the beast and the false prophet placed into the lake of fire prior to Satan being placed in the abyss.[157]

The Nations Attack Jerusalem or The Remaking of Jerusalem (Zech 1:7-16; Rev 20:4-15)

John conflated the two EID tablets that consisted of Gog and Magog on the Ezekiel side and the nations attacking Jerusalem on the Isaiah side. The combined story easily fits within the context of Zechariah 1:13-6 in that the nations who went out of the their way to attack Jerusalem combined with the city of Jerusalem being rebuilt and the city being favored by God and being faithful to God. John keeps the Ezekiel-Isaiah Draft's imagery of the righteous reading the book and that the unrighteous who do not read the book will be destroyed. Thus the story of Gog and Magog becomes the basis for the first and second resurrection found in Revelation 20:4-15.[158]

The Remaking of Jerusalem (Zech 1:1-6; Rev 21:1 - 22:5)

The story of Gog and Magog tells of a perfect world for the believers and a not-so-perfect world for the nations. The story of God remaking the heavens and earth and the New Jerusalem tells of a holy people within the city and a city that brings healing to the nations.[159] It is the perfect place for both the righteous and the unrighteous, and it happens to be the last two remaining wax tablets that John has to fit within Zechariah 1:1-6.[160] All John had to do was a little bit of conflating of the two by placing the Isaiah portion first so that the recreation of the universe begins the process of the city of God descending. He then defines the city as the New Jerusalem, named by combining the Holy City of Jerusalem and the creation of the new heaven and earth. He defines the people in it as those who obey the commandments of God and who will live forever.[161] He also defines it as a place where God and men will dwell forever as it should have been from the beginning.[162]

---

152 Zech 1:9-11; Rev 7:13-5; see "Z9 - The Zechariah Draft Version of the Second Coming (Part 3a)" on page 126.

153 Isa 11:15-6; Rev 9:14; see "Z9 - The Zechariah Draft Version of the Second Coming (Part 3a)" on page 126.

154 See "The Crossing of the Jordan River" on page 140 and "The Story of One Wax Tablet" on page 162.

155 See "Satan Defeated in Heaven and the Great Dragon Locked in the Abyss and How Satan Got so Many Names" on page 87.

156 Rev 20:1-3; see "Z9 - The Zechariah Draft Version of the Second Coming (Part 3b)" on page 127.

157 "Jesus Defeats the Beast on Earth" on page 213.

158 See "Z9 - God's Cities Will Once Again Flow with Prosperity (Part 4)" on page 128.

159 Ezek 47:12; Rev 22:2; see "Z9 - The Return Home (Part 2)" on page 130.

160 See "Z9 - The Return Home (Part 1)" on page 129 and "Z9 - The Return Home (Part 2)" on page 130.

161 Rev 21:4, 7.

162 Rev 21:3.

John finishes the creation of the primary content for the ZrD in the same way he begun the ZrD as seen in the text he selected to start with:

> *It will happen in that day, that I will seek to destroy all the nations that come against Jerusalem.*

> *I will pour on David's house, and on the inhabitants of Jerusalem, the spirit of grace and of supplication; and they will look to me whom they have pierced; and they shall mourn for him, as one mourns for his only son, and will grieve bitterly for him, as one grieves for his firstborn.*[163]

Final Thoughts

Ezekiel may be seen as the backbone to Revelation,[164] but the process used to construct the ZrD is the key to how the bulk of Ezekiel got arranged in the way that it is found in Revelation today. As this chapter has shown, many of the major items found in Revelation today owe their very existence to the process that John used to write the ZrD. If John would have used another book as the key to the process of the EID, it would have been a completely different story than what we find today.

The question that we must ask is, "Did John plan out the EID and ZrD as one draft, or did it just develop that way in the process?" If it was planned, then it was a major accomplishment in just being able to retain the content that he used to write the ZrD. If this was a serendipitous process either by inspiration or by pure luck, the process of the ZrD is no less amazingly simple and yet sufficient enough to confuse scholars for 19 centuries.

---

163 Zech 12:9-10; Rev 1:7.
164 Ian Boxall The Revelation of St John London: Continuum & Peabody MA: Hendrickson (2006) p. 254

The Zechariah Approximation Draft

John began the ZrD with the EID comprised of two columns of wax tablets. One column represented the Ezekiel account of punishment for sin and the other column represented the Isaiah account representing a new beginning with Jesus. John used Zechariah 1:1 - 12:10 as a key to shuffle the EID wax tablets as well as a source for content to bulk up the EID. The process John used was to read Zechariah 1:1 - 12:10 backwards, focusing on the sections rather than the individual words. As he came across each section in Zechariah, John moved the wax tablets that had similar content and began to create a new wax tablet by conflating the content from the wax tablet moved and the Zechariah passage that caused the tablet to be moved. When John came across tablets that did not fit into the Zech 1:1 - 12:10 he either conflated or appended them with its EID parallel wax tablet. .

The end result of the ZrD was a single column of wax tablets that told a story in the vertical. All of the wax tablets used in the ZrD were new tablets formed in the conflated or modified existing tablets. The ZrD process was labor intensive and as a result, John in the later drafts will only insert wax tablets or add content to blank portions of a wax tablet.

How to Read the Following Charts

The construction of the ZrD should be viewed as a two step process. First, John isolated a passaged from Zechariah and moved the wax tablet(s) from the EID that conformed to the Zechariah passage. Second, John took a new wax tablet and conflated the content of the EID wax tablet moved with the content of the Zechariah passage used.

To illustrate the process most of the charts in the Zechariah Approximation Draft will have a title showing the major step used to create the wax tablet, the key text used to move the EID wax tablet and conflated with the moved wax tablet. The key text is the quotation from Zechariah that John used in its the construction. The two boxes containing a number (EP4 and IP4) represent the EID wax tablet(s) moved and used to create the new wax tablets. When the text is grayed out that means that the content was not used to create the wax tablet. The chart on the very bottom is the same chart used to show the source text used within a draft and the text in Revelation that the source material used.

The Four Chariots (Horsemen)/First Four Seals (Z4 -- Part 1)

An explanation of the chart.

Key Text:

The quotation of the verse(s) used as a key.

EP4 The Judgments by the Nations	IP4 The Judgments by Jesus
• The nations will strike in thirds (Ezek 5:2).	• Jesus will strike in thirds (Ezek 5:16-7).
• God's people give evil decrees (Ezek 5:6-10).	• God's people receive evil decrees (Isa 10:1-19).
• The day of the Lord (Ezek 7:7) where God will destroy those without the mark of God on their forehead (Ezek 9:1-11).	• The day of THE LORD (Isa 13:9) where God will darken the sky (Isa 13:10; Ezek 32:7-10).

Jesus Will Strike in Thirds (Ezek 5:16-7) and Zechariah 6:1-8	The Four Horsemen/Chariots (Zech 6:1-8; Rev 6:1-8)
	The First Horseman (Zech 6:3; Rev 6:2)
Zech 6:8 The third chariot with white horses. Zech 5:16 He will send evil arrows.	6:2 A white horse. He had a bow.
	The Second Horseman/Chariot (Zech 6:2; Rev 6:4)
Zech 6:2 The first chariot with red horses. Isa 27:1 A great sword.	6:4 A red horse. He had a great sword.

How John Made the Zechariah Draft (Part 1)

The Ezekiel-Isaiah Draft (The Wax Tablet View)

Below is a depiction of how John organized the wax tablets at the end of the EID. The left side represents the judgment against Israel for disobeying God and the right side represents those who followed Jesus.

Ezekiel Side	Isaiah Side

Ezekiel Introduce (Ezek 1:1-3)

EP1 Ezekiel's Experience in Heaven • God on the throne (Ezek 1:26-2:2). • The living creatures (Ezek 1:4-26). • The scroll (Ezek 2:8 - 3:3).	**IP1 Isaiah's Experience in Heaven** • God on the throne (Isa 6:1). • The seraphim (Isa 6:2-7). • The altar that removes iniquity (Isa 6:6-7).
EP2 Ezekiel's Mission • Gods do not hear or understand (Ezek 3:4-7). • Say, "Thus says the Lord" (Ezek 2:4; 3:27).	**IP2 Isaiah's Mission** • God's people do not hear or understand (Isa 6:9-10). • Until the cities are waste without inhabitant (Isa 6:10).
EP3 Ezekiel Appointed as a Watchman • God's people are like briers, thorns, and scorpions (Ezek 2:6), God hardens Ezekiel's head (Ezek 3:8-9). • Ezekiel appointed as a watchman (Ezek 3:16-27). • End of three ministries and its relation to the siege of Jerusalem (Ezek 4:5-8).	**IP3 The New Seed (Jesus the Child)** • When a tenth of the city is burned God will raise up a new holy seed (Isa 6:10-13). • The sign of a woman with child (Isa 7:14). • Three phases of the child's life is connected to the destruction of Jerusalem (Isa 7:14 - 10:34).
EP4 The Judgments by the Nations • The nations will strike in thirds (Ezek 5:2). • God's people give evil decrees (Ezek 5:6-10). • The day of the Lord (Ezek 7:7) where God will destroy those without the mark of God on their forehead (Ezek 9:1-11).	**IP4 The Judgments by Jesus** • Jesus will strike in thirds (Ezek 5:16-7). • God's people receive evil decrees (Isa 10:1-19). • The day of the Lord (Isa 13:9) where God will darken the sky (Isa 13:10; Ezek 32:7-10).
EP5 The Glory of God Flees Jerusalem • Babylon comes, the glory of God flees (Ezek 10:1- 22). • Israel at war with nations (Ezek 11:1-13). • The Israelites are taken to all nations (Ezek 11:16 - 12:28). • They kill the souls that should not die (Ezek 13:1-23).	**IP5 The Glory of God in Heaven (Jesus the True Morning Star)** • The glory of God triumphs in heaven (Isa 14:1- 12). • The nations are at peace (Isa 14:18). • The remnant of Israel returns (Isa 14:32). • [No parallel]
EP6 Jerusalem the Mother of God's Children • The harlot wears expensive clothing (Ezek 16:10-1). • The harlot kills God's children (Ezek 16:20). • The harlot is the mother of God's children (Ezek 16:20).	**IP6 Jesus as Eliakim the Father of God's Children** • Eliakim wears expensive clothing (Isa 22: 21). • Eliakim saves God's children (Isa 22:21). • Eliakim is the father of God's children (Isa 22:21).
EP7 Tyre • Wealth from trading with other nations (Ezek 27:12-22). • [No parallel] • Their riches became what ruined them (Ezek 27:27). • Merchants lamenting Tyre's destruction (Ezek 27:27-28:2).	**IP7 Tyre (Jesus, a Certain King)** • Wealth from trading with other nations (Isa 23:1-17). • Tyre's destruction 70 years after certain king (Isa 23:15-7). • Post-destruction's wealth will be righteousness (Isa 23:18). • Saints rejoicing over Tyre's destruction (Isa 25:1-6)
EP8 The Slaying of the Great Dragon • With a sword (Ezek 29:8). • The great dragon finds comfort in his army (Ezek 32:31).	**IP8 Jesus Slays the Great Dragon** • The rod of his mouth (Isa 11:4), a great sword (Isa 27:1) • Jesus musters his army from the whole world (Isa 11:10-6).
EP9 Jerusalem Attacked by Gog and Magog • Nations come from the north to destroy Jerusalem and God destroys the nations (Ezek 38:1 - 39:29).	**IP9 Jerusalem Attacked by a Multitude of Nations** • Nations come from all over the world to destroy Jerusalem and God destroys the nations (Isa 29:1-21).
EP10 The City of God • Jerusalem will be a city that God and the righteous will live in (Ezek 40:1 - 48:35).	**IP10 The Holy City of Jerusalem** • Various descriptions of the Holy City of Jerusalem scattered throughout Isaiah.

How John Made the Zechariah Draft (Part 2)

The Process Used to Shuffle the Isaiah Draft Wax Tablets

In this illustration the left two columns represent the order and process in which John dealt with the EID wax tablets shown in part 1. The right column represents how the wax tablets were moved to satisfy the content found in the left column.

The Order and Process John Moved the Wax Tablets	The Tablets John Moved or Used

Z1 **Whom They Have Pierced They Shall Mourn (Zech 12:10; Rev 1:9)**
John began a new wax tablet with Zechariah 12:10 at the beginning.

Z2 **Oratories to God's People (Zech 7:1-12:9; Rev 2:1 - 3:22)**
John conflated the wax tablets EP2 and IP2 to form the template for the letters of the seven churches.

John took the whole wax tablet IP6 and a phrase in IP7 as the first unique content to the seven churches.

EP2	Ezekiel's Mission
IP2	Isaiah's Mission
IP6	Jesus as Eliakim
IP7	Tyre (Jesus as a Certain King)

Z3 **The Coronation of Joshua the High Priest (Zech 6:9-15; Rev 4:1 - 5:14)**
John conflated both Ezekiel's and Isaiah's experience in heaven and then adds the coronation of Jesus.

EP1	Ezekiel's Experience in Heaven
IP1	Isaiah's Experience in Heaven

Z4 **The Four Chariots and the Four Winds (Zech 6:1-8; Rev 6:1-8; 8:7 - 9:21)**
John took the two wax tablets (EP4, IP4) and made IP4 the four chariots and appended EP4 afterwards making it the four winds.

IP4	The Judgments by Jesus
EP4	The Judgments by the Nations

Z5 **The Two Women in the Basket (Zech 5:5-11; Rev 12:1-17; 17:1-18)**
John took the only two passages in the EID containing women and made them parallel each other.

IP3	The New Seed (Jesus the Child)
EP6	Jerusalem the Harlot

Z6 **The Flying Scroll (Zech 5:1-4; Rev 10:1-11)**
John split the scroll from EP1(Ezek 2:8 - 3:3) leaving a portion in the coronation of Jesus scene and moving the rest to this location.

EP1	Ezekiel and the Scroll
IP7	Tyre (Jesus, a Certain King)

Z7 **Jerusalem Will Be Blessed, Joshuah the High Priest, and the Two Anointed (Zech 2:1 - 4:15; Rev 11:1 - 12:17)**
John took the wax tablets (EP3, EP5, IP3, IP5) and creatively infused Zechariah 2:1 - 4:15 to form the 42 month, 1,260 day, 3½ day parallel (see "Z7 - The Zechariah-Encoded Parallel: How it Was Built (Part 1)" on page 117).

EP3	Ezekiel Appointed as a Watchman	IP3	The New Seed
EP5	The Glory of God Flees Jerusalem	IP5	Babylon Pursues God's Glory

Z8 **The Four Horns (Zech 1:18-20; Rev 16:1 - 18:19)**
John made the four horns by copying the four winds from EP4 and changing them from affecting a third to affecting all.

EP4	Judgment by the Nations (John copied)
EP6	Jerusalem the Harlot

Z9 **The Return Home (1:1-17; Rev 18:20 - 20:15)**
John used Zechariah 1:1-17 to tell the following stories:
- God calls his son to return to him (Zech 1:3; EP8).
- God, after 70 years, is angry with the nations (Zech 1:12, IP8, EP9, IP).
- God's cities will once again flow with prosperity (1:17, EP9, IP9, EP10, IP10).

EP7	Tyre		
IP7	Tyre (Jesus, a Certain King) (Isa 23:15-7; 25:1-6)		
EP8	God Slays the Great Dragon	IP8	Jesus Slays the Great Dragon
EP9	Attacked by Gog and Magog	IP9	Jerusalem Attacked by the Nations
IP10	The Holy City of Jerusalem		
EP10	The City of God		

Z1 - The Zechariah Draft Prologue

The Calling of John

The ZrD prologue is derived from three sources. First the chain of custody of the scroll from God to Jesus (Rev 5:1-2, 7-8) and given to the mighty angel and finally to John (Rev 10:1-2; 9-10). Second, the content from Zechariah 12:10 which began the ZrD. Third, the introduction of Ezekiel from the EID.

Content Found in Ezekiel		Content Found in Revelation	
		The Chain of Custody of the Vision (Rev 1:1)	
		1:1	This is the Revelation of Jesus Christ, which God gave him to show to his servants the things which must happen soon, which he sent and made known by his angel to his servant, John.
Zech 12:9	It will happen in that day, that I will seek to destroy all the nations that come against Jerusalem.		
Zech 12:10	I will pour on David's house . . . and they will look to me whom they have pierced; and they shall mourn for him, as one mourns for his only son, and will grieve bitterly for him, as one grieves for his firstborn.	1:7	Every eye will see him, including those who pierced him. All the tribes of the earth will mourn over him. Even so, Amen.
		John's Location (Rev 1:9-10)	
Ezek 1:1	I was among the captives by the river Chebar.	1:9	I was on . . . Patmos.
Ezek 1:3	Ezekiel the priest.	1:9	Because of God's Word . . . of Jesus Christ.
Ezek 1:3	THE LORD's word came expressly to Ezekiel the priest.	1:10	I was in the spirit on THE LORD's day, and I heard behind me a loud voice.

> **A Loud Voice Like a Trumpet Speaking - 1A**
> I heard behind me **a loud voice, like a trumpet speaking with me** (1:10 connects to 4:1)

Content Found in Ezekiel		Content Found in Revelation	
Ezek 1:25	There was a voice.	1:12	I turned to see the voice that spoke with me.
Ezek 1:24	~~I heard the noise of their wings like~~ the noise of great waters, like the voice of the Almighty.	1:15	His voice was like the voice of many waters.
Ezek 1:27	There was brightness around him.	1:16	His face was like the sun shining at its brightest.
Ezek 1:28	As the appearance of the rainbow that is in the cloud in the day of rain, so was the appearance of the brightness all around.		
Ezek 1:28	Ezekiel falls down before God.	1:17	When I saw him, I fell at his feet like a dead man.
Ezek 2:1	He said to me, Son of man, stand on your feet, and I will speak with you.		
Ezek 2:3	THE LORD's hand was there on me.	1:17	He laid his right hand on me, saying.
Isa 44:2	"Don't be afraid, Jacob my servant"	1:17	Don't be afraid.

Z2 - How The Seven Churches Were Formed

The structure of the letters of the seven churches were formed by merging the content found in the EID's second set of wax tablets outlining Ezekiel's and Isaiah's mission.

EP2	Ezekiel's Mission
	• Gods do not hear or understand (Ezek 3:4-7).
	• Say, "Thus says The Lord" (Ezek 2:4; 3:27).

IP2	Isaiah's Mission
	• God's people do not hear or understand (Isa 6:9-10).
	• Until the cities are waste without inhabitant (Isa 6:10)

The resulting template that John created by conflating the two wax tablets (EP2 and IP2) can be seen in the table below.

	Content Found in the Isaiah Draft	The Structure of the Seven Churches (Rev 2:1-3:22)
Isa 6:11	Cities	Each letter written to a city 1:11; 2:1, 8, 12, 18; 3:1, 7, 14
Ezek 2:4; 3:11, 27	When you speak to them say, "Thus says The Lord."	Ezekiel was told to say, "Thus says The Lord" before he would speak. For John, he begins each letter to the seven churches with a description of Jesus and the phrase, "Thus says."

The ZrD was written to the city of Jerusalem and Rome. Each letter contained a message to the unrighteous and a message to the righteous.

	Alpha and Omega Parallel		The Seven Churches
21:6; 22:6	True and faithful witness	3:14	Laodicea
21:7; 22:13	The Alpha and Omega		
22:13	The first and the last	2:8	Smyrna
21:7; 22:13	I am the beginning and end		

Scripture	Greek (Thus says)
Ezek 2:4	Τάδε λέγει
2:1, 8, 12, 18; 3:1, 7, 14	Τάδε λέγει

	Content Found in the Isaiah Draft	The Structure of the Seven Churches (Rev 2:1-3:22)
Ezek 2:3, 5	Ezekiel sent to God's rebellious people.	The essence of five of the seven letters to the churches are that God's people are in some sort of rebellion and thus corrective measures are made.
Isa 6:11	"Lord how long?"	The tone of the seven letters is that whatever is going to happen will occur soon (Rev 2:5; 10, 16, 21-24; 3:3, 9-11).
Isa 6:11	"Until cities are waste without inhabitant."	Each of the seven letters have a connection with the finality of the believer connected with their martyrdom.
Ezek 3:5-7 Isa 6:9-10	God's people cannot hear or understand what Ezekiel will say to them even though he speaks their language and is not a stranger.	He who has an ear, let him hear what the spirit says to the churches (Rev 2:7, 11, 17, 29; 3:6, 13, 22).

Z2 - The Letter to the City of Jerusalem: The Message to the Unrighteous -- Part 1

The content in part 1 and part two represent the possible content to the letter (or message) to the city of Jerusalem that can be found in the ZrD. It is possible that some of the content was not used in the ZrD's prototype to the letter of the seven churches and then in a later draft moved into the seven letters. Therefore what is in part 1 and part 2 is the most verbose the message could have been and not what was in the ZrD.

Content Found in Zechariah		The Message to the Seven Churches (Rev 2:1-3:22)
		The Church in Ephesus (Rev 2:1-7)
"It shall come to pass that, as you were a curse among the nations, house of Judah, and house of Israel, so will I save you, and you shall be a blessing. Don't be afraid. Let your hands be strong."	2:7 22:2-3	To him who overcomes I will give to eat from the tree of life, which is in the paradise of my God. In the middle of its street. On this side of the river and on that was the tree of life, bearing twelve kinds of fruits, yielding its fruit every month. The leaves of the tree were for the healing of the nations. There will be no curse any more.
Zech 8:13-7 For the THE LORD says: "As I thought to do evil to you, when your fathers provoked me to wrath," says the THE LORD, "and I didn't repent; so again have I thought in these days to do good to Jerusalem and to the house of Judah. Don't be afraid. These are the things that you shall do: speak every man the truth with his neighbor. Execute the judgment of truth and peace in your gates, and let none of you devise evil in your hearts against his neighbor, and love no false oath: for all these are things that I hate," says THE LORD.	2:2-7	"I know your works, and your toil and perseverance, and that you can't tolerate evil men, and have tested those who call themselves apostles, and they are not, and found them false. You have perseverance and have endured for my name's sake, and have not grown weary. But I have this against you, that you left your first love. Remember therefore from where you have fallen, and repent and do the first works; or else I am coming to you swiftly, and will move your lamp stand out of its place, unless you repent. But this you have, that you hate the works of the Nicolaitans, which I also hate.
		The Church in Pergamum (Rev 2:12-7)
Zech 7:5 Speak to all the people of the land, and to the priests		
Zech 7:5 When you fasted and mourned . . . for these seventy years, did you at all fast to me, really to me?		
Zech 7:6 When you eat, and when you drink, don't you eat for yourselves, and drink for yourselves? Aren't these the words which the THE LORD proclaimed by the former prophets, when Jerusalem was inhabited and in prosperity, and its cities around her, and the south and the lowland were inhabited?'"	2:20	You tolerate the woman, Jezebel, who calls herself a prophetess. She teaches and seduces my servants to commit sexual immorality, and to eat things sacrificed to idols.

Z2 - The Letter to the City of Jerusalem: The Message to the Unrighteous -- Part 2

Content Found in the Zechariah and Numbers	The Message to the Seven Churches (Rev 2:1-3:22)
	The Church in Pergamum (Rev 2:12-7)
Zech 7:5 Speak to all the people of the land, and to the priests.	
Zech 7:5 When you fasted and mourned . . . for these seventy years, did you at all fast to me, really to me?	
Zech 7:6 When you eat, and when you drink, don't you eat for yourselves, and drink for yourselves?	**2:14** Some who hold the teaching of Balaam, who taught Balak to throw a stumbling block before the children of Israel, to eat things sacrificed to idols.
Aren't these the words which THE LORD proclaimed by the former prophets, when Jerusalem was inhabited and in prosperity, and its cities around her, and the south and the lowland were inhabited?'"	**2:20** You tolerate the woman, Jezebel, who calls herself a prophetess. She teaches and seduces my servants to commit sexual immorality, and to eat things sacrificed to idols.
The Story of Balaam (Num 22:1 - 31:18)	
The Counsel of Balaam	***The Teaching of Balaam***
Num 22:1 to Balaam counsels Balak into letting the Israelites **25:5; 31:16** eat food sacrificed to idols and have sexual relationships with pagan women. Therefore letting the Israelites perform sinful actions as the cause of God cursing them.	**2:14** Some who hold the teachings of Balaam, who taught Balak to throw a stumbling block before the children of Israel, to eat things sacrificed to idols.
Evil Performed in Front of the Righteous	***Righteous in Front of Unrighteousness***
Num 25:6 Two brothers brought a Midianite woman in front of Moses, the Tent of Meeting and the entire congregation.	**2:13** "I know your works and where you dwell, where Satan's throne is. You hold firmly to my name, and didn't deny my faith in the days of Antipas my witness."
The Wicked are Killed and the Righteous Prevail	***The Righteous are Killed and the Wicked Prevail***
Num 25:7-8 Phinehas . . . took a spear in his hand. He went after the man of Israel into the pavilion, and thrust both of them through, the man of Israel, and the woman through her body.	**2:13** Antipas, the faithful servant killed.
The Israelites were spared because of Phinehas' actions.	**2:13-4** The believers followed the teachings of Balaam.
Moses Wages War Against Those Who Sided with Balaam and Balak	***Jesus Will Wage War Against Those Who Sided With Balaam and Balak***
Num 31:1-18 God has Moses avenge the Israelites for what the Midianites (and Balaam) have done to them.	**2:16** Repent therefore, or else I am coming to you quickly, and I will make war against them with the sword of my mouth.

Z2 - The Letter to the City of Jerusalem: The Message to the Righteous

The letter (or message) to the city of Jerusalem probably began with something similar to the following:

Write a letter to the righteous in the city of Jerusalem with the following message:

The first and the last says this:

"I will send Jesus and . . . [See below]

EP6 Jerusalem the Mother of God's Children	IP6 Jesus as Eliakim the Father of God's Children
• The harlot wears expensive clothing (Ezek 16:10-1). • The harlot kills God's children (Ezek 16:20). • The harlot is the mother of God's children (Ezek 16:20).	• Eliakim wears expensive clothing (Isa 22: 21). • Eliakim saves God's children (Isa 22:21). • Eliakim is the father of God's children (Isa 22:21).

Content Found in the Ezekiel-Isaiah Draft		**Content Found in Revelation**	
		The Church in Philadelphia (Rev 3:7-13)	
Isa 22:21	He will be a father to the inhabitants of Jerusalem, and to the house of Judah.	22:16	I, Jesus . . . . I am the root and the offspring of David.
Isa 22:22	I will lay the key of David's house on his shoulder. He will open, and no one will shut. He will shut, and no one will open.	3:7	He who is true, he who has the key of David, he who opens and no one can shut, and who shuts and no one opens, says these things: . . . .
Isa 22:23	I will fasten him like a nail in a sure place. He will be a throne of glory to his father's house.	3:12	I will make him a pillar in the temple of my God.
Isa 22:25	"In that day . . . the nail that was fastened in a sure place will give way. It will be cut down, and fall. The burden that was on it will be cut off, for"	3:10	Because you kept my command to endure, I also will keep you from the hour of testing, which is to come on the whole world, to test those who dwell on the earth.

EP4 The Judgments by the Nations	IP4 The Judgments by Jesus
• The nations will strike in thirds (Ezek 5:2). • God's people give evil decrees (Ezek 5:6-10). • The day of the Lord (Ezek 7:7) where God will destroy those without the mark of God on their forehead (Ezek 9:1-11).	• Jesus will strike in thirds (Ezek 5:16-7). • God's people receive evil decrees (Isa 10:1-19). • The day of the Lord (Isa 13:9) where God will darken the sky (Isa 13:10; Ezek 32:7-10).

		The Church in Smyrna (Rev 2:8-11)	
Rev 22:13	The first and the last	2:8	The first and the last says this:
Isa 10:1	Woe to those who decree unrighteous decrees (Jacob / Israel; see 9:8), and those who write oppressive decrees.	2:9	"I know your works, oppression, and your poverty (but you are rich), and the blasphemy of those who say they are Jews, and they are not, but are a synagogue of Satan.
Isa 10:2	To deprive the needy from justice, and to rob the poor among my people of their rights.		
Isa 10:4	They [those who issue evil decrees] will only bow down under the prisoners, and will fall under the slain.	2:10	The devil is about to throw some of you into prison, that you may be tested. Be faithful to death.
Isa 10:20	God's people will continue to lean on God.	2:9	Be faithful to death.

Z2 The Letter to the City of Rome: The Message to the Righteous

The initial reward and plea to the church in Laodicea came from Isaiah's description of the wages and purchases of a people in the post-destruction city of Tyre. The text in Revelation has been modified and shifted in later drafts but the core elements remain the same for its origin in Isaiah.

EP7 Tyre	IP7 Tyre (Jesus, a Certain King)
• Wealth from trading with other nations (Ezek 27:12-22)	• Wealth from trading with other nations (Isa 23:1-17)
• [No parallel]	• Post-destruction's wealth will be righteousness (Isa 23:18).
• Merchants lamenting, Tyre's destruction (Ezek 27:27-28:2).	• Saints rejoicing over Tyre's destruction (Isa 25:1-6).

Content Found in the Isaiah Draft	Content Found in Revelation
	The Church in Laodicea (3:14-22)
Isa 23:18 Her merchandise and her wages will be holiness to THE LORD. It will not be treasured nor laid up.	3:17 Because you say, I am rich, and have gotten riches, and have need of nothing;
	3:18 I counsel you to buy from me gold refined by fire, that you may become rich;
Isa 23:18 for her merchandise will be for those who dwell before THE LORD,	
to eat sufficiently,	3:20 I will come in to him, and will dine with him, and he with me.
and for durable clothing.	3:18 White garments, that you may clothe yourself, and that the shame of your nakedness may not be revealed

Z2 - The Ezekiel-Isaiah Draft Content for the Seven Churches

The content for the church of Philadelphia is from the wax tablet IP7. The tablet was likely moved during the formation of the ZrD prototype to the seven churches because we do not find any trace of Isa 22:21-5 beyond what we would expect in parallel formation to the church in Philadelphia. We do find EP6 used to form the first half of the harlot passage (Rev 17:1-18).

EP6 Jerusalem the Mother of God's Children	IP6 Jesus as Eliakim the Father of God's Children
• The harlot wears expensive clothing (Ezek 16:10-1).	• Eliakim wears expensive clothing (Isa 22: 21).
• The harlot kills God's children (Ezek 16:20).	• Eliakim saves God's children (Isa 22:21).
• The harlot is the mother of God's children (Ezek 16:20).	• Eliakim is the father of God's children (Isa 22:21).

Content Found in the Ezekiel-Isaiah Draft	Content Found in Revelation
	The Church in Philadelphia (Rev 3:7-13)
Isa 22:21 He will be a father to the inhabitants of Jerusalem, and to the house of Judah.	22:16 I, Jesus . . . . I am the root and the offspring of David.
Isa 22:22 I will lay the key of David's house on his shoulder. He will open, and no one will shut. He will shut, and no one will open.	3:7 He who is true, he who has the key of David, he who opens and no one can shut, and who shuts and no one opens, says these things:
Isa 22:23 I will fasten him like a nail in a sure place. He will be a throne of glory to his father's house.	3:12 I will make him a pillar in the temple of my God.
Isa 22:25 "In that day . . . the nail that was fastened in a sure place will give way. It will be cut down, and fall. The burden that was on it will be cut off, for"	3:10 Because you kept my command to endure, I also will keep you from the hour of testing, which is to come on the whole world, to test those who dwell on the earth.

Z3 - The Coronation of Joshua/Jesus: The First Draft (Part 1)

After inserting the prologue and the four churches, John conflated the first two parallel wax tablets from the EID.

EP1	Ezekiel's Experience in Heaven
	• God on the throne (Ezek 1:26-2:2).
	• The living creatures (Ezek 1:4-26).
	• The scroll (Ezek 2:8 - 3:3).

IP1	Isaiah's Experience in Heaven
	• God on the throne (Isa 6:1).
	• The seraphim at worship (Isa 6:2-3).
	• The seraphim and the altar that removes sin (Isa 6:6-7).

John Encounters God in Heaven

In the EID, John's encounter with God in heaven is a mixture of elements from Ezekiel and Isaiah with the ordering of the material following the Isaiah account. From the Ezekiel account we get the images of heaven such as God sitting on his throne with a rainbow around the throne. We get the primary descriptions of the four living creatures as well as the imagery of the crystal expanse. From the Isaiah account we get the worship element to the four living creatures as well as slight adjustments.

Content Found in Ezekiel and Isaiah			Content Found in Revelation (Ordered by Isaiah and Then Revelation)
			A Loud Voice Like a Trumpet Speaking - 1B After these things ... **the first voice that I heard, like a trumpet speaking with me** (4:1 from 1:10)
Isa 6:1	I saw THE LORD sitting on a throne.	4:2	There was a throne set in heaven, and one sitting on the throne.
Ezek 1:28	A rainbow around the throne.	4:3	A rainbow around the throne.
Ezek 1:26	Throne appearance like sapphire.	4:3	Throne appearance like jasper.
Ezek 1:22	Crystal expanse.	4:6	Sea of glass like crystal.
Ezek 1:5	The living creatures with four faces.	4:6	Four living creatures.
Ezek 1:6 Isa 6:2	Each having four faces. The seraphim had one face.	4:6	Each having one face.
Ezek 1:10	Face of a lion, ox, man and eagle.*	4:7	Face of a lion, calf, man, and eagle.
Ezek 1:6 Isa 6:2	Each having four wings. Each having six wings.	4:8	Each having six wings.
Ezek 1:18	Full of eyes all around.	4:8	Full of eyes around and within
Isa 6:3	They said "Holy, holy, holy is THE LORD . . . ."	4:8	They said "Holy, holy, holy is THE LORD . . . ."
Isa 6:3	"The whole earth is filled with his glory."	4:8	God created all things.

* Arranged in the order found in Revelation 4:7.

Z3 - The Coronation of Joshua/Jesus: The First Draft (Part 2)

John, in creating the ZrD, made at least two separate versions of the coronation of Jesus. The first was the conflation of the two wax tablets (EP1 and EP2). Below represents the first phase of John creating the coronation of Jesus by conflating the EID account of John's encounter with God in heaven and the coronation of Joshua the high priest in Zechariah 6:9-15. The second version will be made when John encounters the flying scroll narrative later in the ZrD construction process.

The Key Text of Zechariah:

6:9 The The Lord's word came to me, saying, 6:10 "Take of them of the captivity, even of Heldai, of Tobijah, and of Jedaiah, and come the same day, and go into the house of Josiah the son of Zephaniah, where they have come from Babylon. 6:11 Yes, take silver and gold, and make crowns, and set them on the head of Joshua the son of Jehozadak, the high priest; 6:12 and speak to him, saying, "The Lord says, 'Behold, the man whose name is the Branch: and he shall grow up out of his place, and he shall build The Lord's temple; 6:13 even he shall build the Lord's temple; and he shall bear the glory, and shall sit and rule on his throne; and he shall be a priest on his throne; and the counsel of peace shall be between them both. 6:14 The crowns shall be to Helem, and to Tobijah, and to Jedaiah, and to Hen the son of Zephaniah, for a memorial in The Lord's temple. 6:15 Those who are far off shall come and build in The Lord's temple; and you shall know that The Lord has sent me to you. This will happen, if you will diligently obey The Lord, your God's voice.'"

EID Wax Tablets Used

EP1	Ezekiel's Experience in Heaven
	• God on the throne (Ezek 1:26-2:2).
	• The living creatures (Ezek 1:4-26).
	• The scroll (Ezek 2:8 - 3:3).

IP1	Isaiah's Experience in Heaven
	• God on the throne (Isa 6:1).
	• The seraphim (Isa 6:2-7).
	• The altar that removes iniquity (Isa 6:6-7).

	Content Found in Ezekiel and Isaiah		Content Found in Revelation (Ordered by Isaiah, Revelation)
Ezek 2:10	It was written within and without.	5:1	The scroll written inside and outside.
Isa 6:8	"Whom shall I send, and who will go for us?"	5:2	"Who is worthy to open the scroll . . . ?"
Ezek 3:1-3	Ezekiel told to take the scroll and eat it. It will taste sweet to the mouth.	5:7	Then he [Jesus] came, and he took it out of the right hand of him who sat on the throne.
		10:9-10	John told to take the scroll and eat it. It was sweet to the lips.
Isa 6:6	Altar, coal touching lips purifies.	5:8-9	Altar and Jesus' death.
Isa 6:6	Coal touching lips cleanses Isaiah of sin.	5:9	Jesus' death cleanses believers of sin.
Zech 6:11	Make crowns and put them on the head of Joshua.	19:12	On his head are many crowns.
Zech 6:12	He shall build The Lord's temple.		[This became the major point of the Exodus Draft.]
Zech 6:13	He shall sit and rule on his throne.	3:21	He who overcomes, I will give to him to sit down with me on my throne, as I also overcame, and sat down with my Father on his throne.
Zech 6:14	Crowns shall be given to [four individuals] for a memorial in the temple.	5:10	[He] made us kings and priests to our God, and we will reign on the earth.
			[This is most likely the place where we have the elders wearing crowns and sitting on their thrones as Rev 3:21 suggests.]
Zech 6:15	Those who are far-off shall come and build The Lord's temple.	5:9	Out of every tribe, language, people, and nation.
Ezek 1:28	The appearance of a rainbow. The appearance of brightness all around him.	10:1	A rainbow on his head. His face was like the sun.
Zech 6:13	He shall bear all glory.	5:13	To him be the glory and dominion forever and ever.
Ezek 1:28	Ezekiel falls down before God.	5:8	The four living creatures and the 24 elders fell down before the Lamb.
		5:14	The four living creatures and the elders fell down and worshiped Jesus.
		1:17	When I saw him, I fell at his feet like a dead man.

Z4 - The Four Chariots (Horsemen)/First Four Seals (Part 1)

John took the attacks by Jesus and all the content found in IP4 from the EID to construct the four chariots. How John did it was to first modernize the four chariots into four horsemen and wrapped content from Ezekiel 5:16-7 and Isaiah 27:1 to the colors of the four horses. He then appended the rest of the content from IP4 after the four horsemen. This action that John performed became the final resting spot for the first six seals as well as the bulk of the content of the first six seals found in Revelation today.

The Key Text of Zechariah:

6:1 *Again I lifted up my eyes, and saw, and behold, four chariots came out from between two mountains; and the mountains were mountains of brass.* **6:2** *In the first chariot were red horses; in the second chariot black horses;* **6:3** *in the third chariot white horses; and in the fourth chariot dappled horses, all of them powerful.* **6:4** *Then I asked the angel who talked with me, "What are these, my lord?"*

EP4	The Judgments by the Nations
	• The nations will strike in thirds (Ezek 5:2).
	• God's people give evil decrees (Ezek 5:6-10).
	• The day of the Lord (Ezek 7:7) where God will destroy those without the mark of God on their forehead (Ezek 9:1-11).

IP4	The Judgments by Jesus
	• Jesus will strike in thirds (Ezek 5:16-7).
	• God's people receive evil decrees (Isa 10:1-19).
	• The day of The Lord (Isa 13:9) where God will darken the sky (Isa 13:10; Ezek 32:7-10).

Jesus Will Strike in Thirds (Ezek 5:16-7) and Zechariah 6:1-8

Zech 6:8	The third chariot with white horses.		
Ezek 5:16	He will send evil arrows.		
Zech 6:2	The first chariot with red horses.		
Isa 27:1	A great sword.		
Zech 6:2	The second chariot with black horses.		
Ezek 5:16	He will break their staff of bread.		
Zech 6:3	The fourth chariot had dappled horses.		
Ezek 5:17	He will kill them with wild animals, pestilence, and the sword.		

The Four Horsemen/Chariots (Zech 6:1-8; Rev 6:1-8)

The First Horseman (Zech 6:3; Rev 6:2)

6:2	A white horse.
	He had a bow.

The Second Horseman/Chariot (Zech 6:2; Rev 6:4)

6:4	A red horse.
	He had a great sword.

The Third Horseman/Chariot (Zech 6:2; Rev 6:5-6)

6:5-6	A black horse.
	Food prices are set for a famine.

The Fourth Horseman/Chariot (Zech 6:3; Rev 6:8)

6:8	A pale horse.
	He had authority to kill them with the sword, with famine, with pestilence, and by wild animals.

Z4 - The Four Chariots (Horsemen)/First Four Seals (Part 2)

The Fifth and Sixth Seal Are Born

As part of the construction of the four chariots (horsemen), John also took the remaining content which was probably part of a wax tablet and appended it to the newly constructed four horsemen. These two sections (God's people receive evil decrees and the day of the Lord) as well as the four horsemen are now referred to as the sixth seals in Revelation.

	God's People Receive Evil Decrees (Isa 10:1-19)		The Fifth Seal (Rev 6:9-11) Also the Church of Smyrna (Rev 2:8-11)
Isa 10:1	Woe to those who decree unrighteous decrees (Jacob/Israel; see 9:8), and those who write oppressive decrees.	2:9	"I know your works, oppression, and your poverty (but you are rich), and the blasphemy of those who say they are Jews, and they are not, but are a synagogue of Satan.
Isa 10:2	To deprive the needy from justice, and to rob the poor among my people of their rights.		
Isa 10:4	They will only bow down under the prisoners, and will fall under the slain.	2:10	The devil is about to throw some of you into prison, that you may be tested. Be faithful to death.
	For all this his anger is not turned away, but his hand is stretched out still.	13:10	If anyone is to go into captivity, he will go into captivity. If anyone is to be killed with the sword, he must be killed.
		6:9	Under the throne of God are the people who were martyred by keeping the commandments.
Isa 10:15-9	God will destroy those who try to deceive God's people illustrated in the burning of all the thorns, briers, and most of the trees.	7:3	Do not harm the trees until all are sealed.
		9:4-7	In the fifth trumpet those with the seal of God on their foreheads as well as the trees and the green grass will not be harmed. The rest will be in torment for five months.
		8:7	One third of the trees were burned up, and all green grass was burned up.
		6:10	Those who martyred the saints will be avenged (see Rev 19:2).
Isa 10:20	God's people will continue to lean on God.	2:9	Be faithful to death.
		6:9	Under the altar of God were the martyrs of the faithful.
		6:11	They were given a white robe and told to rest.

	The Day of the Lord (Isa 13:9-10; Ezek 32:7-10)		The Sixth Seal (Rev 6:12-7)
Isa 13:10 & Joel 2:10	The sun will be darkened . . . the moon will . . . not shine	6:12	The sun became black as sackcloth made of hair and the moon became as blood.
Ezek 32:6	I will also water with your blood.		
Ezek 32:7	I will cover the heavens, and make its stars dark; I will cover the sun with a cloud, and the moon shall not give its light.		
Ezek 32:8	[I will] make its stars dark.		
Isa 13:10	For the stars of the sky and its constellations will not give their light.	6:13	The stars of the sky fell to the earth.
Isa 13:13	God will make the heavens tremble and the earth will be shaken out of place.	6:14	The sky was removed like a scroll when it is rolled up. Every mountain and island were moved out of their places.
Joel 2:10	The earth quakes before them.	16:20	Every island fled away, and the mountains were not found.
Ezek 32:10	Their kings shall be horribly afraid for you.	6:15	The kings of the earth, the princes, the commanding officers, the rich, the strong, and every slave and free person,
Ezek 32:10	They shall tremble at every moment, every man for his own life, in the day of your fall.	6:15	[They] hid themselves in the caves and in the rocks of the mountains.
Isa 13:14-22	They will flee to their own lands.		

Z4 - The Four Winds/First Four Trumpets

The Problem With Displaying How the Four Winds/First Four Trumpets Were Constructed

The four winds in Zechariah are another name for the four chariots (Zech 6:5). John already defined the four chariots as the actions of Jesus from the EID against Jerusalem (Ezek 5:16-7) and made them into the four horsemen. He then used the actions of the nations (Ezek 5:2) and redefined them as the four winds (the first four trumpets in the PVR). John will later form a complex parallel connecting the four attacks by Satan with the first four trumpets as illustrated below. At this stage of the construction of Revelation, John sees Jesus and Satan working together to destroy Jerusalem.

The Key Text of Zechariah:

6:1 *Again I lifted up my eyes, and saw, and behold, four chariots came out from between two mountains; and the mountains were mountains of brass.* **6:2** *In the first chariot were red horses; in the second chariot black horses;* **6:3** *in the third chariot white horses; and in the fourth chariot dappled horses, all of them powerful.* **6:4** *Then I asked the angel who talked with me, "What are these, my lord?"* **6:5** *The angel answered me, "These are the four winds of the sky, which go out from standing before the Lord of all the earth.* **6:6** *The one with the black horses goes out toward the north country; and the white went out after them; and the dappled went out toward the south country."* **6:7** *The strong went out, and sought to go that they might walk back and forth through the earth: and he said, "Go around and through the earth!" So they walked back and forth through the earth.*

EP4	The Judgments by the Nations
	• The nations will strike in thirds (Ezek 5:2).
	• God's people give evil decrees (Ezek 5:6-10).
	• The day of THE LORD (Ezek 7:7) where God will destroy those without the mark of God on their forehead (Ezek 9:1-11).

IP4	The Judgments by Jesus
	• Jesus will strike in thirds (Ezek 5:16-7).
	• God's people receive evil decrees (Isa 10:1-19).
	• The day of the Lord (Isa 13:9) where God will darken the sky (Isa 13:10; Ezek 32:7-10).

The Published Version of the First Four Trumpets and the Four Attacks by Satan

The First Four Trumpets
8:7 **The First Wind/Trumpet**   • A third of the earth was burnt up.   • A third of the trees (Jewish believers).   • All the green grass was burnt up (believers).
8:8-9 **The Second Wind/Trumpet**   • A great burning mountain was thrown into the sea.   • The sea absorbed the mountain.
8:10-1 **The Third Wind/Trumpet**   • A great star fell from the sky.   • The star is called "Wormwood."   • A third of the waters became poisoned.
8:12 **The Fourth Wind/Trumpet**   • A third of the sun, moon, and stars were darkened.

The Four Attacks by Satan
12:17 **The Fourth Attack by Satan**   • Satan waged war against the woman and: • Those who kept God's commandments.   • Those who hold to Jesus' testimony.
12:13-6 **The Third Attack by Satan**   • Satan spewed water from his mouth to destroy the woman and her children.   • The land absorbed the water.
12:7-9 **The Second Attack by Satan**   • Satan thrown to earth.   • Satan's four names.   • Satan is out to deceive the world.
12:1-3 **The First Attack by Satan**   • A third of the stars in the sky are taken. The woman dressed with the sun, the moon under her feet and a crown of twelve stars.

Z4 - Various Judgments That Were Appended to the Four Winds

The Fifth Trumpet and the Sixth Seal Are Born

Just as John appended the material that follows the ZrD version of the four chariots/horsemen he did the same with the material that followed the EID's source of the four winds. The appended material contains content that will be placed primarily in the sixth seal and fifth trumpet. How this section becomes the fifth and sixth trumpet will be told in the next chapter (The Deuteronomy-Joshua Draft).

			Content Found in Revelation
	The Day of the Lord and the Judgment of the Un-righteous (Ezek 7:1-27)		
Ezek 7:1	The end has come on the four corners of the land (or earth).	7:1	I saw four angels at the four corners of the earth.
		9:14	Free the four angels who are bound at the great river Euphrates.
Ezek 7:2-8	Various descriptions of how God is angry with them		
Ezek 7:10	The day . . . it comes and your doom has gone out.	6:17	The great day of his wrath has come; and who is able to stand?
Ezek 7:16	Those who escape shall be on the mountains like doves of the valleys.	6:14	They hid themselves in the caves and in the rocks on the mountains.
Ezek 7:24	The worst nations will possess their houses and their holy places will be profaned.		
Ezek 7:27	The king shall mourn, and the prince shall be clothed in desolation, and the hands of the people of the land shall be troubled.	6:14	The kings of the earth, the princes and everyone else.
Ezek 8:1	In the sixth year, in the sixth month, in the fifth day of the month.	9:15	That hour and day and month and year.
	The Fifth Trumpet (Rev 9:1-12)		
Ezek 9:3	The glory of the God of Israel was gone up from the cherub, whereupon it was, to the threshold of the house: and he called to the man clothed in linen, who had the writer's inkhorn by his side.		
Ezek 9:4	Go through the middle of Jerusalem and set a mark on the foreheads of the men signed and cried over all the abominations that was done.	9:4	They were told that they should not hurt the grass of the earth, neither any green thing, neither any tree, but only those people who don't have God's seal on their foreheads.
Ezek 2:6*	You, son of man, don't be afraid of them, neither be afraid of their words, though briers and thorns are with you, and you do dwell among scorpions: don't be afraid of their words, nor be dismayed at their looks, though they are a rebellious house.	9:5	They were given power not to kill them, but to torment them for five months. Their torment was like the torment of a scorpion, when it strikes a person.

*See "When Wax Tablets Are Placed Together" on page 85 on how these two passages got together.

Z5 - Two Women in the Basket (Part 1)

The Woman With Child (Rev 12:1-17)

The two charts in part 1 and part 2 shows that John first selected the only content from the EID representing women and altered the two passages to conform with Zechariah 5:5-11. He first formed a parallel between the woman with child and the harlot. As a result of the parallel formation he had both women flown away into the wilderness. The woman was taken to the wilderness to be preserved and the harlot was taken to the wilderness to be destroyed.

The Key Text of Zechariah:

5:5 *Then the angel who talked with me came forward, and said to me, "Lift up now your eyes, and see what is this that is appearing."* **5:6** *I said, "What is it?" He said, "This is the ephah basket that is appearing." He said moreover, "This is their appearance in all the land* **5:7** *(and behold, a talent of lead was lifted up); and this is a woman sitting in the middle of the ephah basket."* **5:8** *He said, "This is wickedness" and he threw her down into the middle of the ephah basket; and he threw the weight of lead on its mouth.*

5:9 *Then lifted I up my eyes, and saw, and behold,* **there were two women,** *and the wind was in their wings.* **Now they had wings like the wings of a stork,** *and they lifted up the ephah basket between earth and the sky.* **5:10** *Then I said to the angel who talked with me, "Where are these carrying the ephah basket?"* **5:11** *He said to me,* **"To build her a house in the land of Shinar [Babylon].** *When it is prepared, she will be set there in her own place."*

EP7 Tyre	IP3 **The New Seed (Jesus the Child)**
• Wealth from trading with other nations (Ezek 27:12-22). • [No parallel] • Their riches became what ruined them (Ezek 27:27). • Merchants lamenting Tyre's destruction (Ezek 27:27-28:2).	• When a tenth of the city is burned God will raise up a new holy seed (Isa 6:10-13). • The sign of a woman with child ( ) • Three phases of the child's life is connected to the destruction of Jerusalem (Isa 7:14 - 10:34).

Content Found in Genesis, Isaiah, and Zechariah			**Content Found in Revelation**
		12:1	She is introduced as a pregnant woman in heaven.
Gene 37:9	Joseph's dream where his father was the sun, his mother was the moon and his brothers were the stars.	12:1	A woman clothed with the sun, and the moon under her feet, and on her head a crown of twelve stars.
Isa 9:12	Syria and the Philistines will devour Israel with an open mouth.	12:4	Satan wanted to devour the child.
Isa 14:13	You said in your heart, "I will ascend into heaven! I will exalt my throne above the stars of God! I will sit on the mountain of assembly, in the far north!	12:7	There was war in the sky. Michael [Jesus] and his angels made war on the dragon. The dragon and his angels made war.
Isa 14:14	I will ascend above the heights of the clouds! I will make myself like the Most High!"	12:8	They didn't prevail, neither was a place found for him any more in heaven.
Isa 14:15	Yet you shall be brought down to Sheol, to the depths of the pit.	12:9	The great dragon was thrown down, the old serpent, he who is called the devil and Satan, the deceiver of the whole world. He was thrown down to the earth, and his angels were thrown down with him.
Isa 14:16	Those who see you will stare at you. They will ponder you, saying, "Is this the man who made the earth to tremble, who shook kingdoms;	12:12	Woe to the earth and to the sea, because the devil has gone down to you, having great wrath, knowing that he has but a short time.
Isa 14:16	who made the world like a wilderness, and overthrew its cities; who didn't release his prisoners to their home?"	12:17	The dragon grew angry with the woman, and went away to make war with the rest of her offspring, who keep God's commandments and hold Jesus' testimony.
		12:11	They overcame him because of the Lamb's blood, and because of the word of their testimony. They didn't love their life, even to death.
Zech 6:9-11	The woman was carried in the basket by two stork wings to the land of Shinar (Babylon).	12:14	Two wings of the great eagle were given to the woman, that she might fly into the wilderness to her place, so that she might be nourished for [*42 months (see page 220)*] a time, and times, and half a time, from the face of the serpent.

Z5 - A Woman in the Basket (Part 2)

The Harlot (Rev 17:1-18)

The harlot represents the unfaithful element of Jerusalem and therefore is placed in contrast with the woman in Revelation 12:1-17. The table below is placed in parallel with the woman on the opposing page. However, due to changes in the DnD in the harlot passage (shown in faded text) and the reorganizing of the woman with child passage in the DJD it is harder to reconstruct the parallel. We can, however, align similar content to get a feeling of what the passage might of looked like. The charts on both pages represent an attempt to harmonize the material which may or may not have been part of the ZrD.

Content Found in Ezekiel and Zechariah		Content Found in Revelation (Ordered by Isaiah, Revelation)
	17:1	She is introduced as the harlot on earth
Zech 6:9-11 The woman was carried in the basket by two stork wings to the land of Shinar (Babylon).	17:3	He carried me away in the spirit into a *Babylon* [Babylon (Rome)]. I saw a woman sitting on [a great red dragon] a scarlet-colored animal, full of blasphemous names, having seven heads and ten horns.
Ezek16:10 I clothed you also with embroidered work, and shod you with sealskin, and I dressed you about with fine linen, and covered you with silk.	17:4	The woman was dressed in purple and scarlet, and decked with gold and precious stones and pearls, having in her hand a golden cup full of abominations and the impurities of the sexual immorality of the earth.
Ezek16:11 I decked you with ornaments, and I put bracelets on your hands, and a chain on your neck.		
Ezek 16:16 You took of your garments, and made for yourselves high places decked with various colors, and played the prostitute on them.		
Ezek 16:17 You also took your beautiful jewels of my gold and of my silver, which I had given you, and made for yourself images of men, and played the prostitute with them;		
Ezek16:20 Moreover you have taken your sons and your daughters, whom you have borne to me, and you have sacrificed these to them to be devoured.	17:6	I saw the woman drunken with the blood of the saints, and with the blood of the martyrs of Jesus.

Z6 - The Flying Scroll Alteration

With each scroll having a different result and imagery, John elected to keep the imagery of the Ezekiel scroll and split the content of the scroll using the mighty angel as its author's notation. This allowed him to keep a portion of the scroll before the seals (Rev 5:1-2) and a portion of the scroll prior to the destruction of Jerusalem (Rev 11:1-12). He then included the EID depiction of Jesus representing a certain king and added in the prophecy that the destruction of Jerusalem would take place 70 years after the birth of Jesus and the destruction of Rome would take place 70 years after Jesus' death. However, the adding of the four horns required John to reassess the placement of the Tyre content and therefore he created a second author's notation with the mighty angel and removed the scroll imagery.

The flying scroll destroys the houses of the thieves and liars, so John appended at the end of the judgments to Jerusalem (the seven seals and the first six trumpets) a list of sins with the last sin unique to the city. Jerusalem was assigned the sin of theft and Tyre (Rome) the sin of lying.

Content Found in Ezekiel and Isaiah		Content Found in Revelation (Ordered by Isaiah, Revelation)	
			See "Z4 - Various Judgments That Were Appended to the Four Winds" on page 113 for the previous content.
Zech 5:3-4	Everyone who steals shall be cut off according to it on the one side.	9:21	They didn't repent of their murders, nor of their sorceries, nor of their sexual immorality, **nor of their thefts**.
			Mighty Angel - 1B The mighty angel (10:1 from 5:2)
Ezek 1:28	The appearance of a rainbow. The appearance of brightness all around him.	10:1	A rainbow on his head. His face was like the sun.
		10:2	He had in his hand a little open scroll.
Ezek 3:12	Ezekiel hears the living creatures making loud noises, seven days, saying: "Blessed be The Lord's glory from his place."	10:3-4	John hears the message of the seven thunders but is told not to reveal it to anyone.
Ezek 3:1-3	Ezekiel told to take the scroll and eat it. It will taste sweet to the mouth.	10:9-10	John told to take the scroll and eat it. It was sweet to the lips.
Ezek 3:14	Ezekiel was bitter.	10:9-10	The scroll was bitter to John's stomach.
Ezek 3:16-27	Ezekiel appointed as a watchman to tell everyone	10:11	John is told to tell everyone.
			Mighty Angel - 2A The mighty angel (10:1, 10 to 18:21)
			Mighty Angel - 2B The mighty angel (18:21 from 10:1, 11)
Jer 51:63	It shall be, ~~when you have finished reading this scroll~~, that you shall bind a stone to it, and cast it into the middle of the Euphrates.	18:21	A mighty angel took up a stone like a great millstone and cast it into the sea, saying:
Jer 51:64	Thus shall Babylon sink, and shall not rise again because of the evil that I will bring on her; and they shall be weary.	18:21	"Thus with violence will Babylon, the great city, be thrown down, and will be found no more at all.
Isa 23:15, 17	Tyre will be forgotten 70 years, according to the days of one king . . . after the end of seventy years that The Lord will visit Tyre.		[see "Jesus as the Certain King (Isa 23:15-7; Rev 18:2-6, 22)" on page 29]
Isa 23:16	Take a harp; go about the city . . . . Make sweet melody. Sing many songs, that you may be remembered.	18:22	The voice of harpists, minstrels, flute players, and trumpeters will be heard no more at all in you.
Isa 23:17	She . . . will play the prostitute with all the kingdoms of the world on the surface of the earth.		
Zech 5:3	Then he said to me, "This is the curse that goes out over the surface of the whole land; for everyone who steals shall be cut off according to it on the one side; **and everyone who swears falsely** shall be cut off according to it on the other side.	18:23	With your sorcery **all the nations were deceived**.
Jer 51:49	As Babylon has caused the slain of Israel to fall, so at Babylon shall fall the slain of all the land.	18:24	In her was found the blood of prophets and of saints, and of all who have been slain on the earth.

Z7 - The Zechariah-Encoded Parallel: How it Was Built (Part 1)

To construct the Zechariah-encoded parallel John first formed a complex parallel with the numbers used to illustrate how long the siege of Jerusalem would take place (see "The Length of the Siege of Jerusalem Changed From Years of Sin to Years of Ministry (Ezek 4:5-8; Rev 11:2-3, 9)" on page 20) and extended it to include the Isaiah parallel (wax tablets EP3 and IP3). He then took the first set of numbers (42 months) and integrated the content with chapter 2 of Zechariah. He did the same for the 1,260 days with chapter 3 of Zechariah and the 3½ days with chapter 4 of Zechariah. We can see the process done in the illustration seen below.

A. 42 Months
Measure Jerusalem but not its walls (Zech 2:1-5).
Measure the temple but not its courtyard (Rev 11:1-2).

B.   1,260 Days
Joshua dressed in filthy rags (Zech 3:3).
The two prophets wore sackcloth (Rev 11:3).

C.   3½ Days
The two olive trees and the lampstands represent the work of Joshua and Zerubbabel (Zech 4:11-4).
The two olive trees and the two lampstands, the two prophets do all kinds of miracles from God (Rev 11:4-7).

C'. 3½ Days
The building of the temple on earth and the nations will rejoice (Zech 4:6-10).
The temple is in heaven and the nations will be angry (Rev 11:18-9).

B'.   1,260 Days
Satan kicked out of Jerusalem (Zech 3:1).
Satan kicked out of heaven (Rev 12:3-10).

Sin will be removed from the land (Zech 3:8-10).
Salvation brought to the whole world (Rev 12:10).

A'. 42 Months
God will protect his people and Jerusalem will be loved by all the nations (Zech 2:6-13).
The woman was nourished . . . And the land (nations) rescued her (Rev 12:14-6).

The Available Wax Tablets From the Ezekiel-Isaiah Draft (EID)

The illustration below depicts the wax tablets John used to incorporate Zechariah chapters 2 to 4 with. John simply conflated the content of the tablets with the content of Zechariah. For example, he replaced Babylon (tablet IP6) with Satan in the conflation process.

The Ezekiel-Isaiah Draft Wax Tablets for Part 2

EP3	**Ezekiel Appointed as a Watchman**
	• Ezekiel appointed as a watchman (Ezek 3:16-27).
	• End of three ministries and its relation to the siege of Jerusalem (Ezek 4:5-8).
	• Years of ministry (Ezek 4:5).
	• Years of ministry (Ezek 4:6).
	• Years of ministry (Ezek 4:8).

Content Moved to Form the Four Winds/First Four Trumpets

EP5	**The Glory of God Flees Jerusalem**
	• Babylon comes, the glory of God flees the temple (Ezek 10:1- 22).
	• Israel is at war with nations (Ezek 11:1-13).
	• The Israelites are taken to all nations (Ezek 11:16).
	• They kill the good prophets and give gifts to the evil prophets (Ezek 131-23).

The Ezekiel-Isaiah Draft Wax Tablets for Part 3

IP3	**The New Seed (Jesus the Child)**
	• When a tenth of the city is burned God will raise up a new holy seed (Isa 6:10-13).
	• Three phases of the child's life is connected to the destruction of Jerusalem (Isa 7:14 - 10:).
	• The child as a fetus (Isa 7:14).
	• Before the child can say "father" or "mother" (Isa 8:4).
	• The child will rule (Isa 9:6).

Content Moved to Form the Four Chariots/Horsemen

IP5	**Babylon Chases the Glory of God in Heaven (Jesus the True Morning Star)**
	• Babylon pursues the glory of God in heaven and is defeated (Isa 14:1- 12).
	• The nations are at peace (Isa 14:18).
	• The remnant of Israel returns (Isa 14:32).
	• The righteous returns and the nations are punished (Isa 15:1 - 22:19).

Z7 - The Zechariah Encoded Parallel: The Two Prophets (Part 2)

The text below represents the final process of conflating the EID wax tablets EP3 and EP5 (see part 1) and Zechariah. The end result of the process is the creation most of the content found in Revelation 11:1-12. It is in this portion of the construction of Revelation that we get the two prophets imagery along with the measuring of the temple and not its courtyard.

Content found in Ezekiel, Isaiah and Zechariah		Content in Revelation (Ordered by)	
		Measuring the Temple (Rev 11:1-2)	
Zech 2:1	I lifted up my eyes, and saw, and behold, a man with a measuring line in his hand.	11:1	A reed like a rod was given to me.
Zech 2:2	He said to me, "To measure Jerusalem, to see what is its width and what is its length."	11:1	Someone said, "Rise, and measure God's temple, and the altar, and those who worship in it.
Ezek 10:1-22	The state of the temple before the glory of the Lord flees.		
Zech 2:4	[He] said to him, "Run, speak to this young man, saying, 'Jerusalem will be inhabited as villages without walls."	11:2	Leave out the court which is outside of the temple, and don't measure it,
Ezek 10:1-22	The state of the temple before the glory of the Lord flees.		
Zech 2:4	because of the multitude of men and livestock in it.	11:2	for it has been given to the nations. They will tread the holy city under foot.
Ezek 4:5	Ezekiel laid on his left side for 390 days. Each day represents one year Israel sinned against God.	11:2	The temple courtyard will be trampled by the gentiles for 42 months. Representing the 420 years that the temple been controlled by the Gentiles..
		The Two Prophets (Rev 11:32-13)	
Ezek 4:6	Ezekiel laid on his right side for 40 days. Each day equals one year Judah sinned against God.	11:3	The two witnesses shall testify for 1260 days. Representing 1260 years from the crossing of the Jordan river to the death of Jesus.
Zech 3:3	Now Joshua was clothed with filthy garments	11:3	my two witnesses . . . clothed in sackcloth.
Zech 3:9	The stone that I have set before Joshua; on one stone are seven eyes: behold, I will engrave its engraving,' says THE LORD, 'and I will remove the iniquity of that land in one day.	5:6	[Jesus] having . . . seven eyes.
		5:9	Saints were purchased with [Jesus'] blood.
Zech 4:11	"What are these two olive trees on the right side of the lamp stand and on the left side of it?"	11:4	These are the two olive trees and the two lamp stands,
Zech 4:12	"What are these two olive branches, which are beside the two golden spouts, that pour the golden oil out of themselves?"		
Zech 4:14	"These are the two anointed ones who stand by the Lord of the whole earth."	11:4	Standing before the Lord of the earth.
Ezek13:19	They kill the souls that should not die.	11:7	When [the two prophets] finished their testimony the beast killed them
Ezek 4:8	The sum of the days in Ezek 4:5-6 equals how long the siege of Jerusalem would last.	11:9	The two prophets laid dead in the street for 3½ days with each day representing one year of the siege of Jerusalem in 67-70 CE
Ezek 13:18	The women sew pillows and make kerchiefs for those who hunt souls.	11:10	Those who dwell on the earth rejoiced over the death of the two prophets. They gave gifts to one another.
Ezek 13:19	They give handful of barley and pieces of bread to kill souls		
Ezek 13:23	God will deliver his people out of their hand.	11:12	God breathed life into the two prophets.
Ezek 10:1-22	The glory of God left the temple.	11:13	The two prophets were taken to heaven in front of their enemies.
Ezek 13:23	You will see no more false visions nor practice divination	11:13	The rest were terrified and gave glory to God.
Ezek 10:1-22	The glory of God left the temple	11:17	The temple is in heaven.

Z7 - The Zechariah Encoded Parallel: Satan's Entry into Revelation (Z7 -- Part 3)

The text below represents a snapshot of the ZrD after John conflated the story of the woman, child, the story of Babylon defeated in heaven and the saints return, and the content of Zechariah 2:1 - 4:14. As we can see, John replaced 'Babylon' with 'Satan' ascribed in Isaiah 14 and then conflated the actions of the nations from Isaiah 7:14 - 10:19. The end result is that much of the imagery of Satan found within Revelation came from this single action.

Content found in the ZrD (ordered by Isaiah)		Content Found in Revelation	
		The Aftermath of the Two Prophets Taken to Heaven (Rev 11:13-7)	
Isa 6:10-3	An illustration that even if the oak tree is burned (believers) and a tenth of the city is burned a new crop of believers will be sprouted from the acorns.	11:13	In that day there was a great earthquake, and a tenth of the city fell. Seven thousand people were killed in the earthquake, and the rest were terrified, and gave glory to the God of heaven.
Zech 4:9	Zerubbabel has laid the foundation to the second temple.	11:17	[Jesus laid the foundation of ?] the temple in heaven
		The Sign of the Woman with Child in Heaven (Rev 12:1)	
Isa 7:14	A sign of a woman who is ready to conceive a son that will be named Immanuel.	12:1	A great sign was seen in heaven.
		12:2	She was with child. She cried out in pain, laboring to give birth.
Gen 37:9	"Behold, I have dreamed yet another dream: and behold, the sun and the moon and eleven stars bowed down to me."	12:1	a woman clothed with the sun, and the moon under her feet, and on her head a crown of twelve stars.
Isa 8:4	Before the child knows how to say, 'My father,' and, 'My mother,' the riches of Damascus and the plunder of Samaria will be carried away by the king of Assyria."	12:5	She gave birth to a son . . . . Her child was caught up to God, and to his throne.
		Satan's Third Attack on the Woman and Her Children (Rev 12:12-5)	
Isa 8:5	An army will sweep through Israel like a flood.	12:15	The serpent spewed water out of his mouth after the woman like a river, that he might cause her to be carried away by the stream.
Isa 9:11-6	The army devoured Israel with an open mouth.	12:4	The dragon tried to devour the woman's son.
		12:15	The serpent spewed water out of his mouth is a conflation of and parallel formation of Isa 8:5 and Isa 9:11-6.
Isa 9:6-7	A child is born who will be called Wonderful, Counselor, Mighty God, Everlasting Father, Prince of Peace. His kingdom will reign forever with justice and righteousness.	12:5	She gave birth to a son, a male child who is to rule all nations with a rod of iron.
Isa 14:5	The Lᴏʀᴅ has broken the staff of the wicked, the scepter of the rulers.	2:27	He will rule them with a rod of iron, shattering them like clay pots.
		Satan's First Attack on the Woman and Her Children (Rev 12:3-4)	
Isa 27:1	The dragon that is in the sea.	12:3	Behold, a great red dragon.
Isa 9:15	The tail are the prophets who teaches lies.	12:4	His tail drew one third of the stars in the sky, and threw them to the earth.
Isa 9:16	Those who leads the people astray and those who are led astray are destroyed.	12:9	The deceiver of the whole world.
		Satan's Fourth Attack on the Woman and her Children (Rev 12:17)	
Isa 9:18-9	Their wickedness burns like a fire.	8:7	The first trumpet tells hail mixed with fire and the earth burned up, third of the trees and all of the green grass.
Isa 10:16-9	He will send Assyria to burn the ground and the trees in one day.	12:17	The dragon grew angry with the woman, and went away to make war with the rest of her offspring, who keep God's commandments and hold Jesus' testimony.
	(See "John's First Major Content Alignment Corrections" on page 22)		

Z7 - The Zechariah Encoded Parallel: Satan's Entry into Revelation (Part 4)

The text below represents a snapshot of the ZrD after John conflated the story of the woman, child, the story of Babylon defeated in heaven and the saints return, and the content of Zechariah 2:1 - 4:14. As we can see, John replaced 'Babylon' with 'Satan' ascribed in Isaiah 14 and then conflated the actions of the nations from Isaiah 7:14 - 10:19. The end result is that much of the imagery of Satan found within Revelation came from this single action.

Content found in the ZrD (ordered by Isaiah)		Content Found in Revelation	
		Satan and the War in Heaven (Rev 12:7-9)	
Isa 14:14	Babylon chased the glory of God in heaven.	12:5	Her child was caught up to God and to his throne.
Isa 14:12	How you have fallen from heaven, morning star.	22:16	Jesus as the bright and morning star.
Isa 14:13-4	Babylon defeated the nations on earth and went after God's glory in heaven.	12:9	There was a war in heaven.
Zech 3:1-2	Satan removed from Jerusalem.	12:9	Satan after defeated, he was kicked out of heaven.
Ezek 29:3 Isa 27:1	Pharaoh the great dragon. The great dragon.	12:9	The great dragon.
Isa 14:29 Isa 27:1	The rod that struck you is broken; for out of the serpent's root an adder will emerge, and his fruit will be a fiery flying serpent.	12:9	The old serpent.
Zech 3:1-2	The accuser / devil (Greek), Satan (Hebrew).	12:9	He who is called the devil and Satan.
Zech 3:1	Satan standing at his right hand to accuse him.	12:10	The accuser of our brothers has been thrown down.
Job 1:6-12	Satan in heaven accusing Job.	12:10	Who accuses them before our God day and night.
Isa 14:18-9	The nations will be at peace when Babylon is in Sheol.	12:12-7 20:3 9:11-21 20:7-8	Satan on earth wars against the saints. Satan in prison, the world lives in peace. The release of the angel of the abyss brings war. The release of Satan brings war.
Zech 2:10-3	The nations will join themselves to God and they will be his people.	11:15 12:10	The kingdom of the world becomes the kingdom of God through his anointed one.
Zech 3:9-10	I will remove the iniquity of that land in one day. In that day,' says THE LORD, 'you will invite every man his neighbor under the vine and under the fig tree.'		

The Published Version of the First Four Trumpets and the Four Attacks by Satan

The first four trumpets and the four attacks of Satan form a complex parallel. This can be seen when the four attacks by Satan are compared to the first four trumpets.

First Four Trumpets
8:7   The First Wind / Trumpet • Third of the earth was burnt up. • Third of the trees (Jewish believers). • All the green grass was burnt up (believers).
8:8-9   The Second Wind / Trumpet • A great burning mountain was thrown into the sea. • The sea absorbed the mountain.
8:10-1   The Third Wind / Trumpet • A great star fell from the sky. • The star is called "Wormwood". • Third of the waters became poisoned.
8:12   The Fourth Wind / Trumpet • Third of the sun, moon and stars were darkened .

The Four Attacks by Satan
12:17   The Fourth Attack by Satan • Satan wage war against the woman and: • Those who kept God's commandments. • Those who hold to Jesus' testimony.
12:13-6   The Third Attack by Satan • Satan spewed water from his mouth to destroy the woman and her children. • The land absorbed the water.
12:7-9   The Second Attack by Satan • Satan thrown to earth. • Satan's four names. • Satan is out to deceive the world.
12:1-3   The First Attack by Satan • Third of the stars in the sky taken. The woman dressed with the sun, moon under her feet and a crown of twelve stars.

Z7 - The Zechariah Encoded Parallel: Revelation Chapter 14 is Born (Part 5)

Below represents the text that John did not integrate with Zechariah 2:1 - 4:14 so he simply conflated the Ezekiel and Isaiah text. The end result of the conflation is what we now know as Revelation 14:1-20. In this conflation we get the start of the 144,000 in heaven, two of the three messages acted by and delivered by angels. We also get the beginning of the great harvest.

To see how the Isaiah wax tablets were laid out before the conflation go to "EP5 - The Glory of the Lord Flees Jerusalem" on page 52 and "IP5 - The Glory of the Lord Triumphs in Heaven" on page 53.

Content found in Ezekiel and Isaiah			Content in Revelation (Ordered by)
			The 144,000 in Heaven (Rev 14:1-5)
Isa 14:32	What will they answer the messengers of the nation? That the LORD has founded Zion, and in her the afflicted of his people will take refuge.	14:1-4	The Lamb standing on Mount Zion with the 144,000 representing the first fruits to God and the Lamb.
			The Message of the First Angel (Rev 14:6-7)
Isa 14:32	Oracles to the nations.	14:6	The gospel was spread to the entire world.
Isa 15:1 to 19:17	The oracles to the nations.		
Isa 17:7, 10	People will look to their maker . . . they forgotten God of salvation.	14:7	Fear the Lord . . who made everything.
			The Message of the Second Angel (Rev 14:8)
Isa 21:9	Fallen, fallen is Babylon and all the engraved images of her gods are broken to the ground.	14:8	Babylon the great has fallen, which has made all the nations to drink of the wine of the wrath of her sexual immorality.
			The Great Harvest (Rev 14:14-20)
Ezek 15:2	Son of man	14:14	One sitting like the son of man.
Ezek 15:6	The inhabitants of Jerusalem are connected to the worthless vine.	14:13-6	The saints are connected to the great harvest of grapes.
Ezek 15:7	God will use fire against them.	14:18	An angel who has the power of fire [no fire is used].
Ezek 15:8	God will make the land desolate because they have committed a trespass.	14:19-20	The grapes make the wrath of God which will destroy the harlot and make her desolate (Rev 17:6; 18:5-8).

Z8 - Creating the Four Horns / First Four Bowls (Part 1)

John created the four horns / first four bowls by taking the imagery that affected a third of from the four winds / first four trumpets and copied it to the four horns / first four bowls and had the four horns affect all. The table below illustrates the change and also illustrates how John retained the parallel even after DnD material overwrote portions of the first horn and the fourth horn.

The Key Text of Zechariah:

1:18 *I lifted up my eyes, and saw, and behold, four horns.* *1:19* *I asked the angel who talked with me, "What are these?"*

He answered me, **"These are the horns which have scattered Judah, Israel, and Jerusalem."**

1:20 *The L*ORD *showed me four craftsmen.* *1:21* *Then I asked, "What are these coming to do?"*
He said, "These are the horns which scattered Judah, so that no man lifted up his head; but these have come to terrify them, to cast down the horns of the nations, which lifted up their horn against the land of Judah to scatter it."

The Four Winds / First Four Trumpets	The Four Horns / First Four Bowls
8:7　The First Wind / Trumpet • Third of the earth was burnt up. • Third of the trees (The Jewish believers). • All the green grass was burnt up (gentile believers).	**16:2　The First Horn / Bowl** • The bowl was poured into the earth affecting. • Sores to those who had the mark of the beast. • Sores to those who worshiped his imaged.
8:8-9　The Second Wind / Trumpet • Third of the sea became blood. • Third of the sea creatures died. • Third of the ships destroyed.	**16:3　The Second Horn / Bowl** • All of the sea became blood. • Everything in the sea died.
8:10-1　The Third Wind / Trumpet • Third of the rivers became poisoned. • Third of the springs became poisoned. • Third of the waters became poisoned.	**16:4-7　The Third Horn / Bowl** • All the rivers became blood. • All the springs became blood.
8:12　The Fourth Wind / Trumpet • Third of the sun, moon and stars were darkened.	**16:8-9　The Fourth Horn / Bowl** • The sun scorched the people with great heat (opposite to darkening of the sun).

Z8 - Jerusalem as the Harlot (Part 2)

The depiction of Jerusalem as a harlot and the murderer of God's children became the reason for the four horns (part 1). The harlot also became the antithesis to the woman with child (Rev 12:1-17) where the woman and her children represented the faithful from Israel and the harlot represented evil from Israel.

EP6	Jerusalem the Mother of God's Children	IP6	Jesus as Eliakim the Father of God's Children
	• The harlot wears expensive clothing (Ezek 16:10-1).		• Eliakim wears expensive clothing (Isa 22: 21).
	• The harlot kills God's children (Ezek 16:20).		• Eliakim saves God's children (Isa 22:21).
	• The harlot is the mother of God's children (Ezek 16:20).		• Eliakim the father of God's children (Isa 22:21).

Content Found In Ezekiel and Zechariah	**Content in Revelation**
Zech 5:9 Two wicked women placed into a basket and flown to the wilderness to the land of Shinar.	17:3 He carried me away in the Spirit into a wilderness. I saw a woman sitting on [a red dragon] a scarlet-colored animal, full of blasphemous names, having seven heads and ten horns.
Jerusalem as the Adulterous Bride (Ezek 16:1-63)	***The Harlot (Rev 17:1-18:24)***
Ezek 16:10 I clothed you also with embroidered work, and shod you with sealskin, and I dressed you about with fine linen, and covered you with silk.	17:4 The woman was dressed in purple and scarlet, and decked with gold and precious stones and pearls, having in her hand a golden cup full of abominations and the impurities of the sexual immorality of the earth.
Ezek 16:11 I decked you with ornaments, and I put bracelets on your hands, and a chain on your neck.	
Ezek 16:16 You took of your garments, and made for yourselves high places decked with various colors, and played the prostitute on them.	
Ezek 16:17 You also took your beautiful jewels of my gold and of my silver, which I had given you, and made for yourself images of men, and played the prostitute with them.	
Ezek 16:20 Moreover you have taken your sons and your daughters, whom you have borne to me, and you have sacrificed these to them to be devoured.	17:6 I saw the woman drunken with the blood of the saints, and with the blood of the martyrs of Jesus.
Ezek 16:36 The blood of your children, that you gave to them.	18:24 In her was found the blood of prophets and of saints, and of all who have been slain on the earth."
Ezek 16:37 God will gather all her lovers and they will hate her and strip her naked.	17:16 They will make her desolate, and will make her naked.
Ezek 16:41 They will burn her houses with fire .	17:16 They will burn her utterly with fire.
Ezek 16:53 I will turn again their captivity, the captivity of Sodom and her daughters, and the captivity of Samaria and her daughters, and the captivity of your captives among them.	18:2 She has become a habitation of demons, a prison of every unclean spirit, and a prison of every unclean and hateful bird!
Ezek 16:1-60 Talks about Jerusalem playing the harlot to all nations.	18:3 For all the nations have drunk of the wine of the wrath of her sexual immorality, the kings of the earth committed sexual immorality with her, and the merchants of the earth grew rich from the abundance of her luxury."

Z9 - God Pleads to His People to Return to Him (Part 1)

John places God's call to his people to return to him at the beginning of the wax tablet and then copies the Tyre text from Ezekiel onto the new wax tablet. Since the Isaiah does not add to the Tyre's wealth text, John just ignores the Isaiah text in the copying process.

The Key Text of Zechariah:

1:3 Therefore tell them: The Lord says: 'Return to me,' says The Lord, 'and I will return to you,' says The Lord.

1:13 The Lord answered the angel who talked with me with kind and comforting words. 1:14 So the angel who talked with me said to me, "Proclaim, saying, 'The Lord says: "I am jealous for Jerusalem and for Zion with a great jealousy. 1:15 I am very angry with the nations that are at ease; for I was but a little displeased, but they added to the calamity."

EP7	Tyre
	• Wealth from trading with other nations (Ezek 27:12-22).
	• [No parallel]
	• Their riches became what ruined them (Ezek 27:27).
	• Merchants lamenting, Tyre's destruction (Ezek 27:27-28:2).

IP7	Tyre (Jesus, a Certain King)
	• Wealth from trading with other nations (Isa 23:1-17).
	• Tyre destruction 70 years after a certain king (Isa 23:15-7).
	• Post destruction's wealth will be righteousness (Isa 23:18).
	• Saints rejoicing over Tyre's destruction (Isa 25:1-6).

Content found in Ezekiel and Zechariah			Content in Revelation
Zech 1:3	'Return to me,' says the Lord, 'and I will return to you,.	18:4	I heard another voice from heaven, saying, "Come out of her, my people, that you have no participation in her sins, and that you don't receive of her plagues.
Ezek 27:12	Silver, Iron	18:12	Merchandise of silver, merchandise of iron.
Ezek 27:12	Persons of men, Vessels of brass	18:12-3	Peoples bodies and souls, every vessels mad of brass.
Ezek 27:14	Horses and war horses.	18:13	Horses, chariots
Ezek 27:15	Ivory tusks and ebony.	18:12	Every vessel made of ivory, expensive wood.
Ezek 27:16	Purple and fine linen.	18:12	Purple and fine linen.
Ezek 27:18	Oil	18:13	Olive oil.
Ezek 27:20	Wine of Hellbon	18:13	Wine
Ezek 27:22	Lambs	18:13	Sheep
Ezek 27:22	Chief of all spices, precious stones, and gold.	18:12-3	Spice, precious stones, merchandise of gold.
		18:15	The merchants of these things, who were made rich by her, will stand far away for the fear of her torment, weeping and mourning.
Ezek 22:27	Your riches . . . . shall fall into the heart of the seas in the day of your ruin.	18:17	For in an hour such great riches are made desolate.
Ezek 27:29	All who handled the oar, the mariners, and all the pilots of the sea, shall come down from their ships; they shall stand on the land.	18:17	Every ship master, and everyone who sails anywhere, and mariners, and as many as gain their living by sea, stood far away
Ezek 27:30	and shall cast up dust on their heads, they shall wallow themselves in the ashes.	18:19	They cast dust on their heads.
	[They] shall cause their voice to be heard over you, and shall cry bitterly.		[They] cried, weeping and mourning.
Ezek 27:32	In their wailing they shall take up a lamentation for you . . . "Who is there like Tyre?"	18:18	and cried out as they looked at the smoke of her burning, saying, "What is like the great city?"
Ezek 27:33	When your wares went out of the seas, you filled many peoples; you enriched the kings of the earth with the multitude of your riches and of your merchandise.	18:9	The kings of the earth, who committed sexual immorality and lived wantonly with her, will weep and wail over her, when they look at the smoke of her burning.
		18:11	The merchants of the earth weep and mourn over her, for no one buys their merchandise any more.
Ezek 28:2	Because your heart is lifted up, and you have said, I am a god, I sit in the seat of God, in the middle of the seas; yet you are man, and not God.	18:7	However much she glorified herself. . . . For she says in her heart, 'I sit a queen, and am no widow, and will in no way see mourning.

Z9 - Tyre Will Be Destroyed Seventy Years After a Certain King (Part 2)

Below are the texts that John used to create the first of three stories concerning the judgment against the nations who inflicted damage on Jerusalem.

The Key Text of Zechariah:

1:12 Then the LORD's angel replied, "O LORD, how long will you not have mercy on Jerusalem and on the cities of Judah, against which you have had indignation these seventy years?"

1:13 The LORD answered the angel who talked with me with kind and comforting words. *1:14* So the angel who talked with me said to me, "Proclaim, saying, 'The LORD says: "I am jealous for Jerusalem and for Zion with a great jealousy. *1:15* I am very angry with the nations that are at ease; for I was but a little displeased, but they added to the calamity."

EP7	Tyre
	· Wealth from trading with other nations (Ezek 27:12-22).
	· [No parallel]
	· Their riches became what ruined them (Ezek 27:27).
	· Merchants lamenting, Tyre's destruction (Ezek 27:27-28:2).

IP7	Tyre (Jesus, a Certain King)
	· Wealth from trading with other nations (Isa 23:1-17).
	· Tyre destruction 70 years after a certain king (Isa 23:15-7).
	· Post destruction's wealth will be righteousness (Isa 23:18).
	· Saints rejoicing over Tyre's destruction (Isa 25:1-6).

A Second Author's Notation Created

John, seeing that the Zechariah text contained seventy years, he returned the text used to construct the flying scroll. In so doing he kept the mighty angel author's notation and made some light edits removing any evidence that the text was connected to the scroll.

Content Found in Ezekiel, Isaiah, Jeremiah, and Zechariah		Content Found in Revelation	
		Mighty Angel - 2B The mighty angel (18:21 from 10:10)	
Jer 51:63	It shall be, ~~when you have finished reading this scroll~~, that you shall bind a stone to it, and cast it into the middle of the Euphrates.	18:21	A mighty angel took up a stone like a great millstone and cast it into the sea, saying:
Jer 51:64	Thus shall Babylon sink, and shall not rise again because of the evil that I will bring on her; and they shall be weary.	18:21	"Thus with violence will Babylon, the great city, be thrown down, and will be found no more at all.
Isa 23:15, 17	Tyre will be forgotten seventy years, according to the days of one king . . . after the end of seventy years that the LORD will visit Tyre.		
Isa 23:16	Take a harp; go about the city . . . . Make sweet melody. Sing many songs, that you may be remembered.	18:22	The voice of harpists, minstrels, flute players, and trumpeters will be heard no more at all in you.
Isa 23:17	She . . . will play the prostitute with all the kingdoms of the world on the surface of the earth.		
Zech 5:3-4	everyone who swears falsely shall be cut off according to it on the other side.	18:23	For with your sorcery all the nations were deceived.
Jer 51:49	As Babylon has caused the slain of Israel to fall, so at Babylon shall fall the slain of all the land.	18:24	In her was found the blood of prophets and of saints, and of all who have been slain on the earth.

The Destruction of Tyre and the Saints Praising God and the Eating of a Meal (Isa 25:1-6; Rev 19:1-9).

Below depicts the righteous on a mountain praising God and eating a meal because God destroyed a fortified city. This will eventually be the first part of the second coming in Revelation 19:1-9.

Content Found in Isaiah		Content Found in Revelation	
25:1	The LORD, you are my God. I will exalt you! I will praise your name, for you have done wonderful things, things planned long ago, in complete faithfulness and truth.	19:1 19:2	Hallelujah! Salvation, power, and glory belong to our God True and righteous are his judgments . . . and he has avenged the blood of his servants at her hand." (see Rev 6:9-11).
25:2	[God] made a city into a heap, a fortified city into a ruin,. . . It will never be built.	19:2	For he has judged the great prostitute, who corrupted the earth with her sexual immorality.
25:3	Therefore a strong people will glorify you. A city of awesome nations will fear you.	19:1-5	The righteous praise God and the city that rules the world is destroyed by God.
25:6	In this mountain, The LORD . . . will make all peoples a feast of fat things, a feast of choice wines, of fat things full of marrow, of well refined choice wines.	19:9	Blessed are those who are invited to the marriage supper of the Lamb.

Z9 - The Zechariah Draft Version of the Second Coming (Part 3a)

The ZrD version was a conflation of the Ezekiel and Isaiah account of the second coming. The major change that the ZrD brought into the narrative was the identifying the dragon as Satan and locking him in the abyss. It is later in the DnD that the beast and the lake of fire will be added to Revelation. The text was altered to show that Jesus was the one that locked Satan into the abyss as opposed to an angel (Rev 20:1). This was done to reflect the more probably storyline in the ZrD.

The Key Text of Zechariah:

1:8 "I had a vision in the night, and behold, **a man riding on a red horse,** and he stood among the myrtle trees that were in a ravine; and behind him there were red, brown, **and white horses. 1:9 Then I asked,** 'My lord, what are these?'"
The angel who talked with me said to me, "I will show you what these are."
1:10 **The man** who stood among the myrtle trees **answered,** "They are the ones The Lord has sent to go back and forth through the earth."
1:11 They reported to The Lord's angel who stood among the myrtle trees, and said, "We have walked back and forth through the earth, and behold, all the earth is at rest and in peace."

EP8	The Slaying of the Great Dragon
	• With a sword (Ezek 29:8).
	• The great dragon comforted by his army (Ezek 32:31).

IP8	Jesus Slays the Great Dragon
	• The rod of his mouth (Isa 11:4), a great sword (Isa 27:1).
	• Jesus musters his army from the whole world (Isa 11:10-6).

Content Found In Ezekiel and Isaiah		Content in Revelation
		The Red Horsemen (Rev 6:4)
Zech 1:8 Behold, a man riding on a red horse.	6:4	Another came out, a red horse. To him who sat on it was given power to take peace from the earth, and that they should kill one another. There was given to him a great sword.
Zech 1:8 A man riding on a red horse . . . and behind him were red, brown and white horses.	19:14	The armies which are in heaven followed him on white horses.
Zech 1:9 Then I asked, 'My lord, what are these?"	7:13	One of the elders answered, saying to me, "These who are arrayed in the white robes, who are they, and from where did they come?"
Zech 1:9 The angel who talked with me said to me, "I will show you what these are."	7:14	I told him, "My lord, you know."
Zech 1:10 The man who stood among the myrtle trees answered, "They are the ones The Lord has sent to go back and forth through the earth."		He said to me, "These are those who came out of the great tribulation. They washed their robes, and made them white in the Lamb's blood.
		Crossing the Euphrates River (Rev 9:14; 16:12)
Isa 11:15 His scorching wind he will wave his hand over the river.	9:14	Free the four angels who are bound at the great river Euphrates! (see Rev 7:1 where they are the four angels holding back the four winds)
Isa 11:16 Will cause men to march over in sandals. There will be a highway for the remnant that is left of his people from Assyria.	16:12	The great river, the Euphrates. Its water was dried up, that the way might be prepared for the kings that come from the sunrise.
Isa 27:12 It will happen in that day, that Lord will thresh from the flowing stream of the Euphrates to the brook of Egypt; and you will be gathered one by one, children of Israel.		
		Many of the Saints in Heaven Passages
Isa 12:2 God is my salvation. I will trust, and will not be afraid.	7:10	Salvation be to our God.
Isa 12:3 Therefore with joy you will draw water out of the wells of salvation.	7:17	"The Lamb . . . leads them to springs of waters of life. And God will wipe away every tear from their eyes."
Isa 12:6 Cry aloud and shout, you inhabitant of Zion for the Holy One of Israel is great among you.	14:1	The Lamb standing on Mount Zion.
	14:2	They sounded like many waters and a great thunder.
Isa 12:2 They will sing a song of salvation.	14:3	The sing a new song before the throne.
	14:4	The were redeemed by Jesus.
Isa 12:4 In that day you will say, "Give thanks to the Lord! Call on his name. Declare his doings among the peoples.	14:6	I saw an angel flying in mid heaven, having an eternal Good News to proclaim to those who dwell on the earth, and to every nation, tribe, language, and people.
Isa 12:5 Sing to the Lord for he has done excellent things.	15:3	The sang the song of the Lamb, saying, "Great and marvelous are your works."
Isa 12:6 The Holy One of Israel.	15:4	For you only are holy.

Z9 - The Zechariah Draft Version of the Second Coming (Part 3b)

Below is the continuation of the text from Z9 -- Part 3a. John formed a parallel with the chart in Part 3a, where as God and Jesus are riding a horse and each have a sword. Both have the same enemy, the great dragon, and both have an army. In both passages there are two rivers. One river is what the saints cross to get to Egypt (Isa 11:15-6; 27:12) and the other river is formed by the blood of the Egyptians (Ezek 32:4-5).

Content Found In Ezekiel, Isaiah and Zechariah		Content in Revelation	
		Description of Jesus in the Second Coming (Rev 19:11-15)	
Zech 1:8	White horses.	19:11	Jesus sitting on a white horse.
		19:14	The saints followed Jesus on white horses.
Isa 11:4	[In] righteousness he will judge.	19:11	In righteousness he judges and makes war.
	He will strike the earth with the rod of his mouth.	19:15	Out of his mouth proceeds a sharp, double-edged sword.
Isa 27:1	The Lord with his hard and great and strong sword....		He will rule them with an iron rod.
Isa 11:5	Righteousness will be the belt of his waist.		
	Faithfulness will the belt of his waist.		
Isa 13:1-8	God is mustering a great army from the a distant land to ends of heaven in order to battle the nations.	19:14	The armies which are in heaven followed him on white horses, clothed in white, pure, fine linen.
	The River of Death (Ezek 32:4-5)		***The Slaying of the Great Dragon (Rev 19:17 - 20:3)***
Ezek 32:4	The birds and animals will feast on the dragon's army.		[See Ezek 39:17-20; Rev 19:17-8 below as the rest of the feast of the vulture]
Ezek 32:5	The blood of the dead will be deep enough to swim in.	14:20	The blood was as deep as a horses bridle and as far as 180 miles.
Ezek 32:21	The strong among the mighty shall speak to him out of the middle of Sheol.	20:1	I saw [Jesus] coming down out of heaven, having the key of the abyss and a great chain in his hand.
		20:2	He seized the dragon, the old serpent, which is the devil and Satan, who deceives the whole inhabited earth.
		20:3	and cast him into the abyss, and shut it, and sealed it over him, that he should deceive the nations no more, until the thousand years were finished. After this, he must be freed for a short time.
Ezek 32:31	Pharaoh shall see them, and shall be comforted over all his multitude.	19:19	I saw the [great dragon beast], and the kings of the earth, and their armies, gathered together to make war against him who sat on the horse, and against his army.
Ezek 32:32	Those who are slain by the sword, even Pharaoh and all his multitude.	19:21	The rest were killed with the sword by him who sat on the horse.

Z9 - God's Cities Will Once Again Flow with Prosperity (Part 4)

In the Zechariah Draft (ZrD), the story of Gog and Magog as well as the Isaiah account of the multitude of nations attacking Jerusalem will be conflated to form the foundation of Revelation 20:4-15. If we arrange the Ezekiel and Isaiah content in the order of Revelation we can see how John used the text to provide the primary content of Gog and Magog in Revelation.

EP9	Jerusalem Attacked by Gog and Magog
	• Nations come from the north to destroy Jerusalem and God destroys the nations (Ezek 38:1 - 39:29).

IP9	Jerusalem Attacked by a Multitude of Nations
	• Nations come from all over the world to destroy Jerusalem and God destroys the nations (Isa 29:1-21).

Content Found In the Ezekiel-Isaiah Draft		Content in Revelation
		The First Resurrection (Rev 20:4-6)
Isa 29:18-9 The blind, deaf, and the poor will hear the words of the book and rejoice.	20:4-6	The first resurrection where those who were righteous were found in the book.
		The Attack on Jerusalem
Ezek 38:14 In that day when my people Israel dwells securely, shall you not know it?	20:7	And after the thousand years, Satan will be released from his prison.
		[States that when Satan is locked up in the abyss, Jerusalem will be prosperous and people will dwell safely in it.]
Ezek 38:2 Gog of the land of Magog.	20:8	Gog and Magog mentioned.
Isa 29:8 Multitude of nations.	20:8	Nations from the four corners of the earth.
Ezek 38:18 They shall come against Israel. Isa 29:1 The city where David encamped.	20:9	They went up over the width of the earth, and surrounded the camp of the saints, and the beloved city.
Isa 29:6 They will be destroyed by a devouring fire.	20:9	Fire came down out of heaven from God, and devoured them.
		The Second Resurrection (Rev 20:11-5)
Isa 29:20-1 A book in the context and the unrighteous will be destroyed.	20:11-5	The second resurrection where those who did evil deeds according to a book will be put in the lake of fire.

Z9 - The Return Home (Part 1)

The text below represents a conflation of the last two wax tablets that remained in the EID. The order is set by the text in the published version of Revelation to aid in reading. Most likely the order seen was the order found in the ZrD which will be explained in the construction of the prologue and epilogue found in this chapter.

The Key Text of Zechariah:

1:1 In the eighth month, in the second year of Darius, THE LORD's word came to Zechariah the son of Berechiah, the son of Iddo, the prophet, saying, 1:2 "THE LORD was very displeased with your fathers. 1:3 Therefore tell them: THE LORD says: 'Return to me,' says THE LORD, 'and I will return to you,' says THE LORD. 1:4 Don't you be like your fathers, to whom the former prophets proclaimed, saying: THE LORD says, 'Return now from your evil ways, and from your evil doings;' but they did not hear, nor listen to me, says THE LORD. 1:5 Your fathers, where are they? And the prophets, do they live forever? 1:6 But my words and my decrees, which I commanded my servants the prophets, didn't they overtake your fathers?

EP10 The City of God	**IP10 The Holy City of Jerusalem**
• Jerusalem will be a city that God and the righteous will liven in (Ezek 40:1 - 48:35)	• Various descriptions of the Holy City of Jerusalem scattered throughout Isaiah.

Content Found in Ezekiel, Isaiah and Zechariah		**Content Found in Revelation**	
Isa 65:17	"For, behold, I create new heavens and a new earth; and the former things will not be remembered, nor come into mind.	21:1	I saw a new heaven and a new earth: for the first heaven and the first earth have passed away, and the sea is no more.
Isa 66:22	"For as the new heavens and the new earth, which I will make, shall remain before me."		
Isa 66:20	The holy city Jerusalem.	21:2	I saw the holy city, New Jerusalem, coming down out of heaven from God.
Isa 61:10	God has clothed me . . . as a bride adorns herself with her jewels.		Prepared like a bride adorned for her husband.
Ezek 43:7	God dwells in the temple where his throne is. He will dwell among the people of Israel forever.	21:3	I heard a loud voice out of heaven saying, "Behold, God's dwelling is with people, and he will dwell with them, and they will be his people, and God himself will be with them as their God.
Isa 25:8	The LORD will wipe away tears from off all faces.	21:4	He will wipe away from them every tear from their eyes.
Isa 25:8	He has swallowed up death forever!		Death will be no more; neither will there be mourning, nor crying, nor pain, any more. The first things have passed away."
Isa 42:9	Behold, the former things have happened, and I declare new things.	21:5	He who sits on the throne said, "Behold, I am making all things new."
Isa 25:1	God has done things in complete faithfulness and truth.	21:5	These words of God are faithful and true (also in 22:6).
Isa 44:6	I am the first, and I am the last.	21:6	I am . . . the beginning and end.
Isa 44:3 Isa 55:1	I will pour water on him who is thirsty "Hey! Come, everyone who thirsts, to the waters! Come, he who has no money, buy, and eat! Yes, come, buy wine and milk without money and without price.	21:6	I will give freely to him who is thirsty from the spring of the water of life (also in 22:17).
Ezek 43:7-11	The house of Israel will no longer defile God's name by prostitution, sacrificing to high places and violating God's ordinances.	21:7-8 and 22:15	Those who overcome, they will live in the New Jerusalem. Outside are the dogs, the sorcerers, the sexually immoral, the murderers, the idolaters, and everyone who loves and practices falsehood.
Ezek 40:2	Ezekiel in a vision was carried to a high mountain in Israel where he saw the City of God.	21:10	He carried me away in the Spirit to a great and high mountain, and showed me the holy city, Jerusalem, coming down out of heaven from God.

Z9 - The Return Home (Part 2)

Content Found in Ezekiel, Isaiah and Zechariah		Content Found in Revelation	
Ezek 48:31-4	The city of God has 12 gates named after each of the twelve tribes of Israel, 3 on each side.	21:12	The New Jerusalem has twelve gates named after the twelve tribes of Israel.
		21:13	There are three gates on each side.
Ezek 40:3	[He had] a measuring reed.	21:15	He who spoke with me had for a measure, a golden reed, to measure the city, its gates and its walls
Ezek 40:5	[He measured] the wall, all around and the thickness of the building.		
Ezek 48:16	The city is a square with each side measuring 4,500 cubics* (1.4 miles / 2.3 km).	21:16	The city is a cube with each side measuring 12,012 stadia* (1,380 km / 2,221 km).
Isa 60:19	The sun will be no more your light by day; nor will the brightness of the moon give light to you, but the Lord will be your everlasting light, and your God will be your glory.	21:23	The city has no need for the sun, neither of the moon, to shine, for the very glory of God illuminated it, and its lamp is the Lamb.
Ezek 47:1	The waters came down from under, from the right side of the house, on the south of the altar.	22:1	A river of water of life, clear as crystal, proceeding out of the throne of God and the Lamb.
Zech 14:8	It will happen in that day, that living waters will go out from Jerusalem.		
Ezek 47:12	By the river on its bank . . . shall grow every tree for food whose leaf shall not wither, neither shall its fruit fail. It shall produce new fruit every month . . . its leaf for healing.	22:2	On this side of the river was the tree of life, bearing twelve kinds of fruits, yielding its fruit every month. The leaves of the tree were for the healing of the nations.
Zech 14:11	Men will dwell therein, and there will be no more curse; but Jerusalem will dwell safely.	22:3	There will be no curse any more.

* CB has the length of 1.28 miles, NET has the length as 1.5 miles.

** A stadia equals 607 feet / 192 meters (BDAG, στάδιοί).

Chapter 4: The Deuteronomy-Joshua Draft (DJD)

The Purpose and Scope of the Deuteronomy-Joshua Draft

The Ezekiel side of the EID brought the primary content that depicted Jerusalem's destruction, and the judgments against Israel and its eventual restoration. The Isaiah side of the EID brought hope to the people, through its plethora of descriptions of individuals, God, and Jesus; and portrayed the source material in a positive tone. The ZrD changed everything by mixing things up and then conflating the tablets where many new stories were created, such as: the letters to the two cities (now the seven churches); the seals; the trumpets; the bowls; the two prophets; Satan, and many more. The ZrD also took the role of Joshua the high priest and conveyed it to Jesus, making Jesus the builder of God's new temple in heaven.

The Purpose of the Deuteronomy-Joshua Draft

The stories of Deuteronomy and Joshua were chosen for a variety of reasons; first it is a natural place for John to gravitate to. The ZrD's principle character was Joshua (Jesus) the high priest where John conflated his story with Jesus' story in Revelation. It is natural for John to consider using the most recognizable Joshua (Jesus) in the Hebrew Scriptures—Joshua the son of Nunn. Secondly, the difference in the role of Joshua the high priest and Joshua the son of Nunn is an important consideration. The former is the one that rebuilds the temple and begins the process of restoring God's people to become a righteous people. The latter is the conquerer of the wicked and restorer of God's people to the promised land. Both roles are perfect for depicting Jesus in the book of Revelation (or at least John must have thought as much since he included both in the published version of Revelation).

The Deuteronomy-Joshua Draft (DJD) Simplified (Part 1)

In the Deuteronomy-Joshua Draft (DJD), John took the opposite approach that he had with the ZrD. Instead of reshaping the previous draft to conform to Joshua, John took material from Deuteronomy 29 to Joshua 6 and made it fit to the Zechariah Draft. He did this by adding minor content into the ZrD to tell the story of Deuteronomy 29:1 to Josh 5:11 backwards and using the material from Josh 6:1-27 forwards arriving in Joshua's camp.

The Story Told Backwards

John integrates Joshua 1:16-5:11 with the Zechariah Draft (ZrD) by weaving the storyline backwards, either by using ZrD material or adding distinctive features from Joshua to the ZrD. The end result of John's editing can be seen in the table below.

Story in Deuteronomy 29 to Joshua 5:11	Found in Revelation
The Covenant • They have seen what God has done in the wilderness (Deut 29:1-28). • Those who keep the commandments of God will prosper (Deut 29:9-16). • God will not pardon those who practice idolatry (Deut 29:17-9). • Those who practice idolatry will receive the curses found in Deuteronomy (Deut 29:21).	**The Epilogue** • John is told to publish what he has seen (22:6; see 1:19). • Blessed are those who keep the commandments (22:14). • Idolatry excludes one from the New Jerusalem (22:15). • Those who modify Revelation will receive its plagues (22:18-9).
The Blessing and the Curse • The faithful and return them to the land (Deut 30:1-10). • Who comes from the uttermost part of the heavens (Deut 30:12). • Who comes from beyond the sea (Deut 30:13).	**Gog and Magog** • The faithful reside in Jerusalem again (20:5-10). • The saints came from heaven (20:4-6). • The rest came from the sea (20:11-5).
The Song of Moses • Moses told to write a song which will become the song of Moses (Deut 31:19). • God in front of the Tent of Meeting (Deut 31:15). • A pillar of cloud appeared above the tent's door (Deut 31:15). • God will hide his face from his people if they leave him (Deut 31:18). • God will be angry with his people if they chase idols (Deut 31:16-7).	**The Song of Moses and the Lamb** • They sang the song of Moses and the Lamb (15:3-4). • God in the temple (15:3, 8). • The temple filled with the smoke of God's glory (15:8). • God is never described as being seen. • God is angry (15:1, 7).
Joshua's Camp • They told Joshua that they will go where ever he went (Josh 1:16). • Those that did not listen to Joshua will be put to death (Josh 1:16).	**The 144,000 in Heaven** • They followed the Lamb wherever he went (14:4). • They had been redeemed out of the earth (14:3).
The Two Spies in Jericho • Sent to spy on Jericho (Josh 2:1). • Hunted by the king (Josh 2:2-3). • Hid for three days (Josh 2:22-3). • Came to Joshua's camp (Josh 2:23-4).	**Two Prophets** • Ministered in Jerusalem (11:7). • Killed by the beast (11:7). • Seen dead for three and a half days (11:8-12) • Taken to heaven (11:12).
Priest Crossing the Jordan • A foot in the river and on land (Josh 3:1-15). • Jordan River dried (Josh 3:16-7).	**The Mighty Angel** • Foot in the sea and on land (10:2). • Euphrates River dried (9:13; see parallel in 16:12).
The Circumcision of the Israelites • From the twelve tribes of Israel (Josh 5:1-9). • Circumcised (Josh 5:1-9). • They had a Passover meal (Josh 5:9-11).	**The Sealing of the 144,000** • From the twelve tribes of Israel (7:4-8). • Sealed by God (7:1-3). • Jesus the Passover Lamb (7:7-17).

The Deuteronomy-Joshua Draft (DJD) Simplified (Part 2)
The Rest of the Story Told Forwards

John stopped at the commander of the Lord's narrative and then told the story forward in the ZrD. This allowed John to depict Jerusalem as the new Jericho and the great multitude as the new Israelites.

Story in Joshua 5:13 - 6:27	Found in Revelation
The Commander of the Lord's Army	**Jesus Receives the Scroll**
• Joshua asked who is this person (5:13).	• The search for who is worthy (5:2)
• The person tells Joshua that he is the commander of THE LORD's army (5:14).	• An angel tells John that Jesus is the "Lion who is from the tribe of Judah" (5:5).
• Joshua fell down before the commander of THE LORD's army (5:14).	• The four living creatures and 24 elders fall down before Jesus (5:8, 14)
Joshua Marches Around Jericho	**Jesus Removes the Seals**
• Marches around seven days (6:1-15).	• Removes seven seals (6:1-17; 8:1-6)
• The seventh day he was to march around seven more times (6:16).	• The seventh seal contained seven more judgments (8:1-6).
• The priests blew the trumpets on the seventh time (6:16).	• Seven angels each blew a trumpet (8:6-9:21; 11:15-9).
Jericho Destroyed	**Jerusalem Destroyed**
• The ground shook and the walls collapsed (6:16).	• An earthquake and the city fell (11:13, 19)
• The seven priests blew the trumpets (6:16).	• The seventh angel blew the last trumpet (11:15).
• The people shouted with a great voice (6:16).	• Great voices came from heaven (11:16).
• The priest carried the ark of the covenant around the city (6:16).	• The ark of the covenant is displayed in heaven (11:19).

The Scope of the Deuteronomy-Joshua Draft

In the two prior drafts, we have descriptions of Jesus derived from the Hebrew Scriptures. In the EID, John took various persons in Isaiah 6:1 - 27:13 and ascribed it to Jesus. For the ZrD, John used the imagery of Joshua the high priest and ascribed it to Jesus. John will continue this trend with the DJD, he will take the story of Joshua becoming the new leader of Israel from the last six chapters of Deuteronomy and the first six chapters of Joshua and make it the story of Jesus becoming the new Moses. It is a story of the transition of leadership, from Moses to Joshua, where the faithful pledge their allegiance to Joshua.[1] It is also the story of God's people destroying the city of Jericho so that his people will have a kingdom. It is the story of dire warning, that the people will abandon God and God will unleash his wrath on his people.[2]

Let's Build the Deuteronomy-Joshua Draft (DJD)

The process in which John compiled the DJD is the exact opposite of how he constructed the ZrD, but with a few small twists. In the ZrD, John began the process of writing by adding Zechariah 12:10 on a new wax tablet and read the first twelve chapters of Zechariah backwards. As he read Zechariah, he divided it up into sections (much like a good study Bible would do), and then used those sections to search for content in the EID. When he found matching content, John moved those wax tablets so as to follow Zechariah's storyline. The result was that the bulk of the content and the wax tablets used in the EID were moved

---

1   Deut 39:18 to Josh 1:18.
2   Deut 29:1-28.

to new wax tablets. The process would have been easy if it were done using 21st century tools, but it must have taken John a longer time to complete the ZrD.

The DJD was different, instead of selecting a text to work backward from and forwards in the previous draft, John selected a text to work forward from and started at the end of the ZrD.[3] Instead of rewriting every wax tablet, John added the text between the wax tablets. When he had to change the text, it was the text near the wax tablet he inserted. The process was less traumatic than constructing the ZrD was, but the resulting process transformed the ZrD to something close to the published version of Revelation we have today.

It is possible that John constructed the DJD with a certain agenda in mind, but during the process of importing material from Deuteronomy-Joshua into Revelation he had to change his original plan. Instead of going backwards in the ZrD, he had to stop and instead move forward, overlaying the story backwards with the story going forward. Whether John planned it out from the start of the DJD process or it was a serendipitous act that occurred at the moment, we will never know.

John had a second phase in the DJD—the finishing phase. In this phase, John formed parallels between many passages. It is in the finishing phase that we find major story arcs separated by chapters. These parallels give us great insight into what John was thinking in constructing of Revelation. It is also the part that we will focus on for most of this chapter.

The Lamb of God

One of the more interesting changes that John incorporated into the DJD was the use of the Lamb as a synonym for Jesus. The reason for the DJD's use of the Lamb as Jesus has more to do with the fact that the Greek and Hebrew word for Joshua and Jesus are the same words:

Jesus = Joshua = Ἰησους = יְהוֹשׁוּעַ meaning "The Lord is Salvation"

By using the Lamb as a synonym, it makes it more difficult for the reader/hearer to associate the text of Revelation with the story of Joshua from the Deuteronomy and Joshua books. We know that John used the Lamb as a synonym for Jesus in the DJD for several reasons. First, the DJD is the first draft to include the Passover meal, and the Lamb imagery is not far behind. The second reason is that every place where the DJD directly interacts with Revelation, we have the word "Lamb" instead of Jesus. The last line of evidence is observational when the DJD stops inserting information directly into Revelation the use of the "Lamb" simile for Jesus stops.

The Epilogue is Born

The earliest construction of the epilogue in Revelation began with the process of extracting material from Deuteronomy 29:1-28 and transferring it to a new wax tablet. The passage is a mixture of blessings for the faithful and curses for those who abandoned God. It ends with the dire consequences that those who abandoned God will be given the curses found within Deuteronomy. John simply took the passage of Deuteronomy and transcribed it onto a blank wax tablet, which gives us the first version of the epilogue. However, as we learned in the prior drafts, John likes to tweak the source material to fit the content. The Deuteronomy passage asks the people to reflect upon all that God did in the wilderness for them. In the DJD, John wants the people to reflect upon all that appears in the ZrD/DJD. The Deuteronomy passage

---

3   See "The Deuteronomy-Joshua Draft (DJD) Simplified (Part 1)" on page 132 and "The Deuteronomy-Joshua Draft (DJD) Simplified (Part 2)" on page 133.

tells of a foreigner who will transplant God's people into a barren land which John changes to those who abandoned God. In the DJD however, Jesus will take the faithful to a new land of plenty, expressed in the negative (that he will not take the unfaithful to a land of plenty).[4]

The Birth of the Warning for Those Who Wish to Modify Revelation

The most famous of the passages that John gets from Deuteronomy is the dire warning for readers not to abandon God by chasing after other gods. If they do, they will receive all the curses found within Deuteronomy. John will apply the same message to his book by using ominous terms, which warn that changing his book will bring the plagues within it down upon any soul that does.[5]

Did John originally include this warning in the DJD directed to those who change Revelation or was it for those who practice idolatry and later changed to what we have today? It was probably a dire warning against idolatry since much of Revelation speaks out against that.[6] Then most likely, it later became the warning not to change it. Later in this chapter, and in the last chapter, it will be shown that John put considerable effort into constructing parallels to where they will provide a profound storyline within themselves. John saw that the best way to retain his work for posterity would be to change the dire warning from "practicing idolatry" to "changing Revelation."

Both books place an emphasis on what the book tells the reader. Deuteronomy places an emphasis on the curses' imagery of what the people experienced in Deuteronomy, and Revelation emphasizes the plagues' imagery that people will experience.

The Blessings and the Curses, the Story of Gog and Magog, and the New Jerusalem

The next section that John imports into the DJD from Deuteronomy is where God promises to bring his people back to their land when they are taken into captivity. He promises that if his people are scattered to the uttermost part of the heavens, he will bring them back to their promised land.[7]

God then asks two profound questions to his people, to which they cannot give a response:

> *It is not in heaven, that you should say,*
> *"Who will go up for us to heaven, and bring it to us, and proclaim it to us, that we may do it?"*[8]
> *Neither is it beyond the sea, that you should say,*
> *"Who will go over the sea for us, and bring it to us, and proclaim it to us, that we may do it?"*[9]

The conclusion that God gives in the Deuteronomy passage[10] is to love God and choose life over other gods that will provide only death and the curse.[11] John took the Deuteronomy passage and integrated it with the story of Gog and Magog where he had those who read the book (the righteous) become the martyrs

---

4   Deut 29:22-5; Rev 22:17, 19; See "How the Epilogue Came Into Revelation" on page 136.
5   Deut 29:18-28; Rev 22:18-9; See "How the Epilogue Came Into Revelation" on page 136.
6   Rev 2:14, 20; 9:20;21:8; 22:15.
7   Deut 30:4.
8   Deut 30:12.
9   Duet 30:13.
10 Deut 30:1-20.
11 Deut 30:16-20.

How the Epilogue Came Into Revelation

The chart below shows how John formed Revelation's epilogue by creating a complex parallel with the 29th chapter of Deuteronomy. This is where we get the warning not to alter Revelation (Rev 22:18-9) and where John is to publish Revelation.

Content Found in Deuteronomy		Content Found in Revelation	
The Covenant (Deut 29:1-28)		**The Epilogue (Rev 22:6-21)**	
29:1-5	They have seen all that God has done for the Israelites in the wilderness.	22:6	The conclusion of the book of Revelation. John is told to publish all that he has seen and heard (see Rev 1:19).
29:9-16	Those who keep the commandments of God will prosper.	22:7, 14	Blessed are those who do his commandments, that they may have the right to the tree of life, and may enter in by the gates into the city.
29:17-9	God will not pardon those who practice idolatry and other things that cause his people to turn from him.	22:15	Outside are the dogs, the sorcerers, the sexually immoral, the murderers, the idolaters, and everyone who loves and practices falsehood.
29:22-5	A foreigner will deceive the people and cause the land to become barren.	22:17	Jesus gives the water of life freely.
		22:19	Those who do not follow Jesus will not partake of the tree of life which is in the paradise of God (see Rev 2:7 as the paradise of God; 22:2 used to heal the nations).
29:18-28	God will apply all the curses in Deuteronomy to those who participate with idols.	22:18-9	If anyone modifies Revelation they will suffer the consequences of the plagues contained within the book.

found in heaven, to rule with Jesus for a thousand years.12 Those who did not read the book (the unrighteous), become the dead taken from the sea.13 The two groups are the two groups that tell the story that no one could tell in Deuteronomy.

John showed how the righteous will remain in Jerusalem on earth and how God will protect them when they are attacked by all the nations.[14] He also shows a great defeat of the army that attacks the righteous.[15] However, John needed to transition from the story of Gog and Magog to the New Jerusalem. For the transition, John focused on the act of God commanding his people to love him and the plight of those who obey his commandments and those who disobey his commandments. He formed a new wax tablet where he continued the storyline from Deuteronomy by taking supporting text from the ZrD New Jerusalem narrative and placing it on the new wax tablet. Instead of loving God from Deuteronomy he took the Ezekiel text where God will love them and call them his son.[16] The result is something identical to or close to the published account of the first five four verses describing the New Jerusalem in Revelation.

> I saw a new heaven and a new earth: for the first heaven and the first earth have passed away, and the sea is no more. I saw the holy city, New Jerusalem, coming down out of heaven from God, prepared like a bride adorned for her husband. I heard a loud voice out of heaven saying,
> "Behold, God's dwelling is with people, and he will dwell with them, and they will be his people, and God himself will be with them as their God. He will wipe away from them every tear from their eyes.

---

12   Rev 20:4-6.
13   Rev 20:13.
14   Rev 20:3-10.
15   Rev 20:7-10.
16   Deut 30:16; Rev 21:1-5.

The Blessing and the Curses Told Through the Story of Gog and Magog and the New Jerusalem

he chart below shows how John integrated Deuteronomy 30:1-19 into the story of Gog and Magog and the New Jerusalem. The Ezekiel and Isaiah text is left out in order to emphasize content agreement. The approximation text at the end of this chapter will have the conflation of all three texts.

The Blessing and the Curse in Deuteronomy		Gog and Magog	
30:1-10	God will gather those who obeyed his commandments and return them to their land.	20:5-10	The faithful obeyed the commandments of God (21:4-6) and the faithful now live in Jerusalem on earth.
30:4	If your outcasts are in the uttermost parts of the heavens, from there God will gather you, and from there he will bring you back.	20:4	I saw thrones, and they sat on them, and judgment was given to them. I saw the souls of those who had been beheaded for the testimony of Jesus, and for the word of God.
			They lived and reigned with Christ for a thousand years.
30:11	The commandment is not too distant.	20:3,7	After a thousand years . . . Satan . . . released from the abyss.
		21:6	It is done (see Alpha and Omega parallel).
30:12	Who will go to heaven and return with a message to God?	20:4-6	John proclaims that he saw the outcasts from the uttermost part in heaven (first resurrection).
		21:1-5	John sees and proclaims what he saw in heaven.
30:13	Who will go beyond the sea and return with a message to God?	20:11-5	John reports of seeing the sea giving up the dead for the second resurrection.
30:15	Life and prosperity	20:4-6 21:3-4	The first resurrection where the people are raised and rule with God
			They will live with God and death will be no more.
30:15	Death and evil	20:11-5	The second resurrection where the people go to eternal torment. Note: eternal torment is a product of the DnD.
30:16	Moses commands the people to love God that God might bless you where you live.	20:7-10	God protects his people from the nations that attack them.
		21:1-4	God lives with his people.
		21:5-7	They will be given the water of life and become a child of God.
30:16-9	If the people choose to turn away from God he will denounce them.	20:11-5	These people did not obey the commandments of God (see Rev 20:4-7).
		21:8	Those with sins will not enter the New Jerusalem.

Death will be no more; neither will there be mourning, nor crying, nor pain, any more. The first things have passed away."[17]

John wanted to include the imagery of God denouncing his people for practicing idolatry in the strongest of terms. So he took the imagery from Ezekiel where the sinner cannot enter into the City of God and conflated it with the strongest imagery against idolatry in Isaiah.[18] The end result is that we have the conclusion of the first eyewitness account of John describing the New Jerusalem.

21:5 *He who sits on the throne said, "Behold, I am making all things new." He said, "Write, for these words of God are faithful and true."* **21:6** *He said to me, "It is done! I am the [first and the last]. I will give freely to him who is thirsty from the spring of the water of life.* **21:7** *He who overcomes, I will give him these*

---

17   Rev 21:1-4.
18   Ezek 43:7-11; Isa 44:1-10.

Adding to the Zechariah Draft (Part 1)

Below represents the text that John did not integrate with Zechariah 2:1 - 4:14––he simply conflated the Ezekiel and Isaiah text. The end result of the conflation is what we now know as Revelation 14:1-20. In this conflation we get the start of the 144,000 in heaven, and two of the three messages acted out and delivered by angels. We also get the beginning of the great harvest.

To see how the Isaiah wax tablets were laid out before the conflation go to "EP5 - The Glory of the Lord Flees Jerusalem" on page 52 and "IP5 - The Glory of the Lord Triumphs in Heaven" on page 53. The likelihood that the content below came from the leftover content from the original EID content appended in order to free that wax tablet to be reused again is high. If that scenario is correct then John probably had room at the top of the tablet for the DJD-inserted material.

Content Found in the DJD Material			Content Found in Revelation (Ordered by)
			The 144,000 in Heaven (Rev 14:1-5)
Isa 14:32	What will they answer the messengers of the nation? That The Lord has founded Zion, and in her the afflicted of his people will take refuge.	14:1	The Lamb standing on Mount Zion with the 144,000.
Deut 31:30	The song of Moses taught by Moses	14:3	The Song of the Lamb that only the people know.
Josh 1:16	All that you have commanded us we will do, and wherever you send us we will go.	14:4	These are those who follow the Lamb wherever he goes.
Josh 1:18	Whoever rebels against your commandment, and doesn't listen to your words in all that you command shall himself be put to death. Only be strong and courageous.		These were redeemed by Jesus from among men, the first fruits to God and to the Lamb. In their mouth was found no lie, for they are blameless.
			The Message of the First Angel (Rev 14:6-7)
Isa 14:32	Oracles to the nations	14:6	The gospel was spread to the entire world.
Isa 15:1 - 19:17	The oracles to the nations		
Isa 17:7, 10	People will look to their maker . . . their forgotten God of salvation.	14:7	Fear The Lord . . . who made everything.
			The Message of the Second Angel (Rev 14:8)
Isa 21:9	Fallen, fallen is Babylon and all the engraved images of her gods are broken to the ground.	14:8	Babylon the great has fallen, which has made all the nations to drink of the wine of the wrath of her sexual immorality.
			The Great Harvest (Rev 14:14-20)
Ezek 15:2	Son of man	14:14	One sitting like the son of man.
Ezek 15:6	The inhabitants of Jerusalem are connected to the worthless vine.	14:13-6	The saints are connected to the great harvest of grapes.
Ezek 15:7	God will use fire against them.	14:18	An angel who has the power of fire [no fire is used].
Ezek 15:8	God will make the land desolate because they have committed a trespass.	14:19-20	The grapes make the wrath of God which will destroy the harlot and make her desolate (Rev 17:6; 18:5-8).

---

things. I will be his God, and he will be my son. Outside are the dogs, the sorcerers, the sexually immoral, the murderers, the idolaters, and everyone who loves and practices falsehood."[19]

---

19   Rev 21:5-7 with a few modifications. The "alpha and omega and beginning and end" was replaced with "the first and the last" from Isa 44:6. Rev 21:8 was replaced with Rev 22:15 which reflects what John originally had in the DJD. The Rev 21:8 text is a DnD adaptation interjecting the second death into Revelation.

Adding to the Zechariah Draft (Part 2)

The Song of Moses and the Lamb

John created a new wax tablet that told the story of the making of the song of Moses by ascribing it to the Lamb (Jesus) as well as telling the story backwards. This allowed John to pick up the story in Revelation 14:1-5 as seen below.

The Song of Moses in Deuteronomy		The Song of Moses and the Lamb	
Deut 31:19	Moses was told to write a song which will become the song of Moses.	15:3-4	They sang the song of Moses, and the Song of the Lamb.
Deut 31:18	God will hide his face on that day.		God is not seen.
Deut 31:16-7	God will be angry when his people forsake him and chase after idols.	15:1, 7	The wrath of God
Deut 31:15	Moses and Joshua (Jesus) in the Tent of Meeting.	15:3, 8	Song of Moses and Jesus . . . God in the temple.
	A pillar of cloud appeared above the tent's door.	15:8	The temple was filled with the smoke of the glory of God.

The Song of Moses and the Lamb/Jesus

The next detectable passage that John used to create the DJD was the story of where God instructs Moses to write a song and teach it to his people. The setting is God at the tent of meeting and there is a pillar of clouds that appears above the tent's door. It speaks of a time when God's people will chase after idols and that God will forsake them and hide his face from them.[20] John took this material and turned it into the prelude to the seven bowls, in which God is inside the temple full of wrath. The song of Moses and the Lamb is sung by the people and the temple door is closed until all the judgments are done.

The placement of the story and the story being primarily composed of new material tells us that the story was probably written on a new wax tablet and that tablet was inserted into the ZrD where it resides today in the published version of Revelation. The distance from the last detectable place where John used Deuteronomy shows us that John was strategic in his placement of Deuteronomy and Joshua.

The order that the story is rendered in the song of Moses into the DJD tells us that John wanted to continue the story into the next section. This can be seen in how he reverses the story of the Song of Moses and has that song sung in an earlier portion of Revelation and a later portion of the DJD's construction process.[21] This is the first example of John setting a meter that will allow the reader to follow the story backwards.

The People Swear Allegiance to the Lamb/Jesus

We are now in the first chapter of the book of Joshua where Moses is dead, God swears his allegiance to Joshua, and the people swear their allegiance to the Lamb/Jesus/Joshua. God tells Joshua that he will go

---

20 Deut 31:16-8.
21 See "Adding to the Zechariah Draft (Part 1)" on page 138 on how John reverses the order of the Song of Moses' story (Rev 15:1-8) and continues the song in Rev 14:3.

before them and the people tell Joshua that wherever he will send them, they will follow. There is a loyalty pledge that they will obey the commandments of God and kill those that do not.

John makes the Lamb/Jesus into the Joshua figure in the DJD, and places him on Mount Zion instead of Mount Nebo. John will continue the song of Moses from the previous section, but refer to it as a song that no one knows except the 144,000.[22] The people are described as following the Lamb wherever they go and that they have committed no sins.

Since we are going backwards in the ZrD and forwards in the content from Deuteronomy and Joshua that John selected, this section will be revised and redefined. The 144,000 represent a conflation of those from Ezekiel which had their forehead marked, and those who were circumcised when the Israelites crossed the Jordan River. Therefore, the 144,000 could only be males, but it should be noted that there are no females mentioned in Revelation in a positive light. The woman found in Revelation 12 represents the righteous element of Jerusalem versus the unrighteous element of Jerusalem known as the harlot.

The Sending of the Two Spies Into Jericho/Jerusalem

As we continue along in Joshua, the story picks up when Joshua sends two spies into Jericho where they bed for the night in Rahab's house. The king of Jericho found out about the two spies and sought after them. The two spies hid from the king with Rahab's help, and at nightfall they took flight to the mountains and hid there for three days.

For John, integrating the story of the two spies was simple. John already had the two prophets from the ZrD and they were in the perfect place.[23] All John needed to do was to change two lines of text. The first was to change the text from the EID, "they kill the souls that should not die" to "the two prophets were killed by the king of the abyss,"[24] thus forming an opposite to the story of the two spies. The second was to add in the line "the two prophets laid dead in the streets for three days" in contrast to "the two spies hiding in the mountains for three days." Both accounts agree with the storyline that their returning to the saints' camp started the Israelites to cross the Jordan River. The difference was that the two spies walked on their own two feet and the two prophets were resurrected and taken to heaven.[25]

The Crossing of the Jordan River

How John implements the crossing of the Jordan River, the circumcision of those who were born in the wilderness, and the passover meal, will explain how many of the features of Revelation are constructed. Since John is editing the ZrD backwards as he imports content forward in Joshua, he is looking for opportunities and ease of inserting the material. Therefore, he prefers to insert a new wax tablet between the wax tablets instead of rewriting the wax tablets. He also will move content from the edges of the wax tablets

---

22   Deut 34:1-12; Josh 1:1-18; Rev 14:1-5.
23   Rev 11:1-11. See "How John Modified the Two Prophets as the Two Spies" on page 141.
24   Rev 11:7 has "the beast from the abyss" which was in the DJD the "king from the abyss" (see Rev 9:11 "they have over them as king the angel of the abyss" which is Satan (Rev 20:1-3)).
25   Josh 6:22; Rev 11:11-2.

How John Modified the Two Prophets as the Two Spies

The table below shows the two prophets' section of the Zechariah-encoded parallel and what John had to do to make the two prophets' imagery conform with the two spies sent to Jericho. The result was that a small amount of text was erased, and details of the two prophets being killed by the king of the abyss instead of the King of Jericho was inserted.

	Content Found in the DJD Material		Content Found in Revelation (Ordered by)
			Measuring the Temple (Rev 11:1-2)
Zech 2:1	I lifted up my eyes, and saw, and behold, a man with a measuring line in his hand.	11:1	A reed like a rod was given to me.
Zech 2:2	He said to me, "To measure Jerusalem, to see what is its width and what is its length."	11:1	Someone said, "Rise, and measure God's temple, and the altar, and those who worship in it.
Ezek 10:1-22	The state of the temple before the glory of THE LORD flees.		
Zech 2:4	[He] said to him, "Run, speak to this young man, saying, 'Jerusalem will be inhabited as villages without walls.'"	11:2	Leave out the court which is outside of the temple, and don't measure it,
Ezek 10:1-22	The state of the temple before the glory of THE LORD flees.		
Zech 2:4	because of the multitude of men and livestock in it.	11:2	for it has been given to the nations. They will tread the holy city underfoot.
Ezek 4:5	Ezekiel laid on his left side for 390 days. Each day represents one year Israel sinned against God.	11:2	The temple courtyard will be trampled by the gentiles for 42 months, representing the 420 years that the temple been controlled by the Gentiles.
			The Two Prophets (Rev 11:32-13)
Ezek 4:6	Ezekiel laid on his right side for 40 days. Each day equals one year Judah sinned against God.	11:3	The two witnesses shall testify for 1,260 days. Representing 1,260 years from the crossing of the Jordan River to the death of Jesus.
Zech 3:3	Now Joshua was clothed with filthy garments.	11:3	my two witnesses . . . clothed in sackcloth.
Zech 4:11	"What are these two olive trees on the right side of the lamp stand and on the left side of it?"	11:4	These are the two olive trees and the two lamp stands,
Zech 4:12	"What are these two olive branches, which are beside the two golden spouts, that pour the golden oil out of themselves?"		
Zech 4:14	"These are the two anointed ones who stand by THE LORD of the whole earth."	11:4	standing before THE LORD of the earth.
Ezek 13:19	~~They kill the souls that should not die.~~	11:7	When [the two prophets] finished their testimony the king of the abyss killed them.
Josh 2:2-3	The king of Jericho [wanted them]		
Ezek 4:8	The sum of the days in Ezek 4:5-6 equals how long the siege of Jerusalem would last.	11:9	The two prophets laid dead in the street for 3½ days with each day representing one year of the siege of Jerusalem in 67-70 CE. [No change made by John in the DJD.]
Josh 2:22-3	The two spies hid in the mountains for three days.		
Ezek 13:18	The women sew pillows and make kerchiefs for those who hunt souls.	11:10	Those who dwell on the earth rejoiced over the death of the two prophets. They gave gifts to one another.
Ezek 13:19	They give handfuls of barley and pieces of bread to kill souls.		
Ezek 13:23	God will deliver his people out of their hand.	11:12	God breathed life into the two prophets.
Ezek 10:1-22	The glory of God left the temple.	11:13	The two prophets were taken to heaven in front of their enemies.
Josh 2:23-4	The two prophets returned to Joshua's camp.	14:1-5	The original camp of the saints. [No change by John].
Ezek 13:23	You will see no more false visions nor practice divination.	11:13	The rest were terrified and gave glory to God.
Ezek 10:1-22	The glory of God left the temple.	11:17	The temple is in heaven.

that touch the blank wax tablets being inserted. Nothing illustrates this methodology of John better than how John integrates the crossing of the Jordan to the first Passover meal in the promised land.

As with every time that John has the source text to import and the previous draft in front of him, he needs to decide where to insert the material. We have seen many times that he finds something that begins the alignment process and then builds from there. In the case of the Jordan River crossing, John focused on the material between the wax tablet containing the four winds and the wax tablet containing the mighty angel and the seven thunders.[26]

He decided first to make the mighty angel perform the priestly duty of placing one foot in the water and the other foot on land, simulating the priests crossing the Jordan River.[27] He then moved the entire wax tablet (or a major portion of it) which contained a description of the saints crossing the Euphrates River.[28] He then moved the content pertaining to the saints' crossing and placed it on a new wax tablet.

The Circumcision of Those Born in the Wilderness

With the crossing of the river behind him, John needed to handle the portion that dealt with the circumcision of those who were born in the wilderness. John once again decided that it would be best to place the story of the circumcision on a new wax tablet and insert it between the four chariots/first four seals and the four winds/first four trumpets.[29] In the published version of Revelation, this will become the sealing of the 144,000 (12,000 from each of the twelve tribes) on earth. The major difference is that in Joshua they were circumcised, while in Revelation they receive the seal of God on their foreheads. The difference has to do with Rev 9:4 where those with the mark of God on their forehead are protected. However, the sealing of the forehead could have been changed later as part of a parallel formation which we will discuss later in this chapter.

The First Passover Meal in the Promised Land

John continued the narrative from Joshua of the first Passover meal and appended it to the wax tablet that contained the sealing of the 144,000. It was a few lines of text whereas Jesus is depicted as the Lamb and the believers celebrate Passover without Passover being mentioned. This is probably due to the realization that John cannot depict Jesus as the Lamb if there was also mentioned of a meal where lamb was served.

John also has the gentiles in the promised land as opposed to the Jews who were circumcised. John is depicting many things in the imagery of the two passages together. The first is that he, in just a few paragraphs, describes the sum of all believers from the crossing of the Jordan River to the final resting place of

---

26   See "Z4 - Various Judgments That Were Appended to the Four Winds" on page 113 and "Z6 - The Flying Scroll Alteration" on page 116 to see how the wax tablets were laid out, before John changed the mighty angel to have one foot in the sea and the other on land. Also note that the portion of the wax tablet containing Revelation 18:21-4 was moved to a later place in the ZrD. Therefore the flying scroll wax tablet containing the mighty angel was the upper portion seen in "The Flying Scroll Alteration (Z6)."

27   Josh 4:15-8; Rev 10:1-2 for the mighty angel with a foot on land and a foot in the water. Rev 9:13-5; 16:12 (as a parallel) for the Euphrates River drying up.

28   See "Z9 - The Zechariah Draft Version of the Second Coming (Part 3a)" on page 126 and "Z9 - The Zechariah Draft Version of the Second Coming (Part 3b)" on page 127 on what the wax tablet probably looked like. Note that the section containing the description of Jesus in the second coming was either not part of the wax tablet or was removed from the wax tablet sometime in the ZrD or DJD process.

29   See "Inserting Between the Wax Tablets" on page 144.

all believers in heaven. He does this by depicting the two groups; the Jews which are the first fruits,[30] and the next generation of believers who follow the commandments of God and serve the Lamb.[31]

The Commander of the Lord's Army

The next noticeable text that John imports from Joshua into the ZrD is Joshua's encounter with the commander of the Lord's army. In this encounter, Joshua confronts a man and after a few questions, finds out that he is talking to the commander of the Lord's army. In a scene reminiscent of the burning bush scene from Exodus (but backwards), Joshua finds out the place is holy and so removes his shoes.[32]

The Lion From the Tribe of Judah

John does something different when incorporating the commander of the Lord's army into the ZrD. Instead of the Lamb imitating the actions of Joshua, John has the Lamb imitating the actions of the commander of the Lord's army. The difference is that although Joshua is the one who leads the Israelites into battle in Joshua; the scene imported into the ZrD is the commander of the Lord's army. First, John introduces Jesus with a title worthy of the commander of the Lord's army. He is called the Lion who is of the tribe of Judah to contrast the Lamb imagery of being sacrificed.[33]

It is important to note that this was the furthest that John imported the selected Deuteronomy-Joshua material into the ZrD. It is also the first place in Revelation where we encounter John's use of the synonym "the Lamb" for Jesus. As we have discussed earlier, John consistently uses "Lamb" when importing material from Deuteronomy-Joshua and therefore it is the most preferred synonym of Jesus used in the DJD.

The Worship Scene of Jesus

John includes a similar worship scene that Joshua had with the commander of the Lord's army by appending various imagery of people worshiping the Lamb and falling before him. The imagery must have been simple; what we have today is primarily derived after the parallel development performed later in the DJD and the imagery added in the DnD.

The worship scene is also in the same area that the EID would have placed it. If it survived to the DJD then it would have been an alignment point for Joshua. If it was moved from this section, John would have probably remembered that this is where it would have been. Either way, the DJD improved on the worship scene of Jesus.

John's First Deuteronomy-Joshua Draft Dilemma

As we have seen in the EID and the ZrD, John had a few issues trying to conform the text of the previous draft with the pattern that he is applying the source material to. In the EID, John had to realign a few texts to merge content and limit the complete destruction of Egypt from three times to one time.[34] In the ZrD,

---

30 Rev 14:4.
31 Rev 12:17.
32 Exod 3:5; Josh 5:15.
33 Rev 5:5-10.
34 See "John's First Major Content Alignment Corrections" on page 22.

Inserting Between the Wax Tablets

John created the DJD by starting at the end of the ZrD and integrating Deuteronomy 29:1 to Joshua 5:13 backwards. From there John integrated Joshua 6:1-27 forwards into the ZrD as shown below. The solid boxes represents the text (wax tablets) from the ZrD and the dashed line boxes represents the wax tablets John inserted and in the order that he inserted them (DJ1 being the first). The two dashed line boxes that contain two items (DJ6 and DJ7, DJ5 and DJ8) represents one wax tablet in which John added content going backwards in the ZrD and then appended the content to the wax tablet when John went forwards in the ZrD.

Z3 - The Coronation of Jesus the High Priest (Zech 6:9-15; Rev 4:1 - 5:8)

DJ6 - The Commander of the Lord's Army (Josh 5:13-5; Rev 5:9-14)
- Jesus given a title "The Lion who is of the tribe of Judah." (Josh 5:14; Rev 5:5).
- They were in a holy place and all worshiped him. (Josh 5:14-5; Rev 5:8-14).

   DJ7 - The Destruction of Jericho (Josh 6:1 - 8; Rev 6:9-17)
   - Created the seven seals imagery as seven marches around Jericho (Rev 5:1; 6:1-17; 8:1-6).
   - Made existing content into two additional seals (Rev 6:9-17).

Z4.1 - The Four Chariots/First Four Seals (Zech 6:1-8; Rev 6:1-17)

DJ5 - Entering the Promised Land (Josh 4:1 - 5:12; Rev 7:1-17)
- The sealing of the 144,000 on their foreheads in lieu of circumcision (Josh 5:1-8; Rev 7:1-8).
- The passover meal (Josh 5:9-12; Rev 7:9-17).

   DJ8 - The Seventh Day March (Josh 6:1-16; Rev 8:1-6)
   - There was silence (Josh 6:10; Rev 8:1).
   - The seal contained the seven trumpets (Josh 6:10-15; Rev 8:1-2).
   - The four winds became the seven trumpets with angels representing priests (Josh 6:10-6; Rev 8:1-9:21).

Z4.2 - The Four Winds/First Four Trumpets (Zech 6:1-8; Rev 8:7 - 9:11)

DJ4 - Crossing the Jordan River (Josh 3:1-17; Rev 9:13-21)
- The great river Euphrates dried up and an army walks across it (Josh 3:1-17; Rev 9:14; 16:12).
- Added "right foot on the sea, and his left on the land" as the priests carrying the ark and crossing the Jordan (Josh 3:13, 5; Rev 10:2).

Z6 - The Flying Scroll (Zech 5:1-4; Rev 10:1-11)

Z7.1 - The Two Prophets (Zech 2:1 - 4:14; Rev 11:1-12)

   DJ9 - The Destruction of Jericho (Josh 6:11-27; Rev 11:15-9)
   - Modified that the city was destroyed by fire to destroyed by an earthquake to conform with the destruction of Jericho (Josh 6:20; Rev 11:13).
   - The seventh trumpet blown (Josh 6:20; Rev 11:15).
   - Great voices in heaven are heard (Josh 6:20; Rev 11:15).
   - The ark of the covenant is seen (Josh 6:12; Rev 11:18).

Z7.2 - The Woman, the Child, and Satan (Zech 2:1 - 4:14; Rev 11:1-12)

DJ3 - The Allegiance to Joshua (Josh 1:1-18; Rev 14:1-5)
- They followed the Lamb (Josh 1:16; Rev 14:4).
- They obeyed his commandments (Josh 1:16-8; Rev 14:4-5).

Z7.3 - Non-Zechariah Encoded Passage (Zech 2:1 - 4:14; Rev 14:1-20)

DJ2 - The Song of Moses (Deut 31:15-9; Rev 15:1-8)
- Song of Moses and the Lamb (Deut 31:18; Rev 15:3-5).
- God was angry and hid in the tabernacle until the judgments were complete (Deut 31:15-8; Rev 15:6-8).

Z8 - The Four Horns (Zech 1:18-20; Rev 16:1 - 17:18)

Z9 - The Return Home (Zech 1:1-17 ; Rev 18:20 - 22:5)

DJ1 - Follow God or Receive the Curses in This Book (Deut 29:1-28; Rev 22:6-21)
- They have seen all of what God will do (Deut 29:1-5; Rev 22:6).
- Remain faithful and prosper or practice idolatry and fail (Deut 29:9-19; Rev 22:7, 14-5).
- The curses in this book (Deut 29:18-28; Rev 22:18-9).

DJD Starts Here

Left margin: The Final Days of Moses to Joshua Crossing the Jordan River (Deuteronomy 29:18 to Joshua 5:15)

Right margin: The Destruction of Jericho (Joshua 5:13 - 6:27)

John had content from Zechariah that did not fit the content from the EID, so John created the encoded parallel.[35] At this stage of the process, John could have continued the same process of importing the Deuteronomy-Joshua text into the ZrD by continuing to insert the material from Joshua backwards into the ZrD. The ZrD was set up for such a literary task because it began with the message of the two cities—Jerusalem and Rome. Each of the cities had a message to the believers which foretold their destruction, however there was no means of which to incorporate the seven marches around Jericho and the seven marches within the last march.

Therefore, John had two choices, first, he could continue backwards as he had been doing and either create the material needed to simulate Joshua's defeat of Jericho, or somehow incorporate the four horsemen and four trumpets into something similar to Joshua's march around Jericho. His second option was to precede importing the material found in Joshua in a forward action overlaying material that was already written. By doing this he could let both the four horsemen text and the four trumpet text stay where they were located in the ZrD. With modest changes he can tell the story of Joshua and still be satisfied that he is being true to the process of the importation pattern he uses.

The Retelling of the Story of the Conquest of Jericho

John recreated the conquest of Jericho by making a few subtle changes to the text which resulted in major changes to Revelation's storyline. The first thing John needed to decide was what will be the city of Jericho and how to handle the seven marches around the city of Jericho where the seventh march contained seven more marches. John decided that Jerusalem should represent Jericho as told in the city that the two prophets ministered in.[36]

The Recreation of the Seven Days of Marches Around the City of Jericho

One thing we can say with certainty about the DJD, is that John wanted to incorporate the imagery of how God told Joshua to defeat Jericho. We read in just a few verses of Joshua what in Revelation will span for chapters and reshape the ZrD, to one step closer to the PVR.

> **6:2** THE LORD *said to Joshua, "Behold, I have given Jericho into your hand, with its king and the mighty men of valor.* **6:3** *All of your men of war shall march around the city, going around the city once. You shall do this six days.* **6:4** *Seven priests shall bear seven trumpets of rams' horns before the ark. On the seventh day, you shall march around the city seven times, and the priests shall blow the trumpets.* **6:5** *It shall be that when they make a long blast with the ram's horn, and when you hear the sound of the trumpet, all the people shall shout with a great shout; and the city wall shall fall down flat, and the people shall go up, every man straight in front of him."*[37]

To recreate the imagery of the seven days of marches around Jericho, John had to create a literary device to represent the imagery of Joshua's army marching around Jericho. The path that John took was to create seven seals around the scroll and infused the meaning of each seal with the tablet containing the four

---

35 See "Z7 - The Building of the Encoded-Complex Parallel (Zech 2:1 - 4:14; Rev 11:1 - 12:17)" on page 86.

36 John describes the city "where also their Lord was crucified" (Rev 11:8) which definitely referred to Jerusalem.

37 Josh 6:2-5.

How John Recreates Joshua's March on Jericho

Revelation duplicates the basic structure of Joshua's march against Jericho with a few changes. When Joshua marched around the city of Jericho for the first six days there was only the blowing of the trumpets, whereas each seal that Jesus opened contained a judgment. Likewise, on the last day of the march on Jericho, Joshua's army marched around Jericho six times and nothing happened, while in Revelation the angel blowing the trumpet became a judgment. The final blast of the trumpet, however, is shared by both accounts where there is a blast of the trumpet(s), a shout, and the walls came down.

Actions of Joshua's Army

Day	Joshua Performed
1	Marched around Jericho.
2	Marched around Jericho.
3	Marched around Jericho.
4	Marched around Jericho.
5	Marched around Jericho.
6	Marched around Jericho.
7	• Seven priests with seven trumpets (Josh 6:8). • Joshua told to be silent until all the trumpets are blown (Josh 6:10).
1	Marched around Jericho.
2	Marched around Jericho.
3	Marched around Jericho.
4	Marched around Jericho.
5	Marched around Jericho.
6	Marched around Jericho.
7	Marched around Jericho and trumpets blown.

Actions of Jesus in Revelation

Seal	Jesus Performed
1	Opened a seal (Rev 6:1).
2	Opened a seal (Rev 6:3).
3	Opened a seal (Rev 6:5).
4	Opened a seal (Rev 6:7).
5	Opened a seal (Rev 6:9).
6	Opened a seal (Rev 6:12).
7	• Seven angels with seven trumpets (Rev 8:2). • There was a half hour of silence (Rev 8:1).
1	Trumpet Blown (Rev 8:7).
2	Trumpet Blown (Rev 8:8).
3	Trumpet Blown (Rev 8:10).
4	Trumpet Blown (Rev 8:12).
5	Trumpet Blown (Rev 9:1).
6	Trumpet Blown (Rev 9:13).
7	Trumpet Blown (Rev 11:15) and the Ark of the Covenant is shown (Rev 11:19).

horsemen and the judgment scenes connected to them.[38] Each of the horsemen became a seal and the rest of the judgments not used to create the four horsemen became the fifth and sixth seal. The seventh just needed to be a stub containing a statement of seven more things.

At this stage of the DJD, the material used to create the fifth seal was more than what is in the fifth seal today.[39] It is only through parallel formation that the fifth seal lost the material and gained other material. This is to be expected since John will create a whole storyline writing in the horizontal, the fifth church's

---

38   The approximation draft material that John used to create the six seals can be seen in "Z4 - The Four Chariots (Horsemen)/First Four Seals (Part 1)" on page 110 and "Z4 - The Four Chariots (Horsemen)/First Four Seals (Part 2)" on page 111.

39   Rev 6:9-11; See "The Material Appended to the Four Horsemen in the Zechariah Draft" on page 148.

story will continue to the fifth seal, to the fifth trumpet, and to the fifth bowl, with its conclusion found in the destruction of the harlot.[40]

The sixth seal was already well-defined in the ZrD and therefore changed the least in the process of creating the seven seals and seven trumpets. All John had to do was to put a statement that signified that a seal was opened.[41]

Since the creation of the seven seals were the first of the judgments, John will use them as a template for the construction of the seven trumpets and seven bowls. He will assign the first four judgments as individual actions and the fifth judgment as a snapshot of the conditions for the saint and/or the sinner. The fifth seal is the trigger mechanism for the sixth judgment.

The sixth judgment is the story of how the first four judgments are acted upon. In Revelation, the first four seals are the actions that were performed in the sixth seal and likewise the first four trumpets are actions performed in the sixth trumpet. We will see how this unfolds as we peer into the judgments more closely.

The Creation of the Seventh Seal

The creation of the seventh seal was rather simple for John. He already established the mighty angel as a priest by imitating the crossing of the Jordan River. So John kept the imagery by including the angels as priests holding the seven trumpets. John also included the commandment by God to Joshua by keeping everyone silent until the trumpets are blown.[42] The result is that the seventh seal begins with the following text:

> *When he opened the seventh seal, there was silence in heaven for about half an hour. I saw the seven angels who stand before God, and seven trumpets were given to them.*[43]

At this point, John just needed to make minor changes so that each of the four winds became a blast of a trumpet.

The Creation of the Fifth and Sixth Trumpets

The creation of the fifth and sixth trumpets is an example of how John uses language like any modern writer with a word processor would, except in John's case he used a wax tablet. The fifth and sixth trumpets' formation is better seen than explained, and therefore the reader is encouraged to see how John moved around the text in the illustrations found on page 150 and page 151.

---

40   In the fifth church, Jesus tells the parishioners that they are dead, asleep, and need to wake up and keep the commandments (Rev 3:2-3). In the fifth seal, the saints who are martyred come from beneath the throne of God in heaven and because they kept the commandments they can rest (Rev 6:9-11). The saints in the fifth seal are pleading with Jesus to avenge their deaths on earth (Rev 6:10-1). The fifth trumpet has the unfaithful on earth in agony, desiring death (Rev 9:5,10). With the fifth bowl, the sinners are found above the beast's throne on earth and are suffering in severe agony, and they blaspheme God in heaven (Rev 16:10-1). The finality of the story is when the saints are in heaven witnessing God destroy the harlot and thereby avenging them (Rev 19:1-8) and Jesus defeating the beast's army (Rev 19:11-21).

41   See "The Material Appended to the Four Horsemen in the Zechariah Draft" on page 148.

42   Josh 6:10.

43   Rev 8:1-2.

The Material Appended to the Four Horsemen in the Zechariah Draft
Source Material for the Fifth and Sixth Seal

As part of the construction of the four chariots (horsemen), John also took the remaining content (which was probably part of a wax tablet) and appended it to the newly constructed four horsemen. These two sections (God's people receive evil decrees and the day of the Lord) as well as the four horsemen, are now referred to as the sixth seals in Revelation.

God's People Receive Evil Decrees (Isa 10:1-19)		The Fifth Seal (Rev 6:9-11) Also the Church of Smyrna (Rev 2:8-11)	
Isa 10:1	Woe to those who decree unrighteous decrees (Jacob/Israel; see 9:8), and those who write oppressive decrees.	2:9	"I know your works, oppression, and your poverty (but you are rich), and the blasphemy of those who say they are Jews, and they are not, but are a synagogue of Satan.
Isa 10:2	To deprive the needy from justice, and to rob the poor among my people of their rights.		
Isa 10:4	They will only bow down under the prisoners, and will fall under the slain.	2:10	The devil is about to throw some of you into prison, that you may be tested. Be faithful to death.
	For all this his anger is not turned away, but his hand is stretched out still.	13:10	If anyone is to go into captivity, he will go into captivity. If anyone is to be killed with the sword, he must be killed.
		6:9	Under the throne of God are the people who were martyred by keeping the commandments.
Isa 10:15-9	God will destroy those who try to deceive God's people, illustrated in the burning of all the thorns, briers, and most of the trees.	7:3	Do not harm the trees until all are sealed.
		9:4-7	In the fifth trumpet those with the seal of God on their foreheads as well as the trees and the green grass will not be harmed. The rest will be in torment for five months.
		8:7	One third of the trees were burned up, and all green grass was burned up.
		6:10	Those who martyred the saints will be avenged.
Isa 10:20	God's people will continue to lean on God.	2:9	Be faithful to death.
		6:9	Under the altar of God were the martyrs of the faithful.
		6:11	They were given a white robe and told to rest.

The Day of the Lord (Isa 13:9-10; Ezek 32:7-10)		The Sixth Seal (Rev 6:12-7)	
Isa 13:10 Joel 2:10	The sun will be darkened . . . the moon will . . . not shine.	6:12	The sun became black as sackcloth made of hair and the moon became as blood.
Ezek 32:6	I will also water with your blood.		
Ezek 32:7	The stars withdraw from shining.		
Ezek 32:7	The moon shall not give its light.		
Ezek 32:8	[I will] make its stars dark.		
Isa 13:10	For the stars of the sky and its constellations will not give their light.	6:13	The stars of the sky fell to the earth.
Isa 13:13	God will make the heavens tremble and the earth will be shaken out of place.	6:14	The sky was removed like a scroll when it is rolled up. Every mountain and island were moved out of their places.
Joel 2:10	The earth quakes before them.	16:20	Every island fled away, and the mountains were not found.
Ezek 32:8	I will cover the heavens.		
Ezek 32:10	Their kings shall be horribly afraid for you.	6:15	The kings of the earth, the princes, the commanding officers, the rich, the strong, and every slave and free person.
Ezek 32:10	They shall tremble at every moment, every man for his own life, in the day of your fall.	6:15	[They] hid themselves in the caves and in the rocks of the mountains.
Isa 13:14-22	They will flee to their own lands.		

The Seventh Trumpet: How and Why it Was Placed

The placement of the seventh trumpet came about by many converging factors. There is the association between Joshua's destruction of Jericho and Jesus' destruction of Jerusalem. In both cases, it brought about the ushering of God's people to a new kingdom. For Joshua's defeat of Jericho, it became the first conquest that secured the nation of Israel and for the destruction of Jerusalem it transitioned the kingdom of the world to the kingdom of God.[44]

There is a chronological order that John must account for—he must have the destruction of Jerusalem placed after the death and resurrection of Jesus. Since the two prophets in the ZrD were a depiction of Jesus, John had to place the blowing of the seventh trumpet after the two prophets' death, resurrection, and ascension.[45] Likewise, he also has to account for the chronological order of Jericho. For example, in an earlier modification of the DJD, John conflated the ZrD's depiction of the two prophets with the two spies Joshua sent into Jericho.[46] Therefore the blowing of the seventh trumpet must be placed after the two prophets' narrative.

He could not place the seventh trumpet imagery inside the story of the woman, child, and Satan because that would interrupt the complex parallel between the four attacks by Satan and the first four trumpets.[47] So the only place he could have placed the seventh trumpet narrative is somewhere between the death, resurrection, and ascension of the two prophets and the woman, child, and Satan narrative.

So John started with a new wax tablet and moved the text from Isaiah (in which if a tenth of the city is burned God would raise up a new seed) and copied it onto the wax tablet.[48] Since he was describing the destruction of Jericho whose walls collapsed upon the priest blowing the horn, John changed the city being destroyed by fire to being destroyed by an earthquake.[49] By placing the earthquake scene first on the wax tablet John began the story to form a complex parallel with the destruction of the city of Jericho.[50] This is why the seventh trumpet is out of order with the story of Joshua and in the ExD we will see how John created two earthquake scenes for the two prophets' and seventh trumpet's narrative.[51]

The Finishing Phase

The placement of the seventh trumpet and the depiction of the destruction of Jerusalem was the last of the Deuteronomy-Joshua material that John imported. The DJD at this point was disjointed in that there were seven seals and seven trumpets but there were only four horns (the ZrD prototype of the seven bowls). The

---

44 Rev 11:15; 12:10.
45 Rev 11:7, 11-2.
46 See "DJ13 - The Two Prophets (Rev 11:1-12)" on page 178.
47 See ."DJ9 - The First Four Trumpets (Rev 8:7-12)" on page 175.
48 To see how the wax tablets were arranged prior to the DJD, see "Z7 - The Zechariah Encoded Parallel: The Two Prophets (Part 2)" on page 118 and "Z7 - The Zechariah Encoded Parallel: Satan's Entry into Revelation (Z7 -- Part 3)" on page 119.
49 Isa 6:10-3; Rev 11:13; Josh 6:20; see "The Final Blast of the Trumpets Told Backwards" on page 154.
50 See "The Final Blast of the Trumpets Told Backwards" on page 154.
51 See "God Coming in the Clouds" on page 198.

The Deuteronomy-Joshua Draft's Version of the Fifth and Sixth Trumpet (Part 1)

Below represents the material that came over with the content John used to form the four winds in the ZrD. In the DJD the four winds become the first four trumpets which was an easy change for John to do. However the text used to form the fifth and sixth trumpet required a few changes. The first was to remove the material that John used to form the sixth seal (Rev 6:14, 17). The second was to move the material that formed the fifth trumpet to be placed above the sixth trumpet.

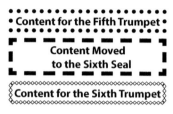

• Content for the Fifth Trumpet •

Content Moved to the Sixth Seal

Content for the Sixth Trumpet

Content Found in Revelation

The Day of the Lord and the Judgment on the Unrighteous (Ezek 7:1-27)

Ezek 7:1	The end has come on the four corners of the land (or earth).	7:1	I saw four angels at the four corners of the earth.
		9:14	Free the four angels who are bound at the great river Euphrates.
Ezek 7:2-8	Various descriptions on how God is angry with them.		
Ezek 7:10	The day . . . it comes and your doom has gone out.	6:17	The great day of his wrath has come; and who is able to stand?
Ezek 7:16	Those who escape shall be on the mountains like doves of the valleys.	6:14	They hid themselves in the caves and in the rocks on the mountains.
Ezek 7:24	The worst nations will posses their houses and their holy places will be profaned.		
Ezek 7:27	The king shall mourn, and the prince shall be clothed in desolation, and the hands of the people of the land shall be troubled.	6:14	The kings of the earth, the princes and everyone else.
Ezek 8:1	In the sixth year, in the sixth month, in the fifth day of the month.	9:15	That hour and day and month and year.

The Fifth Trumpet (Rev 9:1-12)

Ezek 9:3	The glory of the God of Israel was gone up from the cherub, whereupon it was, to the threshold of the house, and he called to the man clothed in linen, who had the writer's inkhorn by his side.		
Ezek 9:4	Go through the middle of Jerusalem and set a mark on the foreheads of the men signed and cried over all the abominations that was done.	9:4	They were told that they should not hurt the grass of the earth, neither any green thing, neither any tree, but only those people who don't have God's seal on their foreheads.
Ezek 2:6*	You, son of man, don't be afraid of them, neither be afraid of their words, though briers and thorns are with you, and you do dwell among scorpions; don't be afraid of their words, nor be dismayed at their looks, though they are a rebellious house.	9:5	They were given power not to kill them, but to torment them for five months. Their torment was like the torment of a scorpion, when it strikes a person.

* See "When Wax Tablets Are Placed Together" on page 85 on how Ezek 9:4 and Ezek 2:6 came together.

The Deuteronomy-Joshua Draft's Version of the Fifth and Sixth Trumpet (Part 2)

The Placement and Content of the Fifth Seal

The content from the ZrD that was used to create the fifth trumpet came from the bottom of the material after the four winds. John simply moved the material up to become the fifth trumpet.

		The Fifth Trumpet (Rev 9:1-12)	
		9:1	The fifth angel sounded.
Ezek 9:4	Go through the middle of Jerusalem and set a mark on the foreheads of the men signed and cried over all the abominations that were done.	9:4	They were told that they should not hurt the grass of the earth, neither any green thing, neither any tree, but only those people who don't have God's seal on their foreheads.
Ezek 2:6	You, son of man, don't be afraid of them, neither be afraid of their words, though briers and thorns are with you, and you do dwell among scorpions; don't be afraid of their words, nor be dismayed at their looks, though they are a rebellious house.	9:5	They were given power not to kill them, but to torment them for five months. Their torment was like the torment of a scorpion, when it strikes a person.

The Placement and Content of the Sixth Trumpet

John created the sixth trumpet with the remaining content from part 1 (on the left page) and inserted a passage from the EID that included a scene very much like the Israelites crossing the Jordan River.

		9:13	The sixth angel sounded . . .
Ezek 7:1	The end has come on the four corners of the land (or earth).	7:1	I saw four angels at the four corners of the earth.
Isa 11:15	His scorching wind he will wave his hand over the river Will cause men to march over in sandals	9:14	Free the four angels who are bound at the great river Euphrates! (See Rev 7:1 where they are the four angels holding back the four winds.)
Isa 11:16	There will be a highway for the remnant that is left of his people from Assyria.		The great river, the Euphrates. Its water was dried up, that the way might be prepared for the kings that come from the sunrise.
Isa 27:12	It will happen in that day, that the Lord will thresh from the flowing stream of the Euphrates to the brook of Egypt; and you will be gathered one by one, children of Israel.		
Ezek 8:1	In the sixth year, in the sixth month, in the fifth day of the month.	9:15	That hour and day and month and year.

DJD provided an epilogue but had no real prologue. For that, John had to change the text outside of the process of how he processed the source material.

Since John is working outside of a process it makes it difficult to follow the same order that John used in creating this portion of the DJD. However, we can explain what he did at various stages and how it affected the development of the DJD.

From the Four Horns to the Seven Bowls

The construction of the seven bowls is a great example of how John used parallels to build its content. As mentioned earlier, the four trumpets and the four horns are synonyms, and although the creation of the four horns/first four bowls were essentially copied from the four winds/first four trumpets in the ZrD,[52] it did not mean that John wanted their names to be a synonym to each other.

We can only guess what the decision-making process was that went into the redefining of the horns to bowls. The reasoning that I follow is that the trumpets also represent a Jewish symbol of the temple and represent the 144,000. The choice of the bowls was made to represent temple items but are also synonymous with the cup of the Lord's supper and the cup of the wrath of God. Both contained or represented the blood of a martyr and faithfulness.

The process of creating the seven bowls was rather straightforward. John first leveraged the song of Moses and the Lamb imagery and made minor tweaks to the text. He then continued the same process he used to create the four winds. He copied or moved the relevant material from the trumpets and changed the word "third" to the word "all." To add spice to the copy, John did two things, first, whatever the trumpet affected the bowl's contents were poured upon. He also interwove the two with an action in the temple ceremony with an action (dumping the censure on the earth) in the ceremony matched with the same imagery in the seventh bowl's contents being dumped on the earth. Likewise, in the ceremony where the bowls were launched, the temple is shut until all judgments are completed and we see the temple open at the end of the seventh trumpet.[53]

The Creation of the Alpha and Omega Parallel

The alpha and omega parallel was initially created by John trying to form parallels with three sections of the DJD; the Gog and Magog narrative; the New Jerusalem narrative; and the epilogue. We know this by the abundance of common content between all three of the sections as well as common content unique to any two of the sections. As a result of the parallel formation John created the earliest prototype of the alpha and omega parallel.[54] At one point in time during the process, John needed more names for God and thus he created two synonyms to "the first and last" from Isaiah 44:6, the first being "the alpha and omega," and the second being "the beginning and end."

Later in the process, John needed to create a prologue to Revelation that would match the size of the epilogue. The best solution to bulking up the ZrD prologue was to form a parallel with the epilogue. In that parallel John had three primary speakers: the first was God; the second was Jesus; and the third was an angel.[55]

John is in full parallel-building mode and as such he formed a parallel with the prologue and the messages to the DJD's prototype of the seven churches. He began each letter with a description of God saying some-

---

52   See "Z8 - The Creation and Placement of the Four Horns/First Four Bowls (Zech 1:18-21; Rev 16:1-9)" on page 92.
53   See "The Structure and Content of the Seven Trumpets and the Seven Bowls" on page 307 which contains all illustrations stated in this paragraph.
54   See "The Alpha Version of the Alpha and Omega Parallel" on page 156.
55   Rev 1:1; to see how John formed the parallel between the prologue and epilogue see "DJ1 - The Prologue (Rev 1:1-20)" on page 167 and "DJ24 - The Epilogue (Rev 22:6-21)" on page 166.

Retaining Symmetry With the Seals and the Trumpets in Revelation

The chart below shows how John aligned and grouped the seven seals with the seven trumpets. The three woes, for example, divided the trumpets into three groups. The first group is the first four trumpets which John wanted the reader to see as a group the same way the reader would naturally see the four horsemen as a group.

John also formed a break or intermission between the sixth and seventh seal and the sixth and seventh trumpet. Both intermissions have a sealing or sending portion for one set of believers and a martyrdom portion where the group is in heaven.

Actions of Joshua's Army	**Actions of Jesus in Revelation**
Seven Seals	***Seven Trumpets***
The First Seal/Horseman (Rev 6:1-2).	First Trumpet (Rev 8:6-7).
The Second Seal/Horseman (Rev 6:3-4).	Second Trumpet (Rev 8:8-9).
The Third Seal/Horseman (Rev 6:5-6).	Third Trumpet (Rev 8:10-1).
The Fourth Seal/Horseman (Rev 6:7-8).	Fourth Trumpet (Rev 8:12-3).
	First Woe (Rev 8:13)
The Fifth Seal (Rev 6:9-11)	**Fifth Trumpet (Rev 9:1-11)**
• The saints are martyred (Rev 6:9).	• The unfaithful wished they were dead (Rev 9:6).
• They are given a robe (Rev 6:11).	• They were given a scorpion sting (Rev 9:5, 10).
• They are told that they have to rest until the number is complete (Rev 6:11).	• They were in agony for five months (Rev 9:5).
	Second Woe (Rev 9:12)
The Sixth Seal (Rev 6:12-7)	**Sixth Trumpet (Rev 9:13-21)**
• The kings and mighty men hid themselves in the mountains from God and the Lamb (Rev 6:15-7).	• A large army that came from the kings of the world are gathered for the day of God (Rev 16:12-4).
Intermission	***Intermission***
144,000 on Earth (Rev 7:1-8)	**John Sent (10:1-11)**
• A loud angel gives the seal of God (Rev 7:1).	• A loud angel gives John the scroll to eat (10:3).
• Until all receive the mark on their forehead (Rev 7:3).	• Until the voice of the seventh angel (10:7).
Great Multitude in Heaven (Rev 7:9-17)	**The Two Prophets on Earth (11:1-12)**
• They were martyrs (7:14).	• They were killed (11:7).
• They are in heaven (7:15).	• They were taken to heaven (11:12).
	The Third Woe (Rev 11:14)
The Seventh Seal (Rev 8:1-6)	**The Seventh Trumpet (Rev 11:14-9)**
• Begins in silence (Josh 6:10; 8:1).	• Begins with a trumpet and a great voice in heaven [spoke] (Josh 6:16; Rev 11:15).

The Final Blast of the Trumpets Told Backwards

John created the seventh seal by leveraging a complex parallel found in Joshua 6:20, and then forming a complex parallel with the content. The first illustration below shows that the ark of the covenant is mentioned in the first half of the chapter, prior to the walls collapsing and how John could have used the complex parallel to form the order of the items, to create a complex parallel in Revelation.

The Selection From Joshua	How John Constructed the Complex Parallel
The Ark of the Covenant	
The Ark of the Covenant mentioned prior to Josh 6:20 (Josh 6:4-12).	A. The Ark of the Covenant (not used after Josh 6:12)
	B. The people shouted (Josh 6:20).
The Complex Parallel in Joshua 6:20	C. The priests blew the trumpets (Josh 6:20).
A. The people shouted.	D. The wall fell down flat (Josh 6:20).
B. The priests blew the trumpets.	D′. Severe earthquake and a tenth of the city fell (Rev 11:13).
B′. ~~When the people heard the sound of the trumpet.~~	C′. The angel blew the seventh trumpet (Rev 11:15).
A′. ~~The people shouted with a great shout.~~	B′. Great voices in heaven followed (Rev 11:15).
The Last Part of Joshua 6:20	A′. The ark of the covenant was seen (Rev 11:19).
The wall fell down flat.	

The table below shows how John incorporated the story of Joshua (the seventh trumpet) into Revelation. Note how John transformed the EID rendition of Isaiah 6:10-3 from the burning of the city to an earthquake. This is an example of how John changes imagery when a new source requires it.

From Isaiah and Joshua		In Revelation (Ordered by)	
Isa 6:10-3	An illustration that even if the oak tree is burned (believers) and a tenth of the city is burned, a new crop of believers will be sprouted from the acorns.	11:13	In that day there was a great earthquake, and a tenth of the city fell. Seven thousand people were killed in the earthquake, and the rest were terrified, and gave glory to the God of heaven.
Josh 6:20	The wall fell down flat.		
		11:14	The second woe is past. Behold, the third woe comes quickly.
Josh 6:20	The priests blew the trumpets.	11:15	The seventh angel sounded,
Josh 6:20	The people shouted.		and great voices in heaven followed, saying, "The kingdom of the world has become the kingdom of our Lord, and of his Christ. He will reign forever and ever!"
Josh 6:4-12	The ark of the covenant is mentioned.	11:19	The ark of the covenant is seen.

thing and a description of Jesus performing an act of redemption. It was probably at this point where John created the two synonyms: the alpha and omega; and the beginning and end.

When John was done with the alpha and omega formation, it was likely close to perfect. That soon changed when John added in the ExD and the DnD though. Those two actions will forever alter the three alpha and omega parallels to the point that no two parallels agree with each other. Additionally, one is incoherent to the point that a reader disconnected from the other two would not be able to tell if it is the angel or Jesus that declares himself as the alpha and omega.[56] Why and how the alpha and omega parallel

---

56   Rev 22:6-16.

became malformed will be answered in the next two chapters[57] but what we can ascertain is that the alpha and omega parallel was not as important as many other parallels that John formed. One possibility is that he thought he would have time to realign the three, but either never had the time or simply forgot. Every writer experiences moments like this, so it is not a statement to belittle his literary skills, but more of a shared experience of all writers.

The Beginning of the Beatitudes

The beatitudes began with the formation of the alpha and omega parallel but it took a different route than the alpha and omega parallel did. This illustrates how parallels may be formed in a draft and how other actions in the construction process distorts a perfect parallel. The beatitudes began with the construction of the epilogue in the DJD where John reduced seven verses, explaining that those who keep the commandments of God will prosper[58] into a beatitude and adding the ultimate prize in Revelation—living in the New Jerusalem.[59] This gave us the following beatitude:

> *Blessed are those who do his commandments, that they may have the right to the tree of life, and may enter in by the gates into the city.*[60]

John, through the process of parallel formation, combined the imagery of the beatitude with the reward for those listening to the book. Unfortunately, the bulk of the beatitude was overwritten by the next two drafts that John did (ExD and DnD material grayed out). However we can still see that it had a similar concept to the original beatitude:

> ***Blessed*** and holy is he who has part in the first resurrection. Over these, the second death has no power, but they will be priests of God and of Christ, and *will reign with him one thousand years.*[61]

He then made another parallel between the epilogue and prologue which is very similar to the epilogue's version, plus the reward from the church in Ephesus:

> *Blessed is he who reads and those who hear the words of the prophecy, and keep the things that are written in it, for the time is at hand. I will give to eat from the tree of life, which is in the paradise of my God.*[62]

John will eventually make seven beatitudes. Each of the beatitudes are in themselves a complete literary structure that will be strategically placed but awkwardly blended into the passage. This gives the reader a feeling that they were plopped down into the manuscript.[63] In reality, many of them were made because of a parallel formation, but the parallel is not as apparent as in the case of the Gog and Magog and epi-

---

57   See "Transitioning From the Deuteronomy-Joshua Draft to the Exodus Draft" on page 201 Citations to the ExD and the DnD.

58   Deut 29:9-16.

59   The chart "The Alpha Version of the Alpha and Omega Parallel" on page 156 shows how John laid out the material discussed in this section.

60   Rev 22:14.

61   Rev 20:6; see "The Alpha Version of the Alpha and Omega Parallel" on page 156.

62   Rev 1:3; 2:6 were originally combined but were later separated. To view how the original beatitude was formed see the following two charts: "DJ24 - The Epilogue (Rev 22:6-21)" on page 166 and "DJ1 - The Prologue (Rev 1:1-20)" on page 167.

63   Rev 1:3; 14:13; 16:15; 19:6; 20:6; 22:7, 14.

The Alpha Version of the Alpha and Omega Parallel

The chart below represents the common content found in at least two out of the three sections from the DJD's version of the Gog and Magog, New Jerusalem, and epilogue narratives. Each of the three sections has a book, a section of writing, a statement against idolatry, and a place for those who follow God and those who follow idols. As a result of parallel formation, each of the three sections contributed to the construction of the alpha and omega parallel. The Gog and Magog section contributed the statement that "God is the true witness" by pointing out that he is the only one that can tell these things (Deut 30:12-3; Rev 1:1). The DJD's version of the New Jerusalem narrative added that the unbelievers are permanently expelled from New Jerusalem (Ezek 43:7-11; Deut 29:17-9; Rev 22:15).

The epilogue most likely added the Isaiah 46:3, 6 content to make a case against idolatry and to provide Jesus, who is a non-foreigner, to take his people to a land of living water. At some point in the insertion of Isa 44:6 John needed to increase the number of names for God and decided to create two synonyms to "the first and the last." The first was "the alpha and the omega" which are the first and last letters of the Greek alphabet and the second was "the beginning and end."

DJD Gog and Magog		New Jerusalem		DJD Epilogue	
Isa 29:18-9	The blind, deaf, and poor will hear the words of the book.	Rev 21:5	God says write these words.	Rev 22:6-10	Publish this book.
				Deut 29:1-5	The people have seen everything in this book.
Deut 30:12	Who will come from heaven and tell you?	Rev 21:5	God's words are faithful and true.	Rev 22:6	God's words are true and faithful.
Deut 30:13	Who will return from beyond the sea and tell you?		[All information in Revelation is provided by God (Rev 1:1). Therefore the story told in Revelation is literally "God's testimony."]		
Rev 20:4-6	The righteous that were raised from the dead came from heaven (Rev 6:9-11).				
Rev 20:13	The unrighteous that were raised came from the sea.				
Deut 30:11	The commandment is not too distant.	Rev 21:6	It is done.	Rev 22:7	I come quickly.
		Rev 21:6	The alpha and omega.	Rev 22:13	The alpha and omega (synonym).
			[Not found]	Isa 44:6	The first and the last (Rev 22:13).
		Rev 21:6	The beginning and the end	Rev 22:13	The beginning and the end (synonym).
Rev 20:4-6	Blessed are those who obeyed the book.	Rev 21:6	God will give water to him who is thirsty.	Rev 22:14	Blessed are those who do his commandments, that they may have the right to the tree of life, and may enter in by the gates into the city.
Rev 20:7-11	They lived in Jerusalem and are protected by God.	Rev 22:7	He who overcomes, I will give him these things.... [the rest of the context tells about the New Jerusalem and its wealth].		
Isa 29:6	The blind, deaf, and poor will hear the words of the book.			Rev 22:17	Jesus give water to him who is thirsty.
				Deut 29:9-16	Those who obey the commandments of God will prosper.
Deut 30:1-10	God will gather those who obeyed his commandments.			Isa 44:3	Jesus will give water to him who is thirsty.
Deut 30:15	Life and prosperity.			Deut 29:17-9	A foreigner will deceive the people and cause the land to become barren.
Isa 29:20-1	The book will be the context in which the unrighteous are destroyed.	Rev 22:15	Outside are the dogs, the sorcerers, the sexually immoral, the murderers, the idolaters, and everyone who loves and practices falsehood.	Deut 29:17-9	God will not pardon those who practice idolatry.
Deut 30:16-9	If they turn away from God, he will denounce them.	Ezek 43:7-11	Those who defile God cannot enter the city of God.		

The Omega Version of the Alpha and Omega Parallel

Below represents what the final product of the alpha and omega parallel looks like in the PVR. As we can see, no two parallels agree and much of the content found in the New Jerusalem and Epilogue parallels have drifted into the letters to the seven churches. We can also see how later drafts altered the parallel (designated as ExD, DnD).

The Prologue & Seven Churches		New Jerusalem		Epilogue	
		21:5	He who sits on the throne spoke.	22:6	The angel spoke.
1:4	God and his throne.	21:5	God and his throne.	22:3	God and his throne.
1:5 3:21	Jesus. Jesus has a throne.			22:3	Jesus and his throne.
1:5	Faithful and true (also in 3:14).	21:5	Faithful and true.	22:6	Faithful and true.
1:7	He is coming in the clouds.	21:6	It is done.	22:12	Behold I come quickly.
	Various rewards in the seven churches.			22:12	My reward is with me, to repay to each man according to his work.
1:8	Alpha and omega.	21:6	Alpha and omega.	22:13	Alpha and omega.
1:8	Who was, who is and who is to come [ExD, see page 192].				
1:17	First and last (also in 2:8).				First and the last.
		21:6	The beginning and end.		The beginning and end.
2:7	To him who overcomes.	21:7	He who overcomes.	22:14	Keeps commandments.
2:7	He may eat from the tree of life.	21:6	He may freely drink from the spring of the water of life.	22:1	River of life flowing from the throne of God.
				22:2	Tree of life on the bank of the river of life.
				22:14	May eat from the tree of life.
				22:17	He who is thirsty, let him come. He who desires, let him take the water of life freely.
	The sinners are: • Those who kill believers (2:10). • The sexually immoral (2:14, 20). • The idolaters (2:14, 20). • The liars (2:2; 3:9).	21:8	The sinners are: • The cowardly [DnD]. • The unbelieving [DnD]. • The sinners [DnD]. • The abominable {DnD}. • The murderers. • The sexually immoral. • The sorcerers. • The idolaters. • All liars.	22:15	The sinners are: • The murderers. • The sexually immoral. • The sorcerers. • The idolaters. • Everyone who lives and practices falsehood.
2:11	The faithful will not be harmed by the second death [DnD, page 213].	21:8	They will go to the lake of fire [DnD, see page 213].	22:15	They will not be allowed to enter into the New Jerusalem.
	Descriptions: • Descriptions of the root and shoot of Jesse. • Jesus as the bright and morning star.			22:16	Jesus is: • The root and offspring of David. • The bright and morning star.

logue narratives we already discussed (while others are obvious, such as the two angels that John worships in Revelation).[64]

The Prologue and Epilogue

The ZrD prologue was sparse in content[65] and the DJD's epilogue was many times its size. The two had no continuity of message and it made the DJD appear unbalanced. John opted to fix the problem by forming a simple parallel between the prologue and the epilogue, so he lined up the two wax tablets and made tweaks from one side to the other until the epilogue and prologue agreed.[66]

The DJD's prototype of the prologue and epilogue had three primary speakers, and when they spoke, their voice was that of a trumpet. We know this for several reasons, such as the chain of custody found in the first verse of the PVR where the vision is created by God who gave it to Jesus and he gave it to an angel and finally it was given to John. Since we have the three speaking in the prologue, it is likely that they were speaking in the order that the first verse of Revelation portrays. We also have the ambiguity of the first author's notation John created in Revelation. In the PVR, John has the angel speak to him with a voice like a trumpet and the conversation picks up again when John is taken to heaven.[67] It is the second part of the author's notation where John describes the voice not in terms of who was speaking, but in terms that it was the first that sounded like a trumpet.[68] He could have easily said that it was the angel but he left it generic and thus we have the only time in Revelation where an author's notation is non-specific. A more likely scenario is that he had each of them speak like a trumpet and just erased the first one.

The last clue is in comparing all three of the alpha and omega parallels and reverse engineering the drafts.[69] We find that the order of two of the three parallels begin with God speaking and declaring himself as the alpha and omega.[70] The third parallel has an angel doing the speaking, but it is likely the event of a parallel formation with the first angel John worships in the second coming narrative.[71] Because of the parallel formation the reader can easily conclude that the angel is also the "alpha and omega, the first and the last, and the beginning and end."[72]

What is important to note, is that John did not bring the three speakers found in the prologue and epilogue to the New Jerusalem's alpha and omega parallel. This is an example of how in a single draft he did not always refresh a parallel. What it means is that it was likely perfect at one time but the process demands too much attention for it to be perfect in all phases of the construction of a draft or even book.

---

64   See "The Alpha Version of the Alpha and Omega Parallel" on page 156 and "How John Worshiped the Second Angel" on page 223.

65   See "Z1 - The Zechariah Draft Prologue" on page 102.

66   To see how John aligned the content in the epilogue and prologue see "DJ24 - The Epilogue (Rev 22:6-21)" on page 166 and "DJ1 - The Prologue (Rev 1:1-20)" on page 167.

67   Rev 1:10; 4:1.

68   Rev 4:1.

69   See "The Omega Version of the Alpha and Omega Parallel" on page 157

70   Rev 1:8, 21:6.

71   Rev 22:13.

72   If one just reads Rev 22:6-21, the structure and flow of the epilogue gives the reader the sense that the angel is speaking when claiming to be the alpha and omega, and not Jesus or God.

The Prologue, the Seven Churches and the Epilogue

John continues to build content through parallel building and parallel hopping. He uses the prologue to form the descriptive sayings of God prior to the "Thus says the Lord" passages that God instructed Ezekiel to say in the first draft of Revelation.[73] Most likely, the phrases "the true and faithful witness," "the alpha and omega," "the first and the last," and "the beginning and the end" were all used in the salutation found in the DJD's prototype of the letters to the seven churches with only two surviving today.[74] John also had three descriptions of Jesus which he used in constructing the DJD's prototype to the seven churches and then made it to the prologue and finally the epilogue where it survived in the PVR:

> *I, Jesus, have sent my angel to testify these things to you for the assemblies.*
> *I am the root and the offspring of David;*
> *the Bright and Morning Star.*[75]

John will maintain a parallel between the prologue and the seven churches until the PVR, however, he will only make minor changes between the prologue and epilogue. This shows that to John, the alpha and omega parallel was not key to the story but to the building of content.

The DJD's prototype of the prologue and epilogue had God speak first, Jesus second, and the spirit third. It likely had the angel dictate the letters to John. This would satisfy the chain of custody found in the first verse of Revelation in which the message began with God, then Jesus, then an angel and finally to John. If the angel dictated each letter to the seven churches to John we should see evidence that shows the angel is speaking to all the churches. We find that evidence in the closing of each letter to the seven churches with the phrase:

> *He who has an ear, let him hear what the Spirit says to the assemblies.*[76]

We also have the angel in the prologue who tells John to write to the seven churches[77] and Jesus who tells John that he has sent his "angel to testify these things to you for the assemblies."[78] Theses are items that shows that the story was in flux.

The Seven Churches

Expanding the judgments from four to seven also meant that John needed to expand the four messages, to the righteous and to the unrighteous, in the cities of Jerusalem and Tyre.[79] With the expansion of the letters from four to seven came the problem of how to fill the three letters with content. John's solution was to take content from one church and copy it to another church with subtle alterations. That is why

---

73   See "Z2 - How The Seven Churches Were Formed" on page 103.

74   See "Z2 - How The Seven Churches Were Formed" on page 103.

75   Rev 22:16.

76   Rev 2:7, 11, 17, 29; 3:6, 13, 22.

77   Rev 1:11.

78   Rev 22:16.

79   See "Z2 - The Oratories to God's People as the Birth of the Letters to Seven Churches (Zech 7:1 - 12:8; Rev 2:1 - 3:22)" on page 67.

we have two stories of Balaam and Balak, two stories of the synagogue of Satan, and two stories relating to the Nicolaitans.[80]

The problem with forming the DJD's prototype of the letter to the seven churches is that it is almost impossible to know who they are addressed to. The DJD for example does not make it clear who Revelation is written to. Is it written to all believers, both Jews and gentiles, or is it written to all Jews who obey the commandments of God and follow the Lamb?[81] One thing for certain in the PVR as well as the DJD's version of the letters to the seven churches is how much of it is connected to Jewish imagery. Was the imagery part of the way John wrote or was it addressed to cities outside of Israel? Unfortunately, we cannot answer these questions with any certainty.

The strongest case is that the DJD's seven cities were Jewish cities that killed all the believers. As a result the destruction of the seven cities was a recreation of Joshua defeating the Canaanite cities. This would be consistent with the two later drafts and the PVR.

The Expanding of the ZrD's Story of Satan

The ZrD's story of Satan was very simple; Satan pursues Jesus from heaven to earth and back to heaven, where Jesus defeats him. As a result he is thrown to the earth for a short while, and during this time he tries to destroy believers on earth. After he accomplishes his goal Satan has one last battle with Jesus and he is finally placed in the abyss.[82]

The Two Stories of Satan and the Two Stories of God's People

The DJD gave John an opportunity to greatly expand the story of Satan by creating two stories of Satan.[83] One story has Satan victorious over the destruction of the city of Jerusalem and the other has Satan defeated by God when he attacked Jerusalem. Both scenarios had Satan locked away in the abyss and later released. After his release he assembles a huge army against Jerusalem. The difference between the two stories is the behavior of the inhabitants of Jerusalem, and what happens to them as a result. When the inhabitants are wicked they are destroyed by Satan and when they are righteous, God comes down and destroys him. Therefore what John is telling us is really two stories, one of defeat and one of victory based upon the success or failure of the other.

When the inhabitants are wicked, John has God and Jesus ally with Satan to destroy Jerusalem. John has Jesus and Satan ally against the wicked in Jerusalem by nesting the seven trumpets (actions of Satan) within the seventh seal (actions of Jesus). When the believers are righteous, Jesus defeats Satan[84] and God defeats Satan.[85] This is why the sixth seal, sixth trumpet, sixth bowl, the second coming, and the story of Gog and

---

80   See "The Meaning of Duplicate Content" on page 161.
81   Rev 12:17.
82   See "The Creation of Satan in the Zechariah Draft" on page 86.
83   See "Satan's Story" on page 294 for a more detailed account.
84   The ZrD and the DJD prototype of the second coming was a battle with Satan. In the DJD, it is Jesus who battles against Satan's army and thereby protecting some of all believers (martyrs).
85   Rev 20:7-15.

The Meaning of Duplicate Content

In Revelation duplicate content means John used parallel formation to bulk up a newly expanded section. The seven churches is one place where John expanded them to seven messages and therefore needed a way to create new content. The best way was to take imagery from one message and put it in another.

Ephesus	Smyrna	Pergamum	Thyatira	Sardis	Philadelphia	Laodicea
Nicolaitans (2:6).		Nicolaitans (2:15).				
	Synagogue of Satan (2:9).				Synagogue of Satan (3:9).	
They reject false teachers (2:2-3).		Balaam and Balak teaches to eat things sacrificed to idols and sexual immorality (2:14).	Jezebel teaches to eat things sacrificed to idols and sexual immorality (2:20-1).			
				Some will walk with Jesus in white (3:4).		Jesus wishes them to buy from him white garments (3:18).
					A door always open.	Jesus wants to open their door.

Magog have many common elements, such as: the rallying of a large army and the army in various stages of defeat.[86]

There is one interesting quirk with the two stories of Satan being locked up in the abyss. In the second story, it is an angel who locks Satan in the abyss with a chain and key,[87] while in the first account it is Satan himself who is given the key to free himself from the abyss.[88]

The New Timeline for Satan

The arranging of the wax tablets to form the two stories of Satan tells us that John himself struggled with the story of Satan within the DJD.[89] What we can tell is that in the PVR the two stories of Satan are really two timelines. The first timeline represents the time of crossing the Jordan to the time of Jesus and the destruction of Jerusalem. In John's mind that was a ballpark number of a thousand years. So when Jesus defeated Satan in the DJD's prototype of the second coming, Satan would be locked away for another

---

86   The best way to read them is in the following order: the amassing of the army by Satan (Rev 16:12-16), the engagement of the army (Rev 9:13-21), the counter-attacks by Jesus and God in the sixth seal (Rev 6:12-7) in the second coming (Rev 19:11 - 12:3) and God versus Satan, Gog, and Magog (Rev 20:4-15).

87   Rev 20:1-3.

88   Rev 9:1-2.

89   Note how the the four attacks of Satan are arranged in order for the two stories of Satan to form a parallel (see "Satan's Story" on page 294). This indicates that at one time John had the story of the woman, child, and Satan within the story of Gog and Magog.

thousand years.[90] This time, however, the resurrected believers now live in the city and have remained holy to God.[91] Satan, fresh out of prison, repeats his last major military action only this time to be defeated by God and never mentioned again in Revelation.[92]

How John changed the timeline back a thousand years prior to Jesus was to have the angel Michael (who defeated Satan over the body of Moses) defeat Satan in heaven.[93] John had that angel (or an angel) lock Satan away for a thousand years only to be released just in time to kill Jesus on earth[94] and seventy years later he would destroy Rome.[95] In the space of a thousand years, seventy years would seem like a short time.

The two stories of Satan is an example of how by following the way John is writing we can glean much more about the book of Revelation than we could glean by simply reading the final product. The way that John arranged the tablets also tells us that he struggled in how he wanted to tell the story as well. Ultimately he settled upon laying the wax tablets in such a way so that parallels were not broken.[96]

The Story of One Wax Tablet

We have seen how content sometimes jumps from one wax tablet to another,[97] but sometimes content jumps from one wax tablets to multiple wax tablets. This is the story of one such tablet and how its content jumped to many wax tablets.

Joshua and the Crossing of the Jordan River

If you will tell the story of Joshua going into the promised land you will need a scene of a river that has stopped, which the people can cross over. John had such a river taken from Isaiah in the EID. The tone and imagery is the reverse of Joshua's crossing of the Jordan River with the whole of Israel fleeing Egypt to conquer the people in the promised land. We have a remnant of Israel crossing a faraway river, returning to conquer the Egyptians:

> **11:15** THE LORD *will utterly destroy the tongue of the Egyptian sea; and with his scorching wind he will wave his hand over the river, and will split it into seven streams, and cause men to march over in sandals.* **11:16** *There will be a highway for the remnant that is left of his people from Assyria, like there was for Israel in the day that he came up out of the land of Egypt.*[98]

It is no surprise that John would use the Isaiah passage as his source passage for the crossing of the Jordan because its ultimate source was the crossing of the Jordan River by Joshua.[99] This is common to see when this writing style is used. We have already seen in the EID that the bulk of the draft was leveraging the parallel that Isaiah made of Ezekiel and John tweaked the two to produce a third story. In the DnD we will see

---

90   Rev 20:1-3.
91   Rev 20:4-6.
92   Rev 20:7-15.
93   Rev 12:7-9; Jude 9;
94   Rev 11:7 "the beast that comes up out of the abyss" was "They have over them as king the angel of the abyss" (Rev 9:11) in the DJD referring to Satan (Rev 20:1-3; 9:1-2).
95   See "Jesus as the Certain King (Isa 23:15-7; Rev 18:2-6, 22)" on page 29.
96   See "Satan's Story" on page 294.
97   See "When Wax Tablets Are Placed Together" on page 85 to see how content jumps from one wax tablet to another.
98   Isa 11:15-6.
99   Josh 3:16-7.

that Daniel copied the worship scene imagery from Ezekiel and John uses the imagery to enhance John's worship scene with Jesus.[100]

How The Content of the Wax Tablet Was Distributed

I will conclude the finishing phase of the DJD with a story of one wax tablet and how John scattered its content throughout the DJD, rather than with everything he did, because the finishing phase covered in this chapter is by no means exhaustive.

When John took the content of one wax tablet to create the imagery of the twelve tribes crossing the Jordan River he took the entire wax tablet because the content that John needed was in the center of the wax tablet. The problem for John was what to do with the wax tablet that had a blank spot in the middle. John's solution was to strip out the content of the wax tablet and distribute it to other places in Revelation. The great sword went to the red horse in the second seal and the rest was divided up to the newly inserted wax tablets in the DJD.

When the PVR is examined in light of its use of the book of Isaiah one can visualize someone with a pair of scissors cutting out sections of Isaiah and placing them into Revelation.[101] In reality, it was methodical, as we learned in the EID and in later drafts, it was distributed based upon a pattern. With the Euphrates River tablet it went through a process akin to cutting it up with a pair of scissors and distributing it throughout Revelation.

Final Thoughts

John's use of Deuteronomy and Joshua profoundly shaped the PVR and yet the two books are probably the least known of the sources used to construct Revelation. It is the draft that brought so many dimensions to Revelation itself and will become the platform for the next two drafts to come.

The process in constructing the DJD teaches us that the rules or methodology in creating a draft can be altered in direction but not in practice. It shows us that a draft need not be a selection of content from a single book in the Hebrew Scriptures, but can be something as simple as the selection of the life story of a famous person in the Hebrew Scriptures.

Perhaps the most profound observation of the DJD (and the creation of each draft) is the ease in which John creates the book of Revelation by applying rules and methodology. The process gives us something that the reader associates with the Hebrew Scriptures, but in a way that makes it nearly impossible to connect it to a single source in the Hebrew scriptures.

---

100 See "Daniel's Ezekiel Draft and Revelation's Ezekiel and Daniel Draft" on page 221.
101 See "How John Distributed the Content From One Wax Tablet in the Deuteronomy-Joshua Draft" on page 164.

How John Distributed the Content From One Wax Tablet in the Deuteronomy-Joshua Draft

The content below represents the wax tablet that John created in the ZrD for the second coming scene (see). It contained the scene of a river crossing similar to the crossing of the Jordan River by John. John then took the content and moved it where he wanted it to go and found himself left with a wax tablet that had a blank portion in its center.

John's solution for the blank spot in the center of the wax tablet was to distribute the bulk of the content with the newly created DJD material and provide the imagery for the rider of the red horse.

Content Found in the DJD Material		Content Found in Revelation	
		The Red Horseman (Rev 6:4)	
Zech 1:8	Behold, a man riding on a red horse.	6:4	Another came out, a red horse. To him who sat on it was given power to take peace from the earth, and that they should kill one another. There was given to him a great sword.
Isa 27:1	THE LORD with his hard and great and strong sword....		
Zech 1:8	A man riding on a red horse . . . and behind him were red, brown and white horses.	19:14	The armies which are in heaven followed him on white horses.
Zech 1:9	Then I asked, 'My lord, what are these?'	7:13	One of the elders answered, saying to me, "These who are arrayed in the white robes, who are they, and from where did they come?"
Zech 1:9	The man who stood among the myrtle trees answered, "They are the ones THE LORD has sent to go back and forth through the earth."		He said to me, "These are those who came out of the great tribulation. They washed their robes, and made them white in the Lamb's blood.
		Crossing the Euphrates River (Rev 9:14; 16:12)	
Isa 11:15	His scorching wind he will wave his hand over the river.	9:14	Free the four angels who are bound at the great river Euphrates! (see Rev 7:1 where they are the four angels holding back the four winds).
Isa 11:16	Will cause men to march over in sandals. There will be a highway for the remnant that is left of his people from Assyria.		
Isa 27:12	It will happen in that day, that THE LORD will thresh from the flowing stream of the Euphrates to the brook of Egypt; and you will be gathered one by one, children of Israel.	16:12	The great river, the Euphrates. Its water was dried up, that the way might be prepared for the kings that come from the sunrise.
		The Great Multitude in Heaven (Rev 7:9-17)	
Isa 12:1	God was angry with them but he comforted them.		
Isa 12:2	God is my salvation. I will trust, and will not be afraid.	7:10	Salvation be to our God.
Isa 12:3	Therefore with joy you will draw water out of the wells of salvation.	7:17	"The Lamb . . . leads them to springs of waters of life. And God will wipe away every tear from their eyes."
		The 144,000 in Heaven (Rev 14:1-5)	
Isa 12:6	Cry aloud and shout, you inhabitants of Zion, for the Holy One of Israel is great among you.	14:1	The Lamb standing on Mount Zion.
		14:2	They sounded like many waters and a great thunder.
Isa 12:2	They will sing a song of salvation.	14:3	They sing a new song before the throne.
		14:4	The were redeemed by Jesus.
Isa 12:4	In that day you will say, "Give thanks to THE LORD! Call on his name. Declare his doings among the peoples.	14:6	I saw an angel flying in mid-heaven, having an eternal good news to proclaim to those who dwell on the earth, and to every nation, tribe, language, and people.
		The Song of Moses and the Lamb (Rev 15:1-8)	
Isa 12:5	Sing to THE LORD for he has done excellent things.	15:3	They sang the song of the Lamb, saying, "Great and marvelous are your works."
Isa 12:6	The Holy One of Israel.	15:4	For you only are holy.

The Deuteronomy-Joshua Draft Approximation Text

The DJD approximation draft is arranged according to the chart below. To help the reader understand the way John incorporated the material from Deuteronomy and Joshua, the major sections will contain the Deuteronomy and Joshua descriptions and their Revelation equivalent.

DJ1	**The Prologue (Rev 1:1-20)**
DJ2	**The Letters to the Seven Churches (Rev 2:1 - 3:22)**
DJ3	**The Throne of God (Rev 4:1-11)**
DJ4	**The Coronation of Jesus (Rev 5:1-14)** • The commander of the Lord's army (Josh 5:13-4; Rev 5:5-8, 14). • Joshua marches around Jericho seven times (Josh 6:1-5; The seals created in Rev 6:1-17;8:1-6).
DJ5	**The First Four Seals (Rev 6:1-8)**
DJ6	**The Fifth and Sixth Seal (Rev 6:9-17)**
DJ7	**The Sealing of God's People and the Passover (Rev 7:1-17)** • The circumcision of those born in the wilderness (Deut 3:5:1-9; Rev 7:1-8). • The first Passover meal in the promised land (Deut 5:9-11; Rev 7:7-17). • The seventh march contained seven more marches around Jericho (Josh 6:16; Rev 8:1-6).
DJ8	**The Seventh Seal (Rev 8:1-6)** • The seven priests with the seven trumpets (Josh 6:16; Rev 8:1). • The moment of silence (Josh 6:16; Rev 8:1).
DJ9	**The First Four Trumpets (Rev 8:7-12)**
DJ10	**The Fifth Trumpet (Rev 9:1-12)**
DJ11	**The Sixth Trumpet and the Crossing of the River (Rev 9:13-21)** • The crossing of the Jordan River (Josh 3:16-7; Rev 9:13; 16:12).
DJ12	**The Mighty Angel (Rev 10:1-11)** • The priest has a foot on land and a foot in the river (Josh 3:1-15; Rev 10:2).
DJ13	**The Two Prophets (Rev 11:1-13)** • Similar to the two spies sent to Jericho (Josh 2:1-24; Rev 11:7-12).
DJ14	**The Seventh Trumpet (Rev 11:14-9)** • The seventh trumpet is created (Josh 6:16; Rev 11:13-9).
DJ15	**The Woman, Child, and Satan (Rev 12:1-17)**
DJ16	**The Song of Moses (Rev 14:1 - 15:8)** • They sung the song of Moses (Deut 31:30; Rev 14:3). • The swore allegiance to Jesus (Josh 1:16; Rev 14:3-4). • Moses was told to write a song (Deut 31:19; Rev 15:3-4). • God in front of the tent of meeting (Deut 31:15; Rev 15:3, 8). • God will hide his face from them if they leave him (Deut 31:18).
DJ17	**The Seven Bowls (Rev 16:1-21)**
DJ18	**The Harlot (Rev 17:1-18)**
DJ19	**The City of Babylon (Rev 18:1 - 19:8)**
DJ20	**Jesus Defeats Satan (Rev 19:11 - 20:3)**
DJ21	**Gog and Magog (Rev 20:4-15)** • The faithful will return home (Deut 30:1-10; Rev 20:5-10). • The witnesses that come from the uttermost part of heaven (Deut 30:12; Rev 20:4-6). • The witnesses from beyond the sea (Deut 30:13; Rev 20:13).
DJ22	**The New Jerusalem (Rev 21:1 - 22:5)**
DJ23	**The Epilogue (Rev 22:6-21)** • They have seen what God will do in Revelation (Deut 29:1-5; Rev 22:6). • Remain faithful and prosper or practice idolatry and fail (Deut 29:9-19; Rev 22:7, 14-5). • The curses in this book (Deut 29:18-28; Rev 22:18-9).

John Inserted the Content of Deuteronomy 29:1 to Joshua 6:5 Into the ZrD Backwards

The Destruction of Jericho Inserted Into the ZrD (Joshua 6:1-16)

John Began Here

DJ24 - The Epilogue (Rev 22:6-21)

John created the epilogue by adding a wax tablet to the end of the ZrD and incorporating Deuteronomy 29:1-28 into it. John will later will form a parallel with the prologue (the chart on the right page) which will cause the size of the prologue and epilogue to increase as information is copied from one to the other in order to form a solid parallel.

Content Found in the DJD Material			Content Found in Revelation (Ordered by)
			The throne of God and the Lamb will be in it, and his servants serve him.
			God Speaks
Isa 25:1	God has done things in complete faithfulness and truth.	22:6	These words of God are faithful and true (also in 22:6).
Deut 29:1-5	They have seen all that God has done for the Israelites in the wilderness.	22:6	The conclusion of the book of Revelation. John is told to publish all that he has seen and heard (see Rev 1:19).
		22:12	Behold, I come quickly. My reward is with me, to repay to each man according to his work.
Isa 44:6	I am the first, and I am the last.	22:13	I am the alpha and omega (synonym), the first and the last, the beginning and end. (synonym).
Deut 29:9-16	Those who keep the commandments of God will prosper.	22:7	Blessed is he who keeps the words of the prophecy of this book.
Ezek 47:12	By the river on its bank . . . shall grow every tree for food whose leaf shall not wither, neither shall its fruit fail. It shall produce new fruit every month . . . its leaf for healing.	22:14	Blessed are those who do his commandments, that they may have the right to the tree of life, and may enter in by the gates into the city.
Isa 44:3	I will pour water on him who is thirsty.		
Isa 55:1	"Everyone who thirsts, to the waters! Come, he who has no money, buy, and eat! Yes, come, buy wine and milk without money and without price.		
			Jesus Speaks
		22:16	I, Jesus, have sent my angel to testify these things to you for the assemblies.
		22:16	I am the root and the offspring of David; the bright and morning star.
			The Angel Speaks
		22:17	The spirit and the bride say, "Come!" He who hears, let him say, "Come!"
Deut 29:18-28	God will apply all the curses in Deuteronomy to those who participate with idols.	22:18-9	If anyone modifies Revelation they will suffer the consequences of the plagues contained within the book.

DJ1 - The Prologue (Rev 1:1-20)

The prologue was constructed by forming a simple parallel with the epilogue. The table below is a reconstruction of the DJD prologue by first forming a simple parallel with the DJD epilogue and aligning content found within the prologue and the seven churches.

Content Found in the DJD Material		**Content Found in Revelation (Ordered by)**
	1:1	This is the Revelation of Jesus Christ, which God gave him to show to his servants the things which must happen soon, which he sent and made known by his angel to his servant, John.
Ezek 1:1 I was among the captives by the river Chebar.	1:9	I was on . . . Patmos.
Ezek 1:3 Ezekiel the priest.	1:9	because of God's Word . . . of Jesus Christ.
Ezek 1:3 THE LORD's word came expressly to Ezekiel the priest.	1:10	I was in the spirit on THE LORD's day, and I heard behind me a loud voice.
		Voice Like a Trumpet - 1A I heard behind me **a loud voice, like a trumpet speaking with me** (1:10 connects to 4:1)
		God Speaks
	1:5	Faithful witness [as Jesus in the PVR].
	1:19	Write therefore the things which you have seen, and the things which are, and the things which will happen hereafter.
Zech 12:10 I will . . . . and they will look to me whom they have pierced; and they shall mourn for him, as one mourns for his only son.	1:7	Behold, [I, God] am coming and every eye will see him, including those who pierced him. All the tribes of the earth will mourn over him. Even so, Amen.
	1:8	I am the alpha and omega.
	1:17	I am the first and the last (Jesus in the DnD).
	1:8	I am . . . the beginning and end (altered in the ExD).
	1:3	Blessed is he who reads and those who hear the words of the prophecy [content overwritten by the DnD].
	2:6	To him who overcomes I will give to eat from the tree of life, which is in the paradise of my God.
		Jesus Speaks
	1:12	Jesus spoke.
Isa 14:10 Jesus as the root of Jesse.	22:16	I am the root and the offspring of David;
Isa 14:12 Babylon as the morning star.		the bright and morning star.
		The Angel Speaks
	22:17	The spirit and the bride say, "Come!" He who hears, let him say, "Come!" He who is thirsty, let him come.
		Write therefore the things which you have seen, and the things which are, and the things which will happen hereafter;

Reconstructing the Deuteronomy-Joshua Draft Version of the Seven Churches

The greatest challenge of the DJD is in reconstructing its version of the letters to the seven churches. The difficulty is in not knowing who they were addressed to and the order in which they were arranged. As a result, only the content will be displayed and placed in the order that is found in the PVR. This is done to make it easy for the reader to connect the content with Revelation and yet flexible enough for the reader to form their own theory as to who or what the letters are addressed to.

DJ2 - The Letter to the Seven Churches (Rev 2:1-11)

The church in Ephesus derives much of its description from the ZrD and from the alpha and omega parallel.

The Church in Ephesus (Rev 2:1-7)

Rev 22:13 I am the beginning and the end.

[The beginning and end says this.]

Zech 8:13-7 For THE LORD says: "As I thought to do evil to you, when your fathers provoked me to wrath," says THE LORD, "and I didn't repent; so again have I thought in these days to do good to Jerusalem and to the house of Judah. Don't be afraid. These are the things that you shall do: speak every man the truth with his neighbor. Execute the judgment of truth and peace in your gates, and let none of you devise evil in your hearts against his neighbor, and love no false oath: for all these are things that I hate," says THE LORD.

2:2-7 "I know your works, and your toil and perseverance, and that you can't tolerate evil men, and have tested those who call themselves apostles, and they are not, and found them false. You have perseverance and have endured for my name's sake, and have not grown weary. But I have this against you, that you left your first love. Remember therefore from where you have fallen, and repent and do the first works; or else I am coming to you swiftly, and will move your lampstand out of its place, unless you repent. But this you have, that you hate the works of the Nicolaitans, which I also hate.

Rev 22:14 Blessed are those who do his commandments, that they may have the right to the tree of life, and may enter in by the gates into the city.

2:7 To him who overcomes I will give to eat from the tree of life, which is in the paradise of my God.

The Church in Smyrna (Rev 2:8-11)

Rev 22:13 The first and the last.

2:8 The first and the last says this:

Isa 10:1 Woe to those who decree unrighteous decrees (Jacob/Israel; see 9:8), and those who write oppressive decrees;

2:9 "I know your works, oppression, and your poverty (but you are rich), and the blasphemy of those who say they are Jews, and they are not, but are a synagogue of Satan.

Isa 10:2 To deprive the needy from justice, and to rob the poor among my people of their rights.

Isa 10:4 They [those who issue evil decrees] will only bow down under the prisoners, and will fall under the slain.

2:10 "I know your works, oppression, and your poverty (but you are rich), and the blasphemy of those who say they are Jews, and they are not, but are a synagogue of Satan.

DJ2 - The Letter to the Seven Churches (Rev 2:12-29)

John created the bulk of the text for Pergamum by retelling the story of Balak and Balaam backwards and opposite.

			The Church in Pergamum (Rev 2:12-7)
	The Counsel of Balaam		***The Teaching of Balaam***
Num 22:1 to 25:5; 31:16	Balaam counsels Balak into letting the Israelites eat food sacrificed to idols and have sexual relationships with pagan women, therefore letting the Israelites' sinful actions be the cause of God cursing them.	2:14	Some who hold the teaching of Balaam, who taught Balak to throw a stumbling block before the children of Israel, to eat things sacrificed to idols.
	Evil Performed in Front of the Righteous		***Righteousness in Front of Unrighteousness***
Num 25:6	Two brothers brought a Midianite woman in front of Moses, the Tent of Meeting, and the entire congregation.	2:13	"I know your works and where you dwell, where Satan's throne is. You hold firmly to my name, and didn't deny my faith in the days of Antipas my witness."
	The Wicked Are Killed and the Righteous Prevail		***The Righteous is Killed and the Wicked Prevail***
Num 25:7-8	Phinehas . . . took a spear in his hand. He went after the man of Israel into the pavilion, and thrust both of them through, the man of Israel, and the woman through her body.	2:13	Antipas, the faithful servant, is killed.
	The Israelites were spared because of Phinehas' actions.	2:13-4	The believers followed the teaching of Balaam.
	Moses Wages War Against Those Who Sided with Balaam and Balak		***Jesus Will Wage War Against Those Who Sided With Balaam and Balak***
Num 31:1-18	God has Moses avenge the Israelites for what the Midianites (and Balaam) have done to them.	2:16	Repent therefore, or else I am coming to you quickly, and I will make war against them with the sword of my mouth.

John created the bulk of the text that forms the church of Thyatira by tweaking Ezekiel 16:20, 37 and Isaiah 11:4; 14:12.

			The Church in Thyatira (Rev 2:18-29)
Ezek 16:37	God will gather all her lovers and they will hate her and strip her naked.	2:22	Behold, I will throw her into a bed, and those who commit adultery with her.
Ezek 16:20	Moreover you have taken your sons and your daughters, whom you have borne to me, and you have sacrificed these to them to be devoured.	2:23	I will kill her children with death, and all the assemblies will know that I am he who searches the minds and hearts. I will give to each one of you according to your deeds.
Isa 11:4	With righteousness he will judge the poor, and decide with equity for the humble of the earth.	2:26	He who overcomes, and he who keeps my works to the end, to him I will give authority over the nations.
	He will strike the earth with the rod of his mouth, and with the breath of his lips he will kill the wicked.	2:27	He will rule them with a rod of iron, shattering them like clay pots; as I also have received of my father:
Isa 14:12	Babylon is the morning star.	2:28	and I will give him the morning star.
		2:29	He who has an ear, let him hear what the spirit says to the assemblies.

DJ2 - The Letter to the Seven Churches (Rev 3:7-18)

The Church in Philadelphia (Rev 3:7-13)

Isa 22:21	He will be a father to the inhabitants of Jerusalem, and to the house of Judah.	22:16	I, Jesus . . . . I am the root and the offspring of David.
Isa 22:22	I will lay the key of David's house on his shoulder. He will open, and no one will shut. He will shut, and no one will open.	3:7	He who is true, he who has the key of David, he who opens and no one can shut, and who shuts and no one opens, says these things:
Isa 22:23	I will fasten him like a nail in a sure place. He will be a throne of glory to his father's house.	3:12	I will make him a pillar in the temple of my God.
Isa 22:25	"In that day . . . the nail that was fastened in a sure place will give way. It will be cut down, and fall. The burden that was on it will be cut off.	3:10	Because you kept my command to endure, I also will keep you from the hour of testing, which is to come on the whole world, to test those who dwell on the earth.

The Church in Laodicea (3:14-22)

Isa 23:18	her merchandise and her wages will be holiness to THE LORD. It will not be treasured nor laid up	3:17	Because you say, "I am rich, and have gotten riches, and have need of nothing;"
		3:18	I counsel you to buy from me gold refined by fire, that you may become rich.
Isa 23:18	for her merchandise will be for those who dwell before THE LORD,		
	to eat sufficiently,	3:20	I will come in to him, and will dine with him, and he with me.
	and for durable clothing."	3:18	White garments, that you may clothe yourself, and that the shame of your nakedness may not be revealed.

DJ3 - The Throne of God (Rev 4:1-11)

John's encounter with God on his throne remains unchanged since the ZrD.

Content Found in the DJD Material		Content Found in Revelation (Ordered by Isaiah and then Revelation)	
		Voice Like a Trumpet - 1B After these things . . . **the first voice that I heard, like a trumpet speaking with me** (4:1 from 1:10)	
Isa 6:1	I saw THE LORD sitting on a throne.	4:2	There was a throne set in heaven, and one sitting on the throne.
Ezek 1:28	A rainbow around the throne.	4:3	A rainbow around the throne.
Ezek 1:26	Throne's appearance like sapphire.	4:3	Throne's appearance like jasper.
Ezek 1:22	Crystal expanse.	4:6	Sea of glass-like crystal.
Ezek 1:5	The living creatures with four faces.	4:6	Four living creatures.
Ezek 1:6 Isa 6:2	~~Each having four faces~~ The seraphim had one face.	4:6	Each having one face.
Ezek 1:10	Face of a man, lion, ox, and eagle.	4:7	Face of a lion, calf, man, and eagle.
Ezek 1:6 Isa 6:2	~~Each having four wings.~~ Each having six wings.	4:8	Each having six wings.
Ezek 1:18	Full of eyes all around.	4:8	Full of eyes around and within.
Isa 6:3	They said "Holy, holy, holy is THE LORD . . . . "	4:8	They said "Holy, holy, holy is THE LORD . . ."
Isa 6:3	"The whole earth is filled with his glory."	4:8	God created all things.

DJ4 - The Coronation of Jesus (Rev 5:1-14)

In the DJD, John conflated the coronation of Jesus with the commander of the Lord's army text. This is the first place where Jesus is referred to as the Lamb and the farthest place where John directly imported the Deuteronomy-Joshua text into Revelation.

Content Found in the DJD Material			Content in Revelation (Ordered by Isaiah and then Revelation)
Ezek 2:10	It was written within and without.	5:1	The scroll written inside and outside.
Isa 6:8	"Whom shall I send, and who will go for us?"	5:2	"Who is worthy to open the scroll?"
Deut 30:4	If your outcasts are in the uttermost parts of the heavens, from there God will gather you, and from there he will bring you back.	5:3	No one in heaven above, or on the earth, or under the earth, was able to open the book, or to look in it.
Deut 30:12	Who will go beyond the sea and return with a message to God?	5:4	And I wept much, because no one was found worthy to open the book, or to look in it.
Josh 5:14	The commander of the Lord's Army.	5:5	One of the elders said to me, "Don't weep. Behold, the lion who is of the tribe of Judah, the Root of David, has overcome; he who opens the book and its seven seals."
Josh 5:14	Joshua fell on his face to the earth, and worshiped, and asked him, "What does my lord say to his servant?"	5:6	I saw in the middle of the throne and of the four living creatures, and in the middle of the elders, a Lamb standing.
Ezek 3:1-3	Ezekiel is told to take the scroll and eat it. It will taste sweet to the mouth.	5:7	Then he [Jesus] came, and he took it out of the right hand of him who sat on the throne.
		5:8	The four living creatures and the 24 elders fell down before the Lamb.
Isa 6:6	Altar, coal touching lips purifies.	5:8-9	Altar and Jesus' death.
Isa 6:6	Coal touching lips cleanses Isaiah of sin.	5:9	Jesus' death cleanses believers of sin.
Zech 6:11	Make crowns and put them on the head of Joshua.	19:12	On his head are many crowns.
Zech 6:12	He shall build THE LORD's temple.		[This became the major point of the Exodus Draft.]
Zech 6:13	He shall sit and rule on his throne.	3:21	He who overcomes, I will give to him to sit down with me on my throne, as I also overcame, and sat down with my father on his throne.
Zech 6:14	Crowns shall be given to [four individuals] for a memorial in the temple.	5:10	[Jesus] made us kings and priests to our God, and we will reign on the earth.
			[This is most likely the place where we have the elders wearing crowns and sitting on their thrones as Rev 3:21 suggests.]
Zech 6:15	Those who are far off shall come and build THE LORD's temple.	5:9	Out of every tribe, language, people, and nation.
Deut 30:12	Who will go beyond the sea and return with a message to God?	5:13	I heard every created thing which is in heaven, on the earth, under the earth, on the sea, and everything in them, saying, "To him who sits on the throne, and to the Lamb be the blessing, the honor, the glory, and the dominion, forever and ever! Amen!"
Ezek 1:28	Ezekiel falls down before God.	5:14	The four living creatures and the elders fell down and worshiped Jesus.
		1:17	When I saw him, I fell at his feet like a dead man.

DJ5 - The First Four Seals (Rev 6:1-8)

John recreated the seven days that Joshua and his army marched around Jericho with the imagery of seven seals wrapped around a scroll. He then used the synonym "the lamb" to represent Jesus (Joshua and Jesus in both Hebrew and Greek are the same word) and prefixed each of the ZrD texts with the opening of a seal.

The Key Text of Joshua:

6:3 All of your men of war shall march around the city, going around the city once. You shall do this six days. **6:4** Seven priests shall bear seven trumpets of rams' horns before the ark. On the seventh day, you shall march around the city seven times, and the priests shall blow the trumpets.

Content Found in the DJD Material		The First Four Seals (Rev 6:1-8)	
		The First Seal/Horseman (Zech 6:3; Rev 6:2)	
Josh 6:3	The seven days march around Jericho.	6:1	I saw the lamb open one of the seven seals.
Zech 6:8	The third chariot with white horses.	6:2	A white horse.
Ezek 5:16	He will send evil arrows.		He had a bow.
		The Second Seal/Horseman (Zech 6:2; Rev 6:4)	
Josh 6:3	The seven days march around Jericho.	6:3	When he opened the second seal.
Zech 6:2	The first chariot with red horses.	6:4	A red horse.
Isa 27:1	A great sword.		He had a great sword.
		The Third Seal/Horseman (Zech 6:2; Rev 6:5-6)	
Josh 6:3	The seven days march around Jericho.	6:5	When he opened the third seal.
Zech 6:2	The second chariot with black horses.	6:5-6	A black horse.
Ezek 5:16	He will break their staff of bread.		Food prices are set for a famine.
		The Fourth Seal/Horseman (Zech 6:3; Rev 6:8)	
Josh 6:3	The seven days march around Jericho.	6:7	When he opened the fourth seal.
Zech 6:3	The fourth chariot had dappled horses.	6:8	A pale horse.
Ezek 5:17	He will kill them with wild animals, pestilence, and the sword.		He had authority to kill them with the sword, famine, pestilence, and wild animals.

DJ6 - The Fifth and Sixth Seal (Rev 6:9-17)

John made the fifth and sixth seals by using the remainder of the text that was moved in conjunction with the text used to form the four horsemen, and divided it up into two judgments. John then made the fifth and sixth seals as templates for the fifth and sixth trumpets and bowls.

	Content Found in the DJD Material		**The Fifth Seal (Rev 6:9-11)**
			Also the Church of Smyrna (Rev 2:8-11)
Josh 6:3	The seven days march around Jericho	6:9	When he opened the fifth seal
Isa 10:1	Woe to those who decree unrighteous decrees (Jacob/Israel; see 9:8), and those who write oppressive decrees;	2:9	"I know your works, oppression, and your poverty (but you are rich), and the blasphemy of those who say they are Jews, and they are not, but are a synagogue of Satan.
Isa 10:2	To deprive the needy from justice, and to rob the poor among my people of their rights.		
Isa 10:4	They will only bow down under the prisoners, and will fall under the slain.	2:10	The devil is about to throw some of you into prison, that you may be tested. Be faithful to death.
	For all this his anger is not turned away, but his hand is stretched out still.	13:10	If anyone is to go into captivity, he will go into captivity. If anyone is to be killed with the sword, he must be killed.
		6:9	Under the throne of God are the people who were martyred by keeping the commandments.
Isa 10:15-9	God will destroy those who try to deceive God's people, illustrated in the burning of all the thorns, briers, and most of the trees.	7:3	Do not harm the trees until all are sealed.
		9:4-7	In the fifth trumpet those with the seal of God on their foreheads as well as the trees and the green grass will not be harmed. The rest will be in torment for five months.
		8:7	One third of the trees were burned up, and all green grass was burned up.
		6:10	Those who martyred the saints will be avenged (see
Isa 10:20	God's people will continue to lean on God.	2:9	Be faithful to death.
		6:9	Under the altar of God were the martyrs of the faithful.
		6:11	They were given a white robe and told to rest.

			The Sixth Seal (Rev 6:12-7)
Josh 6:3	The seven days march around Jericho	6:12	I saw when he opened the sixth seal.
Isa 13:10 Joel 2:10	The sun will be darkened . . . the moon will . . . not shine.	6:12	The sun became black as sackcloth made of hair and the moon became as blood.
Ezek 32:6	I will also water with your blood		
Ezek 32:7	The stars withdraw from shining.		
Ezek 32:7	The moon shall not give its light.		
Ezek 32:8	[I will] make its stars dark.		
Isa 13:10	For the stars of the sky and its constellations will not give their light.	6:13	The stars of the sky fell to the earth.
Isa 13:13	God will make the heavens tremble and the earth will be shaken out of place.	6:14	The sky was removed like a scroll when it is rolled up. Every mountain and island were moved out of their places.
Joel 2:10	The earth quakes before them.	16:20	Every island fled away, and the mountains were not found.
Ezek 32:8	I will cover the heavens.		
Ezek 32:10	Their kings shall be horribly afraid for you.	6:15	The kings of the earth, the princes, the commanding officers, the rich, the strong, and every slave and free person.
Ezek 32:10	They shall tremble at every moment, every man for his own life, in the day of your fall.	6:15	[They] hid themselves in the caves and in the rocks of the mountains.
Isa 13:14-22	They will flee to their own lands.		

DJ7 - The Sealing of God's People and the Passover (Rev 7:1-17)

John created the imagery of the crossing of the Jordan River with his version of the circumcision of all males who were born in the wilderness and the first Passover meal in the promised land. John recreated the circumcision imagery from Joshua by conflating the twelve tribes from Joshua with the marking of the faithfuls' foreheads from Ezekiel.

For John to create the first Passover meal in the promised land he could not conflate Jesus as the Lamb with the Passover meal. So he instead alludes to the Passover meal with the waving of the palm branches and revealing that they will never hunger again.

Content Found in the DJD Material		The Sealing of the 144,000 and the Great Multitude
		The Sealing of the 144,000 on Earth (Rev 7:1-8)
Ezek 7:1	The end has come on the four corners of the land (or earth).	7:1	After this, I saw four angels standing at the four corners of the earth, holding the four winds of the earth, so that no wind would blow on the earth, or on the sea, or on any tree.
		7:2	I saw another angel ascend from the sunrise, having the seal of the living God. He cried with a loud voice to the four angels to whom it was given to harm the earth and the sea,
Josh 5:1-8 Ezek 3:8 Ezek 9:4	Joshua circumcised every male who was not circumcised. Ezekiel's head was hardened. God spared the life of those with the mark on their forehead.	7:3	saying, "Don't harm the earth, neither the sea, nor the trees, until we have sealed the bondservants of our God on their foreheads!"
Josh 4:1- 5:8	The twelve tribes of Israel had males from each tribe that were not circumcised.	7:4	I heard the number of those who were sealed, 144,000, sealed out of every tribe of the children of Israel:
		7:5	of the tribe of Judah were sealed twelve thousand, of the tribe of Reuben twelve thousand, of the tribe of Gad twelve thousand,
		7:6	of the tribe of Asher twelve thousand, of the tribe of Naphtali twelve thousand, of the tribe of Manasseh twelve thousand,
		7:7	of the tribe of Simeon twelve thousand, of the tribe of Levi twelve thousand, of the tribe of Issachar twelve thousand,
		7:8	of the tribe of Zebulun twelve thousand, of the tribe of Joseph twelve thousand, of the tribe of Benjamin twelve thousand.
		The Great Multitude in Heaven (Rev 7:9-17)
Josh 5:9-11	The first meal in the promised land was the Passover meal.	7:9	After these things I looked, and behold, a great multitude, which no man could count, out of every nation and of all tribes, peoples, and languages, standing before the throne and before the Lamb, dressed in white robes, with palm branches in their hands.
Isa 12:2	God is my salvation. I will trust, and will not be afraid.	7:10	They cried with a loud voice, saying, "Salvation be to our God, who sits on the throne, and to the Lamb!"
Zech 1:9	Then I asked, 'My lord, what are these?'	7:13	One of the elders answered, saying to me, "These who are arrayed in the white robes, who are they, and from where did they come?"
Zech 1:9	The angel who talked with me said to me, "I will show you what these are."	7:14	I told him, "My lord, you know."
Zech 1:10	The man who stood among the myrtle trees answered, "They are the ones The Lord has sent to go back and forth through the earth."	7:14 7:15	He said to me, "These are those who came out of the great tribulation. They washed their robes, and made them white in the Lamb's blood. Therefore they are before the throne of God, they serve him day and night.
Isa 49:10	They shall not hunger nor thirst; neither shall the heat nor sun strike them:	7:16	They will never be hungry, neither thirsty any more; neither will the sun beat on them, nor any heat;
Isa 49:10 Isa 12:3	for he who has mercy on them will lead them. He will guide them by springs of water. Therefore with joy you will draw water out of the wells of salvation.	7:17	for the Lamb who is in the middle of the throne shepherds them, and leads them to springs of waters of life. And God will wipe away every tear from their eyes."

DJ8 - The Seventh Seal (Rev 8:1-6)

The seventh seal was made by conflating the imagery of the seventh march around Jericho, and turning it into a container to include all seven trumpets. The silence given in the seventh seal was originally the silence before the trumpets were blown (Josh 6:10; Rev 8:1).

Content Found in the DJD Material		Content Found in Revelation	
		The Seventh Seal (Rev 8:1-6)	
Josh 6:3	The seven days march around Jericho	8:1	When he opened the seventh seal,
			there was silence in heaven for about half an hour.
Josh 6:10	Joshua commanded the people, saying, "You shall not shout, nor let your voice be heard, neither shall any word proceed out of your mouth, until the day I tell you to shout. Then you shall shout."		
Josh 6:4	On the seventh day, you shall march around the city seven times, and the priests shall blow the trumpets.	8:2	I saw the seven angels who stand before God, and seven trumpets were given to them.
		8:6	The seven angels who had the seven trumpets prepared themselves to sound.

DJ9 - The First Four Trumpets (Rev 8:7-12)

The first four trumpets formed a complex parallel with the four attacks by Satan against the woman and child. As a result of the parallel formation many of the elements used to construct the first four trumpets were overwritten with the text from the attacks by Satan found in Revelation 12:1-17.

The Four Attacks by Satan

12:17 The Fourth Attack by Satan
• Satan wages war against the woman and:
  • Those who kept God's commandments.
  • Those who hold to Jesus' testimony.
 	
12:13-6 The Third Attack by Satan
• Satan spewed water from his mouth to destroy the woman and her children.
• The land absorbed the water.
 	
12:7-9 The Second Attack by Satan
• Satan is thrown to earth.
• Satan's four names
• Satan is out to deceive the world.
 	
12:1-3 The First Attack by Satan
• A third of the stars in the sky are taken.
• The woman dressed with the sun, moon under her feet, and a crown of twelve stars

First Four Trumpets

8:7 The First Angel Blew the Trumpet
• Third of the earth was burnt up:
  • Third of the trees (Jewish believers)
  • All the green grass was burnt up (believers).
 	
8:8-9 The Second Angel Blew the Trumpet
• A great burning mountain was thrown into the sea.
• The sea absorbed the mountain.
 	
8:10-1 The Third Angel Blew the Trumpet
• A great star fell from the sky.
• The star is called "Wormwood."
• Third of the waters became poisoned.
 	
8:12 The Fourth Angel Blew the Trumpet
• Third of the sun, moon, and stars were darkened .

DJ10 - The Fifth Trumpet (Rev 9:1-12)

John created the fifth trumpet similarly to how he created the fifth seal: he used text moved to create the first four trumpets. He expands the text of the fifth trumpet by telling the story of Satan being released from the abyss and adding additional content from the four attacks by Satan. John then adds in what is likely Roman Soldiers in a victory parade.

	Content Found in the DJD Material		**Content Found in Revelation**
			The Fifth Trumpet (Rev 9:1-12)
Josh 6:3	The seven days march around Jericho.	9:1	The fifth angel sounded.
Rev 20:1	I saw an angel coming down out of heaven, having the key of the abyss and a great chain in his hand.		I saw a star from the sky which had fallen to the earth. The key to the pit of the abyss was given to him.
Rev 20:2	He seized the dragon, the old serpent, which is the devil and Satan, who deceives the whole inhabited earth, and bound him for a thousand years,	9:2	He opened the pit of the abyss, and smoke went up out of the pit, like the smoke from a burning furnace. The sun and the air were darkened because of the smoke from the pit.
Rev 20:3	and cast him into the abyss, and shut it, and sealed it over him, that he should deceive the nations no more, until the thousand years were finished.	9:3	Then out of the smoke came locusts on the earth, and power was given to them, as the scorpions of the earth have power.
Ezek 2:6	Israelites are like scorpions.		
Ezek 9:3	The glory of the God of Israel was gone up from the cherub, whereupon it was, to the threshold of the house: and he called to the man clothed in linen, who had the writer's inkhorn by his side.	9:4	They were told that they should not hurt the grass of the earth, neither any green thing, neither any tree, but only those people who don't have God's seal on their foreheads.
Ezek 9:4	Go through the middle of Jerusalem and set a mark on the foreheads of the men signed and cried over all the abominations that was done.	9:5	They were given power not to kill them, but to torment them for five months. Their torment was like the torment of a scorpion, when it strikes a person.
Ezek 2:6	You, son of man, don't be afraid of them, neither be afraid of their words, though briers and thorns are with you, and you do dwell among scorpions: don't be afraid of their words, nor be dismayed at their looks, though they are a rebellious house.		
Ezek 5:10	Therefore the fathers shall eat the sons within you, and the sons shall eat their fathers. [They will do anything to live.]	9:6	In those days people will seek death, and will in no way find it. They will desire to die, and death will flee from them. [They will do anything to die.]
	[John in Revelation ascribes the symbol of the locust to the Roman army dressed in parade attire.]	9:7-9	The shapes of the locusts were like horses prepared for war. On their heads were something like golden crowns, and their faces were like people's faces. They had hair like women's hair, and their teeth were like those of lions. They had breastplates, like breastplates of iron. The sound of their wings was like the sound of chariots, or of many horses rushing to war.
Rev 12:4	Imagery of Satan using his tail.	9:10	They have tails like those of scorpions, and stings. In their tails they have power to harm men for five months.
Rev 12:15	Imagery of Satan using his mouth.		
Rev 11:7	The [king] beast of the abyss killed the two prophets.	9:11	They have over them as king the angel of the abyss.

DJ11 - The Sixth Trumpet (Rev 9:13-21)

The sixth trumpet was formed by adding an angel sounding a trumpet and the crossing of the account found in Joshua 3:1-17 of the Israelites crossing the Jordan River. Since the Isaiah account of the saints crossing the Euphrates River was conceptually the same as the Israelites crossing the Jordan River, John kept the Isaiah account.

	Content Found in the DJD Material		Content Found in Revelation
Josh 6:3	The seven days march around Jericho	9:13	The sixth angel sounded.
			I heard a voice . . .
Isa 11:15	THE LORD will utterly destroy the tongue of the Egyptian sea; and with his scorching wind he will wave his hand over the River, and will split it into seven streams, and cause men to march over in sandals.	9:14	saying to the sixth angel who had the trumpet, "Free the four angels who are bound at the great river Euphrates!"
		16:12	the Euphrates. Its water was dried up, that the way might be prepared for the kings that come from the sunrise.
Isa 11:16	There will be a highway for the remnant that is left of his people from Assyria, like there was for Israel in the day that he came up out of the land of Egypt.		
Ezek 8:1	In the sixth year, in the sixth month, in the fifth day of the month.	9:15	The four angels were freed who had been prepared for that hour and day and month and year, so that they might kill one third of mankind.
Zech 5:3	Everyone who steals shall be cut off according to it on the one side; and everyone who swears falsely shall be cut off according to it on the other side.	9:21	They didn't repent of their murders, nor of their sorceries, nor of their sexual immorality, nor of their thefts.

DJ12 - The Mighty Angel (Rev 10:1-11)

John added the imagery of the priests crossing the Jordan River––where the priests had one foot on land and the other foot on water––and applied it to the mighty angel.

	Content Found in the DJD Material		Content in Revelation (Ordered by Isaiah, Revelation)
			The Mighty Angel - 1B The mighty angel (10:1 from 5:2)
Ezek 1:28	The appearance of a rainbow. The appearance of brightness all around him.	10:1	A rainbow on his head. His face was like the sun.
Ezek 2:9	When I looked, behold, a hand was stretched out to me; and, behold, a scroll of a book was therein;	10:2	He had in his hand a little open scroll.
Josh 3:13-7	Imagery of the priests stepping into the water with one foot and causing the Jordan River to be dry. Thus one foot touches the water and the other was on land.		He set his right foot on the sea, and his left on the land.
Ezek 3:12	Ezekiel hears the living creatures making loud noises, seven days, saying: "Blessed be THE LORD'S glory from his place."	10:3-4	John hears the message of the seven thunders but is told not to reveal it to anyone.
Ezek 3:1-3	Ezekiel told to take the scroll and eat it. It will taste sweet to the mouth.	10:9-10	I went to the angel, telling him to give me the little scroll.
Ezek 3:14	Ezekiel was bitter.		He said to me, "Take it, and eat it up. It will make your stomach bitter, but in your mouth it will be as sweet as honey."
Ezek 3:4	He said to me, son of man, go to the house of Israel, and speak my words to them.	10:11	They told me, "You must prophesy again over many peoples, nations, languages, and kings."
Ezek 3:16-27	Ezekiel is appointed as a watchman to tell everyone.		
			The Mighty Angel - 2A The mighty angel (10:1, 10 to 18:21)

DJ13 - The Two Prophets (Rev 11:1-12)

The two prophets narrative were only lightly modified to support the story of Joshua sending two spies into Jericho. The significant change was having the two prophets killed by the king of the abyss (Josh 2:2; Rev 11:7) which was Satan (see "Satan's Story" on page 294).

	Content Found in the DJD Material		Content in Revelation (Ordered by)
			Measuring the Temple (Rev 11:1-2)
Zech 2:1	I lifted up my eyes, and saw, and behold, a man with a measuring line in his hand.	11:1	A reed like a rod was given to me.
Zech 2:2	He said to me, "To measure Jerusalem, to see what is its width and what is its length."	11:1	Someone said, "Rise, and measure God's temple, and the altar, and those who worship in it.
Ezek 10:1-22	The state of the temple before the glory of The Lord flees.		
Zech 2:4	[He] said to him, "Run, speak to this young man, saying, 'Jerusalem will be inhabited as villages without walls.'"	11:2	Leave out the court which is outside of the temple, and don't measure it,
Ezek 10:1-22	The state of the temple before the glory of The Lord flees.		
Zech 2:4	because of the multitude of men and livestock in it.	11:2	for it has been given to the nations. They will tread the holy city under foot.
Ezek 4:5	Ezekiel laid on his left side for 390 days. Each day represents one year Israel sinned against God.	11:2	The temple courtyard will be trampled by the gentiles for 42 months, representing the 420 years that the temple has been controlled by the Gentiles.
			The Two Prophets (Rev 11:3-13)
Ezek 4:6	Ezekiel laid on his right side for 40 days. Each day equals one year Judah sinned against God.	11:3	The two witnesses shall testify for 1,260 days, representing 1,260 years from the crossing of the Jordan River to the death of Jesus.
Zech 3:3	Now Joshua was clothed with filthy garments.	11:3	my two witnesses . . . clothed in sackcloth.
Zech 4:11	"What are these two olive trees on the right side of the lamp stand and on the left side of it?"	11:4	These are the two olive trees and the two lamp stands,
Zech 4:12	"What are these two olive branches, which are beside the two golden spouts, that pour the golden oil out of themselves?"		
Zech 4:14	"These are the two anointed ones who stand by The Lord of the whole earth."	11:4	standing before The Lord of the earth.
Ezek13:19 Josh 2:2	They kill the souls that should not die. The king of Jericho sought the two spies.	11:7	When [the two prophets] finished their testimony the king of the abyss killed them.
Ezek 4:8	The sum of the days in Ezek 4:5-6 equals how long the siege of Jerusalem would last.	11:9	The two prophets laid dead in the street for 3½ days with each day representing one year of the siege of Jerusalem in 67-70 CE.
Josh 2:15, 22	The two spies hid for three days in the mountains.		The two prophets laid dead in the street for 3½ days.
Ezek 13:18	The women sew pillows and make kerchiefs for those who hunt souls.	11:10	Those who dwell on the earth rejoiced over the death of the two prophets. They gave gifts to one another.
Ezek 13:19	They give handfuls of barley and pieces of bread to kill souls.		
Ezek 13:23	God will deliver his people out of their hand.	11:12	God breathed life into the two prophets.
Ezek 10:1-22	The glory of God left the temple.	11:13	The two prophets were taken to heaven in front of their enemies.
Ezek 13:23	You will see no more false visions nor practice divination.	11:13	The rest were terrified and gave glory to God.

DJ14 - The Seventh Trumpet (Rev 11:13-9)

The seventh trumpet was created from the final imagery of the destruction of Jericho. John took the trumpet blast, the shout, and the ark of the covenant, and appended them to the destruction of the city. John also altered the city's destruction from being destroyed by fire to being destroyed by an earthquake, in order to match the story of Joshua's destruction.

	Content Found in the DJD Material		Content in Revelation (Ordered by)
			The Aftermath of the Two Prophets Taken to Heaven (Rev 11:13-7)
Isa 6:10-3	An illustration that even if the oak tree is burned (believers) and a tenth of the city is burned, a new crop of believers will be sprouted from the acorns.	11:13	In that day there was a great earthquake, and a tenth of the city fell. Seven thousand people were killed in the earthquake, and the rest were terrified, and gave glory to the God of heaven.
Josh 6:5	It shall be that when they make a long blast with the ram's horn, and when you hear the sound of the trumpet,	11:15	The seventh angel sounded,
	all the people shall shout with a great shout.		and great voices in heaven followed, saying,
			"The kingdom of the world has become the kingdom of our Lord, and of his Christ. He will reign forever and ever!"
Josh 6:6	Take up the ark of the covenant.	11:19	God's temple that is in heaven was opened, and the ark of the Lord's covenant was seen in his temple.

DJ15 - The Woman, Child, and Satan (Rev 12:1-17)

The text below represents a snapshot of the ZrD after John conflated the story of the woman, child, the story of Babylon defeated in heaven and the saints' return, and the content of Zechariah 2:1 - 4:14. As we can see, John replaced "Babylon" with "Satan," as ascribed in Isaiah 14, and then conflated the actions of the nations from Isaiah 7:14 - 10:19. The end result is that much of the imagery of Satan found within Revelation came from this single literary action.

Content Found in the DJD Material (ordered by Isaiah)		Content Found in Revelation	
		The Sign of the Woman With Child in Heaven (Rev 12:1)	
Isa 7:14	A sign of a woman who is ready to conceive a son that will be named Immanuel.	12:1	A sign of a woman who is ready to conceive a son that will be named Immanuel.
Isa 8:4	Before the child knows how to say, "My father," and, "My mother," the riches of Damascus and the plunder of Samaria will be carried away by the king of Assyria."	12:5	She gave birth to a son . . . . Her child was caught up to God, and to his throne.
		Satan's Third Attack on the Woman and Her Children (Rev 12:12-5)	
Isa 8:5	An army will sweep through Israel like a flood.	12:15	The serpent spewed water out of his mouth after the woman like a river, that he might cause her to be carried away by the stream.
Isa 9:11-6	The army devoured Israel with an open mouth.	12:4	The dragon tried to devour the woman's son.
		12:15	The serpent that spews water out of his mouth might be a conflation of the Isa 8:5 and Isa 9:11-6 passage.
Isa 9:6-7	A child is born who will be called Wonderful, Counselor, Mighty God, Everlasting Father, Prince of Peace. His kingdom will reign forever with justice and righteousness.	12:5	She gave birth to a son, a male child who is to rule all nations with a rod of iron.
Isa 14:5	THE LORD has broken the staff of the wicked, the scepter of the rulers.	2:27	He will rule them with a rod of iron, shattering them like clay pots.
		Satan's First Attack on the Woman and Her Children (Rev 12:3-4)	
Isa 27:1	The dragon that is in the sea.	12:3	Behold, a great red dragon [in heaven].
Isa 9:15	The tails are the prophets who teach lies.	12:4	His tail drew one third of the stars in the sky, and threw them to the earth.
Isa 9:16	Those who lead the people astray and those who are led astray are destroyed.	12:9	The deceiver of the whole world.
		Satan's Fourth Attack on the Woman and Her Children (Rev 12:17)	
Isa 9:18-9	Their wickedness burns like a fire.	8:7	The first trumpet tells of hail mixed with fire and the earth burned up, a third of the trees and all of the green grass
Isa 10:16-9	He will send Assyria to burn the ground and the trees in one day. (See "John's First Major Content Alignment Corrections" on page 22.)	12:17	The dragon grew angry with the woman, and went away to make war with the rest of her offspring, who keeps God's commandments and holds Jesus' testimony.

DJ16 - The Song Of Moses (Rev 14:1 - 15:8)

John integrated the song of Moses (Deut 31:15-30) and the people swearing allegiance to Joshua/Jesus (Josh 1:1-18) into Revelation. As a result, the core of Revelation 15:1-8 was created.

Content Found in the DJD Material		Content in Revelation (Ordered by)	
		The 144,000 in Heaven (Rev 14:1-5)	
Isa 14:32	What will they answer the messengers of the nation? That THE LORD has founded Zion, and in her the afflicted of his people will take refuge.	14:1	The Lamb standing on Mount Zion with the 144,000.
Deut 31:30	The song of Moses taught by Moses.	14:3	The Song of the Lamb that only the people know.
Josh 1:16	All that you have commanded us we will do, and wherever you send us we will go.	14:4	These are those who follow the Lamb wherever he goes.
Josh 1:18	Whoever rebels against your commandment, and doesn't listen to your words in all that you command shall himself be put to death. Only be strong and courageous.		These were redeemed by Jesus from among men, the first fruits to God and to the Lamb. In their mouth was found no lie, for they are blameless.
		The Message of the First Angel (Rev 14:6-7)	
Isa 14:32	Oracles to the nations.	14:6	The gospel was spread to the entire world.
Isa 15:1 to 19:17	The oracles to the nations.		
Isa 17:7, 10	People will look to their maker . . . their forgotten God of salvation.	14:7	Fear the Lord . . . who made everything.
		The Message of the Second Angel (Rev 14:8)	
Isa 21:9	Fallen, fallen is Babylon and all the engraved images of her gods are broken to the ground.	14:8	Babylon the great has fallen, which has made all the nations to drink of the wine of the wrath of her sexual immorality.
		The Great Harvest (Rev 14:14-20)	
Ezek 15:2	Son of man.	14:14	One sitting like the son of man.
Ezek 15:6	The inhabitants of Jerusalem are connected to the worthless vine.	14:13-6	The saints are connected to the great harvest of grapes.
Ezek 15:7	God will use fire against them.	14:18	An angel who has the power of fire [no fire is used].
Ezek 15:8	God will make the land desolate because they have committed a trespass.	14:19-20	The grapes make the wrath of God which will destroy the harlot and make her desolate (Rev 17:6; 18:5-8).
Ezek 32:5	The blood of the dead will be deep enough to swim in.	14:20	The blood was as deep as a horse's bridle and as far as 180 miles.
	The Song of Moses		**The Song of Moses and the Lamb**
Deut 31:19	Moses told to write a song which will become the song of Moses.	15:3-4	They sang the song of Moses, and the song of the Lamb.
Deut 31:18	God will hide his face on that day.		God is not seen.
Deut 31:16-7	God will be angry when his people forsake him and chase after idols.	15:1, 7	The wrath of God.
Deut 31:15	Moses and Joshua (Jesus) in the Tent of Meeting.	15:3, 8	Song of Moses and Jesus . . . God in the temple.
	A pillar of cloud appeared above the tent's door.	15:8	The temple was filled with the smoke of the glory of God.

DJ17 - The Seven Bowls (Rev 16:1-9)

Since the seven bowls were primarily a product of duplicating the seven trumpets and changing the quantity from a "third" to "all," the chart below shows the DJD version of the seven trumpets as the source material. The faded text represents what was placed in from a later draft. The bracketed text represents the probable DJD text.

Content Found in the Seven Trumpets	Content Found in the Seven Bowls
The First Trumpet (Rev 8:7)	***The First Bowl (Rev 16:2)***
8:7 The first sounded, and there followed hail and fire, mixed with blood, and they were thrown to the earth. One third of the earth was burned up, and one third of the trees were burned up, and all the green grass was burned up.	16:2 The first went, and poured out his bowl into the earth, and it became a harmful and evil sore on the people who had the mark of the beast, and who worshiped his image.
The Second Trumpet (Rev 8:8-9)	***The Second Bowl (Rev 16:3)***
8:8-9 The second angel sounded, and something like a great burning mountain was thrown into the sea. One third of the sea became blood, and one third of the living creatures which were in the sea died. One third of the ships were destroyed.	16:3 The second angel poured out his bowl into the sea, and it became blood as of a dead man. Every living thing in the sea died.
The Third Trumpet (Rev 8:10-1)	***The Third Bowl (Rev 16:4-7)***
8:10 The third angel sounded, and a great star fell from the sky, burning like a torch, and it fell on one third of the rivers, and on the springs of the waters.	16:4 The third poured out his bowl into the rivers and springs of water, and they became blood.
8:11 The name of the star is called "Wormwood." One third of the waters became wormwood. Many people died from the waters, because they were made bitter.	16:5 I heard the angel of the waters saying, "You are righteous, who are and who were, you Holy One, because you have judged these things.
	16:6 For they poured out the blood of the saints and prophets, and you have given them blood to drink. They deserve this."
	16:7 I heard the altar saying, "Yes, Lord God, the Almighty, true and righteous are your judgments."
The Fourth Trumpet (Rev 8:12)	***The Fourth Bowl (Rev 16:8-9)***
8:12 The fourth angel sounded, and one third of the sun was struck, and one third of the moon, and one third of the stars; so that one third of them would be darkened, and the day wouldn't shine for one third of it, and the night in the same way.	16:8 The fourth poured out his bowl on the sun, and it was given to him to scorch men with fire.
	16:9 People were scorched with great heat, and people blasphemed the name of God who has the power over these plagues. They didn't repent and give him glory.

DJ17 - The Seven Bowls (Rev 16:10-16)

John copied elements from the fifth and sixth trumpets to make the fifth and sixth bowls. The likely reason why John did not produce a full copy of the fifth and sixth trumpet was due to space. It is likely that all of the bowls fit onto a single wax tablet whereas the trumpets likely inhabited two or more wax tablets.

Content Found in the Seven Trumpets	*Content Found in the Seven Bowls*
The Fifth Trumpet (Rev 9:1-11)	***The Fifth Bowl (Rev 16:10-1)***
9:1 The fifth angel sounded, and I saw a star from the sky which had fallen to the earth. The key to the pit of the abyss was given to him.	16:10 The fifth poured out his bowl on the throne of the [angel of the abyss] beast, and his kingdom was darkened. They gnawed their tongues because of the pain,
9:2 He opened the pit of the abyss, and smoke went up out of the pit, like the smoke from a burning furnace. The sun and the air were darkened because of the smoke from the pit.	16:11 and they blasphemed the God of heaven because of their pains and their sores. They didn't repent of their works.
9:3 Then out of the smoke came locusts on the earth, and power was given to them, as the scorpions of the earth have power.	
9:4 They were told that they should not hurt the grass of the earth, neither any green thing, neither any tree, but only those people who don't have God's seal on their foreheads.	
9:6 In those days people will seek death, and will in no way find it. They will desire to die, and death will flee from them.	
9:10 They have tails like those of scorpions, and stings. In their tails they have power to harm men for five months.	
9:11 They have over them as king the angel of the abyss. His name in Hebrew is "Abaddon," but in Greek, he has the name "Apollyon."	
The Sixth Trumpet (9:13-21)	***The Sixth Bowl (Rev 16:12-6)***
9:13-4 The sixth angel sounded. I heard a voice from the horns of the golden altar which is before God, saying to the sixth angel who had the trumpet, "Free the four angels who are bound at the great river Euphrates!"	16:12 The sixth poured out his bowl on the great river, the Euphrates. Its water was dried up, that the way might be prepared for the kings that come from the sunrise.
9:15-6 The four angels were freed who had been prepared for that hour and day and month and year, so that they might kill one third of mankind.	
20:8 The number of the armies is as the sand of the sea.	
9:17-9 Thus I saw the horses in the vision, and those who sat on them, having breastplates of fiery red, hyacinth blue, and sulfur yellow; and the horses' heads resembled lions' heads. Out of their mouths proceeded fire, smoke, and sulfur. By these three plagues were one third of mankind killed: by the fire, the smoke, and the sulfur, which proceeded out of their mouths. For the power of the horses is in their mouths, and in their tails. For their tails are like serpents, and have heads, and with them they harm.	16:13 I saw coming out of the mouth of the dragon, and out of the mouth of the beast, and out of the mouth of the false prophet, three unclean spirits, something like frogs;
	16:14 for they are spirits of demons, performing signs; which go out to the kings of the whole inhabited earth, to gather them together for the war of that great day of God, the Almighty.
	16:16 He gathered them together into the place which is called in Hebrew, Megiddo.

DJ17 - The Seven Bowls (Rev 16:17-20)

To create the seventh bowl, John used parallel formation with the seventh trumpet. The result is that John had two destructions for the city of Jerusalem.

The Seventh Trumpet (Rev 11:13-9)

11:13   In that day there was a great earthquake, and a tenth of the city fell. Seven thousand people were killed in the earthquake, and the rest were terrified, and gave glory to the God of heaven.

11:15   The seventh angel sounded, and great voices in heaven followed, saying, "The kingdom of the world has become the Kingdom of our Lord, and of his Christ. He will reign forever and ever!"

11:19   The ark of the covenant is seen.

The Seventh Bowl (Rev 16:17-21)

16:17   The seventh poured out his bowl into the air. A loud voice came out of the temple of heaven, from the throne, saying, "It is done!"

16:19   The great city was divided into three parts, and the cities of the nations fell. [Jerusalem] Babylon the great was remembered in the sight of God, to give to her the cup of the wine of the fierceness of his wrath.

16:20   Every island fled away, and the mountains were not found (See Rev 6:14).

DJ18 - The Harlot (Rev 17:1-18)

The account of the harlot did not change since the ZrD. The harlot in the DJD was another symbol for Jerusalem. It is not until the DnD that John merged the harlot with Tyre/Babylon to equate to Rome.

Content Found in the DJD Material		Content Found in Revelation	
Jerusalem as the Adulterous Bride (Ezek 16:1-63)		**The Harlot (Rev 17:1-18:24)**	
Zech 5:9	Two wicked women placed into a basket and flown to the wilderness to the land of Shinar.	17:3	He carried me away in the spirit into a wilderness. I saw a woman sitting on [a red dragon] a scarlet-colored animal, full of blasphemous names, having seven heads and ten horns.
Ezek 16:10	I clothed you also with embroidered work, and shod you with sealskin, and I dressed you about with fine linen, and covered you with silk.	17:4	The woman was dressed in purple and scarlet, and decked with gold and precious stones and pearls, having in her hand a golden cup full of abominations and the impurities of the sexual immorality of the earth.
Ezek 16:11	I decked you with ornaments, and I put bracelets on your hands, and a chain on your neck.		
Ezek 16:16	You took off your garments, and made for yourselves high places decked with various colors, and played the prostitute on them.		
Ezek 16:17	You also took your beautiful jewels of my gold and of my silver, which I had given you, and made for yourself images of men, and played the prostitute with them.		
Ezek 16:20	Moreover you have taken your sons and your daughters, whom you have borne to me, and you have sacrificed these to them to be devoured.	17:6	I saw the woman drunken with the blood of the saints, and with the blood of the martyrs of Jesus.
Ezek 16:36	The blood of your children, that you gave to them.	18:24	In her was found the blood of prophets and of saints, and of all who have been slain on the earth."
Ezek 16:37	God will gather all her lovers and they will hate her and strip her naked.	17:16	They will make her desolate, and will make her naked.
Ezek 16:41	They will burn her houses with fire.	17:16	They will burn her utterly with fire.
Ezek 16:53	I will turn again their captivity, the captivity of Sodom and her daughters, and the captivity of Samaria and her daughters, and the captivity of your captives among them.	18:2	She has become a habitation of demons, a prison of every unclean spirit, and a prison of every unclean and hateful bird!
Ezek 16:1-60	Talks about Jerusalem playing the harlot to all nations.	18:3	For all the nations have drunk of the wine of the wrath of her sexual immorality, the kings of the earth committed sexual immorality with her, and the merchants of the earth grew rich from the abundance of her luxury."

DJ19 - The City of Babylon (Rev 18:4-19)

This section remained unchanged since the first draft.

Content Found in the DJD Material		Content Found in Revelation	
Zech 1:3	"Return to me," says THE LORD, "and I will return to you,"	18:4	I heard another voice from heaven, saying, "Come out of her, my people, that you have no participation in her sins, and that you don't receive of her plagues.
Ezek 27:12	Silver, Iron.	18:12	Merchandise of silver, merchandise of iron
Ezek 27:13	Persons of men, vessels of brass.	18:12-3	People's bodies and souls, every vessel made of brass
Ezek 27:14	Horses, war horses.	18:13	Horses and chariots.
Ezek 27:15	Ivory tusks, ebony.	18:12	Every vessel made of ivory, expensive wood
Ezek 27:16	Purple, fine linen.	18:12	Purple, fine linen
Ezek 27:18	Oil.	18:13	Olive oil.
Ezek 27:20	Wine of Hellbon.	18:13	Wine.
Ezek 27:22	Lambs.	18:13	Sheep.
Ezek 27:22	Chief of all spices, precious stones, gold.	18:12-3	Spice, precious stones, merchandise of gold.
		18:15	The merchants of these things, who were made rich by her, will stand far away for the fear of her torment, weeping and mourning.
Ezek 22:27	Your riches . . . shall fall into the heart of the seas in the day of your ruin.	18:17	For in an hour such great riches are made desolate.
Ezek 27:29	All who handled the oar, the mariners, and all the pilots of the sea, shall come down from their ships; they shall stand on the land	18:17	Every ship master, and everyone who sails anywhere, and mariners, and as many as gain their living by sea, stood far away.
Ezek 27:30	and shall cast up dust on their heads, they shall wallow themselves in the ashes.	18:19	They cast dust on their heads.
	[They] shall cause their voice to be heard over you, and shall cry bitterly.		[They] cried, weeping and mourning.
Ezek 27:32	In their wailing they shall take up a lamentation for you . . . "Who is there like Tyre?"	18:18	and cried out as they looked at the smoke of her burning, saying, "What is like the great city?"
Ezek 27:33	When your wares went out of the seas, you filled many peoples; you enriched the kings of the earth with the multitude of your riches and of your merchandise.	18:9	The kings of the earth, who committed sexual immorality and lived wantonly with her, will weep and wail over her, when they look at the smoke of her burning.
		18:11	The merchants of the earth weep and mourn over her, for no one buys their merchandise any more.
Ezek 28:2	Because your heart is lifted up, and you have said, I am a god, I sit in the seat of God, in the middle of the seas; yet you are man, and not God.	18:7	However much she glorified herself. . . For she says in her heart, "I sit a queen, and am no widow, and will in no way see mourning."

DJ19 - The City of Babylon (Rev 18:21-4)

This section remained unchanged from the ZrD with the possible exception of the removal of Isa 23:15, 17 which could have happened in the ZrD or a later draft.

Content Found in the DJD Material		Content Found in Revelation
		Mighty Angel - 2B The mighty angel (18:21 from 10:10).
Jer 51:63	It shall be, ~~when you have finished reading this scroll~~, that you shall bind a stone to it, and cast it into the middle of the Euphrates.	18:21	A mighty angel took up a stone like a great millstone and cast it into the sea, saying,
Jer 51:64	Thus shall Babylon sink, and shall not rise again because of the evil that I will bring on her; and they shall be weary.	18:21	"Thus with violence will Babylon, the great city, be thrown down, and will be found no more at all."
Isa 23:15, 17	Tyre will be forgotten seventy years, according to the days of one king . . . after the end of seventy years that THE LORD will visit Tyre.		[Removed in either the ZrD or the DJD.]
Isa 23:16	Take a harp; go about the city . . . . Make sweet melody. Sing many songs, that you may be remembered.	18:22	The voice of harpists, minstrels, flute players, and trumpeters will be heard no more at all in you.
Isa 23:17	She . . . will play the prostitute with all the kingdoms of the world on the surface of the earth.		
Zech 5:3-4	Everyone who swears falsely shall be cut off according to it on the other side.	18:23	For with your sorcery all the nations were deceived.
Jer 51:49	As Babylon has caused the slain of Israel to fall, so at Babylon shall fall the slain of all the land.	18:24	In her was found the blood of prophets and of saints, and of all who have been slain on the earth.
Isa 25:1	THE LORD, you are my God. I will exalt you! I will praise your name, for you have done wonderful things, things planned long ago, in complete faithfulness and truth.	19:1 19:2	Hallelujah! Salvation, power, and glory belong to our God. True and righteous are his judgments . . . and he has avenged the blood of his servants at her hand. (see Rev 6:9-11).
Isa 25:2	[God] made a city into a heap, a fortified city into a ruin . . . It will never be built.	19:2	For he has judged the great prostitute, who corrupted the earth with her sexual immorality.
Isa 25:3	Therefore a strong people will glorify you. A city of awesome nations will fear you.	19:1-5	The righteous praise God and the city that rules the world is destroyed by God.

DJ20 - Jesus Defeats Satan (Rev 19:1 - 20:3)

This section was changed in the DJD when John removed a wax tablet from the second coming narrative, which he used to create the crossing of the Jordan River narrative. As a result the content has been reduced significantly from the ZrD (see "How John Distributed the Content From One Wax Tablet in the Deuteronomy-Joshua Draft" on page 164).

Content Found in the DJD Material		**Content Found in Revelation**	
Isa 25:6	In this mountain, THE LORD . . . will make all peoples a feast of fat things, a feast of choice wines, of fat things full of marrow, of well-refined choice wines.	19:9	Blessed are those who are invited to the marriage supper of the Lamb.
			Description of Jesus in the Second Coming (Rev 19:11-5)
Isa 11:4	[In] righteousness he will judge.	19:11	In righteousness he judges and makes war.
	He will strike the earth with the ~~rod~~ of his mouth.	19:15	Out of his mouth proceeds a sharp, double-edged sword.
Isa 27:1	THE LORD with his hard and great and strong sword. . .		He will rule them with an iron rod.
Isa 11:5	Righteousness will be the belt of his waist.	19:8	It was given to her that she would array herself in bright, pure, fine linen: for the fine linen is the righteous acts of the saints.
Isa 11:5	Faithfulness will be the belt of his waist.	19:11	He who sat on it is called Faithful and True.
Isa 13:1-8	God is mustering a great army from a distant land to the ends of heaven in order to battle the nations.	19:14	The armies which are in heaven followed him on white horses, clothed in white, pure, fine linen.
			The Slaying of the Great Dragon (Rev 19:17 - 20:3)
Ezek 32:4	The birds and animals will feast on the dragon's army.		[See Ezek 39:17-20; Rev 19:17-8 below as the rest of the feast of the vulture.]
Ezek 32:21	The strong among the mighty shall speak to him out of the middle of Sheol.	20:1	I saw [Jesus] coming down out of heaven, having the key of the abyss and a great chain in his hand.
		20:2	He seized the dragon, the old serpent, which is the devil and Satan, who deceives the whole inhabited earth,
		20:3	and cast him into the abyss, and shut it, and sealed it over him, that he should deceive the nations no more, until the thousand years were finished. After this, he must be freed for a short time.
Ezek 32:31	Pharaoh shall see them, and shall be comforted over all his multitude.	19:19	I saw the [great dragon beast], and the kings of the earth, and their armies, gathered together to make war against him who sat on the horse, and against his army.
Ezek 32:32	Those who are slain by the sword, even Pharaoh and all his multitude,	19:21	The rest were killed with the sword of him who sat on the horse.

DJ21 - Gog and Magog (Rev 20:4 - 15)

The Gog and Magog narrative was shaped by the DJD in how it was organized in three primary ways. It added the righteous coming from heaven and the unrighteous coming from the sea. It added that Satan will be released after a thousand years and he will lead the army in his failed attempt to destroy Jerusalem. It also added a beatitude to the narrative for those who follow the commandments of God.

Content Found in the DJD Material		Content Found in Revelation (Ordered By)	
			The First Resurrection (Rev 20:4-6)
Isa 29:18-9	The blind, deaf, and the poor will hear the words of the book and rejoice.	20:4	I saw thrones, and they sat on them, and judgment was given to them. I saw the souls of those who had been beheaded for the testimony of Jesus.
Deut 30:1-10	God will gather those who obeyed his commandments and return them to their land.		
Deut 30:4	If your outcasts are in the uttermost parts of the heavens, from there God will gather you, and from there he will bring you back.		
Rev 22:14	Blessed are those who do his commandments.	20:6	Blessed are those who do his commandments.
Deut 30:11	The commandment is not too distant.		They lived and reigned with Christ for a thousand years.
Deut 30:12	Who will go to heaven and return with a message to God?		[The saints come from heaven in Rev 6:9-11.]
			The Attack on Jerusalem
Ezek 38:14	In that day when my people of Israel dwells securely, shall you not know it?	20:7	And after the thousand years, Satan will be released from his prison.
			[States that when Satan is locked up in the abyss, Jerusalem will be prosperous and people will dwell safely in it.]
Ezek 38:2	Gog of the land of Magog.	20:8	Gog and Magog mentioned.
Isa 29:8	Multitude of nations.	20:8	Nations from the four corners of the earth.
Ezek 38:18 Isa 29:1	They shall come against Israel. The city where David encamped.	20:9	They went up over the width of the earth, and surrounded the camp of the saints, and the beloved city.
Isa 29:6	They will be destroyed by a devouring fire.	20:9	Fire came down out of heaven from God, and devoured them.
			The Second Resurrection (Rev 20:11-5)
Isa 29:20-1	A book in the context and the unrighteous will be destroyed.	20:12	The dead were judged out of the things which were written in the books, according to their works.
Deut 30:13	Who will go beyond the sea and return with a message to God?	20:13	The sea gave up the dead who were in it. Death and Hades gave up the dead who were in them.

DJ22 - The New Jerusalem (Rev 21:1 - 22:5)

The first part of the New Jerusalem was modified by the creation of the alpha and omega parallel while the rest of the New Jerusalem passage was untouched. The alpha and omega parallel could have been formed to fill in blank space between the Isaiah's holy city Jerusalem and Ezekiel's city of God.

Content Found in the DJD Material	Content Found in Revelation (Ordered by)
Isa 65:17 "For, behold, I create new heavens and a new earth; and the former things will not be remembered, nor come into mind."	21:1 I saw a new heaven and a new earth: for the first heaven and the first earth have passed away, and the sea is no more.
Isa 66:22 "For as the new heavens and the new earth, which I will make, shall remain before me."	
Isa 66:20 The holy city Jerusalem	21:2 I saw the holy city, New Jerusalem, coming down out of heaven from God.
Isa 61:10 God has clothed me . . . as a bride adorns herself with her jewels.	Prepared like a bride adorned for her husband.
Ezek 43:7 God dwells in the temple where his throne is. He will dwell among the people of Israel forever.	21:3 I heard a loud voice out of heaven saying, "Behold, God's dwelling is with people, and he will dwell with them, and they will be his people, and God himself will be with them as their God.
Isa 25:8 THE LORD will wipe away tears from off all faces.	21:4 He will wipe away from them every tear from their eyes.
Isa 25:8 He has swallowed up death forever!	Death will be no more; neither will there be mourning, nor crying, nor pain, anymore. The first things have passed away.
Isa 42:9 Behold, the former things have happened, and I declare new things.	21:5 He who sits on the throne said, "Behold, I am making all things new."
Isa 25:1 God has done things in complete faithfulness and truth.	21:5 These words of God are faithful and true (also in 22:6).
Isa 44:6 I am the first, and I am the last.	21:6 I am . . . the beginning and end.
Isa 44:3 I will pour water on him who is thirsty. Isa 55:1 "Hey! Come, everyone who thirsts, to the waters! Come, he who has no money, buy, and eat! Yes, come, buy wine and milk without money and without price."	21:6 I will give freely to him who is thirsty from the spring of the water of life (also in 22:17).
Ezek 43:7 to 43:11 The house of Israel will no longer defile God's name by prostitution, sacrificing to high places and violating God's ordinances.	21:7-8 Those who overcome, God will give him the New Jerusalem. Those that don't follow God's ordinances ("cowardly, unbelieving, sinners, murderers, sexually immoral, liars" etc.)
Ezek 40:2 Ezekiel in a vision was carried to a high mountain in Israel where he saw the city of God.	21:10 He carried me away in the Spirit to a great and high mountain, and showed me the holy city, Jerusalem, coming down out of heaven from God,
Ezek 48:31 to 48:34 The city of God has twelve gates named after each of the twelve tribes of Israel, three on each side.	21:12 The New Jerusalem has twelve gates named after the twelve tribes of Israel. 21:13 There are three gates on each side.
Ezek 40:3 [He had] a measuring reed.	21:15 He who spoke with me had for a measure, a golden reed, to measure the city, its gates, and its walls.
Ezek 40:5 [He measured] the wall, all around and the thickness of the building.	
Ezek 48:16 The city is a square with each side measuring 4,500 cubics.	21:16 The city is a cube with each side measuring 12,012 stadia.
Isa 60:19 The sun will be no more your light by day; nor will the brightness of the moon give light to you, but THE LORD will be your everlasting light, and your God will be your glory.	21:23 The city has no need for the sun, neither of the moon, to shine, for the very glory of God illuminated it, and its lamp is the Lamb.
Ezek 47:1 The waters came down from under, from the right side of the house, on the south of the altar.	22:1 A river of water of life, clear as crystal, proceeding out of the throne of God and the Lamb.
Zech 14:8 It will happen in that day, that living waters will go out from Jerusalem;	
Ezek 47:12 By the river on its bank . . . shall grow every tree for food whose leaf shall not wither, neither shall its fruit fail. It shall produce new fruit every month . . . its leaf for healing.	22:2 On this side of the river was the tree of life, bearing twelve kinds of fruits, yielding its fruit every month. The leaves of the tree were for the healing of the nations.
Zech 14:11 Men will dwell therein, and there will be no more curse; but Jerusalem will dwell safely.	22:3 There will be no curse any more.

DJ23 - The Epilogue (Rev 22:6-21)

The epilogue was a blank wax tablet used by John to add in content from Deuteronomy 29:1-28. The tablet was altered in the finishing phase of the DJD where John formed parallels with the Gog and Magog, the New Jerusalem and the prologue narratives. The chart below represents the finalized version of the DJD.

Content Found in the DJD Material			Content Found in Revelation (Ordered by)
			The throne of God and of the Lamb will be in it, and his servants serve him.
			God Speaks
Isa 25:1	God has done things in complete faithfulness and truth.	22:6	These words of God are faithful and true (also in 22:6).
		22:12	Behold, I come quickly. My reward is with me, to repay to each man according to his work.
Isa 44:6	I am the first, and I am the last.	22:13	I am the alpha and omega (synonym), the first and the last, the beginning and end. (synonym).
Ezek 47:12	By the river on its bank . . . shall grow every tree for food whose leaf shall not wither, neither shall its fruit fail. It shall produce new fruit every month . . . its leaf for healing.	22:14	Blessed are those who do his commandments, that they may have the right to the tree of life, and may enter in by the gates into the city.
Isa 44:3			
Isa 55:1	I will pour water on him who is thirsty.		
	"Hey! Come, everyone who thirsts, to the waters! Come, he who has no money, buy, and eat! Yes, come, buy wine and milk without money and without price.		
Ezek 43:7 to 43:11	The house of Israel will no longer defile God's name by prostitution, sacrificing to high places, and violating God's ordinances.	22:15	Outside are the dogs, the sorcerers, the sexually immoral, the murderers, the idolaters, and everyone who loves and practices falsehood.
			Jesus Speaks
		22:16	I, Jesus, have sent my angel to testify these things to you for the assemblies.
		22:16	I am the root and the offspring of David; the bright and morning Star.
			The Angel Speaks
		22:17	The spirit and the bride say, "Come!" He who hears, let him say, "Come!" He who is thirsty, let him come.
Deut 29:22-5	A foreigner will deceive the people and cause the land to become barren.	22:17	He who is thirsty, let him come. He who desires, let him take the water of life freely.
		22:19	If anyone takes away from the words of the book of this prophecy, may God take away his part from the tree of life, and out of the holy city, which are written in this book.
Deut 29:18-28	God will apply all the curses in Deuteronomy to those who participate with idols.	22:18-9	If anyone modifies Revelation they will suffer the consequences of the plagues contained within the book.

Chapter 5: The Exodus Draft (ExD)

The Purpose of the Exodus Draft

The Deuteronomy-Joshua draft (DJD) depicted Jesus as the new Joshua from the end of Moses' life to the destruction of Jericho (Jerusalem). The Exodus Draft (ExD) depicts the story of Moses and Aaron, from the burning bush to the building of the tabernacle. It is the story for a new generation of believers that are no longer tied to a genealogy or to a nation but to the human race who obey the commandments of God and Jesus. They are known as the great multitude.[1] John, in the ExD, will convey all the rights and privileges found in Exodus, such as being called a kingdom of priests to the nations to the kingdom of priests to God. Central to how John depicts the great multitude to the Exodus story is the servicing of the tabernacle, where the tabernacle items' imagery is directly connected to the believers. The amazing portion of the ExD is that John will incorporate the vast majority of the changes found in the ExD into the blank areas of the wax tablets he added in the DJD.[2]

The ExD also became the draft in which John will form hundreds of parallels to tell different threads for each of the churches, God, Jesus and Satan. Many of which can be found in the last chapter of the book, Reading in the Horizontal.

This draft will be different than the three previous drafts in that there will not be an approximation draft the the ExD. The reason for this is space requirements more than anything else. To create an approxima-

---

1   The great multitude is a term taken from Rev 7:9: "After these things I looked, and behold, **a great multitude**, which no man could count, out of every nation and of all tribes, peoples, and languages, standing before the throne and before the Lamb, dressed in white robes, with palm branches in their hands." In this book the term "great multitude" will also refer to the seven churches (Rev 2:1 - 3:22) and those who follow the commandments of God and the Lamb (Rev 12:17). They are distinguished by having the white robes and participating in the new temple in heaven. The great multitude is different from the 144,000 which represents the faithful from the crossing of the Jordan River to the death of Jesus (Rev 7:1-8; 11:1-12) in that they are the ones with the seal of God on their forehead.

2   See "Inserting Between the Wax Tablets" on page 144 for the places where John added wax tablets in the DJD.

tion draft properly, there needs to be two approximation drafts, one prior to parallel formation and one after parallel formation. Since the draft itself is not complex compared to the ZrD and the DJD and the primary modifications are shown in this chapter itself, an approximation draft is really not required. It is easy to see that the ExD transformed the DJD into something closer to the PVR than without it.

Let's Build the Exodus Draft

The basic methodology that John used to construct the ExD followed a simple formula. It began with John introducing the new name of God bearing the same level of grandeur as the burning bush narrative from Exodus.[3] John introduced his book as a way in which all believers are now considered to be priests of God, and as a result to the new era he provides a new set of commandments. John then overlaid the servicing of the tabernacle on the day of atonement onto the blank portions of the wax tablets that were inserted into the DJD.

As a result of all of the changes, John had to alter the seven letters from being addressed to Jews in Israel to being addressed to believers from the great multitude. John employed various writing techniques to bulk up the seven churches and to spread that content to much of the book of Revelation. This was the final finishing stage before he went onto the next draft.

Moses, the Burning Bush, and the Name of God

One of the famous scenes in Exodus is when Moses and God have their first encounter. God gets Moses' attention by having a burning bush that is not being consumed. The two have a dialogue and the high point of the dialogue is when Moses receives a new name of God for Moses to tell the Israelites.

> *Moses said to God,*
> *"Behold, when I come to the children of Israel, and tell them, 'The God of your fathers has sent me to you,' and they ask me, 'What is his name?' What should I tell them?"*

> *God said to Moses,*
> *"I AM WHO I AM," and he said, "You shall tell the children of Israel this: 'I AM has sent me to you.' " God said moreover to Moses, "You shall tell the children of Israel this, 'THE LORD, the God of your fathers, the God of Abraham, the God of Isaac, and the God of Jacob, has sent me to you.' This is my name forever, and this is my memorial to all generations. Go, and gather the elders of Israel together, and tell them, 'THE LORD, the God of your fathers, the God of Abraham, of Isaac, and of Jacob, has appeared to me, saying, "I have surely visited you, and seen that which is done to you in Egypt; and I have said, I will bring you up out of the affliction of Egypt to the land of the Canaanite, the Hittite, the Amorite, the Perizzite, the Hivite, and the Jebusite, to a land flowing with milk and honey.' "[4]*

In the ExD, John will transform the name of God: "I AM WHO I AM" with the name of "who is and who was and who is to come"[5] and will thereby create a name that spans the complete story of Revelation. He will scatter God's new name in five places in Revelation and only being assigned to God.[6] By doing this,

---

3   Exod 3:1-22.
4   Exod 3:13-7.
5   Rev 1:4, 8; 4:8.
6   Rev 1:4, 8; 4:8; 11:17; 16:5.

John is giving a new name for God in hopes that the readers will follow the words of Revelation as the Israelites followed the words of Moses.

It is also important to note that in scattering the new name of God, "who is, and who was, and who is to come," John is leaving a trail for us in parallel development. We can see that John created a parallel with the prologue and the encounter with God on the throne in heaven. Both the prologue and the encounter in heaven have God on his throne, the seven spirits, God's new name, Jesus, and all believers becoming priests and a kingdom to God.[7] In the case of the prologue and the encounter with God in heaven, the order does not follow a simple or complex parallel but is rather a means of forming content agreement. This might suggest a practice of distributing and copying the desired parallel items prior to parallel formation or a radical change in one of the two parallels. We can also see how John connected the encounter with God passage and the seventh trumpet by having the 24 elders worshiping the phrase in both accounts. Last, he made a parallel between the seventh trumpet and the third bowl by copying a single sentence.[8]

The Believers Became the Kingdom of Priests to God

In John's vision, the ExD needed something more than just a new name for God, it needed a new purpose for the believer as well. So John decided to make all believers priests by extracting the following content from Exodus:

> "This is what you shall tell the house of Jacob, and tell the children of Israel:
>> 'You have seen what I did to the Egyptians,
>> and how I bore you on eagles' wings,
>> and brought you to myself.
>
> Now therefore,
>> if you will indeed obey my voice,
>> and keep my covenant,
>> then you shall be my own possession from among all peoples;
>> for all the earth is mine;
>> and you shall be to me a kingdom of priests, and a holy nation.'
>
> These are the words which you shall speak to the children of Israel."[9]

John then conflates the new name of God with the imagery that Israel will be a king of priests, and a holy nation to all believers becoming a kingdom and priests to God. Thereby he weaves two very important sections from Exodus into Revelation as seen in the following text:

> John, to the seven churches that are in Asia:
>> Grace to you and peace, from God, who is and who was and who is to come;
>> and from the seven spirits who are before his throne;
>> and from Jesus Christ, the faithful witness, the firstborn of the dead,
>> and the ruler of the kings of the earth.

---

7   Rev 1:4-6; 4:1-5:14.
8   Rev 1:4, 8; 4:8; 11:17; 16:5.
9   Exod 19:3-6.

First Exodus Overlay: Moses' Journey to Mount Sinai -- Part 1

In the Exodus draft (ExD), John incorporates the highlights of Moses' journey to Mount Sinai as his journey to heaven. The difference for John is that in Exodus it was a few chapters, while in Revelation John overlaid the content on wax tablets that were being rewritten or inserted as a result of the DJD.

What is significant here, is that John now defines all believers as a kingdom of priests to God (Ezek 19:6; Rev 1:6) and that the believers need to be sanctified for God's visitation. He then illustrates the intensity of the lightning and thunder by utilizing more dramatic descriptions and placing the imagery of them in the seventh position of each judgment.

Moses and Mount Sinai in Exodus		John's Vision in Revelation	
		The Prologue (Rev 1:1-10)	
19:4	You have seen what I did to the Egyptians, and how I bore you on eagles' wings, and brought you to myself.	12:14	Two wings of the great eagle were given to the woman, that she might fly into the wilderness to her place, so that she might be nourished for [42 months].
19:5	If you will indeed obey my voice, and keep my covenant, then you shall be my own possession from among all peoples; for all the earth is mine.	1:3	Blessed is he who reads and those who hear the words of the prophecy, and keep the things that are written in it, for the time is at hand.
3:14	God said to Moses, "I AM WHO I AM," and he said, "You shall tell the children of Israel this: 'I AM has sent me to you.'"	1:4	Who is and who was and who is to come.
		1:8	The Lord God, "who is and who was and who is to come, the Almighty."
19:6	You shall be to me a kingdom of priests, and a holy nation.	1:6	[Jesus] made us to be a kingdom, priests to his God and Father; to him be the glory and the dominion forever and ever. Amen.
19:9	Behold, I come to you in a thick cloud, that the people may hear when I speak with you.	1:7	Behold, he is coming with the clouds, and every eye will see him.
Sanctify the People		***The Message to the Seven Churches***	
19:10	THE LORD said to Moses, "Go to the people, and sanctify them today and tomorrow, and let them wash their garments.	1:11	"What you see, write in a book and send to the seven assemblies: to [the seven churches]."
	and be ready against the third day; for on the third day THE LORD will come down in the sight of all the people on Mount Sinai.	1:19	Write therefore the things which you have seen, and the things which are, and the things which will happen hereafter.
19:13	A trumpet sounds.	1:10	A loud voice, like a trumpet saying (see Rev 1:11).
19:14	Moses went down from the mountain to the people, and sanctified the people; and they washed their clothes.	1:5	Jesus who loves us, and washed us from our sins by his blood.
19:15	He said to the people, "Be ready by the third day. Don't have sexual relations with a woman."	2:13-4, 20	Unrighteous commit sexual immorality.
		14:4	These are those who were not defiled with women, for they are virgins.

First Exodus Overlay: Moses' Journey to Mount Sinai -- Part 2

Moses and Mount Sinai in Exodus	John's Vision in Revelation
Moses Taken up to Mount Sinai	***John Taken up to Heaven and the 24 Elders in Heaven (Rev 4:1-5:14)***
19:16 On the third day, when it was morning, there were thunders and lightnings, and a thick cloud on the mountain, and the sound of an exceedingly loud trumpet.	4:1 After these things I looked and saw a door opened in heaven, and the first voice that I heard, like a trumpet speaking with me.
19:17 Moses led the people out of the camp to meet God, and they stood at the lower part of the mountain.	4:4 Around the throne were 24 thrones. On the thrones were 24 elders sitting, dressed in white garments, with crowns of gold on their heads.
19:18 All of Mount Sinai smoked, because THE LORD descended on it in fire; and its smoke ascended like the smoke of a furnace, and the whole mountain quaked greatly.	4:5 Out of the throne proceeded lightnings, sounds, and thunders [from the EID, see "EP1 - Ezekiel's Experience in Heaven - Without the Scroll" on page 38].
When the sound of the trumpet grew louder and louder, Moses spoke, and God answered him by a voice.	5:9-10 Jesus washed all believers with his death (a parallel formation with Rev 1:5-6 from Exod 19:14).
	The Great Multitude in Heaven and the Seventh Seal (Rev 7:9-8:6)
	7:9 After these things I looked, and behold, a great multitude, which no man could count . . . dressed in white robes, with palm branches in their hands.
	7:14 These are those who came out of the great tribulation. They washed their robes, and made them white in the Lamb's blood.
	8:5 There followed thunders, sounds, lightnings, and an earthquake.
	The Two Prophets in Heaven and the Seventh Trumpet (Rev 11:13-9)
	11:19 Lightnings, sounds, thunders, an earthquake, and great hail followed.
	The Seventh Bowl (Rev 16:17-21)
	16:18 There were lightnings, sounds, and thunders; and there was a great earthquake, such as was not since there were men on the earth, so great an earthquake, so mighty.
	16:20 Every island fled away, and the mountains were not found.
	16:21 Great hailstones, about the weight of a talent, came down out of the sky on people.

The Overlaying of Exodus 19:3-6 in Revelation

John takes the imagery of Israel being flown out of Egypt on eagle wings to become a kingdom of priests from Ezekiel 19:3-4 and incorporates it into Revelation. First he redefines Jerusalem as the new Egypt (Rev 11:8). Second, he adds in the imagery of Moses and Aaron delivering the ten plagues by a subtle change in the two prophet narrative (Rev 11:6). Third, John takes the imagery of the eagles rescuing Israel and rewrites the imagery of the woman being flown into the wilderness by a stork to being flown into the wilderness by an eagle (Rev 12:14). Fourth, John uses the eagle flying imagery as a means of delivering a powerful message of woe to Jerusalem's destruction (Rev 8:13, 9:12, 11:14). Fifth, John, shows how the kingdom of world becomes the kingdom of God through his Christ (Exod 19:5; Rev 11:15; 12:10). Sixth, John uses 'Christ' to connect the world as the kingdom of God and assigns all believers to the role of a priest (Exod 19:6; Rev 1:5-6) and later demonstrates the believers from the entire world as the priests (Rev 7:15).

The Key Text of Exodus:

19:3 "*This is what you shall tell the house of Jacob, and tell the children of Israel: 19:4 'You have seen what I did to the Egyptians, and how I bore you on eagles' wings, and brought you to myself. 19:5 Now therefore,* if you will indeed obey my voice, and keep my covenant, then you shall be my own possession from among all peoples; for all the earth is mine; *19:6* and you shall be to me a kingdom of priests, and a holy nation.'"

Egypt (Exod 19:4) Defined as Jerusalem (Rev 11:8)

Rev 11:8   The great city, which spiritually is called Sodom and Egypt, where also their Lord was crucified.

What God Did to the Egyptians (Exod 19:4) as the Ten Plagues (Exod 7:14 - 12:36; Rev 11:6)

Rev 11:6   These have the power to shut up the sky, that it may not rain during the days of their prophecy. They have power over the waters, to turn them into blood [Exod 7:14-24], and to strike the earth with every plague, as often as they desire.

God Carries Them On Eagle Wings to Himself (Exod 19:4) for the Righteous

Rev 12:14   Two wings of the great eagle were given to the woman, that she might fly into the wilderness to her place, so that she might be nourished for a time, and times, and half a time, from the face of the serpent.

God Carries Them On Eagle Wings to Himself (Exod 19:4) for the Unrighteous

Rev 8:13   I saw, and I heard an eagle, flying in mid-heaven, saying with a loud voice, "Woe! Woe! Woe for those who dwell on the earth, because of the other voices of the trumpets of the three angels, who are yet to sound!"

Rev 9:12   The first woe is past. Behold, there are still two woes coming after this.

Rev 11:14   The second woe is past. Behold, the third woe comes quickly.

All the Earth's is God (Exod 19:5) Through Christ (Rev 11:15; 12:10)

Rev 11:15   "The kingdom of the world has become the Kingdom of our Lord, and of his Christ. He will reign forever and ever!"

Rev 12:10   Now the salvation, the power, and the Kingdom of our God, and the authority of his Christ has come.

The Faithful Shall Be a Kingdom of Priests (Exod 19:6)

Rev 1:5-6   Jesus Christ, the faithful witness, the firstborn of the dead, and the ruler of the kings of the earth. To him who loves us, and washed us from our sins by his blood; and he made us to be a Kingdom, priests to his God and Father; to him be the glory and the dominion forever and ever.

Rev 7:9   After these things I looked, and behold, a great multitude, which no man could count, out of every nation and of all tribes, peoples, and languages, standing before the throne and before the Lamb, dressed in white robes, with palm branches in their hands.

Rev 7:15   Therefore they are before the throne of God, they serve him day and night in his temple. He who sits on the throne will spread his tabernacle over them.

To him who loves us, and washed us from our sins by his blood;
and he made us to be a kingdom, priests to his God and Father;
to him be the glory and the dominion forever and ever. Amen.[10]

John will then take God's dire warning from Exodus, "If you will indeed obey my voice and keep my covenant, then you . . ." and apply it to the content of the seven churches with the future promised land of the New Jerusalem.[11] In so doing, John will transform the messages from cities connected to the 144,000 to cities and messages connected with the great multitude.

John is not one to waste a good text so he utilizes the imagery of God flying the Israelites to the promised land on wings of eagles to three woes interlaced within the trumpets,[12] which is the tool that destroys Jerusalem and takes them into captivity. He will also use the imagery of the eagle wings as a means of preserving the Israelites similarly to the Exodus content.[13] In this way he takes the Roman symbol of the eagle and conflates it with the symbol of the eagle in Exodus.

The Sanctifying of the New Believers

John continues the imagery of Moses and Mount Sinai by communicating how the people should sanctify themselves before God comes in the clouds. The two things that are mentioned in this process is the washing of the clothes and the abstaining from sexual relations with women.[14]

The Washing of the Clothes

There are two parts to the washing of the clothes in Revelation. First they are washed through the blood of Jesus that is connected with his death.[15] Second, the only people given a white robe are martyrs.[16] Those that are not given a white robe will have their names blotted out of God's book, which is an allusion to God's punishment of those who made the golden calf when Moses was on Mount Sinai.[17]

To best understand how Revelation depicts the believer and the white robe is to read it vertically, since it was written in the horizontal.[18] In this manner we can observe how the storyline progresses from the saints on earth who are told to remain faithful, to the saints with Jesus at the second coming.

Abstaining From Sexual Activity With Women

The second way that Moses was to sanctify the Israelites was to have them abstain from sexual activity with women.[19] The churches already contained warnings against sexual immorality and examples of saints who abstained from sexual activity with women. So John applied this to praise those who remained virgins as

---

10   Rev 1:4-6.
11   Exod 19:5; Rev 2:2-6, 10, 13-6, 24-5; 3:2-4, 10.
12   Rev 8:12; 9:11; 11:13
13   Rev 12:14; Exod 19:4.
14   Exod 19:10, 15.
15   Rev 1:5; 5:9-10.
16   Rev 6:9-11; 7:9-15; 19:1-8 (as the second part to Rev 6:9-11).
17   Rev 3:5; Exod 32:31-5.
18   See "The Story of the Fifth Church" on page 282.
19   Exod 19:15.

the 144,000 in heaven.[20] As a result of emphasizing the believers as males who are priests and who abstain from sexual relationships with women, we have no examples of married men or any women at all in heaven. The only place where a woman is depicted in a positive light is the mention of the woman who gave birth to the child, which is a symbol that represents the righteous element of Jerusalem.[21] Whether John intended the finished product to exclude married men and/or females to such an extent, we will never know. He may not have even realized the bigger picture of what he was writing or he may actually have had no clue about the impact of excluding righteous women in Revelation. He might have wanted to depict salvation for strictly male virgins or simply imply that it applied only to the 144,000. His true underlying intention, however, is something we are unable to assess.

God Coming in the Clouds

By overlaying Moses' visit to Mount Sinai, John is actually preparing the believer for God's coming in the clouds.[22] We have already seen that for the believer, having their robes washed contains two components: the first is the robe and the second is the act of washing. The washing of the robe is done by Jesus but for the believer to obtain the robe they must sacrifice their life.[23]

In Exodus, we read that on the third day of preparations, God came in a cloud with thunders and lightnings and as it came closer the trumpet became louder and louder.[24] How John transformed this scene was by having the days represent the judgments so that the first day represented the seals, the second day represented the trumpets, and the third day represented the bowls. He then created the sense that God is coming by intensifying the thunder and lightning—the enhancement of this imagery served as a foreshadowing of God's arrival. This was done for two reasons: the first is that he could not add the trumpet into the mix because he already had the seven trumpets and it would seem odd to have the trumpets mixed in with the seals and bowls. So John opted instead to add an earthquake and hail to the thunders and lightnings, in order to intensify the scene.[25]

An oddity of John appending the earthquake imagery on each of the seven judgments is found in the seventh trumpet, where John has an earthquake scene both prior to and after the seventh trumpet.[26] The seventh bowl, however, does a better job of integrating the two together.[27] The oddity of the seventh trumpet was most likely due to how John formed the passage by constructing the conquest of Jericho backwards.[28]

John kept the trumpet imagery from Exodus and made it the voice of God, Jesus, and the angel forming a chain of custody as defined in the first verse in Revelation, and we have each one speaking in the pro-

---

20   Rev 2:13-4, 20.

21   In Rev 12:1-17, the woman is found in heaven and is always protected by God and pursued by Satan.

22   Rev 1:4, 7 (see "DJ1 - The Prologue (Rev 1:1-20)" on page 167 as it originally was applied to God); 22:7, 12.

23   Rev 1:5-6; 5:9-11; 7:9-17.

24   Exod 19:16-9.

25   The seventh seal: "There followed thunders, sounds, lightnings, and an earthquake (Rev 8:5)."

    The seventh trumpet: "Lightnings, sounds, thunders, an earthquake, and great hail followed (Rev 11:19)."

    The seventh bowl: "There were lightnings, sounds, and thunders; and there was a great earthquake, such as was not since there were men on the earth . . . . Great hailstones, about the weight of a talent, came down out of the sky on people (Rev 16:18, 21)."

26   Rev 11:13, 19.

27   Rev 16:17-21.

28   See "The Seventh Trumpet: How and Why it Was Placed" on page 149.

logue.[29] Also, there is no reason why John would have defined the speaker as "the first voice that I heard, like a trumpet speaking with me"[30] when every other author's notation is very specific. Furthermore, the word "first" implies that there is a second to follow.

The Decalogue and the Ten Commandments: Synonyms of Distinction

The term *Decalogue* is used by the Jewish tradition to signify that the commandments received by Moses on the mountain are just ten of many. The ten commandments are used by the Christian tradition to define the significant commandments and thereby ignore the lesser commandments. For the purpose of this book the terms are used interchangeably without emphasis of one tradition over the other.

The Commandments of God and the Story of the Golden Calf Retold

The story of Moses receiving the commandments at Mount Sinai covers eleven chapters and consists of the Decalogue and all the information to build and construct the tabernacle, the priestly clothing, and all of the worship practices.[31] As Moses received all the instructions from God, the Israelites created a golden calf to worship.[32] The actions of the Israelites angered God so much that he was going to destroy them all and start over with a new people. Fortunately for the Israelites, Moses was able to calm God down enough so as not to destroy his people.[33]

When Moses came down from the mountain he was so furious that he broke the stone tablets that God had made for his people.[34] At the end of the golden calf episode we find out that God keeps a book which has the names of his people written within it, and that he blots out the names of those who sinned against him.[35]

John will focus the storyline in Revelation on the righteous obeying the commandments of God over and over again. This is not to ignore that all of the drafts prior to the ExD contained commandments for the people to follow, but instead to emphasize the importance to obey the commandments. In two of the spots in Revelation John will redefine God's book as a carrot and a stick. In the message to the church in Sardis it is a carrot where Jesus threatens to blot out their names from the book.[36] In the New Jerusalem it is the Lamb's book of life containing the names of the righteous.[37]

John incorporated a surprisingly large portion of the tabernacle imagery into Revelation, and in the next section we will go into more detail as to just how he does this.

---

29   God speaks in Rev 12:1, the angel speaks in Rev 1:10-1, and Jesus speaks in Rev 1:12-20.
30   Rev 4:1.
31   Exod 21:1 - 31:18.
32   Exod 32:1- 35.
33   Exod 31:11-4.
34   Exod 31:15-20.
35   Ezek 32:33-5.
36   Rev 3:5.
37   Rev 21:27.

Ezekiel's Exodus Draft

John is not the only one that had an Exodus draft. The book of Ezekiel is essentially the book of Exodus from Moses ascending to mount Sinai to the finish of the tabernacle modernized to reflect Babylonian captivity. The table below represents items that are common elements that Exodus and Ezekiel share.

Content Found in Exodus	Content Found in Ezekiel
Moses is taken up in a cloud (Exod 19:1-25) • THE LORD said to Moses, "Behold, I come to you in a thick cloud (19:9)." On the third day, when it was morning, there were thunders and lightnings, and a thick cloud on the mountain, and the sound of an exceedingly loud trumpet (19:16).	***Ezekiel is Taken up in a Cloud (Ezek 1:4)*** • I looked, and behold, a stormy wind came out of the north, a great cloud, with flashing lightning, and a brightness around it, and out of the middle of it as it were glowing metal, out of the middle of the fire (Ezek 1:4).
Moses sent to God's rebellious people • Moses sent to God's rebellious people (32:7-8). • God gave Moses the Decalogue on two tablets written on both sides. (32:15-6). • In anger Moses broke the tablets (32:19).	***Ezekiel Sent to God's Rebellious People (2:3 - 3:27)*** • Ezekiel sent to God's rebellious people (2:3-7). • God gave Ezekiel a scroll written on two sides to eat. It contained the "lamentations, and mourning, and woe (2:8 - 3:3)." • It was sweet to the lips when Ezekiel ate the scroll (2:8 -3:3).
Moses and God dealing with Israel's Sin / Idolatry (32:19 - 33:23) • Moses makes the Israelites consume the golden calf (32:20). • The glory of God descended upon the tent of meeting (33:1-23).	***God Has Ezekiel Relay How Israel Will Be Destroyed Because of Their Sin / Idolatry (4:1- 20:32)*** • Ezekiel told to make barley cakes baked from human dung. That is what the Israelites will eat (4:9-17). • The Glory flees the temple in Jerusalem (10:1-22).
Moses Builds the Tabernacle (25:1 - 31:17; 35:1 - 40:38) • Twelve stones for the priest breastplate (28:17-20). • Sacrifices are performed (29:38-46). • God lives in the tabernacle (40:34-8).	***The City of God Will Be Built (40:1 - 48:35)*** • Twelve stones of creation identical to Exodus (28:13). • Sacrifices are performed (40:42; 44:11). • God lives in the city of God (43:7).

Isaiah a Third Generation Draft of Exodus
and Revelation as a Second, Third, and Fourth Generation Draft of Exodus

As seen in the Ezekiel-Isaiah Draft chapter in this book, a large portion of Isaiah is the story of Ezekiel but modified where as there are two groups of God's people. The likely reason for the parallel is that the author of Isaiah 6:1 - 29:24 made a simple parallel to the whole of Ezekiel and formed each element into an opposite. This makes Isaiah 6:1 - 29:24 a third generation of the Exodus account of Moses ascending to Mount Sinai to the construction of the tabernacle. Because of how the author forms a parallel with its source the text dramatically changes from one generation to another. It is easy to see how Ezekiel is a second generation to the Exodus narrative but it would be impossible to connect the Isaiah narrative derived from Ezekiel to connect it with Ezekiel's source with out the transition of Ezekiel.

How the text changes from generation to generation of writings represent the greatest power of the writings. When the reader reads a second or third generation text they experience the familiarity of the first generation text without the reader directly connecting it to its source.

For us, the readers, the power of identifying the sources of a text enriches our understanding of what the author is trying to convey unparalleled today. For the first time we can say with certainty how many of the symbols came into Revelation and what they mean. We can, as this book has demonstrated, write a narrative that closely follows what the original author wrote line by line. Such is the power of the GLR methodology. Imagine what we can do by producing a literary genetic structure of the whole of scripture.

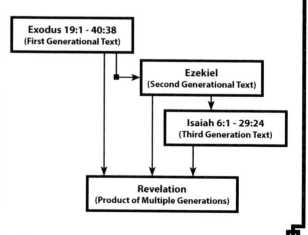

The Temple and the Tabernacle as Synonyms

In Revelation the tabernacle and the temple are synonymous in that they both portray the place where God is. Therefore this chapter will use the words interchangeably.

The Servicing of the Tabernacle in Heaven

The second primary storyline that John adds to the DJD is that of the servicing of the tabernacle. By making the believers a kingdom of priests to God, John began creating the infrastructure of a new temple in heaven.[38] To do this, John takes the reader on a journey of the priest servicing the tabernacle on the Day of Atonement (Yom Kippur) which is the one day that the priest can enter into the Most Holy Place.[39] However for the most part, instead of focusing on the priest performing the activities he will focus on the instruments and the offerings by connecting them with the believers. By focusing on the instruments John does not have to retain the same priest for the duration of the servicing of the tabernacle description.

Transitioning From the Deuteronomy-Joshua Draft to the Exodus Draft

With the tabernacle service being overlaid on the DJD, John had to make many changes to the text in order for the tabernacle service to become the ExD. The first and most significant change John made was to have Jesus, rather than God, as the significant speaker in the prologue. In the DJD, God was the first speaker who gave the message to Jesus and he told the angel to write the message that will be delivered to John.[40] The problem that John had was how to change the text so that it reflects the first step into the tabernacle (caring for the seven lampstands/the Menorah). John could not have God as the central priest to himself, so the text was changed to make Jesus the central figure with the backdrop of the seven lampstands.[41] As a result, the alpha and omega parallel was broken,[42] the worship scene became a falling down as though he was dead scene,[43] and imagery applied to God became imagery applied to Jesus.[44]

The changes were not solely related to the transition of the DJD to the ExD but also can be seen in the different sub drafts within the ExD. As with the previous draft (DJD), the ExD will have a finishing phase in which John will construct parallels and those parallels will shape the prologue. Those changes will be addressed later in this chapter.

The Servicing of the Menorah

The seven lamps are to remain always lit but through the evenings they are unattended and may sometimes go out. So when the priest would enter the tabernacle, the first thing he would do is relight the lamps that

---

38   See "The Day of Atonement and the Tabernacle -- Part 1" on page 204 and "The Day of Atonement and the Tabernacle -- Part 2" on page 205.

39   Lev 16:1-34; see "The Day of Atonement and the Tabernacle -- Part 1" on page 204 and "The Day of Atonement and the Tabernacle -- Part 2" on page 205.

40   Rev 1:1.

41   Rev 1:12-3, 19-20.

42   The phrase "first and the last" which were part of the original alpha and omega parallel (Rev 1:8; 21:6; 22:13) became a description of Jesus and moved to Rev 1:17.

43   Rev 1:17.

44   In Ezek 1:28 - 2:2.

burned out. In Revelation, we have Jesus attending to the seven lampstands and their significance is that they are each the symbol of one of the seven churches (to such an extent that the removal of one would be akin to the removal of the church from the kingdom of God).[45]

Since the priesthood is now expanded to include believers all over the world, John will need to address the message to the cities to include gentile cities as well. However, John will keep the content of the message to the seven churches from prior drafts and only tweak the content of a few of the letters.

How John will shape and organize the seven churches and connect them to the whole of Revelation will be addressed later when we discuss the ExD's finishing phase. This is because there are many parallels that connect the seven churches to other content in Revelation. Those parallel formations will have a stronger effect on the seven churches than the Menorah has, due to its construction.

The Servicing of the Bread on the Table of the Bread of Presence

The table of the bread of presence in Exodus is a small table that held two stacks of six loaves of bread, which were similar in shape to a pancake. Each loaf of bread represented one tribe of Israel and its purpose was to nourish the priests as they performed their duties in the tabernacle. For John to incorporate the table of the bread of presence into the ExD he needed symbols that already conveyed the similar meanings and numbers.

The result is that John took the four living creatures from the EID and combined them with the elders and their thrones from the ZrD. He then limited the living creatures from an indeterminate number to the specific quantity of four.[46] Likewise, he limited the number of elders to 24, where twelve of them would represent the twelve tribes of Israel and the other twelve would represent the twelve apostles.[47] John organized the elders to correspond to the living creatures via a ratio of six (elders) to one (living creature). In this manner he satisfied the loaves of bread being stacked six high. For the nourishing portion, he conflated the two by performing worship ceremonies to God and Jesus.[48]

Making the changes to create similar imagery to the table of the bread of presence was not without its problems. In the ZrD, John had a nice flow in the storyline where he ended the message to the cities with the following quotation:

> *He who overcomes, I will give to him to sit down with me on my throne, as I also overcame, and sat down with my Father on his throne.*[49]

From there he picked up the storyline with God sitting on the throne and the living creatures worshiping him. In the following chapter we have Jesus' coronation in which he gathers people from all over the world to become leaders.[50] The end result is that we have a promise to believers that if they overcome they can

---

45   Rev 2:5.
46   Ezek 1:5; Rev 4:7.
47   Rev 1:4.
48   Lev 25:5-9.
49   Rev 3:21.
50   Rev 5:1-14; see "Z3 - The Coronation of Jesus as the High Priest (Zech 6:9-15; Rev 5:1-14)" on page 74 on how the ZrD depicted the coronation of Jesus.

sit at the throne similar to how Jesus sits on the throne. We have a progression from God on his throne, to Jesus on his throne, to finally the elders on their thrones.

Where the ExD ruined the flow is with the placement of the verse where the elders prepare the incense. In the ZrD they were only a verse apart. In the ExD, John needed them to be farther apart but was limited as to how far back he could push the elders. He could not place them with the material that related to the seven churches because that is covered by the menorah. So the farthest back he could move the elders was only one chapter earlier, where God is sitting on his throne. As a result, the elders were placed around the throne of God prior to the coronation of Jesus, which breaks the chain of God giving Jesus a throne and Jesus giving the elders their thrones. So John removed the imagery of Jesus receiving a throne in the coronation of Jesus, but forgot to remove the promise alluded to earlier, regarding the believers.[51]

The Four Living Creatures and the 24 When Used Together

In Revelation, when the four living creatures and the 24 elders are used in the same text it is with regard to worship. As we progressed through the ExD, the audience and the praise chorus grows. The first encounter with the four living creatures and the 24 elders is just them with God on his throne and the seven spirits of God. In the next encounter, Jesus is added.[52] The next two encounters have to do with the great multitude and the 144,000 in heaven. However, John will make one very important change. The number of the elders is removed from both the great multitude and the 144,000 in heaven narratives, which is most likely due to John seeing the 144,000 in heaven as representing the twelve tribes of Israel and the other twelve representing the twelve apostles.[53] In the last two scenes all 24 elders are mentioned as well as the four living creatures and the context that they are in represent all believers (the 144,000 and the great multitude) in heaven.[54] This is logical since the 24 elders wear the robes of the martyrs and satisfy the promise that Jesus gave to the believers.[55]

The Four Living Creatures Only

When the four living creatures are mentioned alone they are connected to the dispensing of the judgments, namely the first four seals and one of the four living creatures giving the bowl to the angels dispensing the seven bowls.[56] This is probably a carryover from the EID where the seraph takes the coal from the altar and touches Isaiah's lips so that he will be purified[57] (which would indicate that the judgment scenes are for the purification of Jerusalem).

---

51 Rev 3:21.
52 Rev 5:8-11.
53 The only place where the twelve tribes of Israel and the apostles are used together is found in the New Jerusalem (Rev 21:12-21) which is connected to its residents.
54 Rev 11:16; 19:4.
55 Rev 4:4; 19:8, 14. Note: one of the descriptions of the angels can be viewed as they are wearing the martyr's clothing (Rev 15:6). This could indicate that in the ZrD the dispensers of the judgments were the elders via a similar process where the seraphim gave John the coal to his lips to purify him (Rev 6:4-8).
56 Rev 6:1-8; 15:7.
57 Isa 6:4-8.

The Day of Atonement and the Tabernacle -- Part 1

The whole of Revelation is connected in some way with the servicing of the tabernacle. So to understand Revelation one needs to understand how the tabernacle was set up and how it was serviced.

The tabernacle was the portable temple that God instructed Moses to build, and was the center of Israelites' lives. In Exodus, it was the place where God lived and the source of the Israelites' comfort for their forty-year trek through the wilderness. By day a cloud appeared to provide shade to the people from the hot sun. By night it provided light and warmth through the fire in heaven (Exod). It was the place where the manna appeared (a divine source of food in the wilderness). To the people of Moses, it was their center of worship and the place where God resides.

In Exodus and Leviticus, God defined the form, function, and furniture of the tabernacle as well as the duties of the priest and the timing of the events. In Exodus, the shape of the tabernacle was 45 feet by 15 feet long and 15 feet tall (13.7m x 4.6 m x 4.6m) (Exod 26:1, 15-29). The tabernacle had two sections, the larger room (30 feet by 15 feet/9.1 m x 4.6 m) was called the Holy Place and contained three pieces of furniture. The first was the golden lampstand that had seven lamps that were always burning (Exod 25:31-40; 37:17-24). The second was the table for the bread of presence that contained the twelve loaves placed in two stacks, with each loaf representing a tribe from Israel (Exod 25:23-30). The third piece of furniture in the tabernacle was the altar of incense where the priest would burn incense and sprinkle sacrificial blood on the altar (Exod 30:1-5; 37:25-9).

The second room in the tabernacle was the Most Holy Place which was in the form of a cube that measured 15 feet by 15 feet by 15 feet (4.6m x 4.6m x 4.6m) into which the high priest was only allowed to enter once a year. Inside the room was the ark of the covenant (Exod 25:10-22; 37:1-9).

The Servicing of the Tabernacle in Revelation

In Revelation the emphasis is not on the priest servicing the tabernacle but rather on the items in the tabernacle that relate to the sacrifice of Jesus and the believers. Below is a diagram of the tabernacle which is numbered in order as it relates to how the temple is serviced in Revelation.

The Menorah

① **The Servicing of the Golden Lampstand (Rev 1:11 - 3:22)**

In Leviticus	In Revelation
• A single lampstand containing seven lamps (Exod 25:32-5)	• There are seven lampstands each representing a church (Rev 1:20; 2:5 - indicating that they were separate).

The Day of Atonement and the Tabernacle -- Part 2

The Table of the Bread of Presence

② **The Servicing of the Table for the Bread of Presence (Rev 4:1-11)**

In Leviticus	In Revelation
• The purpose of the bread is to represent the sons of Israel [twelve tribes] and to provide nourishment to the priest as he performs his tabernacle duties (Lev 24:5-9).	• The loaves of bread are represented by the 24 elders which are divided into four groups of six (Rev 4:4-8). Although it is not stated directly in Revelation it is assumed that twelve of the elders represent the twelve tribes of Israel and the other twelve elders represent the twelve apostles (see text). They provide nourishment to God through their worship roles which they perform constantly before him (Rev 4:8-11; 7:11-2; 14:3; 19:3).

The Altar of Incense

The Day of Atonement and Revelation have many common elements as well as many differences. The chart below represents the common elements such as the high priest making his own sacrifice, the clothing, and the blood sprinkled on the altar. Revelation, however, uses the imagery in a different way as seen in the following chart.

The Day of Atonement (Lev 16:11-34)	③ Jesus as the Preparing of the Incense (Rev 5:1 - 6:17)	④ The Great Multitude as the Burning of the Incense (Rev 7:9 - 9:22)	⑤ The 144,000 as the Cleansing of the Tabernacle (Rev 15:1-8)
• High priest makes atonement for himself (Lev 16:11).	• Jesus died (Rev 5:6, 9).	• They were martyred (Rev 7:9, 14).	• Saints in heaven singing the song of Moses and the Lamb (Rev 14:1-5; 15:1-4).
• Censer full of coals of the fire from off the altar and sweet ingredients (Lev 16:12).	• Altar originally had coals (Isa 6:5-8; Rev 5:8-11). • Incense was mixed with the blood of Jesus and the prayers of the saints (Rev 5:8-11).	• Censer filled with the fire of the altar (Rev 8:5). • Contained the prayers of the saints (Rev 8:4).	• Those who overcame the beast was like a sea of glass mixed with fire (Rev 15:2; connected with the wrath of God in Rev 15:1). • Censer filled with the wrath of God (Rev 15:7).
• Holy linen.	• Wore a robe with a golden sash around his chest (1:13)	• They were given white robes (Rev 6:11; 7:13-5).	• Seven angels wearing pure, bright linens, and a golden sash around their chests (15:5).
• The blood was sprinkled on the altar of God seven times (Lev 16:14).	• Jesus' blood (Rev 1:5; 5:8-10). • The seven seals (Rev 6:1-17; 8:1-6).	• The great multitude as martyrs (Rev 7:9-17). • The seven trumpets (Rev 8:7 - 9:21; 11:13-7)	• The 144,000 in heaven with Jesus (Rev 14:1-5). • The seven bowls (Rev 16:1-21).

⑥ **The Entering in the Most Holy Place (Rev 21:1 - 22:5)**

In Exodus 25:10-22; 26:15-30 37:1-9	In Revelation
• The Most Holy Place was in the shape of a cube (15' x 15' x 15') and it is the place where God dwells (Exod 26:26-30).	• The New Jerusalem is the Most Holy Place as evident by the fact that it forms a cube and it is the place where God and Jesus live (Rev 21:6).

The Absence of the Four Living Creatures and the 24 Elders in the New Jerusalem

The last scene which depicts the four living creatures and the 24 elders is found in Revelation 19:1-8 where the saints praise God for the destruction of Babylon/Tyre/Rome. This is due to John writing the story in the horizontal and simply ending it prior to the second coming.[58] In John's eyes, the believers who were martyred become rulers shortly after.[59] Thus the need for the 24 elders representing the end state of the believers is no longer needed.

John's use of the 24 elders is significant in that it provides the imagery of all believers, the 144,000, and the great multitude, as indistinguishable. This gives us a glimpse of a time when followers of Jesus made no distinction between those with Jewish heritage and those with gentile heritage. This can be seen in the New Jerusalem, where the only distinction between the two groups is within their physical description. The gates of the New Jerusalem are named after the twelve tribes of Israel and he added that the New Jerusalem has twelve foundations named after the twelve apostles.[60]

The Servicing the Altar of Incense and the Entering the Most Holy Place

The Day of Atonement (Yom Kippur) is the most important event for the tabernacle because it is the one day in which all the sins of Israel are atoned for and the only day that the high priest can enter into the Most Holy Place.[61] It is the day of two sacrifices, incense preparation, the sprinkling of the blood on the altar of God seven times, and the day where the priests wash their clothes after each activity.

John will initially weave the entire activity that the previous paragraph describes into four places in the DJD. Three of the four places are placed on blank spots created from the DJD inserting new tablets prior to the three judgments scenes. The fourth is a simple tweak which makes the square New Jerusalem into a cube, just like the Most Holy Place.[62]

In what amounts to less text inserted into the draft than the whole of this section, John created a way of making an eternal covenant in the lives of those who live in the New Jerusalem.[63] Edits within the process of creating Revelation are seldom easy (often causing more work to be done afterwards) and this one was no exception. John now had to create names and attributes for the old holy seed (those who obeyed the commandments of God) and the new holy seed (those who obey the commandments of God and Jesus).

God and Jesus Become the Temple

One of the more interesting changes in the ExD is the transformation of the temple of God being a physical structure in Ezekiel to God and Jesus becoming the actual temple. This was done to solve a variety of new issues that John created with the making the New Jerusalem into the most holy place. Such as, placing a temple with in the temple for God to live in. This would make God living in a box smaller than the box that the believers living in. The second problem, John had been the temple in the second temple period and in Revelation. One had the continuance of sacrifices of animals and in Revelation it is the sacrifices of

---

58   See ."The Story of the Fifth Church" on page 282.
59   Rev 20:6.
60   Rev 21:12-4.
61   Lev 16:1-34.
62   Rev 21:16.
63   Lev 16:34. The New Jerusalem becomes the most holy place where the high priests (all believers) never leave the temple.

humans[64] and their praising God to nourish him.[65] Since there is no longer any death in the New Jerusalem[66] John opted on the nourishing of God by leveraging the believers as priests already developed in the ExD.[67] To solve the God in a smaller box than the believers' box problem, John made God and Jesus larger than the box (the New Jerusalem) of the believers by making them the sole source of light on the New Earth. This was all done by the simple altering of a few lines of the New Jerusalem narrative.[68]

Moses, Aaron, and the Ten Plagues

John even included the story of Moses, Aaron, and the ten plagues into the ExD by simply expanding the description of the two prophets. He gave the two prophets the power to call down any plagues from heaven and the second plague that is mentioned is the first of the ten plagues from Exodus.[69]

The first plague assigned to the two prophets is actually connected with the prophet Elijah, but the reason John added it is not known. It could be that he wanted the two prophets to represent the most noble of the Israelite's heritage or it could be because he wanted to distract the reader from the source he was using, though it was probably a little of both. One thing is certain though, in this style of writing we should realize how quickly symbols expand in meaning. Therefore we should also realize how limiting a symbol to a single meaning ignores the intent of the author.

The Birth of the 144,000 and the Great Multitude

Up until now, the book of Revelation is written to Jews with judgment against those that ignored Jesus and a reward for those who obeyed him. The distinction was more than just simply following Jesus but actually was those who existed before Jesus and were faithful to God and those who existed after Jesus and obeyed God and Jesus. In the EID this was the old seed and the new seed,[70] but that is hardly descriptive enough for what John does in Revelation. John settled on two names: the 144,000 and the great multitude. The 144,000 represented the faithful who came from the twelve tribes of Israel from the time of the crossing of the Jordan River by Joshua to the death of Jesus.[71] The great multitude represented the faithful from all walks of life who obey the commandments of God and Jesus.[72]

The Creation of the 144,000

The creation as well as the source of the name for the 144,000 came from the first scene after Joshua crossed the Jordan River. In this scene Joshua circumcised all males from the twelve tribes of Israel (all having been born in the wilderness), and reporting that only 12,000 from each tribe were faithful.[73]

---

64 See "The Day of Atonement and the Tabernacle -- Part 2" on page 205.
65 See "The Servicing of the Bread on the Table of the Bread of Presence" on page 202.
66 Rev 21:4.
67 See "The Believers Became the Kingdom of Priests to God" on page 193.
68 Rev 21:23-5.
69 "They had the power over the waters, to turn them into blood" (Rev 11:6; Exod 7:17).
70 See "The End of One Ministry and the Birth of Another (Ezek 4:5-8; Isa 6:13-9:19)" on page 18.
71 Rev 7:1-8; 14:1-5.
72 Rev 7:9-17; Rev 12:17.
73 Rev 7:1-8.

Since John needed a termination place for the 144,000 he chose to use another scene from the DJD where the people pledge their allegiance to Joshua/Jesus on Mount Zion[74] (the very first scene after the woman, Satan, and the child narrative).[75] The placement was ideal in that it did not disrupt the complex parallel between the first four trumpets and the four attacks by Satan.[76] It also came after the child (Jesus) was taken to heaven to rule with God.[77] Through this simple change, we now have the very first scene in which believers are in heaven.

The Creation of the Great Multitude

The great multitude is a term used in this book to describe the followers of Jesus. John provides a multitude of descriptions such as the seven churches,[78] those from every language, tribe, race, and nation.[79] He even equates the twelve apostles on an equal footing with the twelve tribes of Israel.[80] However, John does not provide a term for this group of believers, but nonetheless it is well-defined and distinct from the 144,000. For example, the 144,000 have the seal of God on their foreheads,[81] while the foreheads of the great multitude do not. The great multitude wears the white robes[82] which is not an image that exists in the 144,000 narratives.

The creation of the story of the 144,000 was a very linear process, which is easy for us to follow today. The story of the great multitude was a different case. To construct the story of the great multitude, John needed a beginning much like the beginning of the 144,000. John elected to use the child (Jesus) found in the woman, child, and Satan narrative. This is because, in the EID, the child was the new holy seed for a new crop of believers to replace the old set of believers.[83] The woman, child, and Satan narrative also describes the four attacks by Satan against the woman, child, and a new set of believers who follow the commandments of God and the Lamb. Although it does not supply the text for the destruction of all believers, the complex parallel it forms with the first four trumpets does.[84] The storyline was just too shallow for a literary parallel. John needed a storyline of significance for the end of the great multitude, much like the storyline for the end of the two prophets.

To create the story of the final days for those who come from all countries, languages, and races, John needed a way for them to come from all parts of the world. For John, this was as simple as taking the Isaiah text where the children of God will come from all parts of the world and changing it to the gospel has been preached to the entire world.[85] From there it was a simple process of producing a story with the finality of the believers which represents the great harvest where all believers have been killed off and harvested to heaven.[86]

---

74   Rev 14:1-5.
75   Rev 12:17.
76   Rev 12:1-17.
77   Rev 12:4-5.
78   Rev 2:1 - 3:22.
79   Rev 7:9.
80   Rev 21:14.
81   Rev 7:1-3.
82   Rev 6:9-11; 7:9-17; 19:1-8.
83   See "The End of One Ministry and the Birth of Another (Ezek 4:5-8; Isa 6:13-9:19)" on page 18.
84   Rev 12:17 has its complex parallel element in the first trumpet (Rev 8:7; see "Satan's Story" on page 294).
85   Rev 7:9.
86   Rev 14:6-20.

To bring the story back to where it all began, John modified the first Passover in the promised land from Joshua 5:9-11 to make it where all of the great multitude now reside. Since the primary purpose of the ExD was to produce a new people of God and to service a new temple in heaven, John made the great multitude the wearers of the priestly garb and the 144,000 took on the role of those outside the new priesthood.[87]

The Seven Letters a Transition From Jewish Cities to Gentile Cities?

The ZrD had the letters addressed to Jerusalem and to Rome[88] and the DJD could have been addressed to seven cities in Israel.[89] The ExD is different because it is a transition between the DJD and the DnD where the churches represented Israelite cities and in the PVR they represent gentile cities. We can only guess as to who they were addressed to but not in specifics as to the city that they belong to.

The Changing of the Prologue

The ExD forced John to restructure the prologue on multiple levels. The greatest of these changes had to do with the servicing of the seven candlesticks (the menorah). Obviously it would look silly to have God become his own priest. So that left Jesus or the angel as his only choices. As we see in the PVR, Jesus became the priest servicing the seven lampstands and God's speaking role is reduced to background noise.

The act of making Jesus the caretaker of the seven lampstands made Jesus also the caretaker of the seven churches. As such, the way the letters were addressed in the previous drafts with a statement about God and the phrase "thus says" appended to it was changed to the statements about Jesus and the phrase "thus says" appended to it. This fundamental change caused imagery attributed to God, such as "the first and the last," and the "faithful witness," to now be attributed to Jesus.[90] It also caused the chain of custody of the vision to no longer reflect the prologue as it did in the DJD.[91]

The Organizing of the Seven Churches

The content of the seven churches will not be addressed in this chapter but will be addressed in the chapter on Horizontal Reading. The reason for this is that the seven churches must have changed so many times making it difficult to reconstruct the order and process. The chapter on Horizontal Reading touches a number of parallels formed with the seven churches showing the scope and scale of the parallels that John formed. With each parallel formed the seven churches became organized with greater and greater precision as well as providing us with a wealth of interpretative insight not possible without the understanding of the parallel formations. As a result the formation of the seven churches is best addressed outside the scope of this chapter.

Final Thoughts

The ExD shows us that John can overlay a story onto Revelation and work within the blank spots of the tablets added by the DJD. It also shows that John can take the last draft which is derived from the trans-

---

87   Rev 7:9-17.
88   See "Defining the Content and the Recipients of the Letters to the Churches" on page 71.
89   See "The Seven Churches" on page 159.
90   Rev 1:5, 17; see "The Creation of the Alpha and Omega Parallel" on page 152.
91   Rev 1:1. See "DJ1 - The Prologue (Rev 1:1-20)" on page 167.

ferring the leadership from Moses to Joshua found in Deuteronomy and Joshua and add in the story from the commissioning of Moses to the construction of the tabernacle. The ExD also shows us how much just a little content added into a blank spot profoundly shapes the DJD in such a way that it is very difficult to detect the DJD's source and importation pattern of Deuteronomy and Joshua.

The ExD for the first time acknowledges believers outside of the Jewish people to include all peoples from every tribe, language, and race.[92] The ExD also makes all believers, those who follow Jesus, as priests as well as the sacrifice so as to keep the eternal covenant of the Day of Atonement.[93] John also sees Jesus as the transition figure for the faithful Jews (the 144,000) and the faithful gentiles.

The ExD could have very been the last draft that John planned prior to publication, why else spend the time forming parallels. It is worth noting that if he did publish the ExD instead of the next draft we would not have any concept of a enemy on earth or a place of eternal torment. The harlot would still be depicted as a different aspect of Jerusalem and many other minor things such as the imagery of Jesus that comes from Daniel. It is also worth noting that the ExD was in better shape than the DnD and if he spent the time refining the ExD instead of adding in the DnD he would have given us one of the better written books in the Christian Scriptures as opposed to one of the worse written books in the Christian Scriptures.

---

92   Rev 7:9-17.
93   Lev 16:34.

Chapter 6: The Daniel Draft (DnD)

The Daniel Draft's (DnD) primary purpose is twofold: first it is to provide an earthly adversary second in rank to Satan and being organizationally parallel to Jesus. Second it is to provide context for when the events in Revelation will take place. Therefore, as we investigate how the DnD was constructed and the major changes John made to Daniel, we will get clues who the beast is and when the end of the world will occur.

Let's Build the Daniel Draft

The way John constructed the DnD is similar to how he constructed the ExD, except for that the storyline revolves around the beast. To do this, John selected elements from the book of Daniel and Enoch and established a method with which to integrate the content into the ExD. As a result of this tinkering, he created many author's notations and revised much of the text. The additions and changes will have their own purpose to the story and may be used later to accommodate additional text from Daniel. Because of this, we will see more of the drafts within the DnD as they take shape and this will give us a glimpse of the editorial process throughout the writing of the DnD.

The Debut of the Beast

The beast and his servant, whom we will refer to as the false prophet, comes from the book of Daniel. In fact, when you lay Daniel and Revelation side by side there is not much difference between the two accounts besides some light editing.[1] However, John will translate the imagery Daniel used to predict the beast, into numbers for us as readers to use to predict the beast. This is similar to how Ezekiel transformed

---

1   See "The Creation of the Beast and the False Prophet -- Part 1" on page 214, "The Creation of the Beast and the False Prophet -- Part 2" on page 215, and "The Creation of the Beast and the False Prophet -- Part 3" on page 217.

the number of days he lay on his left and right side (when prophesying the days of the Babylonian siege of Jerusalem) into numbers that would represent the days of the Roman siege of Jerusalem.[2]

In this section we will cover the process of how the beast scenes were added into Revelation, rather than trying to identify who the beast is. Identifying the beast will be covered in a later portion of this chapter. After all, the identity of the beast should be determined by analyzing the entirety of Revelation, rather than just playing number games with the figure 666.[3]

How the Beast Is Organizationally on the Same Level as Jesus

The role of the beast and the role of Jesus reflect each other on a fundamental and organizational perspective; Jesus receives his crown and authority from God, just as the beast receives his crown and authority from Satan.[4] John's selections from Daniel,and his subtle changes, and the shifting of the text, provide a parallel between the beast and the coronation of Jesus narrative. John took the passage of Jesus sitting on the throne, moved it, transformed it to reflect the beast, and then added that the throne came from Satan.[5] He then filled in empty text: he took the details of the 100 million who service God from Daniel, and transformed it into the 100 million angels who worship Jesus in the coronation of Jesus narrative.[6] At the end of the beast narrative John writes that those who wish to live will have to worship the beast.[7] The end scenario is that Jesus purchased his people with their lives and as a result they worship him while the beast forces the people to worship him in order for them to purchase the goods required for their survival.[8]

The Beast Defeats Jesus on Earth

John made changes outside of the Daniel text to provide imagery of both the beast defeating Jesus and Jesus defeating the Beast. As we have previously discussed, one of the symbolic meanings of the two prophets is that they mean Jesus.[9] So it is not surprising that John took what was originally defined as the "king of the abyss" (Satan)[10] and with a small edit made it the beast that slays the two prophets (Jesus).[11] Of course, this change was not made without a literary cost resulting from it. For one thing, it gave the beast two distinctly different origins—one from the sea and the other from the abyss.[12] For another, John did not have to change the king of the abyss who is an angel, as in Satan to become the beast.[13]

---

2   See "The Length of the Siege of Jerusalem Changed From Years of Sin to Years of Ministry (Ezek 4:5-8; Rev 11:2-3, 9)" on page 20.

3   Rev 13:18.

4   Jesus receives authority from God, Rev 2:26-7, The beast receives his authority from Satan, Rev 13:1-2.

5   Zech 6:13; see "The Coronation of Jesus and the Coronation of the Beast" on page 218.

6   Dan 7:10; Rev 5:11. See "The Scattering of the Daniel Text" on page 219.

7   Rev 13:15-7.

8   Jesus died to purchase the believers' lives and thus the universe worships him (Rev 5:9-14). The beast forces the people on earth to worship him, through the false prophet's efforts, so that they can buy food (Rev 13:12-7).

9   In the EID Jesus was connected to the location of the two prophets (see "The End of One Ministry and the Birth of Another (Ezek 4:5-8; Isa 6:13-9:19)" on page 18) and in the ZrD, John clearly wanted the two prophets to be associated with Jesus (see "The Creation of the Two Prophets" on page 91).

10   See "The Two Stories of Satan and the Two Stories of God's People" on page 160.

11   Rev 11:7.

12   The beast coming from the abyss can be found in Rev 11:7; 17:8. The beast who came from the sea can be found in Dan 7:2 and Rev 13:1.

13   See Rev 9:11; 20:1-3 and "Satan's Story" on page 294.

Jesus Defeats the Beast on Earth

To provide symmetry to the act of the beast defeating Jesus, John also changed who Jesus defeated in the second coming by changing it from Satan[14] (originally the great dragon[15]) into the beast.[16] However, as we shall see, there were many more changes that shaped the PVR.

The Creation of the Second Death

In the middle of the passage that John used to create the beast and the false prophet was one of God judging the beast and the false prophet. For John's purposes, this passage was out of place and did not fit the storyline well, so he had to distribute its content throughout Revelation.[17] Out of those wayward verses came the concept of eternal punishment and the great judgment, in which the outcome was already determined.[18]

John took the obvious depiction of the beast and the little horn thrown into the fire (with the rest of the animals being preserved for a period) and turned it into the beast and the false prophet being thrown into the lake of fire (with the rest being killed).[19] This small change of the text created a separation between Satan being locked up in the abyss and the defeat of the great dragon's army (now the beast's army) and therefore allowed John to present a clean story of Satan, and Satan's defeat by God, which we will discuss later in this chapter.

Daniel's scene of the books being open also fit into the Gog and Magog narrative. In both the EID and the DJD, we have two groups of people and a book which the righteous read and the unrighteous ignore, and as a result the righteous are preserved and the unrighteous are destroyed.[20] Once again, with simple edits John transformed both of the stories to conform with the Daniel narrative. He included the scene where the righteous are the first to be resurrected, seated atop thrones, to rule with Jesus for a thousand years, because they resisted the beast, his image, and his mark.[21]

The second resurrection is where John places the books being opened and where the judgment is set. As a result, all those who are judged in the second resurrection are tossed into the second death (the lake of fire) in which there is no end to their torment.[22]

---

14 See "The Destruction of the Dragon and the Two Riders of the Red and White Horses (Zech 1:7-16; Rev 19:11-21)" on page 95.

15 See "EP8 - The Slaying of the Great Dragon" on page 58 and "IP8 - Jesus Slays the Great Dragon With a Great Sword" on page 59.

16 To see how John incorporates Dan 7:11-2 into the second coming see "The Creation of the Beast and the False Prophet -- Part 3" on page 217.

17 See "The Scattering of the Daniel Text" on page 219.

18 See Dan 7:10-2 in "The Scattering of the Daniel Text" on page 219 and "The Creation of the Beast and the False Prophet -- Part 3" on page 217.

19 See Dan 7:10-2 in "The Scattering of the Daniel Text" on page 219 and "The Creation of the Beast and the False Prophet -- Part 3" on page 217.

20 Dan 7:10; 12:1-2 "at that time your people shall be delivered, everyone who shall be found written in the book. Many of those who sleep in the dust of the earth shall awake, some to everlasting life, and some to shame and everlasting contempt."

21 Dan 7:9; Rev 20:4-6.

22 Rev 20:11-5.

The Creation of the Beast and the False Prophet -- Part 1

The adding of the beast into Revelation was a simple matter of copying the seventh chapter of Daniel onto a new wax tablet with only slight changes to the text. In constructing the beast narrative, John focuses on the beast's power and how he will ultimately prevail over the saints.

	Content Found in Daniel		Content Found in Revelation
The Vision of the Four Beasts (Dan 7:2-7)		***The Beast (Rev 13:1-10)***	
7:2	The beast came from the sea.	13:1	The beast came from the sea.
7:4	The first was like a lion.	13:2	He had a mouth like a lion.
7:5	The second was like a bear.	13:2	He had feet like a bear.
7:6	The third was like a leopard.	13:2	He was a leopard.
7:7	The fourth was strong and destroyed anything left.	13:4-7	He destroyed all nations and the saints.
7:7	The last beast had ten horns.	13:1	He had ten horns.
7:8	He devoured up the other three horns.	13:4-7	He destroyed all nations.
7:8	He spoke great things.	13:5	He spoke blasphemous things against God.
7:25	He shall speak words against the Most High, and shall wear out the saints of the Most High.	13:5	A mouth speaking great things and blasphemy was given to him.
7:25	He shall think to change the times and the law; and they shall be given into his hand until a time and times and half a time.	13:5	Authority to make war for forty-two months* was given to him.
The Fourth Beast Explained (Dan 7:8, 20-1)		***The False Prophet (Rev 13:11-15)***	
7:16	The interpretation of these things	13:18	Here is wisdom. He who has understanding . . . . His number is 666.
7:8	There came up among them another horn, a little one, before which three of the first horns were plucked up by the roots: and behold, in this horn were eyes like the eyes of a man, and a mouth speaking great things.	13:11	I saw another beast coming up out of the earth. He had two horns like a lamb, and he spoke like a dragon.
7:20	Concerning the ten horns that were on its head, and the other horn which came up, and before which three fell, even that horn that had eyes, and a mouth that spoke great things, whose look was more stout than its fellows.	13:12	He exercises all the authority of the first beast in his presence.
7:21	I saw, and the same horn made war with the saints, and prevailed against them;	13:12-7	This section describes how the false prophet will defeat the saints.

> **Here is Wisdom - 1A**
> Here is wisdom. He who has understanding (13:18 connects to 17:9)

The Creation of the Beast and the False Prophet -- Part 2

John rewrote a large portion of the harlot passage in Rev 17:1-18 by using the beast narrative from Daniel. This was done for three reasons: the first was to set the stage for God and the beast to work together on the destruction of the harlot. The second was to provide the means of determining who the beast was. The third was to provide another author's notation to point the reader towards the beast's ultimate outcome.

Content Found in Ezekiel, Zechariah and Daniel		**Content Found in Revelation**	
Zech 5:9	Two wicked women placed into a basket and flown to the wilderness to the land of Shinar.	17:3	He carried me away in the spirit into a wilderness. I saw a woman sitting on a ~~red dragon~~ scarlet-colored animal, full of blasphemous names, having seven heads and ten horns.
Ezek 16:10	I clothed you also with embroidered work, and shod you with sealskin, and I dressed you about with fine linen, and covered you with silk.	17:4	The woman was dressed in purple and scarlet, and decked with gold and precious stones and pearls, having in her hand a golden cup full of abominations and the impurities of the sexual immorality of the earth.
Ezek 16:11	I decked you with ornaments, and I put bracelets on your hands, and a chain on your neck.		
Ezek 16:16	You took off your garments, and made for yourselves high places decked with various colors, and played the prostitute on them.		
Ezek 16:17	You also took your beautiful jewels of my gold and of my silver, which I had given you, and made for yourself images of men, and played the prostitute with them;		
Ezek 16:20	Moreover you have taken your sons and your daughters, whom you have borne to me, and you have sacrificed these to them to be devoured.	17:6	I saw the woman drunken with the blood of the saints, and with the blood of the martyrs of Jesus.
			Here Is Wisdom - 1B Here is the mind that has wisdom (17:9 from 13:18).
7:17	These great animals, which are four, are four kings, who shall arise out of the earth.	17:9	The seven heads are seven mountains on which the woman sits.
7:23	The fourth animal shall be a fourth kingdom on earth, which shall be diverse from all the kingdoms, and shall devour the whole earth, and shall tread it down, and break it in pieces.	17:10	They are seven kings. Five have fallen, the one is, the other has not yet come. When he comes, he must continue a little while.
7:24	As for the ten horns, out of this kingdom shall ten kings arise: and another shall arise after them; and he shall be diverse from the former, and he shall put down three kings.	17:11	The beast that was, and is not, is himself also an eighth, and is of the seven; and he goes to destruction.
		17:12	The ten horns that you saw are ten kings who have received no kingdom as yet, but they receive authority as kings, with the beast, for one hour.
7:21	I saw, and the same horn made war with the saints, and prevailed against them;	17:14	These will war against the Lamb, and the Lamb will overcome them, for he is the lord of lords, and king of kings, and those who are with him are called chosen and faithful.
			Lord of Lords, King of Kings - 1A Lord of lords, and king of kings (17:14 connects to 19:16)
Ezek 16:37	God will gather all her lovers and they will hate her and strip her naked.	17:16	They will make her desolate, and will make her naked.
Ezek 16:41	They will burn her houses with fire.	17:16	They will burn her utterly with fire.

The last place where John adds in the second death is in the New Jerusalem narrative in which he contrasts the plight of the righteous living with God in the New Jerusalem and all others living in the lake of fire.[23] When John changed the narrative to include the lake of fire, he both expanded the number of sins and reduce the severity of the sins that will cause one to enter the lake of fire. Before it was sins such as murder and idolatry and now they also include cowardly, and unbelieving.[24]

The second death was a major change within the DnD, and resulted in additional literary issues to attend to, since all previous drafts had, at the worst, a state of non-torment such as Sheol,[25] and at the least a state of being denied entry into the New Jerusalem.[26] Therefore, John had to either keep the incongruent passages or change the previous draft texts to conform to the new punishment known as the lake of fire. Unfortunately for John (but fortunately for our purposes), he was not successful in changing all instances of death and exclusion from the New Jerusalem texts into inclusion in the lake of fire texts. We have already seen in the alpha and omega parallel examples of such texts that John missed.[27] He also missed a few more such as how we are told that only the believers live in the New Jerusalem[28] and everyone else lives in the lake of fire.[29] However, we are also told that the nations outside of the New Jerusalem can enter the New Jerusalem, providing that their names are written in the Lamb's book of life.[30] The passage continues on to depict the river of life and the tree of life that brings healing to all the nations, which is something that indicates there are nations outside of the New Jerusalem before it is directly stated that there are.[31] These missed changes are understandable, since the end of a book is always the last part to get edited, and this indicates that the final proofreading process (which would have caught these editorial oversights) was skipped due to a rush to publication.

The last place where John adds in the second death in Revelation results from forming a complex parallel with a few verses from 1 Enoch. John probably focused on the river of blood and used the descriptions from 1 Enoch, and realized that he could reshape the bulk of the fourteenth chapter of Revelation by 1 Enoch 100:1-9.[32] This is how we get the details of how deep the river of blood is and the imagery of the angels coming from heaven to perform the harvest of the wicked. John changes it from representing Jerusalem as a barren vineyard that will be burned up into a fruitful harvest of the saints that were killed off by the wicked.[33] Both 1 Enoch and John have imagery of the saints resting from their labors and thus protected by God.[34] They both have the commonality of three speakers: for 1 Enoch it is three woes that speak, and for Revelation it is three angels.[35] Regarding the second death passage, both the first woe speaking and

---

23   Rev 21:6-8.

24   Rev 21:8. To see how the lists of sins compare with the alpha and omega parallel see "The Omega Version of the Alpha and Omega Parallel" on page 157.

25   Ezek 32:21; see "It Takes Two to Slay the Great Dragon (EP8, IP8)" on page 30.

26   Ezek 43:7-11; Rev 21:7-8;22:15.

27   See "The Creation of the Alpha and Omega Parallel" on page 152.

28   Ezek 43:7-11; Rev 21:7-8;22:15.

29   Rev 21:23-4; 22:2.

30   Rev 21:24-7; the Lamb's book of life is probably from the ExD (see "The Commandments of God and the Story of the Golden Calf Retold" on page 199).

31   Rev 22:1-5, 15.

32   See "Revelation's Use of 1 Enoch" on page 226.

33   Ezek 15:2-8; Rev 14:14-20; see "EP5 - The Glory of the Lord Flees Jerusalem" on page 52 and "IP5 - The Glory of the Lord Triumphs in Heaven" on page 53.

34   1 En 100:5; Rev 14:2; see "Revelation's Use of 1 Enoch" on page 226.

35   John used three angels instead of three woes because he either had the three woes separating the major divisions of the trumpets (Rev 8:13; 9:12; 11:14) or he had them separated by three angels and merely swapped the angels for the woes. A third possibility is

The Creation of the Beast and the False Prophet -- Part 3

John rewrote a large portion of the DJD's version of the second coming in order to make sure that the descriptions of Jesus were more in line with the book of Daniel's descriptions of God. Instead of having the great dragon (Satan) as the principle enemy in the second coming, the beast became the enemy that Jesus faces.

Normally the author's notation would serve as break in the original source text. Yet in the table below the author's notation is in the center of the Daniel text. The reason for this is a later change which required John to shift the Daniel material prior to the Lord of Lord's author's notation (see "The Descriptions of Jesus, John's Worshiping of the Two Angel, and Broken Parallels (Dan 10:1-21; Rev 1:9-17; 19:9-21; 22:6-15)" on page 222).

Content Found in the Daniel Draft Material		Content Found in Revelation	
Zech 1:8	A white horse	19:11	and behold, a white horse
Isa 11:4	[In] Righteousness he will judge.		In righteousness he judges and makes war.
Dan 10:6	his eyes as flaming torches	19:12	His eyes are a flame of fire,
Zech 6:11	Make crowns and put them on the head of Joshua.		and on his head are many crowns.
Isa 13:1-8	God is mustering a great army from the distant land to the ends of heaven in order to battle the nations.	19:14	The armies which are in heaven followed him on white horses.
Dan 7:9	His clothing was white as snow.		[They were] clothed in white, pure, fine linens.
Isa 11:4	He will strike the earth with the rod of his mouth.	19:15	Out of his mouth proceeds a sharp, double-edged sword, that with it he should strike the nations.
		19:15	He will rule them with an iron rod.
		19:15	He treads the wine press of the fierceness of the wrath of God, the Almighty.
			Lord of Lords, King of Kings - 2B Here is the mind that has wisdom (19:16 from 17:14).
Dan 7:13	I saw in the night visions, and behold, there came with the clouds of the sky one like a son of man.	19:16	He has on his garment and on his thigh a name written, "KING OF KINGS, AND LORD OF LORDS."
Ezek 39:17	Speak to the birds of every sort, and to every animal of the field, assemble yourselves, and come; gather yourselves on every side to my sacrifice that I do sacrifice for you, even a great sacrifice on the mountains of Israel, that you may eat meat and drink blood.	19:17	I saw an angel standing in the sun. He cried with a loud voice, saying to all the birds that fly in the sky, "Come! Be gathered together to the great supper of God."
Ezek 39:18	You shall eat the flesh of the mighty, and drink the blood of the princes of the earth.	19:18	[Vultures] may eat the flesh of kings, the flesh of captains, the flesh of mighty men, and the flesh of horses and of those who sit on them, and the flesh of all men, both free and slave, and small and great.
Ezek 39:20	You shall be filled at my table with horses and chariots, with mighty men, and with all men of war.		
Ezek 32:31	Pharaoh shall see them, and shall be comforted over all his multitude, even Pharaoh and all his army, slain by the sword.	19:19	I saw the beast, and the kings of the earth, and their armies, gathered together to make war against him who sat on the horse, and against his army.
Ezek 32:21	The strong among the mighty shall speak to him out of the middle of Sheol with those who help him: they are gone down, they lie still, even the uncircumcised, slain by the sword.	19:20	The beast was taken, and with him the false prophet who worked the signs in his sight, with which he deceived those who had received the mark of the beast and those who worshiped his image. These two were thrown alive into the lake of fire that burns with sulfur.
Dan 7:11	I saw even until the animal was slain, and its body destroyed, and it was given to be burned with fire.		
Dan 7:12	As for the rest of the animals, their dominion was taken away: yet their lives were prolonged for a season and a time.	19:21	The rest were killed with the sword of him who sat on the horse, the sword which came out of his mouth. All the birds were filled with their flesh.

The Coronation of Jesus and the Coronation of the Beast

John decided to present the beast on the same organizational level as Jesus. He did so by forming a simple parallel between the coronation of Jesus in Revelation 5:1-14 and the content from Daniel that created Revelation 13:1-18. He will first remove the text added in the ZrD and move it to Revelation's beast narrative as seen below.

Found in the Zechariah and Revelation Parallel		Found in Revelation	
Zech 6:13	He shall sit and rule on his throne.	13:2	The dragon gave him his power, his throne, and great authority.
Rev 3:21	He who overcomes, I will give to him to sit down with me on my throne, as I also overcame, and sat down with my Father on his throne.		

John replaced the text shown in the table above with the text from Daniel in the table below.

Found in Daniel		Found in Revelation	
Dan 7:10	Before him: thousands of thousands ministered to him, and ten thousand times ten thousand stood before him.	5:11	I heard something like a voice of many angels around the throne, the living creatures, and the elders; and the number of them was ten thousands of ten thousands, and thousands of thousands.
Dan 7:14	There was given him dominion, and glory, and a kingdom, that all the peoples, nations, and languages should serve him: his dominion is an everlasting dominion, which shall not pass away, and his kingdom which shall not be destroyed.	5:13	"To him who sits on the throne, and to the Lamb be the blessing, the honor, the glory, and the dominion, forever and ever! Amen!"

The end result is that we have the coronation of Jesus and the coronation of the beast following the same pattern. Unfortunately the two passages do not form a clean parallel with each other, which either indicates later modifications caused the parallel to become malformed or that the parallel was never completed. Either way, the two passages show how John wanted to create symmetry between the two organizational hierarchies: the management under God and the management under Satan.

Found in the Coronation of Jesus Narrative		Found in the Coronation of the Beast Narrative	
5:1	God on the throne.	13:4	Satan on his throne.
5:2	"Who is worthy to open the book, and to break its seals?"	13:4	"Who is like the beast? Who is able to make war with him?"
5:3	No one in heaven above, or on the earth, or under the earth, was able to open the book, or to look in it.	13:1	The beast came from the sea.
		13:6	The beast spoke blasphemy against those in heaven.
5:8-9	The four living creatures and the 24 elders sang a new song.	13:5	A mouth speaking great things and blasphemy was given to him.
The Death of Jesus		***The Death of the Beast***	
5:10	"He [Jesus] bought us for God with your blood, out of every tribe, language, people, and nation, and made us kings and priests to our God, and we will reign on the earth."	13:3	The beast was mortally wounded.
		13:7	He made war with the saints from every tribe, language, people, and nation.
			The false prophet made everyone worship the beast or they will not be able to purchase food.
5:11-4	All creation worships Jesus because he was slain to receive power.	13:12-7	The beast died and came back from the dead. As a result, all those who did not keep the commandments of God worshiped the beast.

The Scattering of the Daniel Text

The table below illustrates how four verses from Daniel get scattered throughout the book of Revelation. It also illustrates that John used text from Daniel as content filler, since it did not directly fit within the storyline that John had.

Found in Daniel			Found in Revelation
Dan 7:9	I saw until thrones were placed	20:4	I saw thrones [believers sitting on them].
		4:4	24 elders on their thrones (also in 5:10).
Dan 7:9	and one who was ancient of days sat	4:2-3	God sitting on the throne from the EID.
Dan 7:9	his clothing was white as snow and the hair of his head like pure wool.	1:14	His head and his hair were white as white wool, like snow.
Dan 7:9	His throne was fiery flames, and its wheels burning fire.	1:14	His eyes were like a flame of fire (also in 2:18; 19:12).
		1:15	His feet were like burnished brass, as if it had been refined in a furnace (also in 2:18).
Dan 7:10	Before him: thousands of thousands ministered to him, and ten thousand times ten thousand stood before him.	5:11	I heard something like a voice of many angels around the throne, the living creatures, and the elders; and the number of them was ten thousands of ten thousands, and thousands of thousands;
Dan 7:10	The judgment was set, and the books were opened.	20:12	The books were open.
			The context is all about a judgment in which all those who are being judged will be sent to the lake of fire (20:11-5).
Dan 7:11	I saw even until the animal was slain, and its body destroyed, and it was given to be burned with fire.	19:20	The beast was taken, and with him the false prophet who worked the signs in his sight, with which he deceived those who had received the mark of the beast and those who worshiped his image. These two were thrown alive into the lake of fire that burns with sulfur.
Dan 7:12	As for the rest of the animals, their dominion was taken away: yet their lives were prolonged for a season and a time.	19:21	The rest were killed with the sword of him who sat on the horse, the sword which came out of his mouth. All the birds were filled with their flesh.

---

the last angel speaking are judgment scenes against the sinners. This is where John defines the scene where God will judge the wicked by casting them into eternal torment with the Lamb and the angels who witness the event.[36]

The Removal of Gog and Magog's Vulture Scene

The original location of the vultures feasting imagery, which is found in the second coming, comes from the story of Gog and Magog.[37] One likely reason for this scene to have been moved was the need to insert the second resurrection text after the destruction of Gog and Magog. The reason for this is the lack of transition from the defeating of Satan and the second death—there would be no reason for the vultures to feast on Satan's army. The other reason is more practical. If John moved the vultures feasting on Gog and Magog's army, then he would have room to add in the second resurrection narrative.

---

that they were all eagles taken from the ExD (see "The Believers Became the Kingdom of Priests to God" on page 193).

36   1 En 100:7; Rev 14:9-12; see "Revelation's Use of 1 Enoch" on page 226.

37   See "EP9 - Jerusalem Attacked by Gog and Magog" on page 60.

The Expanding of the 42-Month Parallel

John expanded the 42-month parallel by a simple exchange of the phrase "time, times, and a half of time" (meaning 3½) from Daniel 7:25 (Rev 13:5) with 42 months (3 1/2 years) from Revelation 12:14-6. He also added in the imagery of the dragon (Satan) giving the beast the power to do these things and thus making Satan the ultimate destroyer of God's people on earth. This provided the perfect symmetry of God being defeated on earth by the dragon (Satan) destroying all his followers and Satan being destroyed by God (Rev 20:8-15) with the events of Jesus being killed by the beast on earth (Rev 11:7) and defeating the beast on earth again (Rev 19:11-21).

A. 42 Months
Measure Jerusalem but not its walls (Zech 2:1-5).
Measure the temple but not its courtyard (Rev 11:1-2).

B. 1,260 Days
Joshua dressed in filthy rags (Zech 3:3).
The two prophets wore sackcloth (Rev 11:3).

C. 3½ Days
The two olive trees and the lampstands represent the work of Joshua and Zerubbabel (Zech 4:11-4).
The two olive trees and the two lampstands, the two prophets do all kinds of miracles from God (Rev 11:4-7).

C.' 3½ Days
The building of the temple on earth and the nations will rejoice (Zech 4:6-10).
The temple is in heaven and the nations will be angry (Rev 11:18-9).

B.' 1,260 Days
Satan kicked out of Jerusalem (Zech 3:1).
Satan kicked out of heaven (Rev 12:3-10).

Sin will be removed from the land (Zech 3:8-10).
Salvation brought to the whole world (Rev 12:10)

A.' 42 Months (Before the Daniel Draft)
God will protect his people and Jerusalem will be loved by all the nations (Zech 2:6-13).
The woman was nourished . . . And the land (nations) rescued her (Rev 12:14-6).

A.' 42 Months (After the Daniel Draft)
God will protect his people and Jerusalem will be loved by all the nations (Zech 2:6-13).
They worshiped the dragon, because he gave his authority to the beast, and they worshiped the beast, saying, "Who is like the beast? Who is able to make war with him?" A mouth speaking great things and blasphemy was given to him. Authority to make war for 42 months was given to him. He opened his mouth for blasphemy against God, to blaspheme his name, and his dwelling, those who dwell in heaven (Rev 13:4-6).

The benefit of adding and enhancing the vulture narrative in the second coming scene is that it gave John more material to separate the beast being thrown into the lake of fire and Satan being thrown into the abyss.[38] It also infused humor into Revelation, since John portrays the feast enjoyed by the martyred saints in heaven with the feast enjoyed by vultures upon the defeat of the beast's army.[39] After all, of the two feasts, which one would you prefer to go to?

---

38   Dan 7:10 into Rev 20:12. See "The Scattering of the Daniel Text" on page 219.
39   Rev 19:9; 17-21.

Daniel's Ezekiel Draft and Revelation's Ezekiel and Daniel Draft

The author of Daniel also derived a portion of Daniel's text from Ezekiel's encounter with God. The chart below shows how Daniel used Ezekiel and added to the storyline, and how John took from both Ezekiel and Daniel and added to the storyline as well.

	Found in Ezekiel		Found in Daniel		Found in Revelation
1:1-3	Ezekiel a captive, giving lots of dates and Ezekiel located by a river.	10:1-4	Daniel a captive, giving lots of dates and Daniel was located by a river.	1:9-10	John a captive on an island in the Mediterranean receiving the vision on the Lord's day
		10:5	I lifted up my eyes . . . a man clothed in linen, whose thighs were adorned with pure gold of Uphaz:	1:13	A son of man, clothed with a robe reaching down to his feet, and with a golden sash around his chest.
1:14	The living creatures ran and returned as the appearance of a flash of lightning.	10:6	His body also was like the beryl, and his face as the appearance of lightning.	4:2-3	and one sitting on the throne that looked like a jasper stone and a sardius.
1:16	The appearance of the wheels and their work was like a beryl:	7:9	I saw until thrones were placed, and one who was ancient of days sat: . . . his throne was fiery flames, and its wheels burning fire.	1:16	His face was like the sun shining at its brightest.
1:27	[God had] the appearance of fire within it all around, from the appearance of his waist and upward; and from the appearance of his waist and downward I saw it as the appearance of fire, and there was brightness around him.				I
1:24	I heard the noise of their wings like the noise of great waters, like the voice of the Almighty.	10:6	The voice of his words like the voice of a multitude.	1:15	His voice was like the voice of many waters.
		7:9	His clothing was white as snow, and the hair of his head like pure wool.	1:13	One like a son of man, clothed with a robe reaching down to his feet, and with a golden sash around his chest
				1:14	His head and his hair were white as white wool, like snow.
		10:7	His eyes as flaming torches	1:14	His eyes were like a flame of fire.
1:7	[The living creatures' feet] sparkled like burnished brass.	10:7	His arms and his feet like burnished brass	1:15	His feet were like burnished brass, as if it had been refined in a furnace.
1:25	There was a voice above the expanse that was over their heads.	10:9	Yet heard I the voice of his words.	1:12	I turned to see the voice that spoke with me.
1:28	When I saw it, I fell on my face, and I heard a voice of one that spoke.	10:9	When I heard the voice of his words, then was I fallen into a deep sleep on my face, with my face toward the ground.	1:17	When I saw him, I fell at his feet like a dead man.
2:1	He said to me, son of man, stand on your feet, and I will speak with you.	10:10	Behold, a hand touched me, which set me on my knees and on the palms of my hands.	1:17	He laid his right hand on me, saying, "Don't be afraid."
2:3	He said to me, son of man, I send you to the children of Israel.	10:21	I will tell you that which is inscribed in the writing of truth.	1:11	Write in a book and send it to the seven churches.

How John Worshiped the First Angel

At one point in the DnD, John took the second coming narrative and overlaid it with imagery from Daniel to form a complex parallel with it. As a result, a falling down scene occurred in which John will define the being who he worships as an angel.

Found in Daniel		Found in Revelation	
Dan 10:1	Great warfare	19:19-21	The great battle between Jesus and the beast.
Dan 10:3	Daniel fasts for three weeks.	19:17-8	The vultures are told to come so that they may feast on the beast's army.
Dan 10:6	I lifted my eyes and saw . . .	19:11	I saw the heaven open . . .
Dan 10:6	His eyes as flaming torches.	19:12	His eyes are a flame of fire.
Dan 10:9	Yet heard I the voice of his words; and when I heard the voice of his words, then was I fallen into a deep sleep on my face, with my face toward the ground.	19:10	I fell down before his feet to worship him.
Dan 10:19	Don't be afraid.	19:10	Don't do that.
Dan 10:21	That which is inscribed in the writing of truth	19:9	Write . . . "These are true words of God."

The Descriptions of Jesus, John's Worshiping of the Two Angel, and Broken Parallels (Dan 10:1-21; Rev 1:9-17; 19:9-21; 22:6-15)

Daniel, Revelation and Isaiah have one thing in common, they all have an Ezekiel draft phase. For Daniel, the tenth chapter is very similar to Ezekiel's encounter with God. They both were nearby a river, they were both seeing lighting, a booming voice and a falling down before the speaker scene. John, through parallel formation, conflated the two[40] which brought in new descriptions for Jesus. Such as his eyes being like flaming torches and his hands and feet like brass. John also added in Dan 7:9 into the prologue which gave Jesus the imagery of wearing a white robe and hair white as wool.[41]

John also made a second parallel formation with Dan 10:1-21, but this time it was a complex parallel with the second coming narrative. That is why, much of Jesus' descriptions are the same between the prologue and the second coming narrative. It is also the reason John worships an angel in the second coming narrative[42] and how both passages have John write something.[43] It also began a chain of events that will cause many malformed parallels to come for John.

The results of the two parallel formations from Dan 10:1-21 allows us to provide a logical order in how several passages were construction. We can safely say that complex parallel formation with the second coming narrative occurred after the primary beast narrative from Daniel was completed. We know this because of how the "Lord of Lords" author notation text was shifted around.[44] In a normal author's notation the text

---

40   See "Daniel's Ezekiel Draft and Revelation's Ezekiel and Daniel Draft" on page 221.
41   Rev 1:13-4.
42   Rev 19:9-10; see "How John Worshiped the First Angel" on page 222.
43   Dan 10:21; Rev 1:17; 19:9.
44   See how John has Dan 7:9 prior to the author's notation "Lord of Lords, King of Kings in "The Creation of the Beast and the False Prophet -- Part 3" on page 217. With the complex parallel formed between the second coming and Daniel 10:1-21, John placed most of the descriptions of Jesus prior to the Lord of Lord, King of Kings author's notation (Rev 19:16).

How John Worshiped the Second Angel

The worshiping of the second angel was created by John trying to form a parallel with John worshiping the first angel. The table below shows how the content of the two worship scenes align themselves to each other. However, it should be noted that there is only content agreement and not a well-formed parallel formation (something we have seen consistently in the previous drafts).

	John Worships the First Angel		John Worships the Second Angel
19:9	He said to me, "These are true words of God."	22:6	He said to me , "These words are faithful and true."
		22:6	The Lord God of the spirits of the prophets sent his angel to show to his bondservants the things which must happen soon.
19:10	I fell down before his feet to worship him.	22:8	I fell down to worship before the feet of the angel who had shown me these things.
19:10	He said to me, "Look! Don't do it!"	22:9	He said to me, "See you don't do it."
	"I am a fellow bondservant with you and with your brothers who hold the testimony of Jesus. Worship God, for the testimony of Jesus is the Spirit of Prophecy."	22:9	I am a fellow bondservant with you and with your brothers, the prophets, and with those who keep the words of this book. Worship God."
19:9	He said to me, "Write,"	22:10	He said to me, "Don't seal up the words of the prophecy of this book, for the time is at hand."
19:11-21	Jesus' second coming.	22:7	"Behold, I come quickly. Blessed is he who keeps the words of the prophecy of this book."

is placed after the author's notation. The most likely candidate is the complex parallel formation between Dan 10:1-21 and the second coming narrative.[45]

The formation of the complex parallel between Dan 10:1-21 and the second coming narrative became the driving force for John's second worship scene with an angel and providing us with evidence that John never fully refreshed the alpha and omega parallel.[46] Not to say that the alpha and omega parallel was not important to John, but rather something that he might have wanted to finish last in the construction of Revelation. Since to of the three alpha and the omega passages live in the prologue and the epilogue which are the most worked passages in a book. Every author knows that the beginning of the story must captivate the reader and the end of the story must bring the reader to a satisfying reward to their effort in reading it. A poor beginning and an unresolved ending takes away from the potential readership and that is why authors will spend considerable effort into the beginning and end of a story.

The two direct parallel formations with Dan 10:1-21 and the subsequent parallel formation that created the second angel that John worshiped created an interesting quirk in Revelation in who John does and does not worship. John is before God and Jesus on multiple occasions and witnesses many worship ceremonies where they are the center.[47] However, he worships the two angels and both of them tell him not to do

---

45

46 See "How John Worshiped the Second Angel" on page 223 for the specifics on how John was in the process of forming a parallel with the two worshiping angel scenes. See the parallels in the two charts, "The Alpha and Omega Parallel: The Prologue and the Second Coming" on page 320 and "The Alpha and Omega Parallel: The New Jerusalem and the Epilogue" on page 321, for a visualization of how the second coming narrative affected the alpha and omega parallel.

47 Rev 1:17; 4:8-11; 5:8-14; 7:9-15; 14:1-5; 15:1-4; 19:1-6.

The Complex Parallel Between the Prologue and the Epilogue

John formed a complex parallel between the prologue and the epilogue by creating John's second worship scene with an angel. The complex parallel was never finalized and as a result left many parallel elements not fully connected. For example, in Rev 1:-8, it is God speaking while in Rev 22:6-13 it is the angel quoting either God or Jesus. The context is uncertain. A finishing phase would had cleared up the ambiguity.

A. What will happen soon (Rev 1:1).

   B. Blessed is he who reads, hears and obeys Revelation (Rev 1:3).

   C. The coming of God (or Jesus?: "Those who pierced him" in Rev 1:7):
   - Behold, He is coming (Rev 1:7).
   - Everyone will see him, including those who pierced him (Rev 1:7).
   - The alpha and omega (Rev 1:7-8).

   D. John's encounter with Jesus:
   - Jesus spoke to him (Rev 1:9, 11-7).
   - John fell down before Jesus (1:17).
   - "Don't be afraid" (Rev 1:17).
   - Write what you see and hear (Rev

   D′. John's encounter with the second angel he worships:
   - The angel spoke to John (Rev 22:5-7).
   - John fell down and worships the angel (Rev 22:8).
   - "Don't do that" (Rev 22:9).
   - Published what you wrote (Rec 22:10).

   C′. The coming of Jesus (or God (Rev 22:6-7)):
   - Behold he will come quickly (Rev 22:12).
   - He will repay to each man their work (Rev 22:12).
   - He is the alpha and omega (Rev 22:13).

   B′. Cursed is he that changes this book, they will not receive its blessing (Rev 22:18-9).

A′. Jesus will come soon (Rev 22:20-1).

---

that.[48] When one contrasts it to the falling down before Jesus narrative in the prologue, it does not appear to be a worship scene but rather a compromise between Ezekiel's and Daniel's account.[49]

After the parallel formation between the prologue and Daniel, John tried to refresh the complex parallel between the prologue and the seven churches. In this parallel formation, John stopped mid way giving us evidence that, at least in this case, complex parallel formation start from the middle and work outward.[50] Why he stopped, we may never know, it could have been that he wanted to retain the three door segue parallel,[51] it could have put off later because it required more changes in the prologue than space on the wax tablet. Perhaps he was simply distracted. The fact remains, it was started and was never finished.

The infusion of new descriptions of Jesus from Dan 10:1-21 and the writing of a scroll changed the prologue and provided the changing of two additional parallels. The first parallel that was affected prologue

---

48   Rev 19:9-10; 22:6-11. See "How John Worshiped the First Angel" on page 222 and "How John Worshiped the Second Angel" on page 223.

49   Ezek 1:28; Dan 10:9; see "Daniel's Ezekiel Draft and Revelation's Ezekiel and Daniel Draft" on page 221.

50   See "The Prologue and the Seven Churches Complex Parallel" on page 233.

51   "The Open Door, The Closed Door, And What Is Behind the Door" on page 293.

and epilogue. In the DJD, the prologue and the epilogue formed a simple parallel[52] whereas in the DnD, John changed the prologue and epilogue to form a complex parallel. He begins the prologue with the beatitude to all those who read, hear, and obey Revelation and a curse on those who change Revelation. In the middle, John has a scene of one coming and the declaration of being the alpha and the omega. The last scene, John falls down before a heavenly being and is told to write / publish what he has written.[53]

It is important to note that the epilogue was not a benefactor to the names and descriptions of Jesus derived from prior parallel formations between the prologue and the second coming narrative with Daniel 10:1-21. The changes to the epilogue are more like spot edits whereas the changes to the prologue were substantial requiring a new wax tablet. To fix the epilogue, John would have to start with a new wax tablet and time to produce quality parallel formations with the prologue and the second coming narrative with the epilogue. John never devoted the energy to fix the epilogue.

How John performed parallel formation with Dan 10:1-21 allows us to produce a logical order of construction on multiple passages and what happens when there is no finishing phase. In all passages affected by the parallel formation with Dan 10:1-21 there is a feeling that it was a rough draft and not something one would expect from a professional writer. From the perspective of the mechanics of the process of writing Revelation, the roughness results of fitting material in the blank spots of the wax tablet and not rewriting the material on new wax tablets.

Satan and Jesus as Allies and the Origin of the 200 Million Horsemen

Ever since the first draft of Revelation there were the actions of the nations and the actions of God working together against Israel. They were the earliest version of the first four seals and the first four trumpets.[54] This parallel was so strong that John placed the text from Ezekiel to the Isaiah side of the Ezekiel-Isaiah parallel and changed the actions of God to the actions of Jesus.[55] In the ZrD, Satan entered into the book of Revelation and John had the actions of the nations become the actions of Satan.[56] The relationship between the seals as actions of Jesus (by his opening each one up) and the trumpets as actions by Satan became linked together when John nested the seven trumpets inside the seventh seal.[57] The relationship between the seals and the trumpets may have shifted but they were never broken, so it is not surprising that John would continue this link into the DnD.

The DnD was somewhat of a chaotic draft in that John sets down text so that there is content agreement and perhaps has the intent to turn them into parallels in the future. He also shifts material around as seen by how verses get scattered, as well as by the number of author's notations created in the DnD. Apparently, at one point in time John had the following phrase associated with the second coming as the number of riders on horseback:

> *A fiery stream issued and came out from before him: thousands of thousands ministered to him, and ten thousand times ten thousand stood before him: the judgment was set, and the books were opened.*[58]

52   See "DJ1 - The Prologue (Rev 1:1-20)" on page 167 and "DJ24 - The Epilogue (Rev 22:6-21)" on page 166.

53   See "The Complex Parallel Between the Prologue and the Epilogue" on page 224.

54   See "EP4 - The Judgments by the Nations - Part 1" on page 46 and "IP4 - The Judgments by Jesus - Part 1" on page 47.

55   See "John's First Major Content Alignment Corrections" on page 22.

56   See "The Creation of Satan in the Zechariah Draft" on page 86.

57   See "The Retelling of the Story of the Conquest of Jericho" on page 145.

58   Dan 7:10.

Revelation's Use of 1 Enoch

At some point in the construction of the Daniel draft, John integrated 1 Enoch 100:1-9 with what is now Revelation 14:6-20 backwards. However, he made a few changes, such as instead of three woes he had three messages given by angels.

Found in 1 Enoch (From APOT)		Found in Revelation	
100:1-3	And the horse shall walk up to the beast in the blood of sinners, and the chariot shall be submerged to its height.	14:20	The wine press was trodden outside of the city, and blood came out of the wine press, even to the bridles of the horses, as far as 1,600 stadia.
100:4	In those days the angels shall descend into the secret places and gather together into one place all those who brought down sin, and the Most High will arise on that day of judgment to execute great judgment amongst sinners.	14:14-9	Angels descending for the great harvest of the righteous
100:5	And over all the righteous and holy he will appoint guardians from amongst the holy angels to guard them as the apple of an eye, until he makes an end of all wickedness and all sin, and though the righteous sleep a long sleep, they have nought to fear.	14:13	I heard a voice from heaven saying, "Write, 'Blessed are the dead who die in the Lord from now on.'" "Yes," says the Spirit, "that they may rest from their labors; for their works follow with them."
100:7	Woe to you, sinners, on the day of strong anguish, ye who afflict the righteous and burn them with fire: Ye shall be requited according to your works.	14:9-12	Another angel, a third, followed them, saying with a great voice, "If anyone worships the beast and his image, and receives a mark on his forehead, or on his hand, he also will drink of the wine of the wrath of God, which is prepared unmixed in the cup of his anger. He will be tormented with fire and sulfur in the presence of the holy angels, and in the presence of the Lamb. The smoke of their torment goes up forever and ever. They have no rest day and night, those who worship the beast and his image, and whoever receives the mark of his name. Here is the perseverance of the saints, those who keep the commandments of God, and the faith of Jesus."
100:8	Woe to you, ye obstinate of heart, who watch in order to devise wickedness: Therefore shall fear come upon you and there shall be none to help you.	14:8	Another, a second angel, followed, saying, "Babylon the great has fallen, which has made all the nations to drink of the wine of the wrath of her sexual immorality."
100:9	Woe to you, ye sinners, on account of the words of your mouth, and on account of the deeds of your hands which your godlessness has wrought, in blazing flames burning worse than fire shall ye burn.	14:6	I saw an angel flying in mid-heaven, having an eternal good news to proclaim to those who dwell on the earth, and to every nation, tribe, language, and people. He said with a loud voice, "Fear the Lord, and give him glory; for the hour of his judgment has come. Worship him who made the heaven, the earth, the sea, and the springs of waters!"

At a later time when John was working on the size of the army in the sixth trumpet John made it 200 million horsemen, where 100 million represented the army of Jesus on horseback and the other 100 million represented the horsemen in Satan's (or the beast's) army.[59]

This may seem speculative, and to a point it is, but there are several things that would lead us to theorize that this is the most likely scenario. First, John is in a literary flux when he associates Satan with the trumpets (as well as the beast with the trumpets) by making them both come from the abyss. Likewise, he experiences the same problem with the sixth seal in that he has Satan and the beast involved with the amassing of a great army. It is likely that he wants us to see Satan's army and the beast's army as the same and that is why he has both Satan and the beast as the ones organizing the great army from all nations.[60] By keeping the trumpets generic, John does not have to worry about those places where he described the beast coming from the abyss and those where he described Satan as coming from the abyss.

However, the trumpets are not the actions of Satan alone, but are contained in the seventh seal which is opened by Jesus. Thus they are a joint action by heaven (Jesus) and earth (Satan). All John had to do was double the 100 million horsemen and make the total army consist of 200 million horsemen.[61]

Obviously, the final resting spot was for the 100 million to be part of the attempted parallel formation between the coronation of Jesus and the coronation of the beast. So we can also set the attempted parallel after the 200 million horsemen were created.

God and the Beast as Allies

John is now setting up the Revelation storyline to have similarly ranking foes battle each other, and dissimilar ranking foes forming an alliance with each other. We have already seen this in how Jesus and Satan work together to destroy Jerusalem and now we will see how God and the beast work together.

The Merging of the Harlot and Tyre to Become Rome

One of the more significant structural changes in the DnD is the merging of the harlot and the city of Tyre into a single entity called the harlot. Up until the DnD, the harlot and Tyre were two separate cities which each had their own judgment and purpose. The problem that John faced is that he already has Jesus and Satan team up together to destroy Jerusalem. It would not make sense for him to have God and the beast also team up to defeat Jerusalem. The only option that was before him was to have the beast and God defeat Tyre (Rome), but the problem that John faced was how, exactly, to do that. The solution that John came up with was to merge the harlot and Tyre into one city. The following text delves into the story of how he did just that.

John took the beast narrative derived from Daniel, created an author's notation of "Here is wisdom" and moved it to the bottom of the harlot passage. He then made three modifications to the harlot passage prior to the appended beast narrative. The first was to modify the text of the harlot being flown into the wilderness on the wings of the great red dragon to being carried into the wilderness by the scarlet-colored beast.[62]

---

59   Rev 9:16.
60   Rev 16:12-6; Rev 20:7-10.
61   Rev 9:16.
62   Rev 17:3; see "The Creation of the Beast and the False Prophet -- Part 2" on page 215.

The second was to directly connect the harlot to Babylon by attaching a sign to her forehead which identified her as Babylon.[63] Third, John added a little introduction as to how the beast and the harlot were linked together. In that story, John changes the source of the beast as coming from the abyss after the small change he made in the two prophets' narrative, as opposed to the beast coming from the sea.[64]

The Changes to the Bowls

Now that John has conflated the harlot and Tyre as one city, all he needed to do was to make sure the beast is represented in the seven bowls. So John overlaid the first, fifth, and sixth bowl with the beast's imagery.[65] However, he kept the imagery of Satan gathering a huge army in the sixth seal in order to agree with the description of the synagogue of Satan (the gathering of Satan) which is found in the sixth church.[66]

John also modified the seventh bowl so that the city of Babylon is destroyed as a result of the judgments.[67] This quick edit caused a problem in that it is the only instance where Babylon is destroyed by an earthquake,[68] which is the same event that occurs with Jerusalem.[69] This is a situation we would expect to see when things are conflated at the last minute, without a final editing phase.

God's Defeat by Satan and God's Victory Over Satan

John also created a story where Satan defeats God on earth and God defeats Satan on earth. The problem for John was how to set up Satan's defeat of God on earth. It was easy for John to have the beast kill Jesus by just a simple word change,[70] but how do you show God defeated? The answer for John was to associate Satan with the defeating of God on earth and the blaspheming of everything in heaven. What made this solution more palatable for John was that it was a simple swap of a few words. All John had to do was to swap the words "a time, times, and half a time" from Daniel, with "42 months" and thereby expanding the 42-month parallel.[71] Since a time, times, and half a time is a fancy way of saying 3½, and 42 months is another way of saying 3½ (years) the swapping of the text changed nothing in the meaning but everything in the parallel. John now has the beginning of the 42-month parallel with the temple on earth as the place where God lives and the end of the second element of the 42-month parallel where the temple is in heaven being blasphemed by the beast on earth. In other words, God, and all that he set up on earth, has been defeated.

John already had a story about God defeating Satan when he created the two stories of Satan in the DJD,[72] where after a thousand years, Satan was released and gathered an army to defeat Jerusalem once again. All John needed to do was to simply edit it to support the DnD by having Satan thrown into the lake of fire.[73]

---

63   Rev 17:5.

64   Beast from the abyss in Rev 11:7; The beast from the sea Dan 7:2; Rev 13:1.

65   Rev 16:2, 10-1, 13.

66   Rev 16:13. See "The Story of the Sixth Church" on page 287 on why the description of Satan was maintained.

67   Rev 16:19.

68   The harlot is destroyed by fire (Rev 17:16; 18:18-9;) and by a millstone (Rev 18:21).

69   Rev 11:13, 19.

70   See "The Beast Defeats Jesus on Earth" on page 212.

71   See "The Expanding of the 42-Month Parallel" on page 220.

72   Rev 20:7-11; see "The New Timeline for Satan" on page 161.

73   Rev 20:10.

By doing this, John created a whole new story from the revised slaying of the dragon narrative to the PVR's slaying of the beast narrative as previously discussed.[74]

The Believers Versus the Beast and the Harlot

The believers verses the beast and the harlot have two phases, first is their defeat, and second is their victory. In both their defeat and victory, the believers maintain a passive role apart from their faithfulness to the commandments of God and their following Jesus. On earth, they are destroyed by the beast and the false prophet because of their faithfulness.[75] In Revelation, the saints on earth final act of resisting the beast, the false prophet, and the harlot is by obeying the commandments of God and follow Jesus into martyrdom.[76] In heaven, the saints get to witness the victory over the harlot and the beast.[77]

The End is Soon

The conclusion to the book of Daniel are the answers to the perplexing questions of what will be the end and when will it come? For Daniel he is told that the words are sealed until the end of time and blessed is the one who waits till the end.[78] For John, he will take the four key verses and integrate them into the mighty angel passage with the emphasis that the events will happen very soon. We see this in the following passage in how the angel swears that all will happen soon:

> **10:4** *When the seven thunders sounded, I was about to write; but I heard a voice from the sky saying, "Seal up the things which the seven thunders said, and don't write them."*
>
> **10:5** *The angel whom I saw standing on the sea and on the land lifted up his right hand to the sky,* **10:6** *and swore by him who lives forever and ever, who created heaven and the things that are in it, the earth and the things that are in it, and the sea and the things that are in it, that there will no longer be delay,* **10:7** *but in the days of the voice of the seventh angel, when he is about to sound, then the mystery of God is finished, as he declared to his servants, the prophets.* **10:8** *The voice which I heard from heaven, again speaking with me, said, "Go, take the book which is open in the hand of the angel who stands on the sea and on the land."*

The placement of the verses and the declaration from the mighty angel swearing an oath that the events seen in Revelation will happen really soon tells us that John wanted the readers to believe that the book was written prior to the destruction of Jerusalem. The selection of texts used to write Revelation tells us that Jerusalem has already been destroyed. Why else would the first draft be based upon Ezekiel, which primary message is the destruction of Jerusalem and the rebuilding of the city of God?

This also explains why the chain of custody of the vision from God to Jesus to an angel and finally to John remained in Revelation even though much of Revelation changed so dramatically that we have to look to the passing of the scroll before the chain of custody is exhibited.

---

74 See "Jesus Defeats the Beast on Earth" on page 213.
75 Rev 11:7; 13:7-17; 14:9-12; 20:4-6.
76 Rev 17:9-14.
77 Rev 19:1-21.
78 Dan 12:5-13.

The Mighty Angel Tells John it Will Happen Soon

The final modifications to the mighty angel passage are: the declaration that the events will happen very soon (Dan 12:6-9; Rev 10:5) and its extension to the destruction of the temple narrative on earth (Dan 12:11; Rev 11:1-3; 13:5-8). By those two actions, John declares the point in which he received the vision.

	Content Found in Ezekiel, Joshua, and Daniel		**Content Found in Revelation (Ordered by Revelation)**
Ezek 1:28	The appearance of a rainbow. The appearance of brightness all around him.	10:1	A rainbow on his head. His face was like the sun.
		10:2	He had in his hand a little open scroll.
Josh 3:13-7	Imagery of the priests stepping into the water with one foot and causing the Jordan River to be dry. Thus one foot touches the water and the other was on land.		He set his right foot on the sea, and his left on the land.
Ezek 3:12	When the seven thunders sounded, Ezekiel hears the living creatures making loud noises, seven days, saying: ~~"Blessed be the Lord's glory from his place."~~	10:4	I was about to write; but I heard a voice from the sky saying, "Seal up the things which the seven thunders said, and don't write them."
Dan 12:3	But you, Daniel, shut up the words, and seal the book, even to the time of the end.		
Dan 12:6-7	Daniel mentions men and describes what they are doing or where they are at.	10:5	The angel whom I saw standing on the sea and on the land lifted up his right hand to the sky.
Dan 12:7	I heard the man clothed in linen, who was above the waters of the river, when he held up his right hand and his left hand to heaven, and swore by him who lives forever that it shall be for a time, times, and a half;	10:6	[The angel] swore by him who lives forever and ever, who created heaven and the things that are in it, the earth and the things that are in it, and the sea and the things that are in it, that there will no longer be delay,
Dan 12:9	He said, "Go your way, Daniel; for the words are shut up and sealed until the time of the end."	10:7	but in the days of the voice of the seventh angel, when he is about to sound, then the mystery of God is finished, as he declared to his servants, the prophets.
Ezek 3:1-3	Ezekiel told to take the scroll and eat it. It will taste sweet to the mouth.	10:9-10	I went to the angel, telling him to give me the little scroll.
Ezek 3:14	Ezekiel was bitter.		He said to me, "Take it, and eat it up. It will make your stomach bitter, but in your mouth it will be as sweet as honey."
Ezek 3:4	He said to me, son of man, go to the house of Israel, and speak my words to them.	10:11	They told me, "You must prophesy again over many peoples, nations, languages, and kings."
Ezek 3:16-27	Ezekiel appointed as a watchman to tell everyone		
Dan 12:11	From the time that the continual burnt offering shall be taken away, and the abomination that makes desolate set up,	11:1-2	A reed like a rod was given to me. Someone said, "Rise, and measure God's temple, and the altar, and those who worship in it. Leave out the court which is outside of the temple, and don't measure it, for it has been given to the nations. They will tread the holy city under foot for 42 months (1,260 days).
		13:5-8	A mouth speaking great things and blasphemy was given to him. Authority to make war for 42 months (1,260 days) was given to him. He opened his mouth for blasphemy against God, to blaspheme his name, and his dwelling, those who dwell in heaven. It was given to him to make war with the saints, and to overcome them. Authority over every tribe, people, language, and nation was given to him. All who dwell on the earth will worship him, everyone whose name has not been written from the foundation of the world in the book of life of the Lamb who has been killed.
	there shall be 1,290 days.	11:3	I will give power to my two witnesses, and they will prophesy 1,260 days, clothed in sackcloth.

The Two Publication Dates of Revelation and Who Is the Beast?

Revelation has two publication dates: one is when the author wishes the reader to believe it was published and the other is when the book was actually published. For a seer to predict the future the seer's credibility is founded on how he predicted the past. For John, all the texts selected and its emphasis of the texts were associated with the destruction and restoration of Jerusalem. However, in no place in Revelation does he refer to Jerusalem's destruction as having occurred in the past. In every instance that he refers to the destruction of Jerusalem, it is as a future event. The conflation of the mighty angel text with Daniel's end-of-time text tells us that John wanted the readers to believe that the book of Revelation was published some time prior to the destruction of Jerusalem.[79]

For us to determine when the book was published for the world to see, we need to look at what John reveals to us in terms of a chronology and then overlay it on top of what we know in the historical setting. For that we need the prediction of the "who is the beast" narrative that John provides us with:

> **17:6** *I saw the woman drunken with the blood of the saints, and with the blood of the martyrs of Jesus. When I saw her, I wondered with great amazement.* **17:7** *The angel said to me, "Why do you wonder? I will tell you the mystery of the woman, and of the beast that carries her, which has the seven heads and the ten horns.* **17:8** *The beast that you saw was, and is not; and is about to come up out of the abyss and to go into destruction . . . .* **17:9** *Here is the mind that has wisdom. The seven heads are seven mountains on which the woman sits.* **17:10** *They are seven kings. Five have fallen, the one is, the other has not yet come. When he comes, he must continue a little while.* **17:11** *The beast that was, and is not, is himself also an eighth, and is of the seven; and he goes to destruction.* **17:12** *The ten horns that you saw are ten kings who have received no kingdom as yet, but they receive authority as kings, with the beast, for one hour.* **17:13** *These have one mind, and they give their power and authority to the beast.*

If we set John's relative chronology with the emperor prior to the destruction of Jerusalem we get the emperor Vespasian who was the general that was responsible for ending the first Jewish revolt of 67-70 CE before becoming the emperor of Rome.[80] However, the year that Vespasian became emperor is known as the year of the four emperors in which upon the death of Nero there was a battle for the throne and consequently there were many political and military actions for Vespasian.[81] When Vespasian was coronated he made his two sons co-emperors. He left his elder son Titus in charge of finishing the rebellion and his 16-year-old son with just the honorary title.[82] When Vespasian died, Titus assumed the throne and reigned for two years before he died as well, and then Domitian became the ruler of Rome.[83] The chronology of Domitian fits nicely inside the chronology of the beast passage provided by John.

What About 666?

The phrase "let him calculate the number of the beast, for it is the number of a man. His number is six hundred sixty six" was filler to finish the wax tablet, rather than some numerical puzzle that many books

---

79 See "The Mighty Angel Tells John it Will Happen Soon" on page 230.
80 Jones, Brian W. *The Emperor Domitian* (New York: Routledge Inc., 1993),
81 Jones, *The Emperor Domitian*, 18-9.
82 Jones, *The Emperor Domitian*, 18-9.
83 Jones, *The Emperor Domitian*, 46.

on Revelation delight in speculating about. The most obvious answer is that the number 666 refers to the person in the sixth seal, the sixth trumpet, and the sixth bowl. Domitian would have fit within being the person for each of the sixth judgments as the co-emperor during the destruction of Jerusalem and the one who will be part of the predictive destruction of Rome in 105 CE.

By following the author's notation trail of "here is wisdom" we get a clearer picture of the beast that goes beyond the numbers of 666.[84] As discussed in the previous section, Domitian seems the most likely candidate and from the perspective of when John wishes the reader to believe Revelation was written, the choice becomes obvious.

Who Was the False Prophet?

The false prophet was a literary element that John carried over from Daniel, and used to balance the two prophets and the beast and the false prophet. In all reality, John probably had no idea who the false prophet would be because that was a future event in Revelation.

The State of the Daniel Draft

In a perfect literary world we would expect a few things during the process of writing the book of Revelation. First, that the earlier the draft occurred the more likely it is to be malformed by new content formed in later drafts. This is because the later the parallels occur the more likely they will overwrite the earlier parallels. We would also expect that the later parallels would be the most solid of all of the parallels in the book. Even if the author was inexperienced in writing books, by the time the author reaches the end of the book, or in this case the last draft, the author should have gained more experience.

What we find in the DnD is a mixture of good parallels and parallels that look more like information being staged prior to parallel formation. The first three churches and the beast narrative would represent a well-formed parallel.[85] The formation of the two angels that John worshiped is another example of a solid parallel and another example of something that breaks the alpha and omega parallel. The complex parallel centered on Jesus' description found in the prologue and the seven churches was never finished and was likely the last parallel created.[86] The coronation of Jesus narrative and the coronation of the beast narrative was prepped to become a parallel but it was never finalized.[87]

One major problem (and one we should expect as a byproduct of this writing method) is word definition. If the mechanism for writing is to use many texts from many centuries and incorporate them into one's writing, we would expect to have common words that have a wide range of meanings and having many places where they are ambiguous. We see this in how John uses the Greek word γῆ (meaning earth or land). He uses it over 80 times in Revelation and as Edmondo Lupieri has noted it has a wide range of meanings and in some places—where its meaning is critical to understanding the passage—it is ambiguous.[88] This ambiguity obviously would have been reduced during several passes of an editing process.

---

84   Rev 13:8 and 17:9 form an author's notation (see "The Creation of the Beast and the False Prophet -- Part 1" on page 214 and "The Creation of the Beast and the False Prophet -- Part 2" on page 215) which goes beyond the numbers game of 666.

85   See "The First Three Churches and the Primary Beast Narrative" on page 276.

86   See "The Prologue and the Seven Churches Complex Parallel" on page 233.

87   See "Satan and Jesus as Allies and the Origin of the 200 Million Horsemen" on page 225.

88   Edmondo F. Lupieri *A Commentary on the Apocalypse of John* (Grand Rapids, Mich.: Eerdmans, 2006), 103-4.

The Prologue and the Seven Churches Complex Parallel

Below is the last complex parallel between the prologue and the seven churches. The parallel is built after Daniel 10:6 was added in Revelation. We can see that John started in the middle and worked outward in his parallel formation. At one point he stopped in forming a complex parallel between prologue and the seven churches.

**A Partial Complex Parallel Between the Seven Churches (Rev 2:1-3:22)
and the Prologue (Rev 1:1-20)**

A. *Faithful witness* (1:5) [no match with Head of God's creation].

    B. [No Match -- perhaps key of Death and Hades (1:18)].

        C. Seven spirits of God (1:4), seven stars (1:20).

            D. God his father (1:6); Eyes like a flame of fire, feet like burnished brass (1:15).

                E. **Has a sharp two-edged sword out of his mouth (1:16).**

                F. First and the last was dead and came to life (1:18).

                    G. Has the seven stars and seven candlesticks (1:20).

                    G'. Has the seven stars and seven candlesticks (2:1).

                F'. First and the last, was dead and came to life (2:9).

                E'. Has a sharp two-edged sword out of his mouth (2:12).

            D'. Son of God (2:18); **Eyes like a flame, feet like burnished brass (2:18).**

        C'. Has seven spirits of God and the seven stars (3:1).

    B'. Has the key of David (3:7).

A'. *Faithful* and true *witness* (3:14) the Head of God's creation (3:14).

Other things would have been avoided if John spent the time to proofread Revelation. The proofreading alone would have removed much of the barbaric Greek from Revelation. It also would have fixed some glaring issues in Revelation, such as making it clearer who it is that claims to be the "alpha and omega" in the Epilogue.[89] As every student soon learns, and every author knows, every pass on a work makes it that much better.

Why Was the Daniel Draft Rushed?

Panic must have entered John's mind when he found out that Domitian was assassinated, in the same way that a director would panic if his main actor died before filming ended on his movie. Out of many possibilities, John elected to have the beast slain by the sword and raised from the dead.[90] It is at this point that John rushed the book into publication. Unfortunately, publishing a book then was far different than how it is now. Today, all we have to do is push a button and a book is published, but back then it was a long and laborious process. Each book had to be faithfully copied by hand with crude writing instruments, and at a painfully slow pace. To make matters worse, if the purpose of Revelation was for profit then John need-ed to have many copies produced, since in a time where copyrights didn't exist, any book could be copied

---

89   Depending upon how one reads Rev 22:6-16 it could be the angel John tries to worship or Jesus who is declaring to be the alpha and omega. To see how John had the wax tablets arrange when creating the alpha and omega parallel (see "DJ24 - The Epilogue (Rev 22:6-21)" on page 166 and "DJ1 - The Prologue (Rev 1:1-20)" on page 167 for how they were initially placed and "The Alpha and Omega Parallel" on page 314).

90   Rev 13:3, 12, 14.

and sold by someone who wasn't the author. Due to this, the initial printing of a book had to produce as many copies as afforded by the author.

The most natural question we have about the poor quality of the DnD is why it was poor and what could have caused this. The answer is simple and no different than today. If someone is working on a book about an obscure part of the world, or about an obscure person, and suddenly the subject of the book is receives fame overnight and is constantly broadcasted in the news, then the temptation is to rush the book out, regardless of if it is finished or not. Whether John already had in his mind that Domitian would be the beast or whether the events of the daily news led him to that conclusion, we will never really know, but we can understand why the events occurred as they did. The taking of current events and interpreting it as ushering the coming of Jesus has been practiced by Christians for almost twenty centuries and John was definitely not the first to do so.

Revelation as the Key to the Past

John had at least one more phase planned for the book of Revelation and one day I hope to complete and publish it. In all of the statements that I have made about John and his rushing the book to publication I want the reader to understand that John was not a poor writer. John was trying to write the most complex book ever written in a style that most of the Hebrew Scriptures were written in. I have no doubt that if he would have finished it the way he was capable of doing, it would have been accepted by a larger body of Christians than it has been.

With that said, John, by not finishing Revelation, gave us the key to reverse engineer the bulk of the Hebrew Scriptures and many books in the Christian Scriptures. For the first time in history we can look at previous versions of the Hebrew and Christian Scriptures and like we have seen in this book, we can experience what the writers experienced as though we are looking over their shoulders. To that we owe it all to John and the eagerness to publish his work.

Chapter 7: The Published Version of Revelation

The following represents what John delivered to the scribes with many differences. The first is that, Revelation was written in Greek and the text presented is written using a modified public domain version of the Bible. Secondly, his version had no spaces, punctuation, upper and lower case and paragraph separators. It was tablet after tablet which contained line after line of Greek letters from end to end of Greek text. Much like a word puzzle where the purpose is to find words and circle in the horizontal, vertical or diagonal. The text in this presentation of the draft has all the modern conveniences that make reading easier.

The last major difference is the quality of the grammar. Since John had no time to take what was a document written in the horizontal and convert it to a document written in the vertical the writing seems choppy. The translator on the other hand has time to do two things, first look at how the Greek was constructed and secondly leverage the insight and struggles from previous translations. Second, to produce a translation free of grammatical errors while being somewhat true to the original text.

Contents

The Prologue (Rev 1:1-20)   **238**

    The Chain of Custody of the Vision (Rev 1:1-3) 238

    John Provides Background to His Message (Rev 1:4-8) 238

    Where John Was (Rev 1:9-10) 238

The Seven Churches (Rev 2:1 - 3:22)   **239**

    The Message to the First Church in Ephesus (Rev 2:1-7) 239

    The Message to the Second Church in Smyrna (Rev 2:8-11) 239

    The Message to the Third Church in Pergamum (Rev 2:12-7) 239

    The Message to the Fourth Church in Thyatira (Rev 2:18-29) 240

    The Message to the Fifth Church in Sardis (Rev 3:1-6) 240

    The Message to the Sixth Church in Philadelphia (Rev 3:7-13) 240

    The Message to the Seventh Church in Laodicea (Rev 3:14-22) 241

John's Encounter with God in Heaven (Rev 4:1-11)   **241**

The Removing of the Seals (Rev 6:1 - 8:5)   **243**

    The Opening of the First Seal (Rev 6:1-2) 243

    The Opening of the Second Seal (Rev 6:3-4) 243

    The Opening of the Third Seal (Rev 6:5-6) 243

    The Opening of the Fourth Seal (Rev 6:7-8) 243

    The Opening of the Fifth Seal (Rev 6:9-11) 244

    The Opening of the Sixth Seal (Rev 6:12-7) 244

    The Intermission: The 144,000 Sealed on Earth (Rev 7:1-8) 244

    The Intermission: The Great Multitude in Heaven (Rev 7:9-17) 245

    The Opening of the Seventh Seal (Rev 8:1-5) 245

The Seven Trumpets (Rev 8:6 - 11:19)   **246**

    The First Trumpet (Rev 8:6-7) 246

    The Second Trumpet (Rev 8:8-9) 246

    The Third Trumpet (Rev 8:10-1) 246

    The Fourth Trumpet (Rev 8:12-13) 246

    The Fifth Trumpet (Rev 9:1-12) 246

    The Sixth Trumpet (Rev 9:13-21) 247

    The Intermission: The Two Prophets (Rev 11:1-14) 248

        Their Ministry (Rev 11:1-6) 248

        Their Martyrdom (Rev 11:7-10) 248

        Their Resurrection and Ascension into Heaven (Rev 11:11-4) 248

    The Seventh Trumpet (Rev 11:15-9) 249

The Woman, Child, and Satan (Rev 12:1-17)   **249**

The War in Heaven (Rev 12:7-9) 249

The War on Earth (Rev 12:10-7) 250

The Beast (Rev 13:1-10)   **250**

The False Prophet (Rev 13:11-8)   **251**

The 144,000 in Heaven (Rev 14:1-5)   **251**

The Message of the Three Angels (Rev 14:6-12) 251

The Great Harvest of the Saints (Rev 14:13-20)   **252**

The Seven Bowls (Rev 16:1-20)   **253**

The First Bowl (Rev 16:2) 253

The Second Bowl (Rev 16:3) 253

The Third Bowl (Rev 16:4-5) 254

The Fourth Bowl 254

The Fifth Bowl. 254

The Sixth Bowl 254

The Seventh Bowl 254

Who is the Beast 255

The War Against the Saints on Earth. 255

Who is the Harlot and What are the Ten Horns. 255

The Destruction of the Harlot and the Beast (Rev 19:1-21)   **257**

The Destruction of the Harlot and the Marriage of the Lamb (Rev 19:1-9). 257

The First Angel John Worships (Rev 19:9-10). 258

Jesus Avenges the Saints: The Destruction of the Beast (Rev 19:11-21). 258

The Final Defeat of Satan (Rev 20:1-15)   **259**

Satan Imprisoned for a Thousand Years (Rev 20:1-3) 259

The First Resurrection: The Saints will Rule with Jesus (Rev 20:4-6). 259

Satan is Released from the Abyss (Rev 20:7-10) 259

The Second Resurrection: Satan and His Followers are Placed in the Lake of Fire (Rev 20:11-5). 259

The New Heaven, the New Earth and the New Jerusalem (Rev 21:1 - 22:5)   **260**

The Epilogue (Rev 22:6-21)   **261**

The Second Angel that John Worships (Rev 22:6-11) 261

Jesus Speaks (Rev 22:12-6). 262

The Spirit, Jesus and John Speaks (Rev 22:17-21) 263

The Prologue (Rev 1:1-20)

The Chain of Custody of the Vision (Rev 1:1-3)

1:1 This is the Revelation of Jesus Christ, which God gave him to show to his servants the things which must happen soon, which he sent and made known by his angel to his servant, John, *1:2* who testified to God's word, and of the testimony of Jesus Christ, about everything that he saw.

1:3 Blessed is he who reads and those who hear the words of the prophecy, and keep the things that are written in it, for the time is at hand.

John Provides Background to His Message (Rev 1:4-8)

1:4 John, to the seven churches that are in Asia: Grace to you and peace, from God, who is and who was and who is to come; and from the seven Spirits who are before his throne; *1:5* and from Jesus Christ, the faithful witness, the firstborn of the dead, and the ruler of the kings of the earth. To him who loves us, and washed us from our sins by his blood; *1:6* and he made us to be a Kingdom, priests to his God and Father; to him be the glory and the dominion forever and ever. Amen.

1:7 Behold, he is coming with the clouds, and every eye will see him, including those who pierced him. All the tribes of the earth will mourn over him. Even so, Amen.

> *1:8* "I am the Alpha and the Omega," says the Lord God, "who is and who was and
> who is to come, the Almighty."

Where John Was (Rev 1:9-10)

1:9 I John, your brother and partner with you in oppression, Kingdom, and perseverance in Christ Jesus, was on the isle that is called Patmos because of God's Word and the testimony of Jesus Christ. *1:10* I was in the Spirit on the Lord's day, and I heard behind me a loud voice, like a trumpet *1:11* saying,

> "What you see, write in a book and send to the seven churches:
> to Ephesus, Smyrna, Pergamum, Thyatira, Sardis, Philadelphia,
> and to Laodicea."

Jesus Tending to the Seven Churches (Rev 1:12-20)

1:12 I turned to see the voice that spoke with me. Having turned, I saw seven golden lampstands. *1:13* And among the lampstands was one like a son of man, clothed with a robe reaching down to his feet, and with a golden sash around his chest. *1:14* His head and his hair were white as white wool, like snow. His eyes were like a flame of fire. *1:15* His feet were like burnished brass, as if it had been refined in a furnace. His voice was like the voice of many waters. *1:16* He had seven stars in his right hand. Out of his mouth proceeded a sharp two-edged sword. His face was like the sun shining at its brightest. *1:17* When I saw him, I fell at his feet like a dead man.

He laid his right hand on me, saying,

"Don't be afraid. I am the first and the last, **1:18** and the Living one. I was dead, and behold, I am alive forevermore. Amen. I have the keys of Death and of Hades. **1:19** Write therefore the things which you have seen, and the things which are, and the things which will happen hereafter; **1:20** the mystery of the seven stars which you saw in my right hand, and the seven golden lampstands. The seven stars are the angels of the seven churches. The seven lampstands are seven churches.

The Seven Churches (Rev 2:1 - 3:22)

The Message to the First Church in Ephesus (Rev 2:1-7)

2:1 "To the angel of the church in Ephesus write:

"He who holds the seven stars in his right hand, he who walks among the seven golden lampstands says these things:

2:2 "I know your works, and your toil and perseverance, and that you can't tolerate evil men, and have tested those who call themselves apostles, and they are not, and found them false. **2:3** You have perseverance and have endured for my name's sake, and have not grown weary. **2:4** But I have this against you, that you left your first love. **2:5** Remember therefore from where you have fallen, and repent and do the first works; or else I am coming to you swiftly, and will move your lampstand out of its place, unless you repent. **2:6** But this you have, that you hate the works of the Nicolaitans, which I also hate. **2:7** He who has an ear, let him hear what the Spirit says to the churches. To him who overcomes I will give to eat of the tree of life, which is in the Paradise of my God.

The Message to the Second Church in Smyrna (Rev 2:8-11)

2:8 "To the angel of the church in Smyrna write:

"The first and the last, who was dead, and has come to life says these things:

2:9 "I know your works, oppression, and your poverty (but you are rich), and the blasphemy of those who say they are Jews, and they are not, but are a synagogue of Satan. **2:10** Don't be afraid of the things which you are about to suffer. Behold, the devil is about to throw some of you into prison, that you may be tested; and you will have oppression for ten days. Be faithful to death, and I will give you the crown of life. **2:11** He who has an ear, let him hear what the Spirit says to the churches. He who overcomes won't be harmed by the second death.

The Message to the Third Church in Pergamum (Rev 2:12-7)

2:12 "To the angel of the church in Pergamum write:

"He who has the sharp two-edged sword says these things:

2:13 "I know your works and where you dwell, where Satan's throne is. You hold firmly to my name, and didn't deny my faith in the days of Antipas my witness, my faithful one, who was killed among you, where Satan dwells. **2:14** But I have a few things against you, because you have there some who hold the teaching of Balaam, who taught Balak to throw a stumbling block before the children of Israel, to eat things sacrificed to idols, and to commit sexual immorality. **2:15** So you also have some who hold to the teaching of the Nicolaitans likewise. **2:16** Repent therefore, or else I am coming to you quickly, and I will make war against them with the sword of my mouth. **2:17** He who has an ear, let him hear what the Spirit says to the churches. To him who overcomes, to him I will give of the hidden manna, and I will give him a white stone, and on the stone a new name written, which no one knows but he who receives it.

The Message to the Fourth Church in Thyatira (Rev 2:18-29)

2:18 "To the angel of the church in Thyatira write:

"The Son of God, who has his eyes like a flame of fire, and his feet are like burnished brass, says these things:

2:19 "I know your works, your love, faith, service, patient endurance, and that your last works are more than the first. **2:20** But I have this against you, that you tolerate your woman, Jezebel, who calls herself a prophetess. She teaches and seduces my servants to commit sexual immorality, and to eat things sacrificed to idols. **2:21** I gave her time to repent, but she refuses to repent of her sexual immorality. **2:22** Behold, I will throw her into a bed, and those who commit adultery with her into great oppression, unless they repent of her works. **2:23** I will kill her children with Death, and all the churches will know that I am he who searches the minds and hearts. I will give to each one of you according to your deeds. **2:24** But to you I say, to the rest who are in Thyatira, as many as don't have this teaching, who don't know what some call 'the deep things of Satan,' to you I say, I am not putting any other burden on you. **2:25** Nevertheless, hold that which you have firmly until I come. **2:26** He who overcomes, and he who keeps my works to the end, to him I will give authority over the nations. **2:27** He will rule them with a rod of iron, shattering them like clay pots; as I also have received of my Father: **2:28** and I will give him the morning star. **2:29** He who has an ear, let him hear what the Spirit says to the churches.

The Message to the Fifth Church in Sardis (Rev 3:1-6)

3:1 "And to the angel of the church in Sardis write:

"He who has the seven Spirits of God, and the seven stars says these things:

"I know your works, that you have a reputation of being alive, but you are dead. **3:2** Wake up, and keep the things that remain, which you were about to throw away, for I have found no works of yours perfected before my God. **3:3** Remember therefore how you have received and heard. Keep it, and repent. If therefore you won't watch, I will come as a thief, and you won't know what hour I will come upon you. **3:4** Nevertheless you have a few names in Sardis that did not defile their garments. They will walk with me in white, for they are worthy. **3:5** He who overcomes will be arrayed in white garments, and I will in no way blot his name out of the book of life, and I will confess his name before my Father, and before his angels. **3:6** He who has an ear, let him hear what the Spirit says to the churches.

The Message to the Sixth Church in Philadelphia (Rev 3:7-13)

3:7 "To the angel of the church in Philadelphia write:

"He who is holy, he who is true, he who has the key of David, he who opens and no one can shut, and who shuts and no one opens, says these things:

3:8 "I know your works (behold, I have set before you an open door, which no one can shut), that you have a little power, and kept my word, and didn't deny my name. **3:9** Behold, I give of the synagogue of Satan, of those who say they are Jews, and they are not, but lie. Behold, I will make them to come and worship before your feet, and to know that I have loved you. **3:10** Because you kept my command to endure, I also will keep you from the hour of testing, which is to come on the whole world, to test those who dwell on the earth. **3:11** I am coming quickly! Hold firmly that which you have, so that no one takes your crown. **3:12** He who overcomes, I will make him a pillar in the temple of my God, and he will go out from there no more. I will write on him the name of my God, and the name of the city of my God, the new Jerusalem, which comes down out of heaven from my God, and my own new name. **3:13** He who has an ear, let him hear what the Spirit says to the churches.

The Message to the Seventh Church in Laodicea (Rev 3:14-22)

3:14 "To the angel of the church in Laodicea write:

"The Amen, the Faithful and True Witness,
the Head of God's creation, says these things:

3:15 "I know your works, that you are neither cold nor hot. I wish you were cold or hot. **3:16** So, because you are lukewarm, and neither hot nor cold, I will vomit you out of my mouth. **3:17** Because you say, 'I am rich, and have gotten riches, and have need of nothing;' and don't know that you are the wretched one, miserable, poor, blind, and naked; **3:18** I counsel you to buy from me gold refined by fire, that you may become rich; and white garments, that you may clothe yourself, and that the shame of your nakedness may not be revealed; and eye salve to anoint your eyes, that you may see. **3:19** As many as I love, I reprove and chasten. Be zealous therefore, and repent. **3:20** Behold, I stand at the door and knock. If anyone hears my voice and opens the door, then I will come in to him, and will dine with him, and he with me. **3:21** He who overcomes, I will give to him to sit down with me on my throne, as I also overcame, and sat down with my Father on his throne. **3:22** He who has an ear, let him hear what the Spirit says to the churches."

John's Encounter with God in Heaven (Rev 4:1-11)

4:1 After these things I looked and saw a door opened in heaven, and the first voice that I heard, like a trumpet speaking with me, was one saying,

> "Come up here,
>   and I will show you the things which must happen after this."

4:2 Immediately I was in the Spirit. Behold, there was a throne set in heaven, and one sitting on the throne **4:3** that looked like a jasper stone and a sardius. There was a rainbow around the throne, like an emerald to look at. **4:4** Around the throne were twenty-four thrones. On the thrones were twenty-four elders sitting, dressed in white garments, with crowns of gold on their heads. **4:5** Out of the throne proceed lightnings, sounds, and thunders. There were seven lamps of fire burning before his throne, which are the seven Spirits of God. **4:6** Before the throne was something like a sea of glass, similar to crystal. In the midst of the throne, and around the throne were four living creatures full of eyes before and behind. **4:7** The first creature was like a lion, and the second creature like a calf, and the third creature had a face like a man, and the fourth was like a flying eagle. **4:8** The four living creatures, each one of them having six wings, are full of eyes around and within. They have no rest day and night, saying,

> "Holy, holy, holy is the Lord God, the Almighty,
>> who was and who is and who is to come!"

4:9 When the living creatures give glory, honor, and thanks to him who sits on the throne, to him who lives forever and ever, **4:10** the twenty-four elders fall down before him who sits on the throne, and worship him who lives forever and ever, and throw their crowns before the throne, saying,

> **4:11** "Worthy are you, our Lord and God, the Holy One,
>> to receive the glory, the honor, and the power,
>> for you created all things,
>> and because of your desire they existed,
>> and were created!"

The Coronation of Jesus in Heaven (Rev 5:1-14)

5:1 I saw, in the right hand of him who sat on the throne, a book written inside and outside, sealed shut with seven seals. **5:2** I saw a mighty angel proclaiming with a loud voice,

> "Who is worthy to open the book,
>> and to break its seals?"

5:3 No one in heaven above, or on the earth, or under the earth, was able to open the book, or to look in it. **5:4** And I wept much, because no one was found worthy to open the book, or to look in it. **5:5** One of the elders said to me,

> "Don't weep.
>
> Behold, the Lion who is of the tribe of Judah,
>> the Root of David, has overcome;
>> he who opens the scroll and its seven seals."

5:6 I saw in the midst of the throne and of the four living creatures, and in the midst of the elders, a Lamb standing, as though it had been slain, having seven horns, and seven eyes, which are the seven Spirits of God, sent out into all the earth. **5:7** Then he came, and he took it out of the right hand of him who sat on the throne. **5:8** Now when he had taken the book, the four living creatures and the twenty-four elders fell down before the Lamb, each one having a harp, and golden bowls full of incense, which are the prayers of the saints. **5:9** They sang a new song, saying,

> "You are worthy to take the book, and to open its seals:
>> for you were killed, and bought us for God with your blood,
>> out of every tribe, language, people, and nation,
>
> **5:10** and made us kings and priests to our God,
>> and we will reign on earth."

5:11 I saw, and I heard something like a voice of many angels around the throne, the living creatures, and the elders; and the number of them was ten thousands of ten thousands, and thousands of thousands; **5:12** saying with a loud voice,

> "Worthy is the Lamb who has been killed to receive the power,
>   wealth, wisdom, strength, honor, glory, and blessing!"

5:13 I heard every created thing which is in heaven, on the earth, under the earth, on the sea, and everything in them, saying,

> "To him who sits on the throne,
>   and to the Lamb be the blessing,
>   the honor, the glory, and the dominion, forever and ever! Amen!"

5:14 The four living creatures said, "Amen!" The elders fell down and worshiped.

The Removing of the Seals (Rev 6:1 - 8:5)

The Opening of the First Seal (Rev 6:1-2)

6:1 I saw that the Lamb opened one of the seven seals, and I heard one of the four living creatures saying, as with a voice of thunder, "Come and see!" **6:2** And behold, a white horse, and he who sat on it had a bow. A crown was given to him, and he came forth conquering, and to conquer.

The Opening of the Second Seal (Rev 6:3-4)

6:3 When he opened the second seal, I heard the second living creature saying, "Come!" **6:4** Another came forth, a red horse. To him who sat on it was given power to take peace from the earth, and that they should kill one another. There was given to him a great sword.

The Opening of the Third Seal (Rev 6:5-6)

6:5 When he opened the third seal, I heard the third living creature saying, "Come and see!" And behold, a black horse, and he who sat on it had a balance in his hand. **6:6** I heard a voice in the midst of the four living creatures saying,

> "A choenix of wheat for a denarius,
>   and three choenix of barley for a denarius!
> Don't damage the oil and the wine!"

The Opening of the Fourth Seal (Rev 6:7-8)

6:7 When he opened the fourth seal, I heard the fourth living creature saying, "Come and see!" **6:8** And behold, a pale horse, and he who sat on it, his name was Death. Hades followed with him. Authority over one fourth of the earth, to kill with the sword, with famine, with death, and by the wild animals of the earth was given to him.

The Opening of the Fifth Seal (Rev 6:9-11)

6:9 When he opened the fifth seal, I saw underneath the altar the souls of those who had been killed for the Word of God, and for the testimony of the Lamb which they had. **6:10** They cried with a loud voice, saying,

> "How long, Master, the holy and true,
> until you judge and avenge our blood on those who dwell on the earth?"

6:11 A long white robe was given to each of them. They were told that they should rest yet for a while, until their fellow servants and their brothers, who would also be killed even as they were, should complete their course.

The Opening of the Sixth Seal (Rev 6:12-7)

6:12 I saw when he opened the sixth seal, and there was a great earthquake. The sun became black as sackcloth made of hair, and the whole moon became as blood. **6:13** The stars of the sky fell to the earth, like a fig tree dropping its unripe figs when it is shaken by a great wind. **6:14** The sky was removed like a scroll when it is rolled up. Every mountain and island were moved out of their places. **6:15** The kings of the earth, the princes, the commanding officers, the rich, the strong, and every slave and free person, hid themselves in the caves and in the rocks of the mountains. **6:16** They told the mountains and the rocks,

> "Fall on us, and hide us from the face of him who sits on the throne,
> and from the wrath of the Lamb,
> **6:17** for the great day of his wrath has come;
> and who is able to stand?"

The Intermission: The 144,000 Sealed on Earth (Rev 7:1-8)

7:1 After this, I saw four angels standing at the four corners of the earth, holding the four winds of the earth, so that no wind would blow on the earth, or on the sea, or on any tree. **7:2** I saw another angel ascend from the sunrise, having the seal of the living God. He cried with a loud voice to the four angels to whom it was given to harm the earth and the sea, **7:3** saying,

> "Don't harm the earth, neither the sea, nor the trees,
> until we have sealed the bondservants of our God on their foreheads!"

> **7:4** I heard the number of those who were sealed,
> one hundred forty-four thousand,
> sealed out of every tribe of the children of Israel:

> **7:5** of the tribe of Judah were sealed twelve thousand,
> of the tribe of Reuben twelve thousand,
> of the tribe of Gad twelve thousand,

> **7:6** of the tribe of Asher twelve thousand,
> of the tribe of Naphtali twelve thousand,
> of the tribe of Manasseh twelve thousand,

7:7 of the tribe of Simeon twelve thousand,
of the tribe of Levi twelve thousand,
of the tribe of Issachar twelve thousand,

7:8 of the tribe of Zebulun twelve thousand,
of the tribe of Joseph twelve thousand,
of the tribe of Benjamin were sealed twelve thousand.

The Intermission: The Great Multitude in Heaven (Rev 7:9-17)

7:9 After these things I looked, and behold, a great multitude, which no man could number, out of every nation and of all tribes, peoples, and languages, standing before the throne and before the Lamb, dressed in white robes, with palm branches in their hands. *7:10* They cried with a loud voice, saying,

"Salvation be to our God, who sits on the throne, and to the Lamb!"

7:11 All the angels were standing around the throne, the elders, and the four living creatures; and they fell on their faces before his throne, and worshiped God, *7:12* saying, "Amen! Blessing, glory, wisdom, thanksgiving, honor, power, and might, be to our God forever and ever! Amen."

7:13 One of the elders answered, saying to me,

"These who are arrayed in white robes,
who are they, and from where did they come?"

7:14 I told him, "My lord, you know."

He said to me,

"These are those who came out of the great tribulation.
They washed their robes,
and made them white in the Lamb's blood.
7:15 Therefore they are before the throne of God,
they serve him day and night in his temple.
He who sits on the throne will spread his tabernacle over them.
7:16 They will never be hungry,
neither thirsty any more;
neither will the sun beat on them, nor any heat;
7:17 for the Lamb who is in the midst of the throne shepherds them,
and leads them to springs of waters of life.
And God will wipe away every tear from their eyes."

The Opening of the Seventh Seal (Rev 8:1-5)

8:1 When he opened the seventh seal, there was silence in heaven for about half an hour. *8:2* I saw the seven angels who stand before God, and seven trumpets were given to them. *8:3* Another angel came and stood over the altar, having a golden censer. Much incense was given to him, that he should add it to the prayers of all the saints on the golden altar which was before the throne. **8:4** The smoke of the incense, with the prayers of the saints, went up before God out of the angel's hand. **8:5** The angel took the censer, and he filled it with the fire of the altar, and threw it on the earth. There followed thunders, sounds, lightnings, and an earthquake.

The Seven Trumpets (Rev 8:6 - 11:19)

The First Trumpet (Rev 8:6-7)

8:6 The seven angels who had the seven trumpets prepared themselves to sound. **8:7** The first sounded, and there followed hail and fire, mixed with blood, and they were thrown to the earth. One third of the earth was burnt up, and one third of the trees were burnt up, and all green grass was burnt up.

The Second Trumpet (Rev 8:8-9)

8:8 The second angel sounded, and something like a great burning mountain was thrown into the sea. One third of the sea became blood, **8:9** and one third of the living creatures which were in the sea died. One third of the ships were destroyed.

The Third Trumpet (Rev 8:10-1)

8:10 The third angel sounded, and a great star fell from the sky, burning like a torch, and it fell on one third of the rivers, and on the springs of the waters. **8:11** The name of the star is called "Wormwood." One third of the waters became wormwood. Many people died from the waters, because they were made bitter.

The Fourth Trumpet (Rev 8:12-13)

8:12 The fourth angel sounded, and one third of the sun was struck, and one third of the moon, and one third of the stars; so that one third of them would be darkened, and the day wouldn't shine for one third of it, and the night in the same way. **8:13** I saw, and I heard an eagle, flying in mid heaven, saying with a loud voice,

> "Woe! Woe! Woe for those who dwell on the earth,
>> because of the other voices of the trumpets of the three angels,
>> who are yet to sound!"

The Fifth Trumpet (Rev 9:1-12)

9:1 The fifth angel sounded, and I saw a star from the sky which had fallen to the earth. The key to the pit of the abyss was given to him. **9:2** He opened the pit of the abyss, and smoke went up out of the pit, like the smoke from a burning furnace. The sun and the air were darkened because of the smoke from the pit. **9:3** Then out of the smoke came forth locusts on the earth, and power was given to them, as the scorpions of the earth have power. **9:4** They were told that they should not hurt the grass of the earth, neither any green thing, neither any tree, but only those people who don't have God's seal on their foreheads. **9:5** They were given power not to kill them, but to torment them for five months. Their torment was like the torment of a scorpion, when it strikes a person. **9:6** In those days people will seek death, and will in no way find it.

They will desire to die, and death will flee from them. **9:7** The shapes of the locusts were like horses prepared for war. On their heads were something like golden crowns, and their faces were like people's faces. **9:8** They had hair like women's hair, and their teeth were like those of lions. **9:9** They had breastplates, like breastplates of iron. The sound of their wings was like the sound of chariots, or of many horses rushing to war. **9:10** They have tails like those of scorpions, and stings. In their tails they have power to harm men for five months. **9:11** They have over them as king the angel of the abyss. His name in Hebrew is "Abaddon," but in Greek, he has the name "Apollyon."

9:12 The first woe is past. Behold, there are still two woes coming after this.

The Sixth Trumpet (Rev 9:13-21)

9:13 The sixth angel sounded. I heard a voice from the horns of the golden altar which is before God, **9:14** saying to the sixth angel who had one trumpet,

> "Free the four angels who are bound at the great river Euphrates!"

9:15 The four angels were freed who had been prepared for that hour and day and month and year, so that they might kill one third of mankind. **9:16** The number of the armies of the horsemen was two hundred million. I heard the number of them. **9:17** Thus I saw the horses in the vision, and those who sat on them, having breastplates of fiery red, hyacinth blue, and sulfur yellow; and the heads of lions. Out of their mouths proceed fire, smoke, and sulfur. **9:18** By these three plagues were one third of mankind killed: by the fire, the smoke, and the sulfur, which proceeded out of their mouths. **9:19** For the power of the horses is in their mouths, and in their tails. For their tails are like serpents, and have heads, and with them they harm. **9:20** The rest of mankind, who were not killed with these plagues, didn't repent of the works of their hands, that they wouldn't worship demons, and the idols of gold, and of silver, and of brass, and of stone, and of wood; which can neither see, nor hear, nor walk. **9:21** They didn't repent of their murders, nor of their sorceries, nor of their sexual immorality, nor of their thefts.

The Intermission: The Mighty Angel, the Seven Thunders and John (Rev 10:1-11)

10:1 I saw a mighty angel coming down out of the sky, clothed with a cloud. A rainbow was on his head. His face was like the sun, and his feet like pillars of fire. **10:2** He had in his hand a little open scroll. He set his right foot on the sea, and his left on the land. **10:3** He cried with a loud voice, as a lion roars. When he cried, the seven thunders uttered their voices. **10:4** When the seven thunders sounded, I was about to write; but I heard a voice from the sky saying,

> "Seal up the things which the seven thunders said,
> and don't write them."

10:5 The angel whom I saw standing on the sea and on the land lifted up his right hand to the sky, **10:6** and swore by him who lives forever and ever, who created heaven and the things that are in it, the earth and the things that are in it, and the sea and the things that are in it, that there will no longer be delay, **10:7** but in the days of the voice of the seventh angel, when he is about to sound, then the mystery of God is finished, as he declared to his servants, the prophets. **10:8** The voice which I heard from heaven, again speaking with me, said,

> "Go, take the scroll which is open in the hand of the angel who stands on the sea and
> on the land."

10:9 I went to the angel, telling him to give me the little book.

He said to me,

> "Take it, and eat it up. It will make your stomach bitter,
> but in your mouth it will be as sweet as honey."

10:10 I took the little book out of the angel's hand, and ate it up. It was as sweet as honey in my mouth. When I had eaten it, my stomach was made bitter. **10:11** They told me,

> "You must prophesy again over many peoples, nations, languages, and kings."

The Intermission: The Two Prophets (Rev 11:1-14)

Their Ministry (Rev 11:1-6)

11:1 A reed like a rod was given to me. Someone said, "Rise, and measure God's temple, and the altar, and those who worship in it. **11:2** Leave out the court which is outside of the temple, and don't measure it, for it has been given to the nations. They will tread the holy city under foot for forty-two months. **11:3** I will give power to my two witnesses, and they will prophesy one thousand two hundred sixty days, clothed in sackcloth." **11:4** These are the two olive trees and the two lampstands, standing before the Lord of the earth. **11:5** If anyone desires to harm them, fire proceeds out of their mouth and devours their enemies. If anyone desires to harm them, he must be killed in this way. **11:6** These have the power to shut up the sky, that it may not rain during the days of their prophecy. They have power over the waters, to turn them into blood, and to strike the earth with every plague, as often as they desire.

Their Martyrdom (Rev 11:7-10)

11:7 When they have finished their testimony, the beast that comes up out of the abyss will make war with them, and overcome them, and kill them. **11:8** Their dead bodies will be in the street of the great city, which spiritually is called Sodom and Egypt, where also their Lord was crucified. **11:9** From among the peoples, tribes, languages, and nations people will look at their dead bodies for three and a half days, and will not allow their dead bodies to be laid in a tomb. **11:10** Those who dwell on the earth rejoice over them, and they will be glad. They will give gifts to one another, because these two prophets tormented those who dwell on the earth.

Their Resurrection and Ascension into Heaven (Rev 11:11-4)

11:11 After the three and a half days, the breath of life from God entered into them, and they stood on their feet. Great fear fell on those who saw them. **11:12** I heard a loud voice from heaven saying to them, "Come up here!" They went up into heaven in the cloud, and their enemies saw them. **11:13** In that day there was a great earthquake, and a tenth of the city fell. Seven thousand people were killed in the earthquake, and the rest were terrified, and gave glory to the God of heaven. **11:14** The second woe is past. Behold, the third woe comes quickly.

The Seventh Trumpet (Rev 11:15-9)

11:15 The seventh angel sounded, and great voices in heaven followed, saying,

> "The kingdom of the world has become the Kingdom of our Lord,
>   and of his Christ.
> He will reign forever and ever!"

11:16 The twenty-four elders, who sit on their thrones before God's throne, fell on their faces and worshiped God, *11:17* saying:

> "We give you thanks, Lord God, the Almighty,
>   the one who is and who was;
>   because you have taken your great power, and reigned.

> *11:18* The nations were angry,
>   and your wrath came,
>   as did the time for the dead to be judged,
>   and to give your bondservants the prophets,
>   their reward, as well as to the saints,
>   and those who fear your name,
>   to the small and the great;
>   and to destroy those who destroy the earth."

11:19 God's temple that is in heaven was opened, and the ark of the Lord's covenant was seen in his temple. Lightnings, sounds, thunders, an earthquake, and great hail followed.

The Woman, Child, and Satan (Rev 12:1-17)

12:1 A great sign was seen in heaven: a woman clothed with the sun, and the moon under her feet, and on her head a crown of twelve stars. *12:2* She was with child. She cried out in pain, laboring to give birth. *12:3* Another sign was seen in heaven. Behold, a great red dragon, having seven heads and ten horns, and on his heads seven crowns. *12:4* His tail drew one third of the stars of the sky, and threw them to the earth. The dragon stood before the woman who was about to give birth, so that when she gave birth he might devour her child. *12:5* She gave birth to a son, a male child, who is to rule all the nations with a rod of iron. Her child was caught up to God, and to his throne. *12:6* The woman fled into the wilderness, where she has a place prepared by God, that there they may nourish her one thousand two hundred sixty days.

The War in Heaven (Rev 12:7-9)

12:7 There was war in the sky. Michael and his angels made war on the dragon. The dragon and his angels made war. *12:8* They didn't prevail, neither was a place found for him any more in heaven. *12:9* The great dragon was thrown down, the old serpent, he who is called the devil and Satan, the deceiver of the whole world. He was thrown down to the earth, and his angels were thrown down with him.

The War on Earth (Rev 12:10-7)

12:10 I heard a loud voice in heaven, saying,

> "Now the salvation, the power,
>> and the Kingdom of our God,
>> and the authority of his Christ has come;
>> for the accuser of our brothers has been thrown down,
>> who accuses them before our God day and night.

> **12:11** They overcame him because of the Lamb's blood,
>> and because of the word of their testimony.

> They didn't love their life,
>> even to death.

> **12:12** Therefore rejoice, heavens,
>> and you who dwell in them.

> Woe to the earth and to the sea,
>> because the devil has gone down to you,
>> having great wrath,
>> knowing that he has but a short time."

12:13 When the dragon saw that he was thrown down to the earth, he persecuted the woman who gave birth to the male child. **12:14** Two wings of the great eagle were given to the woman, that she might fly into the wilderness to her place, so that she might be nourished for a time, and times, and half a time, from the face of the serpent. **12:15** The serpent spewed water out of his mouth after the woman like a river, that he might cause her to be carried away by the stream. **12:16** The earth helped the woman, and the earth opened its mouth and swallowed up the river which the dragon spewed out of his mouth. **12:17** The dragon grew angry with the woman, and went away to make war with the rest of her seed, who keep God's commandments and hold Jesus' testimony.

The Beast (Rev 13:1-10)

13:1 Then I stood on the sand of the sea. I saw a beast coming up out of the sea, having ten horns and seven heads. On his horns were ten crowns, and on his heads, blasphemous names. **13:2** The beast which I saw was like a leopard, and his feet were like those of a bear, and his mouth like the mouth of a lion. The dragon gave him his power, his throne, and great authority. **13:3** One of his heads looked like it had been wounded fatally. His fatal wound was healed, and the whole earth marvelled at the beast. **13:4** They worshipped the dragon, because he gave his authority to the beast, and they worshipped the beast, saying,

> "Who is like the beast?

> Who is able to make war with him?"

13:5 A mouth speaking great things and blasphemy was given to him. Authority to make war for forty-two months was given to him. **13:6** He opened his mouth for blasphemy against God, to blaspheme his name, and his dwelling, those who dwell in heaven. **13:7** It was given to him to make war with the saints, and to overcome them. Authority over every tribe, people, language, and nation was given to him. **13:8** All who dwell on the earth will worship him, everyone whose name has not been written from the foundation of the world in the book of life of the Lamb who has been killed.

> *13:9* If anyone has an ear,
> let him hear.

> *13:10* If anyone is to go into captivity,
> he will go into captivity.

> If anyone is to be killed with the sword,
> he must be killed.

> Here is the endurance and the faith of the saints.

The False Prophet (Rev 13:11-8)

13:11 I saw another beast coming up out of the earth. He had two horns like a lamb, and he spoke like a dragon. *13:12* He exercises all the authority of the first beast in his presence. He makes the earth and those who dwell in it to worship the first beast, whose fatal wound was healed. *13:13* He performs great signs, even making fire come down out of the sky to the earth in the sight of people. *13:14* He deceives my own people who dwell on the earth because of the signs he was granted to do in front of the beast; saying to those who dwell on the earth, that they should make an image to the beast who had the sword wound and lived. *13:15* It was given to him to give breath to it, to the image of the beast, that the image of the beast should both speak, and cause as many as wouldn't worship the image of the beast to be killed. *13:16* He causes all, the small and the great, the rich and the poor, and the free and the slave, to be given marks on their right hands, or on their foreheads; *13:17* and that no one would be able to buy or to sell, unless he has that mark, the name of the beast or the number of his name. *13:18* Here is wisdom. He who has understanding, let him calculate the number of the beast, for it is the number of a man. His number is six hundred sixty-six.

The 144,000 in Heaven (Rev 14:1-5)

14:1 I saw, and behold, the Lamb standing on Mount Zion, and with him a number, one hundred forty-four thousand, having his name, and the name of his Father, written on their foreheads. *14:2* I heard a sound from heaven, like the sound of many waters, and like the sound of a great thunder. The sound which I heard was like that of harpists playing on their harps. *14:3* They sing a new song before the throne, and before the four living creatures and the elders. No one could learn the song except the one hundred forty-four thousand, those who had been redeemed out of the earth. *14:4* These are those who were not defiled with women, for they are virgins. These are those who follow the Lamb wherever he goes. These were redeemed by Jesus from among men, the first fruits to God and to the Lamb. *14:5* In their mouth was found no lie, for they are blameless.

The Message of the Three Angels (Rev 14:6-12)

14:6 I saw an angel flying in mid heaven, having an eternal Good News to proclaim to those who dwell on the earth, and to every nation, tribe, language, and people. *14:7* He said with a loud voice,

> "Fear the Lord, and give him glory;
> for the hour of his judgment has come.

Worship him who made the heaven,
the earth, the sea, and the springs of waters!"

14:8 Another, a second angel, followed, saying,

"Babylon the great has fallen,
which has made all the nations to drink of the wine of the wrath of her sexual
immorality."

14:9 Another angel, a third, followed them, saying with a great voice,

"If anyone worships the beast and his image,
and receives a mark on his forehead, or on his hand,

14:10 he also will drink of the wine of the wrath of God,
which is prepared unmixed in the cup of his anger.

He will be tormented with fire and sulfur in the presence of the holy angels, and in the
presence of the Lamb.

14:11 The smoke of their torment goes up forever and ever.

They have no rest day and night,
those who worship the beast and his image,
and whoever receives the mark of his name.

14:12 Here is the patience of the saints,
those who keep the commandments of God,
and the faith of Jesus."

The Great Harvest of the Saints (Rev 14:13-20)

14:13 I heard the voice from heaven saying,

"Write, 'Blessed are the dead who die in the Lord from now on.'"

"Yes," says the Spirit,
"that they may rest from their labors;
for their works follow with them."

14:14 I looked, and behold, a white cloud; and on the cloud one sitting like a son of man, having on his
head a golden crown, and in his hand a sharp sickle. 14:15 Another angel came out from the temple, crying
with a loud voice to him who sat on the cloud, "Send forth your sickle, and reap; for the hour to reap has
come; for the harvest of the earth is ripe!" 14:16 He who sat on the cloud thrust his sickle on the earth, and
the earth was reaped.

14:17 Another angel came out from the temple which is in heaven. He also had a sharp sickle. 14:18 Another
angel came out from the altar, he who has power over fire, and he called with a great voice to him who had
the sharp sickle, saying,

"Send forth your sharp sickle,
and gather the clusters of the vine of the earth,
for the earth's grapes are fully ripe!"

14:19 The angel thrust his sickle into the earth, and gathered the vintage of the earth, and threw it into the great wine press of the wrath of God. *14:20* The wine press was trodden outside of the city, and blood came out from the wine press, even to the bridles of the horses, as far as one thousand six hundred stadia.

The Song of Moses and The Lamb (Rev 15:1-8)

15:1 I saw another great and marvellous sign in the sky: seven angels having the seven last plagues, for in them God's wrath is finished. *15:2* I saw something like a sea of glass mixed with fire, and those who overcame the beast, his image, and the number of his name, standing on the sea of glass, having harps of God. *15:3* They sang the song of Moses, the servant of God, and the song of the Lamb, saying,

> "Great and marvellous are your works, Lord God, the Almighty!
>> Righteous and true are your ways, you King of the nations.
>
> *15:4* Who wouldn't fear you, Lord,
>> and glorify your name?
>
> For you only are holy.
>
> For all the nations will come and worship before you.
>
> For your righteous acts have been revealed."

15:5 After these things I looked, and the temple of the tabernacle of the testimony in heaven was opened. *15:6* The seven angels who had the seven plagues came out, clothed with pure, bright linen, and wearing golden sashes around their breasts.

15:7 One of the four living creatures gave to the seven angels seven golden bowls full of the wrath of God, who lives forever and ever. *15:8* The temple was filled with smoke from the glory of God, and from his power. No one was able to enter into the temple, until the seven plagues of the seven angels would be finished.

The Seven Bowls (Rev 16:1-20)

16:1 I heard a loud voice out of the temple, saying to the seven angels, "Go and pour out the seven bowls of the wrath of God on the earth!"

The First Bowl (Rev 16:2)

16:2 The first went, and poured out his bowl into the earth, and it became a harmful and evil sore on the people who had the mark of the beast, and who worshiped his image.

The Second Bowl (Rev 16:3)

16:3 The second angel poured out his bowl into the sea, and it became blood as of a dead man. Every living thing in the sea died.

The Third Bowl (Rev 16:4-5)

16:4 The third poured out his bowl into the rivers and springs of water, and they became blood. **16:5** I heard the angel of the waters saying,

> "You are righteous,
>   who are and who were,
>   you Holy One,
>   because you have judged these things.
> **16:6** For they poured out the blood of the saints and the prophets,
>   and you have given them blood to drink. They deserve this."

16:7 I heard the altar saying,

> "Yes, Lord God, the Almighty, true and righteous are your judgments."

The Fourth Bowl

16:8 The fourth poured out his bowl on the sun, and it was given to him to scorch men with fire. **16:9** People were scorched with great heat, and people blasphemed the name of God who has the power over these plagues. They didn't repent and give him glory.

The Fifth Bowl

16:10 The fifth poured out his bowl on the throne of the beast, and his kingdom was darkened. They gnawed their tongues because of the pain, **16:11** and they blasphemed the God of heaven because of their pains and their sores. They didn't repent of their works.

The Sixth Bowl

16:12 The sixth poured out his bowl on the great river, the Euphrates. Its water was dried up, that the way might be prepared for the kings that come from the sunrise. **16:13** I saw coming out of the mouth of the dragon, and out of the mouth of the beast, and out of the mouth of the false prophet, three unclean spirits, something like frogs; **16:14** for they are spirits of demons, performing signs; which go forth to the kings of the whole inhabited earth, to gather them together for the war of that great day of God, the Almighty.

16:15 "Behold, I come like a thief. Blessed is he who watches, and keeps his clothes, so that he doesn't walk naked, and they see his shame." **16:16** He gathered them together into the place which is called in Hebrew, Megiddo.

The Seventh Bowl

16:17 The seventh poured out his bowl into the air. A loud voice came forth out of the temple of heaven, from the throne, saying, "It is done!" **16:18** There were lightnings, sounds, and thunders; and there was a great earthquake, such as was not since there were men on the earth, so great an earthquake, so mighty. **16:19** The great city was divided into three parts, and the cities of the nations fell. Babylon the great was remembered in the sight of God, to give to her the cup of the wine of the fierceness of his wrath. *16:20* Every island fled away, and the mountains were not found. *16:21* Great hailstones, about the weight of a talent, came down out of the sky on people. People blasphemed God because of the plague of the hail, for this plague is exceedingly severe.

The Harlot, The Beast and the Children of God

17:1 One of the seven angels who had the seven bowls came and spoke with me, saying, "Come here. I will show you the judgment of the great prostitute who sits on many waters, *17:2* with whom the kings of the earth committed sexual immorality, and those who dwell in the earth were made drunken with the wine of her sexual immorality." *17:3* He carried me away in the Spirit into a wilderness. I saw a woman sitting on a scarlet-colored animal, full of blasphemous names, having seven heads and ten horns. *17:4* The woman was dressed in purple and scarlet, and decked with gold and precious stones and pearls, having in her hand a golden cup full of abominations and the impurities of the sexual immorality of the earth. *17:5* And on her forehead a name was written,

> "MYSTERY, BABYLON THE GREAT,
>   THE MOTHER OF THE PROSTITUTES
>   AND OF THE ABOMINATIONS OF THE EARTH."

17:6 I saw the woman drunken with the blood of the saints, and with the blood of the martyrs of Jesus. When I saw her, I wondered with great amazement. *17:7* The angel said to me, "Why do you wonder? I will tell you the mystery of the woman, and of the beast that carries her, which has the seven heads and the ten horns. *17:8* The beast that you saw was, and is not; and is about to come up out of the abyss and to go into destruction. Those who dwell on the earth and whose names have not been written in the book of life from the foundation of the world will marvel when they see that the beast was, and is not, and shall be present.

Who is the Beast

17:9 Here is the mind that has wisdom. The seven heads are seven mountains, on which the woman sits. *17:10* They are seven kings. Five have fallen, the one is, the other has not yet come. When he comes, he must continue a little while. *17:11* The beast that was, and is not, is himself also an eighth, and is of the seven; and he goes to destruction. *17:12* The ten horns that you saw are ten kings who have received no kingdom as yet, but they receive authority as kings, with the beast, for one hour.

The War Against the Saints on Earth

17:13 These have one mind, and they give their power and authority to the beast. *17:14* These will war against the Lamb, and the Lamb will overcome them, for he is Lord of lords, and King of kings. They also will overcome who are with him, called and chosen and faithful."

Who is the Harlot and What are the Ten Horns

17:15 He said to me,

> "The waters which you saw, where the prostitute sits,
>   are peoples, multitudes, nations, and languages.

17:16 The ten horns which you saw, and the beast,
these will hate the prostitute, and will make her desolate,
and will make her naked,
and will eat her flesh,
and will burn her utterly with fire.

17:17 For God has put in their hearts to do what he has in mind,
and to be of one mind,
and to give their kingdom to the beast,
until the words of God should be accomplished.

17:18 The woman whom you saw is the great city,
which reigns over the kings of the earth."

The Great City of Babylon (Rev 18:21-24)

18:1 After these things, I saw another angel coming down out of the sky, having great authority. The earth was illuminated with his glory. *18:2* He cried with a mighty voice, saying, "Fallen, fallen is Babylon the great, and she has become a habitation of demons, a prison of every unclean spirit, and a prison of every unclean and hateful bird! *18:3* For all the nations have drunk of the wine of the wrath of her sexual immorality, the kings of the earth committed sexual immorality with her, and the merchants of the earth grew rich from the abundance of her luxury."

18:4 I heard another voice from heaven, saying, "Come out of her, my people, that you have no participation in her sins, and that you don't receive of her plagues, *18:5* for her sins have reached to the sky, and God has remembered her iniquities. *18:6* Return to her just as she returned, and repay her double as she did, and according to her works. In the cup which she mixed, mix to her double. *18:7* However much she glorified herself, and grew wanton, so much give her of torment and mourning. For she says in her heart, 'I sit a queen, and am no widow, and will in no way see mourning.' *18:8* Therefore in one day her plagues will come: death, mourning, and famine; and she will be utterly burned with fire; for the Lord God who has judged her is strong. *18:9* The kings of the earth, who committed sexual immorality and lived wantonly with her, will weep and wail over her, when they look at the smoke of her burning, *18:10* standing far away for the fear of her torment, saying, 'Woe, woe, the great city, Babylon, the strong city! For your judgment has come in one hour.' *18:11* The merchants of the earth weep and mourn over her, for no one buys their merchandise any more; *18:12* merchandise of gold, silver, precious stones, pearls, fine linen, purple, silk, scarlet, all expensive wood, every vessel of ivory, every vessel made of most precious wood, and of brass, and iron, and marble; *18:13* and cinnamon, incense, perfume, frankincense, wine, olive oil, fine flour, wheat, sheep, horses, chariots, and people's bodies and souls. *18:14* The fruits which your soul lusted after have been lost to you, and all things that were dainty and sumptuous have perished from you, and you will find them no more at all. *18:15* The merchants of these things, who were made rich by her, will stand far away for the fear of her torment, weeping and mourning; *18:16* saying, 'Woe, woe, the great city, she who was dressed in fine linen, purple, and scarlet, and decked with gold and precious stones and pearls! *18:17* For in an hour such great riches are made desolate.' Every shipmaster, and everyone who sails anywhere, and mariners, and as many as gain their living by sea, stood far away, *18:18* and cried out as they looked at the smoke of her burning, saying, 'What is like the great city?' *18:19* They cast dust on their heads, and cried, weeping and mourning, saying, 'Woe, woe, the great city, in which all who had their ships in the sea were made rich by reason of her great wealth!' For in one hour is she made desolate.

>*18:20* "Rejoice over her, O heaven, you saints, apostles, and prophets; for God has judged
>   your judgment on her."

18:21 A mighty angel took up a stone like a great millstone and cast it into the sea, saying,

>"Thus with violence will Babylon,
>   the great city, be thrown down,
>   and will be found no more at all.
>
>*18:22* The voice of harpists, minstrels, flute players, and trumpeters
>   will be heard no more at all in you.
>
>No craftsman, of whatever craft,
>   will be found any more at all in you.
>
>The sound of a mill will be heard no more at all in you.
>
>*18:23* The light of a lamp will shine no more at all in you.
>
>The voice of the bridegroom and of the bride will be heard no more at all in you;
>
>for your merchants were the princes of the earth;
>   for with your sorcery all the nations were deceived.
>
>*18:24* In her was found the blood of prophets
>   and of saints,
>   and of all who have been slain on the earth."

The Destruction of the Harlot and the Beast (Rev 19:1-21)

The Destruction of the Harlot and the Marriage of the Lamb (Rev 19:1-9)

19:1 After these things I heard something like a loud voice of a great multitude in heaven, saying,

>"Hallelujah! Salvation, power, and glory belong to our God:
>   *19:2* for true and righteous are his judgments.
>
>For he has judged the great prostitute,
>   who corrupted the earth with her sexual immorality,
>   and he has avenged the blood of his servants at her hand."

19:3 A second said,

>"Hallelujah! Her smoke goes up forever and ever."

19:4 The twenty-four elders and the four living creatures fell down and worshiped God who sits on the throne, saying,

>"Amen! Hallelujah!"

19:5 A voice came forth from the throne, saying,

"Give praise to our God, all you his servants,
> you who fear him,
> the small and the great!"

19:6 I heard something like the voice of a great multitude, and like the voice of many waters, and like the voice of mighty thunders, saying, "Hallelujah! For the Lord our God, the Almighty, reigns! **19:7** Let us rejoice and be exceedingly glad, and let us give the glory to him. For the marriage of the Lamb has come, and his wife has made herself ready." **19:8** It was given to her that she would array herself in bright, pure, fine linen: for the fine linen is the righteous acts of the saints.

The First Angel John Worships (Rev 19:9-10)

19:9 He said to me,

"Write,

'Blessed are those who are invited to the marriage supper of the Lamb.'"

He said to me,

"These are true words of God."

19:10 I fell down before his feet to worship him. He said to me,

"Look! Don't do it!

I am a fellow bondservant with you and with your brothers who hold the testimony of Jesus.

Worship God, for the testimony of Jesus is the Spirit of Prophecy."

Jesus Avenges the Saints: The Destruction of the Beast (Rev 19:11-21)

19:11 I saw the heaven opened, and behold, a white horse, and he who sat on it is called Faithful and True. In righteousness he judges and makes war. **19:12** His eyes are a flame of fire, and on his head are many crowns. He has names written and a name written which no one knows but he himself. **19:13** He is clothed in a garment sprinkled with blood. His name is called "The Word of God." **19:14** The armies which are in heaven followed him on white horses, clothed in white, pure, fine linen. **19:15** Out of his mouth proceeds a sharp, double-edged sword, that with it he should strike the nations. He will rule them with an iron rod. He treads the wine press of the fierceness of the wrath of God, the Almighty. **19:16** He has on his garment and on his thigh a name written,

"KING OF KINGS, AND LORD OF LORDS."

19:17 I saw an angel standing in the sun. He cried with a loud voice, saying to all the birds that fly in the sky,

"Come! Be gathered together to the great supper of God,
> **19:18** that you may eat the flesh of kings,
> the flesh of captains,
> the flesh of mighty men,
> and the flesh of horses and of those who sit on them,

and the flesh of all men,
both free and slave, and small and great."

19:19 I saw the beast, and the kings of the earth, and their armies, gathered together to make war against him who sat on the horse, and against his army. **19:20** The beast was taken, and with him the false prophet who worked the signs in his sight, with which he deceived those who had received the mark of the beast and those who worshiped his image. These two were thrown alive into the lake of fire that burns with sulfur. **19:21** The rest were killed with the sword of him who sat on the horse, the sword which came forth out of his mouth. All the birds were filled with their flesh.

The Final Defeat of Satan (Rev 20:1-15)

Satan Imprisoned for a Thousand Years (Rev 20:1-3)

20:1 I saw an angel coming down out of heaven, having the key of the abyss and a great chain in his hand. **20:2** He seized the dragon, the old serpent, which is the devil and Satan, who deceives the whole inhabited earth, and bound him for a thousand years, **20:3** and cast him into the abyss, and shut it, and sealed it over him, that he should deceive the nations no more, until the thousand years were finished. After this, he must be freed for a short time.

The First Resurrection: The Saints will Rule with Jesus (Rev 20:4-6)

20:4 I saw thrones, and they sat on them, and judgment was given to them. I saw the souls of those who had been beheaded for the testimony of Jesus, and for the word of God, and such as didn't worship the beast nor his image, and didn't receive the mark on their forehead and on their hand. They lived, and reigned with Christ for a thousand years. **20:5** The rest of the dead didn't live until the thousand years were finished. This is the first resurrection. **20:6** Blessed and holy is he who has part in the first resurrection. Over these, the second death has no power, but they will be priests of God and of Christ, and will reign with him one thousand years.

Satan is Released from the Abyss (Rev 20:7-10)

20:7 And after the thousand years, Satan will be released from his prison, **20:8** and he will come out to deceive the nations which are in the four corners of the earth, Gog and Magog, to gather them together to the war; the number of whom is as the sand of the sea. **20:9** They went up over the breadth of the earth, and surrounded the camp of the saints, and the beloved city. Fire came down out of heaven from God, and devoured them. **20:10** The devil who deceived them was thrown into the lake of fire and sulfur, where the beast and the false prophet are also. They will be tormented day and night forever and ever.

The Second Resurrection: Satan and His Followers are Placed in the Lake of Fire (Rev 20:11-5)

20:11 I saw a great white throne, and him who sat on it, from whose face the earth and the heaven fled away. There was found no place for them. **20:12** I saw the dead, the great and the small, standing before the throne, and they opened books. Another book was opened, which is the book of life. The dead were judged out of the things which were written in the books, according to their works. **20:13** The sea gave up the dead who were in it. Death and Hades gave up the dead who were in them. They were judged, each one according to his works. **20:14** Death and Hades were thrown into the lake of fire. This is the second death, the lake of fire. **20:15** If anyone was not found written in the book of life, he was cast into the lake of fire.

The New Heaven, the New Earth and the New Jerusalem (Rev 21:1 - 22:5)

21:1 I saw a new heaven and a new earth: for the first heaven and the first earth have passed away, and the sea is no more. **21:2** I saw the holy city, New Jerusalem, coming down out of heaven from God, prepared like a bride adorned for her husband. **21:3** I heard a loud voice out of heaven saying,

> "Behold, God's dwelling is with people,
>> and he will dwell with them,
>> and they will be his people,
>> and God himself will be with them as their God.

21:4 He will wipe away from them every tear from their eyes.

> Death will be no more;
>> neither will there be mourning,
>> nor crying,
>> nor pain,
>> any more.

> The first things have passed away."

21:5 He who sits on the throne said,

"Behold, I am making all things new."

He said,

"Write, for these words of God are faithful and true."

21:6 He said to me,

> "It is done!
> I am the Alpha and the Omega,
>> the Beginning and the End.
> I will give freely to him who is thirsty from the spring of the water of life.
> **21:7** He who overcomes,
>> I will give him these things.
> I will be his God,
>> and he will be my son.
> **21:8** But for the cowardly, unbelieving, sinners,
>> abominable, murderers, sexually immoral,
>> sorcerers, idolaters, and all liars,

their part is in the lake that burns with fire and sulfur,
which is the second death."

21:9 One of the seven angels who had the seven bowls, who were loaded with the seven last plagues came, and he spoke with me, saying,

"Come here. I will show you the wife, the Lamb's bride."

21:10 He carried me away in the Spirit to a great and high mountain, and showed me the holy city, Jerusalem, coming down out of heaven from God, **21:11** having the glory of God. Her light was like a most precious stone, as if it were a jasper stone, clear as crystal; **21:12** having a great and high wall; having twelve gates, and at the gates twelve angels; and names written on them, which are the names of the twelve tribes of the children of Israel. **21:13** On the east were three gates; and on the north three gates; and on the south three gates; and on the west three gates. **21:14** The wall of the city had twelve foundations, and on them twelve names of the twelve Apostles of the Lamb. **21:15** He who spoke with me had for a measure, a golden reed, to measure the city, its gates, and its walls. **21:16** The city lies four-square, and its length is as great as its breadth. He measured the city with the reed, Twelve thousand twelve stadia. Its length, breadth, and height are equal. **21:17** Its wall is one hundred forty-four cubits, by the measure of a man, that is, of an angel. **21:18** The construction of its wall was jasper. The city was pure gold, like pure glass. **21:19** The foundations of the city's wall were adorned with all kinds of precious stones. The first foundation was jasper; the second, sapphire; the third, chalcedony; the fourth, emerald; **21:20** the fifth, sardonyx; the sixth, sardius; the seventh, chrysolite; the eighth, beryl; the ninth, topaz; the tenth, chrysoprasus; the eleventh, jacinth; and the twelfth, amethyst. **21:21** The twelve gates were twelve pearls. Each one of the gates was made of one pearl. The street of the city was pure gold, like transparent glass. **21:22** I saw no temple in it, for the Lord God, the Almighty, and the Lamb, are its temple. **21:23** The city has no need for the sun, neither of the moon, to shine, for the very glory of God illuminated it, and its lamp is the Lamb. **21:24** The nations will walk in its light. The kings of the earth bring the glory and honor of the nations into it. **21:25** Its gates will in no way be shut by day (for there will be no night there), **21:26** and they shall bring the glory and the honor of the nations into it so that they may enter. **21:27** There will in no way enter into it anything profane, or one who causes an abomination or a lie, but only those who are written in the Lamb's book of life.

22:1 He showed me a river of water of life, clear as crystal, proceeding out of the throne of God and of the Lamb, **22:2** in the middle of its street. On this side of the river and on that was the tree of life, bearing twelve kinds of fruits, yielding its fruit every month. The leaves of the tree were for the healing of the nations. **22:3** There will be no curse any more. The throne of God and of the Lamb will be in it, and his servants serve him. **22:4** They will see his face, and his name will be on their foreheads. **22:5** There will be no night, and they need no lamp light; for the Lord God will illuminate them. They will reign forever and ever.

The Epilogue (Rev 22:6-21)

The Second Angel that John Worships (Rev 22:6-11)

22:6 He said to me,

"These words are faithful and true.

The Lord God of the spirits of the prophets sent his angel to show to his bondservants the things which must happen soon."

22:7 "Behold, I come quickly.

Blessed is he who keeps the words of the prophecy of this book."

22:8 Now I, John, am the one who heard and saw these things. When I heard and saw, I fell down to worship before the feet of the angel who had shown me these things.

22:9 He said to me,

"See you don't do it!

I am a fellow bondservant with you and with your brothers, the prophets, and with those who keep the words of this book. Worship God."

22:10 He said to me,

"Don't seal up the words of the prophecy of this book,
for the time is at hand.

22:11 He who acts unjustly,
let him act unjustly still.

He who is filthy,
let him be filthy still.

He who is righteous,
let him do righteousness still.

He who is holy, let him be holy still."

Jesus Speaks (Rev 22:12-6)

22:12 "Behold, I come quickly.

My reward is with me,
to repay to each man according to his work.

22:13 I am the Alpha and the Omega,
the First and the Last,
the Beginning and the End.

22:14 Blessed are those who do his commandments,
that they may have the right to the tree of life,
and may enter in by the gates into the city.

22:15 Outside are the dogs, the sorcerers, the sexually immoral, the murderers, the idolaters, and everyone who loves and practices falsehood.

22:16 I, Jesus, have sent my angel to testify these things to you for the churches.

I am the root and the offspring of David;
the Bright and Morning Star."

The Spirit, Jesus and John Speaks (Rev 22:17-21)

22:17 The Spirit and the bride say, "Come!" He who hears, let him say, "Come!" He who is thirsty, let him come. He who desires, let him take the water of life freely. **22:18** I testify to everyone who hears the words of the prophecy of this book, if anyone adds to them, may God add to him the plagues which are written in this book. **22:19** If anyone takes away from the words of the book of this prophecy, may God take away his part from the tree of life, and out of the holy city, which are written in this book. **22:20** He who testifies these things says, "Yes, I come quickly."

Amen! Yes, come, Lord Jesus.

22:21 The grace of the Lord Jesus Christ be with all the saints. Amen.

Chapter 8: Reading in the Horizontal

A Different Way to Read Revelation

Despite being a short book, Revelation is rather difficult to read and understand. This is largely due to it being an unfinished work. A key element in beginning to understand Revelation is its construction; it was written in the horizontal. In today's modern world of computers, we can compare text side by side and discover how the parallel formation was constructed. By doing this we are able to unlock the mysteries of this previously confusing text.

In this chapter we will see the stories of Revelation presented in the horizontal, and as a result will be able to follow many story lines that would have never been able to otherwise be seen. Presented in this chapter are ways in which John arranged the wax tablets to write the stories inside the vision of Revelation. Since these are the stories that John spent the majority of his time creating, they should be the ones analyzed the most by those interested in the book of Revelation.

The Finishing Phase

The draft chapters in this book tell how each draft was constructed, but they do not really go into any detail on how the finishing phase went. All authors have a refinement process for their work, and John was no exception. The only difference is that the method with which he refined his work is unlike the way the vast majority of other writers' methods. For John, the refinement phase is a parallel formation within the text instead of from outside sources. This chapter gives the reader a sense of the scope and scale of the parallels which John incorporated.

It also should be noted that while this chapter covers many of the major parallels, it is not an exhaustive list. The ones I decided to include created a good balance of complexity and diversity, and is sufficient for our purposes. They should appeal to both the first time reader of Revelation and those that spent decades studying it. For me, on a personal level, they are the stories that I love to return to and yearn to discover more about.

Reading the Seven Churches

The seven letters to the seven churches appear short and simple on a surface level. That is the impression that most readers who read the book of Revelation have. After the last letter, there is only one additional mention of the churches (in the last chapter of Revelation).[1] The letters seem to follow a straight forward and formulaic style, with a few items that connect some of the letters together. Depending on how attentive the reader is during their reading, they will be able to pick up on the connection between elements in every letter to various parts of Revelation. As a result, the letters will either be ignored or incredible license will be used when interpreting them.

For the commentary writer on the book of Revelation, the seven churches are a nightmare to cover. It is impossible to cover the letters of the seven churches without showing how they interact with the rest of Revelation. Likewise, covering the sections that are connected with each of the seven letters will make the commentary repetitive and bloated. Traditionally, commentaries tend to focus on the text of the seven letters and not much more. They compensate by giving detailed information about the city and defining the Greek words, but there is always a distinct disconnect between the letters and the book of Revelation. It is akin to explaining the American Civil War by describing how the railroad functioned during the time, without mentioning the fact that trains were used by both sides of the war, and the manner in which each side utilized the trains.

Each of the letters have their own story to tell, but they are also a part of many different stories that John is telling. Some of the stories are found within the letters to the seven churches while others span huge portions of the book of Revelation itself. The stories of the seven churches in this section are only a portion of the many stories within Revelation.

The Structure of the Church Letters

There are many ways to slice and dice the seven letters to the churches. In this chapter we will break them down in the same way John did. We know that we are employing the same method of dissection because of how he connected the letters with other sections within Revelation.

Each letter contains three primary sections: the salutation, the body of the letter, and the closing. Additionally, each section contains two subsections. This provided John with a wide range of literary possibilities.

The Salutation

Each letter begins with a salutation that contains the location of the church and associates the church with one of the spirits connected to one of the lamp stands.[2] Each salutation also contains a description of Jesus with the phrase, "Thus says." The description of Jesus is also repeated in the body of all the letters, except the letter to Sardis, thereby giving each letter a personal touch. This would suggest that at one time

1   Rev 22:16.
2   Rev 1:20; 2:1, 8, 12, 18; 3:1, 7, 14.

A Difference of Perspective

Each letter contains two perspectives of the church that is being written to. One perspective is from an inside or outside perspective of the church. The other perspective reflects the church's physical state as seen from Jesus' perspective.

The Church	Internal / External Perspective	Jesus' Perspective
Ephesus	The do not tolerate false teaching (2:2).	They lost their first love (2:4).
Smyrna	They are poor (2:9).	They are rich (2:9).
Pergamum	They had Antipas* who was faithful (2:13).	They are being taken by the Nicolaitans** (2:14-5).
Thyatira	They are growing in love, faith, and deeds (2:19).	They are straying with Jezebel (2:20).
Sardis	They are alive (3:1).	They are dead (3:2).
Philadelphia	They have little power (3:8).	Those with power will bow down before them (3:9).
Laodicea	They are rich (3:17).	They are poor (3:17).

*Antipas is composed of two Greek words, anti (against - BDAG, ἀντί.) and pas (everyone - BDAG, πᾶς).

**Nicholaitans are composed of two words, Nichos (victory - BDAG, νῖκος) and laos (people - BDAG, λαός).

---

the letter to Sardis was similar to the seven churches, but for some reason the body or the salutation was changed. There are two likely scenarios for this: the first, is that John had the following phrase in the original salutation and in the original body:

3:1 *"He who has the seven spirits of God . . . says these things:"*

3:4 *Nevertheless you have a few names in Sardis that did not defile their garments. They will walk with me in white, for they are worthy.* **3:5** *I will in no way blot his name out of the book of life, and I will confess his name before my Father, and before his angels.*

John, when reversing the phrases "He who has an ear, let him hear" and "He who overcomes" in the last four churches[3] simply moved the following text between Rev 3:4-5 to produce what we have today:

3:4 *Nevertheless you have a few names in Sardis that did not defile their garments. They will walk with me in white, for they are worthy.* **3:5** *He who overcomes will be arrayed in white garments, and I will in no way blot his name out of the book of life, and I will confess his name before my Father, and before his angels.* **3:6** *He who has an ear, let him hear what the Spirit says to the churches.*

By shifting the text around we get a repetition of the idea that those who have not strayed are able to walk with Jesus in white robes and that those who overcome will walk in white robes. The repetition is more understandable when the text is shifted, than when it is written in a single sitting.

The second scenario is that John had two accounts of walking with the angels, one with Jesus, and one with God.[4] The text containing Jesus' angels was removed to include the "He who overcomes" phrase as seen in the first scenario. This scenario is also easy to visualize and is consistent with John's simple tweaking of the text.

---

3   This will be discussed more in the section dealing with the salutation.
4   Rev 3:4-5.

The First Four Churches (Rev 2:1-29)

Ephesus (Rev 2:1-7)	Smyrna (Rev 2:8-11)	Pergamum (2:12-7)	Thyatira (2:18-29)
2:1 "**To the angel of the church in** Ephesus write: "He who holds the seven stars in his right hand, he who walks among the seven golden lampstands **says these things:**	**2:8** "**To the angel of the church in** Smyrna write: "The first and the last, who was dead, and has come to life **says these things:**	**2:12** "**To the angel of the church in** Pergamum write: "He who has the sharp two-edged sword **says these things:**	**2:18** "**To the angel of the church in** Thyatira write: "The Son of God, who has his eyes like a flame of fire, and his feet are like burnished brass, **says these things:**
2:2 "**I know your works**, and your toil and perseverance, and that you can't tolerate evil men, and have tested those who call themselves apostles, and they are not, and found them false. **2:3** You have perseverance and have endured for my name's sake, and have not grown weary. **2:4** **But I have this against you**, that you left your first love. **2:5** Remember therefore from where you have fallen, and repent and do the first works; or else I am coming to you swiftly, and will move your lampstand out of its place, unless you repent. **2:6** But this you have, that you hate the works of the **Nicolaitans**, which I also hate.	**2:9** "**I know your works**, oppression, and your poverty (but you are rich), and the blasphemy of those who say they are Jews, and they are not, but are a **synagogue of Satan**. **2:10** Don't be afraid of the things which you are about to suffer. Behold, the devil is about to throw some of you into prison, that you may be tested; and you will have oppression for ten days. Be faithful to death, and I will give you the crown of life.	**2:13** "**I know your works** and where you dwell, where Satan's throne is. You hold firmly to my name, and didn't deny my faith in the days of Antipas my witness, my faithful one, who was killed among you, where Satan dwells. **2:14** **But I have a few things against you**, because you have there some who hold the teaching of Balaam, who taught Balak to throw a stumbling block before the children of Israel, **to eat things sacrificed to idols, and to commit sexual immorality**. **2:15** So you also have some who hold to the teaching of the **Nicolaitans** likewise. **2:16** Repent therefore, or else I am coming to you quickly, and I will make war against them with the sword of my mouth.	**2:19** "**I know your works**, your love, faith, service, patient endurance, and that your last works are more than the first. **2:20** **But I have this against you**, that you tolerate your woman, Jezebel, who calls herself a prophetess. She teaches and seduces my servants **to commit sexual immorality, and to eat things sacrificed to idols**. **2:21** I gave her time to repent, but she refuses to repent of her sexual immorality. **2:22** Behold, I will throw her into a bed, and those who commit adultery with her into great oppression, unless they repent of her works. **2:23** I will kill her children with Death, and all the churches will know that I am he who searches the minds and hearts. I will give to each one of you according to your deeds. **2:24** But to you I say, to the rest who are in Thyatira, as many as don't have this teaching, who don't know what some call 'the deep things of Satan,' to you I say, I am not putting any other burden on you. **2:25** Nevertheless, hold that which you have firmly until I come.
2:7 **He who has an ear, let him hear what the Spirit says to the churches**. To him who overcomes I will give to eat of the tree of life, which is in the Paradise of my God.	**2:11** **He who has an ear, let him hear what the Spirit says to the churches. He who overcomes** won't be harmed by the second death.	**2:17** **He who has an ear, let him hear what the Spirit says to the churches. To him who overcomes**, to him I will give of the hidden manna, and I will give him a white stone, and on the stone a new name written, which no one knows but he who receives it.	**2:26** **He who overcomes**, and he who keeps my works to the end, to him I will give authority over the nations. **2:27** He will rule them with a rod of iron, shattering them like clay pots; as I also have received of my Father: **2:28** and I will give him the morning star. **2:29** **He who has an ear, let him hear what the Spirit says to the churches.**

The Last Three Churches (Rev 3:1-22)

Sardis (3:1-6)	Philadelphia (3:7-13)	Laodicea (3:14-22)
3:1 **"And to the angel of the church in** Sardis write: "He who has the seven Spirits of God, and the seven stars **says these things:**	*3:7* "**To the angel of the church in** Philadelphia write: "He who is holy, he who is true, he who has the key of David, he who opens and no one can shut, and who shuts and no one opens, **says these things:**	*3:14* "To the angel of the church in Laodicea write: "The Amen, the Faithful and True Witness, the Head of God's creation, **says these things:**
"**I know your works**, that you have a reputation of being alive, but you are dead. *3:2* Wake up, and keep the things that remain, which you were about to throw away, for I have found no works of yours perfected before my God. *3:3* Remember therefore how you have received and heard. Keep it, and repent. If therefore you won't watch, I will come as a thief, and you won't know what hour I will come upon you. *3:4* Nevertheless you have a few names in Sardis that did not defile their garments. They will walk with me in white, for they are worthy.	*3:8* "**I know your works** (behold, I have set before you an open door, which no one can shut), that you have a little power, and kept my word, and didn't deny my name. *3:9* Behold, I give of **the synagogue of Satan,** of those who say they are Jews, and they are not, but lie. Behold, I will make them to come and worship before your feet, and to know that I have loved you. *3:10* Because you kept my command to endure, I also will keep you from the hour of testing, which is to come on the whole world, to test those who dwell on the earth. *3:11* I am coming quickly! Hold firmly that which you have, so that no one takes your crown.	*3:15* "**I know your works**, that you are neither cold nor hot. I wish you were cold or hot. *3:16* So, because you are lukewarm, and neither hot nor cold, I will vomit you out of my mouth. *3:17* Because you say, 'I am rich, and have gotten riches, and have need of nothing;' and don't know that you are the wretched one, miserable, poor, blind, and naked; *3:18* I counsel you to buy from me gold refined by fire, that you may become rich; and white garments, that you may clothe yourself, and that the shame of your nakedness may not be revealed; and eye salve to anoint your eyes, that you may see. *3:19* As many as I love, I reprove and chasten. Be zealous therefore, and repent. *3:20* Behold, I stand at the door and knock. If anyone hears my voice and opens the door, then I will come in to him, and will dine with him, and he with me.
3:5 **He who overcomes** will be arrayed in white garments, and I will in no way blot his name out of the book of life, and I will confess his name before my Father, and before his angels. *3:6* **He who has an ear, let him hear what the Spirit says to the churches.**	*3:12* **He who overcomes,** I will make him a pillar in the temple of my God, and he will go out from there no more. I will write on him the name of my God, and the name of the city of my God, the new Jerusalem, which comes down out of heaven from my God, and my own new name. *3:13* **He who has an ear, let him hear what the Spirit says to the churches.**	*3:21* **He who overcomes,** I will give to him to sit down with me on my throne, as I also overcame, and sat down with my Father on his throne. *3:22* **He who has an ear, let him hear what the Spirit says to the churches."**

The Body

Each letter has a body that is divided into two portions, the first portion contains an internal or external conflict the church is faced with. Ephesus, Smyrna, and Philadelphia experience external conflict while Sardis and Laodicea experience internal conflict. Pergamum and Thyatira experience both internal and external conflict. The second portion of each letter has a call to sacrifice spoken in terms of what the church must do to repent or to retain their faithfulness. Ephesus, Pergamum, Thyatira, Sardis, and Laodicea are told what they must do to be faithful to Jesus, and Smyrna and Philadelphia are told that the path they are on is the correct path.

Five of the seven churches have common content between the salutation and the body. In the salutation of the letter to the Ephesians, for example, Jesus is shown with the seven lampstands,[5] and in the body of the letter Jesus threatens to remove their lampstand unless they repent.[6] In the salutation of the letter to Pergamum, Jesus is introduced with a sword emanating from his mouth, and in the body of the letter, Pergamum is told that if they don't repent they will face the sword of his mouth.[7] The letter to Smyrna has Jesus introduced as the "first and the last, who was dead and has come to life" in the salutation.[8] In the body of the letter of Smyrna, Jesus uses the salutation to assure them that they would be raised from the dead.[9] Jesus, in the letter to Thyatira, is introduced as having eyes of fire and uses that imagery to encourage Thyatira by telling them that he will judge them according to their mind and heart[10] which signifies a special vision or knowledge. Philadelphia is the last church in which the salutation and the body of the letter is connected by a key that opens and closes a door.[11]

Sardis and Laodicea are the two exceptions which have no direct literary connections between the salutation and the body of the letter. In the letter to Laodica there is one possible connection; one could connect his title "true and faithful witness" with his need to dine with Laodicea to share the truth with them.[12] For Sardis, however, the connection between the salutation and the body of the letter simply does not exist.[13]

The body of each letter have two perspectives on each of the seven churches. One perspective is formed by those within or outside of the church and the other perspective is formed by Jesus. In most cases they are opposite to each other, such as how the church in Smyrna is seen to be poor but is actually rich. The church in Philadelphia has enemies who see them as having little power, but they will one day be seen as having great power by their enemies. The church in Laodicea is rich but Jesus sees them as poor.[14]

The Closing

The last section of each letter is the closing which contains two subsections, "the general call" and the "call to overcome." The general call is John's way of saying that the message to the specific church is the message

---

5   Rev 2:1.
6   Rev 2:5.
7   Rev 2:12, 16.
8   Rev 2:8.
9   Rev 2:10.
10   Rev 2:18, 23.
11   Rev 3:7-8.
12   Rev 3:14, 20.
13   See the explanation in "The Salutation" on page 266 on how Sardis' salutation and its body was connected and then altered.
14   See "A Difference of Perspective" on page 267 for all the references.

The Spiritual State of the Seven Churches in the Form of a Complex Parallel

The illustration below shows how John used a complex parallel to form the spiritual state of the seven churches. In so doing, John created four separate church groups: the completely lost, the completely faithful, the mixed, and the example church.

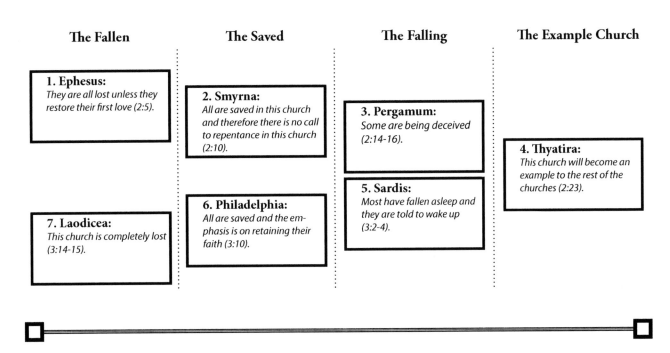

The Fallen

1. Ephesus:
They are all lost unless they restore their first love (2:5).

7. Laodicea:
This church is completely lost (3:14-15).

The Saved

2. Smyrna:
All are saved in this church and therefore there is no call to repentance in this church (2:10).

6. Philadelphia:
All are saved and the emphasis is on retaining their faith (3:10).

The Falling

3. Pergamum:
Some are being deceived (2:14-16).

5. Sardis:
Most have fallen asleep and they are told to wake up (3:2-4).

The Example Church

4. Thyatira:
This church will become an example to the rest of the churches (2:23).

to all believers as seen in the phrase "He who has an ear, let him hear what the spirit says to the churches."[15] Since each of the seven churches are all facing the challenge to remain faithful unto death, John includes a reminder of what the believer must do to obey Jesus:

> *13:8 All who dwell on the earth will worship him, everyone whose name has not been written from the foundation of the world in the book of life of the Lamb who has been killed. 13:9 **If anyone has an ear, let him hear**. 13:10 If anyone is to go into captivity, he will go into captivity. If anyone is to be killed with the sword, he must be killed. Here is the endurance and the faith of the saints.*[16]

The call to overcome is the reward that each church will receive if they overcome. The vast majority of the rewards are found scattered throughout the pages of Revelation. There are a few rewards that are not found anywhere in Revelation such as the "hidden manna"[17] and Jesus confessing their names before the father.[18] Those with no matches are indicators that at one time they had a match and in the course of writing Revelation, John removed their complements.

The strangest portion of the closing is that the first three churches have the general call first and the call to overcome second, while the rest of the churches have the call to overcome first and the general call sec-

---

15 Rev 2:7, 11, 17, 29; 3:6, 13, 22.
16 Rev 13:8-10.
17 Rev 2:17.
18 Rev 3:5.

How the Churches and the Seals Interact With Each Other (Part 1)

The diagram below shows how the letters of the seven churches are broken down and how the conflict of each church connects to its respective seal. The reward for repenting or continuing in their faithfulness is a token that is found in the seal previous to the numerical order of the church. For the church in Ephesus the reward is that they will not lose their candlestick in heaven (2:20), which is the state of heaven before the seals.

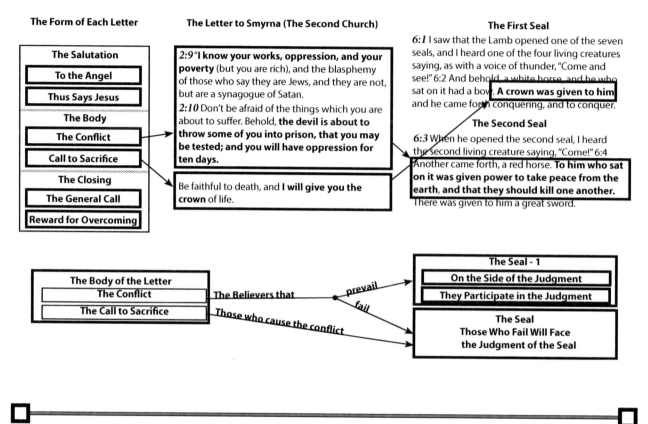

The Form of Each Letter

| The Salutation |
| To the Angel |
| Thus Says Jesus |
| **The Body** |
| The Conflict |
| Call to Sacrifice |
| **The Closing** |
| The General Call |
| Reward for Overcoming |

The Letter to Smyrna (The Second Church)

2:9 "**I know your works, oppression, and your poverty** (but you are rich), and the blasphemy of those who say they are Jews, and they are not, but are a synagogue of Satan.

2:10 Don't be afraid of the things which you are about to suffer. Behold, **the devil is about to throw some of you into prison, that you may be tested; and you will have oppression for ten days.**

Be faithful to death, and **I will give you the crown** of life.

The First Seal

6:1 I saw that the Lamb opened one of the seven seals, and I heard one of the four living creatures saying, as with a voice of thunder, "Come and see!" 6:2 And behold, a white horse, and he who sat on it had a bow. **A crown was given to him** and he came forth conquering, and to conquer.

The Second Seal

6:3 When he opened the second seal, I heard the second living creature saying, "Come!" 6:4 Another came forth, a red horse. **To him who sat on it was given power to take peace from the earth, and that they should kill one another.** There was given to him a great sword.

| **The Body of the Letter** |
| The Conflict |
| The Call to Sacrifice |

The Believers that

prevail

fail

Those who cause the conflict

| **The Seal - 1** |
| On the Side of the Judgment |
| They Participate in the Judgment |

| **The Seal** |
| **Those Who Fail Will Face the Judgment of the Seal** |

---

ond. The reason for the reversal of order was to distinguish the first three churches as one group and the last four churches as another. The first three churches are grouped with the beast which can be seen in how John forms a complex parallel with the first three churches and the primary beast narrative.[19] The last four churches John intended them to be associated with the harlot but did not construct solid parallels similar to the first three churches and the beast. The likely culprit was the story of the fifth, sixth, and seventh church (which will be discussed later in this chapter) made it more difficult to form parallels between the last four churches and the harlot.

The Spiritual State of the Seven Churches

The template for defining the seven churches was not enough for John. John organized the seven churches into a complex parallel which showed the various stages of their salvation. The first and the last church he had totally lost; the second church and the sixth church were problem free. The third and the third-to-last church represented two stages of falling away. The middle church was going to be the example church in her destruction.[20]

19   "The First Three Churches and the Beast" on page 275
20   See "The Spiritual State of the Seven Churches in the Form of a Complex Parallel" on page 271.

How the Churches and the Seals Interact With Each Other (Part 2)

The purpose of the diagram below is to illustrate what the seven churches and seven seals offset looks like. Note that the ordering of the church's reward and conflict are reversed in order to make it easier to visualize the offset.

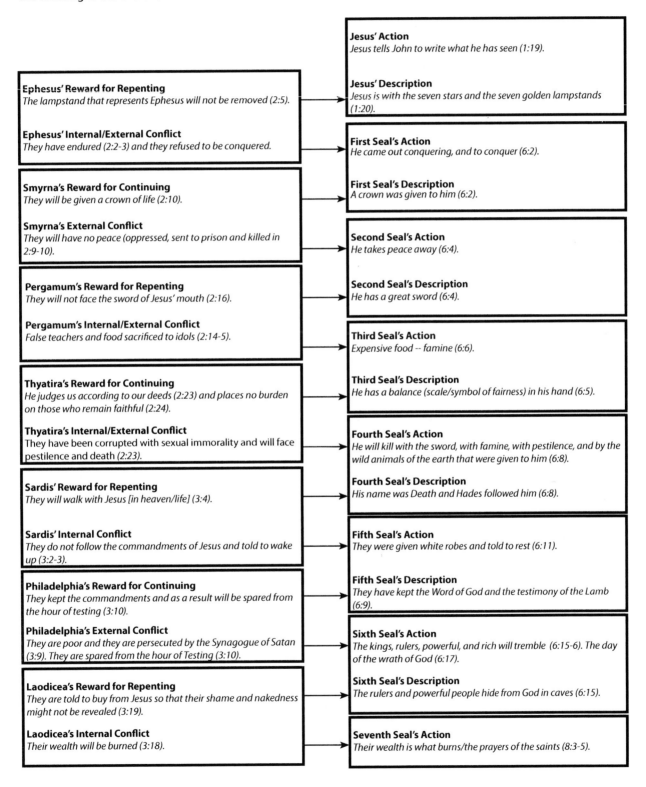

Jesus' Action
Jesus tells John to write what he has seen (1:19).

Jesus' Description
Jesus is with the seven stars and the seven golden lampstands (1:20).

Ephesus' Reward for Repenting
The lampstand that represents Ephesus will not be removed (2:5).

Ephesus' Internal/External Conflict
They have endured (2:2-3) and they refused to be conquered.

First Seal's Action
He came out conquering, and to conquer (6:2).

First Seal's Description
A crown was given to him (6:2).

Smyrna's Reward for Continuing
They will be given a crown of life (2:10).

Smyrna's External Conflict
They will have no peace (oppressed, sent to prison and killed in 2:9-10).

Second Seal's Action
He takes peace away (6:4).

Second Seal's Description
He has a great sword (6:4).

Pergamum's Reward for Repenting
They will not face the sword of Jesus' mouth (2:16).

Pergamum's Internal/External Conflict
False teachers and food sacrificed to idols (2:14-5).

Third Seal's Action
Expensive food -- famine (6:6).

Third Seal's Description
He has a balance (scale/symbol of fairness) in his hand (6:5).

Thyatira's Reward for Continuing
He judges us according to our deeds (2:23) and places no burden on those who remain faithful (2:24).

Thyatira's Internal/External Conflict
They have been corrupted with sexual immorality and will face pestilence and death (2:23).

Fourth Seal's Action
He will kill with the sword, with famine, with pestilence, and by the wild animals of the earth that were given to him (6:8).

Fourth Seal's Description
His name was Death and Hades followed him (6:8).

Sardis' Reward for Repenting
They will walk with Jesus [in heaven/life] (3:4).

Sardis' Internal Conflict
They do not follow the commandments of Jesus and told to wake up (3:2-3).

Fifth Seal's Action
They were given white robes and told to rest (6:11).

Fifth Seal's Description
They have kept the Word of God and the testimony of the Lamb (6:9).

Philadelphia's Reward for Continuing
They kept the commandments and as a result will be spared from the hour of testing (3:10).

Philadelphia's External Conflict
They are poor and they are persecuted by the Synagogue of Satan (3:9). They are spared from the hour of Testing (3:10).

Sixth Seal's Action
The kings, rulers, powerful, and rich will tremble (6:15-6). The day of the wrath of God (6:17).

Sixth Seal's Description
The rulers and powerful people hide from God in caves (6:15).

Laodicea's Reward for Repenting
They are told to buy from Jesus so that their shame and nakedness might not be revealed (3:19).

Laodicea's Internal Conflict
Their wealth will be burned (3:18).

Seventh Seal's Action
Their wealth is what burns/the prayers of the saints (8:3-5).

How John Connected the Scroll to the Judgments in Revelation

John takes the three items found written in the scroll from Ezekiel 2:10 and applies them to the three judgments in Revelation. The seven seals represent the mourning, as in depicting that Jesus and the believers as dead. The trumpets represent the woes in how they are separated by the three woes. The result of the bowls is the destruction and lamentation of the harlot.

Rev 5:1 . . . *a book written inside and outside, sealed shut with seven seals.*

Ezek 2:9 *When I looked, behold, a hand was put forth to me; and, behold, a scroll of a book was therein;* **2:10** *He spread it before me: and it was written within and without; and there were written therein lamentations, and mourning, and woe.*

The Mourning	The Woes	The Lamentations
The First Four Seals (6:1-8)	**The First Four Trumpets (8:7-12)**	**The Effects of the Bowls (18:1-24)**

The Mourning	The Woes	The Lamentations
The Fifth Seal (6:9-11) **6:9** When he opened the fifth seal, I saw underneath the altar the souls of those who had been killed for the Word of God, and for the testimony of the Lamb which they had. **6:10** They cried with a loud voice, saying, "How long, Master, the holy and true, until you judge and avenge our blood on those who dwell on the earth?" **6:11** A long white robe was given to each of them. They were told that they should rest yet for a while, until their fellow servants and their brothers, who would also be killed even as they were, should complete their course.	**The First Woe (8:13)** **8:13** I saw, and I heard an eagle, flying in mid heaven, saying with a loud voice, "Woe! Woe! Woe for those who dwell on the earth, because of the other voices of the trumpets of the three angels, who are yet to sound!".	**18:9** The kings of the earth, who committed sexual immorality and lived wantonly with her, will weep and wail over her, when they look at the smoke of her burning, **18:10** standing far away for the fear of her torment, saying, 'Woe, woe, the great city, Babylon, the strong city! For your judgment has come in one hour.' **18:11** The merchants of the earth weep and mourn over her, for no one buys their merchandise any more;
	The Fifth Trumpet (9:1-11)	**18:15** The merchants of these things, who were made rich by her, will stand far away for the fear of her torment, weeping and mourning; **18:16** saying, 'Woe, woe, the great city, she who was dressed in fine linen, purple, and scarlet, and decked with gold and precious stones and pearls! **18:17** For in an hour such great riches are made desolate.' Every shipmaster, and everyone who sails anywhere, and mariners, and as many as gain their living by sea, stood far away, **18:18** and cried out as they looked at the smoke of her burning, saying, 'What is like the great city?' **18:19** They cast dust on their heads, and cried, weeping and mourning, saying, 'Woe, woe, the great city, in which all who had their ships in the sea were made rich by reason of her great wealth!' For in one hour is she made desolate.
The Sixth and Seventh Seals (6:12-17, 8:1-6) **Note: The Seventh Seal becomes the Seven Trumpets so only the opening of the seal will be cited.**	**The Second Woe (9:12)** **9:12** The first woe is past. Behold, there are still two woes coming after this.	
	The Sixth Trumpet (9:1-11) **The Little Scroll (10:1-11)** **The Two Prophets (11:1-13)**	
	The Third Woe (11:14) **11:14** The second woe is past. Behold, the third woe comes quickly.	
	The Seventh Trumpet (11:14-19)	

The First Three Churches and the Beast

John connected the first three churches with the beast narrative in Revelation 13:1-17 by forming a complex parallel and using synonyms as a means of connecting the two. The church in Ephesus forms a simple parallel with the false prophet, the church in Smyrna forms a complex parallel with the middle portion of the beast narrative. The church in Pergamum forms a simple parallel with the first third of the beast narrative. John is in effect making the parallel formation of the first three churches a complex parallel where the parallel formation itself is a complex parallel.

The First Three Churches in Revelation			The Beast Narrative in Revelation 13:1-18	
	The Church in Ephesus (Rev 2:1-7)		***The False Prophet (Rev 13:11-7)***	
2:2	They tested those who call themselves apostles (syn: prophets) and found them to be false.	13:11-7	The [false prophet (syn: apostles; see 19:20)] deceives everyone.	
	[Note: The apostles spoke on Jesus' behalf. Jesus died and rose again.]	13:12	The false prophet spoke for the beast who had a fatal wound that was healed.	
2:3	They endured for Jesus' name's sake.	13:17	They have succumbed to the name of the beast.	
2:7	If they overcome they will be able to eat of the tree of life.	13:17	No one will eat without the mark of the beast.	
	The Church in Smyrna (Rev 2:8-11)		***The Middle Portion of the Beast Narrative (Rev 13:8-10)***	
2:9	They are oppressed by the synagogue of Satan.	13:10	Here is the endurance of the saints.	
2:10	They will be taken to prison (syn: captivity) and some will be killed.	13:10	If anyone is to go into captivity, he will go into captivity. If anyone is to be killed with the sword, he must be killed.	
2:11	He who has an ear let him hear.	13:9	If anyone has an ear let him hear.	
2:11	If they overcome they will not be harmed by the second death (in Rev 20:14-5 everyone not in the book of life will go to the second death).	13:8	Everyone who worships the beast will not be in the book of life.	
	The Church in Pergamum (Rev 2:12-7)		***The Dragon and the Beast (Rev 13:2-7)***	
2:13	Where Satan's throne is.	13:2	Where the dragon's throne is.	
2:13	Antipas (meaning: against everyone) who was killed.	13:3	The beast was fatally wounded.	
2:16	They eat food sacrificed to idols.	13:4	Everyone worshiped the beast.	
	Those who are not faithful will face the sword of Jesus' mouth (from Rev 19:15 where Jesus will war against the beast),	13:4	Who will war against the beast.	

By John forming the spiritual state of the seven churches' complex parallel he caused content to become positionally fixed and thereby made it difficult to shift the letters around. For the reader, it provides an additional storyline that must be figured out to understand.

The Seven Churches and the Seven Seals

The seven churches and the seven seals form a unique relationship with each other. The body of each message maps back to a seal, one in a simple parallel and the other in the form of an offset to a simple parallel. The conflict that each church faces in each letter forms a simple parallel with the content of its respective seal. The call to sacrifice found in each letter is connected to the seal that is numerically one less than what it parallels. For example, the letter to the second church has a call to action which can be attributed to the first seal, and likewise the call to sacrifice found in the third church is connected to the second seal, and so on. For the first church, the call to sacrifice is connected to something tangible in heaven prior to the seven seals.[21]

By forming the two parallels between the seven churches and the seven seals, John is telling three stories. He is telling the story of what happens when the saints prevail, the story of what happens when the parishioners fail, and what will happen to those who inflict the crises on the believer.

By comparing the two sets of parallels between the seven churches and the seven seals we can also see John's creativeness as well as his intent in what the symbols meant. For example, the fifth church, Sardis, is told to wake up and obey the commandments and in the fifth seal, the saints are given a white robe and told to rest (the synonym for "sleep" and the antonym for "wake up"). Sardis' reward for its obedience is that they will walk with Jesus in white robes and the judgment of the fourth seal (the offset parallel) is that death and Hades follows the fourth horsemen. John is saying, in both of the parallels, that if they obey the commandments of Jesus they will walk with him and will be able to rest later, to recuperate for whatever happens to them on earth. If they rest on earth, however, then they will walk with death and Hades will be their resting place.

The fourth church, Thyatira, is also an easy parallel to both figure out and to visualize. The internal conflict they face is sexual immorality and they are told that they will face death and disease if they do not repent. The fourth seal or horseman is the color associated with sickness[22] and it will destroy with the sword, famine, death, and wild animals. Thyatira's call to sacrifice is to remain holy and as a result Jesus will not add to their burden, which fits nicely with the imagery of the third seal in which the writer of the horse has a scale.

Other associations can be made and some are more subjective than others, but at one time they were all strong parallels and later changes to the churches caused the parallels to become malformed. We always must remember that a parallel was a snapshot in time and a malformed parallel is a change to that snapshot.

The First Three Churches and the Primary Beast Narrative

The first three churches and the primary beast narrative form a complex parallel because the first church and the last section of the beast narrative align. Each of the three churches have many points in which they form parallels with the beast narrative and each of those parallels alternate. Ephesus forms a simple parallel with the last portion of the beast narrative and Smyrna forms a complex parallel with the middle portion of the beast narrative. The church in Pergamum forms a simple parallel to the beast narrative. To add an additional layer of complexity, the parallel elements between Ephesus and the beast are opposites, the parallel between Smyrna and the beast are complements, and the parallel between Pergamum and the beast are opposites. By doing this, John is in effect creating a parallel within a parallel by using parallels. This is not the first time that John did it though, he did it in the Zechariah-encoded parallel as well.[23]

John does something else different in the first three churches and the beast narrative in that he forms the primary parallels by using synonyms such as Satan and the dragon, prison and captivity, and apostle and prophet. He also forms a connection between the three churches and the beast narrative in which the read-

---

21   See "How the Churches and the Seals Interact With Each Other (Part 1)" on page 272 and "How the Churches and the Seals Interact With Each Other (Part 2)" on page 273.
22   BDAG, χλωρός.
23   See "Z7 - The Building of the Encoded-Complex Parallel (Zech 2:1 - 4:14; Rev 11:1 - 12:17)" on page 86.

The Church In Ephesus Versus the False Prophet

The church in Ephesus is complimented on how they test apostles and found them to be false as well as their hatred for the Nicolaitans (Greek meaning victory by the people or in this case victory by the world). The beast narrative shows how the people all over the world will worship the beast or else face death. The means by which the people will be deceived is the false prophet (Rev 16:13;19:20; 20:10) which is a synonym to "apostle" used in the Ephesus narrative.

The Church in Ephesus (Rev 2:1-7)	The False Prophet (Rev 13:11-18)
• They tested those who call themselves apostles (syn: prophets) and found them to be false (2:2).	• The [false prophet (syn: apostles; see 19:20)] deceives everyone (13:11-7).
• [Allusion to: The apostles spoke on Jesus behalf. Jesus died and rose again.]	• The false prophet spoke for the beast who had a fatal wound that was healed (13:12).
	• They have succumbed to the name of the beast (13:17).
• They endured for Jesus' name's sake (2:3).	• No one will eat without the mark of the beast (13:17).
• If they overcome they will be able to eat of the tree of life (2:7).	

2:1 "To the angel of the church in Ephesus write:

"He who holds the seven stars in his right hand, he who walks among the seven golden lampstands says these things:

2:2 "I know your works, and your toil and perseverance, and that you can't tolerate evil men, and have tested those who call themselves apostles, and they are not, and found them false. 2:3 You have perseverance and have endured for my name's sake, and have not grown weary. **2:4** But I have this against you, that you left your first love. **2:5** Remember therefore from where you have fallen, and repent and do the first works; or else I am coming to you swiftly, and will move your lampstand out of its place, unless you repent. **2:6** But this you have, that you hate the works of the Nicolaitans, which I also hate. **2:7** He who has an ear, let him hear what the Spirit says to the churches. To him who overcomes I will give to eat of the tree of life, which is in the Paradise of my God.

13:11 I saw another beast coming up out of the earth. He had two horns like a lamb, and he spoke like a dragon. 13:12 He exercises all the authority of the first beast in his presence. He makes the earth and those who dwell in it to worship the first beast, whose fatal wound was healed. **13:13** He performs great signs, even making fire come down out of the sky to the earth in the sight of people. **13:14** He deceives my own people who dwell on the earth because of the signs he was granted to do in front of the beast; saying to those who dwell on the earth, that they should make an image to the beast who had the sword wound and lived. **13:15** It was given to him to give breath to it, to the image of the beast, that the image of the beast should both speak, and cause as many as wouldn't worship the image of the beast to be killed. **13:16** He causes all, the small and the great, the rich and the poor, and the free and the slave, to be given marks on their right hands, or on their foreheads; **13:17** and that no one would be able to buy or to sell, unless he has that mark, the name of the beast or the number of his name. **13:18** Here is wisdom. He who has understanding, let him calculate the number of the beast, for it is the number of a man. His number is six hundred sixty-six.

---

er has to go to another passage in order to understand. Such as they will not be harmed by the second death in Smyrna and in the beast narrative they are in the Lamb's book of life.[24] When put all together, this is John's writing at its best with the least amount of changes in either text.

These three parallels between the first three churches and the beast narrative are great examples in how we can use parallel formation to interpret the text as John intended us to. These parallels allow us to bracket in the possible meanings to certain text as well as exclude interpretations. When passages have more than one set of parallels, such as the first three churches have with the first three seals, we can narrow down the range of possibilities of interpretations even more. As with all parallels, when one is formed on an existing

---

24   Rev 2:11; 13:8; 20:14-5.

parallel it causes the earlier parallel formation to become malformed. How John makes parallels also gives us a clue as to what the malformed parallel looked like in the past.

Ephesus Verses the Second Beast / False Prophet (Rev 2:1-7; 13:11-7)

Ephesus is introduced as a strong church that tests whether apostles are true are not. Those who they test are found to be false. There seems to be not a care in the world for the church of Ephesus, but in fact according to Jesus they are completely lost because they lost their first love.[25] Without knowing the parallel to this passage we are left with only guesses that sound scholarly, but with knowing the parallel and how the two passages interact, we can complete story. The other side to the story in Ephesus is the story of the second beast / false prophet in the primary beast narrative. John is using synonyms to connect the two stories: apostles in Ephesus, and the false prophet in the beast narrative. Although it should be stated that nowhere in the primary beast narrative does the word prophet exist, but he is referred to as the false prophet in elsewhere in Revelation.[26]

The parallel reveals a whole new dimension to the story found in Ephesus. It reveals that the reward for persevering is eating the food from the New Jerusalem in the afterlife and yielding to the false prophet is eating food in this life. It is all in whose name do they follow, the name of the beast or Jesus' name. John is not talking about traveling apostles or even a church for that matter, but how believers should deal with the false prophet. He is depicting a world in which all the people will follow the beast and the saints will have to decide to live on earth and follow the beast or die on earth and live in the New Jerusalem. The Nicolaitans represent victory of the people[27] and that is why Jesus and the Ephesians hate their efforts.[28]

The question that still remains is what is their first love and why is it so important in the battle between the false prophet and Ephesus? The answer can be found in how John defines the followers of Jesus:

> *12:10 I heard a loud voice in heaven, saying, "Now the salvation, the power, and the Kingdom of our God, and the authority of his Christ has come; for the accuser of our brothers has been thrown down, who accuses them before our God day and night. 12:11 **They overcame him because of the Lamb's blood, and because of the word of their testimony. They didn't love their life, even to death**.*[29]

John is telling the Ephesians that it is not enough to reject the false prophet and endure the suffering. They need to love Jesus more than their own lives. If they do this then they will be allowed to eat from the tree of life in the New Jerusalem.[30]

Smyrna Taken into Captivity (Rev 2:8-11; 13:8-10)

The church in Smyrna faces the synagogue of Satan, who will throw some of them into prison and kill others. Jesus' only advice is that church be faithful to the end and take comfort in the fact that just as he was raised from the dead they will also be raised from the dead. Smyrna is told that in no way will they face the second death.

---

25   Rev 2:4.
26   Rev 16:13; 19:20; 20:10.
27   See individual definitions in BDAG, νῖκος and BDAG, λαός
28   Rev 2:6.
29   Rev 12:10-1.
30   Rev 22:14.

The Church in Smyrna and the Beast Narrative

John formed a complex parallel between the church in Smyrna and the beast narrative (see "The First Three Churches and the Beast" on page 275). The chart below represents the text John used to construct the parallel and to point out that the beast narrative (Rev 13:8-10) was created from Smyrna's content.

The Church in Smyrna (Rev 2:8-11)	Where the Saints Go (Rev 13:8-10)
• They are oppressed by the synagogue of Satan (2:9). • They will be taken to prison (syn: captivity) and some will be killed (2:10). • He who has an ear let him hear (2:11). • If they overcome they will not be harmed by the second death (2:11; see Rev 20:14-5 book of life is connected with the second death).	• Here is the endurance of the saints (13:10). • If anyone is to go into captivity, he will go into captivity. If anyone is to be killed with the sword, he must be killed (13:10). • If anyone has an ear let him hear (13:9). • Everyone who worships the beast will not be in the book of life (13:8).

2:8 "To the angel of the church in Smyrna write:

"The first and the last, who was dead, and has come to life says these things:

2:9 "I know your works, oppression, and your poverty (but you are rich), and the blasphemy of those who say they are Jews, and they are not, but are a synagogue of Satan. 2:10 Don't be afraid of the things which you are about to suffer. Behold, the devil is about to throw some of you into prison, that you may be tested; and you will have oppression for ten days. Be faithful to death, and I will give you the crown of life. **2:11** He who has an ear, let him hear what the Spirit says to the churches. He who overcomes won't be harmed by the second death.

13:8 All who dwell on the earth will worship him, everyone whose name has not been written from the foundation of the world in the book of life of the Lamb who has been killed. **13:9** If anyone has an ear, let him hear. **13:10** If anyone is to go into captivity, he will go into captivity. If anyone is to be killed with the sword, he must be killed. Here is the endurance and the faith of the saints.

The Original Source Parallel Formation of the Church in Smyrna

Below is the original source material that John used to construct the core text that became the church in Smyrna. By comparing the parallel between Smyrna and the beast and the source text it is not difficult to see how John came up with the synagogue of Satan.

	From Isaiah		What it Became in Revelation
Isa 10:1	Woe to those who decree unrighteous decrees (Jacob/Israel; see 9:8), and those who write oppressive decrees;	2:9	"I know your works, oppression, and your poverty (but you are rich), and the blasphemy of those who say they are Jews, and they are not, but are a synagogue of Satan.
Isa 10:2	To deprive the needy from justice, and to rob the poor among my people of their rights.		
Isa 10:4	They [who issue evil decrees] will only bow down under the prisoners, and will fall under the slain.	2:10	"I know your works, oppression, and your poverty (but you are rich), and the blasphemy of those who say they are Jews, and they are not, but are a synagogue of Satan.

The beast narrative is effectively the same story as Smyrna but it is told backwards and in synonyms.[31] The bulk of the parallel comes from the parallel formation that was used to create Smyrna.[32] Although with parallel formation, content can come from both sides of the parallel where one or both elements are conflated. Take the synagogue of Satan for example, in which John conflated the things they did from Isaiah 10:1 and Satan and the beast making war against the saints.[33] John will also solidify the imagery when he forms the parallels with the sixth church, Philadelphia, which also includes the synagogue of Satan.[34]

Some texts just cannot be derived from parallel formation such as the ten days in prison found in the letter to Smyrna. The reason for this is that the numbers are geared towards the time that John is writing and not from a text. John redid the numbers from Ezekiel's prophesy over the destruction of Jerusalem to conform with the 3½ year siege of Jerusalem by the Romans. My guess is that the parallel between the first three churches and the beast narrative was among the very last parallels written before publication. John used the ten days to symbolize ten years until Jesus would come again. This is just like what he did in the 1,260 day parallel, which represented the number of years of Israel's ministry.[35] This is based upon the book being published in 96 CE and upon the end of the world in 105 CE from the "days of a certain king prophesy" John used from Isaiah.[36]

Pergamum Lives with Satan (Rev 2:12-7; 13:1-7)

The church in Pergamum is where Satan lives and for the most part they did well, until their member Antipas (Greek meaning "against everyone") died. Now as a result the church is being seduced by the likes of Balaam and Balak. The letter to Pergamum originally was a parallel formation with Numbers' account of Moses, the Israelites, Balaam, and Balak.[37]

John creates a simple parallel with Pergamum and the beast narrative by using the throne of the dragon and the conquest of the saints. Like the other two parallels between the churches and the beast, John uses a synonym for Satan: the dragon. John also contrasts the person Antipas (against everyone) and the beast by focusing on both of the deaths and the beast's resurrection. It is Antipas who was the person responsible for keeping the church together and it was his death that allowed the parishioners to wander away from the faith. The opposite to Antipas' death is the beast in that his death and resurrection are responsible for deceiving the world.

John uses the imagery from Numbers' story of Balaam and Balak, where the Israelites ate food sacrificed to idols and had sex with foreign women,[38] and equates it with worshiping the beast. He also adds in the Nicolatains as representing the whole world being deceived.

---

31   See "The First Three Churches and the Beast" on page 275.

32   Isa 10:1-4; Rev 2:9-10; see "The Original Source Parallel Formation of the Church in Smyrna" on page 279.

33   Isa 10:1; Rev 13-5-7. See

34   See "The Story of the Sixth Church" on page 287.

35   See "The Length of the Siege of Jerusalem Changed From Years of Sin to Years of Ministry (Ezek 4:5-8; Rev 11:2-3, 9)" on page 20.

36   See "Jesus as the Certain King (Isa 23:15-7; Rev 18:2-6, 22)" on page 29.

37   See "Satan, Balaam, and Phinehas (Num 22:1 - 25:18; Rev 2:13-5)" on page 89.

38   See "Satan, Balaam, and Phinehas (Num 22:1 - 25:18; Rev 2:13-5)" on page 89.

The Church in Pergamum and the Beast Narrative

John forms a simple parallel between the church in Pergamum and the first portion of the beast narrative. The parallel like the other two churches and the beast parallel contains an element based upon the synonyms, Satan and the dragon. It contains a contrast on what happens when the righteous dies and what happens when the beast dies and comes back to life. It concludes with the question: "Who will war against the beast?" It even provides the answer, that it will be Jesus.

The Church in Pergamum (Rev 2:12-7)	The Dragon and the Beast's Throne (Rev 13:1-7)
• Where Satan's throne is (2:13).	• Where the dragon's throne is (13:2)
• Antipas (meaning: against everyone) who was killed (2:13).	• The beast was fatally wounded (13:3).
• They eat food sacrificed to idols (2:14).	• Everyone who worshiped the beast (13:4) will receive food (13:17).
• Those who are not faithful will face the sword of Jesus' mouth (2:16 from Rev 19:15 where Jesus will war against the beast).	• Who will war against the beast (13:4).

2:12 "To the angel of the church in Pergamum write:

"He who has the sharp two-edged sword says these things:

2:13 "I know your works and where you dwell, where Satan's throne is. You hold firmly to my name, and didn't deny my faith in the days of Antipas my witness, my faithful one, who was killed among you, where Satan dwells. **2:14** But I have a few things against you, because you have there some who hold the teaching of Balaam, who taught Balak to throw a stumbling block before the children of Israel, to eat things sacrificed to idols, and to commit sexual immorality. **2:15** So you also have some who hold to the teaching of the Nicolaitans likewise. **2:16** Repent therefore, or else I am coming to you quickly, and I will make war against them with the sword of my mouth. **2:17** He who has an ear, let him hear what the Spirit says to the churches. To him who overcomes, to him I will give of the hidden manna, and I will give him a white stone, and on the stone a new name written, which no one knows but he who receives it.

13:1 Then I stood on the sand of the sea. I saw a beast coming up out of the sea, having ten horns and seven heads. On his horns were ten crowns, and on his heads, blasphemous names. **13:2** The beast which I saw was like a leopard, and his feet were like those of a bear, and his mouth like the mouth of a lion. The dragon gave him his power, his throne, and great authority. **13:3** One of his heads looked like it had been wounded fatally. His fatal wound was healed, and the whole earth marvelled at the beast. **13:4** They worshipped the dragon, because he gave his authority to the beast, and they worshipped the beast, saying,

"Who is like the beast? Who is able to make war with him?"

13:5 A mouth speaking great things and blasphemy was given to him. Authority to make war for forty-two months was given to him. **13:6** He opened his mouth for blasphemy against God, to blaspheme his name, and his dwelling, those who dwell in heaven. **13:7** It was given to him to make war with the saints, and to overcome them. Authority over every tribe, people, language, and nation was given to him.

Conclusion to the Three Churches and the Beast Parallel

The three churches and the beast parallel represent John's parallel formation at his best. He both connects the two passages and yet obfuscates his parallel by using synonyms which the reader has to be aware of the whole text of Revelation in order to make the connections with. The manner and consistency cannot be attributed to a random spontaneous combustion of a literary development but through skill and effort.

The three parallels are in themselves a complex parallel by how the structure is formed. The first parallel, Ephesus and the false prophet, forms a simple parallel and the second parallel between Smyrna and the middle section of the beast narrative forms a complex parallel. The last parallel between Pergamum and the first section of the beast narrative forms a simple parallel. When the three parallels are combined, the structure itself forms a complex parallel with the parallels of simple, complex, and simple parallel.

The three churches and the beast parallel also allows us to see how John altered the original beast narrative and the three churches narrative to create the parallel. For example, to formulate the parallel between the church of Smyrna and the beast narrative, John used the text of the letter to Smyrna as the source material for the beast narrative. For the church of Ephesus, John used the false prophet narrative as the source of the parallel formation with the letter to Ephesus. For the genetic literary reconstruction critic, it is the perfect example of how perfect parallels enable us to produce an order of construction to a given passage. It also allows us to see how parallel formation distorts earlier parallel formation. In this case, how the internal parallel formation of the letters to the first three churches changed the DnD parallel formation of the beast and little horn.

The Story of the Fifth Church

John wrote the story of the fifth church (Sardis) in the horizontal. The story includes the fifth church, the fifth seal, the story of the great multitude in heaven, the fifth trumpet, the fifth bowl plus a beatitude connected to the sixth bowl, the avenging of the saints by both God and Jesus, the imprisonment of Satan, and the first and second resurrection. It is the story of the plight of all believers and the plight of all nonbelievers told with rich imagery which makes the fifth church's horizontal reading the most complex in Revelation. It is John at his very best in the writing of Revelation and thus a preview of what Revelation could have been if he had time to finish it.

The fifth church's horizontal reading will be covered by the major themes of each parallel and some of the imagery will be repeated in different themes. This is not a reflection of John as a writer but a limitation of me as a writer and of us as readers whose mindsets are bound in the vertical. The best way to read it in the horizontal is to read the text in its entirety found on the next two pages. The following text will highlight the major themes and threads that John wrote.

What is Living and What is Dying?

The journey begins for both saint and sinner in the congregation of the Sardis where a once great people in God's eyes are slowly drifting away from God by not obeying his commandments. Most are no longer alive as Jesus sees it. John is writing the story of how these two groups will separate over time to become the two extreme groups depicted in the fifth church's parallel. To weave the story together, John will use two sets of parallels for each story. The first is the story of the fall of the saints on earth depicted by their martyrdom and the rise of the sinners depicted by their blaspheming against God.[39] The second part is God and Jesus avenging the saints by destroying those who destroyed the saints and finalizing the saints and sinners outcome, placing the saints as rulers and the sinners into the lake of fire.[40]

John weaves the story together in terms of opposites and locational differences. The story begins with Jesus telling those in Sardis that they who are now living on earth think they are alive but they are in fact dead because they no longer keep the commandments.[41] In the next horizontal reading, John shows that those in heaven are martyrs because they kept the commandments of God and they are, for the first time, recorded in the Christian scriptures as believers living in heaven prior to the resurrection.[42] John is capitalizing on

39   Rev 16:10.
40   Rev 20:4-6, 11-5.
41   Rev 3:2.
42   Rev 6:9-11.

word play showing that those living on earth are actually dead and those killed on earth are actually living in heaven. What separates the two groups is whether they will keep the commandments of God or not.

John continues the wordplay of the living and the dead to the fifth trumpet, where those who do not have the seal of God on their foreheads are living on earth in severe pain. So severe is the pain that they wished that they were dead. John is now adding another contrast in which those who are alive on earth wish that they were actually dead. In the fifth seal, John now has a world in which all who are on earth are non-believers and are in severe pain and yet they blaspheme God.[43]

John's finality of both the state of the believer and the state of the non-believer is that the believer is raised from the dead to rule with God and Jesus for a thousand years in the first resurrection. The non-believer is raised from the dead to spend all eternity in a lake of fire where they feel nothing but pain. The two plights are defined by whether one keeps the commandments of God and Jesus and as such, their name is retained in the Lamb's book of life.

Rising to One's Height and Descending to One's Depth

One of the messages that John is trying to convey in the fifth church's parallel is how the two groups rise with those who they follow. Those that follow God can only rise to a level less than God as seen in how they are depicted as being beneath the throne of God.[44]

For those who follow Satan the story is different because Satan is depicted as a transient being and God is depicted as a fixed point in which all reality is under his control.[45] At no point in Revelation is there a scenario where those who follow God rise above God and everything depicted in Revelation is the result of God's action. Satan is depicted as existing within a framework and as such, only has a limited amout of interaction with the world, and at certain times can wage war against the saints. We see the debut of Satan in the story of the fifth church parallel in the fifth trumpet in which the angel of the abyss (Satan) is released from the abyss and as a result he rises with all of his minions, depicted as scorpions, to inflict pain on the world.

We find by the time of the fifth bowl, all the followers of Satan have vanquished the believers on earth and therefore the judgment of the bowl is poured on the throne of the beast, and as a result his kingdom is darkened. The fifth trumpet has Satan bringing darkness into the world from the depths of the abyss and the fifth bowl has the darkness taking over the world. The spreading of the darkness results in pain for all who share the kingdom of Satan and the beast.

The height of those who follow Satan is only pain and suffering whereas the height of those who served God is comfort and rest.[46] What would happen if the story was in reverse, where those who were martyrs actually ruled the way God intended? John gives us the answer by having Satan locked away once again in the abyss for a thousand years and the saints rule for the same length of time that Israel ruled. When Sa-

---

43   Rev 16:10.
44   Rev 6:9.
45   Satan is defeated in heaven and thrown to earth (Rev 12:7-9). He is placed in the abyss for a thousand years (Rev 20:1-3). His final destination is in the lake of fire (Rev 20:10). God is depicted as the prime reality for heaven and earth. He sets all things in motion (Rev 1:1), is the creator of all things (Rev 4:11), destroys the earth and all that can bee seen in the heavens (Rev 21:1). He even has the power to stop death and remove all tears (Rev 21:2).
46   Rev 16:10.

The Fifth Church Parallel Part 1

The Fifth Church (Rev 3:1-6)	The Fifth Seal (Rev 6:9-11), Saints (Rev 7:9-17)	The Fifth Trumpet (Rev 9:1-11)
• Spoken from heaven to the earth (3:1).	• Beneath the throne in heaven (6:9)	• On earth
• Living but dead to Jesus (3:1).	• Dead but alive with Jesus (6:9)	• Alive on earth but desire death (9:5-6)
• Wake up and obey (3:2).	• Obeyed and now can rest (6:9-11)	• Obey and live without pain (9:4-6).
• Jesus seeks commitment (3:2).	• They seek justice against all on earth (6:10).	• Pain from the king of the Abyss (9:2).
• They don't know when (3:3).	• When the numbers are complete (6:11)	• In torment for five months (9:5).
• Walk with Jesus in white robes (3:5).	• They are given white robes (6:11).	• Locust had a crown & breastplate (9:7-10).

3:1 "And to the angel of the church in Sardis write:

"He who has the seven Spirits of God, and the seven stars says these things:

"I know your works, that you have a reputation of being alive, but you are dead. **3:2** Wake up, and keep the things that remain, which you were about to throw away, for I have found no works of yours perfected before my God. **3:3** Remember therefore how you have received and heard. Keep it, and repent. If therefore you won't watch, I will come as a thief, and you won't know what hour I will come upon you. **3:4** Nevertheless you have a few names in Sardis that did not defile their garments. They will walk with me in white, for they are worthy. **3:5** He who overcomes will be arrayed in white garments, and I will in no way blot his name out of the book of life, and I will confess his name before my Father, and before his angels. **3:6** He who has an ear, let him hear what the Spirit says to the churches.

6:9 When he opened the fifth seal, I saw underneath the altar the souls of those who had been killed for the Word of God, and for the testimony of the Lamb which they had. **6:10** They cried with a loud voice, saying,
"How long, Master, the holy and true, until you judge and avenge our blood on those who dwell on the earth?"

6:11 A long white robe was given to each of them. They were told that they should rest yet for a while, until their fellow servants and their brothers, who would also be killed even as they were, should complete their course.

7:9 After these things I looked, and behold, a great multitude, which no man could number, out of every nation and of all tribes, peoples, and languages, standing before the throne and before the Lamb, dressed in white robes, with palm branches in their hands. **7:10** They cried with a loud voice, saying,
"Salvation be to our God, who sits on the throne, and to the Lamb!"

7:11 All the angels were standing around the throne, the elders, and the four living creatures; and they fell on their faces before his throne, and worshipped God, **7:12** saying, "Amen! Blessing, glory, wisdom, thanksgiving, honour, power, and might, be to our God forever and ever! Amen."

7:13 One of the elders answered, saying to me, "These who are arrayed in white robes, who are they, and from where did they come?"
7:14 I told him, "My lord, you know."
He said to me,
"These are those who came out of the great tribulation. They washed their robes, and made them white in the Lamb's blood.

7:15 Therefore they are before the throne of God, they serve him day and night in his temple. He who sits on the throne will spread his tabernacle over them. **7:16** They will never be hungry, neither thirsty any more; neither will the sun beat on them, nor any heat; **7:17** for the Lamb who is in the midst of the throne shepherds them, and leads them to springs of waters of life.

9:1 The fifth angel sounded, and I saw a star from the sky which had fallen to the earth. The key to the pit of the abyss was given to him. **9:2** He opened the pit of the abyss, and smoke went up out of the pit, like the smoke from a burning furnace. The sun and the air were darkened because of the smoke from the pit. **9:3** Then out of the smoke came forth locusts on the earth, and power was given to them, as the scorpions of the earth have power. **9:4** They were told that they should not hurt the grass of the earth, neither any green thing, neither any tree, but only those people who don't have God's seal on their foreheads. **9:5** They were given power not to kill them, but to torment them for five months. Their torment was like the torment of a scorpion, when it strikes a person. **9:6** In those days people will seek death, and will in no way find it. They will desire to die, and death will flee from them. **9:7** The shapes of the locusts were like horses prepared for war. On their heads were something like golden crowns, and their faces were like people's faces. **9:8** They had hair like women's hair, and their teeth were like those of lions. **9:9** They had breastplates, like breastplates of iron. The sound of their wings was like the sound of chariots, or of many horses rushing to war. **9:10** They have tails like those of scorpions, and stings. In their tails they have power to harm men for five months. **9:11** They have over them as king the angel of the abyss. His name in Hebrew is "Abaddon," but in Greek, he has the name "Apollyon."

The Fifth Church Parallel Part 2

The Fifth Bowl (Rev 16:10-1)	The Saints Avenged (Rev 19:1-8)	Satan Bound (Rev 20:1-6)
• At the beast's throne on earth (16:10). • Living in extreme pain (16:10). • They did not repent of their death (16:11). • They blaspheme God in heaven (16:11). • Jesus will come like a thief (16:15). • They are naked (16:15).	• A great multitude in heaven (19:1). • They are praising God (19:1-6). • She was judged by her deeds (19:2). • They have been avenged (19:2). • Prior to Jesus' coming (19:11-18). • They are given a robe (19:8).	• Satan in the Abyss, Saints on thrones (20:1-4). • Saints rule for a 1,000 years (20:4). • They were judged by their deeds (20:4-15). • Satan's army is destroyed.

16:10 The fifth poured out his bowl on the throne of the beast, and his kingdom was darkened. They gnawed their tongues because of the pain, **16:11** and they blasphemed the God of heaven because of their pains and their sores. They didn't repent of their works.

16:15 "Behold, I come like a thief. Blessed is he who watches, and keeps his clothes, so that he doesn't walk naked, and they see his shame."

19:1 After these things I heard something like a loud voice of a great multitude in heaven, saying,
"Hallelujah! Salvation, power, and glory belong to our God: **19:2** for true and righteous are his judgments. For he has judged the great prostitute, who corrupted the earth with her sexual immorality, and he has avenged the blood of his servants at her hand."

19:3 A second said,
"Hallelujah! Her smoke goes up forever and ever."

19:4 The twenty-four elders and the four living creatures fell down and worshipped God who sits on the throne, saying, "Amen! Hallelujah!"

19:5 A voice came forth from the throne, saying,
"Give praise to our God, all you his servants, you who fear him, the small and the great!"

19:6 I heard something like the voice of a great multitude, and like the voice of many waters, and like the voice of mighty thunders, saying,
"Hallelujah! For the Lord our God, the Almighty, reigns! **19:7** Let us rejoice and be exceedingly glad, and let us give the glory to him. For the marriage of the Lamb has come, and his wife has made herself ready."

19:8 It was given to her that she would array herself in bright, pure, fine linen: for the fine linen is the righteous acts of the saints.

20:1 I saw an angel coming down out of heaven, having the key of the abyss and a great chain in his hand. **20:2** He seized the dragon, the old serpent, which is the devil and Satan, who deceives the whole inhabited earth, and bound him for a thousand years, **20:3** and cast him into the abyss, and shut it, and sealed it over him, that he should deceive the nations no more, until the thousand years were finished. After this, he must be freed for a short time.

20:4 I saw thrones, and they sat on them, and judgment was given to them. I saw the souls of those who had been beheaded for the testimony of Jesus, and for the word of God, and such as didn't worship the beast nor his image, and didn't receive the mark on their forehead and on their hand. They lived, and reigned with Christ for a thousand years. **20:5** The rest of the dead didn't live until the thousand years were finished. This is the first resurrection. **20:6** Blessed and holy is he who has part in the first resurrection. Over these, the second death has no power, but they will be priests of God and of Christ, and will reign with him one thousand years.

20:11 I saw a great white throne, and him who sat on it, from whose face the earth and the heaven fled away. There was found no place for them. **20:12** I saw the dead, the great and the small, standing before the throne, and they opened books. Another book was opened, which is the book of life. The dead were judged out of the things which were written in the books, according to their works. **20:13** The sea gave up the dead who were in it. Death and Hades gave up the dead who were in them. They were judged, each one according to his works. **20:14** Death and Hades were thrown into the lake of fire. This is the second death, the lake of fire. **20:15** If anyone was not found written in the book of life, he was cast into the lake of fire.

tan is released again from prison and raises an army to destroy Jerusalem once more, God steps in and destroys his army and casts him into the second death. John shows the heights and depths of the journey of the believer and the non-believer, showing the range that each group can reach and thus providing a clear distinction to the reader as to which group they should be a part of.

The Anger of the Righteous and the Unrighteous

Both the righteous and the unrighteous cry out to God or Jesus over their situation. The righteous seek to be avenged for those who have killed them and the unrighteous blaspheme God because of the pain that has been inflicted on them.[47] The righteous were martyred for their obeying the commandments of God by those who rejected the commandments of God. The result is that God avenges the righteous by destroying the harlot/Babylon with the saints observing the whole operation. Jesus will avenge the saints by destroying the beast, the false prophet, and their army before the saints as well.[48]

When Parallels Fail: The Story of the White Robes

So far our discussion of the fifth church parallel has remained confined to the fifth judgments, the story of God and Jesus avenging the saints, and the story of the first and second resurrection. The stories are direct and both easy to follow and easy for John to have segmented. The problem is that there are stories that the fifth church parallel, sixth church parallel, and the seventh church parallel have but do not fit in any of their respective judgments. John's solution was to redefine the Passover narrative from the DJD and make it part of the story for the fifth, sixth, and seventh church parallel. It also completed the parallel between the two stories of Satan.[49]

The fifth church depicts the faithful as keeping their white robes pure. The fifth seal shows Jesus giving them their white robes and telling them to rest until their numbers are complete and only then will they be avenged. The trumpet and the fifth bowl are focused on the plight of the unbeliever and therefore they do not have a story which contains receiving a white robe. John continued the story of the fifth seal by modifying the story of the great multitude. He made it the vision of heaven, and of what will happen when their numbers are complete. We see an untold number of people who have been martyred, coming from all walks of life, and living a life of comfort while servicing the temple in front of the throne of God.

The great multitude in heaven narrative contains imagery that the fifth, sixth, and seventh church contains and that does not fit within the fifth, sixth, and seventh trumpet. It may not have been a satisfying parallel, but nonetheless it was a satisfying story in the horizontal, as well as making the two stories of Satan a satisfying parallel when the texts were shifted into their proper location.[50]

John had a similar problem with fitting the story of the white robes in the fifth and seventh bowls as well. His solution was to add a beatitude containing content from the fifth and sixth church at the end of the sixth bowl. The solution and placement were similar to where the story of the great multitude in heaven was placed.

---

47   Rev 6:9-11; 16:10.
48   Rev 19:1-21.
49   See "Satan's Story: Told Two Ways" on page 296.
50   See "Satan's Story: Told Two Ways" on page 296.

John concludes the story of the white robes by having the saints observe the destruction of Babylon and the beast that forms Revelation 19:1-21 today. In both actions, the saints are just observers. It is only in the first resurrection in which the saints become the rulers of Jerusalem for a thousand years.[51]

The Story of the Fifth Church as Revelation was Intended to Be

So far we have only covered major themes within the fifth church parallel and not an exhaustive analysis of all that John did. There are many more ways to look at the content of the fifth church parallel and many more passages that can be added to the fifth church parallel. The purpose of this section is to provide the reader with the means of understanding the importance of reading in the parallel when it comes to the book of Revelation and many other books in the Bible. The fifth parallel is the best instance of storytelling that John does in Revelation.

It also causes us to wonder what Revelation might have been if he spent the time to finish it, and whether it was the best he could do or the best that he did? For me, I am torn between the two. If he would have finished it, it would have been much more difficult to have discovered how John wrote Revelation. For the world, he would have given us a piece of literature that would have been more universally accepted.

The Story of the Sixth Church

The sixth church, Philadelphia, is one of two churches in which Jesus finds nothing wrong. The imagery found in the church of Philadelphia is that their door is open by Jesus using the key of David and the conflict they face from the synagogue of Satan. They are encouraged to continue in their faith and as a reward they will become a fixed pillar in God's temple.[52] The core of the text that formed the imagery of the church in Philadelphia comes from the EID and the changes outside of the initial source text is a product of parallel formations.[53]

The Synagogue of Satan

The synagogue of Satan is the main opponent of the two faithful churches in Revelation, Smyrna and Philadelphia.[54] In both cases they are referring to the same foe but in two different ways. Before we can go on we need to first define the Greek meaning for synagogue, it can be a Jewish place of worship or a gathering.[55] We also need to make sure that we are able to explain the phrase "they claim to be Jews but they lie."[56] With an expanded definition of synagogue and this phrase in mind we can examine the sixth seal, sixth trumpet, sixth bowl, the second coming, and the story of Gog and Magog. What we find is in all accounts they are connected to the amassing of an army that is connected to the wrath of God.[57] The story of Gog and Magog and the sixth bowl, Satan is actively seeking allies through the vehicle of lies.[58] The first six trumpets are connected with the actions of Satan from the ZrD and continued to the published ver-

---

51 Rev 20:4-6.
52 Rev 3:7-12.
53 Isa 22:20-5; Rev 3:7-12; see "IP6 - Jesus as the Father of God's Children (Isa 22:20-5)" on page 55.
54 Rev 2:9; 3:9.
55 BDAG, συναγωγή.
56 Rev 3:9.
57 Rev 6:12-7; 9:13-21; 16:12-6; 20:7-10.
58 Rev 16:13-4; 20:8.

sion.[59] Therefore the likely candidate for the synagogue of Satan is the gathering of the armies of the world to defeat the saints.

The question is "How are they Jews?" and the answer is found in how they compete with God for worship as well as their similarities. Satan gives the throne to the beast just as God gives the throne to Jesus.[60] Both God and Jesus are worshiped and likewise Satan and the beast are worshiped.[61] One set is authentic while the other has to deceive and it is in that way, that they claim to be Jews but they are not.

Becoming a Fixed Pillar

Philadelphia's reward for overcoming is that they will be a fixed pillar in God's temple. This may seem strange but it is the result of parallel formation from the original source text. John took the core of the Eliakim text from Isaiah and made it into the church in Philadelphia.[62] Within Isaiah there is the depiction of vessels that would hang from nails in the temple and the strain would cause them to fall down and thus the burden would be removed.[63] John took the imagery of the nails and wall and made it a floor and pillars and then applied it to the reward for Philadelphia overcoming.[64] John then had a problem because nowhere in any of the sixth judgments or the other sections can a pillar be inserted without a profound alteration of the text. So John elected to use the great multitude narrative, which is between the sixth and seventh bowl to add in the imagery that the saints are always at the altar of God in the temple.[65]

Kept From the Hour of Testing

John further connects the sixth church with the sixth seal, the sixth trumpet, and the sixth bowl by alternating hour and day on each one.[66] It is a subtle change but it also shows how detail oriented John is in the parallel's development. Another subtle change is that one can read the order of the sixth judgments backwards and the story progresses in a chronological order.

The Story of the Seventh Church

The seventh church (Laodicea) is noted for being the only church that Jesus has nothing good to say about.[67] It is also noted for being a wealthy church that is not concerned with heavenly wealth and therefore Jesus pleads with Laodicea to purchase from him gold refined through fire as well as white garments so that they will not become naked or ashamed.[68] If they buy from Jesus then they will be able to sit down on their thrones and in the same way that Jesus sits on his throne before God.[69] John takes the refining by fire, the white robes, and the thrones and then weaves them into the great multitude in heaven, the seventh seal,

---

59   See "Satan's Story" on page 294.

60   Rev 3:21; 13:1-5.

61   Rev 4:8-11; 5:11-4; 13:1-5.

62   Isa 22:20-5; Rev 3:7-12; see "IP6 - Jesus as the Father of God's Children (Isa 22:20-5)" on page 55.

63   Isa 20:24-5.

64   Rev 3:12.

65   Rev 7:14-7.

66   Rev 3:10; 6:17; 9:15 ; 16:14.

67   Rev 3:14-22.

68   Rev 3:18.

69   Rev 3:21.

the seventh trumpet, a beatitude, the seventh bowl, the marriage of the Lamb, and the first resurrection.[70] This allows us to compare them side by side in order to deduce what John wants the readers to understand.

Buy From Jesus Gold Refined By Fire and White Garments (Rev 3:18)

The desire of Jesus for the church in Laodicea is that they buy from him gold refined by fire and white garments. What Jesus is actually telling the church in Laodicea is that it is his desire to be a martyr. Every scene depicting the saints being given a white robe in Revelation are all martyr scenes.[71] This makes the purchase of the gold refined by fire and the purchase of the white robe the same price as in their death. The gold refined by fire is really the additive of the prayers of the saints to the incense that burned in a gold censure. Of the two cases that mention the prayers of the saints, they are connected with a death scene, the first being Jesus and the second being the great multitude.[72] There is a possible refinement scene for the city of Babylon which is depicted as burning forever.[73]

If They Overcome They Will Sit on Their Thrones Next to God (Rev 3:21)

The reward for overcoming is that the believer will be able to sit on their throne around the throne of God as Jesus does. John uses the 24 elders to represent the believers sitting down at their thrones, or near the throne of God, until the saints actually get to sit on their thrones and then the imagery of the 24 elders are no longer needed in Revelation.[74] John also equates the price of sitting on the throne as the same as the gold refined by fire and the white robe, which is their martyrdom. He further expands on the actual cost of serving Jesus by letting the reader understand that only those believers who did not take the mark of the beast or worship the beast.[75] The reader would easily connect the cost of not worshiping the beast or receiving the mark of the beast with the denial of the ability to purchase food.[76]

John also shows in the seventh trumpet that the kingdom of the world became the kingdom of God through his Christ.[77] Although in the parallel formation, John does not have Jesus sitting on the throne, he does place him (as the child) in the next chapter and then repeats the phrase "the kingdom of the world has become the kingdom of God through his Christ."[78]

Wealth and Earthquakes

The church in Laodicea is depicted as extremely wealthy to the point that they think they can fix any crisis. The seventh seal, seventh trumpet, and seventh bowl have an earthquake theme in which the intensity of the earthquake imagery increases to the point that it is the greatest earthquake in human history.[79] The reason why John connected them into a theme is that in 60 CE Laodicea was destroyed by an earthquake.

---

70   See "The Seventh Church Parallel Part 1" on page 292 and "The Seventh Church Parallel Part 2" on page 293.
71   Rev 6:9-11; 7:9-17; 19:1-8.
72   Rev 5:6-11; 8:9-5.
73   Rev 19:3.
74   Rev 4:4, 10; 7:11-7; 11:16; 14:3;19:3. The saints finally get to sit on their thrones in Rev 20:4-6 where they will rule for a thousand years.
75   Rev 20:4.
76   Rev 13:15-7.
77   Rev 11:15.
78   Rev 12:4-5, 10-1.
79   Rev 8:5; 11:19; 16:18.

The Sixth Church Parallel Part 1

The Sixth Church (Rev 3:7-13)	The Sixth Seal (Rev 6:12-7; 7:13-7)	The Sixth Trumpet (9:13-21)
• Door is always open (3:7).	• The sky is taken away from their foes (6:12-4).	• The river is bound (9:14-5).
• The synagogue (gathering) of Satan (3:9).	• Their enemy's enemy is God and Jesus (6:17).	• A 200,000,000 army is their enemy (9:16).
• Jesus loves them (3:9).	• Their enemies will face Jesus' wrath (6:17).	• They love sin (9:20-1).
• Kept from the hour of testing (3:10)	• Their enemies face great day of wrath (6:17).	• The hour that killed a third of mankind (915).

3:7 "To the angel of the church in Philadelphia write:

"He who is holy, he who is true, he who has the key of David, he who opens and no one can shut, and who shuts and no one opens, says these things:

3:8 "I know your works (behold, I have set before you an open door, which no one can shut), that you have a little power, and kept my word, and didn't deny my name. **3:9** Behold, I give of the synagogue of Satan, of those who say they are Jews, and they are not, but lie. Behold, I will make them to come and worship before your feet, and to know that I have loved you. **3:10** Because you kept my command to endure, I also will keep you from the hour of testing, which is to come on the whole world, to test those who dwell on the earth. **3:11** I am coming quickly! Hold firmly that which you have, so that no one takes your crown. **3:12** He who overcomes, I will make him a pillar in the temple of my God, and he will go out from there no more. I will write on him the name of my God, and the name of the city of my God, the new Jerusalem, which comes down out of heaven from my God, and my own new name. **3:13** He who has an ear, let him hear what the Spirit says to the churches.

6:12 I saw when he opened the sixth seal, and there was a great earthquake. The sun became black as sackcloth made of hair, and the whole moon became as blood. **6:13** The stars of the sky fell to the earth, like a fig tree dropping its unripe figs when it is shaken by a great wind. **6:14** The sky was removed like a scroll when it is rolled up. Every mountain and island were moved out of their places. **6:15** The kings of the earth, the princes, the commanding officers, the rich, the strong, and every slave and free person, hid themselves in the caves and in the rocks of the mountains. **6:16** They told the mountains and the rocks,
"Fall on us, and hide us from the face of him who sits on the throne, and from the wrath of the Lamb, **6:17** for the great day of his wrath has come; and who is able to stand?"

7:13 One of the elders answered, saying to me,
"These who are arrayed in white robes, who are they, and from where did they come?"

7:14 I told him, "My lord, you know."

He said to me,
"These are those who came out of the great tribulation. They washed their robes, and made them white in the Lamb's blood.
7:15 Therefore they are before the throne of God, they serve him day and night in his temple. He who sits on the throne will spread his tabernacle over them. **7:16** They will never be hungry, neither thirsty any more; neither will the sun beat on them, nor any heat; **7:17** for the Lamb who is in the midst of the throne shepherds them, and leads them to springs of waters of life. And God will wipe away every tear from their eyes."

9:13 The sixth angel sounded. I heard a voice from the horns of the golden altar which is before God, **9:14** saying to the sixth angel who had one trumpet,

"Free the four angels who are bound at the great river Euphrates!"

9:15 The four angels were freed who had been prepared for that hour and day and month and year, so that they might kill one third of mankind. **9:16** The number of the armies of the horsemen was two hundred million. I heard the number of them. **9:17** Thus I saw the horses in the vision, and those who sat on them, having breastplates of fiery red, hyacinth blue, and sulfur yellow; and the heads of lions. Out of their mouths proceed fire, smoke, and sulfur. **9:18** By these three plagues were one third of mankind killed: by the fire, the smoke, and the sulfur, which proceeded out of their mouths. **9:19** For the power of the horses is in their mouths, and in their tails. For their tails are like serpents, and have heads, and with them they harm. **9:20** The rest of mankind, who were not killed with these plagues, didn't repent of the works of their hands, that they wouldn't worship demons, and the idols of gold, and of silver, and of brass, and of stone, and of wood; which can neither see, nor hear, nor walk. **9:21** They didn't repent of their murders, nor of their sorceries, nor of their sexual immorality, nor of their thefts.

The Sixth Church Parallel Part 2

The Sixth Bowl (Rev 16:12-5)	The Second Coming of Jesus (Rev 19:11-21)	Gog and Magog (Rev 20:7-10)
• The river dried up (16:12). • An army from every kingdom (16:13-4). • Followed Satan and demons (16:13-4). • Great day of God (16:14).	• Heaven opens up (19:11). • Army of Jesus and the army of the beast (19:11-21). • They love Jesus (19:9).	• The Abyss is opened (20:7). • Army of Gog and Magog (20:8). • God loves Jerusalem (20:9). • Satan is tormented everyday (20:10).

16:12 The sixth poured out his bowl on the great river, the Euphrates. Its water was dried up, that the way might be prepared for the kings that come from the sunrise. **16:13** I saw coming out of the mouth of the dragon, and out of the mouth of the beast, and out of the mouth of the false prophet, three unclean spirits, something like frogs; **16:14** for they are spirits of demons, performing signs; which go forth to the kings of the whole inhabited earth, to gather them together for the war of that great day of God, the Almighty.

16:15 "Behold, I come like a thief. Blessed is he who watches, and keeps his clothes, so that he doesn't walk naked, and they see his shame." **16:16** He gathered them together into the place which is called in Hebrew, Megiddo.

19:11 I saw the heaven opened, and behold, a white horse, and he who sat on it is called Faithful and True. In righteousness he judges and makes war. **19:12** His eyes are a flame of fire, and on his head are many crowns. He has names written and a name written which no one knows but he himself. **19:13** He is clothed in a garment sprinkled with blood. His name is called "The Word of God." **19:14** The armies which are in heaven followed him on white horses, clothed in white, pure, fine linen. **19:15** Out of his mouth proceeds a sharp, double-edged sword, that with it he should strike the nations. He will rule them with an iron rod. He treads the wine press of the fierceness of the wrath of God, the Almighty. **19:16** He has on his garment and on his thigh a name written,
"KING OF KINGS, AND LORD OF LORDS."

19:17 I saw an angel standing in the sun. He cried with a loud voice, saying to all the birds that fly in the sky,
"Come! Be gathered together to the great supper of God,
19:18 that you may eat the flesh of kings, the flesh of captains, the flesh of mighty men, and the flesh of horses and of those who sit on them, and the flesh of all men,
both free and slave, and small and great."

19:19 I saw the beast, and the kings of the earth, and their armies, gathered together to make war against him who sat on the horse, and against his army. **19:20** The beast was taken, and with him the false prophet who worked the signs in his sight, with which he deceived those who had received the mark of the beast and those who worshiped his image. These two were thrown alive into the lake of fire that burns with sulfur. **19:21** The rest were killed with the sword of him who sat on the horse, the sword which came forth out of his mouth. All the birds were filled with their flesh.

20:7 And after the thousand years, Satan will be released from his prison, **20:8** and he will come out to deceive the nations which are in the four corners of the earth, Gog and Magog, to gather them together to the war; the number of whom is as the sand of the sea. **20:9** They went up over the breadth of the earth, and surrounded the camp of the saints, and the beloved city. Fire came down out of heaven from God, and devoured them. **20:10** The devil who deceived them was thrown into the lake of fire and sulfur, where the beast and the false prophet are also. They will be tormented day and night forever and ever.

The Seventh Church Parallel Part 1

The Seventh Church	Saints in Heaven and the Seventh Seal (Rev 7:9-8:5)	The Seventh Trumpet (Rev 11:15-9)
• Purchase gold refined in fire (3:18). • They need buy white garments (3:18). • They will sit with Jesus on their thrones (3:21).	• Saint's prayers burned in gold censure (8:3). • The martyrs received the white robes (7:9-15). • They served God at his temple/throne (7:15-7).	• [Not mentioned] • [Not mentioned] • Jesus' rule, 24 elders sitting on thrones before God (11:15-6).

3:14 "To the angel of the church in Laodicea write:

"The Amen, the Faithful and True Witness, the Head of God's creation, says these things:

3:15 "I know your works, that you are neither cold nor hot. I wish you were cold or hot. **3:16** So, because you are lukewarm, and neither hot nor cold, I will vomit you out of my mouth. **3:17** Because you say, 'I am rich, and have gotten riches, and have need of nothing;' and don't know that you are the wretched one, miserable, poor, blind, and naked; **3:18** I counsel you to buy from me gold refined by fire, that you may become rich; and white garments, that you may clothe yourself, and that the shame of your nakedness may not be revealed; and eye salve to anoint your eyes, that you may see. **3:19** As many as I love, I reprove and chasten. Be zealous therefore, and repent. **3:20** Behold, I stand at the door and knock. If anyone hears my voice and opens the door, then I will come in to him, and will dine with him, and he with me. **3:21** He who overcomes, I will give to him to sit down with me on my throne, as I also overcame, and sat down with my Father on his throne. **3:22** He who has an ear, let him hear what the Spirit says to the churches."

7:9 After these things I looked, and behold, a great multitude, which no man could number, out of every nation and of all tribes, peoples, and languages, standing before the throne and before the Lamb, dressed in white robes, with palm branches in their hands. **7:10** They cried with a loud voice, saying, "Salvation be to our God, who sits on the throne, and to the Lamb!"

7:11 All the angels were standing around the throne, the elders, and the four living creatures; and they fell on their faces before his throne, and worshipped God, **7:12** saying, "Amen! Blessing, glory, wisdom, thanksgiving, honor, power, and might, be to our God forever and ever! Amen."

7:13 One of the elders answered, saying to me, "These who are arrayed in white robes, who are they, and from where did they come?"

7:14 I told him, "My lord, you know."

He said to me, "These are those who came out of the great tribulation. They washed their robes, and made them white in the Lamb's blood. **7:15** Therefore they are before the throne of God, they serve him day and night in his temple. He who sits on the throne will spread his tabernacle over them. **7:16** They will never be hungry, neither thirsty any more; neither will the sun beat on them, nor any heat; **7:17** for the Lamb who is in the midst of the throne shepherds them, and leads them to springs of waters of life. And God will wipe away every tear from their eyes."

8:1 When he opened the seventh seal, there was silence in heaven for about half an hour. **8:2** I saw the seven angels who stand before God, and seven trumpets were given to them. **8:3** Another angel came and stood over the altar, having a golden censer. Much incense was given to him, that he should add it to the prayers of all the saints on the golden altar which was before the throne. **8:4** The smoke of the incense, with the prayers of the saints, went up before God out of the angel's hand. **8:5** The angel took the censer, and he filled it with the fire of the altar, and threw it on the earth. There followed thunders, sounds, lightnings, and an earthquake.

11:15 The seventh angel sounded, and great voices in heaven followed, saying,

"The kingdom of the world has become the Kingdom of our Lord, and of his Christ.
He will reign forever and ever!"

11:16 The twenty-four elders, who sit on their thrones before God's throne, fell on their faces and worshiped God, **11:17** saying:

"We give you thanks, Lord God, the Almighty, the one who is and who was; because you have taken your great power, and reigned.
11:18 The nations were angry, and your wrath came, as did the time for the dead to be judged, and to give your bondservants the prophets, their reward, as well as to the saints, and those who fear your name, to the small and the great; and to destroy those who destroy the earth."

11:19 God's temple that is in heaven was opened, and the ark of the Lord's covenant was seen in his temple. Lightnings, sounds, thunders, an earthquake, and great hail followed.

The Seventh Church Parallel Part 2

The Seventh Bowl (Rev 16:15-21)	The Marriage of the Lamb (Rev 19:3-8)	The First Resurrection (Rev 20:4-6)
• The results of not buying (16:15-21).	• Babylon refined in fire (19:3).	• They did not buy from the beast (20:4).
• They keep their clothes (16:15).	• The saints are given a robe (19:8).	• They were given a thrown to rule (20:4).
• The ruling nation is destroyed (16:19).	• God rules the nations (19:4-7).	• They ruled with Jesus for 1,000 years (20:5-6).

16:15 "Behold, I come like a thief. Blessed is he who watches, and keeps his clothes, so that he doesn't walk naked, and they see his shame."

16:17 The seventh poured out his bowl into the air. A loud voice came forth out of the temple of heaven, from the throne, saying, "It is done!" **16:18** There were lightnings, sounds, and thunders; and there was a great earthquake, such as was not since there were men on the earth, so great an earthquake, so mighty. **16:19** The great city was divided into three parts, and the cities of the nations fell. Babylon the great was remembered in the sight of God, to give to her the cup of the wine of the fierceness of his wrath. **16:20** Every island fled away, and the mountains were not found. **16:21** Great hailstones, about the weight of a talent, came down out of the sky on people. People blasphemed God because of the plague of the hail, for this plague is exceedingly severe.

19:3 A second said, "Hallelujah! Her smoke goes up forever and ever."

19:4 The twenty-four elders and the four living creatures fell down and worshiped God who sits on the throne, saying, "Amen! Hallelujah!"

19:5 A voice came forth from the throne, saying, "Give praise to our God, all you his servants, you who fear him, the small and the great!"

19:6 I heard something like the voice of a great multitude, and like the voice of many waters, and like the voice of mighty thunders, saying, "Hallelujah! For the Lord our God, the Almighty, reigns! **19:7** Let us rejoice and be exceedingly glad, and let us give the glory to him. For the marriage of the Lamb has come, and his wife has made herself ready."

19:8 It was given to her that she would array herself in bright, pure, fine linen: for the fine linen is the righteous acts of the saints.

20:4 I saw thrones, and they sat on them, and judgment was given to them. I saw the souls of those who had been beheaded for the testimony of Jesus, and for the word of God, and such as didn't worship the beast nor his image, and didn't receive the mark on their forehead and on their hand. They lived, and reigned with Christ for a thousand years. **20:5** The rest of the dead didn't live until the thousand years were finished. This is the first resurrection. **20:6** Blessed and holy is he who has part in the first resurrection. Over these, the second death has no power, but they will be priests of God and of Christ, and will reign with him one thousand years.

Instead of receiving help from the empire, the residents elected to reconstruct the city using their own resources.[80] John is capitalizing on the history of Laodicea's ability to recover from their earthquake and provide a backdrop in which the greatest city cannot recover from their earthquake.[81]

The Open Door, The Closed Door, And What Is Behind the Door

John, in the previous church, Philadelphia, has their door always open and he depicts Laodicea as closing their door.[82] For Laodicea, John offers a carrot in which those who overcome will be sitting on their own thrones around the throne of God.[83] John then uses the door as a means to segue into the heaven scene where we have God sitting on his throne and the 24 elders sitting on their thrones around the throne of

---

80   *Ann.* 14.27.
81   Rev 16:18.
82   Rev 3:8, 20.
83   Rev 3:21.

God.[84] This is yet another way in which John connected the 24 elders as representing the fulfillment of the promise for their overcoming.

Satan's Story

The story of Satan cannot be fully understood by simply using a concordance and finding all of the places where Satan appears in Revelation. That is because John uses synonyms for Satan such as "dragon" and the "deceiver."[85] John also connects the story of Satan not just with synonyms but also with actions or events that Satan participates in, such as being thrown to earth or being sealed up into the abyss. Thereby, understanding how John formed parallels with Satan is critical in the understanding of how John wants the reader to understand Satan's story.

Many readers of Revelation may be surprised that there are two stories of Satan in Revelation. One story is where Satan defeats Jerusalem and God's people and the other is where Satan tries to defeat Jerusalem and God destroys him.[86] As such, much of the symbols connected to the two stories of Satan becomes more like guesswork connected to a theological or historical-critical position than from a consistent methodology based upon the writer's writing style.

How John Formed the Story of Satan

The two stories of Satan are formed by arranging the wax tablets into two columns. The first column contains Revelation 7:1 - 9:21 and the second column contains Rev 20:1-6; 12:1-17; 20:7-15. The second column is clearly marked as Satan, making it easy for the reader to associate the actions of Satan with the text. The first column is connected to Satan by the four attacks by Satan and the first four trumpets complex parallel and the angel who is the king of the abyss being released with a key. When the two columns of wax tablets are laid side by side we get the equivalent of two stories of Satan as well as two stories of the saints.[87]

The Sealing of the 144,000 and the Sealing of Satan for a Thousand Years (Rev 7:1-8; 20:1-3)

John begins both parallels with a period of peace. For the saints it begins with the circumcision of the Israelites when they cross the Jordan River.[88] For the world it begins when Satan is sealed away for a thousand years in the abyss.[89] From the perspective of John, the thousand years lasted from the time of the Jordan River crossing to the conception of Jesus.[90] We know this by how the parallel is structured where the saints are not harmed until Satan is released from the abyss.[91]

---

84   Rev 4:1-4.

85   Rev 12:9; 20:2.

86   See "Satan's Story: Told Two Ways" on page 296.

87   See "Satan's Story: Told Two Ways" on page 296.

88   Rev 7:1-8; see "The Crossing of the Jordan River" on page 140 and "The Circumcision of Those Born in the Wilderness" on page 142.

89   Rev 20:1-3, 7.

90   From a chronological point of view, Satan first appears with the conception of Jesus and the woman found in Rev 12:1-3.

91   Satan being released from the abyss in Rev 7:1-3; 9:1-2, 4-5, 11; 20:3, 7. Satan amassing a huge army in Rev 9:13-9 and in Rev 20:20:8.

The Three Door Segue

One of the more interesting ways that John connects two of the churches and segues into a heaven is by the use of a door imagery. The church in Philadelphia is righteous and thus Jesus keeps its door always open (Rev 3:7) while the church of Laodicea keeps their door shut to Jesus (Rev 3:20). In order to entice Laodicea to open their door Jesus tells them that they will receive the right to sit down at his throne as he overcame and sat down at his father's throne. After the promise, John shows the reader what is behind the door that is open for Philadelphia and Laodicea keeps closed (Rev 4:1-4). The three door segue is an example of how John transitions using a parallel as a segue.

Door Always Open (Rev 3:7)	Door Always Shut (Rev 3:20-1)	What Is Behind the Door (Rev 4:1-4)
"He who is holy, he who is true, he who has the key of David, he who opens and no one can shut, and who shuts and no one opens, says these things:	**3:20** Behold, I stand at the door and knock. If anyone hears my voice and opens the door, then I will come in to him, and will dine with him, and he with me.	**4:1** After these things I looked and saw a door opened in heaven, and the first voice that I heard, like a trumpet speaking with me, was one saying, "Come up here, and I will show you the things which must happen after this."
	The Promise (Rev 3:21)	***The Reward (Rev 4:2-4)***
	3:21 He who overcomes, I will give to him to sit down with me on my throne, as I also overcame, and sat down with my Father on his throne.	**4:2** Immediately I was in the Spirit. Behold, there was a throne set in heaven, and one sitting on the throne **4:3** that looked like a jasper stone and a sardius. There was a rainbow around the throne, like an emerald to look at. **4:4** Around the throne were twenty-four thrones. On the thrones were twenty-four elders sitting, dressed in white garments, with crowns of gold on their heads.

The Martyrdom of Believers and Their 1,000 Year Reign (Rev 7:9-17; 20:4-6)

Did John intend for the two parallels to reflect one story or two? It is likely that he had two separate stories in mind, one in which the Jews reigned in Israel for a thousand years and they became corrupt. As a result Satan was released from prison and destroyed Jerusalem first and then went after the saints second. Satan was then imprisoned a second time and the new crop of believers reigned over Jerusalem for a thousand years, keeping the inhabitants of Jerusalem holy.

What is important to note about the two stories of the saints in heaven is that the Revelation 20:4-6 story does not have Satan in it. This is an indicator that it likely had Satan in it but was overwritten by the beast content from the DnD.[92] Although we may not be able to recover the original narrative containing Satan, we can at least recognize that somehow Satan was part of the narrative.

The First Four Trumpets and the Four Attacks By Satan Against the Woman

The first four trumpets and the four attacks by Satan form a complex parallel and therefore to tell the story correctly we must follow the story of one and go backwards in the other. The story we will go forward in

---

92   Dan 7:9; Rev 20:4-6; see "The Creation of the Second Death" on page 213.

Satan's Story: Told Two Ways

The chart below represents the final form of the "Two Babylonian Captivities" with Satan replacing Babylon from the Zechariah Draft. The left column ("Satan is Victorious") tells the story from Ezekiel 6:1-12:28 of Jerusalem being destroyed because of their unfaithfulness. The right column ("Satan is Defeated") tells the story of Satan being defeated, beginning with Satan first residing in heaven and then losing a war in heaven (Rev 12:3-9 from Isa 14:12-18) to his imprisonment (Rev 20:1-3 from Isa 14:12-18) and his eventual freedom where he repeats the same action against the saints in Jerusalem but fails (Rev 20:7-10) only to be permanently placed in the second death.

The center section is a complex parallel that represents the attacks by Satan against the believers. Within this section the parallel letterings are arranged in chronological order. The parallel is unique in that it is only visible by inserting Rev 12:1-17 between Rev 20:6 and Rev 20:7. The formation shows us that John does not need contiguous content for each side of the parallel but he can use sections to form a parallel.

Satan is Victorious	Satan is Defeated
The 144,000, the Great Multitude, and the Six Trumpets (7:1-9:21)	**Chapter 20 with Chapter 12 Inserted**

The Angel Holding Back the Four Winds (7:1-8)
- The four angels that hold back the four winds (7:1-2).
- So that they do not hurt the earth, sea, or trees until the 144,000 is sealed (7:3-8).

The Angel with Keys to the Abyss (20:1-4)
- An angel sealed Satan in the abyss for 1,000 years (20:1-2).
- So he cannot deceive the world (20:3-4).

Great Multitude is in Heaven (7:14-17)
- They came from the great tribulation (7:14-17).

The First Resurrection (20:4-6)
- The souls of those beheaded and those who did not worship the beast lived and reigned with Jesus for 1,000 years.

First Trumpet (8:7)
- Hail and fire mixed with blood was thrown down to the earth. A third of the earth and trees burnt up and all the green grass. — **D**
- From Ezek 5:2 where a "third part burns in the fire in the midst of the city."

A' The woman clothed with the sun, the moon under her feet, and twelve stars, then came Satan who with his tail sweeps a third of the stars from the sky (12:1-6).

Second Trumpet (8:8-9)
- A great burning mountain was thrown into the sea. A third of the sea became blood, a third of the living creatures in the sea died, and a third of the ships destroyed. — **C**
- From Ezek 5:2 where a third part was scattered to the wind

B' There was a war in heaven and the one called the Great Dragon, the Old Serpent, the Devil, and Satan was kicked out of heaven with his angels to deceive the world (12:7-9).

Third Trumpet (8:10-1)
- A great star fell from the sky, burning like a torch (8:10). — **B**
- Turned a third of the rivers and springs bitter and many people died from the bitter waters (8:10-1).

C' The serpent spewed out water from his mouth so that the woman might be carried with it but the earth opened and swallowed up the water (12:15-6).

Fourth Trumpet (8:12)
- A third of the sun, moon, and stars were struck. They were darkened by day and night by a third. — **A**
- From Ezek 5:2 where a third was struck with a sword.

D' The dragon grew angry with the woman, and made war against her offspring who keeps God's commandments and holds Jesus' testimony (12:17).

Fifth Trumpet (9:1-12)
- An angel opens the keys to the abyss (9:1-2).
- Their king is the angel from the king of the abyss (9:11).

Satan Released From His Prison (20:7)
- He is released from the abyss (see 20:3, 7).

A Huge Army Is Assembled (9:13-9)
- The four angels were freed to kill a third of mankind (9:15).
- Their army was 200,000,000 (9:16).
- The army used fire from their mouths to destroy and their tails to do damage (9:17-9).

Satan Gathers a Huge Army (20:7-10)
- They are from the four corners of the earth (20:7).
- Their numbers are like the sands of the sea (20:8).
- They surrounded the camp of the saints and the beloved city (20:9).
- Fire came down from heaven and destroyed them (20:9).

They Did Not Repent of Their Deeds (9:20-21)
- The rest of humanity did not repent from their evil deeds (9:20-21).

The Great White Throne Judgment (20:11-15)
- The dead were judged according to their works--these are the unbelievers and are thrown in the lake of fire.

is the story of the four attacks by Satan because they are in chronological order and the first four trumpets are in reverse chronological order.

The Twelve Tribes Conceived in Heaven and Deceived by Satan (Rev 8:12; 12:1-6)

The depiction of the woman clothed with the sun, moon under her feet, and a crown of twelve stars is taken from Joseph's dream in which he saw Jacob (later named Israel) as the sun, Joseph's mother as the moon and his brothers as the stars.[93] John conflates Joseph's dream with the sign of the woman with child from Isaiah and places them both in heaven.[94]

What John is saying here is that Satan deceived a third of Israel, represented by the sweeping a third of the stars with his tail.[95] The imagery of the tail is important to note because it comes from the EID where the tail signifies that those who deceive will lead the people into destruction.[96]

When the first attack by Satan is compared to the fourth trumpet we get a complementary picture in which a third of Israel (the sun, moon, and stars) are struck and they never shine the same way again.[97] This is a spiritual story of Israel illustrated with a cosmological backdrop in which he will retain this imagery in the remaining attacks by Satan and the first three trumpets.

The War in Heaven and the Falling Star (Rev 8:10-1; 12:7-9)

John tells the story of Satan's war in heaven two ways. The first is in terms of the actual war with Michael and his angels in heaven in which he is soundly defeated and is thrown to earth. The second is told from a cosmological perspective in which a great star falls from the heavens and poisons the drinking water. As a result many are killed. The first story is concerned with what Satan does in heaven and the second with what Satan does on earth.

The war in heaven and the falling star parallel also tells us that John forms parallels by similar concepts as well as synonyms. Satan receives multiple names and one of them is the "deceiver of the whole world" and the fallen star is named "Wormwood" (a bitter tasting plant) making a third of the water bitter.

What we can derive from comparing the two stories is that Satan is the fallen star. The result of the falling star making the water bitter which kills a third of mankind is really Satan's deception upon the world. Like the first attack by Satan and the fourth trumpet, the story is told from a cosmological perspective rather than in terms of a simple descriptive manner.

The Land Absorbs the Water and the Sea Absorbs the Mountain (Rev 8:8-9; 12:15-6)

John provides us with a story in which Satan tries to destroy the woman and her children by drowning them with water spewed from his mouth. The earth however, rescued the woman and her children by absorbing the water. The imagery that we receive in the third attack by Satan is that Satan was not successful in destroying all of the woman's children.

---

93 Gen 37:9-10.
94 Rev 12:1-2; See
95 Rev 12:4.
96 Isa 9:15-6; Rev 12:4 see "Z7 - The Zechariah Encoded Parallel: Satan's Entry into Revelation (Z7 -- Part 3)" on page 119.
97 Rev 8:12.

The Sealing of the 144,000 and the Sealing of Satan for a Thousand Years (Rev 7:1-8; 20:1-3)

John begins both parallels with a period of peace. For the saints it begins with the circumcision of the Israelites when they crossed the Jordan River (Rev 7:1-8; see "The Circumcision of Those Born in the Wilderness" on page 142). For the world it begins when Satan is sealed away for a thousand years in the abyss (Rev 20:1-3, 7). From the perspective of John, the thousand years was from the time of the Jordan River crossing to the conception of Jesus (Rev 12:1-3). We know this by how the parallel is structured and that the saints are not harmed until Satan is released from the abyss (Rev 7:1-3; 9:1-5, 11; 20:3, 7).

The Angel Holding Back the Four Winds (Rev 7:1-8)	The Angel with the Keys to the Abyss (Rev 20:1-3)
• An angel ascends with the seal of the living God (7:2).	• An angel descends, having the key to the abyss (20:1).
• The angel cried with a loud voice to the angels holding back the four winds (7:2).	• The angel seized the dragon and bound him (20:2).
• The 144,000 sealed with the seal of the living God (7:2-3).	• Satan locked away for a thousand years (20:2).
• Harm will come after everyone receives the seal of God (7:3).	• Satan will deceive the nations after he is released (20:3).

7:1 After this, I saw four angels standing at the four corners of the earth, holding the four winds of the earth, so that no wind would blow on the earth, or on the sea, or on any tree. **7:2** I saw another angel ascend from the sunrise, having the seal of the living God. He cried with a loud voice to the four angels to whom it was given to harm the earth and the sea, **7:3** saying, "Don't harm the earth, neither the sea, nor the trees, until we have sealed the bondservants of our God on their foreheads!" **7:4** I heard the number of those who were sealed, one hundred forty-four thousand, sealed out of every tribe of the children of Israel: **7:5** of the tribe of Judah were sealed twelve thousand, of the tribe of Reuben twelve thousand, of the tribe of Gad twelve thousand, **7:6** of the tribe of Asher twelve thousand, of the tribe of Naphtali twelve thousand, of the tribe of Manasseh twelve thousand, **7:7** of the tribe of Simeon twelve thousand, of the tribe of Levi twelve thousand, of the tribe of Issachar twelve thousand, **7:8** of the tribe of Zebulun twelve thousand, of the tribe of Joseph twelve thousand, of the tribe of Benjamin were sealed twelve thousand.

20:1 I saw an angel coming down out of heaven, having the key of the abyss and a great chain in his hand. **20:2** He seized the dragon, the old serpent, which is the devil and Satan, who deceives the whole inhabited earth, and bound him for a thousand years, **20:3** and cast him into the abyss, and shut it, and sealed it over him, that he should deceive the nations no more, until the thousand years were finished. After this, he must be freed for a short time.

The story found in the second trumpet is the complete opposite in that there is a great mountain that fell from the sky and was absorbed by the sea. In this story, John tells us what happened to those who were not killed: they were simply absorbed by all the nations in the form of being taken into slavery.

Satan Wars Against Those who Keep God's Commandments and Jesus' Testimony (Rev 8:7; 12:17)

The last attack by Satan is when he wars against those who obey the commandments of God and hold to Jesus' testimony. The way it is constructed is the same as the other four attacks by Satan. The first four trumpets make a complex parallel in that the attacks by Satan tells the first part of the story and the trumpet tells the second part. In the fourth attack by Satan we have the beginning of his campaign against those who follow the commandments of God and Jesus' testimony. The first trumpet tells the story in which Satan defeated those who obey the commandments of God and Jesus' testimony. It is depicted through imagery as a third of the trees burned (the faithful Jews) and all the green grass (the great multitude).

The Martyrdom of Believers and Their 1,000 Year Reign (Rev 7:9-17; 20:4-6)

Did John intend for the two parallels to reflect one story or two stories? It is likely that he had in mind two separate stories, one in which the Jews reigned in Israel for a thousand years and they became corrupt. As a result Satan was released from prison and destroyed Jerusalem first and then went after the saints second. Satan was then imprisoned a second time and the new crop of believers reigned over Jerusalem for a thousand years, keeping the inhabitants of Jerusalem holy.

What is important to note about the two stories of the saints in heaven is that the Revelation 20:4-6 story does not have Satan in it. This is an indicator that it likely had Satan in it but was overwritten by the beast content from the DnD (see "The Creation of the Second Death" on page 213). Although we may not be able to recover the original narrative containing Satan, we can at least recognize that somehow Satan was part of the narrative.

The Great Multitude in Heaven (Rev 7:9-17)	The First Resurrection (Rev 20:4-6)
• Those in heaven came from the great tribulation (7:9-14). • They will serve God night and day in the temple (7:15).	• Those in heaven were martyred by the beast (20:4). • They will reign with Jesus for a thousand years (20:5-6).

7:9 After these things I looked, and behold, a great multitude, which no man could number, out of every nation and of all tribes, peoples, and languages, standing before the throne and before the Lamb, dressed in white robes, with palm branches in their hands. **7:10** They cried with a loud voice, saying,

"Salvation be to our God, who sits on the throne, and to the Lamb!"

7:11 All the angels were standing around the throne, the elders, and the four living creatures; and they fell on their faces before his throne, and worshiped God, **7:12** saying, "Amen! Blessing, glory, wisdom, thanksgiving, honor, power, and might, be to our God forever and ever! Amen."

7:13 One of the elders answered, saying to me,

"These who are arrayed in white robes, who are they, and from where did they come?"

7:14 I told him, "My lord, you know."

He said to me,

"These are those who came out of the great tribulation.
They washed their robes, and made them white in the Lamb's blood.
7:15 Therefore they are before the throne of God, they serve him day and night in his temple.
He who sits on the throne will spread his tabernacle over them.
7:16 They will never be hungry, neither thirsty any more;
neither will the sun beat on them, nor any heat;
7:17 for the Lamb who is in the midst of the throne shepherds them,
and leads them to springs of waters of life.
And God will wipe away every tear from their eyes."

20:4 I saw thrones, and they sat on them, and judgment was given to them. I saw the souls of those who had been beheaded for the testimony of Jesus, and for the word of God, and such as didn't worship the beast nor his image, and didn't receive the mark on their forehead and on their hand. They lived, and reigned with Christ for a thousand years. **20:5** The rest of the dead didn't live until the thousand years were finished. This is the first resurrection. **20:6** Blessed and holy is he who has part in the first resurrection. Over these, the second death has no power, but they will be priests of God and of Christ, and will reign with him one thousand years.

The First Four Trumpets and the Four Attacks By Satan Against the Woman (Part 1)

The first four trumpets and the four attacks by Satan form a complex parallel and therefore to tell the story correctly we must follow the story of one and go backwards in the other. The story we will go forward in is the story of the four attacks by Satan because they are in chronological order and the first four trumpets are in reverse chronological order.

The Twelve Tribes Conceived in Heaven and Deceived by Satan (Rev 8:12; 12:1-6)

The depiction of the woman clothed with the sun, moon under her feet, and a crown of twelve stars is taken from Joseph's dream in which he saw Jacob (later named Israel) as the sun, Joseph's mother as the moon and his brothers as stars (Gen 37:9-11). John conflates Joseph's dream with the sign of the woman with child from Isaiah and places them both in heaven (Rev 12:4).

What John is saying here is that Satan deceived a third of Israel, represented by the sweeping of a third of the stars with his tail (Rev 12:4). The imagery of the tail is important to note because it comes from the EID where the tail signifies that those who deceive will lead the people into destruction (Isa 9:15-6; Rev 12:4 see "Z7 - The Zechariah Encoded Parallel: Satan's Entry into Revelation (Part 4)" on page 120).

When the first attack by Satan is compared to the fourth trumpet we get a complementary picture in which a third of Israel (the sun, moon, and stars) are struck and they never shine the same way again (Rev 8:12). This is a spiritual story of Israel illustrated with a cosmological backdrop in which he will retain this imagery in the remaining attacks by Satan and the first three trumpets.

The Fourth Trumpet (Rev 8:12-3)	Satan's First Attack (Rev 12:1-6)
• Third of the sun was struck (8:12). • The sun was darkened (8:12).	• Satan swept a third of the 12 stars (12:4). • The woman fled into the wilderness where she was nourished by God (12:6).

8:12 The fourth angel sounded, and one third of the sun was struck, and one third of the moon, and one third of the stars; so that one third of them would be darkened, and the day wouldn't shine for one third of it, and the night in the same way. **8:13** I saw, and I heard an eagle, flying in mid heaven, saying with a loud voice,

"Woe! Woe! Woe for those who dwell on the earth, because of the other voices of the trumpets of the three angels, who are yet to sound!"

12:1 A great sign was seen in heaven: a woman clothed with the sun, and the moon under her feet, and on her head a crown of twelve stars. **12:2** She was with child. She cried out in pain, labouring to give birth. **12:3** Another sign was seen in heaven. Behold, a great red dragon, having seven heads and ten horns, and on his heads seven crowns. **12:4** His tail drew one third of the stars of the sky, and threw them to the earth. The dragon stood before the woman who was about to give birth, so that when she gave birth he might devour her child. **12:5** She gave birth to a son, a male child, who is to rule all the nations with a rod of iron. Her child was caught up to God, and to his throne. **12:6** The woman fled into the wilderness, where she has a place prepared by God, that there they may nourish her one thousand two hundred sixty days.

The First Four Trumpets and the Four Attacks By Satan Against the Woman (Part 2)

The War in Heaven and the Falling Star (Rev 8:10-1; 12:7-9)

John tells the story of Satan's war in heaven two ways. The first is in terms of the actual war with Michael and his angels in heaven in which he is soundly defeated and thrown to earth. The second is told from a cosmological perspective in which a great star falls from the heavens and poisons the drinking water. As a result many are killed. The first story is concerned with what Satan does in heaven and the second with what Satan does on earth.

The war in heaven and the falling star parallel also tells us that John forms parallels by similar concepts as well as synonyms. Satan receives multiple names and one of them is the "deceiver of the whole world" and the fallen star is named "Wormwood" (a bitter tasting plant) making a third of the water bitter.

What we can derived from comparing the two stories is that Satan is the fallen star. The result of the falling star making the water bitter which kills a third of mankind is really Satan's deception upon the world. Like the first attack by Satan and the fourth trumpet the story is told from a cosmological perspective rather than in terms of a simple descriptive manner.

The Third Trumpet (Rev 8:10-1)	Satan's Second Attack (Rev 12:7-9)
• A great star fell on a third of the rivers, springs, and the waters (8:10). • The water became bitter and many people died (8:11).	• Satan lost a war in heaven and was thrown down to earth (Rev 12:9). • Satan becomes the deceiver of the world (Rev 12:9).
8:10 The third angel sounded, and a great star fell from the sky, burning like a torch, and it fell on one third of the rivers, and on the springs of the waters. **8:11** The name of the star is called "Wormwood." One third of the waters became wormwood. Many people died from the waters, because they were made bitter.	**12:7** There was war in the sky. Michael and his angels made war on the dragon. The dragon and his angels made war. **12:8** They didn't prevail, neither was a place found for him any more in heaven. **12:9** The great dragon was thrown down, the old serpent, he who is called the devil and Satan, the deceiver of the whole world. He was thrown down to the earth, and his angels were thrown down with him.

The Land Absorbs the Water and the Sea Absorbs the Mountain (Rev 8:8-9; 12:15-6)

John provides us with a story in which Satan tries to destroy the woman and her children by drowning them with water spewed from his mouth. The earth however, rescues the woman and her children by absorbing the water. The imagery that we see in the third attack by Satan is that Satan was not successful in destroying all of the woman's children.

The story found in the second trumpet is the complete opposite in that there is a great mountain that fell from the sky and absorbed by the sea. In this story, John tells us what happens to those who were not killed: that they were simply absorbed by all the nations in the form of being taken into slavery.

The Second Trumpet (Rev 8:8-9)	Satan's Third Attack (Rev 12:13-6)
• A great burning mountain thrown into the sea (8:8). • Third of the sea became blood (8:8). • Third of the sea life died (8:9).	• Satan spewed water from his mouth to destroy the woman (12:15). • He tried to sweep her away by the stream (12:16). • The earth opened its mouth and swallowed the water (12:16).
8:8 The second angel sounded, and something like a great burning mountain was thrown into the sea. One third of the sea became blood, **8:9** and one third of the living creatures which were in the sea died. One third of the ships were destroyed.	**12:13** When the dragon saw that he was thrown down to the earth, he persecuted the woman who gave birth to the male child. **12:14** Two wings of the great eagle were given to the woman, that she might fly into the wilderness to her place, so that she might be nourished for a time, and times, and half a time, from the face of the serpent. **12:15** The serpent spewed water out of his mouth after the woman like a river, that he might cause her to be carried away by the stream. **12:16** The earth helped the woman, and the earth opened its mouth and swallowed up the river which the dragon spewed out of his mouth.

The Release of Satan From the Abyss (Rev 9:1-12; 20:7)

Prior to forming an army from Gog and Magog, Satan needs to be released from the abyss. The fifth trumpet tells the story of Satan being released and how the believers will be protected from his release. John connects the two stories by mentioning a key, the opening of the abyss, and providing a synonym for Satan as the angel (messenger) who is the king of the abyss.

The Gathering of the Army of Satan (Rev 9:13-9; 20:8-10)

Both accounts have a massive army that gathers and prepares to attack. In the sixth trumpet the massive army is victorious, while in the story of Gog and Magog the army is defeated by God. The difference between the two suggests that John intended to have two stories: the first being a story of how the Jews failed, which led to Jerusalem's destruction, and the second being a story of how those who followed Jesus are successful. If that was true then John intended to have two 1,000 year imprisonments for Satan.

Those Who Keep on Sinning on Earth and Where They Go (Rev 9:20-2; Rev 20:11-5)

The last two parallels tell about the wicked being victorious and being defeated. The sixth trumpet ends depicting a world that continued in their sin. The story of the second resurrection tells of the fate of those who continued in sin by placing them in a state of eternal torment.

The Trumpets and the Bowls

A side-by-side comparison of the seven trumpets and the seven bowls is nothing new, but it only tells part of the story. The seven trumpets and the seven bowls are actually a part of a larger story that contains over a third of the book of Revelation (8 chapters out of 22). It is the story that contains the beginnings of the 144,000 (Rev 7:1-9) to the destruction of the harlot (Rev 17:1-18).

The Formation of the Trumpets and the Bowl

The trumpets and the bowls parallel began in the ZrD when John had to create imagery for the four horns without content unique to the source content found in the previous draft (EID) or from Zechariah. His solution was to take the Zechariah prototype of the first four horns and to copy the judgments, replacing the quantity of a "third," found in the trumpets to "all" found in the bowls.[98] The DJD expanded the number of judgments from four to seven and as a result John continued the process by copying the last three trumpets and making them the last three bowls. It was in the ExD that the trumpets and the bowls parallel, depicted in this section, was at its best.

John had no problem with the bowls being a copy of the trumpets because from the ZrD to the ExD, the woman and the harlot were two aspects of Jerusalem. The woman and her children represented those who still follow God and Jesus.[99] The harlot represented those who were responsible for the death of God's children. John just saw Satan destroying the righteous representing a third of Israel and God destroying those who destroyed the righteous, representing two-thirds or all that remained in Jerusalem.

---

98   See "Z8 - The Creation and Placement of the Four Horns/First Four Bowls (Zech 1:18-21; Rev 16:1-9)" on page 92.
99   Rev 12:17.

At the time of the ExD, the seals, trumpets, and bowls were all actions against the city of Jerusalem. The seals were actions by Jesus, the trumpets were actions by Satan, and the bowls were actions by God. John had Jesus and Satan team up together to destroy Jerusalem. John also had Satan defeat God's people in the trumpets, only to have God defeat Satan's kingdom in the bowls.

The DnD altered portions of the trumpets and the bowls parallel in a few areas but left the bulk of it untouched. The harlot passages representing Jerusalem were overwritten with passages from Daniel, the harlot was changed from Jerusalem to represent Rome by including the city of Tyre/Babylon narrative. Additionally, a few of the bowls were overwritten to include the beast narrative.

The alterations by the DnD suggests that John tried to maintain the trumpet and the bowls parallels while also creating additional parallels that contained the trumpets and the bowls. What we have in the PVR provides us with a solid foundation in ascertaining what John was trying to accomplish in the formation of the parallel and how we can leverage what we understand in this parallel to other portions of Revelation.

The 144,000 and the Great Multitude

The story of the seven trumpets and the seven bowls begins with two groups of faithful believers. The first group is the 144,000 comprised of twelve thousand from each of the twelve tribes of Israel.[100] The second group is the great multitude comprised of people from all over the world.[101] Both groups have many similarities and differences in which this section will cover.

The Similarities Between the 144,000 and the Great Multitude

Both groups follow Jesus through extremes. The 144,000 follow Jesus by not lying and not having sexual relationships with women, while the great multitude followed Jesus to their martyrdom.[102] They each have a section in which an unspecified group of elders are part of their worshiping scene before Jesus.[103] The likely cause for the numbers of the elders not being specified is that the twenty four elders represent the twelve tribes of Israel and the twelve apostles. John wanted the great multitude to reflect that they came from the twelve apostles and the 144,000 came from the twelve tribes of Israel.[104]

The144,000 and the great multitude each have a scene in heaven and a scene on earth. The 144,000 is depicted as the first on earth and the first in heaven.[105] The great multitude is defined as the last group in heaven and the last group on earth. We know that they are the last group in heaven because of their activity. In the fifth seal, the believers are martyrs under the altar of God pleading with Jesus to judge those who killed them.[106] Jesus gives the martyrs a white robe and tells them to rest until their numbers are complete.[107] When they are depicted again, the martyrs are wearing the white robes and they are actively engag-

---

100 Rev 7:1-8.
101 Rev 7:9.
102 Rev 7:9, 14; 14:1-5. Note: The 144,000, can be seen from two perspectives: in the two stories of Satan they are faithful from the time of the Jordan River crossing to the destruction of Jerusalem. In the story of the trumpets and the bowls they are those who are from the twelve tribes of Israel and follow Jesus wherever they go (Rev 14:4).
103 Rev 7:11, 13; 14:3.
104 Rev 7:1-17.
105 Rev 7:1-3 suggests that the 144,000 are prior to the calamities on earth. Rev 14:4 defines the 144,000 as the first fruits in heaven.
106 Rev 6:9-10.
107 Rev 6:11.

The First Four Trumpets and the Four Attacks By Satan Against the Woman (Part 3)

Satan Wars Against Those Who Keep God's Commandments and Jesus' Testimony (Rev 8:7; 12:17)

The last attack by Satan is that he wars against those who obey the commandments of God and hold to Jesus' testimony. It is constructed in the same fashion as the other four attacks by Satan, and the first four trumpets make a complex parallel in that the attacks by Satan tells the first part of the story and the trumpet tells the second part. In the fourth attack by Satan we are presented with the beginning of his campaign against those who follow the commandments of God and Jesus' testimony. The first trumpet tells the story in which Satan defeated those who obey the commandments of God and Jesus' testimony as being depicted as a third of the trees (the 144,000) and all the green grass (the great multitude) burned.

The First Trumpet (Rev 8:6-7)	The Fourth Attack by Satan (Rev 12:17)
• Hail and fire mixed with blood thrown to the earth (8:7).	• The dragon grew angry with the woman and went to war with her and her offspring.
• The green grass and a third of the trees burned (8:7; See 7:1-3; 9:4).	• Those that kept the commandments of God and follow Jesus.

8:6 The seven angels who had the seven trumpets prepared themselves to sound. **8:7** The first sounded, and there followed hail and fire, mixed with blood, and they were thrown to the earth. One third of the earth was burnt up, and one third of the trees were burnt up, and all green grass was burnt up.

12:17 The dragon grew angry with the woman, and went away to make war with the rest of her seed, who keep God's commandments and hold Jesus' testimony.

The Release of Satan From the Abyss (Rev 9:1-12; 20:7)

Prior to forming an army from Gog and Magog, Satan needs to be released from the abyss. The fifth trumpet tells the story of Satan being released and how the believers will be protected from him after his release. John connects the two stories by incorporating a key, the opening of the abyss, and providing a synonym for Satan as the angel who is the king of the abyss.

The Fifth Trumpet as the Opening of the Abyss (Rev 9:1-19)	Satan Released from the Abyss (Rev 20:7)
• The key to the abyss was given to the fallen star (9:1).	• Satan originally locked in the abyss (20:1-3).
• The fallen star opened the abyss with the key (9:2).	• After 1,000 years Satan will be freed (20:7).

9:1 The fifth angel sounded, and I saw a star from the sky which had fallen to the earth. The key to the pit of the abyss was given to him. **9:2** He opened the pit of the abyss, and smoke went up out of the pit, like the smoke from a burning furnace. The sun and the air were darkened because of the smoke from the pit. **9:3** Then out of the smoke came forth locusts on the earth, and power was given to them, as the scorpions of the earth have power. **9:4** They were told that they should not hurt the grass of the earth, neither any green thing, neither any tree, but only those people who don't have God's seal on their foreheads. **9:5** They were given power not to kill them, but to torment them for five months. Their torment was like the torment of a scorpion, when it strikes a person. **9:6** In those days people will seek death, and will in no way find it. They will desire to die, and death will flee from them. **9:7** The shapes of the locusts were like horses prepared for war. On their heads were something like golden crowns, and their faces were like people's faces. **9:8** They had hair like women's hair, and their teeth were like those of lions. **9:9** They had breastplates, like breastplates of iron. The sound of their wings was like the sound of chariots, or of many horses rushing to war. **9:10** They have tails like those of scorpions, and stings. In their tails they have power to harm men for five months. **9:11** They have over them as king the angel of the abyss. His name in Hebrew is "Abaddon," but in Greek, he has the name "Apollyon."

9:12 The first woe is past. Behold, there are still two woes coming after this.

20:7 And after the thousand years, Satan will be released from his prison.

Note the Context of Satan's Imprisonment:

20:1 I saw an angel coming down out of heaven, having the key of the abyss and a great chain in his hand. **20:2** He seized the dragon, the old serpent, which is the devil and Satan, who deceives the whole inhabited earth, and bound him for a thousand years, **20:3** and cast him into the abyss, and shut it, and sealed it over him, that he should deceive the nations no more, until the thousand years were finished. After this, he must be freed for a short time.

The Gathering of the Army of Satan (Rev 9:13-9; 20:8-10)

Both accounts have a massive army that gathers and prepares for attack. The massive army is victorious in the sixth trumpet, while the army is defeated by God in the story of Gog and Magog. The difference between the two suggests that John intended to have two stories, the first being how the Jews failed, which led to Jerusalem's destruction, and the second being how those who followed Jesus are successful. If that were true then John intended to have two 1,000 year imprisonments for Satan.

A Huge Army Is Assembled (Rev 19:13-9)	Satan Gathers a Huge Army (Rev 20:8-10)
• The four angels freed the four winds of the earth and the great Euphrates River (9:14-5; see 7:1-3). • The army numbered 200,000,000 (9:16). • Fire proceeded out of their mouths (9:17; from the abyss in 9:1-11).	• Satan deceived the nations from the four corners of the earth (20:8). • The army number is as the sand of the sea (20:8). • Fire came down from heaven by God (20:9).

9:13 The sixth angel sounded. I heard a voice from the horns of the golden altar which is before God, **9:14** saying to the sixth angel who had one trumpet,

"Free the four angels who are bound at the great river Euphrates!"

9:15 The four angels were freed who had been prepared for that hour and day and month and year, so that they might kill one third of mankind. **9:16** The number of the armies of the horsemen was two hundred million. I heard the number of them. **9:17** Thus I saw the horses in the vision, and those who sat on them, having breastplates of fiery red, hyacinth blue, and sulfur yellow; and the heads of lions. Out of their mouths proceed fire, smoke, and sulfur. **9:18** By these three plagues were one third of mankind killed: by the fire, the smoke, and the sulfur, which proceeded out of their mouths. **9:19** For the power of the horses is in their mouths, and in their tails. For their tails are like serpents, and have heads, and with them they harm.

20:8 and he will come out to deceive the nations which are in the four corners of the earth, Gog and Magog, to gather them together to the war; the number of whom is as the sand of the sea. **20:9** They went up over the breadth of the earth, and surrounded the camp of the saints, and the beloved city. Fire came down out of heaven from God, and devoured them. **20:10** The devil who deceived them was thrown into the lake of fire and sulfur, where the beast and the false prophet are also. They will be tormented day and night forever and ever.

Those Who Keep on Sinning on Earth and Where They Go (Rev 9:20-2; Rev 20:11-5)

The last two parallels tell about the wicked being victorious and being defeated. The sixth trumpet ends by depicting a world that continued in their sin revealed by their works. The story of the second resurrection tells of the fate of those who continued in sin by placing them in a state of eternal torment.

They Would Not Repent of Their Deeds (Rev 9:20-21)	The Great White Throne Judgment (Rev 20:8-10)
• The rest of mankind (9:20). • They did not repent of their evil deeds (9:20-1).	• Those who were raised in the first resurrection (20:12; see 20:6). • They were judged by their evil deeds (20:12-5).

9:20 The rest of mankind, who were not killed with these plagues, didn't repent of the works of their hands, that they wouldn't worship demons, and the idols of gold, and of silver, and of brass, and of stone, and of wood; which can neither see, nor hear, nor walk. **9:21** They didn't repent of their murders, nor of their sorceries, nor of their sexual immorality, nor of their thefts.

20:11 I saw a great white throne, and him who sat on it, from whose face the earth and the heaven fled away. There was found no place for them. **20:12** I saw the dead, the great and the small, standing before the throne, and they opened books. Another book was opened, which is the book of life. The dead were judged out of the things which were written in the books, according to their works. **20:13** The sea gave up the dead who were in it. Death and Hades gave up the dead who were in them. They were judged, each one according to his works. **20:14** Death and Hades were thrown into the lake of fire. This is the second death, the lake of fire. **20:15** If anyone was not found written in the book of life, he was cast into the lake of fire.

ing in servicing the temple in heaven, which suggests that their numbers are complete.[108] The placement of the great multitude in heaven is also prior to the seventh seal which contains the seven trumpets and is the means of judging those who martyred the saints.[109]

To complement the last of the great multitude in heaven and form an opposite to the first of the 144,000 on earth, John created the last of the great multitude on earth and placed it after the 144,000 in heaven.[110] How we know this is by comparing the parallels and following the symbols. When we lay the two passages that relate to the 144,000 side by side, we can see the whole life cycle of the 144,000 from the first days on earth to the last days in heaven.[111] It is only when we take the two sections after the 144,000 narratives and compare them to each other that we see the last of the great multitude in heaven and the last of the great multitude on earth.[112] They both begin with the same place "every nation, tribe, language, and people"[113] with the saints in heaven coming from there and as a result the gospel was spread to them. In the last of the great multitude section on earth we have the complement to the fifth seal, where because they are now dead they can rest from their service on earth.[114]

In two passages that form the great multitude, we have a temple scene in heaven. The first passage has the great multitude in heaven temple where the great multitude serves God and the Lamb.[115] The second passage has the temple in heaven where a command is issued that begins the great harvest on earth.[116] The result of the great harvest on earth is a river of blood stretching 156 miles (251.2 km) at 5.5 feet (1.68 m) which is used to produce blood for the wine of God's wrath.[117] The imagery of blood and wine is also found with the harlot getting drunk of the blood of the saints.[118] Therefore we can conclude that the great harvest as well as the river of blood is actually the same thing. The harlot kills the saints and gets drunk from their blood, and when the last of the saints on earth are martyred, the blood turns into the cup of God's wrath against the harlot.

The Differences Between the 144,000 and the Great Multitude

There are differences between the 144,000 and the great multitude other than the obvious ones already mentioned. The 144,000 have the seal of God on their foreheads[119] and there is no mention of the great multitude having a seal on their foreheads. Likewise, the great multitude are given the white robes[120] with no mention of the 144,000 wearing white robes. The 144,000 has the seal of God on their forehead as a result of the DJD conflating passages regarding the destruction of Jerusalem from Ezekiel and the first circumcision after crossing the Jordan in Joshua.[121] Those who had the seal of God on their forehead were

---

108 Rev 7:9-17.

109 Rev 8:1-6.

110 Rev 14:6-20.

111 Rev 7:1-8; 14:1-5; see "The Beginning of the 144,000 on Earth and the Last of the 144,00 in Heaven" on page 309.

112 Rev 7:9-17; 14:6-20; see "The Last of the Great Multitude in Heaven and the Last of the Great Multitude on Earth" on page 310.

113 Rev 7:9; 14:6.

114 Rev 6:9-11; 14:13.

115 Rev 7:9-17; see Rev 7:15.

116 Rev 14:14-20.

117 Rev 14:19.

118 Rev 17:6.

119 Rev 7:1-3; 9:4.

120 Rev 3:4-5, 18; 6:11; 7:9, 13-4; 19:8, 14.

121 See "DJ7 - The Sealing of God's People and the Passover (Rev 7:1-17)" on page 174.

The Structure and Content of the Seven Trumpets and the Seven Bowls

The chart below shows the context in which the seven trumpets and the seven bowls were placed, as well as the content shared between the two sets of judgments. It should be noted that it reflects the published version and not the ExD's version, but it still illustrates that the bowls were copied from the trumpets.

The Context

The Seven Trumpets	The Seven Bowls
The 144,000 on Earth (7:1-8)	**The 144,000 in Heaven (14:1-5)**
The Great Multitude in Heaven (7:9-17)	**The Great Multitude on Earth (14:6-20)**
The Burning of the Incense in Heaven (8:1-5)	**The Burning of the Incense in Heaven (15:1-8)**
The Seven Trumpets (8:7- 9:21; 11:13-9) · For each of the trumpets, when an angel blows the trumpet, it affects the same part of the physical universe that the bowl affects, except it generally affects only a third.	**The Seven Bowls (16:1-20)** · The bowls are poured on what the trumpets affect. The difference is that the trumpets affect a third and the bowls affect all.
The Woman, Child and Satan (12:1-17)	**The Harlot and the Beast (17:1-18)**

The Seven Trumpets (Actions by Satan)	The Seven Bowls (Actions by God)
The First Trumpet (8:7) · Fire and hail mixed with blood was thrown to earth. · A third of the earth and trees were burned up and all the grass was burned up as well.	**The First Bowl (16:2)** · Poured on the earth · Painful sores to those who followed the beast
The Second Trumpet (8:8-9) · A great mountain was thrown into the sea. · A third of the sea became blood, a third of the sea creatures died, and a third of the ships were destroyed.	**The Second Bowl (16:3)** · Poured into the sea · Everything in the sea died.
The Third Trumpet (8:10-11) · A great star fell on a third of the rivers and springs of waters. · A third of the waters became bitter and many died.	**The Third Bowl (16:4-7)** · Poured into the rivers and springs of waters. · Rivers and streams turned to blood because they killed the saints.
The Fourth Trumpet (8:12) · A third of the sun, moon, and stars were struck. · The sun, moon, and stars were darkened by a third.	**The Fourth Bowl (16:8-9)** · Poured on the sun · They were scorched and they refused to give God glory.
The Fifth Trumpet (9:1-12) · The angel opened the pit to the Abyss. · The sun was darkened and those without the seal of God on their forehead suffered great pain.	**The Fifth Bowl (16:10-1)** · Poured on the throne of the Beast. · His kingdom was darkened and his people in great pain
The Sixth Trumpet (9:13-21) · Freed the four angels who bound to the Euphrates. · An army of 200 million killed a third of mankind.	**The Sixth Bowl (16:12-6)** · Poured on the great river Euphrates. · The river dried up and a great army from the whole world gathered for the Great Day of God.
The Seventh Trumpet (11:15-19) · Great voices in heaven · The temple was opened in heaven. · Lightning, sounds and thunder with an earthquake.	**The Seventh Bowl (16:17-20)** · Poured into the air · A loud voice came from the temple. · Lightning, sounds, and thunder with a great earthquake

The 144,000 and the Great Multitude Depicted in Revelation

The illustration below depicts the flow from the 144,000 as the faithful crossing the Jordan River (Rev 7:1-8) to the death of the two prophets (Jesus) and their uniting as a group in heaven (Rev 14:1-5). The great multitude is depicted as beginning with the conception of Jesus (Rev 12:1), progressing to the last believer on earth (Rev 14:6-20), and ending with a scene similar to the 144,000 in heaven (Rev 7:9-11; 14:1-5). Both sets of stories reflect each group's origin and their finality both on earth and in heaven with Jesus as the intersection between the two groups as the last of the prophets and the firstborn of the great multitude.

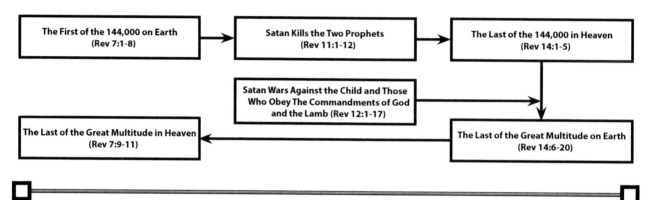

those who were spared from the destruction of Jerusalem.[122] The reason why those who are part of the great multitude wear a robe is that they represent the new priesthood that God is establishing.[123]

Each group has a different style of worship when they are in heaven. The 144,000 sing to God and the Lamb with a song that no one knows.[124] The great multitude join a session to praise God and the Lamb.[125] Both groups are performing before the throne of God and the Lamb, which is depicted in an earthly setting that can be applied to Jerusalem.[126]

John's Placement of the 144,000 and the Great Multitude

The placement of the two 144,000 and great multitude sections is an example of John writing in a circle. The narrative progresses from the first of the 144,000 on earth, to the last of the 144,000 in heaven, to the last of the great multitude on earth, and finally ends with the last of the great multitude found in heaven.[127] At the center of the story are two depictions of Jesus: he is the two prophets who were killed by the beast, and he is the child who was taken to heaven.[128] The two prophets and the child are also depicted similarly to how the 144,000 and the great multitude on earth are. The sealing of the 144,000 on earth and the child are both in their infancy, and the two prophets and the great multitude on earth both depict their final days. This is John's way of telling his readers that Jesus is the transitional figure between both groups.

---

122 Ezek 9:4; Rev 9:4.

123 Rev 1:4-5; see "The Believers Became the Kingdom of Priests to God" on page 193.

124 Rev 14:3.

125 Rev 7:10-2.

126 The 144,000 are before the Lamb on Mount Zion (Rev 14:1) which is another name for Jerusalem. The great multitude is servicing the temple (Rev 7:14-5).

127 Rev 7:1-8; 14:1-20; 7:9-17; see "The 144,000 and the Great Multitude Depicted in Revelation" on page 308.

128 Rev 11:7-8; 12:4-5.

The Beginning of the 144,000 on Earth and the Last of the 144,00 in Heaven

The two sections below show the first of the 144,000 being sealed on earth and the last of the 144,000 in heaven with Jesus. They represent the faithful believers out of the twelve tribes of Israel that crossed the Jordan (see "The Crossing of the Jordan River" on page 140 and "The Circumcision of Those Born in the Wilderness" on page 142) to the death of Jesus.

The First of the 144,000 on Earth (Rev 7:1-8)

7:1 After this, I saw four angels standing at the four corners of the earth, holding the four winds of the earth, so that no wind would blow on the earth, or on the sea, or on any tree. **7:2** I saw another angel ascend from the sunrise, having the seal of the living God. He cried with a loud voice to the four angels to whom it was given to harm the earth and the sea, **7:3** saying, "Don't harm the earth, neither the sea, nor the trees, until we have sealed the bondservants of our God on their foreheads!" **7:4** I heard the number of those who were sealed, one hundred forty-four thousand, sealed out of every tribe of the children of Israel:

7:5 of the tribe of Judah were sealed twelve thousand, of the tribe of Reuben twelve thousand,

of the tribe of Gad twelve thousand,

7:6 of the tribe of Asher twelve thousand, of the tribe of Naphtali twelve thousand, of the tribe of Manasseh twelve thousand,

7:7 of the tribe of Simeon twelve thousand, of the tribe of Levi twelve thousand, of the tribe of Issachar twelve thousand,

7:8 of the tribe of Zebulun twelve thousand, of the tribe of Joseph twelve thousand, of the tribe of Benjamin were sealed twelve thousand.

The Last of the 144,000 in Heaven (Rev 14:1-5)

14:1 I saw, and behold, the Lamb standing on Mount Zion, and with him a number, one hundred forty-four thousand, having his name, and the name of his Father, written on their foreheads. **14:2** I heard a sound from heaven, like the sound of many waters, and like the sound of a great thunder. The sound which I heard was like that of harpists playing on their harps. **14:3** They sing a new song before the throne, and before the four living creatures and the elders. No one could learn the song except the one hundred forty-four thousand, those who had been redeemed out of the earth. **14:4** These are those who were not defiled with women, for they are virgins. These are those who follow the Lamb wherever he goes. These were redeemed by Jesus from among men, the first fruits to God and to the Lamb. **14:5** In their mouth was found no lie, for they are blameless.

The Burning of the Incense

Each of the great multitude scenes ends with the same result, whether it be the last to arrive in heaven or the last of the faithful to be killed on earth. The number requirement has been met and the great multitude can now be avenged.[129] John uses the imagery at the altar of incense to launch the judgments against those who inflicted death on the faithful. Prior to the seven seals, we have the death of Jesus, the preparation of the incense, and a worship scene.[130] For the seven trumpets and the seven bowls we have the martyrdom of everyone in the great multitude, the burning of the incense, and a temple ceremony scene. For each of the temple scenes, the incense is the blood of the martyrs that begins with Jesus and ends with the last of the great multitude.[131]

---

129 Rev 6:9-11.
130 Rev 5:8-14.
131 See "The Altar of Incense" on page 205.

The Last of the Great Multitude in Heaven and the Last of the Great Multitude on Earth

John provides two sections that deal with the great multitude: the first is when they are all in heaven and the second depicts the aftermath of when the great multitude was removed from the earth (Rev 14:6-20). It is only when these two passages are compared side by side that the parallels become apparent to the reader.

The Last of the Great Multitude in Heaven (Rev 7:9-17)	The Last of the Great Multitude on Earth (14:6-20)
• They come from every nation, tribe, and language (7:9).	• The Gospel is preached to every nation, tribe, and language (14:6).
• They worshiped God and the Lamb (7:9-12).	• The people failed to worship God (14:7).
• Martyred for God and serve him without rest (7:13-5).	• The people served the beast and will not rest in the second death (14:9-12).
• Water of life (7:16-7).	• River of death (14:7-20).

7:9 After these things I looked, and behold, a great multitude, which no man could count, out of every nation and of all tribes, peoples, and languages, standing before the throne and before the Lamb, dressed in white robes, with palm branches in their hands. **7:10** They cried with a loud voice, saying, "Salvation be to our God, who sits on the throne, and to the Lamb!"

7:11 All the angels were standing around the throne, the elders, and the four living creatures; and they fell on their faces before his throne, and worshipped God, **7:12** saying, "Amen! Blessing, glory, wisdom, thanksgiving, honor, power, and might, be to our God forever and ever! Amen."

7:13 One of the elders answered, saying to me, "These who are arrayed in the white robes, who are they, and from where did they come?"

7:14 I told him, "My lord, you know."

He said to me, "These are those who came out of the great tribulation. They washed their robes, and made them white in the Lamb's blood. **7:15** Therefore they are before the throne of God, they serve him day and night in his temple. He who sits on the throne will spread his tabernacle over them. **7:16** They will never be hungry, neither thirsty any more; neither will the sun beat on them, nor any heat; **7:17** for the Lamb who is in the middle of the throne shepherds them, and leads them to springs of waters of life. And God will wipe away every tear from their eyes."

14:6 I saw an angel flying in mid heaven, having an eternal Good News to proclaim to those who dwell on the earth, and to every nation, tribe, language, and people. **14:7** He said with a loud voice, "Fear the Lord, and give him glory; for the hour of his judgment has come. Worship him who made the heaven, the earth, the sea, and the springs of waters!"

14:8 Another, a second angel, followed, saying, "Babylon the great has fallen, which has made all the nations to drink of the wine of the wrath of her sexual immorality."

14:9 Another angel, a third, followed them, saying with a great voice, "If anyone worships the beast and his image, and receives a mark on his forehead, or on his hand, **14:10** he also will drink of the wine of the wrath of God, which is prepared unmixed in the cup of his anger. He will be tormented with fire and sulphur in the presence of the holy angels, and in the presence of the Lamb. **14:11** The smoke of their torment goes up forever and ever. They have no rest day and night, those who worship the beast and his image, and whoever receives the mark of his name. **14:12** Here is the perseverance of the saints, those who keep the commandments of God, and the faith of Jesus."

14:13 I heard a voice from heaven saying, "Write, 'Blessed are the dead who die in the Lord from now on.'"

"Yes," says the Spirit, "that they may rest from their labours; for their works follow with them."

14:14 I looked, and behold, a white cloud; and on the cloud one sitting like a son of man, having on his head a golden crown, and in his hand a sharp sickle. **14:15** Another angel came out of the temple, crying with a loud voice to him who sat on the cloud, "Send your sickle, and reap; for the hour to reap has come; for the harvest of the earth is ripe!" **14:16** He who sat on the cloud thrust his sickle on the earth, and the earth was reaped.

14:17 Another angel came out of the temple which is in heaven. He also had a sharp sickle. **14:18** Another angel came out from the altar, he who has power over fire, and he called with a great voice to him who had the sharp sickle, saying, "Send your sharp sickle, and gather the clusters of the vine of the earth, for the earth's grapes are fully ripe!" **14:19** The angel thrust his sickle into the earth, and gathered the vintage of the earth, and threw it into the great wine press of the wrath of God. **14:20** The wine press was trodden outside of the city, and blood came out of the wine press, even to the bridles of the horses, as far as one thousand six hundred stadia.

Understanding the Trumpets and the Bowls

When discussing the seven trumpets and the seven bowls, there are similarities between each of them such as what they affect. There are also similarities between the two that are connected to the seven seals. We have already shown how each of the three judgments have a death, the creation of the incense, and a temple scene prior to the judgments. Like many symbols in Revelation there are more than one aspect to them.

How the Seals, Trumpets, and the Bowls Are Connected to Each Other

There are many aspects amongst the three sets of judgments that should be explored before we go into the simple parallel formed between the seven trumpets and the seven bowls. One such aspect is the principle actor in each of the sets of judgments. The principle actor for the seven seals is Jesus, as seen in his ability to open every seal. The first six trumpets are actions by Satan, as we can see in the two stories of Satan.[132] Since the trumpets are wrapped up in the seventh seal, we can also view the seven trumpets as a team effort between Jesus and Satan to destroy Jerusalem. The seven bowls are actions performed by God as a response to Satan defeating the saints. Just as Jesus and Satan teamed up to destroy Jerusalem, God will team up with the beast to destroy the harlot.[133]

Each of the judgments are connected to the scroll's description from Ezekiel, "there were written therein lamentations, and mourning, and woe." Where the seals represent mourning, the trumpets represent woe, and the bowls represent lamentations. The seven churches and the seven seals form a simple parallel and a simple parallel with an offset centered on the way the parishioners are killed and the way those who killed them are judge.[134] The seven trumpets are divided into three groups separated by a woe, and the end result is the harlot's destruction, along with the lamentations by those who profited from her.[135]

Each set of judgments can be divided into three parts: the fifth seal, fifth trumpet, and fifth bowl, which defines the trigger mechanism that will launch the judgment. The sixth seal, sixth trumpet, and sixth bowl describe various phases of the army and their actions. The first four seals, first four trumpets, and first four bowls provide the details to the army in their respective sixth judgment. The seventh seal, seventh trumpet, and seventh bowl represent the victory of God, with the intensity increasing when read in the vertical.[136]

The last three seals, trumpets, and bowls tell a much broader story that connects the last three churches and chapters 19 and 20 of Revelation. It is the story that contains the path of the righteous and the path of the unrighteous. Their stories are told in the fifth church, sixth church, and seventh church sections in this chapter.

---

132 See "Satan's Story" on page 294.
133 See "Satan and Jesus as Allies and the Origin of the 200 Million Horsemen" on page 225 and "God and the Beast as Allies" on page 227.
134 See "How the Churches and the Seals Interact With Each Other (Part 1)" on page 272 and "How the Churches and the Seals Interact With Each Other (Part 2)" on page 273.
135 See "How John Connected the Scroll to the Judgments in Revelation" on page 274.
136 Rev 11:

Two Temple Ceremonies

John formed two temple ceremonies connected with the death of the believers and the burning of the incense. He did this by creating a complex parallel between the two. This is illustrated in how the verse numbers of the parallel elements (shown below) go in reverse order.

The Burning of the Incense (Rev 8:1-6)	**The Cleansing of the Tabernacle (Rev 15:1 - 16:1)**
• Temple silent for about a half an hour (8:1).	• A loud voice from the temple (16:1).
• Seven angels before God with the trumpets (8:2).	• Seven angels before God with plagues (15:8).
• An angel with a golden censure (8:3).	• One of the four living creatures with a censure (15:7).
• The censure contained incense and the prayers of the saints (8:3-4).	• The censure contained the wrath of God (15:7).
• The prayers of the saints (8:4).	• The song of Moses and the Lamb (15:3-4).
• An angel filled the censure from the fire at the altar of God (8:5).	• Heaven is filled by all those who overcame the beast (15:2).
• Seven angels prepared to sound (8:6).	• Seven angels with the last plagues (15:1).

8:1 When he opened the seventh seal, there was silence in heaven for about half an hour. **8:2** I saw the seven angels who stand before God, and seven trumpets were given to them. **8:3** Another angel came and stood over the altar, having a golden censer. Much incense was given to him, that he should add it to the prayers of all the saints on the golden altar which was before the throne. **8:4** The smoke of the incense, with the prayers of the saints, went up before God out of the angel's hand. **8:5** The angel took the censer, and he filled it with the fire of the altar, and threw it on the earth. There followed thunders, sounds, lightnings, and an earthquake.

8:6 The seven angels who had the seven trumpets prepared themselves to sound.

15:1 I saw another great and marvellous sign in the sky: seven angels having the seven last plagues, for in them God's wrath is finished. **15:2** I saw something like a sea of glass mixed with fire, and those who overcame the beast, his image, and the number of his name, standing on the sea of glass, having harps of God. **15:3** They sang the song of Moses, the servant of God, and the song of the Lamb, saying,

"Great and marvellous are your works, Lord God, the Almighty!

Righteous and true are your ways, you King of the nations.

15:4 Who wouldn't fear you, Lord, and glorify your name?

For you only are holy.

For all the nations will come and worship before you.

For your righteous acts have been revealed."

15:5 After these things I looked, and the temple of the tabernacle of the testimony in heaven was opened. **15:6** The seven angels who had the seven plagues came out, clothed with pure, bright linen, and wearing golden sashes around their breasts.

15:7 One of the four living creatures gave to the seven angels seven golden bowls full of the wrath of God, who lives forever and ever. **15:8** The temple was filled with smoke from the glory of God, and from his power. No one was able to enter into the temple, until the seven plagues of the seven angels would be finished.

16:1 I heard a loud voice out of the temple, saying to the seven angels, "Go and pour out the seven bowls of the wrath of God on the earth!"

The Unique Similarities and Differences Between the Trumpets and the Bowls

John creates the seven bowls, making a simple parallel with the seven trumpets and changing what it affects from a third in the trumpets to all in the bowls.[137] He also made it so that whatever the trumpets affected, the corresponding bowl would be dumped onto.

The trumpets represent the destruction of Jerusalem and the destruction of the faithful from the 144,000 and the great multitude. In the trumpets, the faithful can still be seen as alive and they are associated with the green grass and the trees.[138] The trees represent the 144,000 and the green grass represent the great multitude.[139] When it comes to understanding the trumpets, we need to understand that the story is told both forwards and backwards. Told forwards it is the story of Jesus taking on the role of Joshua in the conquest of Jericho.[140] When read backwards it the story of Joshua sending the two spies into Jericho, to the crossing of the Jordan, the first circumcision, and the first passover meal in the promised land.[141]

The bowls represent the destruction of the harlot after the faithful have been removed from earth. The end result will be the complete destruction of the harlot by God and the beast. In John's way of writing, the third of the earth that is destroyed are the believers and the two-thirds remaining are the "all."

The First Four Trumpets and the First Four Bowls

The best way to describe the first four trumpets and the first four bowls is to include the four attacks by Satan within the parallel. Once we include Satan into the parallel, each story is the same, only told in a different way. In the four attacks by Satan, he launches an attack against the righteous people of Jerusalem (the woman, child, and those who obey God) and fails each time. In the trumpets, Satan is successful and as a result the bowls come into play. The bowls represent God's actions against the harlot because of the slaying of all believers and therefore it affects all.

The parallels will be displayed with the attack by Satan and its complex parallel element in the trumpet and the trumpet's simple parallel element. The first parallel contains the fourth attack by Satan, it is told first and then the first trumpet, and finally the first bowl and the last parallel contains the first attack by Satan, the fourth trumpet and the fourth bowl. The direction of each of the stories is similar to the circle that John forms when he is telling the story of the 144,000 and the great multitude, as discussed earlier in the trumpets and the bowls, only in this case he begins the story on the other side of the circle.

Since each of the parallel charts have sufficient detail describing the parallel as well as the meaning, the narrative portion will defer to the charts. These parallels are small and easy to follow and as a result the explanation can be seen with the parallel itself.

The Fifth, Sixth, and Seventh Trumpet and Bowl Combinations

We have already explained how John wove the fifth, sixth, and seventh trumpets and bowls within the fifth, sixth, and seventh church sections in this chapter. Therefore covering the trumpet and the bowl com-

---

137 See "The Structure and Content of the Seven Trumpets and the Seven Bowls" on page 307.

138 Rev 7:1-3;7:8; 9:4; see "IP4 - The Judgments by Jesus - Part 2" on page 49.

139 The trees represent the one third of Israel that obeyed the commandments of God (Rev 8:8

140 See "The Deuteronomy-Joshua Draft (DJD) Simplified (Part 2)" on page 133.

141 See "The Deuteronomy-Joshua Draft (DJD) Simplified (Part 1)" on page 132.

Satan's Fourth Attack, the First Trumpet, and the First Bowl (Rev 12:17; 8:7; 16:1)

The first four trumpets and the first four bowls form a simple parallel in both the judgments and the details between the respective trumpet and bowl. The tables below show the details of how John formed a simple parallel with at least two elements in each set of judgments.

Satan's Fourth Attack (Rev 12:17)	The First Trumpet (Rev 8:7)	The First Bowl (Rev 16:1)
• The dragon grew angry with the woman and went to war with her and her offspring. • Those that kept the commandments of God and follow Jesus.	• Hail and fire mixed with blood thrown to the earth (8:7). • The green grass and a third of the trees burned (8:7; See 7:1-3; 9:4).	• The first bowl poured on the earth (16:1). • The wicked hit with an evil sore (16:1; See 9:4).
12:17 The dragon grew angry with the woman, and went away to make war with the rest of her offspring, who keep God's commandments and hold Jesus' testimony.	*8:7* The first sounded, and there followed hail and fire, mixed with blood, and they were thrown to the earth. One third of the earth was burned up, and one third of the trees were burned up, and all green grass was burned up.	*16:1* The first went, and poured out his bowl into the earth, and it became a harmful and evil sore on the people who had the mark of the beast, and who worshipped his image

binations again would be redundant, and additionally would not reflect the true scale and scope of these parallels.

The Woman and the Harlot

The woman and the harlot in the ExD are two stories about the city of Jerusalem. The woman and her children reflect the righteous elements and the harlot and her associates reflect the wicked elements. The ExD version of the woman and the harlot also includes Satan as their chief adversary, which makes the parallel easier to construct. However, the DnD overwrote much of the content found in the original harlot passage[142] with a beast narrative from Daniel, and made the harlot represent Rome with a few tweaks that combined the harlot with the city of Tyre.[143] The result of the DnD have many common items found in the woman and the harlot narratives but without an organized parallel structure that links all of them. This would suggest that the previous material had similar content but in the same order as the woman narrative.[144]

The Alpha and Omega Parallel

The alpha and omega parallel is the perfect example of how Revelation is not a finished product and how parallels can become malformed. In the following two pages all three texts that form the alpha and omega parallel and the second coming of Jesus are aligned to show their common content. Of the four sections only the prologue has its verses shifted around to accommodate the order of the other three sections. The end result is that all four sections have content derived from at least another section, and when seen to-

---

142 See "The Creation of the Beast and the False Prophet -- Part 2" on page 215.

143 See "The Merging of the Harlot and Tyre to Become Rome" on page 227.

144 For an example of parallel formation between the woman and the harlot see "Z5 - The Two Aspects of the Same Woman in the Zechariah Draft" on page 79 and "Z5 - The Two Women Flown Into the Wilderness and the Shifting of a Wax Tablet" on page 81.

Satan's Third Attack, the Second Trumpet, and the Second Bowl (Rev 12:15-6; 8:8-9; 16:2)

In this parallel, Satan is trying to destroy the righteous with water, but the land prevents this and aids the woman by absorbing the water. The storyline continues in the second trumpet, where the sea absorbs a giant mountain, and as a result a third of the sea turns to blood (Rev 8:-9). In the second bowl the entire sea turns to blood.

Something to note in this parallel is the orphan element within the second trumpet ("third of the ships"). How and why it became an orphan is the key to connecting the symbols in a meaningful way.

Satan's Third Attack (12:15-6)	The Second Trumpet (Rev 8:8-9)	The Second Bowl (Rev 16:2)
• Satan spewed water from his mouth to destroy the woman (12:15).	• A great burning mountain thrown into the sea (8:8).	• The second poured into the sea (16:2).
• He tried to sweep her away by the stream (12:16).	• Third of the sea became blood (8:8).	• All of the sea became blood (16:2).
• The earth opened its mouth and swallowed the water (12:16).	• Third of the sea life died (8:9).	• Everything in the sea died (16:2).
	• ~~Third of the ships were destroyed (8:9).~~	

12:15 The serpent spewed water out of his mouth after the woman like a river, that he might cause her to be carried away by the stream. *12:16* The earth helped the woman, and the earth opened its mouth and swallowed up the river which the dragon spewed out of his mouth.

8:8 The second angel sounded, and something like a great burning mountain was thrown into the sea. One third of the sea became blood, *8:9* and one third of the living creatures which were in the sea died. One third of the ships were destroyed.

16:2 The second angel poured out his bowl into the sea, and it became blood as of a dead man. Every living thing in the sea died.

Satan's Second Attack, the Third Trumpet, and the Third Bowl (Rev 12:7-9; 8:10-1; 16:4-7)

This parallel depicts Satan defeated in heaven and tossed down to earth where he sets out to deceive the world. In the third trumpet John continues the story by depicting Satan as a great star that fell from the earth, and equates deceiving the people with poisoning the drinking water (see Rev 17:). As a result of the saints killed through Satan's deception, John in the third bowl turns the drinking water into blood (Rev 16:6).

Something to note in this parallel is that John gives names to the multiple variations of Satan and God as well as the falling star. This is an example of how attentive John is in constructing these parallels.

Satan's Second Attack (Rev 12:7-9)	The Third Trumpet (Rev 8:10-1)	The Third Bowl (Rev 16:4-7)
• Satan lost a war in heaven and was thrown down to earth (Rev 12:9).	• A great star fell on a third of the rivers, springs, and the waters (8:10).	• A bowl was poured on the rivers, springs, and water (16:4).
• Satan becomes the deceiver of the world (Rev 12:9).	• The water became bitter and many people died (8:11).	• The judgment is in response to the slaying of the saints (16:6-7).

12:7 There was war in the sky. Michael and his angels made war on the dragon. The dragon and his angels made war. *12:8* They didn't prevail, neither was a place found for him any more in heaven. *12:9* The great dragon was thrown down, the old serpent, he who is called the devil and Satan, the deceiver of the whole world. He was thrown down to the earth, and his angels were thrown down with him.

8:10 The third angel sounded, and a great star fell from the sky, burning like a torch, and it fell on one third of the rivers, and on the springs of the waters. *8:11* The name of the star is called "Wormwood." One third of the waters became wormwood. Many people died from the waters, because they were made bitter.

16:4 The third poured out his bowl into the rivers and springs of water, and they became blood. *16:5* I heard the angel of the waters saying, "You are righteous, who are and who were, you Holy One, because you have judged these things. *16:6* For they poured out the blood of the saints and prophets, and you have given them blood to drink. They deserve this." *16:7* I heard the altar saying, "Yes, Lord God, the Almighty, true and righteous are your judgments."

Satan's First Attack, the Fourth Trumpet, and the Fourth Bowl (Rev 12:1-6; 8:12; 16:8-9)

In this story, John is portraying Israel as a kingdom that came from heaven, deceived by the dragon (Satan), and ultimately blaspheming God. The twelve tribes of Israel is depicted as stars from Joseph's dream in Genesis 37:9. The imagery of the tail comes from Isaiah where the false teachers are called the tail (Isa 9:15-6).

Satan's First Attack (Rev 12:1-6)	The Fourth Trumpet (Rev 8:12)	The Fourth Bowl (Rev 16:8-9)
• Satan swept a third of the twelve stars (12:4). • The woman fled into the wilderness where she was nourished by God (12:6).	• Third of the sun was struck (8:12). • The sun was darkened (8:12).	• The fourth bowl poured on the sun (16:8). • The people were scorched with great heat by the sun (16:9).

12:1 A great sign was seen in heaven: a woman clothed with the sun, and the moon under her feet, and on her head a crown of twelve stars. **12:2** She was with child. She cried out in pain, laboring to give birth. **12:3** Another sign was seen in heaven. Behold, a great red dragon, having seven heads and ten horns, and on his heads seven crowns. **12:4** His tail drew one third of the stars of the sky, and threw them to the earth. The dragon stood before the woman who was about to give birth, so that when she gave birth he might devour her child. **12:5** She gave birth to a son, a male child, who is to rule all the nations with a rod of iron. Her child was caught up to God, and to his throne. **12:6** The woman fled into the wilderness, where she has a place prepared by God, that there they may nourish her one thousand two hundred sixty days.

8:12 The fourth angel sounded, and one third of the sun was struck, and one third of the moon, and one third of the stars; so that one third of them would be darkened, and the day wouldn't shine for one third of it, and the night in the same way.

16:8 The fourth poured out his bowl on the sun, and it was given to him to scorch men with fire. **16:9** People were scorched with great heat, and people blasphemed the name of God who has the power over these plagues. They didn't repent and give him glory.

gether one can easily see the various combinations that resulted from John aligning the wax tablets to form parallels.

At one time all three of the alpha and omega parallels were in a perfect or near perfect state and then various changes caused one parallel to become malformed. For example, it is obvious that John aligned the second coming narrative with the epilogue for the creation of the two times that John worshiped the angel.[145] By making the epilogue conform to the first angel John worshiped, John had to make the words spoken by God into the angel's words. John does this by having the words spoken and then telling the audience that the words are being spoken by an angel. The problem for John is the awkwardness of the epilogue flow because if the reader reads the passage devoid of a theological bias they would assign the phrase "I am the alpha and omega" as spoken by the angel and not by God or Jesus.[146] How John aligned the second coming narrative and the epilogue suggests that John intended Jesus as the speaker but he never gave it the attention that it required.[147] There is evidence that John was going to change the New Jerusalem alpha and omega narrative in the sentence "Write, for these words of God are faithful and true," which has

145 Rev 19:9-10; 22:7-9. See the next two pages for a how the alpha and omega parallels are arranged with the second coming narrative.
146 Rev 22:6-14.
147 Rev 19:11-6.

God speaking in the third person.[148] It is likely that John made that simple modification and then realized that the amount of work was too much or he just got distracted and thus never revised the New Jerusalem narrative.

The alpha and omega parallel for John was problematic, for us it is an aid to reconstruct the logical order of construction after the alpha and omega parallel was formed. With each change to the parallel there was a cause, and by identifying the cause we can assess when it was applied to the alpha and omega parallel. By identifying all of the causes we can then predict the order of construction and verify the prediction by duplicating the process. Once a process has produced results similar to the PVR it can be validated, like what John did, and can give us not just the words of each draft but the ability to relive the writing of the alpha and omega parallel passages.

Final Thoughts

In the draft chapters we saw how John used parallel formation to produce the bulk of his work from Hebrew Scripture sources. In this chapter we saw a significant number of parallels that John constructed for his readers. The combination of the two produce a work that is inherently familiar to the scriptures and intellectually stimulating to all readers. Revelation is such a work that each time it is read or heard new insights can be discovered.

The parallels shown in this chapter are more of a sampling of the major parallels to be found in Revelation. They were chosen for a variety of reasons: first to show a finishing phase that was not shown in the draft chapters; and second, to demonstrate a different way of reading Revelation by providing a rich diversity of parallels.

---

148 Rev 21:5.

The Woman and the Harlot (Part 1)

The parallel between the woman and the harlot was originally formed in the ZrD (see "Z5 - Two Women in the Basket (Zech 5:5-11; Rev 12:1-17; 17:1-18)" on page 78) and expanded in the ExD (see). Unfortunately, the DnD overwrote many of the original parallels when John overwrote much of the harlot narrative with the beast imagery from Daniel (see). The DnD shifted many of the portions of the harlot narrative around to the point that it no longer forms a simple parallel with the woman, child, and Satan narrative. The fact that both passages contain many common elements meant that the material that John overwrote with Daniel material suggests that the text prior to the DnD contained similar text to the DnD but in a different order.

To get a sense of what the parallel looked like prior to the DnD the reader must make a few mental changes in the text as they are reading it. First, substitute Satan for the beast since the beast is a product of the DnD. Second, when reading both narratives, understand that they are referring to two different aspects of Jerusalem. The faithful is found in the woman and child (Rev 12:1-17) and the unfaithful found in the harlot (Rev 17:1-18).

The Woman, Child, and Satan (Rev 12:1-17)	The Harlot, the Beast, and the Saints (Rev 17:1-18)
• A woman with child in heaven clothed with the sun, moon, and twelve stars (12:1-2).	• A harlot who sits on many rivers on earth and is clothed with the wealthiest clothing on earth (17:1, 4).
• Woman is the mother of those who obey God and follow Jesus (12:17).	• The harlot is the mother of all prostitutes and of the abominations of the earth (17:5).
• Satan comes from heaven and descends to earth (12:3-4).	• The beast ascends from the abyss to the earth (17:8).
• Satan has four names, the great dragon, the old serpent, the devil, the deceiver of the whole world (12:9).	• The beast is full of blasphemous names (17:3).
• Satan has seven heads and ten horns (12:3).	• The beast has seven heads and ten horns (17:3).
• Satan takes a third of Israel (Rev 12:1-4; Gen 37:9).	• She seduces all the kingdoms of the world (17:2).
• Satan tries to devour her son (12:4).	• She drinks the blood of God's children (17:6).
• The son becomes a ruler in heaven (12:5).	• The beast becomes a ruler on earth (17:9-12).
• God flies the woman into the wilderness (12:6, 14).	• The beast ~~flies~~ carries the harlot into the wilderness (17:3).
• Satan wars against the saints on earth (12:12-7).	• The beast wars against the saints on earth (17:8).
• Satan tries to destroy the woman with water on earth (12:15-6).	• The beast destroys the harlot with fire on earth (17:16).

The Woman and Harlot Texts ⟶

Where Are the Fifth, Sixth, and Seventh Trumpet and Bowl Parallels?

The fifth, sixth, and seventh trumpet and bowl combinations can be found in the stories of the fifth, sixth, and seventh churches. Since those parallels include the trumpets and the bowls as well as many more parallels, they provide the reader with a greater context.

The Woman and the Harlot (Part 2)

The Woman, Child, and Satan (Rev 12:1-17)	**The Harlot, the Beast, and the Saints (Rev 17:1-18)**

12:1 A great sign was seen in heaven: a woman clothed with the sun, and the moon under her feet, and on her head a crown of twelve stars. **12:2** She was with child. She cried out in pain, labouring to give birth. **12:3** Another sign was seen in heaven. Behold, a great red dragon, having seven heads and ten horns, and on his heads seven crowns. **12:4** His tail drew one third of the stars of the sky, and threw them to the earth. The dragon stood before the woman who was about to give birth, so that when she gave birth he might devour her child. **12:5** She gave birth to a son, a male child, who is to rule all the nations with a rod of iron. Her child was caught up to God, and to his throne. **12:6** The woman fled into the wilderness, where she has a place prepared by God, that there they may nourish her one thousand two hundred sixty days.

12:7 There was war in the sky. Michael and his angels made war on the dragon. The dragon and his angels made war. **12:8** They didn't prevail, neither was a place found for him any more in heaven. **12:9** The great dragon was thrown down, the old serpent, he who is called the devil and Satan, the deceiver of the whole world. He was thrown down to the earth, and his angels were thrown down with him.

12:10 I heard a loud voice in heaven, saying, "Now the salvation, the power, and the Kingdom of our God, and the authority of his Christ has come; for the accuser of our brothers has been thrown down, who accuses them before our God day and night. **12:11** They overcame him because of the Lamb's blood, and because of the word of their testimony. They didn't love their life, even to death.

12:12 Therefore rejoice, heavens, and you who dwell in them. Woe to the earth and to the sea, because the devil has gone down to you, having great wrath, knowing that he has but a short time."

12:13 When the dragon saw that he was thrown down to the earth, he persecuted the woman who gave birth to the male child. **12:14** Two wings of the great eagle were given to the woman, that she might fly into the wilderness to her place, so that she might be nourished for a time, and times, and half a time, from the face of the serpent. **12:15** The serpent spewed water out of his mouth after the woman like a river, that he might cause her to be carried away by the stream. **12:16** The earth helped the woman, and the earth opened its mouth and swallowed up the river which the dragon spewed out of his mouth. **12:17** The dragon grew angry with the woman, and went away to make war with the rest of her seed, who keep God's commandments and hold Jesus' testimony.

17:1 One of the seven angels who had the seven bowls came and spoke with me, saying, "Come here. I will show you the judgment of the great prostitute who sits on many waters, **17:2** with whom the kings of the earth committed sexual immorality, and those who dwell in the earth were made drunken with the wine of her sexual immorality." **17:3** He carried me away in the Spirit into a wilderness. I saw a woman sitting on a scarlet-colored animal, full of blasphemous names, having seven heads and ten horns. **17:4** The woman was dressed in purple and scarlet, and decked with gold and precious stones and pearls, having in her hand a golden cup full of abominations and the impurities of the sexual immorality of the earth. **17:5** And on her forehead a name was written,

"MYSTERY, BABYLON THE GREAT,
THE MOTHER OF THE PROSTITUTES
AND OF THE ABOMINATIONS OF THE EARTH."

17:6 I saw the woman drunken with the blood of the saints, and with the blood of the martyrs of Jesus. When I saw her, I wondered with great amazement. **17:7** The angel said to me, "Why do you wonder? I will tell you the mystery of the woman, and of the beast that carries her, which has the seven heads and the ten horns. **17:8** The beast that you saw was, and is not; and is about to come up out of the abyss and to go into destruction. Those who dwell on the earth and whose names have not been written in the book of life from the foundation of the world will marvel when they see that the beast was, and is not, and shall be present.

17:9 Here is the mind that has wisdom. The seven heads are seven mountains, on which the woman sits. **17:10** They are seven kings. Five have fallen, the one is, the other has not yet come. When he comes, he must continue a little while. **17:11** The beast that was, and is not, is himself also an eighth, and is of the seven; and he goes to destruction. **17:12** The ten horns that you saw are ten kings who have received no kingdom as yet, but they receive authority as kings, with the beast, for one hour.

17:13 These have one mind, and they give their power and authority to the beast. **17:14** These will war against the Lamb, and the Lamb will overcome them, for he is Lord of lords, and King of kings. They also will overcome who are with him, called and chosen and faithful."

17:15 He said to me,
"The waters which you saw, where the prostitute sits, are peoples, multitudes, nations, and languages.
17:16 The ten horns which you saw, and the beast, these will hate the prostitute, and will make her desolate, and will make her naked, and will eat her flesh, and will burn her utterly with fire.
17:17 For God has put in their hearts to do what he has in mind, and to be of one mind, and to give their kingdom to the beast, until the words of God should be accomplished.
17:18 The woman whom you saw is the great city, which reigns over the kings of the earth."

The Alpha and Omega Parallel: The Prologue and the Second Coming

The purpose of this chart and the one on the adjoining page is to show how the alpha and omega looks today and to show clues as to why it was changed. For example, by comparing the second coming, the New Jerusalem, and the epilogue narratives we can see how John changed the main speaker from God to an angel.

The Prologue (Rev 1:1-20)	The Second Coming (Rev 19:9-20)
1:4 . . . God, who is and who was and who is to come; and from the seven Spirits who are before his throne; **1:5** and from Jesus Christ, the faithful witness,	**19:9** He said to me, "Write, 'Blessed are those who are invited to the marriage supper of the Lamb.'" He said to me, "These are true words of God."
1:3 Blessed is he who reads and those who hear the words of the prophecy, and keep the things that are written in it, for the time is at hand.	
1:17 When I saw him, I fell at his feet like a dead man. He laid his right hand on me, saying, "Don't be afraid. I am the first and the last, **1:18** and the Living one. I was dead, and behold, I am alive forever more. Amen. I have the keys of Death and of Hades.	**19:10** I fell down before his feet to worship him. He said to me, "Look! Don't do it! I am a fellow bondservant with you and with your brothers who hold the testimony of Jesus. Worship God, for the testimony of Jesus is the Spirit of Prophecy."
1:19 Write therefore the things which you have seen, and the things which are, and the things which will happen hereafter; **1:20** the mystery of the seven stars which you saw in my right hand, and the seven golden lamp stands. The seven stars are the angels of the seven assemblies. The seven lamp stands are seven assemblies.	
1:7 Behold, he is coming with the clouds, and every eye will see him, including those who pierced him. All the tribes of the earth will mourn over him. Even so, Amen.	**19:11** I saw the heaven opened, and behold, a white horse, and he who sat on it is called Faithful and True. In righteousness he judges and makes war. **19:12** His eyes are a flame of fire, and on his head are many crowns. He has names written and a name written which no one knows but he himself. **19:13** He is clothed in a garment sprinkled with blood. His name is called "The Word of God." **19:14** The armies which are in heaven followed him on white horses, clothed in white, pure, fine linen. **19:15** Out of his mouth proceeds a sharp, double-edged sword, that with it he should strike the nations. He will rule them with an iron rod. He treads the wine press of the fierceness of the wrath of God, the Almighty. **19:16** He has on his garment and on his thigh a name written, "KING OF KINGS, AND LORD OF LORDS."
1:8 "I am the Alpha and the Omega," says the Lord God, "who is and who was and who is to come, the Almighty."	
	19:20 The beast was taken, and with him the false prophet who worked the signs in his sight, with which he deceived those who had received the mark of the beast and those who worshiped his image. These two were thrown alive into the lake of fire that burns with sulfur.
1:1 This is the Revelation of Jesus Christ, which God gave him to show to his servants the things which must happen soon, which he sent and made known by his angel to his servant, John,	

The Alpha and Omega Parallel: The New Jerusalem and the Epilogue

This chart is a continuation of the chart on the adjoining page. It presents the last two parallel formations of the alpha and omega parallel. Its purpose is to show how a few tweaks of the text changes one parallel to another. For example, one can see how there was light editing in who said "faithful and true" (Rev 21:5; 22:6), was it an angel or God?

The New Jerusalem (Rev 21:5-8)	The Epilogue (Rev 22:6-16)
21:5 He who sits on the throne said, "Behold, I am making all things new." He said, "Write, for these words of God are faithful and true."	**22:6** He said to me, "These words are faithful and true. The Lord God of the spirits of the prophets sent his angel to show to his bondservants the things which must happen soon."
	22:7 "Behold, I come quickly. Blessed is he who keeps the words of the prophecy of this book."
	22:8 Now I, John, am the one who heard and saw these things. When I heard and saw, I fell down to worship before the feet of the angel who had shown me these things. **22:9** He said to me, "See you don't do it! I am a fellow bondservant with you and with your brothers, the prophets, and with those who keep the words of this book. Worship God."
	22:10 He said to me, "Don't seal up the words of the prophecy of this book, for the time is at hand. **22:11** He who acts unjustly, let him act unjustly still. He who is filthy, let him be filthy still. He who is righteous, let him do righteousness still. He who is holy, let him be holy still."
21:6 He said to me, "It is done!	**22:12** "Behold, I come quickly. My reward is with me, to repay to each man according to his work.
I am the Alpha and the Omega, the Beginning and the End. I will give freely to him who is thirsty from the spring of the water of life. **21:7** He who overcomes, I will give him these things. I will be his God, and he will be my son.	**22:13** **I am the Alpha and the Omega**, the First and the Last, the Beginning and the End. **22:14** Blessed are those who do his commandments, that they may have the right to the tree of life, and may enter in by the gates into the city.
21:8 But for the cowardly, unbelieving, sinners, abominable, murderers, sexually immoral, sorcerers, idolaters, and all liars, their part is in the lake that burns with fire and sulfur, which is the second death."	**22:15** Outside are the dogs, the sorcerers, the sexually immoral, the murderers, the idolaters, and everyone who loves and practices falsehood.
	22:16 I, Jesus, have sent my angel to testify these things to you for the assemblies. I am the root and the offspring of David; the Bright and Morning Star."

Bibliography

Alter, Robert. *The Art of Biblical Poetry*. New York: Basic Books, 2011.

Aune, David E. *Revelation 1-5*. Nashville, Tenn.: Thomas Nelson Press, 1998.

Beale, G. K., and D. A. Carson. *Commentary on the New Testament Use of the Old Testament*. Grand Rapids, Mich.: Baker Academic, 2007.

Bowen, Nancy R. *Ezekiel*. Nasville, Tenn.: Abingdon, 2010.

Bullinger, E. W. *Figures of Speech Used in the Bible: Explained and Illustrated*. Lodon: Eyre & Spottiswoode, 1898.

Cadbury, Henry J. *The Making of Luke-Acts*. Peobody, Mass.: Hendrickson Publishers, 1999.

Charles, R H. *A Critical and Exegetical Commentary on the Revelation of St. John*. New York: Charles Scribner's Sons, 1920.

Cohen, Shaye J.D., and Joshua J. Schwartz. *Studies in Josephus and the Varieties of Ancient Judaism*. Leiden: Brill, 2007.

Elliott, J. K. *The Collected Biblical Writings of T.C. Skeat*. Leiden: Brill, 2004.

Goldwurn, Hersh. *History of the Jewish People: The Second Temple Era*. Brooklyn: Mesorah Publications, 1982.

Jauhiainen, Marko. *The Use of Zechariah in Revelation*. Tübingen: Mohr Siebeck, 2005.

Jones, Brian W. *The Emperor Domitian*. New York: Routledge Inc., 1993.

Lupieri, Edmondo F. *A Commentary on the Apocalypse of John*. Grand Rapids, Mich.: Eerdmans, 2006.

Neusner, Jacob, and Alan J. Avery-Peck. *The Blackwell Companion to Judaism*. Maiden, Maine: Blackwell, 2003.

Neusner, Jacob, and Alan J. Avery-Peck. *The Routledge Dictionary of Judaism.* New Your: Routledge, 2004.

Osborne, Grant R. *Revelation.* Grand Rapids, Mich.: Baker Academic, 2002.

Roloff, Jürgen. *The Revelation of John: A Continental Commentary.* Minneapolis: Fortress Press, 1993.

Toorn, K. *Scribal Culture and the Making of the Hebrew Bible.* Cambridge, Mass.: Harvard University Press, 2007.

Roberts, Colin H., and T. C. Skeat. *The Birth of the Codex.* London: Oxford University Press, 1983.

Smalley, Stephen S. *The Revelation of John: A Commentary on the Greek Text of the Apocalypse.* Downers Grove , Ill.: IVP Academic, 2005.

Wallace, Daniel B. *Greek Grammar Beyond the Basics.* Grand Rapids, Mich.: Zondervan, 1996.

The Stratification Charts

The following pages shows the relationship between the drafts and the chapters. It is patterned after an archaeological dig in which the draft on the bottom represents the earliest material added to Revelation and the upper most draft layer represents the latest information. The columns represent the various chapters in Revelation. The intersection provides information to what has been added and what page number the reader will find the section containing the information about the addition. For those who have read Revelation, they may be troubled why some material was not covered in a particular draft or why the material seems not right. Many times it is because the concepts were not introduced in the draft. The stratification charts provides an easy way to see if the material was added in a later draft.

For the first time reader, the chart will serve as a means of seeing how Revelation was developed. They provide a quick way to see what the draft will cover as well as how a chapter will change over time in the later drafts.

	Chapter 1	Chapters 2 - 3	Chapter 4	Chapter 5
Daniel Draft (DnD) **Chapter 6**	• Most of the descriptions of Jesus, 222.	• The cities are define, • Parallels formed with the prologue, 222. • The first three cities form a parallel with the beast, 276.		• The 100 million angels worship Jesus, 225.
Exodus Draft (ExD) **Chapter 5**	• God's new name, who was, who is, and who is to come, 192. • God coming in the clouds, • Believers are a kingdom of priests, 193. • Seven lampstands, 201.	• The formation of the offset parallel between the seven churches and the seven seals, 275. • The formation of the complex parallel reflecting the seven churches spiritual states, 272.	• The 24 elders added to this section, 202. • God defined as "who is, was and is to come," 192.	• The preparing of the incense, 204. • The removal of the crowning of the 24 elders, 202.
Deuteronomy - Joshua Draft (DJD) **Chapter 4**	• The alpha and omega parallel, 152. • The chain of custody of the letter, 158.	• Expanded from four churches to seven churches, 159.		• Jesus as the commander of the Lord's army, 143. • The scroll receives seven seals, 145.
Zechariah Draft (ZrD) **Chapter 3**	• Whom they have pierced, 66.	• Four messages or churches defined, 67. • The template for the church letters, 71, 103.	• The first author's notation, 72.	• The splitting of the scroll from Ezekiel, 79. • Jesus as the high priest, 74. • The mighty angel, 74. • The 24 elders, 74.

Ezekiel-Isaiah Draft (EID) **From Isaiah** **Chapter 2**		• Individualize content for:
		  • Smyrna, 49.
		  • Philadelphia, 28.
		  • Laodicea, 29.
		• The phrase "he that has an ear, let him hear", 41.
			• The four living creatures receive a worshiping role, 16.	• The altar, 16.

Ezekiel-Isaiah Draft (EID) **From Ezekiel** **Chapter 2**	• John exiled because he obeyed the commandments of God, 16. • John's falling down experience, 16.	• The phrase "thus says the Lord" defined, 17. • The phrase "he that has an ear, let him hear", 40.	• John in heaven, 15. • God sitting on the throne. • The sea of glass, 16. • The living creatures with four faces, eagle, lion, calf and man, 16.	• The falling down and worshiping scenes, 16. • The two sided scroll, 15.

	Chapter 6	Chapters 7	Chapter 8	Chapter 9
Daniel Draft (DnD) Chapter 6				• The size of the 200,000,000 army, 225.
Exodus Draft (ExD) Chapter 5		• The creation of the 144,000, 207. • The great multitude in heaven, 208. • The temple imagery, 208.	• The burning of the incense • The earthquake, 198	
Deuteronomy - Joshua Draft (DJD) Chapter 4	• The seven seals, 145. • The second horsemen receives the great sword, 163.	• The 12 tribes of Israel, 140. • The sealing of the 144,000, 142. • The passover meal, 142. • The placement of the Isaiah texts, 162.	• The seventh seal with the seven trumpets inside of it, 145. • The period of silence, . • The angels blowing the trumpets, 145.	The crossing of the Euphrates river, 140. The angel from the abyss,160.
Zechariah Draft (ZrD) Chapter 3	• The four horsemen and their colors, 75.	• The elder's question, 95.	• The placement of the trumpets, 75. • The formation of the first four trumpets and the four attacks by Satan, 75.	• The placement of the trumpets, 75. • The placement of the scorpions, 85.
Ezekiel-Isaiah Draft (EID) From Isaiah Chapter 2	• The great sword, 30. • The content of the fifth seal, 22. • The content of the sixth seal, 22.	• The well of salvation, 59. • Do not harm the grass and trees, 22.		
Ezekiel-Isaiah Draft (EID) From Ezekiel Chapter 2	• The content three of the of the four horsemen, 22. • The content of the fifth and sixth seal, 22.		• The idea of three attacks by the nations (prototype of the first four trumpets), 21.	• The core of the fifth trumpet, 22. • The hardening of the forehead, 18, 42. • The scorpions, 18.

	Chapter 10	Chapters 11	Chapter 12	Chapter 13
Daniel Draft (DnD) Chapter 6	• The time is now, 229. • Seal up this book, 229. • The other angels, 229.	• The beast kills the two prophets, 212.		• The description and name of the beast, 211. • The description and name of the false prophet, 211. • The new 42 month parallel element location, 220.
Exodus Draft (ExD) Chapter 5		• The two prophets like Moses and Aaron, 207. • The temple imagery, 201.		
Deuteronomy - Joshua Draft (DJD) Chapter 4	• The mighty angel has one foot in the land and one foot in the sea, 140.	• The king of the abyss kills the two prophets, 140. • The earthquake, 149. • The seventh trumpet, 149. • The ark of the covenant, 149.		
Zechariah Draft (ZrD) Chapter 3	• The placement of the scroll, 79. • The mighty angel, 80.	• The measuring of the temple, 90. • The placement of the two prophets, 91.	• The woman's clothing, 78. • The woman flown to the wilderness, 78. • The placement of Satan, 86. • The encoding chapter 11-12 with Zech 2:1 - 4:14, 86.	
Ezekiel-Isaiah Draft (EID) From Isaiah Chapter 2		• The defining of the three numbers representing years of service to God and relating them to the years of the Roman siege of Jerusalem, 20.	• The sign of a woman with child, 18. • Several attacks by Satan, 21.	
Ezekiel-Isaiah Draft (EID) From Ezekiel Chapter 2	• God appointing John as a watchman, 17.	• The three sets of numbers representing years of sin to days of a siege, 20.		

	Chapter 14	Chapters 15	Chapter 16	Chapter 17
Daniel Draft (DnD) Chapter 6	• The beast imagery added, 213. • The message of the three angels, 226.		• Adding the beast into the seven bowls, 228.	• The imagery of the beast, 227.
Exodus Draft (ExD) Chapter 5	• The 144,000 named, 207. • The gospel is spread to the whole world, 208.	• The temple imagery added, 201.		
Deuteronomy - Joshua Draft (DJD) Chapter 4		• The song of Moses and the lamb, 139. • God angry and hides his face, 139.	• The four horns become the seven bowls, 152. • The seven angels delivering the judgments, 145, 152.	
Zechariah Draft (ZrD) Chapter 3			• The creation of the four horns (first four bowls), 92.	• The harlot taken to the wilderness, 78.
Ezekiel-Isaiah Draft (EID) From Isaiah Chapter 2	• The gathering at mount Zion, 26. • The great harvest scene, 26. • Fallen, fallen is Babylon, 26.			
Ezekiel - Isaiah Draft (EID) From Ezekiel Chapter 2	• The river of blood but not its placement, 31.			• The harlot as Jerusalem who God clothed and who killed their children, 28.

	Chapter 18	Chapters 19	Chapter 20	Chapter 21-22
Daniel Draft (DnD) Chapter 6	• The merging of chapter 17 and 18 to become the harlot, 227.	• The first angel John worships, 222. • The imagery of Jesus in the second coming, 222. • The defeat of the beast, 213.	• The second death, 213. • The Lambs book of life, 213.	• The second death, 213. • Longer list of sins, 213.
Exodus Draft (ExD) Chapter 5				• The height of Jerusalem, 206. • God and Jesus became the temple, 206.
Deuteronomy - Joshua Draft (DJD) Chapter 4			• The sinners come from the sea, 135.	• The creation of the epilogue. 134. • The alpha and the omega parallel, 152. • The book of curses. 135.
Zechariah Draft (ZrD) Chapter 3	• The mighty angel and the millstone, 94.	• The white horses, 95. • Satan defeated by two horsemen, 95.	• Satan imprisoned in the abyss, 87.	• The saints receiving thrones, 74. • No longer will there be a curse, 130.
Ezekiel-Isaiah Draft From Isaiah Chapter 2	• The name of Babylon, 26. • The musicians will never play the songs of Babylon again, 29.	• The imagery of Jesus with a sword coming out of his mouth, 30. • The saints eating a meal watching a great city destroyed, 30.	• The imagery of a book where the good people read it and the bad people don't, 31. • God calling fire from heaven destroying the army of the nations rising up against Jerusalem, 31.	• The holy city of Jerusalem, 34. • Where death is no more, 34. • God wipes away their tears, 34. • The city adorned like a bride, 34
Ezekiel-Isaiah Draft From Ezekiel Chapter 2	• The city of Tyre as the city of Rome, 28. • The wealth of Tyre, 28, 56. • The merchants lament of Tyre's destruction, 56.	• The imagery of the vultures feasting on the army, 30. • The slaying of the great dragon's army and sending the dragon to Sheol, 30.	• The story of Gog and Magog, 31.	• The righteous will be the only ones to enter the City of God, 32. • The City of God has 12 gates named after the twelve tribes of Israel, 32. • A river that brings life and a tree that produces twelve kinds of fruit, 32.